500 extraord[...] islands

1st Edition

By Julie Duchaine, Holly Hughes,
Alexis Lipsitz Flippin, and
Sylvie Murphy

Wiley Publishing, Inc.

Contents

Published by:

Wiley Publishing, Inc.

111 River St.
Hoboken, NJ 07030-5774

ISBN 978-0-470-50070-5

Editor: Jennifer Reilly
Production Editor: Heather Wilcox
Photo Editor: Cherie Cincilla (with special thanks to Susan Barnes)
Interior book design: Melissa Auciello-Brogan
Production by Wiley Indianapolis Composition Services

Front cover photo: France, Normandy: Le Mont Saint Michel with reflection in water © Nagelestock.com/Alamy Images
Back cover photos: Moai on Easter Island, Chile © Russell Kord/Alamy Images; Giant tortoise on the Galápagos © Blickwinkel/Schmidbauer/Alamy Images; Manhattan, New York © Scott Murphy/Ambient Images/PhotoLibrary; Aitutaki Atoll, Cook Islands © Greg Balfour Evans/Alamy Images

For information on our other products and services or to obtain technical support, please contact our Customer Care Department within the U.S. at 877/762-2974, outside the U.S. at 317/572-3993 or fax 317/572-4002.

Wiley also publishes its books in a variety of electronic formats. Some content that appears in print may not be available in electronic formats.

Manufactured in the United States of America

5 4 3 2 1

About the Authors

Julie Duchaine has been a freelance writer for the past 25 years. Most recently, she contributed to *Frommer's 500 Places to See Before They Disappear, Frommer's 500 Places for Food & Wine Lovers,* and *Frommer's 500 Places to Take Your Kids Before They Grow Up.* She lives in Milwaukee.

Holly Hughes has traveled the globe as an editor and writer. A former executive editor of Fodor's Travel Publications, she edits the annual *Best Food Writing* anthology and is the author of the bestselling *500 Places to Take Your Kids Before They Grow Up, 500 Places to See Before They Disappear, 500 Places for Food & Wine Lovers,* and *Frommer's New York City with Kids.* She has also written fiction for middle graders. New York City makes a convenient jumping-off place for her travels with her three children and husband.

Alexis Lipsitz Flippin is a writer and editor who lives in New York City. She is the author of *Frommer's New York City with Kids, Frommer's New York Day by Day, Frommer's Portable Turks & Caicos,* and *Frommer's Portable St. Maarten/St. Martin, Anguilla & St. Barts.*

Sylvie Murphy has lived and worked in Rome as a travel writer and travel guide and currently resides in Kansas City. She is also the author of *Frommer's Day by Day Rome* and a contributor to *Pauline Frommer's Italy.*

Acknowledgments

Julie Duchaine would like to thank her editor, Jennifer Reilly, for her clear, helpful directions and good cheer. It helped a great deal in writing these reviews. **Holly Hughes** thanks her family for crossing every bridge and hopping on every ferry with her. She's grateful to all the other Frommer's writers who shared their own favorite islands—what a great worldwide team you are! And she sends a million thanks to her editor, Jennifer Reilly, for steering this complicated yacht safely into harbor. **Alexis Lipsitz Flippin** says she could not have completed this fascinating and challenging assignment were it not for the unerring good sense, unflagging support, utter graciousness, and reassuring serenity of her editor, Jennifer Reilly. She is a dream to work for. Thanks, too, to her husband, Royce, for his unflagging support. **Sylvie Murphy** would like to thank all her island-junkie friends and family for their extraordinarily helpful tips and insights.

An Invitation to the Reader

In researching this book, we discovered many wonderful places. We're sure you'll find others. Please tell us about them so we can share the information with your fellow travelers in upcoming editions. If you were disappointed with a recommendation, we'd love to know that too. Please write to:

Frommer's 500 Extraordinary Islands, 1st Edition
Wiley Publishing, Inc. • 111 River St. • Hoboken, NJ 07030-5774

An Additional Note

Please be advised that travel information is subject to change at any time—and this is especially true of prices. We therefore suggest that you write or call ahead for confirmation when making your travel plans. The authors, editors, and publisher cannot be held responsible for the experiences of readers while traveling. Your safety is important to us, however, so we encourage you to stay alert and be aware of your surroundings. Keep a close eye on cameras, purses, and wallets, all favorite targets of thieves and pickpockets.

Frommer's Icons

We use six feature icons to help you quickly find the information you're looking for. At the end of each review, look for:

Where to get more information
Nearest airport
Nearest boat service/port
Nearest train station
Driving information
Recommended hotels

Frommers.com

Now that you have this guidebook to help you plan a great trip, visit our website at **www.frommers.com** for additional travel information on more than 4,000 destinations. We update features regularly to give you instant access to the most current trip-planning information available. At Frommers.com, you'll find scoops on the best airfares, lodging rates, and car-rental bargains. You can even book your travel online through our reliable travel booking partners. Other popular features include:

- Online updates of our most popular guidebooks
- Vacation sweepstakes and contest giveaways
- Newsletters highlighting the hottest travel trends
- Podcasts, interactive maps, and up-to-the-minute events listings
- Opinionated blog entries by Arthur Frommer himself
- Online travel message boards with featured travel discussions

About This Book

That Robinson Crusoe fantasy runs deep. Its perpetual appeal lies behind the success of movies and TV shows from *South Pacific* to *Swiss Family Robinson* to *Castaway, Gilligan's Island* to *Lost.* The tried-and-true chat-show quiz—"What five books (or five CDs, or five people) would you take if you were stranded on a desert island?"—causes us all to mentally drift off for a moment, plotting our getaway.

So what is it about islands that makes them so intriguing? Whether it's a tropical speck in the midst of a vast ocean, or a tree-shrouded hummock in the river of a great city, it's still somehow set apart, unique, proud, lonely, even mysterious. The waters around it ineffably define it, in a way that no plot of mainland can be defined. And because effort is required to get there—whether it's simply driving across a bridge or chartering a private plane—once you've reached its shores, you *know* you're somewhere different.

Why These Islands?

As with other books in this *500 Places* series, *500 Extraordinary Islands* began to take shape as a sort of life list—how many islands have you been to, and which have you always dreamed of seeing? When we four writers began this project, we all had our favorite islands to nominate. In some cases, we had to draw straws to decide who'd get the honor of writing about certain beloved places.

But as our final list evolved—500 is a lot of islands, but there were thousands of others we might have included—we found ourselves broadening the definition, expanding our concept of what makes an island alluring. After all, even a peninsula can qualify as an island, if it still *feels* cut off from the land to which it is technically attached, if only at low tide. So many different forces gave birth to these islands—some are the protruding tops of tropical coral reefs or the geothermal peaks of volcanoes, while others were rock-carved by glaciers or softly piled-up silt and sand. Some are entirely man-made; on others, nature now runs wild over ancient relics of habitation.

An entire country—even a continent, like Antarctica—can be considered an island if its character has been defined by its strategic isolation. (Great Britain and Australia tempted us, but we knew we couldn't cover them fairly in a one-page write-up—so we compensated by covering dozens of their outlying islands, fascinating in their own right.) Does an archipelago qualify as a single destination (like the Philippines) or should we treat its various islands separately (as we did with Indonesia)? In compiling our list, we ended up trusting our travelers' instinct—what routes are best developed, and what do most visitors go there for? We debated how to include New Zealand, Japan, and Greece, nations composed of several large islands, each with its own history and character and natural beauty. Rather than give their various islands short shrift, we've sprinkled them liberally throughout the book. Our main criterion was simple: We wanted to offer the 500 islands you'd most want to visit—or perhaps stay on forever.

How This Book Is Organized

Traditional travel guides are usually arranged geographically—but this is no traditional travel guide. As a traveler, you already know what aspects of a destination you're most interested in. That's why we've organized this book to showcase each island's most compelling reason to visit (although certain islands could have fit into any of several chapters). The first chapter, "Beachcomber Islands," is for travelers who always want to chalk up some sun worshiping, snorkeling, and diving. If you find yourself drawn instead to the lush greenery behind the beach, or the rolling farmlands at the island's heart, then the next chapter, "Garden Islands," is for you. Nature lovers who bring their binoculars and cameras on vacation, hoping to spot native birds and animals, should pore over "Wildlife Islands," a rich trove of places where island isolation has allowed endemic species to flourish.

Island isolation is also the key to "Island Escapes"—that chapter highlights islands that are especially quiet, laid-back, relaxing, and off the beaten track. "Treasure Islands" is devoted to island jewels that offer unique, one-of-a-kind qualities. "Pleasure Islands" covers sybaritic spots where nightlife and creature comforts rule; "Leisure Islands" focuses on destinations geared for active travelers, who prime their vacations with sports and outdoor adventures. "Islands of History" looks at islands with a vivid heritage, from bloody battles to pirate raids to literary associations. "Islands of Mystery" are just that—places with a slightly spooky or surreal aura, created by natural phenomena, baffling history, spiritual associations, or native myths.

"Island Cities" celebrates bustling modern cities that are set entirely on islands, whereas "City Islands" looks at island refuges tucked away within various metropolitan areas. "Island Nations" celebrates several self-contained island countries whose history has been defined by their island status. The last chapter, "Ends of the Earth," explores especially remote destinations—hard to get to, but well worth the effort.

Threaded throughout the book, you'll also find our Island Hopping features—overviews of island chains well worth skipping around. Why content yourself with the traditional entry point when the chain's real charm may lie on its smaller, more remote islands?

When it comes time to plan your vacation, flip to the geographic index at the end of the book—that'll help you locate all the islands in geographic proximity to your chosen destination.

A Note on Transport, Tours & Hotels

By definition, an island requires some extra effort to get to. An essential element of every island write-up, therefore, is information on how to reach the place—whether you drive across a bridge, take a ferry or excursion boat, rent a sailboat or kayak, or fly into an island airport. (Sometimes the trip is half the fun!) In some more far-flung cases, tour operators provide the most reliable means of reaching the island, and we've added that information where applicable. Many islands are also highly seasonal in nature, cut off by rough water or harsh weather at certain times of year, all hotels and attractions shut up tight, ferry services closed down. We've made special note when that is the case.

Note that **phone numbers** listed begin with international dialing codes—if you're dialing from within that country, drop the first set of numbers and add 0 before the regional dialing code. (In some cases, a 0 may need to be added or deleted before the regional dialing code when dialing from abroad.) U.S. and Canadian numbers, however, don't list the international prefix, which is 1.

At the end of every write-up, you'll also find a couple of brief recommendations of places to stay while visiting that island. (For more choices and detailed information, consult the corresponding Frommer's guide or www.frommers.com for that destination.) In some cases, it may be the only hotel on that island; in others where there are no lodgings, the best we could do was to suggest a hotel near the ferry docks or bridge. **Hotel rates** are noted in three price ranges—$$$ (expensive), $$ (moderate), and $ (inexpensive)—but that's relative to local hotel rates, which vary wildly around the world. (A $125-per-night motel room in Indonesia would be extravagant, but you'd be lucky to find something minimally decent for that rate in Manhattan.) In the time-honored Frommer's tradition, we list affordable options when available—but when it comes to islands, that's often trumped by the law of supply and demand. If you want to stay on certain islands, you'll have to pay for the privilege. Of course, on other islands the only options are humble indeed—you won't pay much, but don't expect luxury!

1 Beachcomber Islands

Aquatic Playgrounds

1

Fraser Island

Where Sand Is King

Australia

Sand is just sand, right? Well, Fraser Island may change your mind about that. Lying just south of the Great Barrier Reef, this is the world's biggest sand island, an ecological marvel where ancient eucalyptus rainforest actually grows out of dunes up to 240m (787 ft.) high. You'd expect it to have beaches, but to have an uninterrupted surf-foamed Pacific beach running the length of the island for 120km (75 miles)—now that's something special. Only problem is . . . you can't swim there. The currents offshore are just too strong, and the shark population is just too, well, sharky. But there's an easy way around that: Go inland, where Fraser Island offers so many places to swim, it's like nature's biggest water park.

Set into the sand dunes of Fraser Island are more than 100 little freshwater lakes, ringed with dazzling white sand that's pure silica—whiter sand than the big Pacific beach, in fact. Some, like brilliant blue **Lake McKenzie,** sprang up when water filled hardened hollows in the dunes; others, like emerald-green **Lake Wabby,** were created when shifting dunes dammed up a stream. Shallow, swift-flowing **Eli Creek** is as much fun as a lazy river ride—wade up the creek for a mile or two and then let the current carry you back down.

You should, of course, spend some time on **75-Mile Beach**—it's actually a highway you can drive along with a four-wheel-drive vehicle (the only cars allowed

Previous page: Cape Hatteras beach. Above: Fraser Island.

on this island). A rusted wrecked luxury steamship, the ***Maheno,*** sits right on the beach, offering a rare chance for nondivers to see a shipwreck up close; just north of the wreck loom gorgeous erosion-sculpted ocher cliffs called the **Cathedrals.** At the northern end of the beach, you can dip into the ocean in the spalike bubbling waters of the **Champagne Pools** (also called the Aquarium for their tide-pool marine life), shallow pockets of soft sand protected from the waves by a natural rock barrier.

With no towns and few facilities apart from low-profile ecotourism resorts, Fraser Island has been maintained as a no-frills destination for folks who love wildlife better than the wild life. It's a place for camping out, bird-watching, and bush walking through eucalyptus woods and low-lying "wallum" heaths that offer a spectacular wildflower display every spring and summer. Its fringing wetlands feature pristine mangrove colonies and sea-grass beds, where dugongs and swamp wallabies thrive. And from August to October, Fraser Island is one of Australia's best sites for seeing humpback whales returning to Antarctica 486 with their calves in tow (book whale-watching tours, as well as dolphin- or manatee-spotting tours, from local resorts). Dingoes even run wild here, one of the purest populations anywhere—what's more Australian than that? *—HH*

ⓘ **Tourist information,** 262 Urraween Rd., Hervey Bay (✆ **61/7/4215 9855** in Australia, or 1800/811 728; www.frasercoast holidays.info), or www.fraserisland.net.

✈ Hervey Bay (15km/9⅓ miles).

⛴ 45 min. by catamaran or barge from Hervey Bay.

🛏 $$ **Fraser Island Backpackers YHA,** Happy Valley (✆ **61/7/4127 9144;** www.fraserislandco.com.au). $$$ **Kingfisher Bay Resort,** West Coast (✆ **61/7/4120 3333,** or 1800/072 555 in Australia; www.kingfisherbay.com).

2 Aquatic Playgrounds

Koh Phuket

Pearl of the Andaman Coast

Thailand

This classic volcanic island not only has beaches but also has fabulous *views* of beaches—and of shimmering turquoise seas and emerald green hills dotting the horizon. Before Phuket was devastated by the tsunami that struck Indonesia on December 26, 2004, the beautiful island province of Phuket (pronounced Poo-get), on the Andaman Coast of Thailand, enjoyed a bubbling tourism market drawn to its stunning beaches, balmy Indian Ocean seas, and mellow vibe. In fact, during high season, the island's prime beaches were packed with holiday revelers (and some of the island towns, like Patong, took on a certain seedy overdevelopment), and Thailand's largest island quickly went from a hideaway of the beach-loving cognoscenti to the country's leading holiday destination. Then the tsunami struck, killing some 7,000 people in Thailand and virtually wiping out resorts on Phuket's beautiful west coast.

Today this island has rebounded spectacularly from the catastrophe, with most of the destroyed properties rebuilt and new luxury resorts rising up all over the island. The seas are clear, and underwater coral gardens are reputedly back to pre-tsunami splendor (fishermen even report spotting large schools of fish they haven't seen for years).

Phuket is directly connected to the Thailand mainland at the island's northern tip by the **Sarasin Bridge.** Renting a car is the best way to see the island, but driving the cliff-hugging roads on hairpin turns can be heart-stopping—on the roads in Phuket, anything goes. With a car, you can beach-hop the west coast and stop in at **Phuket Town** to shop and see colonial mansions built by the moneyed set when the island economy revolved around tin and rubber production. You can head to the island's last rainforest, located in the **Khao Phra Thaw Royal Wildlife Reserve.** Here you can hike and stand beneath waterfalls and perhaps spot the bloom of the rare Rafflesia—the "corpse flower"—which looks and smells like rotting flesh.

The island's west coast offers the most cinematically beautiful palm-fringed beaches, many of which have starred in such Hollywood films as *The Beach, Rescue Dawn,* and *The Man with the Golden Gun.* **Kata** and **Karon,** on the island's southwest coast, are two of Phuket's finest beaches. Just north of Patong, **Kamala Bay, Surin Beach,** and **Bang Thao Beach** have secluded resorts on smashing beaches for those who want to hit the action in Patong but don't want to sleep there. North of the main resort areas, **Nai Yang,** part of **Sirinat National Park,** has few facilities but a fantastic beach fringed with casuarina pines. A coral reef just offshore makes for great snorkeling.

You can participate in just about any watersports on the island, but the diving around Phuket is particularly world-class. **Fantasea Divers** (✆ **66/7628-1388;** www.fantasea.net) offers dive packages and PADI certification courses in addition to full-day dives around Phuket. **Scuba Cat,** in Patong (✆ **66/7629-3120;** www.scubacat.com), offers a full range of trips for anyone from beginner to expert. The snorkeling is great on Phuket, too, with right-off-the-beach opportunities at places like **Nai Harn Beach** and **Relax Bay.**

You'll have no trouble finding a viewing spot that offers cozy seating and sundowners to watch the red-tinged sun melt into the darkening sea. Of course, if you're after more bustling nightlife, head to the 3km (1¾-mile) beachside strip at **Patong.** Lit up like a seedy Las Vegas in miniature, it's got bars, nightclubs, discos, malls, and such familiar Western chains as Starbucks. It also has hundreds of "hostess" bars, so you may want to take the family elsewhere. —*AF*

ⓘ **Tourism Authority of Thailand** (TAT), 191 Klang Rd., Phuket Town (✆ **66/7621-2213;** www.tourismthailand.org).

✈ Phuket International Airport.

🛏 $$ **Indigo Pearl Resort,** Nai Yang Beach and National Park (✆ **66/7632-7006;** www.indigo-pearl.com). $$$ **Le Royal Meridien Phuket Yacht Club,** 23/3 Viset Rd. (✆ **800/225-5843** in the U.S. and Canada; www.lemeridien.com).

3 Aquatic Playgrounds

The Lido di Venezia

The Lido Shuffle

Italy

Yes, Venice 406 itself is an island, or rather a huddled mass of islands. There's water *everywhere.* Nevertheless, when the Venetians want a day by the sea, they head to another island: the Lido.

While some adventurous tourists make it out to the Venetian lagoon's other islands (p. 420), very few opt to spend their precious days in Venice at the local beach. If you're traveling in the summer, however, know that Venice can get mercilessly muggy and few hotels offer swimming pools. With kids in tow on my last visit, I knew we needed to include a beach day in our vacation. The Lido was the perfect solution.

Centuries ago, the Doge's navy sailed out from this long, thin barrier island, which separates the lagoon from the Gulf of Venice, an arm of the Adriatic Sea. Nowadays it's easily reached by the ACTV waterbus—there's a direct boat from the train station (#35), though the #1 vaporetto also sails over once it's finished cruising the Grand Canal. The lagoon side of the island is traced by a shady promenade with superb Venice views, while a strip of beach runs along the 18km-long (11-mile) gulf front; they're linked by the Gran Viale, which leads from the waterbus landing to the beach.

Facing the sea across palm-lined Lungomare Marconi, you'll find two sister bastions of old-world resort elegance, the **Hotel des Bains** and the **Westin Excelsior;** each has its own private beach, a Riviera-style strand with deck chairs and cabanas. (Visconti's classic film of Thomas Mann's *Death in Venice* was filmed at the Hotel des Bains and its beach.) The more egalitarian public parts of the Lido beach (along Lungomare G. D'Annunzio) are more of a family hangout, though you can expect to see a few topless sunbathers and men in incredibly skimpy Speedos. (And there were my boys in their baggy surfer jams.) The broad strip of fine-grained golden sand was convivially crowded, so we could combine sunbathing with people-watching. Protected by a system of outlying dikes, the waters lapping the beach are calm and shallow, great for youngsters (our youngest was only 4 at the time), and almost ridiculously warm, practically like a bathtub. The bottom's a little sludgy, but blessedly free of the rocks or sharp shells that make wading a problem in the New England waters we were used to.

During the Venice Film Festival every September, the Lido is a hot spot, thanks to the 1930s modernist **Palazzo del Cinema,** and the adjacent Art Deco **Casino,** which has become a secondary venue since it closed for gambling in 1999. —*HH*

ⓘ **Tourist information,** Fondamente San Lorenzo (✆ **39/041/5298711;** www.turismovenezia.it).

✈ Aeroporto Marco Polo.

🛏 $$$ **Locanda Ai Santi Apostoli,** Strada Nuova, Cannaregio (✆ **39/041/5212612;** www.locandasantiapostoli.com). $$ **Pensione Accademia,** Fondamenta Bollani, Dorsoduro (✆ **39/041/5210188;** www.pensioneaccademia.it).

Majorca

Vamos a la Playa

Balearic Islands, Spain

The most recreationally tricked-out of Spain's playground Balearic islands, Majorca is also the largest and most popular of the archipelago. With a holiday atmosphere that lasts almost all year and fun beachy things to do for all ages and tastes, Majorca has much more to offer the active traveler than the one-trick-pony party isle of Ibiza 246 or the tiny, trendy getaway of Formentera 183.

Majorca (note that the island's name is just as often spelled "Mallorca," which is the Catalan version—double *L* or single *J* in the middle, it's the same place) holds the dubious distinction of being one of the global "pioneers" of package tourism. In the 1950s, droves of sun-starved Brits and Germans began streaming in on charter flights, and the trend has never really let up. Majorca remains *the* no-brainer beach getaway for much of northern Europe. When chalky-white, soon-to-be-lobster-toned mainlanders take over the shores of Majorca every summer—and the situation is most extreme in August—Majorca can cease to feel like a place with any kind of cultural identity. However, that's typical of many sunny Mediterranean locales—Spain's Costa Brava and Costa del Sol aren't much different. So what if the best beach real estate has been snapped up by sterile hotels that look like a tangle of beached cruise ships? That kind of in-your-face holiday atmosphere can be great fun as long as you know what to expect. Majorca still has plenty of unspoiled corners along its pretty coastline of pine-backed coves, and if you're looking for a social holiday, you certainly won't be disappointed.

Majorca's capital city of **Palma** is a vibrant and charming metropolis with a population of a quarter million, as well as splendid architecture and colorful street life. From June to August, Majorca's northern and eastern coasts are packed to the gills, as that's where the best beaches are. Party animals should head for **El Arenal,** south of Palma, where the revelry transitions seamlessly from the sand to enormous discos that feel like Oktoberfest-by-the-Sea. North of Palma, you'll find almost exclusively Brits—and lots and lots of merriment—at **Magaluf** beach. Nearby **Santa Ponça** is where the Scottish and Irish go, and the resort's Celtic-themed architecture is supposed to make them feel right at home. **Puerto de Andratx** is not yet overrun with the package tour set, so go now before the buildings and golf course that are underway here draw in the masses. Halfway up the northwest coast, the seaside town of **Valdemossa** is quieter (practically dead at night) and is where Michael Douglas and Catherine Zeta-Jones have a house. Over on the east coast, **Port d'Alcúdia** is an altogether stress-free place, great for families. On any of these beaches, you'll find the full complement of watersports, though **jet skis** remain the most fashionable waterborne thrill on Majorca.

The flip side to the potentially chaotic coastal scene is that Majorca is blessed with the most dramatic interior of any of the Balearics, and exploring that splendid mountain scenery is a highlight that too few visitors take advantage of. You'll need a car to get around even a fraction of the 3,640-sq.-km (1,405-sq.-mile) island. The **Serra de Tramuntana** mountain range dominates the northwest coast—take a day away from the sand to drive up to the island's spectacular highest point, **Puig Major** (1,445m/4,741 ft.). Away from Palma and the coast is also where the best self-catering villas and *agriturismos* are to be found, often in panoramic hilltop locations. —*SM*

ⓘ www.illesbalears.es or www.mallorcaspain.net.

✈ Palma-Sont San Joan.

⛴ From Barcelona (3½ hr.), and from Valencia (4–7 hr.). **Transmediterránea** (✆ **34/90-245-46-45**).

🛏 $$ **Can Furios,** Camí Vell Binibona, Binibona (✆ **34/97-151-57-51;** www.canfurios.com). $$$ **La Residencia,** Son Canals, Deià (✆ **34/97-163-90-11;** www.hotel-laresidencia.com).

5 Aquatic Playgrounds

Grand Bahama Island

Grand Vacationland

The Bahamas

On a map, Grand Bahama Island looks like a razor-tooth saw, its spindly fingers of sand stretching out into the deep blue sea. The history of this island is rife with tales of ships wrecking on the shallow reefs that trace the island's 97km (60-mile) shoreline. Its very name, in fact, is derived from the Spanish phrase for "great shallows": *gran bajamer*.

From the air, the island is distinguished not so much by the landscape as by the seascape, flashing that sumptuous Bahamas blue, which segues from teal to turquoise in a flicker of sunlight. Here in The Bahamas the land and the sea are eternally intertwined. This coral reef archipelago is a low-lying chain of some 700 islands, 2,000 cays, and scores of rocky outcroppings dotted along the southern Atlantic Ocean—see p. 36, 241, and 254 for info on more islands in the chain. The northernmost island of The Bahamas is Grand Bahama, just 84km (52 miles) due east of Palm Beach, Florida.

This 155km (96-mile) island has all the best attributes of a typical Bahamas island (and some say a few of the worst, including overdevelopment, particularly in bustling **Freeport,** the island's largest city). Largely flat, sandy scrubland, Grand Bahama has fine, snow-white beaches; calm, shallow coves perfect for swimming and snorkeling; some of the best **scuba diving** opportunities in the world (The internationally renowned diving school UNEXSO [www.unexso.com] is here); and a well-developed tourist infrastructure in the resort cities, with lots of hotels, restaurants, casinos, golf courses, and watersports operators.

But dig deeper, and you'll discover another, less-frenzied Grand Bahama, one that is rich in history. This was the island, after all, where slaves freed by the British in the pre–Civil War years settled and staked a claim. Many of the older towns on the island were founded by these slaves and still bear their names. Grand Bahama is also the site of some significant Lucayan archaeological sites from a couple of centuries before Columbus threaded these islands in 1492. A Lucayan Indian burial ground is located in the world's largest underground system of limestone caves in what is now **Lucayan National Park.** Descendants of slaves still live on Grand Bahama; the Lucayans were wiped out by disease and hardships brought on by the European expeditions.

Like many other Bahamian islands, Grand Bahama has plenty of quiet pleasures. On its East End are idyllic, unpopulated beaches with names like **Fortune Beach** and **Barbary Beach.** (Of course, if you prefer beaches with a little more action, head to the island's southwest

Lucayan National Park.

coast to popular spots like **Xanadu Beach.**) In **Lucayan National Park,** on the island's north coast, wooden walkways lead through a mangrove swamp to one of The Bahamas' most beautiful beaches, **Gold Rock Beach.** It's a stretch of sand that reaches far into clear, shallow waters, with stingrays painting fleeting shadows on the waves. Even amid the bustle of Freeport you can discover the soul of The Bahamas, in the local straw crafts sold at the **Port Lucaya Marketplace** and the infectious *goombay* music played at Junkanoo celebrations and parades. —*AF*

ⓘ www.bahamas.com.

✈ Nassau (New Providence Island).

🛏 $$$ **Old Bahama Bay,** West End (✆ **242/350-6500;** www.oldbahamabay.com). $$ **Pelican Bay at Lucaya,** Seahorse Rd., Lucaya (✆ **242/373-9550;** www.pelicanbayhotel.com).

Aquatic Playgrounds 6

Isla Todos Santos

Surf's Up!

Mexico

Uninhabited but for shorebirds, sea lions, and harbor seals, tiny Isla Todos Santos is an oasis of peace and serenity in the Bay of Ensenada off Baja's Pacific coast. Just offshore is another story: Here in the cold, clear waters, the surf spits out monster 15m-high (49-ft.) waves during winter swells. The prime reef break is "Killers," where waves can reach heights of 18m (59 ft.) and over. It's found at the northwest tip of the island.

Actually two islands, Sur and Norte, Isla Todos Santos, located 97km (60 miles) below the California/Mexico border, has become such a major spot for giant waves that it has drawn big-time competitions, such as those leading up to the **Billabong XXL Global Big Wave awards** (www.billabongxxl.com), considered the Oscars of big-wave surfing. The surfing world has come a long way since the goofy, giddy days of the famous Windansea Surf Club, formed in the early 1960s by a community of surfers from La Jolla, California. It was this group of surfing fanatics who first discovered, in their *Endless Summer* quests for the perfect wave, the monsters at Isla Todos Santos.

Why such huge waves in a spot where every other nearby beach has waves half the size? Like the perfect storm, the perfect wave is dependent on a number of factors. Surfers say that at Isla Todos Santos, the reef points directly into the mouth of the swells, and a deep underwater canyon works to double the size of any wave that comes its way.

Once the site of abalone farms, the island now has a lovely cove and is also a favorite spot for kayakers, who paddle the bay in the company of dolphins and the occasional whale. **Humboats Kayak Adventures,** in Eureka (✆ **52/707/443-5157;** www.humboats.com), offers combo camping/kayaking expeditions to Isla Todos Santos. Nature rules here, with superb tide-pooling, stargazing, and watching the occasional migrating gray whale cruise by. The fishing is pretty impressive here, too, with exceptional catches of large bonito, rock cod, whitefish, and yellowtail. For fishing expeditions, contact **Ensenada Sportfishing Works** (✆ **52/646/156-5151;** www.ensenadasportfishingworks.com), which offers day and overnight trips and leaves from Ensenada, 19km (12 miles) away.

The island's pristine state can be directly tied to its inaccessibility: Isla Todos Santos can be reached only by boat. (Don't confuse Isla Todos Santos, the island, with Todos Santos, the town—the latter is a coastal town located on the Pacific Coast side of the Baja California peninsula.) And if you come to surf, know that you don't just walk off the beach and catch a wave at Isla Todos Santos—in most cases, you need to be towed to the big reef breaks. If you don't have a boat, you can rent out a *panga* (skiff) with a driver in Ensenada. You can also get information on boats leaving for the island by visiting the **San Miguel Surf Shop,** Avenida López Mateos between Gastelum and Miramar, Ensenada (✆**52/646/178-1007**). Here you can get local surf reports and rent longboards, shortboards, and wet suits (you'll need the last in the frigid waters). *—AF*

ⓘ www.visitmexico.com.

✈ Tijuana or Ensenada (airport being built at press time).

⛴ Ensenada (19km/12 miles).

🛏 $$$ **Casa Natalie,** Carretera Tijuana-Ensenada Km 103.3, Ensenada (✆ **888/562-8254** in the U.S., or 52/646/174-7373; www.casanatalie.com).

7 Aquatic Playgrounds

Marco Island

Mangrove Magic

Ten Thousand Islands, Florida, U.S.

On the map, the southern Gulf Coast of Florida almost looks like it's dissolving into the sea, with a maze of inlets and channels shattering the land into thousands of tiny islands. The largest mass, Marco Island is anchored to the mainland by an extension of Naples's Collier Boulevard, arcing over the water just enough to let boats skim underneath. Even Marco looks half-waterlogged because it's bisected by so many man-made canals.

Marco Island is the gateway to the Ten Thousand Islands, many of them wildlife preserves teeming with dolphins, manatees, shorebirds, alligators, and the elusive Florida panther. Runaway real-estate development in the 1960s turned Marco itself into a condo-packed haven for snowbirds from the Northeast, but what it lacks in historic charm, Marco makes up for in sports options. Granted, most Marcoites—residents as well as visitors—seem content to lounge in front of the high-rise resorts that line the island's **3½-mile-long (5.6km) crescent of sugar-sand beach,** waiting for spectacular sunset views. But boaters and fishermen know that with just a little exploring, you can rediscover what made this island such a draw in the first place.

Game fishing is one of Marco's strong points, whether you go for tarpon, redfish, pompano, and snapper in the islands' calm backwaters, or head out into the Gulf for deep-water prey like grouper, king mackerel, barracuda, and cobia. Show up at the **Marco River Marina,** 951 Bald Eagle Dr. (✆ **877/864-0588** or 239/394-2502; www.marcoriver.com), or the **Cedar Bay Marina,** 725 Elkcam Circle (✆ 239/642-6717; www.cedarbayrentals.com), to rent boats or charter fishing tours; or reserve ahead of time with **Sunshine Tours** (✆ **239/642-5415;** www.sunshinetoursmarcoisland.com), **Six Chuter Charters** (✆ **239/389-1575;** www.sixchutercharters.com), or **Marco Island Sea Excursions** (✆ **239/642-6400;** www.seaexcursions.com).

To penetrate into the heart of the Ten Thousands Islands, however, kayaking or canoeing is your best bet. Just north of Marco Island, there's a self-guided canoe trail around Rookery Bay at the Southwest Florida Conservancy's excellent **Briggs Nature Center,** on Shell Island Road, off Fla. 951 between U.S. 41 and Marco Island (✆ **239/775-8569;** www.conservancy.org), which also has a half-mile boardwalk trail through a pristine example of Florida's disappearing scrublands. At **Collier-Seminole State Park,** east of Marco Island off U.S. 41 (✆ **239/394-3397;** www.floridastateparks.org/Collier-Seminole), you can rent canoes to explore a 13½-mile (22km) canoe trail along the twisting mangrove-lined Blackwater River. For more experienced canoers and kayakers, there's the **Paradise Coast Blueway,** a network of paddling routes marked via GPS waypoints from Everglades City, at the tip of Everglades National Park, up the coast to the fishing village of Goodland, just southeast of Marco Island. Along the route, you'll pass through the mangrove estuary of the **10,000 Islands National Wildlife Refuge** (✆ **239/353-8442;** www.fws.gov/refuges/profiles/index.cfm?id=41555) and the orchid-draped cypress slough of **Fakahatchee Strand State Preserve** (✆ **239/695-4593;** www.floridastateparks.org/fakahatcheestrand), where rangers occasionally lead guided canoe trips. This is what Florida looked like before the condos sprouted, and you'll have it all to yourself. *—HH*

ⓘ **Marco Island Area Chamber of Commerce,** 1102 N. Collier Blvd. (✆ **800/788-6272** or 239/394-7549; www.marcoislandchamber.org).

✈ Naples.

15-mile/24km drive from Naples.

$ **Boat House Motel,** 1180 Edington Place (✆ **800/528-6345** or 239/642-2400; www.theboathousemotel.com). $$ **Olde Marco Inn & Suites,** 100 Palm St. (✆ **877/475-3466** or 239/394-3131; www.oldemarcoinn.com).

Aquatic Playgrounds **8**

Vieques Island

Glow-in-the Dark Swimming

Puerto Rico, U.S.

It's almost like something out of a horror movie—the eerie blue-green glow of the waters around you, responding to every flitting fish and swirling oar. But far from being some ghastly chemical calamity, the phosphorescence of Vieques Bay is a 100% natural phenomenon, and one you have to see to believe.

A beach on Vieques Island.

In 2003, the U.S. Navy closed its installation on the island of Vieques (pronounced Bee-*ay*-kase), off the coast of Puerto Rico, and since then Vieques has begun to boom as an ecofriendly—and still charmingly scruffy—destination. With some 40 palm-lined white-sand beaches, and reefs of antler coral offshore, Vieques—7 miles (11km) off the big island's east coast, only an hour by ferry—has an obvious sand-and-sun appeal. For years, Vieques has been where Puerto Ricans go to get away from the tourists on the main island. Snorkeling, kayaking, and fishing (both spin casting and fly-fishing) are hugely popular here, and the waterfront of the island's main town, **Isabel Segunda,** is lined with watersports operators, all of whom seem to be related to one another and cheerfully share business. That small-town casualness is one of the island's strongest appeals.

On the south coast, the panoramic crescent of **Sun Bay (Sombe) public beach** is a longtime favorite, located near the pretty fishing village of Esperanza, where several watersports outfitters have shops as well. But since the Navy moved out, the beautiful white sands of **Red Beach (Bahia Corcha)** and **Blue Beach (Bahia de la Chiva)** have been opened to the public as well, as part of the huge **Vieques National Wildlife Refuge** (office on Rd. 200, Km 0.4; ✆ **787/741-2138**). The refuge is also a prime destination for superb bird-watching; endangered species such as the sea turtle, the manatee, and the brown pelican inhabit its mangrove wetlands and sea-grass beds.

Vieques's most unique feature is **Mosquito Bay,** just west of Isabel Segunda. It's nicknamed Phosphorescent Bay for the way its waters glow in the dark, thanks to millions of tiny bioluminescent organisms called pyrodiniums (translation from science-speak: "whirling fire"). They're only about one-five-hundredths of an inch in size, but when these tiny swimming creatures are disturbed, they dart away and light up like fireflies, leaving blue-white trails of phosphorescence, clearly

Island Hopping the Turks & Caicos: Barefoot Luxury

Overnight, it seems, this sun-kissed archipelago has become synonymous with tropical island luxury. A nation of low-lying coral islands just below The Bahamas, the TCI seemed content to be a laid-back place where you could soak up the sun and sip a sudsy Turks Head beer in a ramshackle beach shack. Sure, beach bums and divers already knew about these islands: The dry, flat scrubland terrain may be fairly underwhelming, but there was no way those turquoise seas, rich marine life, and luscious white-sand beaches could go unnoticed. It wasn't until the 1990s, however, that the Turks & Caicos took on a new persona. That's when a newly elected government opened its doors to development of the high-end variety. Today on the island of Providenciales, the 19km (12 miles) of **Grace Bay Beach,** the country's most famous stretch of sand, has a lineup of luxury resorts, each one the last word in barefoot luxury. And though said government is gone—its premier forced to resign amid allegations of corruption that included being perhaps a little *too* helpful to developers—the islands have emerged as one of the region's top destinations.

In spite of the ramped-up development, this British Protectorate has managed to retain its laid-back, "no worries" feel; even the upscale resorts have absorbed the warm, wry TCI outlook—no attitude here, thank you. If you're looking for scintillating nightlife—bone-rattling discos, say—you'll be sorely disappointed. On the TCI, the low-key beach-shack-and-cold-beer ethos still reigns. Most visitors island-hop by puddle jumper, although you can charter a boat (pricey) to get from one Caicos island to another, and a ferry runs between Provo and North Caicos, weather depending. This is not to say that visitors can't get their fill of outdoor thrills. You can scuba-dive a vertical undersea wall where the continental shelf drops a heart-stopping mile deep, swim alongside humpback whales and stingrays, cast a line for bonefish, or free-dive 6m (20 ft.) to the sea bottom for fresh conch. **Big Blue Unlimited** (✆ **649/946-5034;** www.bigblueunlimited.com) is one of the islands' top outfitters for watersports; they also offer kayaking eco-tours into North and Middle Caicos.

Here is what you *won't* experience on the Turks & Caicos islands: You won't hear the roar of jet skis or an army of motorboats—the shallow coral reef is part of a protected national park. You won't spend your beach time stepping over sunbathers packed like sardines or fending off pushy hucksters. But if you dream of lying on a parcel of sugary sand encircled by emerald seas, or want nothing more than to spend your days bubbling about a splendid coral reef with mask and snorkel, this is the place for you.

Grace Bay beach lies on the northeast coastline of 98-sq.-km (38-sq.-mile) ❾ **Providenciales (Provo),** the archipelago's most developed island. This is where the action is, with the bulk of the country's lodging, dining, tours, and activities. Still, don't expect a bustling metropolis: Provo remains sleepier than most other Caribbean islands; that's a big part of its charm. The ❿ **Caicos Cays,** also called the Leeward Cays, are gorgeous little spits of sand. Some of these former pirate lairs are now private islands with secluded resorts; others are uninhabited except by day-trippers beachcombing and snorkeling the shallows. Beach cruises among the cays is one of the TCI's most popular activities; **Silver Deep** (✆ **649/946-5612;** www.silverdeep.com) offers a range of excursions that let you snorkel, swim, fish, or hunt for sand dollars.

The projected site of the second TCI boom is ⓫ **North Caicos;** it has lovely secluded beaches and lush tidal flats. A causeway now links North to ⓬ **Middle Caicos,** the largest island in the Turks & Caicos. Middle has a remarkably varied landscape. Soft green slopes overlook beautiful **Mudjin Harbor,** where you can snorkel in bottle-green shallows. **Crossing Place Trail** is a raised 18th-century pathway named for the shallow sandbar that connects Middle and North at low tide. At **Bambarra Beach** the sunlit aquamarine waters stretch long into the horizon. ⓭ **South Caicos,** a still-sleepy fishing community of some 1,200 people, is hearing faint rumblings of tourist development. With its excellent diving and bonefishing opportunities and historic Bermudan-style architecture, "Big South" is an up-and-coming spot.

Separating the Caicos archipelago from the two Turks islands, to the east, is the **Turks Island Passage,** also known as the Columbus Passage. Christopher Columbus sailed into the New World via this waterway, and many historians believe the explorer made landfall on the island of ⓮ **Grand Turk.** Today this small gem of an island, the nation's capital and the keeper of the country's rich heritage, is recovering from a devastating 2008 hurricane. Still standing are the 150-year-old lighthouse, 19th-century Bermudian homes, and abandoned salinas from the salt-raking era. Grand Turk is one of the world's great diving spots, where the dramatically steep "wall" of the continental shelf lies just minutes from shore. **Blue Water Divers** (✆ **649/946-2432;** www.grandturkscuba.com) is one of the area's top dive operators. You can swim in the shallow water with stingrays at nearby ⓯ **Gibbs Cay.**

If getting away from it all is your bottom line, head to tiny ⓰ **Salt Cay** (pop. 60), little more than a spit of sand in turquoise seas. Salt Cay is missing many of the basic accouterments of 21st-century civilization, like ATMs and cars, but don't be fooled by its modest demeanor: People come from around the world to snorkel, dive, and whale-watch in the luminescent green seas and to comb its secluded beaches for flotsam and jetsam. Salt Cay is admittedly small (6.5 sq. km/2½ sq. miles), but it is a place of haunting beauty and enormous heart. —*AF*

ⓘ **Turks & Caicos Tourist Board,** Stubbs Diamond Plaza, Providenciales (✆ **800/241-0824** in the U.S. or 649/946-4970; www.turksandcaicostourism.com).

✈ Providenciales International Airport.

🛏 $$$ **Grace Bay Club,** Providenciales (✆ **800/946-5757** in the U.S., or 649/946-5050; www.gracebayclub.com). $$$ **Parrot Cay** (✆ **877/754-0726** in the U.S., or 649/946-7788; www.parrotcay.como.bz).

discernible on a cloudy, moonless night. (***Note:*** Don't come here during a full moon—you'll see almost nothing.) You can swim in these glowing waters, a sensation that's incredibly cool. **Island Adventures** (✆ **787/741-0720;** www.biobay.com) operates 2-hour nighttime trips in Phosphorescent Bay; you can get even closer to those glow-in-the-dark waters on a nighttime kayak tour offered by **Blue Caribe Kayak** (✆ **787/741-2522;** www.enchanted-isle.com/bluecaribe). —*HH*

ⓘ www.enchanted-isle.com.

✈ Vieques.

Isabel Segunda (1¼ hr. from Fajardo, Puerto Rico).

$$ **The Crow's Nest,** Rte. 201, Barrio, FL (✆ **877/CROWS-NEST** [276-9763] or 787/741-0033; www.crowsnestvieques.com). $$ **Trade Winds Guesthouse,** Calle Flamboyan 107, Esperanza (✆ **787/741-8666;** www.enchanted-isle.com/tradewinds).

Life's a Beach 17

Isla Partida & Isla Espíritu Santo

Paradise in the Sea of Cortez

Mexico

There are beautiful beaches, and then there are beaches that literally take your breath away: Pristine coastal ecosystems where the living inhabitants—here, dolphins, manta rays, seals, and more—are in such elegant sync with their environment that they seem almost airbrushed into the picture. Set inside a quarter-moon crescent of sand ringed by honeycombed cliffs, **Ensenada Grande** is all that and more.

With lusciously clear cerulean seas, Ensenada Grande is just one of several magnificent beaches fronting the Sea of Cortez on **Isla Partida,** an uninhabited, completely uncommercialized island on Mexico's Baja California Sur coast, and its bigger sister island **Isla Espiritu Santo,** also uninhabited and owned by the Nature Conservancy. The two islands are connected by a mere sandbar, and are UNESCO Biospheres. Most itineraries encompass both islands.

Both Isla Partida and Isla Espíritu Santo offer superb, unspoiled beaches and some of the Western Hemisphere's most exceptional sea kayaking, snorkeling, and wildlife-watching opportunities. The conditions are pristine—it's basically you and the sea, sky, and sand. The good news is that it looks like things will stay that way. The Sea of Cortez, also known as the Bay of California, has protected UNESCO World Heritage Site status. The bay contains an astonishing 39% of the world's total number of species of marine mammals and a third of the world's marine cetacean species. As for the islands, both are UNESCO Biosphere reserves.

The best way to see Partida and Espirito Santo islands is on a guided boat trip or island safari, with opportunities to camp out on the islands under the stars. A number of solid tour guides operate out of La Paz, the capital of the state of Baja California Sur—a 2-hour boat ride away from the islands. **Baja Quest** (✆ **52/612/123-5320;** www.bajaquest.com.mx) offers 3- to 5-night sea kayaking and camping expeditions to Espiritu Santo, with lots of time built in for snorkeling the waters and exploring the islands. **Sea & Adventures** (✆ **800/355-7140** in the U.S. or 52/612/123-0559; www.kayakbaja.com) also offers kayaking and camping trips to Espiritu Santo with expert guides.

Baja Camp (www.bajacamp.com) operates overnight camping stays in big, comfortable tents on one of Espiritu Santo's most beautiful beaches, **Ensenada del Candelero,** from June through September out of the marina at La Paz. You can kayak or swim alongside sea lions and seals, snorkel amid manta rays and sharks, and fish for your dinner—a gourmet chef will prepare it for you as you relax with your feet in the sand in a beachside tent, watching the last sunbeams of the day pirouette on the sparkling bay. —*AF*

(i) www.explorebajasur.com.

La Paz.

2-hr. ride from La Paz.

$ **Hotel Mediteranne,** Allende 36, La Paz (✆ **52/612/125-1195;** www.hotelmed.com). $$ **La Concha Beach Resort,** Carretera a Pichilingue Km 5 (✆ **52/612/121-6161;** www.laconcha.com).

18 Life's a Beach

Grand Cayman

Easy Fun Under the Caribbean Sun

Cayman Islands

It's cleaner, safer, and more organized than many other islands in the turquoise Caribbean sea, and if there's one drawback to this state of affairs on Grand Cayman island, it's that you might wonder why you've come all this way for somewhere about as exotic as . . . your own backyard. However, if you're looking for a vacation with reliable sunshine, tropical-cliche beaches, and amazing undersea exploration, in a place that's fun and family-friendly, you could do a lot worse than Grand Cayman. Though Hurricane Ivan inflicted serious damage here in 2004, the rebuilding of the island was an excuse to make some much-needed improvements to many facilities, and Grand Cayman is looking better than ever.

Surrounded by coral reefs and dramatic drop-offs in all directions and endowed with perpetually warm and clear waters, Grand Cayman is a major diving and snorkeling destination—it's said to be the birthplace of recreational Caribbean diving; scuba pioneer Bob Soto opened the island's first dive shop in 1957. What's especially nice is that most sites, marked by moorings in the water, are easily accessible right from the beach—there's no need to spend a bunch of money on boat dive trips. If you do want something organized and guide-accompanied, look no further than the excellent **Red Sail Sports** (✆ **345/945-5965;** www.redsailcayman.com), which has locations all over Grand Cayman. In fact, Red Sail is your one-stop shop for just about every activity under the sun or on the waves: If it's a watersport, they'll either rent you the equipment or take you out for an excursion.

Beach going on Grand Cayman is practically synonymous with spreading your towel and soaking up the scene on the sugary sands of **Seven Mile Beach.** Not only is this the most intrinsically spectacular beach on the island, but it's also where all the action is. Parasailing and jet-skiing are only the tip of the iceberg when it comes to the water-based fun here—the sea is shallow and inviting all along the beach, and you can rent ocean kayaks, aqua trikes, view boards, paddle cats, and paddleboats to explore at your leisure. The calm conditions make this an ideal

Diving in Grand Cayman.

place to teach little ones how to snorkel. After a day playing in the surf and sand, take your pick from the dozens of bars and restaurants (most attached to hotels, which welcome nonguests at their dining facilities) that line the beach.

Other notable beaches on Grand Cayman are **Cemetery Reef** (great for snorkeling), **Smith Cove** (a diminutive strip of sand perfect for swimming and a quiet picnic), and remote **Rum Point,** an oasis of Caribbean seclusion with lots of shady palms and an atmospheric beach cafe.

The classic Cayman wildlife encounter is **Stingray City,** a shallow, open-water site about 3km (1¾ miles) east of the island's northwestern tip where you can dive among and feed near-domesticated stingrays. (Book an excursion through Red Sail Sports or any of the touts on Seven Mile Beach.) It's thrilling, though certainly not without its risks: The animals are not normally aggressive, but they still possess dangerous stingers. —*SM*

ⓘ www.caymanislands.ky.

✈ Grand Cayman–Owen Roberts International.

🛏 $$ **Beach Club Colony Hotel & Dive Resort,** 719 W. Bay Rd., Seven Mile Beach (✆ **345/949-8100;** www.beachclubcolony.ky). $$$ **The Ritz-Carlton,** W. Bay Rd. (✆ **800/241-3333** in the U.S. and Canada or 345/943-9000; www.ritzcarlton.com).

Life's a Beach 19

Anguilla

Love Shack

On my first visit to Anguilla, I was ready to be wowed. This was Anguilla, after all, island of posh resorts and fabulous beaches, and playground of the rich and famous. But once I got off the ferry I felt . . . underwhelmed. Where was the glamour, the pizazz? All I saw were goats munching dry scrub brush, sandy roads with no stoplights, and a flat, dull horizon of *more* scrub brush. Once I arrived at my unprepossessing inn, a place that had obviously seen better days, I felt my heart sinking. It was time to hit the beach, for better or worse.

The sand was blindingly white, the sea a transparent blue. Fronting the beach was a shady stand of palm trees. A lone dog tripped down the beach. Otherwise, the wide, curving strand was empty: no touts, no hawkers, no jet skis buzzing, no radios blaring. Just powdery sand, sparkling turquoise seas, and a goofy-looking dog making his merry way along . . . *one of the most beautiful beaches I've ever seen.* It was noon, I had been in Anguilla all of 1 hour, and it was the start of a full-blown love affair.

Anguilla is many things: It's justly famous for its laid-back luxury hideaways on stunning beaches, with some of the priciest rooms in the region. A British dependency, having been colonized by English settlers in the 17th century, it's also an old-fashioned sort of place, with a modest and unassuming but well-educated, tightly knit community of some 14,000 people. The influence of the Christian Council has successfully kept cruise ships, casinos, and other potential bogeymen at bay. You won't see bus loads of camera-toting visitors being led from one attraction to another. Frankly, Anguilla has few attractions to begin with—if you can call a handful of rickety old colonial relics scattered about "attractions." The Valley, the island's main center, has full-service banks and grocery stores, but it's not a charmer to tour, like Gustavia on neighboring St. Barts 260, which competes with Anguilla for the title of poshest Caribbean island. The landscape is typical coral and limestone; flat, dry scrubland with low-lying salt ponds; and a few hills for panoramic views.

You hit scenic gold when you get to the beaches. Most of the best (Barnes, Maundays, Meads, Rendezvous Bay, Shoal Bay West) are on the west end of the island. **Rendezvous Bay** is a long, curving ribbon of satiny, pale-gold sand that stretches along the bay for 4km (2½ miles). In the northeast, 3km (1¾-mile) **Shoal Bay** is Anguilla's most popular beach, with powder-soft sands and a lively beach bar scene.

The hook—if Anguilla has a "hook" other than wonderful beaches and correspondingly fine watersports activities—is the island's ultracasual, ultrainclusive, sublimely pleasurable **beach shack scene.** Anguilla has some of the finest restaurants in the Caribbean, but if you want to chill out the barefoot way over barbecue and mellow reggae, hit the beach. Even the most uptight financial-services nerd will feel his backbone slip watching a fine Anguilla sunset with his feet in the sand, a beer in the hand, and a grilled lobster smoking on the coals. I don't think I've ever seen anything quite like the **Dune Preserve** (✆ **264/497-2660**). Owned by reggae star and Anguilla native Bankie Banx, the oceanfront bar/restaurant is a beehive of salvaged boats and beach detritus. At Upper Shoal Bay, check out **Gwen's Reggae Bar & Grill** (✆ **264/497-2120**), where Gwen Webster serves barbecued chicken in a shady palm grove with hammocks. Uncle Ernie died in 2007, but a photograph of him watches over the action at **Uncle Ernie's** (✆ **264/497-3907**) on Shoal Bay, where you can get chicken and ribs and cold Red Stripe beer. Down a bumpy road to Junk's Hole is Nat Richardson's **Palm Grove Restaurant** (✆ **264/497-4224**). There you can snorkel in warm, clear seas until your lobster comes off the grill. Some say this is where Brad and Jennifer bid each other adieu. Romance may be fleeting, after all, but true love—we're talking mine for Anguilla—is here to stay. *—AF*

ⓘ **Anguilla Tourist Board** (✆ **264/497-2759;** www.anguilla-vacation.com).

✈ St. Maarten (Princess Juliana International Airport; 16km/10 miles). Small commuter airlines fly into Anguilla's Wallblake Airport from St. Thomas, San Juan, and Antigua.

⛴ Public ferries run between Marigot Bay, St. Martin, and Blowing Point, Anguilla (✆ **264/497-6070**); or privately run charter boats and ferries deliver passengers between Anguilla and the airport in St. Maarten.

🛏 $$$ **CuisinArt Resort,** Rendezvous Bay (✆ **800/943-3210** in the U.S. and Canada or 264/498-2000; www.cuisinartresort.com). $$ **Frangipani Beach Resort,** Meads Bay (✆ **866/780-5165** in the U.S. and Canada or 264/497-6442; www.frangipaniresort.com).

Life's a Beach 20

Ilha de Santa Catarina

Sizzle in Floripa

Brazil

If you're looking for the hottest beach scene on the planet these days, you may want to bypass Miami, San Juan, and Ibiza 246 and head straight to Brazil. Santa Catarina Island (Ilha de Santa Catarina), aka the island of Florianópolis, has become one of the most popular destinations in Brazil, with miles and miles of gorgeous beaches offering world-class surfing.

First, what's the difference between Santa Catarina, Florianópolis, and Floripa? **Florianópolis** the city is the capital of the state of Santa Catarina, about a 1-hour flight from Säo Paolo. Half of the city is also located on the island of Santa Catarina. Island and city together are just referred to as Florianópolis, which people often shorten to Floripa. Floripa is easily accessed via a bridge from the mainland.

Much of Floripa's appeal has to do with its 42—yes, 42—beaches, not a stinker in the bunch. The north end of the island is made up of modern resorts and calm waters; it's an urbanized, heavily touristed beach scene, particularly in the high summer months of December, January, and February. Yet even amid all the action, the beaches are perfectly swimmable, even picturesque. If you like your beaches less trammeled, check out **Santinho,** a quieter spot on the rocky northern coast with a beautiful, expansive beach, the island's only five-star resort, and a quaint village.

Farther south in the center of the island, the **Lagoa da Conceição** is a large lagoon wrapped in sand dune and verdant vegetation. Nearby, the quiet little community of **Lagoa da Conceição** boasts some of the best restaurants in the region. **Barra de Lagoa** has vintage fishing-village charm, more good beaches, and **del Morro de Barra,** a lovely section of town linked by a lagoon (crossed by a hanging bridge) where no cars are allowed. Just to the east are the spectacular beaches of **Galeta, Mole,** and **Joaquina**—wide, sandy strands enveloped in verdant green hills and blessed with large, surfable waves. Mole is a happening hangout for gorgeous bodies and skimpy swimsuits. Lovely Galeta doesn't even bother with the suits: It's the island's only clothing-optional beach.

Farther south toward **Campeche,** the handsome beaches become more rugged and the rolling waves are like catnip to surfers—and the partying goes well into the night here. To the west side of the island facing the mainland, the quaint Azorean fishing village of **Riberão da Ilha** is accessible only via a narrow, winding seaside road with views of the Bahia Sul and the lush hills of the mainland across the bay.

Wherever you are, you won't be far from restaurants and cafes offering delicious regional seafood. Local *camarão* (shrimp) figure prominently on menus, as do local oysters, farmed right here in the seas around Riberão da Ilha. —*AF*

(i) www.braziltour.com.

✈ Florianópolis International Airport.

Rodoviaria buses link Florianópolis with every major city in southern Brazil (✆ **55/48/3222-2260;** www.rodoviariasbr.com.br).

🛏 **Pousade Penareia,** Rua Hermes Guedes da Fonseca 207 (✆ **55/48/3338-1616;** www.pousadapenareia.com.br). $$ **Praia Mole Eco Village,** Estrada Geral da Barra da Lagoa 2001 (✆ **55/48/3239-7500;** www.praiamole.com.br).

21 Life's a Beach

Sanibel Island

Seashells, Seashells, by the Seashore

Florida, U.S.

I'm the sort of beachgoer who could spend the entire day walking up and down the strand, searching for seashells—in fact, once I get started, I hardly notice anything else. Maybe it's because I'm a Midwesterner, but I still get a ridiculous thrill out of finding shells in the sand, even relatively common things like whelks, olives, scallops, sand dollars, and conch. And I've never found a better place to indulge this obsession than down on the Gulf Coast of Florida, where a little apostrophe of coastal keys, attached by a long causeway to Fort Myers, offers the most amazing concentration of seashells I've ever seen.

Sanibel Island is a superb beach destination for other reasons, too—fine sugary white sand and healthy stands of palm trees, the local curbs on high-rises and tacky development, the amount of land devoted to wildlife refuges—but I'll freely admit that it was the shells I went for, and they did not disappoint. Some 200 species of shells can be found on Sanibel's wide, placid beaches. Prime time for shell hunting is February to April or after any storm; low tide is the best time of day. Shells can be sharp, so wear Aqua Socks or old running shoes whenever you go walking on the beach. Just make sure to peer into the shell to check whether living creatures are still inside—Florida law prohibits taking live shells from the beaches.

Shoot, there's even a shell museum here: the **Bailey-Matthews Shell Museum,** 3075 Sanibel-Captiva Rd. (✆**888/679-6450** or 239/395-2233; www.shellmuseum.org), devoted solely to saltwater, freshwater, and land shells. Shells

Fishing on Sanibel Island.

from as far away as South Africa surround a 6-ft. (1.8m) globe in the main exhibit hall, showing their geographic origins. Most important for my purpose, though, was the *Wheel of Fortune*–shaped case identifying shells likely to wash up on Sanibel.

To find really rare shells, you can always head for the adjacent shoals and nearby small islands; **Captiva Cruises** (✆ **239/472-5300;** www.captivacruises.com) runs shelling trips, departing from the South Seas Resort on nearby Captiva Island, and several charter-boat skippers also will take guests on shelling expeditions (you can find several of them at the Sanibel Marina on North Yachtsman Dr., off Periwinkle Way east of Causeway Blvd.). Maybe next time I'll get around to that—I'll just need an extra suitcase to tote all my treasures home. —*HH*

ⓘ **Tourist information,** 1159 Causeway Rd. (✆ **239/472-1080;** www.sanibel-captiva.org).

✈ Fort Myers International (14 miles/23km).

5-mile (8km) drive on Sanibel Causeway (FL 867) from Fort Myers.

$ **Palm View Motel,** 706 Donax St. (✆ **877/472-1606** or 239/472-1606; www.palmviewsanibel.com). $$$ **Sundial Beach Resort,** 1451 Middle Gulf Dr. (✆ **866/565-5093;** www.sundialresort.com).

Life's a Beach **22**

Green Island

Coral Cay Paradise

Australia

Reportedly, the local aboriginal population regarded this 6,000-year-old island as *wunjami*—a place haunted by spirits, to be avoided if possible. But those days are long gone: Reachable by a 45-minute catamaran ride from the mainland city of Cairns, this gorgeous, 15-hectare (37-acre) coral cay island has become a favorite destination for Aussie day-trippers, who come to enjoy the sun, sand, and flora and fauna. Located 27km (17 miles) off the coast of Queensland, Australia, in the middle of the Great Barrier Reef Marine Park, Green Island offers natural beauty—in addition to its spectacular beaches and reefs, it's the only one of the Great Barrier Reef's 300 sand cays with its own rainforest—and some of the world's best snorkeling and scuba diving right off the beach.

Green Island has always emphasized ecofriendly tourism, dating back to its designation as a national park in 1936. Today, it teems with tropical birds, more than 120 species of native plants, and all manner of marine life, from the fish that inhabit the coral gardens ringing the island to the **Marineland Melanesia Aquarium, Museum and Crocodile Farm** (✆ **61/7/4051 4032**), where you can have hands-on encounters with sea turtles and the smallest of the establishment's 30-odd crocs. **Glass-bottom-boat tours** are a specialty here—in fact, Green Island is thought to have been the first place on earth to employ this boating innovation—and the island also boasts the world's oldest underwater observatory. For those inclined to immerse themselves in the surrounding sea, snorkeling and scuba gear can be rented, and diving boat trips to the nearby Great Barrier Reef itself are also available.

Insiders know that the true Green Island experience begins after the last ferry leaves the island at 4:30 each afternoon. Then, the overnight guests of **Green**

Island Resort—the island's sole hotel, as well as the only five-star resort in Queensland—have the little island to themselves. The resort features 46 luxury suites set in the midst of the island's rainforest, and a stay grants access to the underwater observatory, windsurfing, canoeing and snorkeling equipment, a glass-bottom-boat tour, and a guided nighttime nature tour. Scuba instruction and certification is also offered. Guests of the resort can have a great time just exploring on their own, though, as they're given the run of an island with a circumference that can be walked in a little under an hour. In addition to the marine life, guests give particularly high marks to the sunset, the empty stretches of beach, and the opportunity to spot offshore fish feeding at twilight—an event that sharks have been known to attend.

If you're not staying on the resort, you can still visit the island on a day trip—a number of tour operators offer boat trips that include stops on the island. **Great Adventures** (✆ **1800/673-366** or 61/7/4044 9944; www.greatadventures.com.au)—owned by Quicksilver, the same company that owns Green Island Resort—runs day tours to Green Island from Cairns.

With Sydney a good 4 hours away by plane and boat, Green Island remains a bit off the beaten track. And if you're lucky enough to claim the island for your own, you may find yourself hoping the rest of the world heeds the old aboriginal legends and keeps away—at least for a night or two. —*AF*

ⓘ www.destinationqueensland.com or www.queensland.com.sg.

✈ Cairns (4 hr. from Auckland).

45-min. ride from Cairns.

$$$ **Green Island Resort** (✆**1800/673-366** or 61/7/4052 1511; www.greenislandresort.com.au).

23 Unvarnished & Unspoiled

Phu Quoc

Wild & Pungent

Vietnam

There are plenty of island paradises in Southeast Asia (like Bali 201 and Koh Samui 302, to name a few) that have been discovered by Western tourists, but Phu Quoc is not one of them—for now, anyway. Just west of mainland Vietnam in the Gulf of Thailand, this island falls squarely in the category of "go now" destinations around the globe. Resort developers and Vietnamese tourism authorities are grooming Phu Quoc to be the next big ecotourism vacation spot in Southeast Asia. But until modern infrastructure arrives, Phu Quoc is a superauthentic island getaway, where luxury hotels are still very affordable and golf courses are nonexistent, and where touring is done by moped down dusty red-dirt roads that lead to secluded beaches.

Phu Quoc is best suited to those with a sense of adventure and a love of unvarnished culture. While Phu Quoc has some of the best and least trodden beaches in the region, getting to those unspoiled stretches of sand often means renting a scooter and threading your way down unmarked dirt roads or arranging casual rides with local fishermen or motorists. (Even with prearranged boat or four-wheel-drive tours, you never really know what you're going to get, which is certainly half the fun.) Head for the north and northeast part of the island to find the emptiest, most gorgeous beaches. **Ganh**

Dau Beach even has a view of Cambodia, just 18km (11 miles) away. If you do set out on your own exploration of Phu Quoc, always pack a lunch and plenty of water, though even the smallest towns and quietest beaches usually have some sort of restaurant where you can sample the delicious, seafood-rich island cuisine.

The main town on Phu Quoc is **Duong Dong,** on the west coast of the emerald-shaped island, where the airport, seaport, and most hotels and services are located. **An Thoi,** on the southern coast, is the next town of any size; it's a bit too remote to function as a base, but is close to the pristine white-sand beaches of **Bai Sou** and **Bai Kem.** Sprinkled up and down the coasts of Phu Quoc are smaller, less developed villages where visitors can have a truly genuine encounter with island culture. One is **Cua Can,** interesting for its old wooden bridges and where impromptu tours up the Cua Can River can be arranged with local fishermen. For just about anything water-based, **Famous Tony** organizes tours for individual groups (✆ **84/913/197334;** info@tonyanh.com).

Anywhere you visit on Phu Quoc, you'll need to get used to the island's smell. Because Phu Quoc is one of the premier manufacturers of fish sauce in Vietnam, the scent of dried fish literally permeates every corner of the island. If you're interested in touring one of these factories, the largest is **Hung Thanh** (✆ **84/77/846124;** www.hungthanhfishsauce.com.vn), in Duong Dong. Attempting to transport a souvenir bottle of fish sauce out of Phu Quoc is another story: The airlines have banned them because of the risk of breakage and accompanying stench in the cabin and cargo hold!

Because of its limited transportation connections (you can fly here from Ho Chi Minh City or take a ferry from Rach Gia and Ha Tien, on the west coast of Vietnam), Phu Quoc is usually visited as part of a longer trip to Vietnam and Cambodia. When the new international airport is completed—sometime around 2011—more direct flights from more cities will surely bring a new kind of tourism here. —*SM*

ⓘ www.discoverphuquoc.com.

✈ Duong Dong airport (50 min. from Ho Chi Minh City).

⛴ Duong Dong Express from Rach Gia, 2½ hr. (✆ **84/77/3981648;** www.duongdongexpress.com.vn).

🛏 $$ **Cassia Cottage** (✆ **84/77/3848395;** www.cassiacottage.com). $$$ **Grand Mercure La Veranda** (✆ **84/77/3982988;** www.laverandaresort.com).

Unvarnished & Unspoiled 24

Lombok

Not the Next Bali

Indonesia

Travel writers and tourism board officials in search of catchy tag lines love to compare Lombok to Bali 201, that much more famous Indonesian island 40km (25 miles) to the west: Lombok, they say, is "what Bali was like 30 years ago," or "an unspoiled version of Bali." These descriptions are only partly apt. Lombok is predominantly Muslim, whereas Bali gets much of its distinctive flavor from its unique Hindu traditions. Lombok's geography is quite different, and it's generally much drier here than in Bali.

But unlike Bali's well-developed tourism infrastructure, tourism is in its early stages on Lombok: Despite recent resort development, the overall atmosphere that prevails on Lombok is that of an authentic

Indonesian culture, largely undiscovered but welcoming of outsiders, with some excellent beaches and awesome surfing spots thrown into the mix.

The brooding cone of **Gunung Rinjani** (Mount Rinjani, a 3,726m/12,224-ft. stratovolcano) dominates the profile of Lombok, which is shaped a bit like a stingray whose "tail" trails off to the southwest. Hiking to the top of Rinjani is the favorite pursuit of many backpackers who stay on the Gili Islands, off Lombok's west coast. **Mataram** is the largest city on Lombok, where you'll find fascinating local flavor in the streets and markets but not much in the way of Western tourism. Lombok's hotel strip lies to the north of Mataram in an area called **Senggigi.**

Surfers will want to make a beeline for **Kuta** on the south coast (not to be confused with Bali's übertouristy Kuta Beach), which has some of the best waves in the world. At **Grupuk Beach** (in the Kuta area) swimmers can enjoy the calm waters of the cove, while boarders can take outrigger canoes to the waves beyond the point. The biggest waves are usually at rugged **Seger Beach**, 2km (1¼ miles) from Kuta. Offshore, **snorkeling and diving** opportunities abound, and charter boats that can deliver you to prime dive sites are easy and cheap to organize—Gili Islands–based **Blue Marlin Dive** (✆ **62/370/632424;** www.bluemarlindive.com) is a reliable outfitter.

Lombok's interior of gently rolling hills is filled with rural villages and waterfalls that make for fun and edifying day trips when you need a break from the sun and sand. Arts and crafts collectors will find Lombok immensely satisfying, as the island specializes in pottery, baskets, and woven textiles that are still very affordable. All throughout Lombok, you'll also receive a warm and hospitable reception from locals—and especially children, whose smiles are infectious.

Political unrest in Indonesia in the early 21st century had a dramatic impact on the growth of tourism on Lombok, and it's just now beginning to pick up again, as foreign investors pour millions into luxury resorts and golf courses. My advice is to travel to Lombok now, on the cusp of its tourist boom, before it truly becomes another (overcommercialized) Bali. —*SM*

ⓘ www.lombok-network.com.

✈ Mataram-Selaparang.

⛴ Traditional ferry or fast boat from Bali, 2½–5 hr.

🛏 $$$ **The Oberoi Lombok,** Medana Beach, Tanjung (✆ **62/370/638444;** www.oberoilombok.com). $$ **Qunci Villas,** Jalan Raya Mangsit, Senggigi (✆ **62/370/693800;** www.quncivillas.com).

25 Unvarnished & Unspoiled

Tioman Island

Dragon of the Sea

Malaysia

Legend has it that Tioman Island, 58km (36 miles) off Malaysia's east coast, is actually a dragon princess who stopped here to rest, fell in love with the beauty of the place, and never left. It's a sentiment many visitors share. The largest island in a string of volcanic atolls in the South China Sea, Tioman is indeed shaped like a sleeping dragon. Although it's a treasured destination for many Malaysian vacationers, Tioman is still fairly raw and largely undiscovered, with nowhere near the development of sister Malaysian islands Penang 264 and Langkawi 237, on the country's west coast. The business of tourism is a modest one on Tioman, with one large resort and a smattering of understated lodges, chalets perched in the jungle canopy, and traditional huts set in the sand. The island has no asphalt roads (except in the main town of Tekek) or cars (just bikes and four-wheel-drives)—in fact, the most expeditious way to get around is by hopping a boat from one part of the island to the other. The waters surrounding Tioman are part of the protected **Tioman Marine Park.** A controversial marina project that reportedly cut into the fragile coral reef enveloping the island was allowed to move forward and is now open, and the island has been awarded duty-free status. Little Tioman may be on the verge of a development boom.

Tioman Island first entered the global consciousness when the movie *South Pacific* was filmed here in 1958. In its role as the paradisiacal Bali Ha'i, Tioman was trumpeted as one of the most beautiful islands in the world. It's still spectacularly lovely. Emerald cliffs rise dramatically from pale-sand beaches. The fringing coral reef, gin-clear waters, and balmy year-round water temperatures draw divers and snorkelers from around the world. The snorkeling is especially good—even right off the beaches. One of the best places to snorkel is in **Air Batang,** where you can swim amid coral gardens packed with colorful fish and turtles. **Tioman Dive Centre** (✆ **60/9/419-1228;** www.tioman-dive-centre.com) offers dive and snorkeling trips. Scuba professionals **Dive Asia** (Salang and Tekek; ✆ **60/9/419-5017;** www.diveasia.com.my) offers dive safaris and PADI-certified courses.

For such a relatively small island—it's only 22km long and 11km wide (14×6¾ miles)—Tioman is incredibly diverse, a magnificent hodgepodge of rainforest, mist-shrouded granite spires, mangrove swamp forest, and coral reef. Much of the island interior is tangled jungle vegetation and protected nature reserve. The woods are filled with rare and exotic breeds, including the long-tailed macaque, binturong (Asian bearcat), pythons, and some 138 species of birds. Trekking trails through the steamy jungle interior take in waterfalls, rapids, and natural pools.

Note: November to February is monsoon season, with frequent rain showers and rougher seas. —*AF*

ⓘ **Tourism Malaysia** (✆ **60/3/2615-8188;** www.tourismmalaysia.gov.my).

✈ Tekek Airport (40 min. from Singapore).

⛴ From Tanjung Gemok (1 hr., 15 min.), **Fast Ferry Venture** (✆ **60/9/413-1997**). From Mersing (2 hr.), **Blue Water Express** (✆ **60/7/799-5015**).

🛏 $$ **Berjaya Beach, Golf & Spa Resort,** Tioman Island, Pahang Carul Makmur (✆ **60/9/419-1000;** www.berjayahotels-resorts.com). $$$ **JapaMala Resort** (✆ **60/3/4256-6100;** www.japamalaresorts.com).

Unvarnished & Unspoiled

26

Kamaran Island

Red Sea Reefs

Yemen

Kamaran gets its Arabic name, "two moons," for the unusual double reflection of the moon that it's possible to see, just as the moon is rising in the early evening, in the waters off the northern end of the island. Located at the strategic southern tip of the Red Sea, Kamaran was occupied over the centuries by the Portuguese, the Ottoman Empire, and the British, before being handed over to Yemen in the mid–20th century. Interesting remnants of those eras remain scattered over the island, but Kamaran's most compelling draw for visitors is its excellent diving and opportunities to experience a very traditional way of life, practically untouched by tourism.

Long and thin, 108-sq.-km (42-sq.-mile) Kamaran is a mostly flat shelf of sand and rock, unrelieved by vegetation except for some green pastures in the north where wild camels and deer graze. Look in almost any direction, and the panorama consists of two colors: beige and turquoise. Tawny stone buildings left over from Kamaran's most prosperous era, when the Ottomans used it as a quarantine station for pilgrims on their way to Mecca, blend almost imperceptibly into the backdrop of gently rolling dunes. The island's sparse population is divided among three dusty, yet fascinating and friendly, authentic villages where visitors can mix with friendly locals and sample the delicious (and cheap) typical island food.

The coastline of Kamaran descends into the tantalizing, wildlife-rich waters of the **Red Sea:** It's this embarrassment of undersea vitality, contrasting so starkly with the barren scene on land, that makes a visit here so worthwhile for divers and snorkelers. Kamaran is surrounded on three sides by coral reefs, with dense mangroves taking up the fourth side. While the perimeter of Kamaran itself is riddled with places where you can swim among schools of grouper and rays or explore archaeological remains of the island's previous eras, some of the best dive sites lie off such uninhabited nearby islands as **Zubayr** and **Ogban,** which have endless mazes of coral channels and caves and an awesome spectrum of fish, sea turtles, sharks, and dolphins.

Tourism on Kamaran is decidedly primitive: There are no palm-lined drives, no golf courses, no shopping centers. The only "hotel" on the island is really a camp of sorts, Kamaran Tourist Village (see below). Accommodations are seaside *tihama* huts (mud-and-thatch constructions typical of the Red Sea coast) with traditional cots or western-style beds and mosquito nets. Toilets and showers are in another building a short walk away. By day, the tourist village organizes diving excursions and tours (by donkey or by pickup) of Kamaran's historical sights; by night, communal feasts and performances by traditional local musicians bring guests together in the central *mafraj* (sitting room).

This bare-bones state of affairs seems poised to change soon, however, as Egyptian development companies have recently signed agreements with Yemeni officials to invest $500 million in infrastructure and resort facilities on Kamaran. Until those projects are carried out, for anyone not interested in Red Sea diving, or complete peace and quiet in a place that is still culturally authentic, Kamaran can feel desolate, and the sun and moist heat on the Red Sea, need I remind you, are unrelenting. *—SM*

(i) www.kamaran.net.

✈ Kamaran airport, with connections to Sana'a. (Or fly to Sana'a, then drive or bus to Salif and make a 20-min. boat transfer.)

🛏 $$ **Kamaran Tourist Village** (✆ **967/7771-1742;** www.kamaran.net).

Unvarnished & Unspoiled

27

Los Roques

Sail Away

Venezuela

Like La Blanquilla 187, Los Roques enjoys the same sparkling turquoise seas and warm trade winds as its more popular counterparts in the Caribbean. But this island chain is much more gloriously untouched, with rudimentary tourist infrastructure and pristine ecosystems. Largely free of the civil unrest and political upheaval that bedeviled many Latin American nations in the late 20th century, the Venezuelan archipelago of Los Roques offers an embarrassment of riches when it comes to experiencing the Caribbean of old.

The archipelago Los Roques is made up of some 300 islands—224,749 hectares (555,367 acres) of sea and land that includes more than 42 *cayos,* or coral cays, and 250 spectacularly colorful coral reefs. Only a handful of the islands and cays are inhabited. A national park since 1972, the islands of Los Roques compose the largest marine reserve archipelago in the world. Los Roques is protected by not one but two barrier reefs. The archipelago is a sailor's dream; constant winds range from 10 to 15 knots, and the barrier reefs ensure that the waters are protected. In fact, many people charter a crewed sailboat or motored yacht in Los Roques and dip from one jewel-like cay to another, stopping to snorkel or fish in brilliantly clear, warm lagoon waters.

Others take up residence in one of the many family-owned *posadas* (inns) on **Gran Roque,** the largest island in the archipelago and the only island with lodging options (it's also the site of the airport). Strict regulations ensure that the island is not overrun with megaresorts: None of the *posadas* is higher than two floors, and none has more than 15 rooms. A good half of the *posadas* are owned by Italian expats, which explains the island's old-world Mediterranean vibe—cafe menus include such Italian classics as carpaccio. The boat-filled **Gran Roque beach** is a great place to promenade, but it's not the beach you've come from miles away to experience—you find it in the breathtaking little cays strewn throughout the archipelago. A stay in a *posada* lets you enjoy the culture of the island and get your Robinson Crusoe fix, too: Most offer full-service day trip excursions to a lovely, uninhabited cay nearby to which you're delivered by boat, with a picnic basket of food, a cooler of beer, and a big umbrella. Ah, *paradisio*!

The diving and snorkeling in and around Los Roques is world-class. **Lost World Adventures** (✆ **800/999-0558** in the U.S. and Canada or 404/373-5820; www.lostworldadventures.com) offers diving, fishing, and sailing tours in and around the island. Many fishermen come from around the globe to go **bonefishing** in Los Roques; called "the gray ghost of the shoals," the bonefish of Los Roques are big, weighing up to 5.4kg, and spirited. The seas are full of tarpon, jacks, barracuda, tuna, and bonito. Gran Roques is also garnering attention as a terrific **kitesurfing** spot; the constant winds fill billowing sails and send boards skimming across the seas.

Keep in mind that if you plan to charter a boat in Venezuela, the boat should be licensed by the Venezuelan authorities and a Venezuelan *marinero* (mariner) must be onboard. So if you want to explore the Venezuelan archipelagos bareboat (without a crew), you'll need to board the boat in another country—nearby Grenada 57 is a good choice. Otherwise, any boat you hire in Venezuela comes with a crew—not a bad idea if you're unfamiliar with these waters.

The protected status of Los Roques is good news for the future of the islands. Only the northeast corner of the national marine park is allowed to have accommodations for visitors, and the islands have virtually no cars or trucks—people get around largely by golf cart, bicycle, or good old feet. Being on land is a temporary state of being, however; most everyone is lost in a liquid Caribbean dream. —*AF*

ⓘ www.los-roques.com.

✈ Caracas to Gran Roque (35 min.).

⛴ Boat charter from Caracas or Puerto la Cruz (mainland Venezuela).

🛏 $$ **Posada Acuarela** (✆ **58/212/953-6455;** www.posadaacuarela.com). $$ **Posada El Botuto** (✆ **58/416/621-0381;** www.posadaelbotuto.com).

28 Unvarnished & Unspoiled

Nevis

Liming It

The sleepy, laid-back counterpart to its busier, more touristed sister island, St. Kitts 218, Nevis is the unvarnished, unspoiled Caribbean. It's lovely, all right, with bejeweled coral reefs and palm-fringed, white-sand beaches. Still, goats and donkeys roam the largely rural 93-sq.-km (36-sq.-mile) island, and untamed bougainvillea spills onto dirt roads and over colonial windmills. It's no vision of manicured perfection, and for many travelers, that's not a bad thing.

Nevis (pronounced *Nee*-vis) was built on sugar cane, and the 18th-century ruins of the sugar trade can be found all over the island. Nevis, one-half of a two-island federation (the larger St. Kitts is the other half separated from Nevis by a 3.2km/2-mile channel), was under British control for 200 years until it achieved independence in 1983. The island's capital and main port, **Charlestown,** is a living-history relic from colonial times, its streets lined with Georgian-style structures. The island was slowly building a reputation for gracious West Indies–style hospitality when Hurricane Omar hit the region in 2008. Damage from the hurricane closed down the island's largest and swankiest property, the Four Seasons Nevis, and put hundreds of islanders out of work (the resort was scheduled to reopen in summer 2010). The handful of other island properties, many of them small-scale inns charmingly rejiggered from centuries-old sugar plantations, are soldiering on in a weakened world economy.

Still, quiet seclusion has its fans, and Nevis is increasingly on the radar of those rich and discerning folks who are weary of glitzy resorts and who appreciate discreet, character-filled tropical hideaways far from the cruise ship crowds. (It's been called a rustic alternative to St. Barts 260.) Painter Brice Marden recently bought the Golden Rock Plantation Inn, an old sugar plantation that was converted into an inn in 1958.

It doesn't hurt that Nevis is blessed with a stunningly scenic landscape that takes in velvety volcanic peaks, beautiful beaches, and lush rainforest. You can hike up 955m (3,133-ft.) **Mount Nevis** with biologists on fascinating nature hikes through **Top to Bottom** (✆ **869/469-9080;** www.walknevis.com). You can stroll amid vividly hued tropical flora and tangled vines in the **Botanical Gardens of Nevis** (Montpelier Estate; ✆ **869/469-3509;** www.botanicalgardennevis.com). You can take a fabulous

Gardens on Nevis.

snorkel trip on the **MV *Rum*** (✆ **869/469-1060**), cruising the unspoiled reefs along the island's leeward coast. You can head underwater for a dive trip in virgin seas with the pros at **Scuba Safaris** (✆ **869/469-9518;** www.scubanevis.com).

Nevis has a number of fine beaches, including **Oualie,** which lies in a sheltered cove with sunset views, and **Pinney's,** a 4.8km-long (3-mile) stretch of velvety white sand and Caribbean seas. You can sail, windsurf, and fish to your heart's content, or you can golf, hike, and play tennis—but really, put down that tennis racket and put up your feet. Nevis is about succumbing to the island's old-fashioned West Indian charm and meditating on a grain of sand. Taking it easy is called *"liming"* here, and if someone back home asks you what you were doing on Nevis, the proper answer is "Liming!" —*AF*

ⓘ **Nevis Tourism Authority** (✆ **866/55-NEVIS** [556-3847] in the U.S. and Canada or 869/469-7550; www.nevisisland.com).

✈ Antigua (20 min.), St. Maarten (20 min.), and San Juan (60 min.).

⛴ St. Kitts (ferry companies don't take reservations; 45 min.).

🛏 $$$ **Montpelier Plantation,** St. John Figtree (✆ **869/469-3462;** www.montpeliernevis.com). $$ **Oualie Beach Resort,** Oualie Beach (✆ **869/469-9735;** www.oualiebeach.com).

29 Unvarnished & Unspoiled

Padre Island

Sun & Surf, Texas-Style

Texas, U.S.

No, I'm not talking about South Padre Island, which might conjure up images (unpleasant or otherwise) of cheap hotels and raucous bar crawls—a scene best left to college spring breakers. Just to the north lies **Padre Island National Seashore,** a 70-mile (113km) stretch of sand, low dunes, and prairie grasses where south Texans come for fun in the sun and surf. Everything's bigger in the Lone Star State, and Padre Island is doing its part to make the adage ring true: This is the longest section of undeveloped barrier island in the world.

Easily accessed from Corpus Christi or Galveston 352, Padre Island National Seashore is barely a mile wide and bordered by the Gulf of Mexico on the seaward side and the **Laguna Madre** on the landward side. Hairline channels separate Padre Island from Mustang Island to the north and the resort hotels of South Padre to the south. Laguna Madre is a hypersaline lagoon (meaning its salt content is higher than the ocean's), one of only six such lagoons in the world. On both sides of the seashore, the water is warm and salty, which gives everything that floats in it extra buoyancy.

For such a narrow strip of land, Padre Island is teeming with wildlife. Coyotes, badgers, raccoons, opossums, rats, squirrels, and bats make up the diverse **mammal population** among the low grasses.

A sunset over the Gulf of Mexico.

The island is positioned along the **Central Flyway,** a major bird migration route, and many species stop at Padre to winter or to breed and nest. All told, some 350 species of birds have been documented along the national seashore. The rich sea life in the area includes many fish and **sea turtles,** four different species of which nest here. Summertime visitors might be lucky enough to witness the Park Service's hatchling release program of Kemp's Ridley turtles in action. Several species of venomous and nonvenomous snakes live here, too, though they're rarely seen. However, visitors should be on the lookout for three species of poisonous snake: the western diamondback, the massasauga, and the Texas coral snake.

Although it's under the jurisdiction of the National Park Service, don't expect a *totally* pristine encounter with nature here: Vehicles are allowed right on the beach in most places, and you'll likely have to contend with convoys of SUVs on weekends and holidays and whenever the weather's nice. Furthermore, plenty of flotsam from the Gulf of Mexico makes its way to the shores of Padre Island, meaning that avid beachcombers can find treasures like shells and driftwood among the metal, glass, and plastic that washes up here. At the northern end of the seashore, **Malaquite Beach** is the most unspoiled beach in the area—it's closed to vehicular traffic—with simple wood-frame picnic shelters where you can set up for a day of shore exploration. For those wishing to stay a bit longer at Padre Island, the **Bob Hall Pier** area, also at the northern end, is the only part of the island where you'll find hotels and restaurants. —*SM*

ⓘ **Malaquite Visitors Center,** Milepost 0 (✆ **361/949-8068;** www.nps.gov/pais).

✈ Corpus Christi International.

43-mile (69km) drive from Corpus Christi.

$$ **Bahia Mar,** 15201 Windward Dr., Corpus Christi (✆ **361/949-2400;** www.bahiamarsuites.com). $ Camping permits available at park visitor center (see above).

Unvarnished & Unspoiled **30**

Cape Hatteras

Graveyard of the Atlantic

North Carolina, U.S.

Hwy. 12 runs the length of the **Cape Hatteras National Seashore,** and at times this curving two-lane road feels like a ride in an amusement park. Over here you can see the waters of the mighty Pamlico Sound, a huge estuarine breeding ground for marine life. Over there is the mighty Atlantic Ocean, milky whitecaps and sea spray visible above the dune line. You are basically riding a slender thread of blacktop between two massive bodies of water.

Driving Hwy. 12 gives you a good idea of how narrow and fragile this sliver of land is, and how easily a good nor'easter can breach it, sending waves crashing into the sound. Which it does, every so often—this, after all, is how inlets are formed.

The Cape Hatteras National Seashore runs 70 miles (113km) along North Carolina's Outer Banks from Whalebone Junction to Ocracoke Island 351. At the Cape itself, the land juts deep into the ocean where two currents meet—you can actually see the warm, blue Gulf Stream crashing into the chilly Labrador current. The largest lighthouse on the East Coast is here, shining its 1,000-watt beam to mariners maneuvering this elbow of land, but even that powerful beam of light is sometimes not enough: The shifting shoals around Cape Hatteras are littered with the bones of some 2,000 wrecked ships—the reason the area is called "The Graveyard of the Atlantic." Here lie schooners, steamships, warships—even a 987-ton Civil War ironclad, the USS *Monitor,* discovered in 1974.

For today's tourists, however, the Cape Hatteras National Seashore is a water-sports paradise, with small villages separated by miles of undeveloped, unspoiled beaches forever protected against commercial growth. It's one of the East Coast's top beach recreation spots, with plenty of surfing, sailing, windsurfing, fishing, and scuba diving opportunities. For top-notch kite boarding, surfing, and windsurfing lessons and rentals, head to **Kitty Hawk Kites** (✆ **252/986-1446;** www.kittyhawk.com), which has locations on Hatteras Island in Hatteras village, Avon, and Rodanthe. For sportfishing, **Hatteras Harbor Marina** (✆ **800/676-4939;** www.hatterasharbor.com) offers half- and full-day inshore and offshore fishing charters, gear, and bait.

What makes this seashore so captivating is its beautiful wildness, and wild it will stay; only 12% of the island can ever be developed (the rest is protected federal or state parkland or wetlands). The wind is a constant, and currents can be unpredictable. The sea air is pungently salty. The national seashore is, after all, an unprotected strip of sand that stretches out into the Atlantic almost to the Continental Shelf. The land and the sea are in a constant dance; the sand rolls underneath the banks and comes up the other side. Boundaries shift; the bones of old ships disappear.

Coming from the north, the drive down Hwy. 12 takes you past **Oregon Inlet,** where waves crash and tumble on the shoals and fishermen in waders wrestle puppy drum onto the beach. Oregon Inlet was formed in 1846, when the sea split the land in a roaring gale. In between stretches of national seashore are old fishing villages and new beach houses. Wrecked ships figure large in the history of the old lifesaving station at **Chicamacomico;** the original building from 1874 is still on-site, as is the 1911 station, its weather-beaten shingles silvery with age. The black and white stripes of the 1870 **Cape Hatteras Lighthouse,** in Buxton, spiral up the length of the 200-ft. (61m) tower.

Cape Hatteras is an informal, barefoot kind of place. You can easily beach-hop from one stretch of tawny sand to another—just pull into one of the park's beach-access parking lots, cross a wooden boardwalk over dunes of sea oats, and find a spot to lay your towel. The waves, the sand, the seagulls flying overhead: It's all blessedly wild, untamed by little more than the elements. *—AF*

ⓘ www.nps.gov/caha and www.hatterasguide.com.

✈ Norfolk, Virginia (2 hr.).

⛴ Ocracoke (coming from the south, 40 min.; www.ncdot.org/transit/ferry).

🛏 $$ **Breakwater Inn,** 57896 Hwy. 12, Hatteras Village (✆ **877/986-2565** or 252/986-2565). $$ **Comfort Inn,** 46745 NC Hwy. 12, Buxton (✆ **877/424-6423** or 252/995-6100; www.outerbankscomfortinn.com).

Sailing Along 31

Tortola

Bareboatin'

British Virgin Islands

In the opinion of many travelers, a "bareboat" vacation—in which you and your companions charter a sailboat for a week or so, load it with provisions, and head wherever the trade winds and your imagination take you—is the ultimate way to explore any island chain. And there's no better place to launch your own sailing adventure than in the bareboat capital of the world: Tortola, the largest (19×4.8km/12×3 miles) and most populous of the British Virgin Islands.

In terms of convenience, safety, affordability, and sheer number of attractive places to drop anchor, the 60-plus islands and cays of B.V.I. are tailor-made for the do-it-yourself island hopper. The capital of the British Virgin Islands, **Road Town,** nestled on Tortola's mountainous southern coast (the island's beaches are all on the northern, Atlantic side), is home to dozens of charter companies with well-maintained catamarans and single-hulled boats to choose from. (Powerboats and full-sized yachts with crew are also available.) Sail out of the town's well-protected natural harbor, and you'll find yourself a couple of hours away from **Norman** 350, **Peter,** and **Cooper islands,** all awaiting with white-sand beaches, reefs perfect for snorkeling, sheltered coves for anchoring overnight, and waterfront bars and restaurants that cater to the seaborne set. The larger islands of Virgin Gorda 307, to the northeast, and Jost Van Dyke, off Tortola's northern flank, are both less than a day's sail away. Scattered about are scores of uninhabited islets that are yours for the claiming.

The key to any successful bareboat vacation is advance planning. Charter companies all ask you to submit a "sailing resume" proving you have enough experience to handle their boats. The official B.V.I. tourist site, **www.bvitourism.com**, has a long list of reputable charter companies with links to their websites. While prices vary, bareboat vacations tend to be remarkably affordable, typically costing about as much as a cruise. If you're worried about rusty sailing skills, you can charter a boat with an extra sleeping space or two and pay for your own skipper and cook. In addition to knowing the best spots to drop anchor, the crews-for-hire in Tortola are also accustomed to blending in with new boat mates. For a little extra, you can even request a captain who's a certified sailing instructor.

Sailors aren't the only active travelers enjoying Tortola's sparkling seas. Divers and snorkelers have much to explore here, most notably the wreck of the **HMS *Rhone,*** a British Royal Mail steam packet ship that sank here in an October storm in 1867. The wreck lies in depths from 6 to 24m (20–79 ft.) just south of Tortola near Salt Island. Reserve a dive with **Blue Water Divers** (✆ **284/494-2847;** www.bluewaterdiversbvi.com) to the site of the Rhone and other gems of the deep.

For those who prefer to spend their time on solid ground, Tortola has its share of fine resorts and villas, all imbued with the relaxed, friendly, non–theme park atmosphere (no casinos here, thank you!) for which the B.V.I. is known. The beaches on Tortola are actually quite wonderful, from popular **Cane Garden Bay,** wrapped in soft green hills, to the secluded sands of **Long Bay,** where you can swim and snorkel in clear, gentle seas.

With half its income coming from tourism and the other half from the financial industry (the island is headquarters to many of the world's offshore companies), and a currency based on U.S. dollars, Tortola is an enchanting blend of old world and new. And when you're out in the archipelago, the wind filling your sails, it's all yours to discover. —*AF*

ⓘ www.bvitourism.com.

✈ Tortola: Beef Island International Airport, connected to Tortola by the Queen Elizabeth Bridge.

⛴ Regular ferries from St. Thomas, U.S.V.I. (45 min.).

🛏 $ **Ole Works Inn,** Cane Garden Bay (✆ **284/495-4837;** www.quitorymer.com). $$$ **The Sugar Mill,** Apple Bay (✆ **800/462-8834** in the U.S., or 284/495-4355; www.sugarmillhotel.com).

32 Sailing Along

Paros

A Break from Greek Cultural Overload

Greece

Paros should be a required stop on any traveler's itinerary through the Cyclades islands. Not only because it's the archipelago's transportation hub—lying halfway between the more well known islands of Mykonos 245 and Santorini 238—and has great beaches but also because its lack of any single must-see historical sight makes it a sort of cultural free-pass for anyone suffering from antiquities overload (a common affliction in Greece). Make no mistake, Paros has history and some of the islands' quaintest darn villages, but the bulk of your time on Paros is much more likely to be spent sunbathing or learning to windsurf, blissfully unobligated to traipse through yet another hot and dusty archaeological site.

Most visitors arrive by ferry at busy **Parikia**—as Greek port towns go, it's not the most compelling, though it is quite lively. But watersports fans won't much care about staying in town, for Paros is known first and foremost as the **windsurfing capital of Greece.** Thanks to constant, strong winds along the strait between Paros and Naxos 229 (off the east coast of Paros), conditions are excellent from late spring to early fall. Serious windsurfers tend to avoid the peak months of July and August, when all too many "amateurs" take to the water. Go ahead and join them: The free *Paros Windsurfing Guide,* available at tourist offices island-wide, provides resources for equipment rentals and lessons; I like the **F2 Windsurfing Center** on Golden Beach (✆ **30/22840/41878**) and **Santa Maria Surf Club** on Santa Maria Beach (✆ **30/22840/52490**).

If heaving water-logged sails out of the water seems like too much hassle on your Greek holiday, just take yourself and a towel to the beach. The best all-around strip on Paros is 1km-long (⅔-mile) **Chrissi Akti** (Golden Beach), on the island's southeast coast. It's blessed with omnipresent breezes that keep windsurfers happy and tan-seeking landlubbers from feeling too sun-fried on the sand. With smooth and chalky rock formations dividing the bay into pretty coves, **Kolimbithres** is the most picturesque beach on Paros, with basic facilities and snack bars. Rounding out the big three of Paros beaches is **Santa Maria** (also a favorite spot for windsurfers), on the northeast tip of the island. It's very un-Greek-looking in that the fine golden sand stretches back from the water quite a way, and the waves that gently lap at the shoreline are a shallow, clear turquoise.

Venture inland to visit the medieval hill town of **Lefkes** (which also has the island's best hotel, the Lefkes Village Hotel), with its postcard-perfect square and cafes. The fishing village of **Naoussa,** across the bay from Kolimbithres beach, is utterly charming and getting more gentrified by the season as trendy shops and upscale restaurants move in. Art junkies or mineralogists familiar with such masterworks as the *Venus de Milo* may want to check out the defunct marble quarries at **Marathi.** Parian marble was highly prized by the ancient Greeks and Romans alike, who once had hundreds of thousands of slaves working here day and night to export chunks of the luminous white stone for use all over the Mediterranean world. —*SM*

(i) www.parosweb.com or www.paroslife.com.

✈ Paros Airport.

⛴ From Piraeus (3–6 hr.), and other Cyclades islands (1-3 hr.), to Parikia.

🛏 $$ **Hotel Petres,** Naoussa (✆ **30/22840/52467;** www.petres.gr). $$$ **Lefkes Village Hotel,** Lefkes (✆ **30/22840/41827** or 30/210/6748470 during winter; www.lefkesvillage.com).

Sailing Along **33**

Tjörn

Yachting & Trekking Among the Rocks

Sweden

Every summer, yachties and sun seekers from mainland Sweden flock to this island, causing the population to double, from 15,000 to more than 30,000. The rest of the year, the people lucky enough to live and work on Tjörn have one of western Sweden's most diverse recreational areas in their own backyard.

Like so many Scandinavian islands, Tjörn has a coastline defined by countless rocky inlets and infinite offshore skerries. The protected, azure waters of the Skagerrat Strait, which runs from Tjörn's west coast, between Denmark and Norway, to the North Sea, are a magnet for the sailing crowd. The annual **Tjörn Runt** regatta (held in Aug) circles the island and brings with it thousands of colorful boats.

Tjörn's intricate topography also makes for some wonderful exploring, whether along the shore or into the island's wild interior. Trekking is a year-round activity here, taking in such varied scenery as green pastures, dense groves of trees, and unspoiled beaches. While cycling or hiking in the **Tuveslatt** district, you might come across ancient rock carvings and ruins of Stone Age dwellings. Whether you're looking for a protected cove or sandy stretch of shore, Tjörn offers plenty of places to swim in summer. Believe it or not, the water up here does get warm enough in July and August for a dip, though it'll be a bracing one!

Skärhamn, halfway up Tjörn's western coast, is the island's municipal seat and

Tjörn Island and sailboats.

main harbor. The marina swells to capacity in the summer months with the boats of vacationers, and a lively holiday atmosphere permeates the town, which, at 58 degrees north latitude, stays light almost all night long. In fact, the unique quality of light on Tjörn has been drawing artists for centuries. Be sure to visit the very worthwhile **Nordic Watercolour Museum** (Södra hamnen 6; www.akvarellmuseet.org), set in a striking modern building on the water's edge in Skärhamn.

The inhabitants of Tjörn have traditionally drawn their livelihood from the sea. Fishing is as important today as it was in the island's early history, but the construction of the Tjörn Bridge in 1960 greatly facilitated the island's leap from isolated fishing community to thriving community of industry, with the growth of prosperous canning, shipping, and shipbuilding businesses. (With this modernization, too, has come the construction of thousands of summer cottages for vacationing Swedes.) Fortunately, the stewards of Tjörn's growth and progress have been careful to ensure that development does not infringe on the island's natural treasures. *—SM*

(i) www.tjorn.se.

Gothenburg (61km/38 miles).

Tjörn Bridge, 664m (2,178 ft.) to Stenungsund.

$$$ **Salt & Sill Floating Hotel,** Klädesholmen (✆ **46/304/673480;** www.saltosill.se).

Island Hopping The Bahamas Out Islands: Out on the Water

More than 700 islands make up the Bahamas archipelago, but many visitors never venture farther than the two main islands, Grand Bahama and New Providence (Nassau)—and, of course, Paradise Island, a single bridge away from Nassau and home to the massive Atlantis resort. More and more, however, travelers are heading on to a chain of beautiful and historic islands that stretch south from Grand Bahama. Known as The Bahamas' Out Islands—or "the Family Islands," as the tourism department calls them—these silky strands of sand have some of the finest and most pristine natural resources in the entire archipelago: gorgeous beaches and vibrant undersea coral gardens; sublime fishing, diving, and snorkeling; and prime sailing waters. The Out Islands also teem with historic sites, from the ruins of sugar plantations to the Victorian cottages in Dunmore Town, The Bahamas' former capital. Direct flights from the U.S. are now making these tropical isles easier to access, but not to worry: The islands and cays are still remote enough to stay peaceful and secluded and slightly rough-hewn.

Built on a backbone of coral, the Out Islands owe much of their inaccessibility and lack of development to the fringing reefs and shifting shoals that have made navigation dangerous for big ships for hundreds of years.

Sailing by the Abacos.

The closest islands to Grand Bahama are the 26-cay ❸❹ **Abacos,** which have a famously beautiful beach, **Treasure Cay.** The Abacos are a major sailing center, with the largest marina in The Bahamas and a number of celebrated regattas. According to *Cruising World,* The Bahamas are blessed with some of the clearest, cleanest seas to navigate in the world, in large part because of the absence of industry and river runoff. If you're itching to charter a sailboat and get out on the water, contact **Abaco Sailing** (www.abacosailing.com); they also offer lessons. The Abacos have been called "Nantucket under the Palms," for the vintage New England–style clapboard cottages built by the island's first settlers, British Loyalists who fled America in the wake of the War of Independence.

Divers flock to The Bahamas' largest island, ❸❺ **Andros,** which has the third-largest coral reef in the world. Anglers come to battle the fighting bonefish that live in the sparkling shallows. For a fly-fishing expedition in a shallow-draft flats boat, contact **Phillip Rolle's North Andros Fly Fishing** (✆ **242/329-2661;** www.northandrosflyfishing.com). Just beyond the reef is the "Tongue of the Ocean," a steep drop-off that harbors big game, including blue marlin, sailfish, dolphin, wahoo, king fish, mackerel, tuna, snapper, and grouper.

(36) **Eleuthera** may be the Out Islands' most touristed spot, with an international airport that is seeing increasing traffic from major airlines. The long, narrow island (177×4km/110×2½ miles) has lovely sugary-sand beaches ringed by teal water, and colonial-era villages and plantations. Just 3.2km (2 miles) east is (37) **Harbour Island,** a favorite destination of the rich and trendy and the site of the former capital of The Bahamas, **Dunmore Town.** This lovely little village has colorful clapboard homes rimmed by white picket fences and draped in bougainvillea. Harbour Island's most famous beach, **Pink Sand,** is 4.8km (3 miles) of luminous, salmon-hued sand.

For castaway seclusion on magnificent beaches, head to (38) **Cat Island,** 209km (130 miles) southeast of Nassau. Legend has it that the island was named after Arthur Catt, famous British sea captain or notorious pirate; take your pick. Cat Island was settled in the late 1700s by British Loyalists from the Americas who built prosperous cotton plantations here with slave labor. Today the island is littered with the ruins of their 18th-century plantation homes.

The 365 islands and cays that compose the beautiful (39) **Exuma** chain are a sailing paradise, with secluded coves, uninhabited cays, and excellent anchorages. Ecotourism is also big here, with the 456-sq.-km (176-sq.-mile) **Exuma Cays Land and Sea Park** (www.exumapark.info), the Caribbean's first marine fishery reserve.

Some people think (40) **Long Island** may be the prettiest of The Bahamas' Out Islands. It's another slender thread of land, just 97km long by 2.4km wide (60×1½ miles). The beaches are classic strands of Bahamian pink and white sand, lapped by clear, gentle seas. Long Island is also the site of **Dean's Blue Hole,** the world's deepest blue hole, plunging 203m (665 ft.) into the ocean floor. (A blue hole is generally created when the ceiling to a limestone cave collapses in the ocean.) Dean's Blue Hole is a fabulous spot to snorkel: You just paddle in off the white-sand beach with snorkel and flippers; the depth quickly drops from 1.5 to 180m (5–591 ft.). This is also one of the world's prime free-diving spots, and you can take free-diving lessons here from world-record-holder William Trubridge at **Vertical Blue** (www.verticalblue.net).

Rounding out the Out Islands is **Bimini** island, one of the top sport-fishing capitals of the world—it's reviewed separately on p. 242. —*AF*

ⓘ www.myoutislands.com or www.bahamas.com.

✈ Nassau (New Providence Island).

Ferry service between Nassau and Eleuthera, Andros, Harbour Island, and Great Exuma (Bahamas Ferries; ✆ **242/323-2166;** www.bahamasferries.com).

$$ **Green Turtle Club Resort and Marina,** Green Turtle Cay, Great Abaco (✆ **866/528-0539** in the U.S., or 242/365-4271; www.greenturtleclub.com). $$$ **Rock House** (✆ **242/333-2053;** www.rockhousebahamas.com).

Diving's the Thing

Buck Island

Lucky Buck

U.S. Virgin Islands

The largest of the U.S. Virgin Islands, St. Croix 341 has plenty of attractions—relaxing beach resorts, stands of lush rainforest, historic plantation houses, and a thriving rum factory. But many visitors come here mainly to go scuba diving along the drop-offs, reefs, and wrecks that line the island's north coast, or snorkeling around the reefs of the west end. And among St. Croix's many dive sites, it's generally agreed that the premier spot is the pristine marine garden surrounding nearby Buck Island, now owned by the National Park Service. Some divers declare it's the finest dive spot in the whole Caribbean.

A tropical speck lying a mile and a half off St. Croix's northeast coast, Buck Island is only about 1km wide and 1.6km long (⅔×1 mile), but it is nearly surrounded by an elkhorn coral barrier reef—the only elkhorn reef in U.S. waters, in fact. The waters here are so clear, visibility can be up to 30m (98 ft.). There's an underwater snorkeling trail laid out among the grottoes at the eastern end of the island, where the water's only 3.6m (12 ft.) deep and landmarks are clearly marked with underwater signs; sun dapples the submarine labyrinths as a wealth of reef fish, like queen angelfish and smooth trunkfish, flit in and out. There are also two approved mooring spots for scuba divers, where relatively shallow water—9 to 12m (30–39 ft.)—surrounds haystack formations of

A beach on Buck Island.

elkhorn coral. Marked walking trails bisect the island—it'll take about 45 minutes to hike across—where you'll pass through dry tropical forests of tamarind, frangipani, and pigeon-berry trees to get a spectacular oceanview panorama from the island's gentle crest. Hawksbill turtles, leatherback turtles, brown pelicans, and least terns are among the endangered species that thrive along Buck Island's shoreline; be sure to respect their nesting areas when you're enjoying the island's unspoiled white coral beaches.

You can reach the island either by private boat (you must get a permit from the park visitor center in St. Croix's capital, Christiansted) or on a half- or full-day tour by one of the boat operators licensed to serve the island, including **Caribbean Sea Adventures** (✆ **340/773-2628;** www.caribbeanseaadventures.com), **Captain Heinz** (✆ **340/773-3161;** teroro@viapowernet.net), and **Llewellyn Charters** (✆ **340/773-9027**). *—HH*

ⓘ **Buck Island Reef National Monument visitor center,** 2100 Church St., Christiansted (✆ **340/773-1460;** www.nps.gov/buis).

✈ Henry E. Rohlsen Airport, Estate Mannings Bay, St. Croix.

⛴ 8.8km (5½ miles) by boat from Christiansted: 40 min. by motor boat, 1½ hr. by sailboat.

🛏 $$$ **The Buccaneer,** Gallows Bay, St. Croix (✆ **800/255-3881** in the U.S. or 340/712-2100; www.thebuccaneer.com). $ **Holger Danske Hotel,** 1200 King Cross St., Christiansted (✆ **340/773-3600;** www.holgerhotel.com).

42 Diving's the Thing

Bonaire

Friendliest Diving in the Caribbean

Think of Bonaire as the Caribbean, version 2.0—an island of slower paces and authentic encounters, perhaps to try out after you've exhausted the nonstop activities and crowded beaches of other islands like Aruba 261. Boomerang-shaped Bonaire, just 80km (50 miles) north of Venezuela, is desertlike, with just a few stretches of rocky beach, so travelers with a major sunbathing agenda should look elsewhere. However, what draws people here over and over is Bonaire's world-class diving and snorkeling: Its reef-lined western coast is an amazing, uninterrupted chain of shore-accessible sites with turquoise waters. The island's yellow, five-character license plates say it all: "BONAIRE, N.A.—DIVERS PARADISE."

Upon arrival on Bonaire, divers pay a one-time fee of $25 for the **Bonaire National Marine Park** "nature tag." Then, you hit the road and keep your eyes peeled for yellow stone markers pointing the way to one of the island's 53 shore dive sites. Once under the crystal-blue water, feast your eyes on a magnificent array of nearly 500 species of reef fish, sea turtles, rays, sharks, and dolphins. For a diver, Bonaire is pure heaven: Your days are filled with easily accessible, diverse sites, and the island's omnipresent, outgoing outfitters make the practical side of diving—filling tanks, getting tips on where to see whale sharks, and so on—a breeze. With a population of about 10,000, Bonaire is very much a tight-knit community, and one of the best ways to experience this is to get into the local diving culture. For a more targeted approach to diving here, the official website of Tourism Corporation Bonaire (see below) has a comprehensive list of the island's 22 accredited dive operators.

For nondivers, there are still enough natural attractions above the waterline to make for a satisfying short stay. The north half of the island is the hilliest and most scenic: The drive north from the capital of **Kralendijk** takes in turquoise sea on the left and coral cliffs on the right. Along this road, there are lovers' lookouts aplenty, and paths suitable for hiking or biking leading off the shoulder. The wildlife preserve of **Washington Slagbaii National Park** (✆**599/785-0017;** www.washingtonparkbonaire.org) takes up 6,000 hectares (14,826 acres) of northwestern Bonaire: Here you can see tropical birds, visit the romantic black-sand beach of **Boca Chiquito,** and dive into remote bays like **Wajaca,** whose reef shelters turtles and octopuses.

As if the airport terminal—Flamingo International, painted bright pink—weren't enough to tip you off, Bonaire is famous for its **flamingos,** which spend most of their time in the salt flats in the southern part of the island. Slaves once worked to extract salt from here (you can see some remnants of their stone huts nearby), but the salt pans today are run by the International Salt Company, which employs many a local. Also in the south of Bonaire is the island's best area for beach bumming, **Lac Bay,** with its sandy shores, gin-clear waters, and vivid coral reef. One of the most endearing places in the Caribbean is to the northwest—**Donkey Sanctuary** (✆ **599/95/607-607;** www.donkeysanctuary.org), where abandoned or injured animals (originally brought over from Spain for hard labor in the 1600s) are cared for and given a comfortable and loving home on the range. —*SM*

ⓘ **Tourist information,** Kaya Grandi 2, Kralendijk (✆**599/717-8322;** www.tourismbonaire.com).

✈ Flamingo Airport, connections through Aruba, Curaçao, and St. Maarten.

🛏 $$ **The Deep Blue View,** Kaya Diamanta 50, Santa Barbara Heights (✆**599/717-8073;** www.deepblueview.com). $$$ **Harbour Village Bonaire,** Kaya Gobernador N. Debrot 17, Playa Lechi (✆**599/717-7500;** www.harbourvillage.com).

Diving's the Thing **43**

Roatán

Coral Reef Paradise

Bay Islands, Honduras

You know a destination has "arrived" in savvy travel circles when people refer to it only by its first name. *"We're heading to Roatán,"* someone confides, and everyone nods knowingly. That would be Roátan, Honduras, and if you haven't heard of it yet, you soon will: It's the Caribbean in an unspoiled state, with pristine sugary-sand beaches and lush coral reefs. It also has some of the best diving, offered at the cheapest prices, anywhere in the world.

This beautiful tropical island is the argest of the Bay Islands (which include Utila 304 and Guanaja) off the Caribbean coast of Central America. It's 65km (40 miles) long and comprises 127 sq. km (49 sq. miles). Roátan is a serious dive and snorkel destination, with warm, diamond-clear waters that are protected as a marine park. It sits on the second-largest barrier reef in the world, a magnificent necklace of coral that is alive with sponges, turtles, eagle rays, and fish in a paint box of vivid colors. The diverse underwater topography is one of dramatic ridges, channels, and vertical walls.

The island has several dive shops that can get you onto the reef in under 30 minutes. On **West End**—home to the island's best beaches—**Ocean Connections** (www.ocean-connections.com) is a PADI-certified dive center that offers recreational diving, diving courses, and dive packages on Roátan. Its dive center is just 15 minutes away from the coral reef.

On land, the vibe is laid-back and refreshingly unpolished. Visitors shouldn't be surprised if the electricity goes out for a few hours, and the nightlife essentially consists of hanging out, barefoot and sunburned, with new island pals over sundowners. If you get bored with the water activities during the day, you can hit the **iguana reserve** just outside French Harbour—it holds 2,500 iguanas of four distinct species; or go horseback riding through the **Gumbalimba Nature Park,** a forested jungle reserve filled with colorful tropical birds like parrots and native macaws. You can even take a **Jungle Canopy Tour** along several platforms in the park, where the views of forest and sea are superb. For info on all park tours, go to www.gumbalimbapark.com.

The lodging scene here largely comprises small inns and hostels—and a few diving resorts like **Anthony's Key** (see below)—and there is only one spa on the island (at Parrot Tree Plantation, a planned development). But Nikki Beach is opening up one of its upscale resorts in 2010. Roátan also has been targeted by not one but two major cruise lines (Royal Caribbean and Carnival), which are greatly expanding their Roátan presence—by 2010, the island could be visited by some 200 ships and around 700,000 cruise passengers annually. And airlines are now offering direct flights from Miami, Houston, and Newark into the international airport at **Coxen Hole,** the island capital. Prices and crowds on this lovely, supremely relaxed Caribbean outpost remain reasonable for now—but I recommend diving in as soon as you can, before that changes. —*AF*

ⓘ www.hondurastips.honduras.com.

✈ La Ceiba (30 min.).

⛴ La Ceiba (1½ hr.): **M.V. *Galaxy Wave*** (✆ **504/445-1795;** www.safeway maritime.com).

🛏 $$$ **Anthony's Key Resort,** Sandy Bay (✆ **954/929-0090** [U.S.]; www.anthonyskey.com). $$ **Mayan Princess Resort,** West Bay (✆ **504/445-5050;** www.mayanprincess.com).

44 Diving's the Thing

Ambergris Caye

Coral Reef Paradise

Belize

Coral reef systems around the world are under threat; in fact, it's estimated that one-third of all coral reefs in the world may be damaged beyond repair. Nestled in the crook of the arm of Central America is one of the world's most stunning examples of a living, breathing, thriving coral reef—an exquisitely fine-tuned ecosystem that experts say is under threat from rampant development and the destruction of critical mangrove habitat. The degradation of Belize's coral reef would have serious repercussions: The Belize Barrier Reef Reserve System, named a UNESCO World Heritage Site in 1996, is the longest continuous barrier reef in the Northern Hemisphere, 306km (190 miles) of rich and diverse marine habitat less than half a mile

Diving in Ambergris Caye.

offshore. The diving and snorkeling along this reef is first-class, and the water quality and visibility are consistently excellent. It's a vital life source for marine species and a significant habitat for such threatened species as marine turtles, manatees, and the American marine crocodile. It is also the country's top tourist attraction. In 2009, after UNESCO officially placed the reef on its Danger List, the Belize prime minister called it a "wake-up call" for the country.

Among the hundreds of sand cays and atolls strung along Belize's coral reef, the largest island, Ambergris Caye, enjoys a prime position in this marine ecosystem: The island's 40km (25-mile) shoreline runs almost parallel to the barrier reef. Just 15 minutes by puddle jumper from Belize City, Ambergris Caye is the most developed island in the country, home to most of the cays' lodgings and restaurants. But don't expect high-gloss hospitality: A trip to Ambergris Caye is a journey back to an old-fashioned Caribbean, leisurely and laid-back. If a road is paved at all, it's paved with cobblestones. It has neither glitzy nightlife nor megaluxe resorts, but you can get a cold bottle of the local lager, Belikin, for about $2. Ambergris Caye doesn't even have classic Caribbean beaches, more like short spurts of white sand between mangrove forests and sea. Wade into the shallows, and you're up to your ankles in sea grass.

The fishing village of **San Pedro** (pop. 7,000) has grown to be the largest town on Ambergris Caye. This is where the action is—the island hub for restaurants, cafes, and nightclubs—and where most of the islanders live. San Pedro has a funky, joyful vibe, where the sandy streets are filled with bicycles and golf carts, and the occasional taxi.

As for the lack of big, wide classic beaches, do as the locals do: Swim off one of the many piers that extend beyond the sea grass. Or do your swimming during your forays to the coral reef, when you'll be immersed in warm, sparkling blue waters.

The coral reef is the major draw for visitors, and Ambergris has incredibly easy access to world-class dive and snorkel sites. **Shark-Ray Alley** and **Hol Chan Marine Reserve** are two justifiably popular snorkel spots just off the island, where close encounters with green moray eels, groupers, stingrays, and nurse sharks are abundant. Both sites are about 6.4km (4 miles) southeast of San Pedro Town. For reliable scuba diving service, contact **Amigos del Mar** (✆ **501/226-2706;** www.amigosdive.com), **Aqua Dives** (✆ **800/641-2994** in the U.S. and Canada, or 501/226-3415; www.aquadives.com), or **Gaz Cooper's Dive Belize** (✆ **800/499-3002** in the U.S. and Canada, or 501/226-4455; www.divebelize.com). Among the operators who specialize in snorkeling trips here is the very personable Alfonse Graniel and his launch ***Li'l Alfonse*** (✆ **501/226-3537**). —*AF*

ⓘ www.belizetourism.org, www.goambergriscaye.com, or www.ambergriscaye.com.

✈ Belize City to Ambergris Caye (15 min. on Tropic Air or Maya Island Air).

Water taxi (45 min.–1 hr.): **Caye Caulker Water Taxi Association** (✆ **501/223-5752;** www.cayecaulkerwatertaxi.com).

$$ **Tides Beach Resort,** Boca del Rio Dr. (✆ **501/226-2283;** www.ambergriscaye.com/tides). $$$ **Victoria House** (✆ **800/247-5159** in the U.S. or 501/226-2067; www.victoria-house.com).

45 Diving's the Thing

Rock Islands

Really Big Fish

Palau, Micronesia

They almost seem to float on the shimmering surface of Palau's Southern Lagoon, rounded knobs of ancient coral formations mantled in dense emerald-green foliage. Though most of them are uninhabited, this spatter of tiny islands 805km (500 miles) west of the Philippines 452 has become famous among divers for its rich diversity of marine life. The warm blue waters are so clear (up to 30m/98-ft. visibility) that even snorkelers get quite a show, but scuba divers report truly awesome experiences here, with breathtakingly deep drop-offs and immense submarine caverns. Wall-diving sites such as the **Blue Corner, the Blue Holes, the German Channel, the Peleliu Wall,** and the **Ngmelis Drop-Off** have achieved almost legendary status among divers in the know.

It's the big fish that give the Rock Islands their special claim to fame. Commercial fishing has been banned in Palau 454 for more than a decade, and as a result, threatened shark, barracuda, and wrasse species, as well as turtles and dolphins and giant clams, thrive around the island's spectacular reefs. Tallies vary widely, but there are somewhere around 300 islands in the group, spread over some 161km (100 miles) of ocean south of Palau's largest island, **Babeldaob.** Three ocean currents converge here, which means that hundreds of migratory fish species pass in and out of these waters. Several World War II shipwrecks provide underwater landmarks to explore; you can also swim through tunnels in certain islands' coasts to reach inland marine lakes, populated with rare stingless jellyfish, a snorkeling experience you'll never forget.

For a great overview of the Rock Islands, take a speedboat tour from the main tourist town of **Koror,** about 20 minutes from the airport. These tours will whiz you around to secluded coves, jewel-like lagoons, and the most dazzling strips of white-sand beach. When it's time to get down to some serious diving, leading dive-boat operators include **Fish and Fins** (✆ **680/488-2637;** www.fishnfins.com),

Neco's Marine (✆ **680/488-1755;** www.necomarine.com), and **Sam's Tours** (✆ **680/488-7267;** www.samstours.com). For a little variety, you can also try kayaking and sport fishing around the islands; there are plenty of watersports shops in Koror, as well as at the leading resorts.

Exotic as Palau may seem, English is spoken everywhere, and the U.S. dollar is the main currency. You can easily base yourself in Koror, or book a berth on a live-aboard boat such as the *Eclipse* (book through Sam's Tours, above) or the *Ocean Adventure I* and *III* (book through Fish and Fins, above). —*HH*

ⓘ **Palau tourist office** (✆ **680/488-2793;** www.visit-palau.com).

✈ Palau International Airport, Babeldaob Island.

🛏 $$ **Dolphin Bay Resort,** Peleliu Island (✆ **680/345-5555;** www.dolphinbay-resort-peleliu.com). $$$ **Palau Pacific Resort,** Koror (✆ **680/488-2600;** www.palauppr.com).

Diving's the Thing **46**

Onemaba Island

The House Reef Rules

Sulawesi, Indonesia

When Swiss-born diver Lorenz Mäder launched the **Wakatobi Dive Resort** in the mid-1990s, this remote island cluster in the Banda Sea barely registered on the world map of premier dive sites. But that was what Mäder liked about it: Remote and pristine, these Indonesian islands offered warm, clear, shallow waters around superb biodiverse reefs, with no tourist hordes to contend with. If you were serious enough about diving to make the effort to get here, underwater nirvana was yours for the taking. Word quickly spread; eventually no less a submarine authority than Jacques Cousteau pronounced Wakatobi possibly the finest dive site in the world.

The resort itself is set on the scrubby, flat island of Onemaba, which means "long white beach" in the local language—and fittingly, the resort buildings front onto a gorgeous white-sand beach, fringed with nodding palms. What began as a sort of bare-bones destination located in a single traditional longhouse has morphed into a high-end resort for some 50 guests at a time, with private air-conditioned bungalows furnished with canopied beds, soaring teak-beamed ceilings, sleek volcanic stone floors, and huge windows overlooking the sea. Amenities include Internet access, top chefs serving gourmet fusion cuisine, and a private airstrip, where charter flights from Bali 201 arrive bearing resort guests. If you don't want to stay on land, the resort also has its own luxury live-aboard motor yacht, the *MY Pelagian.*

Lodging includes all meals and three daily 70-minute dive expeditions out to the surrounding Wakatobi islands of Wangi, Kaledupa, Tomea, and Binongki, all of which have thriving reefs; there are more than 40 dive sites available, where you can do everything from drift diving to exploring calm coral bowls, pinnacles, and bommies. With a ratio of one guide to every four divers, these outings tend to be highly productive; during a 10-day stay, you can easily rack up 40 hours or more of bottom time. Don't expect fake shipwrecks and artificial seawalls; do expect incredibly healthy reefs with brilliantly colored coral, hard and soft, and an astonishing variety of marine life from clown fish to rays, wrasses, eels, and sharks, including exotics like pygmy sea horses, ghost pipefish, leaf scorpionfish, and cuttlefish.

Even better, Wakatobi Dive Resort has an excellent house reef right off that white beach, a fringing reef that's accessible via tender boat 24 hours a day. Given all the other great dive opportunities here, that house reef is the icing on the cake—but oh, what icing! *—HH*

(i) www.wakatobi.com.

✈ Wakatobi Dive Resort, 2½ hr. from Bali.

🛏 $$ **Wakatobi Dive Resort** (✆ **866/825-3429** in the U.S., or 62/868/1212-2355; www.wakatobi.com).

Storied Sand & Surf

Kos

Temple of Healing

Greece

The world of medicine made a giant leap here in the 4th century B.C. Kos is the birthplace of the father of Western medicine, Hippocrates, whose followers founded the Kos Asklepeion, a healing temple that became a pioneering hospital and medical school specializing in the therapeutic principles laid out by Hippocrates. It was Hippocrates who led the way in separating superstition from fact in the practice of clinical medicine and whose belief in taking a whole-body approach to medicine was light-years ahead of its time. The ruins of the sprawling Asklepeion are among the many archaeological treasures of this, the third-largest island in the Dodecanese chain.

The healing properties of Kos are not limited to its hospitals. This largely flat island, studded with two small peaks, is a sun-splashed, soul-lifting slice of Greek island paradise. It has gorgeous beaches, picturesque villages, and a lively sociability. Tourism is the island's main industry, and the capital, **Kos Town,** can sometimes seem overrun with buzzing beach resorts and besotted youth, but if you get out into the serene countryside, amid ruins and verdant farm fields, colorful villages and rustic tavernas, you get to experience Kos at its most authentic.

Because the island is largely flat, it's easily seen by bicycle, and bikes can be rented throughout the island. You might start your sightseeing by biking along the northern coastline to **Tigaki Beach,** just 10km (6¼ miles) from Kos Town. Tigaki's shallow waters and gentle surf make it a fine beach for families; ditto for **Marmari Beach,** just 10km (6¼ miles) west of Tigaki. For a little more wave action, head just 5km (3 miles) west to **Mastahari,** which has lots of family-owned restaurants fronting the beach. On the south side of the island (which can be reached by bus or car from Kos Town), beautiful **Kefolos** has sparkling seas and ivory sand. It's an easy swim to the small island just off the beach, which holds the monastery of **St. Nicolas.**

The Kos beaches are bliss, but a visit to the **Asklepeion** is a must for visitors to Kos. The ancient ruins lie in an area just 4km (2½ miles) west of Kos Town. The buildings are set dramatically upon four terraces linked by a marble staircase. Among them, the Temple of Asklepeion is a Doric temple that was built in the 2nd century B.C. The Stoa here once housed Hippocrates's medical school.

More antiquities can be found around the port of Kos Town, where excavations of the ancient city have uncovered ruins from a range of civilizations, from the classical-era **Agora** to a 15th-century **castle built by the Knights of St. John.** It's a remarkable architectural timeline tracing this island's rich history. —*AF*

ⓘ www.hippocrates.gr or www.visit greece.gr.

✈ Athens (55 min.).

⛴ Year-round regular ferry service from several islands, including Piraeus (10 hr.), Rhodes (3 hr.), Mykonos (9 hr.), and Syros (6½ hr.). Daily hydrofoils (fast ferries) run in high season between Kos and Rhodes (2 hr.) and other Aegean islands, including Agathonisi (2½ hr.), Kalymnos (35 min.), Leros (1½ hr.), Lipsi (2 hr.), and Patmos (2½ hr.). Reservations: www.ferries.gr.

🛏 $$ **Alice Springs Hotel,** 100 Lambi, Kos Island (✆ **30/22420-23473;** www.alicespringshotel.com). $$$ **Hotel Platanista,** Psalidi, Kos Island (✆ **30/22420-22400;** www.platanista.gr).

Storied Sand & Surf **48**

Santa Maria

The Yellow Island

The Azores, Portugal

Geographically speaking, Santa Maria is an island with a split personality. Half of it is flat as a pancake, with golden beaches and ubiquitous sunshine, while the other half, the eastern end, is hilly and almost wild with lush vegetation and frequent rainfall—and the island only measures 17km (11 miles) end to end. Like all the Azores, Santa Maria is a traditional place and quite remote, but with its sparkling seacoast, upcountry scenery, and truly untouched feel, there's plenty to draw the visitor in search of an offbeat, beachy island destination.

The southernmost of the Azores archipelago, and the closest, along with São Miguel **299**, to the Portuguese mainland, Santa Maria is sometimes called the "Yellow Island" for the vivid hues of sunny yellow wildflowers that bloom here as early as February. But Santa Maria is an island of many colors—it's known for its whitewashed and basalt-trimmed architecture, some of which dates back to the 15th century when the Portuguese first settled here. In the high country, you can't miss the fertile dark-red soil. Santa Maria is also referred to as the "island of the sun" for the indisputable meteorological fact that Santa Maria is drier and has better weather year-round than its fellow Azores.

Despite its diminutive size, Santa Maria has excellent unspoiled beaches that are integral to the island experience here; the bathing areas are basically divided between São Lourenço Bay, on the northeast coast, and Praia Formosa, a wide bay along the southern coast. Swimmers and aesthetes will want to return to **São Lourenço Bay,** again and again. This crescent of soft sand, punctuated by dramatic rocks, and backed by neatly defined vineyards that terrace up to muscular-looking, verdant hills, is one of the most stunning bathing spots in the Azores. But perhaps the best beach for those who love wide expanses of gorgeous sand is **Praia Formosa,** well equipped with watersports and refreshment facilities.

At 590m (1,936 ft.), **Pico Alto** is the highest point on the island, with breathtaking views in every direction. The main town on Santa Maria, **Vila do Porto,** is also the oldest in the Azores, with characteristic winding streets that lead all the way up to a panoramic fortress on a cliff overlooking the port. The village of **Anjos** earned its place on the tourist circuit of Santa Maria by being the first European spot where Christopher Columbus landed on his return from the Americas. There's a bronze statue of Columbus near the chapel of **Ermida de Nossa Senhora dos Anjos,** one of many historic churches on the island, but one that gets special status because it's where the explorer and his crew prayed for continued safe travels. —*SM*

ⓘ www.azores.com.

✈ Santa Maria Airport, connections from São Miguel.

⛴ From São Miguel (4 hr.), twice per week in summer.

🛏 $$ **Hotel Colombo,** Rua Cruz Teixeira, Vila do Porto (✆ **351/296/820200;** www.colombo-hotel.com).

Storied Sand & Surf

49

Rügen

Bathing in the Baltic Sea

Germany

Beautiful island beaches may not be the first thing that comes to mind when you think about Germany, but this Scandinavian-flavored gem is definitely worth a visit for its sand and shore, especially if you have kids in tow. It's already been discovered by thousands of travelers who flock here for long, leisurely summer holidays.

Located in the Baltic Sea off Germany's northeast coast, 976-sq.-km (377-sq.-mile) Rügen Island is Germany's largest island, with enough land to encompass

Children playing on Rügen beach.

family-friendly seaside resorts, sandy beaches, a chalk-cliff coastline, preserved wetlands, and fairy-tale forests. Its location by the sea keeps temperatures temperate and fresh breezes constant, and its northerly latitude extends daylight hours in summer well into the evening; it gets a hundred more hours of sunshine annually than Munich.

Rügen is home to 70,000 people, who live in four towns and scores of municipalities including the capital, Bergen. In the 19th century it was an elegant Baltic spa resort. It continued to be a popular vacation destination after World War II when it was part of the German Democratic Republic (East Germany), and German reunification did nothing to blunt its popularity. Today the population swells to include visitors on holiday enjoying Rügen's numerous recreational opportunities. The long, fine-sand beach and gentle surf in the seaside town of **Binz** make it ideal for small children (it also has dog-friendly and clothing-optional beaches). Hiking and biking trails trace the island along level, well-maintained pathways. You can rent bikes at **Weiradhaus Deutschmann,** which has two offices in Binz (near the railway station and the petrol station; ✆ **49/38393-32420**).

Children of all ages delight in the **Rasender Roland** (www.rasender-roland.com), a kid-size narrow-gauge railroad steam train that travels from **Putbus** (west of Binz) to **Gohren,** with stops at the resort towns of **Sellin** and **Baabe** and at **Jagdschloss,** a 19th-century hunting castle set at the highest point in a 1,200-hectare (2,965-acre) beech forest. In the evenings, folks in Binz stroll down its famous wooden beachside promenade past elegant, beautifully preserved 19th-century villas with Art Nouveau grace notes. If the stars are out, it's an impossibly romantic scene.

You can get to Rügen by traveling over the Rügenbrucke Bridge, which connects the island by road and rail with the city of Stralsund on the mainland, and crosses over the Strelasund. If you don't have a rental car, Rügen has a reliable public bus system (RPNV; ✆ **49/3838-8229-55**). Whether you take a bus or rent a car, a ride in the countryside reveals the island's impressive assortment of vintage palaces *(schloss)* and manor houses, many of which offer accommodations and cultural events. —*AF*

ⓘ www.ruegen.de or www.ostseebad-binz.de.

✈ Berlin (3½ hr. from Rügen).

⛴ **Glewitz ferry** (www.weisse-flotte.com) between Rügen and the mainland (Stahlbrode-Glewitz). **Scandlines** (www.scandlines.com) transports passengers and autos from Sweden (Trelleborg) to Rügen's Sassnitz harbor, about 10km (6¼ miles) north of Binz.

🛏 $$ **Steigenberger Resort Hotel,** Neddesitz 18 (adjacent to Jasmund National Park; ✆ **49/6966-5644-60;** www.ruegen.steigenberger.com). $$$ **Travel Charme Kurhaus Binz,** Strandpromenade 27, Ostseebad Binz (✆ **49/38393-66-50;** www.travelcharme.com).

Storied Sand & Surf

50

Antigua

A Beach for Every Day of the Year

Here's how you might spend a fine day on the eastern Caribbean island of Antigua. It would start in a boat skimming sparkling green seas where you might spot a hawksbill turtle moving gracefully below the glassy surface. You put down anchor when you find the right beach. Will it be a soft crescent of secluded white sand? A palm-fringed gathering spot with lilting calypso rhythms and barbecues smoking? A sheltered cove of sparkling blue water? Take your pick; all are public. You dive into the warm, sun-splashed seas, water so buoyant you practically float atop the waves. You've brought provisions, of course, picnic fare, drinks, and—most important—snorkeling equipment. The coral reef delivers calm, protected waters packed with underwater eye candy. With flippers and snorkel, you commune with parrotfish, angelfish, grouper, sponges and sea fans, and more big, lumbering turtles. A fine day, indeed.

It's been said that Antigua is more or less a beach with an island in the middle. It's also been said that Antigua has a beach for every day of the year. Even if they number only 364, Antigua's beaches would still rank among the Caribbean's finest. (The locals have their secret favorites.) The gentle waves and powdery sand make **Dickenson Bay,** on the northwest coast, popular with families. The kicked-up Atlantic surf at **Half-Moon Bay,** on the island's southeastern coast, is a windsurfer haven. Some of the island's best snorkeling can be had on **Long Bay, Galleon Beach,** and **Pigeon Beach.** If you're looking for great dive sites, head to the southern or eastern shores, where marine life teems among the steep walls and ledges. **Big John's Dive Antigua** (✆ **268/462-DIVE** [462-3483]; http://diveantigua.com), which has PADI-certified instructors and 25 years' experience diving on Antigua, can help arrange many trips.

Antigua is the largest English-speaking nation in the Leeward Islands; the island nation includes Barbuda 182 and Redonda. Throughout the island, you can see the crumbling relics of the island's days as a sugar-processing workhorse for the British Empire. These days, many of the remnants of 18th-century sugar plantations have been converted into tourist properties or lie in splendid ruins in a tangle of lush vegetation. The historic town of **English Harbor** was once the Caribbean headquarters of the British Navy and is now part of the restored **Nelson's Dockyard National Park.** Antigua's not-so-distant colonization (it achieved full independence from Britain in 1981) is evident in the island's lilting British/Caribbean accents and the tradition of afternoon teas. Most of the islanders are descendants of the African slaves the British brought over to work the sugar plantations.

The island's strong sailing tradition is also a likely offshoot of the British occupation, when a young Horatio Nelson arrived in Antigua in the late 18th century to develop the naval facilities and dockyard (he stayed in his quarters on the ship, calling the island "a vile place"). Regattas and races sponsored by local yacht clubs give the island a fizzy, celebratory ambience year-round. Even if you're not a sailor, you can get out on the water any number of ways, from cruises to eco-tours, to speedboat charters.

Antigua has a pretty sophisticated tourism infrastructure and plenty of small-scale luxury resorts, each with its own splendid chunk of beachfront real estate. But if you're the adventurous sort—and even if you're not—it's highly recommended that you take to the water and discover your own little slice of sandy paradise. —*AF*

ⓘ www.antigua-barbuda.org.

✈ V.C. Bird International Airport.

🛏 $$$ **Carlisle Bay Antigua** (✆ **268/484-0000;** www.carlisle-bay.com). $$ **Sibonney Beach Club** (✆ **268/462-0806;** www.caribbean-resort-antigua-hotel-siboney-beach.com).

Storied Sand & Surf **51**

Oahu

The Hawaiian Icon

Hawaii, U.S.

Though it's sometimes dismissed by island aficionados as either too populated or too Vegas-y to be a proper vacation destination, Oahu is in many ways the most Hawaiian island of the archipelago. Legendary, one-of-a-kind sights like Waikiki Beach, Pearl Harbor, and the North Shore surf breaks make Oahu a must-see, even if only for a few days en route to Maui 263, Kauai 88, or the Big Island 242. This is the Hawaii of classic TV and movies, from the tiki idol episode of the *Brady Bunch* to *From Here to Eternity,* with appealing retro-Polynesian style all over the island. In 2008, Oahu also received a very welcome publicity shot in the arm when native son Barack Obama, the pride of Makiki (a neighborhood in the capital city of **Honolulu,** on the south side of Oahu), was elected President of the United States.

Surfers need no more compelling reason to book a trip to Oahu than the promise of being able to ride the waves that crash on the fabled **North Shore.** When winter brings 30-ft. (9m) swells, the world-class breaks of **Waimea Bay,** the **Banzai Pipeline,** and **Sunset Beach** are for experts only. In summer, the waters are much calmer, and these become idyllic snorkeling spots. The funky town of **Haleiwa** is known as Surf City, U.S.A., with all the midcentury memorabilia and hang-loose atmosphere you'd expect—a little kitschy, but fun.

Surfing in Oahu.

Of course, you haven't seen Oahu until you've done **Waikiki beach.** Essentially a suburb of Honolulu, Waikiki's famous pink-sand beach is lined with glitzy hotels, excellent dining and shopping, and great places to people-watch. It's hard to find any kind of Polynesian soul in Waikiki, but the dramatic promontory of **Diamond Head volcano,** at one end of the beach, is an undeniably iconic symbol of Hawaii. All along the beach here are watersports vendors offering everything from snorkeling equipment rentals to outrigger canoe excursions.

Oahu's "day of infamy"—the bombing of **Pearl Harbor** on December 7, 1941—is chillingly recalled at the **USS *Arizona* Memorial** (www.nps.gov/usar). The monument spans the sunken remains of the ship where 1,177 crew members died during the Japanese aerial attack. Also at Pearl Harbor, the enormous **USS *Missouri*** battleship (www.ussmissouri.com), where Japan signed its surrender in 1945 to end World War II, is now open to the public as a museum ship.

Since the 2008 presidential campaign, Obama tourism has become a lucrative addition for island guides—as much a part of the modern Oahu experience as surf lessons on Waikiki beach or visiting the *Arizona* memorial. For a fee, entrepreneurial locals will sell you a map that marks all the places on Oahu where the various generations of Barack's family have ever set foot, and organized tours will take you to the 44th president's favorite burger joint, **Kua 'Aina Sandwich Shop** (66-160 Kamehameha Hwy.; ✆ **808/637-6067**), or bodysurfing spot, **Sandy Beach,** on Oahu's southeastern tip. —*SM*

ⓘ www.gohawaii.com/oahu or www.visit-oahu.com.

✈ Honolulu International.

🛏 $$$ **Royal Hawaiian,** 2259 Kalakaua Ave., Waikiki (✆ **808/923-7311;** www.royal-hawaiian.com). $$ **Waikiki Parc,** Lewers St. (✆ **800/422-0450** or 808/921-7272; www.waikikiparchotel.com).

52 Archipelagos & Atolls

Bazaruto Archipelago

Pearl of the Indian Ocean

Mozambique

Glorious Mozambique is like Rip Van Winkle awakening from a deep sleep. Held back by years of iron-fisted colonial rule, devastating civil wars, and drought, this East African nation is emerging as one of the world's most unspoiled, undiscovered destinations. Among its treasures is the beautiful Bazaruto Archipelago, whose pink-coral beaches and dazzling Indian Ocean seas have been largely untouched by civilization for decades. It's a seascape so magical, so environmentally exquisite, that the government has wisely designated the entire archipelago as a protected national marine park. It's a remarkably forward-thinking directive aimed at maintaining the region's ecological and social integrity.

The archipelago is composed of five islands lying in the Indian Sea off the southern coast of Mozambique: Bazaruto, Benguerua, Margaruque, Banque, and Santa Carolina. **Margaruque** is a private island owned by a Zimbabwean millionaire. **Banque** is tiny and completely undeveloped. The largest island, **Bazaruto,** has voluminous sand dunes whose color changes with the light, from Namibian red to blindingly white. Both Bazaruto and the second-largest island, **Benguerua,** have interiors of glittering freshwater lakes, home to large crocodiles—evidence of the island's ancient past. Benguerua also has high, beautiful dunes, from which you can watch the moon set and the sun rise. One way to experience this amazing landscape is on horseback; **Mozambique Horse Safari** (✆ **258/82-7639249;** www.mozambiquehorsesafari.com) offers day rides on Benguerua's empty white-sand beaches past flocks of flamingos skimming the tidal flats. Cashew nuts, once the country's major export, still grow on indigenous trees on Benguerua, as do wild orange trees, coconut palms, and sisal plants.

The rich and famous haunted **Santa Carolina** island (also known as Paradise Island) from the 1940s to the 1960s, when Mozambique was still a Portuguese colony. Bob Dylan wrote the song "Mozambique" on a piano in the sumptuous 250-room Art Deco **Hotel Santa Carolina;** the piano is now in safekeeping at the Indigo Bay Island Resort (see below) because when the Portuguese abruptly fled the country in 1975, they abandoned the hotel; it now lies in ruins. Rani Resorts, which runs several resorts in Mozambique, have been granted the rights to redevelop the island and plan to re-create the hotel as it was in the 1940s; look for a 2010 opening.

The islands in the Bazaruto archipelago are largely sand, sea, and tropical flora and fauna. There are no towns on the islands, no shops, no streets, and no cars. Tourism is in its infancy here, and large-scale development is not in the cards for the archipelago. The handful of resorts on the islands follow the conservation-minded example of the high-end, low-volume, low-impact bush lodges of Botswana: pampered luxury in pristine surrounds, at a price. Foreigners are not allowed to own land in Mozambique but can build (eco-conscious) concessions with long-term (99-year) leases.

Even though the island "attractions" are few, there's plenty to do here. Activities include superb **deep-sea diving** and **snorkeling** on unspoiled coral reefs; **saltwater fly-fishing;** and **big-game fishing** for whopping marlin, sailfish, king mackerel, and bonito (tag and release, of course). Bazaruto also has the largest remaining population of **dugong** in East Africa. This extremely rare mammal is a sea cow (and relative of the manatee) and though it has been hunted to the brink of extinction, it can be spotted on boat tours. You can arrange any of these activities through your lodging.

It's not difficult to get to Bazaruto. You can fly into the coastal city of **Vilanculos,** on the Mozambique mainland, from Maputo (Mozambique's capital) or Johannesburg, South Africa. Most resorts then arrange for charter flights from Vilanculos to the islands or set up boat transfers. Non–hotel guests are not allowed onto the islands with resort properties. *—AF*

ⓘ www.mozambiquetourism.co.za.

✈ Vilanculos, Mozambique (from Maputo, Mozambique, 1 hr., 20 min.; Johannesburg, South Africa, 2 hr., 30 min.). Charter flights on CFA Air Carters from Maputo.

⛴ Lodges arrange boat transfers (30 min.).

🛏 $$$ **Indigo Bay Island Resort & Spa,** Bazaruto Island (✆ **27/011/658-0063;** www.indigobayresort.com). $$$ **Marlin Lodge,** Benguerua Island (✆ **27/012/460-9410;** www.marlinlodge.co.za).

53 Archipelagos & Atolls

San Blas Islands

Kuna Yala

Panama

Imagine this: The San Blas Islands were once simply a place you passed through on the way to the Panama Canal. Boy, have times changed: The sleepy little San Blas Islands are still sleepy—that's their charm—but these idyllic, sun-dappled tropical isles off the northeast coast of Panama are now a big lure for nature lovers and beach bums. The pristine islands in the Caribbean Sea were even selected one of the top two "best cruising destinations in the world" by *Cruising World* magazine, and CBS's *Survivor* TV show visited one San Blas island, Sapbeinega.

Composed of approximately 365 islands and cays, the San Blas Islands are part of the Comarca de Kuna Yala, an autonomous territory controlled by the native Kunas, who call it Kuna Yala ("Kuna Territory"). Only 60 of the islands are inhabited; the others are largely uninhabited white-sand atolls fringed with palm trees and ringed by pulsing coral reefs and clear, sparkling emerald seas. It's an impossibly gorgeous seascape. The capital of Kuna Yala is the island of **El Porvenir,** a 20-minute flight from Panama City. If you decide to stay in the Porvenir area, head to **Island Perro (Dog Island)** for some great snorkeling just off the beach around the wreck of an old cargo ship. Other top snorkeling spots include the **Cayos Holandes,** a group of remote and largely uninhabited cays in the northeast quadrant of the archipelago.

Some 50,000 Kunas currently live in Panama. One segment of this indigenous tribe lives on just a handful of the islands in thatched-roof villages—theirs is a close-knit community in the most literal sense. The rest of the San Blas islands have an almost primitive, castaway feel, with no one else for miles around. Coral reefs support a vital population of spectacularly hued marine life—you can snorkel-hop from one island to the next with joyous abandon.

One of the most fascinating things to do in the San Blas Islands is take an expedition to a Kuna village and learn more about the Kuna culture. The Kunas move from one island to another in motorized *cayucos* (dugout canoes), and many of the lodges are owned and operated by the Kunas. You can even buy traditional (Keith Haring–like) *mola* embroidered textiles. The Kuna women wear traditional colorful dresses (women travelers should wear one-piece suits or coverups, if possible, to avoid offending the Kunas). **Ancon Expeditions of Panama** (✆ **507/269-9415;** www.anconexpeditions.com) offers solid Kuna Village and San Blas expeditions.

If you're interested in taking combination kayaking and snorkeling trips of the San Blas Islands, contact **Adventuras Panama** (✆ **507/260-0044;** www.aventuras panama.com). Full-service 3- to 21-day sailing trips of the island archipelago are offered by **San Blas Sailing** (✆ **507/314-1800;** www.sanblassailing.com), with plenty of mooring stops to snorkel, swim, and soak up the scenery. —*AF*

ⓘ www.visitpanama.com.

✈ Panama City, then small plane (Air Panama or Aeroperlas) to El Porvenir.

🛏 $$ **Coral Lodge,** near San Blas (✆ **507/232-0200;** www.corallodge.com). $$ **Sapibenega The Kuna Lodge,** Iskardup island (✆ **507/215-1406;** www.sapibenega.com).

Archipelagos & Atolls

54

Turneffe Islands Atoll

Life on the Atoll

Belize

From the shallows to the deep, the marine ecosystem in Belize is so vibrant that the waters pulse with life everywhere you look. For fishermen chasing hard-fighting bonefish in sparkling saltwater flats and divers exploring tropical coral gardens, the Turneffe Atoll is one of the most vital places in the world. In fact, according to the Oceanic Society, which operates a marine research center here on Blackbird Caye, Turneffe is the most biologically diverse atoll in the Western Hemisphere.

At 48km long and 16km wide (30×10 miles), the Turneffe Islands Atoll is the largest of three atolls (coral reefs ringing a shallow lagoon) off the coast of Belize. Some 200 islands, or cayes, make up the atoll, some mere dollops of sugary white sand, others blanketed by mangrove forests or swaying coconut palms. The islands represent the tip of a submerged volcanic rim that rises from deep offshore waters, and the surrounding vertical wall makes for world-class diving with excellent visibility (down to 24–30m/80–100 ft.). Sightings include eagle rays, turtles, green morays, jewfish, nurse and reef sharks, grouper, snapper, and horse-eye jacks. Close by, the **Elbow** offers huge gorgonians and sponges in current-driven drift dives. A little farther out, **Lighthouse Reef** features the famed underwater sites **Half Moon Caye** and **Blue Hole.** It was Jacques Cousteau who blazed the trail to the Blue Hole in 1972. This circular limestone sinkhole, 300m (984 ft.) wide and more than 120m (394 ft.) deep, is actually a massive Ice Age cavern whose roof collapsed to create a cobalt-blue ocean hole. It's filled with giant stalactites and stalagmites and large pelagics, fat groupers, and rays.

You can get to Turneffe by a 2- to 3-hour boat ride from Belize City for day trips on the atoll, or you can take overnights on full-service dive boats operating out of Belize City or Ambergris Caye 44; the **Aggressor Fleet** (www.aggressor.com) offers weekly dive trips to the Turneffe Atoll on the ***Belize Aggressor II*** out of Belize City. But perhaps the most thrilling way to experience Turneffe is to stay at one of the three well-run resorts on the atoll, all of which have excellent fishing and dive operations and offer fishing, dive, and general vacation packages. The oldest (40 years) is the 5.6-hectare (14-acre) private island resort **Turneffe Island Lodge** (see below), considered one of the Caribbean's top saltwater-flats fishing destinations. Blackbird Caye has two resorts: **Turneffe Flats** and **Blackbird Caye Resort.**

Avid divers and anglers have long known about Turneffe, but it's a little off the radar of most mainstream travelers, perhaps because the atoll lies 56km (35 miles) from the mainland, and the tourism infrastructure of this unspoiled landscape is, well, little more than water and sand. Things may be shifting, however. Conservationists are raising warning flags that the balance of this exquisite ecosystem could be tipped in the near future by illegal fishing and the private purchases of public land—slices of the atoll are up for sale. Much is riding on the preservation of these marine habitats: According to the Ocean Society, the expanses of mangrove and sea-grass habitat serve as a huge nursery area for crocodiles, manatees, dolphins, and invertebrates. Underwater sponges provide rich feeding grounds for the endangered hawksbill sea turtle. Endangered and threatened nesting species of birds include the least tern, the roseate tern, and the white crowned pigeon.

If you simply can't get enough of unspoiled coral atolls, head just south of Turneffe to **Glover's Reef.** It was named for the 18th-century British pirate John Glover, who used the atoll as a base from which to plunder passing Spanish galleons. This marine reserve and UNESCO World Heritage Site has a no-fishing zone (over 75% of the area) that ensures a rich and diverse marine life along the 207-sq.-km (80-sq.-mile) coral reef. —*AF*

ⓘ www.travelbelize.org.

✈ Belize City (48–56km/30–35 miles from Turneffe).

Boat transfers to island from airport (about 90 min.).

$$$ **Turneffe Flats,** Blackbird Caye (✆ **888/512-8812** in the U.S. or 501/220-4046; www.tflats.com). $$$ **Turneffe Island Lodge,** Little Caye Bokel (✆ **713/236-7739** [U.S.]; www.turnefferesort.com).

55 Archipelagos & Atolls

Tuvalu

Somewhere in the South Pacific . . .

At the remote coordinates of 9 degrees south latitude and 179 degrees east longitude, Tuvalu may just be the most far-flung independent monarchy in the world. Its name, pronounced Tu-*vah*-loo, means "eight standing together," for the eight islands that originally composed Tuvalu. There are now nine, together covering a grand total of 27 sq. km (10 sq. miles) in area, making it the fourth-smallest country in the world land-wise; the population, at just over 11,000, isn't much bigger. The South Pacific island of Tuvalu is one very remote spot, with little tourism infrastructure, but if you do find your way there—perhaps sailing between Hawaii and the Cook Islands (p. 516) or French Polynesia—you'll find broadly smiling locals and a number of interesting sights and activities to keep you happily occupied as you hop around the atolls.

Five of the islands of Tuvalu are atolls while the other four are the tops of more solid pinnacles of land. None of the islands of Tuvalu reaches an elevation of more than about 4m (13 ft.), and all are covered with sugary white sand and coconut palms. **Funafuti** atoll is the capital of Tuvalu, and its village of **Fogafale** is where the island's few services are to be found. Bicycles are the preferred mode of transportation here and far outnumber motor vehicles. The Australian dollar is the local currency.

Tuvalu's attractions do not include any mountains, hikes, or waterfalls. Instead, it's all about the uninterrupted, bliss-inspiring (and potentially stir-crazy-making) expanses of ocean in every direction, and outstanding snorkeling amid the coral reefs. Great distances of open water separate the islands of Tuvalu, so if you're looking for the truly unspoiled South Pacific, this is it. Tuvaluans perform their Polynesian dances for each other—not outside visitors, though they're welcome, too—and play an ancient ballgame called *te ano* that also involves singing, dancing, and traditional dress.

During World War II, Tuvalu was occupied by the Americans, and this provides a bit of historical sightseeing around the islands. The **remains of warplanes** are nestled in the shrubs along the American-built airstrip on Nanumea; and on that same island, the wrecks of small American landing craft are still visible in the low surf. The principal "archaeological" site on Funafuti is not war-related but Darwin-related: It was here that several holes were bored more than 300m (984 ft.) to prove Darwin's theory on the formation of atolls. The boreholes can still be seen today at the site called **David's Drill,** after the scientist who led the experiment.

Although it's unlikely that tourism will be sufficiently developed here to provide a significant source of income, Tuvalu has benefited greatly from the Internet age: Its national domain suffix **".tv"** is hungrily sought by media corporations worldwide, and Tuvalu is only happy to sell, providing the tiny island nation with millions of site-rights dollars every year. —*SM*

ⓘ www.timelesstuvalu.com or www.tuvaluislands.com.

✈ Funafuti International Airport (connections to Tarawa, Kiribati and Suva, Fiji).

🛏 $$ **Vaiaku Lagi,** Funafuti (✆ **688/20501;** vaiakulagi@gmail.com).

2 Garden Islands

Beautiful Bounty

56

Corfu

Emerald Isle

Greece

If Greece had a nurturing Mother Nature, Corfu would fit the bill. Bathed in sunshine, Corfu is all about man and the natural world coexisting in exquisite, joyful harmony. The warm Mediterranean climate nourishes classic flora that has grown here since Homer's time: olive and fig trees, grapes, and pomegranates. In fact, during Venetian rule, groves of olive trees were planted throughout the island to support the burgeoning olive oil industry; today the island terrain holds some five million olive trees. Fruit trees bearing oranges, lemons, and kumquats cover verdant slopes, and some 600 varieties of wildflowers blanket the hillsides. During harvest season, the air is scented with the perfume of ripened grapes. The weather is so temperate, subtropical even, that banana trees thrive in spots.

The northernmost of the Greek Ionian islands, Corfu—known as Kerkyra in Greek—lies in the Adriatic Sea. Its lush greenness sets it somewhat apart from other Greek islands, but it also has the classic Greek island lineup of stunning beaches, dramatic rocky outcroppings, and picturesque villages. **Paleokastritsa,** the largest beach on the west coast, has two bottle-green bays enclosed by cliffs—James Bond cavorted here in *For Your Eyes Only.* You can snorkel in the tranquil waters off **Kassiopi,** a vintage fishing village on the island's northeast coast.

Aside from its bountiful natural attributes, Corfu has a rich and interesting history. The Phoenicians who first occupied the island made sure their creature comforts were well taken care of and were considered hospitable hosts, reportedly showing Odysseus a fine time. The 400-year reign of the Venetians (which ended at the dawn of the 19th c.) is evident in the handsome neoclassical architecture in **Corfu Town,** the island's capital; its **Old Town** was named a World Heritage Site in 2007. The town dates back to the 8th century B.C., and among its most impressive buildings are three forts designed by esteemed Venetian engineers, built to defend the trading interests of the Republic of Venice against the Ottomans.

The magnificent gardens on the grounds of the neoclassical **Achillion Palace,** high atop Corfu in the village of Gastouri, only look ancient—they were planted amid Greek statuary as a summer retreat for the Empress Elizabeth of Austria (known as "Sisi") in the late 1900s. The palace lost its beloved mistress in 1898, when Sisi was assassinated by an Italian anarchist, and was vandalized during World War II. But today the restored palace and grounds, where vines of purple wisteria drape stone statuary, is one of the island's biggest attractions.

Stop in at a local *taverna* for a taste of classic Mediterranean fare, here and there revealing the Italian influences of the Venetian era, such as *pastitsado,* a meat stew served over pasta. You might wash it down with some of the locally made wines, many produced from the white Kakotrygis and red Petrokoritho grapes grown on island vineyards. And don't leave the island without a bottle of kumquat liqueur, made from the Chinese fruit that has been cultivated on this lush and lovely island since the late 1800s. —*AF*

Previous page: Moorea.

ⓘ http://ionian-islands.com and www.corfuonline.gr.

✈ Athens (50 min.).

⛴ Many lines and ships link Corfu to both Greek and foreign ports, including Igoumenitsou (1–2 hr.), Patras (about 7 hr.), and ports in Italy, such as Ancona, Bari, Brindisi, Trieste, and Venice.

🛏 $$ **Cavalieri,** 4 Kapodistriou (✆ **30/26610/39041;** www.cavalieri-hotel.com). $$$ **Corfu Palace Hotel,** 2 Leoforos Demokratias (✆ **30/26610/39485;** www.corfupalace.com).

57 **Beautiful Bounty**

Grenada

The Spice Island

At one time, Grenada produced more nutmeg than any other spot in the world, except for Indonesia. Richly endowed with ideal conditions for growing tropical fruits and spices, the "Isle of Spice," in the southeastern Caribbean Sea just north of Venezuela, grew more spices per square mile than any other place on earth, kitchen staples like nutmeg, cinnamon, ginger, cloves, bay leaves, and mace. But in 2004, crops in Grenada suffered a devastating hit from Hurricane Ivan (followed, the next year, by a cruel drenching from Hurricane Emily). The storms wiped out 85% of the island's nutmeg trees—Grenada's "black gold" and biggest export, a $20-million industry.

Today, the bounty of the Caribbean is back in full flower on Grenada, which is actually the largest island in the three-island independent nation of Grenada (the other

Grenada.

islands are Carriacou and Petit Martinique). The island interior—a lush oasis of rainforest and mountains—is a riot of blooms, from hibiscus to bougainvillea to frangipani, ringed by classic sugary-sand beaches, some 40 palm-fringed crescents lapped by turquoise seas. Fruit trees hang heavy with mangoes, papaya, carambola, and breadfruit, and sugar cane fields dot the landscape. Nutmeg trees have been replanted, but it's still too early to tell if the industry can rebound to pre-Ivan levels (it takes 7 or 8 years for the trees to bear fruit—and it turns out the farmers may have planted more male trees than female).

If spices are what you're after—nutmeg included—you'll have no trouble finding fresh dried spice packs to take home. Head to **Market Square,** in Grenada's capital **St. George's,** or other marketplaces on the island. You can also tour the old spice estates and processing factories to see just how the local crops go from tree to table. (Cinnamon, interestingly, is extracted from the inner bark of the cinnamon tree.) Take a tour at the **Dougaldston Spice Estate,** just outside Gouyave, a weather-beaten relic from the 19th century. Tours are also offered at the **Nutmeg Processing Stations** in Gouyave and Grenville, the island's largest nutmeg processing factories. But perhaps the island's biggest agritourism attraction is the 17th-century **Belmont Estate** (✆ **473/442-9524;** www.belmontestate.net), a working organic farm where cocoa has replaced nutmeg as the top crop—the estate has allied with the Grenada Chocolate Company to make fine organic dark chocolate. Visitors can tour Belmont's gardens, heritage museum, goat dairy, and the cocoa processing facilities and dine in the estate cafe.

Grenada also has three rum distilleries where the local sugar cane crops are processed and where exotic blends that draw on the island bounty are produced—how about rum flavored with cinnamon and passion fruit? Take a guided tour at the historic **River Antoine Rum Distillery** (✆ **473/442-7109**), the oldest water-propelled distillery in the Caribbean. Sample the potent (70% alcohol) white rum, distilled in much the same way as when the factory was built in 1785.

Of course, you can always leave the touring to others and take advantage of the island's top-notch water-based activities. The diving on Grenada is world-class, and includes the vivid marine life found around the **World War II–era *Bianca C.,*** the largest shipwreck in the Caribbean, which lies a mile offshore. Or you can pick one of the island's lovely beaches—**Grand Anse,** perhaps, or **Anse La Roche**—and simply drift away to the music of the sea and the lingering perfume of spices in the air. —*AF*

ⓘ www.grenadagrenadines.com.

✈ Point Salines International Airport.

🛏 $$ **La Sagesse,** St. Davids (✆ **473/444-6458;** www.lasagesse.com). $$$ **Spice Island Beach Resort,** Grand Anse Beach (✆ **473/444-4258;** www.spiceisland beachresort.com).

Beautiful Bounty **58**

Prince Edward Island

Beyond Green Gables

Canada

Sometimes it gets a bit much, all the Anne of Green Gables hoopla around Prince Edward Island. How can a century-old series of children's books define an entire Canadian province?

Green Gables.

But cross the Confederation Bridge from New Brunswick and drive around PEI's low rolling hills blanketed in trees and crops, and that bucolic past celebrated in Lucy Maud Montgomery's books makes sense after all. Explore beyond the jagged coast with its inlets and historic fishing villages, and you'll discover that small farms make up the island's backbone—one-quarter of Prince Edward Island is dedicated to agriculture, with more than 2,300 individual farms, many of them devoted to the island's most famous crop, potatoes (there's even a Potato Museum in O'Leary). Maybe it's just the Midwesterner in me, but I find this fertile, placid farmland totally alluring.

Relatively flat and compact, Prince Edward Island is a great place to explore by bicycle—it was the first province to complete its section of the **TransCanada Trail,** with the Confederation Trail crossing the island from Tignish in the west to Elmira in the east. Covering 270km (168 miles), the trail is built along the abandoned route of the Prince Edward Island Railway, so it's conveniently level-graded with bridges across gullies and sparkling rivers and boardwalks built over marshy areas. Curving like a snake along the island's spine, it passes through woodlands, wetlands, croplands, and quaint villages, giving you a wonderful cross section of the island terrain.

East of the lively capital, **Charlottetown,** it's worth a detour to visit **Orwell Corner Historic Village** (✆ **902/651-8515;** www.orwellcorner.ca), which recreates life in a small agricultural town in the 1890s. North of Charlottetown, **Prince Edward Island National Park** stretches along the coast of the surprisingly warm Gulf of St. Lawrence, a lovely swath of red-sand beaches, placid inlets, vast salt marshes, and wind-sculpted dunes topped with marram grass. Outside the park, you can get in touch with the island's Acadian heritage at the five **Rusticos:** the coastal villages of North Rustico, South Rustico, Rusticoville, Rustico Harbour, and Anglo Rustico.

Which inevitably brings you to **Cavendish,** the vortex of Anne of Green Gables country. Plenty of tacky amusement parks and motels line this stretch of Route 6, but you really should see the farmstead that

Island Hopping the Florida Keys: Stringing the Pearls

Like a gigantic real-world game of connect-the-dots, the Overseas Highway skips from island to island through the Florida Keys, with 42 bridges linking some 30 islands of this 400-plus-island archipelago. Sure, you can fly directly into Key West or the mid-Keys hub of Marathon, but that almost feels like cheating—there's something intriguing about following that highway all the way through this 150-mile-long (242km) string of islands, like pearls in a necklace.

Built in 1938 to replace Henry Flagler's railroad (which had been destroyed by a hurricane—that's South Florida for you), the Overseas Highway is a jumping-off point for the Keys—most islands are still accessible only by boat, many of them unpopulated. Divers, snorkelers, sport fishermen, and kayakers may depend on the highway to get here—addresses in the Keys generally refer to U.S. 1 mile markers—but as soon as possible they leave its inevitable traffic jams behind and get onto the water. And the farther you go, the more exotic and unspoiled the Florida Keys still seem.

Many divers get no farther than the first large island off the mainland, 59 **Key Largo** (originally Rock Harbor, it was renamed after the 1948 Humphrey Bogart film), where **John Pennekamp Coral Reef State Park** (Mile Marker 102) protects part of the only living coral reef in the continental United States. Glass-bottom boat tours are the classic way for nondiving tourists to view this undersea preserve's shallow waters, populated with 40 species of coral and more than 650 species of fish. For a more serene experience, rent a canoe to paddle through Pennekamp's narrow mangrove channels and tidal creeks. Less well-known is Key Largo's other gem, **Dagny Johnson Key Largo Hammock Botanical State Park** (C.R. 905, off Mile Marker 106), a fascinating remnant of West Indian tropical hardwood hammock (which is an elevated piece of land above a marsh), created by seeds dropped by migratory songbirds flying north from the Caribbean. Over 6 miles (9.7km) of nature trails display 84 protected species of plants and animals, including several rare birds (white-crowned pigeons, mangrove cuckoos, black-whiskered vireos) and an incredible number of butterflies. You can also get close to nature at the **Florida Keys Wild Bird Center** in Tavernier (Mile Marker 93.6), a much-loved sanctuary for injured local birds where you can hike a nature trail; watch pelicans, cormorants, herons, and roseate spoonbills feeding in the shallows; and learn about the Keys ecosystem.

A scrum of marinas and charter-boat operations tells you that sport fishing is king in the next community, Islamorada (actually four islands: Plantation Key, Windley Key, Upper and Lower Matecumbe Keys). From Islamorada, take a ferry or rent a powerboat to visit 60 **Lignumvitae Key** (visitor center at Mile Marker 88.5), another rare fragment of virgin tropical forest. Named for the lignum vitae ("wood of life") trees found there, it still has several lush hammocks which botanists have painstakingly restored so that only truly native species live here. Don't miss the splendid botanical gardens surrounding the park's main structure, the coral rock Matheson House, built in 1919. Past Islamorada, 61 **Long Key**—once Henry Flagler's exclusive fishing retreat—is almost entirely occupied by the 965-acre (391-hectare) **Long Key State Recreation Area,** sited atop the remains of an ancient coral reef. Here you can hike or canoe through several distinct habitats, including beaches where sea turtles nest in season (humans can observe from a respectful distance).

Once you cross Long Key, you've reached the somewhat more laid-back Middle Keys, with its main town of 62 **Marathon** (covering Vaca, Fat Deer, and Grassy Keys). Sun worshipers flock to Sombrero Beach, one of the few really good beaches in the Keys, but for nature lovers the highlight is the **Crane Point Nature Center** (Mile Marker 50), a 64-acre (26-hectare) property containing what is probably the last virgin thatch-palm hammock in North America. The visitor center has some wonderful exhibits on local ecology; walking trails meander through several habitats, from a butterfly meadow to a freshwater pond to stands of red, white, and black mangroves. For a glimpse of vintage Keys life before the highway arrived, take a ferry from Knight's Key (Mile Marker 47) to historic 63 **Pigeon Key,** a palm-fringed 5-acre (2-hectare) island under the old Seven-Mile Bridge where Flagler's railroad workers lived in modest yellow wood-frame cottages. While cars today soar over the water on its modern replacement, the original Seven-Mile Bridge—itself a major engineering feat for its time—has become an alternative route for cycling and other "green" modes of transport; if you have time, you can walk the 2¼ miles (3.5km) over it to Pigeon Key.

Crossing the Seven-Mile Bridge, you'll pass from the Middle Keys to the Lower Keys and soon reach 64 **Bahia Honda** (Mile Marker 37.5), a 524-acre (212-hectare) state park with one of the most beautiful coastlines in South Florida. The whole range of Lower Keys ecosystems are represented here: coastal mangroves, tropical hammocks, beach dunes, and even a small white-sand beach. Bahia Honda is a magnet for bird-watchers, with rare species like reddish egrets, roseate spoonbills, mangrove cuckoos, black-whiskered vireos, and white-crowned pigeons. The most famous residents of 65 **Big Pine Key** are the tiny Key deer: Only about 300 of these delicate creatures exist in the world, two-thirds of them at the **National Key Deer Refuge** (entrance at Mile Marker 30.5). Hit the walking trail through the hammocks in early morning or late evening, when these gentle dog-size creatures come to the rock quarry to drink. You may have started down the Overseas Highway thinking that Key West was your destination; at moments like this, you'll realize it's all about the journey. *—HH*

ⓘ **Key Largo Chamber of Commerce,** U.S. 1 at Mile Marker 106 (✆ **800/822-1088** or 305/451-1414; www.keylargo.org). **Islamorada Chamber of Commerce,** U.S. 1 at Mile Marker 82.5 (✆ **800/322-5397** or 305/664-4503; www.islamoradachamber.com). **Greater Marathon Chamber of Commerce,** U.S. 1 at Mile Marker 53.5 (✆ **800/262-7284** or 305/743-5417; www.floridakeysmarathon.com).

✈ Miami International Airport, Key West International Airport, or Florida Keys Marathon Airport.

🛏 $$ **Conch Key Cottages,** 62250 Overseas Hwy., near Marathon (✆ **800/330-1577** or 305/289-1377; www.conchkeycottages.com). $$$ **Little Palm Island Resort,** 28500 Overseas Hwy., near Little Torch Key (✆ **800/343-8567** or 305/515-4004; www.littlepalmisland.com).

started it all, **Green Gables** (2 Palmers Lane; ✆ **902/963-7874;** www.pc.gc.ca), a solid white mid-19th-century farmhouse with green shutters (and, naturally, green gable points) that belonged to cousins of author Montgomery. Parks Canada owns the site and has meticulously furnished the rooms according to descriptions in the books. Walking trails from the house lead to outdoor settings from the novel such as Lover's Lane and the Haunted Woods.

It's also worth stopping at **Avonlea** (Rte. 6; ✆ **902/963-3050;** www.avonleavillage.com), a "re-creation" of Montgomery's fictional version of Cavendish: Among the faux vintage buildings are a few real historic structures imported from elsewhere in the region, including a schoolhouse where Montgomery once taught and a church she attended. —HH

ⓘ **Tourist office,** Gateway Village, by the Confederation Bridge (✆ **800/463-4734** or 902/368-4444; www.gov.pe.ca or www.tourismpei.com).

✈ Charlottetown.

⛴ Wood Islands (75 min. from Caribou, Nova Scotia).

🛏 $$$ **Barachois Inn,** Church Rd., Rustico (✆ **800/963-2194** or 902/963-2194; www.barachoisinn.com). $$ **Cavendish Beach Cottages,** 1445 Gulf Shore Rd., Cavendish (✆ **902/963-2025;** www.cavendishbeachcottages.com).

Blooming Wonders **66**

Flores

Island of Flowers

The Azores, Portugal

Portugal's Azores islands are beautiful, tranquil, and sparsely inhabited. Flores, the "Flower Island," is blessed with shimmering lakes, hills carpeted with greenery, dramatic *miradouros* (viewpoints) along rocky promontories, and a charmingly bucolic old-world tableau of seaside villages, vintage water mills, and clip-clopping oxcarts. Oh, and tourists are few and far between. Sounds perfect, right?

Well it is—but Flores is also an isolated speck in the middle of the Atlantic Ocean and historically difficult to access, which explains the small, tidy number of inhabitants and visitors to this part of the world. But with air travel picking up between the Azores and the rest of the world—Flores is now just a 4-hour nonstop hop from such cities as Boston and Montreal—it's becoming more and more popular with North American East Coasters.

The Azores, a chain of nine islands strung across 644km (400 miles) of sea, stretches the boundaries of Western Europe deep into the mid-Atlantic. The tiny island of Flores, which lies a good distance away from the other islands in the archipelago, is Europe's westernmost point.

Flores has been called "a garden floating on the foam of the sea" for the flowers that blanket hill and dale in summer, particularly **hydrangeas.** The hydrangea's flower head varies in color according to the acidity of the soil—so the hues of these big, showy blooms can be white, blue, lavender, or dusty pink depending on the soil in which its roots are planted. (In fact, a neighboring island, Faial 491, has so many blue hydrangeas it's often referred to as the "Blue Island.") These and other luxuriant plants thrive here on Flores because of the island's proximity to the Gulf Stream, which makes the climate moderate enough to grow a range of exotica, from wild ferns to Japanese cedars, Brazilian lantana, Asian camellias, and African dragon trees. Neither the hydrangea nor the flower for which the island was named—the yellow-hued cubre—is native: Both were likely introduced by colonists from Europe—whether explorers, pirates, farmers, or whalers—who began arriving in the 15th century.

Flores is nature at its most glorious—from the depths of the island's seven glassy lakes, trimmed in flowers, to the heights of its mountain peaks (**Sete Pes, Burrinha, Marcel,** and the 900m/2,953-ft. **Morro Alto,** the highest point on the island). Waterfalls tumble down island cliffs into the sea; the **Ribeira Grande** waterfall, in Fajazinha, drops some 300m (984 ft.). The **Hotel Ocidental** (see below) is the activities center for the island, offering walking tours, whale-watching excursions, and scuba diving. —*AF*

ⓘ www.visitazores.org or www.visitazores.travel.

✈ João Paulo II Airport on the island of São Miguel (SATA Azores Express; 50 min.).

🛏 $$ **Aldeia da Cuada** (✆ **351/292/590-040;** www.aldeiadacuada.com). $$ **Hotel Ocidental,** av. Dos Baleeiros (✆ **351/292/590-100;** www.hotelocidental.com).

67 Blooming Wonders

Tresco

A Blooming Miracle

The Scilly Isles, U.K.

It lies just 47km (29 miles) across the water from rugged Land's End, Cornwall, from where it takes only 20 minutes to get here by helicopter. You'd think the outlying location would serve up nothing but harsh Atlantic winds and waves, but the Isles of Scilly will surprise you: Thanks to the warm currents of the Gulf Stream, the islands have a unique microclimate where semitropical plants spring lushly from the granite soil. The islands' main export, in fact, is flowers, blooms that appear weeks ahead of their mainland cousins; in summer the isles are simply a mass of colorful blossom.

Of the five inhabited Scilly islands, St. Mary's is the largest, the one where planes land and ferries dock, and there's no doubt it's charming—a fine place to cycle and beachcomb and bird-watch. But if gardening's your passion, head straight for its tiny neighbor Tresco. Only 1.6km wide by 3.2km long (1×2 miles), Tresco is technically private property, but visitors are its bread and butter. Presiding over this island estate, **Tresco Abbey** is an Italianate stone manor built in the 19th century by Tresco's Lord Proprietor Augustus Smith beside the ruined arches and crumbling walls of the old 12th century Benedictine abbey of St. Nicholas. Scilly islanders led a hardscrabble existence from the 15th to the 19th century—the islands' location at the mouth of the Channel left them exposed to every foreign threat from the Spanish Armada to Napoleon's navy—but under Smith's leadership, prosperity finally came to Tresco.

You can't visit the house (Smith's descendants still live there), but the surrounding **Abbey Gardens** (✆ **44/1720/424108**) are the real point of visiting Tresco. Encouraging Scilly farmers to pursue the flower trade, Smith set an example by planting his own showcase gardens, transforming a barren moorland into one of Britain's horticultural showplaces; today it features more than 5,000 species of plants from 80 different countries. Notice the south-facing terraces, which expose the semitropical plants to the

Tresco.

greatest amount of sun, and the system of walls and California pine and cypress trees cleverly arranged to protect the plants in winter when gales of salt air whip over the islands. Plant groups from all Mediterranean-climate regions of the world are represented, from Chile and Mexico to South Africa, New Zealand, and Australia. Don't miss **Valhalla,** a collection of nearly 60 figureheads from ships wrecked around the islands; the gaily painted figures from the past have an eerie quality, each one a ghost with a different story to tell.

If time remains after you visit the gardens, wander around the meadows and coastal fields that surround them, following trails to the bird-rich Great Pool or to unspoiled beaches with heather-shrouded dunes and surprisingly tame seabirds. You can't bring a car to Tresco—the only cars here belong to Tresco Estate staff—but you can rent bikes by the day, the best way to explore this island where the garden is king. —*HH*

ⓘ **Tresco Estate** (✆ **44/1720/422849;** www.tresco.co.uk or www.simplyscilly.co.uk).

✈ Helicopter from Penzance (20 min.).

⛴ Launch from St. Mary's (**Bryher Boats;** ✆ **44/1720/422886**), 20 min.

🛏 $$$ **Island Hotel,** Long Point (✆ **44/1720/422883**). $$ **New Inn,** New Grimsby Quay (✆ **44/1720/422844**).

68 Blooming Wonders

Martinique

France in the Tropics

The local Carib Indians called the island *Madinina*—"The Flower Island"—and if you are here between February and May, you will see Martinique in full bloom. Everything, from bougainvillea and hibiscus to lotus, will be flowering amid dense, intensely green vegetation. Even Christopher Columbus, a man who'd been around the block a time or two, couldn't stop gushing: "This land is the best, the most fertile, the most gentle, and the most charming in the world. It is the most beautiful thing I have ever seen. My eyes never tire of seeing such greenery," he wrote in 1502.

The second-largest island in the West Indies, the 1,101-sq.-km (425-sq.-mile) Martinique is blessed with a hot and humid tropical climate, abundant precipitation, and loamy volcanic soil—all the ingredients for a voluptuous garden ecosystem. The landscape is equally voluptuous, swooping and dipping between volcanic peaks and fertile valleys, a terrain embroidered with fields of sugar cane and pineapple and banana plantations. Two-thirds of the island is protected nature park.

Like many islands in the West Indies, Martinique was colonized by France centuries ago, and today is an overseas department and region of France. The island remains *trés* French: French is the official language (although you'll hear many people speaking a Creole patois), the place names are French, and the food is a delicious marriage of French and Creole cuisines. The French settled the island in 1635, growing sugar cane and importing slaves from Africa to work the plantations. (Reportedly, Christopher Columbus introduced sugar cane to Martinique. Now 12 varieties of sugar cane are grown on 3,035 hectares/7,500 acres of land to make rum *agricole.*) Today, southern Martinique has many of the most popular beaches and gets much of the tourist business, but northern Martinique looks as it might have when the French first arrived, a wild, untouched landscape of rainforest, black-sand beaches, sinuous rivers, waterfalls, and exotic flowers.

Gardens are everywhere on Martinique. Named for its balata gum trees, **Le Jardin de Balata** has hundreds of vivid floral plantings planted by Jean-Philippe Thoze on his grandmother's estate (✆ **596/596/64-48-73;** www.jardindebalata.fr). Thoze has also been transforming the creek gardens of **Habitation Latouche** (✆ **596/596/78-19-19**), in Carbet, a plantation estate whose mansion was destroyed in the horrific 1902 eruption of Mount Pelée, which killed 30,000 people and has been described as the worst volcanic disaster of the 20th century. On the **Céron Plantation** (✆ **596/596/52-94-53**), you can dine in an alfresco restaurant overlooking the ruins of an old mill and beautiful grounds; land that once grew coffee, cocoa, and bananas now grows fields of avocados. The 13-hectare (32-acre) **Clément Plantation** (✆ **596/596/54-62-07**) has a lovely 18th-century Creole plantation house and grounds holding more than 300 plant species. It also has a rum distillery, where you can take a tour and sample the wares.

A note for art lovers: Before there was Tahiti 319, there was Martinique—for painter Paul Gauguin, that is, who lived here for several months where he was inspired to do some 12 paintings of the island and its people, particularly around **Carbet,** his favorite village. A man who appreciated lush landscapes and rich, saturated color, Gauguin was able to capture the island in full, voluptuous flower. —*AF*

ⓘ **Martinique Tourism Authority** (www.martinique.org).

✈ International Martinique Airport Aimé Césaire (connecting flights from San Juan or Miami).

🛏 $$$ **Cap Est Lagoon Resort & Spa,** Quartier Cap Est (✆ **800/633-7411** in the U.S. and Canada or 596/596/54-80-80; www.capest.com). $$ **Diamant Beach Hotel,** Ravine Gens Bois (✆ **596/596/76-16-16;** www.diamant-beach.com).

Wet & Wild **69**

Dominica

Caribbean Green

If you're a moviegoer, maybe you've already been to Dominica—or, at least, to a slightly Disneyfied version of it. Taking advantage of Dominica's unspoiled and soaring, camera-ready natural scenery, some of the lushest sequences in the *Pirates of the Caribbean* franchise were shot here. The real Dominica—an independent commonwealth lying between the French islands of Martinique **68** and Guadeloupe **168**—may not have swashbuckling pirates, but it is a nature lover's paradise, a sort of tropical Switzerland whose mountainous terrain is blanketed in rainforest and partitioned by a seemingly endless supply of rivers and waterfalls.

Sculpted by rainfall and volcanic activity, Dominica (pronounced Dom-in-*ee*-ka) rises from the sea, its brawny contours swathed in green. The traditional Carib name for the island is the apt *Waitukubuli,* meaning "Tall Is Her Body." Careful stewardship, combined with the fact that Dominica is practically beachless, has kept mass tourism and development at bay (and prices much lower than on some neighboring islands). This 751-sq.-km (290-sq.-mile) gem lives up to its nickname, "Nature Isle of the Caribbean," with a wealth of exploration opportunities, from leisurely river cruises to extreme hikes through untouched rainforest and past bubbling hot springs.

Adventurous travelers should make a beeline for **Morne Trois Pitons National Park,** a UNESCO World Heritage Site in the southern half of the island and home to Dominica's greatest hits of nature: tropical forest, rushing waterfalls, and exotic bird life. The inland village of **Laudat** is the best starting point for treks through Morne Trois Pitons; you'll find plenty of guides here (recommended). For an unforgettable rainforest swim, seek out **Emerald Falls.** The higher reaches of Morne Trois Pitons, where Dominica's strangest volcanic phenomena lie, are for experienced hikers only, but those willing to take on the extreme conditions here (slippery trails, steep terrain, and windy exposures) should head for **Boiling Lake,** the second-largest flooded fumarole in the world. Elsewhere on the island, you'll find less challenging hikes, past idyllic waterfalls and swimming holes and arcadian tropical landscapes, but going with a guide is highly recommended here: Arrange one at the office of the **Dominica National Park,** in the Botanical Gardens in Roseau (✆ **767/448-2401**).

Dominica has 365 rivers—one for every day of the year, locals joke—and getting out on these inland waterways is a must. The **Layou** is Dominica's longest, and tube rides past spectacular cliffs and enchanting rainforests are the most popular way to experience it. The primordial, mangrove-lined **Indian River,** which empties in the northern coastal village of Portsmouth, was featured in those eerie, candlelit river scenes in *Dead Man's Chest.* The crystal-clear rivers of Dominica can be lazy or dangerously swift, so be sure to check on conditions before you take the plunge.

The beach scene on Dominica is—let's face it—nonexistent, but there is an interesting swimming site at **Champagne,** where volcanic vents puff steam into the ocean; swimmers have likened the effect to swimming in the bubbly. Also recommended is a **whale-watching** trip. More cetaceans pass through the waters off Dominica than anywhere else in the Caribbean, and you're likely to spot entire pods of great sperm whales, pilot whales, and dolphins. I like the tours offered by the **Anchorage Hotel,** at Castle Comfort (✆ **767/448-2638;** www.anchoragehotel.dm/main/). —*SM*

ⓘ ✆**767/448-2045;** www.dominica.dm.

✈ Canefield Airport and Melville Hall Airport.

⛴ **L'Express des Iles** (www.express-des-iles.com) from Guadeloupe, Martinique, and St. Lucia.

🛏 $$$ **Jungle Bay Resort & Spa,** Point Mulatre (✆ **767/446-1789;** www.junglebaydominica.com). $$ **Sea Cliff Cottages,** Hodges Beach (✆ **767/445-8998;** www.dominica-cottages.com).

70 Wet & Wild

Isla Damas

Window into the Wild

Costa Rica

It may be little more than dense mangrove wetlands threaded by silky estuaries, but Isla Damas packs an ecologically impressive punch in its small 6km (3¾-mile) frame. Isla Damas offers a window into the wild, a steamy estuarine jungle alive with white-faced capuchin monkeys, two- and three-toed sloths, silky anteaters, boa constrictors, crocodiles, Sally lightfoot crabs, caimans, and green iguanas. A variety of bird life thrives here too, including swallows, mangrove wrens, and shorebirds. This is an intricate food web at its source, and Costa Rica at its purest.

Isla Damas lies off the country's central Pacific coast, 5km (3 miles) from the mainland town of Quepos, a good place to base yourself for a boat tour or kayak excursion to the island and neighboring Manuel Antonio National Park, Costa Rica's most popular national park.

Glassy estuaries snake through tangled thickets of coastal mangroves—the lifeblood of many a marine ecosystem. A healthy mangrove forest provides essential habitat and nutrition for numerous marine and terrestrial organisms, including many threatened or endangered species. Mangroves provide refuge and vital nursery grounds for crabs, shrimp, and fish and are a critical feeding and nesting habitat for migratory birds. Isla Damas is a mangrove jackpot, with three types of mangrove forests: white, black, and red.

To get up close to this rich wildlife diorama, you can take one of many excellent covered boat tours out of Quepos into the mangrove lagoons, passing farmland and palm plantations on the way. In addition to the numerous tour operators in Quepos that offer excursions to the island, a number of hotels also arrange boat tours and kayak expeditions to Damas, just 20 minutes by boat from Quepos. More independent sorts can paddle sea kayaks into these protected inland waterways. Operators for kayaking expeditions include **H20 Adventures** (✆ **506/2777-4092;**

A boat tour in Isla Damas.

www.h2ocr.com) and **Rio Tropicales** (✆ **866/722-8273** in the U.S. or 506/2233-6455; www.riostropicales.com). *—AF*

ⓘ www.visitcostarica.com.

✈ Quepos, from San José (Sansa Airlines or Nature Air; 35 min.).

⛴ Private or tour operator boats make the 5km (3-mile) trip from Quepos.

🛏 $$ **La Sirena Hotel,** 50 mt West Banco Nacional, Quepos (✆ **800/493-8426** in the U.S. or 506/2777-0572; www.lasirenahotel.com).

Wet & Wild

71

Ilha Grande

Jungle in the Bay

Brazil

Who says a trip to Rio has to be all about Copacabana and Ipanema? Even the most die-hard hedonists are bound to crave refuge from the city's constant partying, so why not trade the urban jungle for a real one? The nature reserve of Ilha Grande ("Big Island") lies an easy half-day's journey from downtown Rio de Janeiro (and just across the water from Angra dos Reis) and offers fantastic upcountry hikes, gorgeous beaches, and practically zero commercialism. If you're looking to score Brazilian ecotourism insider points, look no further than Ilha Grande. (The wildlife-rich Cagarras Islands 430 are closer to the city but have much less land where you can disembark and explore, and no dining or accommodations.)

Like many South American islands with aggressive native flora, Ilha Grande once housed a notorious prison. In fact, no public visitors were allowed here until after the prison closed, in 1994. What touristic development there is has been low-impact, rustic, and focused on appreciating and protecting the natural environment. All the hotels and restaurants—which are strictly small, independent operations—are in the main town of **Abrãao,** from which the island's many hiking trails and eco-excursions depart. Camping is also possible here, but only at specified sites along the northeast coast (Ensenada las Palmas, Abrãao, and Ensenada des Estrelhas), and at Aracatiba on the northwest coast.

For active travelers, Ilha Grande has a well-signposted system of *trilhas* (trails) out of Abrãao. Most of the hikes require at least a half-day commitment, and it's always wise to hire a guide to accompany you to make sure you don't get lost in the jungle, and to educate you on whether the plants and animals you encounter along the way are friend or foe. Ilha Grande's 193 sq. km (75 sq. miles) comprise one of the most important remaining swaths of Brazilian Atlantic rainforest. It's a teeming ecosystem, with squawking parrots and screaming monkeys in the trees overhead, and iguanas, snakes, and capybaras scurrying and slithering along the jungle floor on either side of the trail.

The classic bragging-rights trek on Ilha Grande is the climb to the top of **Pico do Papagayo.** This 990m (3,248-ft.) monolith (second in height to 1,031m/3,383-ft.-tall **Pico da Pedra d'Agua**) is the island icon, and depending on your vantage point, can resemble any number of creatures, from its namesake *papagayo* (parrot) to a dog, rat, or elephant. The ascent is a challenging and exciting trail past sheer rock faces and into rainforest. Take the T2 *trilha* from Abrãao to **Cachoeira da Feiticeira** ("Waterfall of the Sorceress") for an enchanting hike past a ruined aqueduct and the barred archways of the old quarantine hospital, all evocatively overgrown with heavy vines.

And if all that jungle vegetation gets too intense, just head for one of Ilha Grande's beaches, like **Lopes Mendes** (with great surfing), **Green Lagoon** and **Blue Lagoon** (with calm natural swimming pools where dolphins play), **Dois Rios** (with a virgin stretch of white sand against a forested mountain slope), or the "urban beach" of **Abrãao Cove.** Perhaps the most memorable way to take in the full scale of Ilha Grande's chiseled perimeter, however, is on a full-day ***escuna* sailing tour** around the island. These festive Brazilian schooners are a great way to meet fellow vacationers, so you may even experience a bit of Rio-style fun while onboard. —*SM*

ⓘ www.ilhagrande.com.ar or www.braziltour.com.

✈ Rio de Janeiro-Galeão, then bus to Angra dos Reis.

⛴ From Angra dos Reis (1½ hr.).

🛏 $$$ **Pousada Naturalia,** Abrãao (✆ **55/24/3361-9583;** http://pousadanaturalia.net).

72 Wet & Wild

Isla de Ometepe

Sweetwater Island

Nicaragua

Rising from the "sweet waters" of Lake Nicaragua, Isla de Ometepe is the largest freshwater-lake island in the world. Essentially two volcanic islands connected by a slender sinew of land, the 276km (171-mile) Ometepe is one of the most biodiverse places in the world. The tropical island has two magnificent volcanoes rising from its blue waters—the dormant **Maderas** and the active **Concepción**—and volcanic ash has made the soil exceptionally fertile, nurturing rainforests and crops such as coffee, tobacco, and plantains. The undulating landscape is lush and green, with an amazing range of habitats and species. Lovely, unspoiled, and remote—and certainly a challenge to reach (see below)—Ometepe is being developed as an ecotourism hot spot, with adventure hikes up volcanic slopes, jungle canopy tours, beautiful beaches, and stays on organic farms and plantations—but the industry is in its bare-bones infancy, so expect to rough it a bit. Most tours and activities are arranged through your hotel or inn.

During the Somoza dictatorship, this was prime farmland, much of it owned or controlled by the Somoza family. When the Sandinistas took over the government in the 1980s, the farmland was confiscated and turned into state cooperatives, of which only one or two survive today. Because Ometepe's tourist infrastructure is rudimentary, roads here are potholed, bumpy, and dusty—if you plan to get around on your own, you'll need a 4WD or a motorcycle. Mountain bikes are a good way to see the scenery (bike and motorcycle rentals are available on the island or through your hotel). Your hotel can also arrange to have a car and driver show you around. The island bus system is cheap but slow.

It's highly recommended that you hire a guide to take you on the treks up the volcanoes, especially Concepción, the more strenuous hike. The trails up Concepción are very steep, and the entire hike can take 8 hours; but you do pass atmospheric coffee and banana farms, tropical forest, and scenic viewing points. The hike up Maderas takes less time (6 hr.), ascends through forested terrain (and mud—wear good hiking boots), and ends up at the volcano's crater lake. The forests ringing the volcanoes are the home of mantled howler monkeys and white-faced capuchin monkeys, the Mexican anteater, the Northern naked tail armadillo, and the yellow-necked parrot. For a change of pace, many visitors follow a rough hike with a day or two on the lovely black-sand beach at **Playa San Domingo,** the most "resorty" spot on the island. —*AF*

ⓘ www.visitaometepe.com or www.visitanicaragua.com.

✈ Managua, then bus or express shuttle (or taxi) to Rivas (1–3 hr.); then 5-minute taxi to San Jorge.

⛴ San Jorge (1 hr.) or Granada (3½ hr.) to Moyogalpa: **Transportes Lacustre** (✆ **505/278-8190**) or **Ometepe Tours** (✆ **505/563-4779**).

🛏 $ **Finca Magdalena** (✆ **505/8498-1683;** www.fincamagdalena.com). $$ **Hotel Villa Paraiso** (✆ **505/563-4675;** www.villaparaiso.com.ni).

Wet & Wild **73**

Kiawah Island

Prince of Tides

South Carolina, U.S.

I was stung by a jellyfish once while swimming on the beach at Kiawah Island. Earlier that day, my springer spaniel had jumped into the resort pool, unbidden and definitely unappreciated. Ladies shrieked; kids hooted. Look, the dog was hot—summers get brutal here on the South Carolina coast—and the pool was filled with cool, refreshing water. I dragged my dog by the scruff of his neck and led him onto the big, wide Kiawah beach. We galloped down the dunes into the sparkling seawater and rode the steel-gray swells.

It was only after I got out of the water that I started to scratch. Everything itched, my ears, my arms, my legs. And in the wake of the scratches grew long, purple blotches. My ears started to swell, then my nose. I felt sick to my stomach.

Luckily, a doctor staying at Kiawah gave me medicine that slowed the swelling and eventually tempered the jellyfish bite. But what I remember about that day was not so much the discomfort or the swelling or even the dog jumping in the resort pool. I certainly don't remember seeing a jellyfish. No, it was the softness of the late afternoon air, the vast sweep of the beach, the delicious sparkle of the surf. Dipping into the warm south Atlantic on that big, wide stretch of Kiawah sand was that wonderful. I think of it still.

Just 25 miles (40km) from the antebellum cobblestones of Charleston, Kiawah Island is blessed with copious natural beauty. The island is both magnificently wild and comfortably civilized. The island has some of the finest beaches on the East Coast, but it also has a **maritime forest** tangled with pines, sand palms, and sea myrtle. Live oaks are draped in Spanish moss, and a sea of gold-tinged marsh grass extends to the horizon. Wildlife rustles in the thick brush—fox, deer, river otters, raccoons, bobcats, some 300 species of birds, and 30 species of reptiles and amphibians (including alligators)—and the tidal creeks hold sweet shrimp, crabs, and fish.

In the years before the English colonized this part of the New World, the only inhabitants on the barrier island were the Kiawah Indians. Throughout the 18th century, private owners used the island for growing indigo and raising cattle. Big development arrived here in the 1970s, when an investment group from Kuwait built a handsome resort inn, villas, and a golf course. The group set an early—and remarkably forward-thinking—tone in their commitment to conservation and eco-sensitivity on Kiawah. The island has some 30 miles (48km) of biking and hiking trails that weave through pristine

Kiawah beach.

marshland and more than 100 acres (40 hectares) of **protected parkland and bird sanctuaries.** You can kayak or canoe the shimmering saltwater tidal creeks.

The inn now lies dormant, and a revolving door of private development groups have come and gone; but a new luxury resort has sprung to life, along with seven world-class golf courses. Visitors can stay at the hotel or rent a private villa to access all that Kiawah has to offer. Much of the island is still wild and untamed, including that glorious sweep of southern Atlantic beach, 17 miles (27km) of steel-gray swells and pillowy sand. —*AF*

(i) www.kiawahisland.com.

Charleston International Airport.

25-min. drive from Charleston.

$$$ **The Sanctuary Hotel** at Kiawah Island Golf Resort (✆ **877/683-1234;** www.kiawahresort.com).

Wet & Wild **74**

Livingstone Island

Island with a View

Zambia

It's quite a sight, whether from above or below. But perhaps the best place to see and experience Victoria Falls, one of the great natural wonders of the world, is on Livingstone Island, which sits on the lip of the falls, mere feet away from the roaring curtain of water. For many travelers, a trip to Livingstone Island is the adventure of a lifetime—imagine a place where you can not only picnic above the falls but also take a dip in a calm, crystalline pool just inches from the edge of the abyss.

It was in a dugout canoe on the mighty Zambezi River, accompanied by members of the local tribe, the Kololo, that the Scottish doctor and explorer David Livingstone first glimpsed what the tribesmen called Mosi-Oa-Tunya ("The Smoke that Thunders"). From afar, the massive columns of spray were accompanied by a thunderous pounding. The natives rowed to the tiny island in the middle of the river so that the 42-year-old Livingstone, who had been coming to Africa since he was 27, could get a closer view. Livingstone was enthralled—he called it the most wonderful sight he had ever seen in Africa. "No one can imagine the beauty of the view from anything witnessed in England," he wrote. "It had never been seen before by European eyes; but scenes so lovely must have been gazed upon by angels in their flight."

Livingstone had discovered the largest column of falling water in the world. He named it "Victoria Falls" after Queen Victoria, and the tiny island in the river, known to the natives as Kaseruka, was later named Livingstone in the explorer's honor. The island had been highly revered as sacred burial grounds for tribal chiefs. The constant spray from the falls also made the island very lush, and when Livingstone arrived it was brimming with tropical blooms. He called it "The Garden Island."

Today the view from the island is unparalleled—this, for many visitors, is the best place to see the falls. But it's recommended that you go through one of the local lodgings to do so. (In the dry season, it's possible to walk across the lip of the falls to the island.) Livingstone Island was opened in 1995 exclusively to lodges and tour operators on the Zambian and Zimbabwean sides of the falls for picnics and expeditions during the drier months of July to March. Trips are subject to water levels, and only 12 guests are allowed to visit the island at one time. If you're not staying at a local lodge, you can arrange a trip through an outfitter such as **Wildlife Tours and Safaris** (✆ **260/213/323726;** www.wildsidesafaris.com), which operates morning, lunch, and high-tea trips to the island from its base in the town of Livingstone, Zambia.

The boat trip to the island through the fast-moving currents of the Zambezi is a thrill in itself. Once on the island, you can picnic on the edge of the falls, stand in shallow water just a couple of inches from the lip, and swim in **Devil's Pool,** a gentle bowl of water literally feet from the top of the falls. The lush island can be muddy, and the flowers that greeted Livingstone are largely gone, trampled by elephants; but the spectacle is unforgettable, almost too breathtaking for words. But Livingstone gave it a good shot: "The snow-white sheet seemed like myriads of small comets rushing on in one direction, each of which left behind its nucleus rays of foam."—*AF*

ⓘ **Zambia Tourism Board** (www.zambiatourism.com).

✈ Lusaka, Zambia (Lusaka International Airport) or Livingstone Airport.

🛏 $$$ **The River Club,** Livingstone, Zambia (✆ **44/1980/849160;** www.theriverclubafrica.com). $$$ **Tongabezi** Lodge, Private Bag 31, Livingstone, Zambia (✆ **260/3/327450;** www.tongabezi.com).

75 Wet & Wild

Bora Bora

Romantic Heaven on Earth

Totemic South Pacific mountains slope down to a lagoon striped with bands of deep-blue-green to neon-turquoise water. Around the lagoon, palm-fringed atolls and coral reefs trace a wispy pentagon, and everywhere, suspended boardwalks lead tentacle-like to this island's irresistible lodging cliche, the over-water bungalow (OWB). The whole ensemble is romantic, tropical-getaway perfection: Nothing says "ultimate honeymoon" quite like Bora Bora. The word is out—and has been for some time—about this French Polynesian island's extraordinary natural beauty, and though newlyweds seem to compose the overwhelming majority of vacationers here, Bora Bora's remoteness and high prices have kept the island's luxurious mystique intact.

Enchanting Bora Bora belongs to the exclusive, so-preposterously-gorgeous-it-doesn't-seem-natural club of travel destinations. Even the most jaded of globe-trotters duly drops his jaw when confronted with the spectacle of the lagoon and the iconic silhouette of **Mount Otemanu** in the background. Many visitors, in fact, never get farther than that perfect tableau of paradise—they stick to their OWB love nests and resort dining, signing up for every watersport offered on the crystal-clear lagoon (shark feeding is the signature activity), and admiring the blissful views from parasail harnesses. But excursions to the main island and its lofty interior are how you'll get to the real heart of Bora Bora. Tearing yourself away from the plush lagoon life may seem counterintuitive, but as you ascend the lush slopes and the hum of jet skis fades away, you'll be glad you made the effort.

The basalt pyramid of Mount Otemanu (725m/2,379 ft.) lords over Bora Bora like a petrified Polynesian god, mantled in dense tropical flora. Just next to it, the spike-topped **Mount Pahia** is only slightly lower

Bora Bora.

(660m/2,165 ft.). Treks to the summit regions of either peak are for experienced hikers only and should be undertaken with a guide: Try **Pahia Heights Adventure** (✆ **689/677773**). Otherwise, **4x4 excursions** over the mountain roads of Bora Bora will whisk you up to forested heights and fabulous views—it's a thrill ride and nature discovery outing all in one. A gentler way to feel adventurous and still take in those rapturous island panoramas is by hiking along splendid **Matira Beach** (keep to the road that starts at Hotel Bora Bora and make your way southeast toward Matira Point). The flat, 3km (1¾-mile) walk, skirting Rofau Bay, is probably the most scenic in the South Seas.

However you choose to spend your time on Bora Bora, there is one place you must go before you fly back home: **Bloody Mary's** (✆ **689/9677286**). Part barbecue fish joint, part island watering hole, this beloved spot incorporates elements of the Polynesian to great effect, from the thatched-roof dining room to the sugary-sand floor (you eat barefoot) to the rustic tables and stools made of coconut palm wood. The food, drink, and service are all top-notch. —*SM*

ⓘ **Bora Bora Comité du Tourisme,** Vaitape (✆ **689/677636**); also www.tahiti-tourisme.com.

✈ Bora Bora-Motu Mute (connections to Tahiti, Moorea, Huahine, and Raiatea, on Air Tahiti Nui).

🛏 $$$ **Four Seasons Bora Bora,** Motu Tehotu (✆ **689/603130;** www.fourseasons.com/borabora). $$ **Hotel Maitai,** Matira Point (✆ **689/603000;** www.hotelmaitai.com).

76 Wet & Wild

Hainan Island

The Chinese Hawaii

China

Big and sprawling, China has a wide range of landscapes, but it's hard to picture a tropical island—Polynesian palms, curvy crescents of white sand—in the mix. Yet the "Hawaii of the Orient" does indeed exist, a lovely slice of the tropics floating in the South China Sea in the steamy monsoon zone. Hainan Island's palm-fringed beaches and surfable waves are being discovered by beach bums and surfers and travelers looking to holiday on uncrowded sand. The air is clean, the water is a sparkling blue, and mossy green hills framing sun-dappled beaches present a picture-postcard Polynesian silhouette.

Situated 48km (30 miles) below the country's southernmost tip, Hainan was long China's unloved stepchild, a place of exile for dissidents and undesirables through centuries of dynastic rule. After the Japanese occupation during World War II, Hainan continued to get no respect: Its forests were unceremoniously stripped to plant cash crops in the warm, wet climate. But since tourism became the main source of income, Hainan has been on the upswing. The island is now a regional breadbasket, growing mangoes, coconuts, pineapples, and sugar cane; and succulent tropical fruit is on the menu wherever you go. The island has even been designated the latest space launch center for the country's space program.

In recent years, Chinese mainlanders have helped make Hainan the country's second-most-visited destination. Though these visiting mainlanders disdain basking in the sun à la Coppertoned Westerners, resorts and international hotel chains (Ritz-Carlton, Hilton, Marriott, Crowne Plaza, Holiday Inn, Sheraton) have elbowed their way onto Hainan's comely coastline. The island's capital city, **Haikou,** on Hainan's north coast, is the major entry point. Just 15km (9¼ miles) southwest of the city is the **Haikou Shishan Volcanic Cluster Geopark,** where you can see the 10,000-year-old remnants of volcanic clusters and lush "lava landscapes" that include an ecological garden and a volcanic crater garden. After seeing Haikou and the park, most people head to the port city of **Sanya,** on the island's southern coast, and its national resort district. (A new railway linking Haikou and Sanya is expected to be completed in late 2010.) Twenty-four kilometers (15 miles) east of Sanya is **Yalong Bay,** perhaps the island's prettiest beach; also popular are **Tianya Haijiao** (which is pictured on the Chinese two-yuan note) and **Dadonghai Bay.**

Golf courses are popping up like mushrooms; the island now has 16 courses. And if you've never surfed, this is a good place to learn; **Surfing Hainan** (✆ **86/135/198-00103;** www.surfinghainan.com) provides lessons in prime spots like **Houhai Bay.** If you're a seasoned surfer, know that the best surfing waves arrive in fall and winter—and if you can wait out the typical ankle-biting wavelets of summer, a typhoon sweeping by is guaranteed to kick up some wicked peaks. —*AF*

ⓘ The **People's Government of Hainan Province** (www.hi.gov.cn) or the **China National Tourist Office** (www.cnto.org).

✈ Hong Kong (90 min.) or Shanghai (3 hr.) to Sanya.

Regular train ferries from Guangdong to Haikou and Sanya (11–15 hr.).

$$ **Haikou Treasure Island Hotel,** Lantian Rd. 16, Haikou (✆ **86/898/667-63388;** www.treasureisland-hotel.com). $$$ **The Ritz-Carlton,** Sanya, Yalong Bay National Resort District, Sanya (✆ **86/898/889-88888;** www.ritzcarlton.com/en/Properties/Sanya).

Island Hopping the Apostle Islands: Return to the Wild

Imagine how the old French *voyageurs* felt, gliding in their quiet canoes into this long arm of Lake Superior, between the topmost tip of modern-day Wisconsin and Minnesota's long northern hook. How deftly they must have had to paddle around this scattering of forested islands, flung outward from the Bayfield Peninsula into the world's largest freshwater lake. Early explorers, counting 12 main islands, named them the Apostles—and though modern maps show 22 islands, that old name still seems perfect for the spiritual calm of these densely wooded islands, their sandstone cliffs rising loftily above the lake's cold, cobalt-blue depths.

Being so close to shore, in relatively shallow (though often rough) waters, the Apostles were already settled by the native Ojibwa people; over the next few centuries, loggers, farmers, fishermen, and quarrymen also left their marks. Yet today they stand uninhabited, a playground for kayakers, hikers, sailors, anglers, and campers, with a flourishing second-growth forest of hemlock, white pine, and northern hardwood. Look carefully and you'll still find patches of old-growth forest on the six islands which were reserved for lighthouses, essential for guiding ships through treacherous currents.

The Apostle Islands National Park headquarters lies in the mainland town of Bayfield, but most of the park is accessible only by boat. You can island-hop in relative ease on a narrated 55-mile (89km) island cruise with the **Apostle Islands Cruise Service,** departing from the Bayfield city docks. You can also take the car ferry (a 20-min. ride) from Bayfield to the largest Apostle island, 77 **Madeline Island.** The only inhabited Apostle Island, Madeline is not part of the national park, and has more conventional tourist facilities—restaurants, pubs, shops, marinas, and even a few inns and tourist cabins. Here you can cycle along lakeshore roads, play golf, beachcomb or camp at **Big Bay State Park,** or learn about the French fur trading era at the **Madeline Island Historical Museum,** a set of historic log structures in the village of La Pointe, site of a 17th-century trading post founded by Pierre La Sueur.

Day excursions are also scheduled in summer from Bayfield out to a couple of the most popular islands. You might, for example, visit small 78 **Raspberry Island,** in the heart of the island cluster, where park rangers run guided tours of the restored 1863 lighthouse and lightkeeper's home. Set on a spectacular bluff-top site, the substantial red-roofed white frame house below the square wooden light tower is a historical treasure, carefully furnished to demonstrate what life was like for the 19th-century lightkeepers and their families. Or if beaches are your pleasure, try 79 **Stockton Island,** the second largest in the archipelago, which has 14 miles (23km) of hiking trails and three beautiful sand beaches at Quarry Bay, Presque Isle Bay, and Julian Bay. The most unusual beach curls around Julian Bay, where the "singing" sand squeaks underfoot. Crossing the narrow bridge of sand out to **Presque Isle Point,** gaze around you at a rare geologic feature called a tombolo, a wildlife-rich mosaic of bogs, dunes, lagoons, savannas, and pine forests. Just be careful if you're planning to camp on Stockton—the island is densely populated with black bears, who swim with ease from island to island.

In the spirit of the *voyageurs,* the best way to explore the Apostles is still by kayak—the islands are close enough together that day trips are entirely feasible. Local outfitters offer rentals, kayaking instruction, and guided excursions; having a guide is a huge plus, allowing you to paddle directly to the most interesting beaches, caves, and coves.

Picturesque little 80 **Devil's Island,** lying out on the archipelago's northern fringe, has an impressive set of sea caves in the base of the red sandstone cliffs on its north shore, reachable only via kayak. After exploring them, anchor at the South Landing and follow a 1-mile-long (1.6km) trail winding through a primeval boreal forest of paper birch and balsam fir. Devil's Island also has a lighthouse dating back to 1891, the last-built of the Apostle's chain of lights.

At the western end of the Apostles, the much larger 81 **Sand Island** is a textbook-perfect example of the return of wild nature to previously settled lands. Until very recently, Sand Island was one of the few Apostles with no white-tailed deer, which means you can still see here a lush undergrowth of Canadian yew, the deer's favorite browsing shrub. Hiking the 2-mile (3.2km) trail from the East Bay campground to the Sand Island Lighthouse, you'll pass through an overgrown farm, view the Swallow Point sea caves (reachable only by kayak from the water), journey through a 250-year-old virgin white pine forest, and end up on an overlook with a panoramic view of Lighthouse Bay. The lighthouse itself is a striking octagonal tower of locally quarried sandstone blocks, with a Victorian Gothic-style keepers' house snuggled around its base. In the woods near group campsite "A" on Sand Island, look for a low masonry foundation, the remains of a one-room schoolhouse built long ago for the children of Sand Island's farmers and fishermen—just another historical relic beneath the tangled woodlands of the Apostles. *—HH*

(i) **Apostle Islands National Park visitor center,** 415 Washington Ave., Bayfield (© **715/779-3397;** www.nps.gov/apis).

✈ Hayward, Wisconsin (75 miles/121km); Bessemer, Michigan (75 miles/121km).

Apostle Islands Cruise Service (© **800/323-7619** or 715/779-3925; www.apostleisland.com). **Madeline Island Ferry Service** (© **715/747-2051;** http://madferry.com).

$$ **Bayfield Inn,** 20 Rittenhouse Ave. (© **800/382-0995** or 715/779-3363; www.bayfieldinn.com). $$ **The Inn on Madeline Island,** La Pointe (© **800/822-6315;** www.madisland.com).

TOUR Kayak outfitters include **Living Adventure** (© **866/779-9503** or 715/779-9503; www.livingadventure.com), **Trek and Trail** (© **800/354-8735;** www.trek-trail.com), and **Whitecap Kayak Excursions** (© **906/364-7336;** www.whitecapkayak.com).

Wet & Wild 82

Yakushima

Forest of the Sea

Japan

To the Japanese, Yakushima is a mystical place, and it's little wonder why: The island holds some of the country's oldest living trees, a primeval forest tableau of ancient Japanese cedars *(Yakusugi)*, some more than 3,000 years old. One famous tree, **Johmon Sugi,** is said to be 7,000 years old, with a massive and muscular trunk that measures 16m (52 ft.) around. It's not the only thing on Yakushima that's outsized. Giant loggerhead turtles emerge from the sea to lay their eggs—in 2008 alone there were 5,700 reported turtle landings on the beach at Nagata—3,000 of which lay eggs.

A subtropical island lying off the southern coast of Kyushu 83 in the East China Sea, this World Heritage Site has been called the "Forest of the Sea." This is the place that inspired Hayao Miyazaki's celebrated anime movie, *Princess Mononoke;* one area of the forest, Mononoke-hime no Mori, is even named for Princess Mononoke.

Three-quarters of the island is forested mountains, and the rainy climate keeps things wet and wild; in fact, this is the wettest place in Japan. It's water, water everywhere: Moss blankets the undergrowth, and waterfalls tumble into sun-dappled plunge pools. All this humidity, combined with the fertile volcanic soil, makes for a bonanza of flora, with some 1,900 species and subspecies.

Mountaineering is a popular activity on Yakushima; the season begins in May. Hiking trails lead up to the summit of **Mount Miyanouradake,** the island's highest peak, but you can find trails all over the island. Even though trails are clean and well-marked, it's recommended that you have one of the official Yakushima guides lead you on a hiking trek into the densely wooded mountains.

Most visitors use a rental car to get around the island; agencies are located near the ferry docks and the airport. In high season, a shuttle bus runs from the Yakushima Museum to the entrance to the Arakawa Trail, which leads to the Johmon Sugi tree—the only way to see the ancient cedar. —*AF*

(i) www.jnto.go.jp.

✈ Kagoshima (25 min.).

⛴ Kagoshima into Miyanoura or Anbo port (**Yakushima Ferry;** www.f2.dion.ne.jp/%7Eorita.k/; 4 hr.). Hydrofoil from Kagoshima into Miyanoura or Anbo port (**Cosmo Line;** www.cosmoline.jp; approx. 2 hr.).

🛏 $$$ **JR Hotel,** 136-2 Onoaida (✆ **81/9/9747-2011;** www.jrhotelgroup.com/eng/hotel/eng154.htm). $$ **Yakushima Cottages** (✆ **81/9/9749-8750**).

83 Manicured Gardens

Kyushu

The Samurai Garden Club

Japan

Here in the land of cherry-blossom viewing and ikebana, you'd expect to find a fair number of gardens, especially in semitropical Kyushu, the southernmost of Japan's four main islands, traditionally considered the cradle of Japanese civilization. Indeed, Kyushu has gardens, and beautiful ones they are—but beautiful in a distinctly Japanese way, serene and delicate and artfully designed.

Start in the south in **Kagoshima,** an easygoing city of palm trees, flowering trees, and wide avenues. It's been nicknamed "the Naples of Italy"—like Naples, it sits on a wide bay, Kinko Bay, and even has its own Vesuvius, the active volcano Sakurajima, rising dramatically from water's edge. Historically, Kagoshima was so far from the shoguns of Kyoto and Edo that its ruling clans were powerfully independent, and had much more contact with other nations (it is, after all, closer to Seoul and Shanghai than to Tokyo). The beautiful 300-year-old garden of the Shimadzu clan's estate **Sengan'en** (9700-1 Yoshino-cho; ✆ **81/99/247-1551**) is still the city's biggest attraction. Notice how the garden incorporates Sakurajima and Kinko Bay into its design, a principle known as "borrowed landscape"; a bamboo grove here, an artificial waterfall there, a stone lantern set by a perfectly sited carp pond, all dramatically frame the panorama. It's the last Japanese garden with a *kyokusui,* or poem-composing garden, an idyllic spot where the lord of the manor would challenge guests to complete a poem in the time it took a sake cup to float down a tiny brook.

Sengan'en.

For another window on the samurai past, visit the 18th-century castle town of **Chiran,** standing amid tea plantations 31km (19 miles) south of Kagoshima in Minamikyushu. Along Samurai Lane, lined with moss-covered stone walls, you can visit seven exquisite **small gardens** (✆ **81/99/358-7878**) that warriors built as status symbols around their homes, inspired by journeys to Kyoto and Edo with their feudal lord. Notice how the gardens cunningly imitate in miniature the landscapes in the distance. In some, a tiny pond stands in for the sea, with rocks as mountains and undulating hedges for horizons; others dispense with water altogether and substitute a patch of dazzling white sand, carefully raked into wavelike ripples.

Kyushu's other star garden is up in Kumamoto. Beside historic Kumamoto Castle, **Suizenji Garden** (8-1 Suizenji Koen; ✆ **81/96/383-0074**) is a tiny jewel that was laid out around a spring-fed pond in the 1630s as a tea-ceremony retreat. The design, which took 80 years to complete, is ingenious: 53 miniature landscapes that represent the 53 stages of the ancient Tokaido Highway from Kyoto to Tokyo. You probably won't know them all—not unless you've studied Hiroshige's famous Tokaido wood block prints—but near the garden's entrance you'll see the Nihonbashi (Bridge of Japan), and along the circular path you can't miss the cone-shaped grassy mound that imitates Mount Fuji. Afterward, sip tea in a thatched-roof teahouse overlooking the pond—what you'll really be drinking in is serenity. *—HH*

ⓘ **Kagoshima tourist office,** Kagoshima Chuo train station (✆ **81/99/253-2500**). **Kumamoto tourist office,** Kumamoto station (✆ **81/96/352-3743**); also www.jnto.go.jp.

✈ Kagoshima or Kumamoto.

🚄 Kagoshima (7½ hr. from Tokyo) or Kumamoto (9 hr. from Tokyo, or 1½ hr. by bullet train).

🛏 $$$ **Castle Park Hotel,** 41-1 Shinshoin-cho, Kagoshima (✆ **81/99/224-2200;** www.shiroyama-g.co.jp). $$ **Kumamoto Hotel Castle,** 4-2 Joto-machi, Kumamoto (✆ **81/96/326-3311;** www.hotel-castle.co.jp).

Manicured Gardens **84**

Isle of Gigha

Pocket of Green

Scotland

The Isle of Gigha is, in the native parlance, a "wee place," just 11km (6¾ miles) long and 1.6km (1 mile) wide. The southernmost island in the Inner Hebrides is inhabited by only 150 people and a sprinkling of Highland cows. But even the mighty Vikings considered the island to be a treasure; they used it to stash their plunder wrested from Scandinavian settlements.

This picturesque spot has bays and lochs and seas full of dolphins and seals. But what draws most visitors to Gigha (pronounced *Gee*-ah) are the island's remarkable gardens. It's unusual for rhododendrons and camellias to prosper in a place as wind battered as Scotland's west coast. The Isle of Gigha owes its temperate climate to the island's proximity to the Gulf Stream. But it's not just the warm currents and dry air that help the gardens thrive. Walls that surround and protect the plants most susceptible to wind and cold add to the unique microclimate.

The 20-hectare (49-acre) **Achamore Gardens** (1.6km/1 mile from the ferry dock at Ardminish; ✆ **44/1583/505-267**) has a wildflower meadow, great swaths of rhododendrons and azaleas, and preening peacocks. It's a remarkably dense pocket of green on an island ringed by sandy beaches. In August, the gardens are abloom with lavender hydrangeas, white and yellow daisies, bluebells and pink foxglove, creamy white morning glories, and even blazing red hibiscus.

The gardens were the creation of Col. Sir James Horlick, who owned **Achamore House,** the baronial mansion on the garden grounds, from 1944 to 1972. You can experience the gardens much the way its former owners did by staying in one of the rooms at the Achamore House, now a bed-and-breakfast.

Little Gigha has other enticements, and to see them, do like the locals do and head out on foot on one of several walks detailed in the "Walk Gigha" booklet (available at the Gigha Hotel). You will pass pastures, sand beaches, rocky shores, bracken and bramble-covered hillsides, and heather-clad hilltops. On a clear day you can even see the coast of Antrim in Ireland to the southwest.

Gigha is now owned by its residents, who orchestrated a groundbreaking community buyout in 2002. The community has big plans for the island, including using green energy to help power its electric grid. By the time you read this, Gigha should have Scotland's first community-owned, grid-connected wind farm up and running. It's estimated that the windmills will provide approximately two-thirds of the island's electrical needs. —*AF*

(i) www.gigha.org.uk.

✈ Glasgow (2½ hr. from Tayinloan).

From Tayinloan (**Caledonian Macbrayne ferry; ✆ 44/1475/650-100;** www.calmac.co.uk; 20 min.).

$ **Achamore House Bed and Breakfast** (**✆ 44/1583/505-400;** www.achamorehouse.com). $$ **Gigha Hotel** (**✆ 44/1583/505-254;** www.gigha.org.uk).

85 Manicured Gardens

Mainau

Island Abloom

Germany

It's no wonder plant lovers flock to Mainau from all over the world; the entire island is one big, spectacular garden. A million visitors make the trek annually to this little jewel of green in Lake Constance. The freshwater alpine lake (also spelled Konstanz) lies on the Rhine River at the foot of the Alps and stretches into three northern European countries: Germany, Switzerland, and Austria. With such close proximity to the Alps and the lake's heritage as an Ice Age glacier, it would make sense that the island's growing season——and repertoire of plants—would be limited. But Mainau has long been ambrosia for plant lovers for its miraculous microclimate, which owes much to natural windbreaks and the surrounding waters. These unique conditions nurture plants that normally thrive in warm-weather locations, with something in bloom year-round. Even exotica like orange and lemon trees and palms enjoy a long season here.

The gardens are very much a labor of love, for love is what set in motion the design of the gardens you see today. For centuries, the island was the domain of fervent "gardeners"—Hungarian princes and Baden dukes—from various royal and ducal dynasties, each of whom built upon the botanical construction left by the previous owner. In 1932, the island was a gift

Palace gardens on Mainau.

to Prince Lennart Bernadotte of Sweden from his father in the wake of the prince's marriage to a commoner—which effectively ended his claim to the Swedish throne. Bernadotte chose love over the crown, and in the bargain gained an island home.

It was Prince Lennart (thereafter downsized to Count Lennart) who dedicated himself to reshaping, reorganizing, and modernizing the island. He opened it to the public, and adopted ecofriendly gardening techniques that have earned the garden numerous environmental awards. The Count died in 2004, but the family created a foundation to maintain the island—and his heirs continue to live in the baroque 18th-century **Castle of the Teutonic Order,** the architectural centerpiece of the island.

The 45-hectare (111-acre) island is a pleasure to stroll. Pick up a map and hit the neatly manicured pathways. Among the garden highlights are the **Italian Flower and Water Staircase,** a cascade of flowers and conifers; the Mediterranean-tinged **Arena of Fountains,** a terraced garden surrounded by tropical plants; and the 20,000 roses abloom in the **Rose Gardens.** Kids love the whimsical topiary, Germany's largest **Butterfly Gardens,** and the farm, where ponies, donkeys, sheep, and rare farm breeds live the good life.

Mainau is easy to get to: You can access the island either by tour boat from the town of Constance or by walking across the small footbridge connecting the island to the mainland. The island has four restaurants but no lodging. —*AF*

ⓘ www.mainau.de/htdocs/en/start.htm or www.bodensee.eu.

✈ Friedrichshafen, Zürich, and Altenrhein, then train or bus/car to Mainau.

🚆 Konstanz is on the main Konstanz-Singen-Villingen-Offenburg rail line, the Schwarzwaldbahn, with frequent connections to the major cities of Germany (✆ **49/1805/996-633**).

Bodensee-Schiffsbetrieben (✆ **49/7531/3640-389;** www.bsb-online.com).

$ **Barbarossa,** Obermarkt 8, Constance on Lake Constance (✆ **49/7531/128-990;** www.barbarossa-hotel.com). $$$ **Steigenberger Inselhotel,** Auf der Insel 1, Constance on Lake Constance (✆ **800/223-5652** in the U.S. and Canada, or 49/7531/1250; www.konstanz.steigenberger.com).

86 Lush Life

Moorea

Bali Hai

It is, without exaggeration, one of the most eye-poppingly gorgeous islands in the world. In fact, Moorea is such a stunning South Seas locale that it's been featured in countless movies that aren't even set here. When you actually see it for yourself, you may find it hard to believe that the scenery isn't computer-generated: The jagged mountain contours of Moorea are so dramatically faceted as to seem man-made, and the dense vegetation blanketing every surface of the island has the lush look of green velvet. Writer James Michener called Moorea "a monument to the prodigal beauty of nature" and was so inspired by Moorea's captivatingly good looks that he based the mythical island of Bali Ha'i (in *Tales of the South Pacific*) on this real-life French Polynesian gem.

Nearby Bora Bora 75 and its irresistible lagoon tempt you with ways to get out on the water. Moorea, on the other hand, is more about experiencing nature on the island itself and moving at a slower pace. The island is shaped roughly like a heart, but with two clefts instead of one. Those clefts are **Cook's Bay** and **Opunohu Bay,** both deep, fingerlike bodies of water that are surrounded by soaring, pointed peaks. The trademark mountain on Moorea is **Moua Roa,** the cathedral-like incisor of black stone that rises 880m (2,887 ft.) above sea level at the end of a series of smaller rock "teeth." Equally photogenic is the 830m-tall (2,723-ft.) **Moua Puta,** which has a tiny hole at the top. At 1,207m (3,960 ft.), **Mount Tohiea** is the highest point on the island, but the best peak to climb is **Mount Rotui** (800m/2,625 ft.), which commands the South Pacific's most magnificent vista, from its **Belvedere lookout** over the twin bays of Cook and Oponuhu.

The best way to get around Moorea is by rental car (or numerous outfits on Moorea can provide a four-wheel-drive vehicle and driver/guide for you). The **circle drive** around the island is a must; you can do the quickie version in a few hours, but if you have the time, allow several days to see all the sights along the 62km (39-mile) circuit. Stop for the short hike to **Atiraa waterfall** (near Afareaitu), where the water cascades 32m (105 ft.) down a glistening black rock cliff to a small pool where you can swim. Experienced hikers can also take to Moorea's many nature trails, but be sure to bring plenty of water and bug spray.

Though sea activities aren't nearly as central to vacationers' enjoyment of Moorea as they are on Bora Bora, Moorea still offers plenty of ways to dip into that crystal-clear Polynesian water. For a lazy day on the beach, **Temae Plage Publique** is Moorea's best stretch of public sand. At the **Moorea Dolphin Center** (www.mooreadolphincenter.com), visitors can swim with docile cetaceans. Another unforgettable South Seas adventure, swimming with and petting rays, can be arranged at the **Moorea Lagoonarium,** at Haapiti near the Intercontinental Hotel (✆ **689/563875;** www.dolphinlagoonarium.com).

As for accommodations, luxurious over-water bungalow resorts can be found all along the dramatic northern coast near Cook's Bay and Oponuhu Bay, but the island is also full of casual *fares* (guest houses) for a more authentic Polynesian experience. —*SM*

ⓘ **Moorea Visitors Bureau,** Le Petit Village, Haapiti (✆ **689/562909;** www.gomoorea.com).

✈ Temae airport, connections from Papeete, Tahiti.

⛴ From Papeete, high-speed catamarans (30 min.) arrive at Vaiare (on Moorea's east coast).

🛏 $$$ **Hilton Moorea Lagoon Resort & Spa** (✆ **689/551111;** www.hilton.com). $$ **Hotel Lestipaniers,** in Haapiti (✆ **689/561267;** www.lestipaniers.com).

Lush Life 87

Tutuila

A Yank in the South Seas

American Samoa

One of the newest entrants on the roster of U.S. national parks, and the only one south of the equator, is in the South Pacific island territory of American Samoa. Established in 1988, the **National Park of American Samoa** is spread over several islands in a remote archipelago halfway between Hawaii and New Zealand. Tutuila is the largest and most visited island of the group, with striking coastal landscapes and mountain rainforests, as well as unique opportunities to get close to the millennial traditions of the Samoan people.

The natural harbor town of **Pago Pago,** the capital of American Samoa, is the point of entry to this magnificent natural treasure. Head for the northern coast of Tutuila, where the park areas are located. Do keep in mind that this national park is young and relatively undeveloped: facilities, where they exist, are very basic. Locals still own the land (the park service has a 50-year lease) and subsistence farm on it. In exchange, your reward is the feeling of being the first to discover one of the most untouched paradises in the South Pacific. Much of the rugged coastline may remind you of Big Sur or Oregon, and then, in other places, it transforms into postcard-perfect Polynesia—without the condos and bungalows.

Jagged **Mount Alava** dominates northern Tutuila, and a hiking trail (9.7km/6 miles round-trip) leads up to the 483m (1,585-ft.) peak past glistening ferns, vibrant orchids, and persistent banyan trees, which grow from the top down by invading and eventually strangling the host tree. Because Tutuila is such a small and narrow island (140 sq. km/54 sq. miles total, and less than 4.8km/3 miles wide at this point), the view from the top of Mount Alava encompasses both the north and south sides of the Pacific coast and the deep inlet of Pago Pago harbor. Just east of Mount Alava is the **Amalau Valley,** where verdant hillsides hide away beautiful, ribbon-like waterfalls and a thriving population of flying foxes (a type of fruit bat), which may well swoop overhead. It's a long way from the American mainland, but throughout this exotic and far-flung place you'll spot the brown-and-white signs of the U.S. park service.

Vatia Bay may be Tutuila's most scenic area, however. This finger-shaped inlet is backed by imposing and multifaceted mountains cloaked in green. A steep ridge curves around Vatia's west side, leading to the most photographed spot in Tutuila, the offshore rock feature of **Pola Island.** From Vatia village, there's a trail that goes to a pebbly beach where you'll get the best landside views of Pola. **North Shore Tours** (✆ **684/258-3527**) runs boat tours to the island.

Accommodations in and around the park are few, so you may opt to stay in Pago Pago (which is quite easy; the driving distances and bus services are very manageable on Tutuila). But for a more memorable encounter with the island, consider a home stay with native Samoans in Vatia or another village within the park. The National Park Service website (see below) has more information on what this entails. —*SM*

ⓘ **National Park Service:** Pago Plaza Shopping Center, Pago Pago (✆ **684/633-7082;** www.nps.gov/npsa); also www.amsamoatourism.com.

✈ Pago Pago (connections through Honolulu on Hawaiian Air).

🛏 $$$ **Turtle and Shark Lodge,** Vaitogi, Pago Pago (✆ **684/699-3131;** www.turtleandshark.com).

88 Lush Life

Kauai

The Garden Isle

Hawaii

The opening scenes in the film *Jurassic Park* show a helicopter swooping over an impossibly green, incredibly lush island landscape. Special effects? Computer imaging? Nope, just the mossy backbone of Kauai ringed by the sparkling blue Pacific.

The Hawaiian Islands are all beauties, of course, but Kauai is Hawaii gone native, a tropical Eden blissfully devoid of high-rises and megaresorts. And it should stay that way; a local ordinance has decreed that no building taller than a coconut tree (four stories high) can be built on the island. Kauai is Hawaii unvarnished and almost primeval, with 50 miles (80km) of some of the world's most spectacular beaches, breathtaking cliffside seascapes, and waterfalls tumbling into rainforest jungle. Under 5% of the island is zoned for commercial and residential use; the rest is protected parkland or farmland. This is where many Hawaiians themselves go to relax amid sumptuous and serene natural environs.

Kauai is the ideal spot for those who not only enjoy scenic splendors but can't wait to plunge in. The outdoor adventures here are world-class—and in this climate, you can enjoy them all year-round. You can hike **Waimea Canyon,** the "Grand Canyon of the Pacific," its burnt-red lava beds sculpted by an ancient earthquake. The raw and remote **Na Pali Coast**—with its spectacularly eroded sea cliffs—can be seen by sea kayak or helicopter tour. The all-purpose **Kauai Kayak** (✆ **800/437-3507;** www.kayakkauai.com), with locations in Hanalei and Kapaa, has been taking visitors on guided sea kayak tours of the Na Pali Coast for more than 20 years. It also offers hiking tours (including of the Waimea Canyon), snorkeling tours on the calm **Puupoa Reef** ("The Blue Lagoon") on the Hanalei River, and whale-watching tours. Also highly recommended is **Outfitters Kauai** (✆ **888/742-9887;** www.outfitterskauai.com), which has a tantalizing array of outdoor adventures, such as kayaking Hawaii's largest tropical

Na Pali Coast State Park.

river, the **Wailua,** and hiking through rainforest to a 100-ft. (30m) waterfall. Another well-known general outfitter is **Snorkel Bob's** (several locations; ✆ **800/262-7725;** www.snorkelbob.com), which offers boat tours, snorkel trips, helicopter tours, zipline outings, and even traditional luaus.

Of course, if zip-lining here and adventure trekking there isn't your idea of relaxing, there are plenty of other ways to enjoy Kauai's natural wonders. For some people, lying on the beach will do the trick—and Kauai's beaches are among the world's best. Try the 17-mile (27km) **Polihale State Park,** on the island's west coast, or the beauteous **Anini Beach,** which overlooks a blue lagoon—look (or listen) for **Barking Dogs Beach** nearby, where bare feet walking on sand sounds like dogs barking. Speaking of animals, you may be surprised to see so many chickens and roosters roaming free on the island—local lore has it that when Hurricane Iniki devastated Kauai in 1992, it knocked down a chicken farm. And the freed chickens bred like, well, rabbits. *—AF*

ⓘ **Kauai Visitors Bureau** (www.kauaidiscovery.com).

✈ Honolulu into Lihue, Kauai (40 min.).

🛏 $$ **Hanalei Colony Resort,** 5-7130 Kuhio Hwy., the North Shore (✆ **800/628-3004** or 808/826-6235; www.hcr.com). $$$ **Waimea Plantation Cottages,** 9400 Kaumualii Hwy., Western Kauai (✆ **866/77-HAWAII** [774-2924] or 808/338-1625; www.waimea-plantation.com).

Lush Life **89**

St. Lucia

Colorful Caribbean

Life is lush on this colorful Windward Island in the Eastern Caribbean. Abundant precipitation, rich volcanic soil, and tropical sunshine provide a dynamic breeding ground for flora and fauna. When it rains here, it *really* rains: Clouds turn black, the heavens rumble, and the skies cut loose with a thunderous pounding. And when the sun breaks through, hibiscus and bougainvillea blooms muscle through thick green underbrush. The sweet sounds of birdcall fill the air, and a fine mist lifts off simmering black tar. St. Lucia is a vivid place to be.

Everywhere is color, from saffron frangipani to red spikes of torch ginger to the islanders' traditional dress—a sunny patchwork of blues and oranges and yellows. Roads coil around vine-covered cliffs ringed in blue mist. The island's moss-backed **Pitons,** twin volcanic "plugs" that rise up some 600m (1,969 ft.) out of the sea, are St. Lucia's visual touchstones and everyone's favorite photo prop—neither Piton has a bad side. (Perhaps that's why the local beer is called Piton.)

European explorers first arrived on the island in the 15th century, encountering a tribe of fierce Amerindian warriors known as the Kalinago, who were able to stave off entrenchment by the Europeans until their expulsion to Dominica 69 and St. Vincent 249 in the mid–17th century (a small tribe of descendants still lives on the island's southwest coast). By then, the black volcanic soil of St. Lucia was feeding the region. The island's role as breadbasket to the Windward Islands—not to mention its superb protected harbor—underscored St. Lucia's value to the European settlers. Thus began a 200-year tug of war between the British and the French for control of the island. Although St. Lucia ultimately became a British protectorate and English is widely spoken, it is the French influences that predominate today, from the rich Creole patois to place names to the French-infused cuisine.

A visit to St. Lucia is a plunge into nature at its ripest. At breakfast your morning companions will be scores of gorgeously hued birds hovering, eager to plunge a beak into a pot of honey. (Some resorts give their guests water guns to playfully shoo the birds away.) You can hike one of the many rainforest trails up into the hills and see wild orchids, waterfalls, and rare birds such as the St. Lucia parrot. Amid the dense foliage of the **Forestlere Rainforest Trail** are giant fig trees and ferns. The waters surrounding St. Lucia are home to a thriving and colorful marine world, with divers and snorkelers exploring steep undersea slopes filled with exotic fish, coral, sponges, and turtles.

On **Mount Soufriére** in the Sulphur Springs is what is billed as the "world's only drive-in volcano," active sulfur fields that give off steaming clouds of sulfuric gases reportedly strong enough to tarnish

St. Lucia.

silver jewelry. You can't actually drive into the volcano, which last erupted some 40,000 years ago, but you can watch the action from viewing stations. Consider, if you will, that out of a similar witch's brew of heat and sulfur came the creation of all that surrounds you on lush and lovely St. Lucia. —*AF*

ⓘ **St. Lucia Tourist Board** (✆ **800/465-8242** in the U.S.; www.stlucia.org).

✈ Vieux Fort (Hewannora International Airport).

🛏 $$$ **Anse Chastanet, Soufrière** (✆ **800/223-1108** in the U.S.; www.ansechastanet.com). $$ **Mago Estate Hotel,** Soufrière (✆ **758/459-5880;** www.magohotel.com).

Lush Life 90

Isla del Coco

The Last Paradise

Costa Rica

Isla del Coco (Cocos Island) has no inhabitants, no stores, no hotels or resorts, no cool rum punches waiting at the dock. It's easily one of the most remarkable islands in the Western Hemisphere, however—both a national park and a World Heritage Site. It's a place so full of natural treasures—and so isolated from the civilized world—that it's become an ecological case study, a critical laboratory for research into the marine ecosystem and its evolution. Jacques Cousteau once described it as the most beautiful island in the world. Michael Crichton's book *Jurassic Park: The Lost World*—which told the tale of an insular island untrammeled by civilization—was reportedly inspired by Cocos Island. Cocos is the earth as it used to be.

Cocos has all the physical attributes of a lush volcanic island in the tropics. But it has much more than natural good looks. It's the largest uninhabited island in the world. The only inhabitants are the park rangers who are paid to protect it. It's the only island in the eastern Pacific Ocean with a tropical rainforest and the only cloud forest island in the world. It's also a Ramsars wetlands site of international significance (www.ramsar.org).

Cocos Island is located 483km (300 miles) southwest of Costa Rica. Only around 2,000 tourists visit the island annually (most of them divers or fishermen), and for good reason: The only way to get here is via a 36-hour boat ride from Puntarenas, Costa Rica; you cannot fly in. Most people charter multiday trips on full-service dive boats and yachts (see below for recommended operators).

In spite of its remoteness, Cocos has a storied history of explorers, pirates, and buried treasure. It appeared on a world map as early as 1542, as the Isles de Coques. Today the waters and coral reefs surrounding the island are considered some of the most pristine in the world. Divers consider it among the best places on the planet to view large pelagic species such as sharks, rays, tuna, and dolphins. It has the world's largest population of hammerhead sharks. In fact, the island is considered to be ground zero for the earth's shark population, although the illegal poaching of shark fins in these shark-rich protected waters is threatening Cocos's exquisite marine ecosystem.

More than a thousand different species of flora and fauna are found on the island, many of them endemic. Of its 100 species of birds, the native *espiritu santo,* or Holy Spirit bird, will flutter mystically around your head while you walk. Cocos has some 70 waterfalls to swim in and 235 species of flowering plants that bring vivid color to the mossy jungle backdrop. The island owes its lushness and vivid green vegetation to precipitation: It gets more than 7,000m (275 in.) of rainfall every year. It all adds up to one hot and steamy tropical landscape, a terrain of such richness and vitality that it almost breathes with life. —*AF*

ⓘ www.cocosisland.org.

✈ Puntarenas, Costa Rica.

Aggressor Fleet (www.aggressor.com) charters dive trips to Cocos Island, as does the **Undersea Hunter** (www.underseahunter.com).

$$ **Hotel Alamar,** Paseo de los Turistas, Puntarenas (✆ **506/2661-4343;** www.alamarcr.com).

91 Lush Life

La Palma

Unspoiled Volcanic Gem

Canary Islands, Spain

Brits and northern Europeans who've outgrown the all-night parties of Ibiza 246 and Tenerife 247 need not abandon the idea of a Spanish island holiday: The Canary Islands' La Palma is a completely different kind of getaway, perfect for nature lovers seeking a slower pace in a place that remains off the radar of mass tourism. Nicknamed *La Isla Bonita* ("the pretty island"), La Palma has lush flora and gorgeous volcanic topography and is widely regarded as the most physically beautiful of the seven Islas Canarias.

Built on black volcanic rock, the anvil-shaped island is one of the steepest in the world. La Palma is only 50km (31 miles) long and 30km (19 miles) across at its widest point, though its highest point rises to an elevation of 2,423m (7,949 ft.). The summit of La Palma is a treeless area with rock outcroppings called the **Roque de los Muchachos,** home to a world-renowned astronomical observatory. More often than not, Roque de los Muchachos is above the clouds, which, combined with the island's minimal light pollution, makes for outstanding viewing of the heavens. La Palma's northern end is dominated by the **Caldera de Taburiente,** and one of the most popular activities on La Palma is trekking to the summit and into the **Barranco de las Angustias**—the ominously named "Valley of Fear"—a hikeable canyon that goes right inside the dormant crater. To the south, the lavic ridge of **Cumbre Vieja** is the most volcanically active on the island, having last erupted in the 1970s. (On a doomsday geological note, some scientists hypothesize that a significant future eruption along the Cumbre Vieja, which already has a rift, could cause the entire mass to break off and slip into the ocean, propelling a tsunami westward across the Atlantic.)

A good place to base yourself is the east-coast port town of **Santa Cruz,** the island's most charming inhabited area, but you'll find a wealth of accommodations in the Los Cancajos beach development, just south of Santa Cruz. Cancajos also offers myriad ecotourism services like trekking excursions. All over the island, you'll find smaller, welcoming towns and villages where you can rent simple holiday apartments and have a more authentic experience, sampling Canarian cuisine in local restaurants and partaking of La Palma's excellent and inexpensive red and white wines, made from grapes grown on the island's volcanic slopes.

Before contemplating a trip to La Palma, it's key to bear in mind that this is not your typical Spanish island paradise. The name might conjure up images of sun-drenched beaches, but La Palma is frequently overcast and wet. (Sun seekers hoping to come home with a tan might want to pick another island.) La Palma is well away from the mainland, 200km (124 miles) west of Morocco, and it's in the Atlantic Ocean—not the Mediterranean Sea—so the waters are quite chilly and rough for much of the year and the vegetation denser and more forest-like than what you might associate with Spain. Bottom line: Come to La Palma for its spectacular natural attractions, regardless of the weather, not for lazing on the beach. —*SM*

ⓘ www.turismodecanarias.com.

✈ La Palma airport.

🛏 $$ **Hacienda San Jorge,** Brena Baja (✆ **34/92-218-10-66;** www.hsanjorge.co).

3 Wildlife Islands

Unique Species 92

Kangaroo Island

Marsupial Bliss

Australia

Think of Australia and what do you picture? Koalas and kangaroos. Of course, those iconic Australian marsupials are proudly displayed at wildlife parks and attractions all over Oz. But if you really want to see these unique critters in the wild, there's no place better than the aptly named Kangaroo Island.

It's like a textbook example of the virtues of island isolation. Lying across the strait from metropolitan Adelaide, Kangaroo Island was lucky enough to never be colonized by the dingo, Australia's "native" dog that's really a feral scavenger introduced from Asia some 4,000 years ago. Not even any foxes or rabbits ever arrived to prey on the native animals. There are kangaroos here, but not just any kangaroos—they're a distinct Kangaroo Island species. The underbrush is still primarily native eucalypt scrub, all along the unlandscaped roadsides. To preserve all this, strict regulations monitor what visitors bring on and off the island; tourists are asked to wash the soil off their shoes and car tires, and drivers are encouraged to drive slowly, especially at dusk, when koalas, echidnas, bandicoots, and kangaroos may wander onto the roads.

Of the many preserves on the island (about one-third of the island is a conservation area), you'll score the most wildlife sightings at **Flinders Chase National Park** on the western end of the island. Birders have recorded at least 243 species here; koalas are so common they're almost falling out of the trees (the government has in fact had to take steps to reduce the koala population). Kangaroos, wallabies, and brush-tailed possums are so tame that a barrier was erected around the Rocky River Campground to stop them from carrying away picnickers' sandwiches. Platypuses have been sighted, too, but they're elusive—to see one, you might need to wait next to a stream in the dark for a few hours.

At Cape du Couedic, the southern tip of the park, the hollowed-out limestone promontory called Admiral's Arch is home to a colony of some 4,000 New Zealand fur seals (despite the name, a legitimately native species). Rangers at the southern coast's **Seal Bay Conservation Park** (✆ **61/8/8559 4207**) lead guided tours along boardwalks through the dunes to a beach where Australian sea lions congregate.

Up on the north coast, **Lathami Conservation Park,** just east of Stokes Bay, is a superb place to spot wallabies in the low canopy of casuarina pines. If you want to see Little Penguins—which stand about a foot high—the **National Parks & Wildlife South Australia** (✆ **61/8/8553 2381**) conducts tours of their colonies around Nepean Bay at both Kingscote and Penneshaw. Last but not least, **Clifford's Honey Farm** (✆ **61/8/8553 8295**) is the home of the protected Ligurian honeybee, found nowhere else on earth but on this seemingly magical island. —*HH*

Previous page: A koala on Kangaroo Island.

ⓘ **Tourism Kangaroo Island,** Howard Dr., Penneshaw (✆ **61/8/8553 1185;** www.tourkangarooisland.com.au).

✈ Kangaroo Island (30 min. from Adelaide).

⛴ Penneshaw (40 min. from Cape Jervis, South Australia).

🛏 $$ **Kangaroo Island Lodge,** Scenic Rd., American River (✆ **61/8/8553 7053;** www.kilodge.com.au). $$$ **Ozone Seafront Hotel,** The Foreshore, Kingscote (✆ **61/8/8553 2011;** www.ozonehotel.com).

93 Unique Species

Komodo Island

Here Be Dragons

Indonesia

It takes a tough species to survive on a place like Komodo Island. This jagged volcanic island off the northwest tip of Flores, Indonesia, some 200 nautical miles west of Bali 201, is wickedly hot and dry 8 months of the year—and then the monsoons drench it. Much of the island is rocky and barren, with patches of hardy savanna, mossy bamboo cloud forest on higher ridges, and an orchid-rich tropical forest in the valleys, full of fan palms and other trees that are water-retention specialists.

Not many species can make it here, but the king of the island looks perfect for the job: the Komodo dragon, world's biggest lizard, a scaly monster 2.4 to 3m (8–10 ft.). long that hasn't evolved much in 4 million years. This hefty reptile weighs anywhere from 45 to 150kg, depending on how recently it has gorged on carrion. But it's no mere scavenger: The Komodo lies in wait in the grass, springs out and slashes its victim (Timor deer, wild pigs, buffalo) with powerful serrated teeth, and then lets them struggle off into the bush to die, poisoned by bacteria in the Komodo's saliva. Flicking its forked yellow tongue, the lizard "tastes the air" to detect the scent of rotting flesh, then ambles over to the corpse and feasts. Komodos are not only carnivores but cannibals; they'll even eat their young, who are forced to spend their first few months of life in the rainforest canopy to escape being devoured. (Luckily, they hatch just after the Jan–Feb rainy season, when there's plenty to munch on up there.)

There are nearly 6,000 of these "dragons" (really a giant monitor lizard) on

A komodo on Komodo Island.

Komodo and a few neighboring islands; they're the main attraction for most visitors to **Komodo National Park,** established in 1980 specifically to conserve the Komodo dragon. A viewpoint at Banugulung is baited to draw Komodos for tourist viewing; the hike there and back from the Loh Liang ranger station takes about 2 hours. While most visitors make this a tour-boat stop, if you stay overnight in the spartan ranger stations, you may also catch the dragons basking in the sun in the early morning, raising their body temperatures (they are, after all, cold-blooded) before slinking off to hunt.

While you're waiting for the dragons, you can also get in some great bird-watching, with more than 150 species including sulphur-crested cockatoos, collared kingfishers, and imperial pigeons. The waters between the islands also attract scuba divers to their sea-grass beds, mangrove forests, and coral reefs, fed by a unique confluence of tidal currents; there are more than 1,000 species of fish as well as dugong, sharks, manta rays, whales, dolphins, and sea turtles. Unfortunately, the health of these reefs is increasingly compromised by the local villages' destructive fishing practices. Park entrance fees support conservation efforts, to protect the unique biodiversity of this very special island. —*HH*

ⓘ **Komodo National Park,** Labuanbajo, Indonesia (✆ **62/358-41004;** www.komodonationalpark.org).

✈ Bima (42km/26-mile drive to Sape).

⛴ 57km (35 miles) from Sape (Sumbawa Island) or 42km (26 miles) from Labuanbajo (Flores Island).

🛏 $ Ranger stations at Loh Liang or Loh Buaya (Rinca Island); no advance reservation needed.

TOUR Flores Exotic Tours, Labuanbajo, Flores (✆ **62/385-21824;** www.komodoisland-tours.com). **Floressa Bali Tours** (✆ **62/361-467625;** www.floressatours.com).

Unique Species

94

Borneo

The Wild & the Wealthy of Southeast Asia

If you're going to claim, as Borneo does, to be the "most biodiverse place on Earth," you'd better be able to back that up. Indeed, this astonishingly rich island—the third largest in the world at nearly a quarter of a million square kilometers—is an ecosystem on steroids, whose extraordinary richness even the non–biologically trained can easily comprehend. Dense tropical rainforests carpet nearly all of Borneo and shelter populations of many unusual and endangered species like the Bornean orangutan, the clouded leopard, the Asian pygmy elephant, and the Sumatran rhino. Under the canopy, the explosive colors of tropical flora and the screeching of birds seem too vivid and untamed to be real.

Three nations hold territory on Borneo; the lion's share belongs to **Indonesia,** which calls its portion of Borneo Kalimantan. Nearly a quarter of Borneo, along the northern coast, comprises the states of Sarawak and Sabah, both part of **Malaysia.** The wealthy independent nation of **Brunei Darussalam** is made up of two unconnected states, totaling 6,000 sq. km (2,317 sq. miles), on the north coast. As vast parts of Borneo's interior remain unexplored, this is largely an extreme destination (with ethnic strife, in places, as wild as the animals). For the best of both worlds—Borneo's cultural history as well as its ecology—consider staying in the amenity-filled capital of Brunei, **Bandar Seri Begawan,** and making that your base for forays into the island's visitor-friendly nature parks. Within Brunei itself, **Ulu Temburong National Park** is accessed by an evocative jungle cruise; hearing the calls of proboscis monkeys, gliding past orchids of colors and dimensions you've never seen before, you're in for a wonderful introduction to Borneo's natural treasures.

For a raw adventure into the wilds of Kalimantan, take a river cruise with **Kalimantan Tour Destinations** (© **62/536/32-22099;** www.wowborneo.com). Departing from the Central Kalimantan capital of **Palangkaraya,** these 3- to 5-day journeys aboard refitted *rungkan* vessels navigate jungle waterways to remote villages and past the orangutan habitats protected by the **Borneo Orangutan Survival Fund.** (The simians, like so many of the rare animals and plants on Borneo, are threatened by logging, mining, and hunting.) The Malaysian provinces of Sarawak and Sabah also have a number of outfitters offering ecotourism expeditions, but keep in mind that tourism in general is a new frontier in Borneo: Be sure to get references before booking anything.

After getting to know the wild heart of Borneo, you can get reacquainted with civilization back in Brunei. The centuries-old sultanate contains plenty of glitzy shopping and dining opportunities (though the predominantly Muslim nation is alcohol free) and glittering monuments and museums exalting its royal heritage. Like a gilded saddle on an exotic beast, modern Brunei sits atop the untamed bulk of Borneo. —*SM*

(i) www.tourismbrunei.com.

✈ Bandar Seri Begawan.

🛏 $$ **Rimba Lodge** (© **62/370/682-9957;** www.orangutanexplore.com). **Ulu Ulu Resort,** Temburong, Brunei (© **62/673/244-1791;** www.uluuluresort.com).

95 Unique Species

Channel Islands

Channel-Surfing

California, U.S.

Off the coast of Santa Barbara sits an archipelago of rugged beauty and ecological diversity that proves that the natural treasures of California don't end with the Golden State's sun-kissed coastline. **Channel Islands National Park** consists of five islands—Anacapa, Santa Cruz, Santa Rosa, San Miguel, and Santa Barbara—that offer visitors a chance to see California's Pacific habitats as they once were, and to encounter species of flora and fauna that exist nowhere else on Earth.

Some 150 species of endemic plant and animal have been identified in the Channel Islands, from island foxes and skunks to the Channel Island lizard to a subspecies of a classic California tree, the Torrey pine. As the islands are 20 to 80 miles (32–129km) from the mainland, their isolation for so many millions of years has allowed these diverse life-forms to grow and adapt to their particular environment. Many of the animals and plants here exist on only one of the five islands in the National Park. For instance, there's a bird—the island scrub jay—on Santa Cruz Island that you won't find on Anacapa, Santa Rosa, San Miguel, or Santa Barbara islands, even though only a few miles of ocean separate them.

At 96 square miles (249 sq. km), **Santa Cruz** is the largest of the Channel Islands (and it's the largest island in California) and the one that represents the best cross-section of biological diversity in the archipelago. It's also the most physically impressive, with a coastline of jagged cliffs and a 2,450-foot-tall (747m) peak called Mount Diablo. **Painted Cave,** along the northwest coast, is one of the largest sea caves in the world. Excursion boats take visitors to see the natural attractions that are accessible only by sea, but for those who wish to set foot on the island, the boats also dock at one of two harbors here, from which you can set off on numerous hiking trails of varying length and difficulty.

Positioned in the heart of coastal California's rich biosphere, the Channel Islands' waters are teeming with marine life. One-third of the world's species of cetaceans are regularly spotted in the **Santa Barbara Channel,** including gray, blue, humpback, sperm, orca, and pilot whales and dozens of dolphins and porpoises. Whale-watching—whether from shore observation points or from boat charters from Santa Barbara or Ventura—is possible year-round, though the most popular time is gray whale migration season (Dec–May). Humpbacks and blues are most commonly sighted in the summer. It's also inevitable that you'll see California sea lions or harbor seals any time of year, as the Channel Islands provide well-established colonies for these pinnipeds.

Preservation and maintenance of the Channel Islands' natural resources is strictly supervised: This means that virtually no services exist on the islands apart from a few basic facilities. Visits are day trips or overnight stays at one of several simple campgrounds, the largest being the Scorpion Ranch Campground on eastern Santa Cruz Island, which is open year-round, though reservations are required. —*SM*

ⓘ **Visitor center,** 1901 Spinnaker Dr., Ventura (✆ **805/658-5730;** www.nps.gov/chis).

✈ Santa Barbara Airport (25 miles/40km).

⛴ Transport available through tour operators (see below).

🛏 $ Campgrounds (✆ **877/444-6777** or www.nps.gov). $$$ **Inn of the Spanish Garden,** 915 Garden St., Santa Barbara (✆ **805/564-4700;** www.spanishgarden inn.com).

TOUR Island Packers, 1691 Spinnaker Dr., Ventura (✆ **805/642-1393;** www.islandpackers.com). **Truth Aquatics,** 301 W. Cabrillo Blvd., Santa Barbara (✆ **805/963-3564;** www.truthaquatics.com).

Unique Species **96**

Moresby Island

The Other Galápagos

Queen Charlotte Islands, Canada

The Queen Charlotte Islands are often referred to as the Galápagos (p. 100) of the north; a claim justified by its diverse plant and animal life and rugged landscape. Moresby Island is the second largest in this chain of about 150 off the coast of British Columbia, Canada, and is dominated by the San Christoval Mountains, which peak at about 1,000m (3,280 ft.). Most of the west coast gets dramatic exposure to wind and rain, creating forests that are boggy and stunted, supporting hearty species like western red cedar and hemlock. On the eastern side, you'll find temperate rainforests dominated by western hemlock, Sitka spruce, and western red cedar.

Because of its unique landscape, the island's flora and fauna have evolved differently than that on the mainland—an abundance of unique wildlife is one reason UNESCO named the Queen Charlotte Islands a World Heritage Site. Sightings of bald eagles, cormorants, rhinoceroses, auklets, pacific loons, and grizzly bears are common. (A significant subspecies here is the **black bear,** which is larger than its mainland counterpart.) You can also spot more common animals like Sitka black-tailed deer, raccoons, and beavers. As an added bonus, the island is on a migratory path, so you can catch birds migrating if you visit in the spring or fall.

People come to Moresby primarily to enjoy its unspoiled beauty and wildlife but also for the chance to visit ancient Haidan villages. Sometimes referred to as the Vikings of the Pacific, the Haida were mighty seafarers, and during raiding forays, ranged as far south along the Pacific Coast as Oregon. The Haida were also excellent artists, carvers of both totems and argillite, a slatelike rock that they transformed into tiny totemic sculptures and pendants. The Haida today make up about half of Moresby's population of 1,000. **Gwaii Haanas National Park Reserve and the Haida Heritage site,** which covers the bottom third of the island archipelago, is home to totem poles that have stood for centuries. Perhaps the most famous site in the park is **SGang Gwaay 'Ilnagaay,** or Ninstints, on Anthony Island, an ancient Native village revered as sacred ground by the modern-day Haida.

Since there are no direct roads to Gwaii Haanas, as on much of the island, the only way to get there is by boat or floatplane. Only a small number of tourists are allowed in the park during the day, making this remote spot seem even more isolated. Before going, you are required to make a reservation and register your trip with the park. You'll also be asked to attend an orientation session; call **Super Natural British Columbia** (✆ **800/435-5622**) for details. By far the easiest and most convenient way to visit Gwaii Haanas is by joining a guided tour, however—see below for options. Trips can be long and costly out here, but, for your troubles, you will get stunning views of the wilderness and wildlife, in addition to a chance to soak in a 10,000-year-old culture.

For a less rigorous adventure, **Mosquito Lake** is a popular fishing spot and campsite—a great home base for visitors seeking to enjoy outdoor adventures, just southwest of the town of Sandspit. There, you'll find anglers vying for cutthroat and dolly varden. You can rest assured that the lake is named after World War II fighter planes, rather than the troublesome insect.

Most of the island's population lives in **Sandspit,** located on the northeastern tip. The town is the only area of the island where you'll find paved roads. Before taking to the island's unpaved terrain, be sure to call ✆ **250/637-5323** for road conditions. Otherwise, as on Gwaii Hannas, you'll have to get around by boat or floatplane. *—JD*

ⓘ **Queen Charlotte Visitor Information Center** (✆ **250/559-8316;** www.qcinfo.ca/centre.html).

✈ Sandspit Airport (via Vancouver).

⛴ www.bcferries.com.

🛏 $ **Bayview Garden Bed & Breakfast,** 401 Beach Rd., Sandspit (✆ **250/637-5749;** www.bayviewgardenbandb.com/index.html). $ **Moresby Island Guest House,** 385 Beach Rd., Sandspit (✆ **250/637-5300**).

TOUR Butterfly Tours Great Expeditions (✆ **604/740-7018;** www.butterflytours.bc.ca). **Ecosummer Expeditions** (✆ **800/465-8884** or 250/674-0102; www.ecosummer.com).

Island Hopping the Galápagos Islands: Intimate Encounters with Extraordinary Creatures

Christmas-colored iguanas that swim in the ocean? Seabirds with blue feet the color and texture of a rubber kiddie pool? Hundred-year-old tortoises that look like they've just walked off the set of a dinosaur movie? No wonder Charles Darwin was so taken with the Galápagos Islands. As a destination for lovers of wildlife, or for anyone who needs a thorough cleansing from the rigors of modern life, this pristine and superbly isolated archipelago tops even the safaris of Africa. Among our planet's many outstanding natural wonders, there are none quite so intimate as the encounters with wildlife you'll have in the Galápagos. The unusual animals here, whether reptile, bird, or mammal, are completely unafraid of people, and it's this opportunity to commune with wildness in its most natural, unguarded state that makes the Galápagos such an unforgettable destination.

An iguana on the Galápagos.

The magic of the Galápagos Islands, which straddle the equator 966km (600 miles) west of Ecuador, reveals itself to you slowly. The landforms here aren't exactly beautiful—so don't come here if you're looking for a tropical paradise of endless palm-treed, sandy beaches. With rough volcanic surfaces and scrubby vegetation in many places, the islands in the archipelago have a bizarre, even forbidding, aspect. But once you take your first shore excursion and greet the islands' unique inhabitants as they go about their business, unconcerned about your presence, you'll fall under the same spell that bewitched Darwin. These islands may be the most scientifically important in the world, but on a more basic level, they're also the most delightful.

Due to their particular topography, weather, and sea conditions, each island in the Galápagos is a distinct wildlife habitat, though many species are present on multiple islands. All but a handful of the islands are uninhabited and have no signs of civilization besides some marked trails. Access to most is by sea only and carefully controlled by the Galápagos National Park; touring the archipelago is best done with accredited ship-based outfitters. 97 **Santa Cruz** is the most populated island of the archipelago; its main town, bustling Puerto Ayora, is home to the Charles Darwin Research Station and the famous Galápagos tortoise Lonesome George.

98 **Española** is undoubtedly one of the archipelago's greatest treasures: Here, visitors can walk on a broad, sugary beach where hundreds of adorable sea lions romp, either playfully curious or totally oblivious to their human interlopers; or you can hike

the path that skirts Española's western end, where there are delightful sideshows of seabird antics at every turn. Blue-footed boobies dance and court, frigate birds perform acrobatics, and waved albatrosses take off and land on a windy "airstrip." 99 **Isabela** is the largest island and perhaps the most beautiful. It's made up of six shield volcanoes whose bases fused together above sea level to make up one mountainous island. Isabela's rugged seacoast is riddled with dramatic coves and rock walls where snorkelers and divers can swim right alongside sea turtles, sea lions, and Galápagos penguins. The youngest in the archipelago is 100 **Fernandina,** an otherworldly landscape of black lava where very little vegetation exists. Despite the scant flora, Fernandina supports thriving communities of marine iguanas—basking in the sun, usually underfoot! Flightless cormorants, yet another unusual Galápagos species, which lost its ability to fly because it had no predators, nest on Fernandina every summer. Tiny 101 **Bartolome,** with its gorgeous crescent beach and spiky rock formation in the quiet bay, is the iconic image of the Galápagos, featured in the film *Master and Commander: The Far Side of the World* and countless marketing materials. Sailing between any of the islands, you're likely to spy whales, dolphins, rays, and sharks, or the coolest pelagic fish of them all—the enormous *mola mola,* or ocean sunfish—launching its entire body out of the water.

As the full wealth of the Galápagos Islands can be visited only by sea and with government permits (tour operators arrange these up to a year in advance), it's essential to do your homework and find a reputable outfitter that suits your needs and traveling style. The small cruise ships that sail in the Galápagos are equipped with a full range of ways to explore the archipelago and its wildlife and have more comfortable accommodations, while the intimate catamarans offer more of a "roughing it" type of experience. Most expeditions last from a week to 10 days, though the longer you spend in the Galápagos, the tougher it is to reenter the civilized world. —*SM*

A garza bird on the Galápagos.

(i) www.galapagos.org.

✈ Baltra, the islands' only airport, is served by Aerogal and charter flights from Guayaquil and Quito, Ecuador.

TOUR Geographic Expeditions (✆ **800/777-8183** in the U.S. and Canada; www.geoex.com). **Lindblad Expeditions** (✆ **800/397-3348** in the U.S. and Canada; www.expeditions.com).

Unique Species 

Jersey

Durrell's Island Ark

The Channel Islands, U.K.

Gerald Durrell had worked in zoos—long before he became a well-known nature writer—and he knew they didn't work. So when, in 1959, he set up a park for breeding endangered species, the word "zoo" was never used. Yes, people could visit, but the animals would be housed in humane, naturalistic environments, and individuals bred in captivity would be returned to the wild whenever possible. Durrell's "nonzoo" worked so well, it became the model for modern wildlife parks all over the world.

Raised in an unconventional globe-trotting family (his classic memoir *My Family and Other Animals* is set in Corfu 56), the self-taught Durrell already had quite a menagerie in his older sister's garden in Bournemouth when he finally had enough money to build his dream park. He chose a site across the Channel in Jersey, notable for its salubrious climate. Though Jersey is only 91 sq. km (35 sq. miles), it's like Britain in microcosm, from the bracken-clad cliffs of the north to the broad golden beaches of the south, with an interior plateau of rich farmland and wooded valleys full of songbirds and scampering red squirrels. On the west coast, the wild sandy sweep of St. Ouen's Bay offers a breathtaking vista of dunes, reedy marsh, rock pools, and freshwater ponds.

Today the **Durrell Wildlife Conservation Trust** (Les Augres, Trinity; ✆ **44/1534/860035;** www.durrell.org) lies in the heart of the island, packed onto 13 hectares (32 acres) of gardens and parkland. It's home to some 1,400 mammals, birds, reptiles, and amphibians that Durrell conservationists have brought from around the world—Sumatran orangutans, Western Lowland gorillas, and black Andean bears; Assam pygmy hogs and Mallorcan midwife toads; and all sorts of lemurs and tamarins and pheasants and pigeons. Entrance fees help fund Durrell's conservation projects around the world, so you might as well pay extra for a guided tour (call to arrange one in advance), which may give you access to animals not viewable by the public; you may even get to help with daily feedings.

Durrell's exotics may steal the limelight, but Jersey's native species deserve your attention as well. With an unusually wide fluctuation between high and low tides, Jersey has a broad intertidal zone, rich with shorebirds and sea creatures. The coastal path that circles the island is essential for bird-watchers, from the gulls of the northern cliffs to the skylarks, sand martins, and lapwings of St Ouen's Bay.

And let's not forget Jersey's namesake dairy cows, which you'll see grazing on pasturelands all across the interior. In the heart of St. Lawrence, **Hamptonne Country Life Museum** (La Rue de la Patente; ✆ **44/1534/633374;** www.jerseyheritage.org) is a restored 17th-century farm, built of the island's distinctive rough pink granite, with costumed interpreters, a nature trail, and farm animals—Jersey calves, chickens—just waiting to be hand-fed. *—HH*

ⓘ **Tourist office,** Liberation Place, St. Helier (✆ **44/1534/448800;** www.jersey.com).

✈ Jersey.

⛴ **Condor Ferries** (✆ **44/845/6091026;** www.condorferries.com). St. Helier, from St-Malo (1 hr.), Guernsey (1 hr.), Weymouth (3½ hr.), Poole (3 hr.), Portsmouth (10½ hr.).

🛏 $$ **Les Charrieres Country Hotel,** St. Peter, Jersey (✆ **44/1534/481480;** www.lescharriereshotel.co.uk).

103 Birding Meccas

Phillip Island

The March of the Penguins

Australia

Who doesn't love penguins? Even hard-hearted cynics find it hard to resist those adorable flightless seabirds, waddling across the grainy brown beach in the gathering dusk to snuggle into their burrows on the sand dunes. Australia's most popular animal encounter, the Penguin Parade on Phillip Island spotlights a cast of hundreds of Little penguins, also known as fairy penguins—Australia's only native penguins, foot-high charmers with dark-blue heads, backs, and flippers. Even though the Penguin Parade on Phillip Island has commercialized the experience, with spectators packed into concrete bleachers to watch the nightfall ritual, those plucky little penguins somehow redeem it, night after night.

Phillip Island has all the virtues of convenience—handily connected by causeway to the mainland, it's only a 2-hour drive from Melbourne. Once you get here, you discover that there's a lot more to enjoy than just your cocktail hour with the penguins. On the scrubby, wind-swept Summerland peninsula, just past the **Penguin Parade beach** (✆ **61/3/5951 2820;** www.penguins.org.au), you'll find Australia's largest colony of fur seals mobbed onto the basalt outcropping called (what else?) Seal Rocks, viewable from observation decks on **The Nobbies** headland. Inside the Nobbies visitor center (1019 Ventor Rd.; ✆ **61/3/5951 2883**), monitors display close-ups of the seals, relayed from cameras on Seal Rocks. In the center of the island, cuddly koalas drip from the eucalyptus trees at the **Koala Conservation Center** (Phillip Island Rd. at Ventnor Beach Rd.; ✆ **61/3/5952 1610**). Just north of here, more koalas, as well as wallabies, echidnas, owls, and bats, can be found along the eucalyptus-scented trails of the **Oswin Roberts Woodland** (Cowes-Rhyll Rd.); continue north and east to the protected wetlands of **Rhyll Inlet,** where boardwalks wind through a mangrove estuary teeming with spoonbills, oystercatchers, herons, egrets, cormorants, and the rare bar-tailed godwit and whimbrel. Heading back toward the causeway, turn left to visit tiny Churchill Island, where the restored farmstead at **Churchill Island Heritage Farm** (✆ **61/3/5956 7214**) features ambling Clydesdale draft horses and shaggy red Highland cattle. Then detour south to the rocky heights of **Cape Woolamai,** where trails cross heath lands to fabulous coastal views; from September to April, thousands of short-tailed shearwaters (also known as mutton birds) cover its pink-granite headlands.

The trick to enjoying Phillip Island is avoiding the day-trippers. Staying here overnight helps enormously—that way you can explore the other nature attractions at your leisure, and get to the koalas before midafternoon when the buses arrive. It's also worthwhile to upgrade your Penguin Parade ticket: Book the less-crowded Penguins Plus boardwalk, where rangers provide commentary; the elevated Penguin Sky Box (no children allowed, unfortunately); or the Ultimate Penguin Tour (no children 15 and under), held on a separate, more secluded beach with its own penguins. Or come early for a ranger-guided behind-the-scenes tour of Penguin Parade's research operations. However you do it, in peak season reservations are essential. *—HH*

ⓘ **Visitor center,** 895 Phillip Island Tourist Rd., Newhaven (✆ **61/3/5956 7447;** www.visitphillipisland.com).

✈ Melbourne.

🚗 140km (87-mile) drive from Melbourne.

🛏 $$$ **Glen Isla House,** 230 Church St., Cowes (✆ **61/3/5952 1882;** www.glenisla.com). $ **Seahorse Motel,** 29–31 Church St., Cowes (✆ **61/3/5952 2003;** www.seahorsemotel.com.au).

TOUR Gray Line (✆ **61/3/9663 4455;** www.grayline.com) arranges Penguin Parade day trips.

Birding Meccas **104**

Lord Howe Island

The Lords of Lord Howe Island

Australia

There are a lot of outdoor things to do on a Lord Howe Island holiday—swim in a crystal-clear lagoon, marvel at tropical fish in a coral reef, hike trails through palm and banyan forests—but sooner or later the place turns every visitor into a bird-watcher. Not only does it have a lot of birds, but it has rare birds—and, best of all, they aren't shy of people.

Possibly Australia's best birding site, Lord Howe Island is a carefully preserved nature sanctuary, where only 400 tourists are allowed at a time. Seventy-five percent of the island, including much of the southern mountains and northern hills, is a permanent protected nature reserve. Many of its 350 residents are ancestors of the island's first 18th-century settlers. Life here is slow-paced; people get around on bikes instead of cars and just about everybody diligently recycles.

Lord Howe Island is home to more than 130 bird species, between residents and migratory visitors. There are 14 species of seabird alone, which roost and nest here in huge numbers. Walking trails along the island's ragged east coast offer great views of seabirds such as terns, boobies, noddies, and shearwaters. Star among them is one of the world's rarest birds, the Providence petrel, which nests near the summit of Mount Gower. This sturdy-looking seabird is so trustful of humans that it can sometimes be called out of the air—and might even decide to rest in your lap.

The rarest resident of all is the **Lord Howe Island woodhen,** found nowhere else but Lord Howe Island. This flightless brown bird, about the size of a bantam rooster, is listed as an endangered species, but the combined efforts of Australia's national wildlife service, the Lord Howe Island Board, and the Foundation for National Parks and Wildlife have resulted in a successful breeding program, and they now populate many parts of the island—some have even nested in residents' backyards. The best place to see them is on the 3km (1.75-mile) Little Island trail, where you can also see some beautiful emerald ground doves.

For impressive aerial feats, look to the skies, especially over the tropical forests of the northern hills, and you'll see the beautiful **red-tailed tropic bird,** with its elegant red tail streamers. When courting, it will fly backward, fly in circles, and, for good measure, throw in some vertical displays. It's a splendid sight, and one few birders ever get to see.

A speck off of Australia's east coast, equidistant from Sydney or Brisbane, Lord Howe Island is only a 2-hour plane ride from the mainland. Conveniently, there are just enough hotels on the island to handle all 400 visitors. —*HH*

ⓘ **Visitor center** (✆ **61/2/6563 2114;** www.lordhoweisland.info).

✈ Lord Howe Island.

🛏 $$ **Blue Lagoon Lodge** (✆ **61/2/6563 2006;** www.bluelagoonlodge.com). $$$ **Pinetrees Resort Hotel** (✆ **61/2/6563 2177;** www.pinetrees.com.au).

105 Birding Meccas

Stewart Island

Last Stop for Kiwis

New Zealand

New Zealanders love their national bird, the kiwi; they even proudly refer to themselves as "kiwis" from time to time. But these days it's well-nigh impossible to see one of these funny little flightless brown birds in the wild—that is, except on Stewart Island.

New Zealand's third island is also the farthest south, just across a 30km (19-mile) strait from the South Island 226, with a wonderful temperate climate and so much wildlife you won't believe it. (Only 1% of the island is inhabited.) The Maori name for it is Rakiura, which means "Land of Glowing Skies," referring to the vivid colors of dawn and the twilight skies on this still-unspoiled island. Hiking, kayaking, and diving are the main forms of entertainment here; head for the visitor lodge for **Rakiura National Park** (✆ **64/3/219-0009;** www.doc.govt.nz), only a 5-minute walk up Main Road from the ferry terminal, to get trail information and hut passes. The park encompasses 85% of the island,

Stewart Island.

which means loads of protected wilderness for wildlife, and some outstanding bird-watching: You can easily view uniquely New Zealand species like the kaka, tui, weka, kereru, and korimako, though you probably won't be able to see the nearly extinct kakapo and kokako.

Frequent sightings of the famously shy kiwi are the icing on the cake. All it takes is a little luck—or a little extra effort, like booking a nighttime kiwi-spotting boat tour with **Bravo Adventure Cruises** (✆ **64/3/219-1144**) or **Ruggedy Range Tours** (✆ **64/3/219-1066;** www.ruggedyrange.com). Though kiwis were not originally a nocturnal species, they've come to prefer nighttime forays, to avoid predators. Taking only 15 passengers at a time so as not to spook the kiwis, these 3-hour tours involve prowling the length of remote Ocean Beach with flashlights. The plump, spiky-feathered kiwis can be found poking around the washed-up kelp, sniffing out food with the nostrils located at the end of their long pointed beaks. Darting and skittering about in their ungainly, comical way, the kiwis take a little patience to see, but they're worth it.

Technically, Stewart Island's kiwi is its own species, slightly different from the spotted kiwis and brown kiwis found on the North and South Islands or on Kapiti Island 129; the Stewart Island kiwi has larger legs, a longer beak, and slightly lighter-colored plumage. But on the mainland, kiwi populations are declining at alarming rates, preyed upon by dogs, ferrets, stoats, and feral cats, while their natural habitats—the native forest and scrub—are being converted to pastureland and residential development.

Stoats and ferrets haven't made it over to Stewart Island yet, though, and human settlement is still sparse. For now, the Stewart Island kiwis still have a stable population. Their cousins on the mainland should have it so good. —*HH*

ⓘ **Tourist office,** Red Shed, 12 Elgin Terrace, Oban (✆ **64/3/219-1400;** www.stewartisland.co.nz).

Stewart Island (service from Invercargill, South Island).

Oban, 1 hr. from Bluff, South Island (✆ **64/3/212-7660;** www.stewartislandexperience.co.nz).

$$$ **Port of Call,** Leask Bay Rd. (✆ **64/3/219-1394;** www.portofcall.co.nz). $ **South Sea Hotel,** Elgin Terrace, Oban (✆ **64/3/219-1059;** www.stewart-island.co.nz).

Birding Meccas

The Skelligs

Into the West

Ireland

In high tourist season, scores of tour buses trundle around the Ring of Kerry, a 177km (110-mile) route around the Iveragh Peninsula of County Kerry. Shimmering seacoast views, picturesque fishing villages, thatched-roof cottages, ancient ring forts, moody bog lands, breathtaking mountain panoramas—yep, the Ring of Kerry fulfills every Irish tourism cliché.

But detour off of the main road, N70, and you'll escape the day-trippers and find one of Ireland's most memorable experiences: two tiny offshore islands known as the Skellig Rocks. These pyramid-shaped pinnacles of wind-scoured sandstone jut straight up from the sea, and yet on one of them—craggy Skellig Michael—a crew of Early Christian monks built a monastery on a 200m-high (656-ft.) cliff. And on the other—Small Skellig—vast flocks of seabirds practice their own form of communal living, turning the bare rock pinnacles and cliffs into their summer nesting grounds.

Follow R565 to Portmagee, and then cross the bridge over a marshy channel to **Valentia Island,** where you can learn all about the history, flora, and fauna of these islands at **The Skellig Experience** (see below). Besides a number of artifacts and audiovisual displays, the exhibit features a re-created sea cliff to give you an up-close idea of the seabirds' habitat. From there, you can board a 2-hour cruise with **Skellig Boat Trips** (✆ **353/66/947-6120**) that circles the Skelligs, which lie about 12km (7½ miles) west of Kerry's Atlantic coast. ***Warning:*** The sea crossing can be rough, and is sometimes cancelled when conditions aren't favorable (May–Oct are the best months to visit). If you want to actually get off the boat and climb the 1,000 stone steps to the monastery, which is a World Heritage Site, be sure to take one of the many longer trips offered by boat captains in either Valencia or Portmagee that add a 2-hour stop at **Skellig Michael,** aka The Rock. (Note that only a limited number of people per day are allowed to visit the monastery.)

Though passengers aren't allowed to go onto **Small Skellig** (An Sceilg Bheag in Gaelic), the boats do pull close enough for you to distinguish individual birds and even the details of their nests, resourcefully patched together from fishing nets, bits of rope, plastic bags, and whatever else the birds could find. An estimated 27,000 pairs of gannets live on Little Skellig year-round, the second-largest colony in the world; these massive seabirds, with their black-tipped 2m (6½-ft.) wingspans, can often be seen dive-bombing into the water for fish. Penguin-like black-and-white guillemots perch upright on their cliff-face niches; adorable orange-beaked puffins and petite black storm petrels nestle in tiny crevices, and shearwaters skim dramatically over the surface of the water, while grey seals sun themselves on rocky ledges at the island's base. If you're lucky, you may also see dolphins or even a minke whale from the boat. In its own way, it's just as much of a religious experience as the monastery visit. —*HH*

ⓘ **The Skellig Experience,** Valencia Island (✆ **353/66/947-6306;** www.skelligexperience.com; open Mar–Nov).

✈ Kerry County Airport.

🚆 Killarney Railway Station.

🛏 $$ **Derrynane Hotel,** off N71, Caherdaniel (✆ **353/66/947-5136;** www.derrynane.com). $$ **Earls Court House,** Woodlawn Junction, Muckross Rd., Killarney (✆ **353/64/663-4009;** www.killarney-earlscourt.ie).

107 Birding Meccas

Texel Island

Wadden Sea Eco-Paradise

The Netherlands

When the tides pull out from Texel Island, they leave behind broad glistening mud flats, where the North Sea had been lapping only hours earlier. That enormous displacement of water stirs up so many vital nutrients that a variety of animals thrive here, from plankton to seals to as many as 300 species of birds. Prowl around the flats at low tide and you never know what you'll find crawling about underfoot.

Running along the entire 24km-long (15-mile) North Sea coast of Texel (pronounced *Tess*-uhl)—the largest and most populated of the Wadden Islands archipelago—the Dunes of Texel National Park is a fascinating intertidal ecosystem, from its mud flats to stretches of gently waving marsh grass dotted with sea lavender and sea aster. South of the coastal village of De Koog, the wildlife biologists at the Wadden Islands research center **Ecomare,** Ruijslaan 92 (✆ **31/222/317-741;** www.ecomare.nl), are invaluable guides to this coastal dune system's natural wonders. They not only conduct guided "mud excursions" at low tide but also lead tours of three protected nature reserves: **De Schorren, De Bol,** and **Dijkmanshuizen,** where the bird-watching is superb. Expect to see healthy numbers of spoonbills, oystercatchers, Bewick swans, eider ducks, Brent geese, avocets, marsh harriers, snow buntings, ringed plovers, kestrels, short-eared owls, and bar-tailed godwits. Ecomare also runs a rehab program for birds affected by environmental hazards, particularly oil spills, which are deadly for bird populations: Ecomare estimates that only 10% of birds immersed in oil wash ashore alive—and those that do are given a spin in Ecomare's special bird-washing machine and rehabbed in the sanctuary pool.

Texel Island is a sunny, serene place to get close to wildlife, with much of the island dedicated to nature preserves. Its cinematically picturesque landscape is a mix of sea and mud flat, sand dunes and meadows. But communing with nature isn't the only attraction on Texel: The island has seven charming villages, many with historic 16th- and 17th-century Dutch architecture and cobblestone streets (one, Den Hoom, is enveloped in flowering fields of bulbs in the spring). Den Burg is the central town.

Not all the wildlife on Texel is wild—there are just as many sheep residing here as people (14,000 permanent residents). Texel has been raising prized Texel lamb since the 15th century—the lean, muscular animals are free to roam the heather-rich pastures, and the sea air infuses the lamb meat with a naturally salty flavor. You can be sure to see Texel lamb on the menu at the many celebrated island restaurants, as well as smoked fish and other local specialties.

The 20-minute trip across the Marsdiep Strait to Texel is an attraction in itself, aboard the largest ferry in Netherlands waters, the *Dokter Wagemaker.* From its "panorama deck" you can enjoy 360-degree views of the Wadden Sea and great gulps of invigorating salt air. —*AF*

ⓘ **Tourist office,** Emmalaan 66, Den Burg (✆ **31/222/314-741;** www.texel.net).

✈ Den Helder (small private planes can land on Texel).

⛴ TESO car ferry (✆ **31/222/369-691;** www.teso.nl). From Den Helder, 20 min.

🛏 $$ **Hotel de Lindeboom,** Groeneplaats 14, Den Burg (✆ **31/222/312-041;** www.hotelgroeptexel.nl). $$$ **Hotel Greenside,** Stappeland 6, De Koog (✆ **31/222/327-222;** www.hotelgroeptexel.nl/en/greensidekamers).

108 Birding Meccas

Hawar Island

The Last Frontier

Bahrain

The Persian Gulf doesn't have many undisturbed island habitats left—which makes Hawar Island feel like a last frontier. The largest island in the 130-sq.-km (50-sq.-mile) Hawar Islands archipelago, the long crescent of Hawar Island (full name Jazarit Hawar) has natural wetlands, mud flats, and sea-grass beds of such beauty and environmental purity that scientists from all over the world are drawn to it.

How did the pristine habitat of Hawar and its sister islands survive in a country (and region) that is one of the most densely populated places in the world? After all, the coastline of Bahrain has become so degraded by human activity that the country decided to dredge sand from the Gulf to create new prime waterfront property, a la Dubai. On completion, the seaside city resort of Durrat Al Bahrain, on Bahrain's southern coast, will consist of 13 man-made islands covered with hundreds of villas, hotels, shopping centers, and even an 18-hole golf course; to the north, the Amwaj Islands will contain homes, high-rises, and a marina.

But 25km (16 miles) off the southeast coast, this group of 36 desert islands remains sparsely inhabited, for two critical reasons: isolation and lack of water. The islands of Hawar have no surface or aquifer water, which kept human settlement to a minimum over the years. And Bahrain is taking steps to ensure that they retain their uniquely primeval habitat, even applying for World Heritage Site recognition.

For birds and birders, Hawar is paradise. Hawar Island is a nesting and breeding site for countless birds and provides critical habitat for several endangered species. Hawar has the largest colony in the world of **Socotra cormorants,** some 200,000 birds, as well as large numbers of sooty falcons, white-cheeked terns, linnets, chaffinches, and pied kingfishers. For the latest bird-watching sightings, go to the Bahrain Bird Report (www.hawar-islands.com). To arrange wildlife tours and packages, including bird-watching trips, contact **Alreem Environmental Consultation and Ecotourism** (✆ **973/710868;** www.alreem.com); tours are located under "Ecotourism" on the website.

Few places in the Arabian Gulf have such pristine marine ecosystems, either. Among other species, the seas around Hawar are an important winter feeding ground for the endangered **dugong,** a sea cow related to the manatee. The gentle dugong can live to be 70 years of age, but elsewhere its existence is threatened by hunting and fishing, predators, and human encroachment. If World Heritage status is ultimately conferred, the dugong will have an all-important refuge in Hawar. —*AF*

(i) www.bahraintourism.com or www.hawar-islands.com.

✈ Bahrain International Airport in Muharraq.

⛴ Southern Tourism Company, Ad Dur jetty, Manama (45 min.; www.eskanbank.com/en).

🛏 $$$ **Tulip Inn Hawar Beach Hotel and Resort,** Hawar Island (✆ **973/17-535000;** www.goldentulip.com).

Birding Meccas 

Cape Sable Island

Raw & Wild

Canada

Bedeviled by fog, nor'easters, and hurricanes, Cape Sable Island is nature raw and unfiltered. Known to locals as Cape Island, Cape Sable (not to be confused with Sable Island 125, to the east) lies in the Atlantic Ocean off the southwest coast of Nova Scotia. Over 11km (7 miles) long and 4.8km (3 miles) wide, it's home to some 1,000 residents—fishermen, boat builders, sea captains, and the sons and daughters of sea captains—who live by the whims of the currents and the tides.

Cool Atlantic breezes and warm currents make this island a rich and diverse ecosystem for wildlife, both on land and offshore. A major pit stop for migratory birds in spring and fall, Cape Sable has been designated an Important Bird Area (IBA). It's an essential habitat and breeding ground for shorebirds of every stripe: piping plovers, Atlantic brandt (some 6% of the global species), semipalmated sandpipers, sanderlings, and short-billed dowitchers. In the evening thousands of Atlantic brandt take to the skies en masse after feeding in the salt marshes—on a moonlit night you can see them bobbing on the waves of the Atlantic. The island is also a prime spot for water birds—loons, egrets, herons, sea ducks, and the like—and is the only site in Canada for the American oystercatcher. The prime birdwatching spot is on the island's southern tip at **The Hawk beach,** which has another fascinating attraction: a 1,300-year-old "drowned forest" that reappears at low tide.

Cape Sable Island is easy to get to; it's connected to mainland Nova Scotia by a causeway that crosses a narrow strait known as the Barrington Passage. When the weather kicks off and the fog sets in, this can be a dangerous place for a ship to navigate. In 1860, the Canadian steamer SS *Hungarian* wrecked on the island shoals in a fierce gale, one of the worst maritime disasters in Canadian history. As a result, the next year the first **Cape Sable Lighthouse** was built—at just over 30m (100 ft.) high, it's the tallest lighthouse in Nova Scotia. The lighthouse is located on an offshore islet just south of Cape Sable Island; you can see it from the beach at The Hawk.

Conditions may be rough at times on Cape Sable, but its raw beauty is undeniable, a gothic stew of wind, sea, and fog. Canada's southernmost point has miles of uncrowded white beaches; a shoreline boardwalk runs the length of the island from the tourist office to the wharf at Clarks Harbour, the island's main port. Even the island's main road hugs the coastline in a scenic loop. It seems that no matter where you are on Cape Sable, the sea is front and center. —*AF*

(i) www.capesableisland.ca or www.destinationsouthwestnova.com.

✈ Halifax or Yarmouth, Nova Scotia.

1-hour drive from Yarmouth, Nova Scotia, or 3-hour drive from Halifax.

$ **Island Breeze Inn,** 4 Penny Beach Rd., Cape Sable Island (✆ **902/745-0807;** www.island-breeze-inn.com).

110 Birding Meccas

Pelee Island

The Tropics of Canada

Canada

You can't get much farther south in Canada: Plunked down into Lake Erie, Pelee Island looks as if it had come unmoored from Ontario and was drifting toward Ohio. For migrating birds and butterflies heading north on the Atlantic flyway, it's a welcome sight every spring, the first bit of dry land where they can rest their wings after soaring across the great lake.

Pelee Island Is a freak of nature—but in a good way. Surrounded by warm, shallow waters, it has an unusually warm microclimate for this latitude, and seeds dropped by migrating birds have only added to its biodiversity. (Where else in Canada can you find prickly pear cactus?) Early-19th-century settlers ravaged the island, hacking down its red cedar forests for timber and quarrying its glacier-carved stone, but from the mid-1800s on, farmers moved in to exploit that long growing season, with acres of vineyards thriving in this surprisingly Mediterranean climate. Recently, as more of that deep-soiled farmland has reverted to the wild, the limestone savannas and forests have rebounded magnificently, now covering almost a quarter of the island and harboring species that long ago disappeared from the Ontario mainland. Nutrient-rich local waters attract fish to spawn and raise their young, thus luring to the island's shores large colonies of the water birds that feast on those fish. For visitors, there's not much to do here but enjoy nature, but that slow pace suits the birds to a T.

Just north of the ferry docks, the **Pelee Island Heritage Center** (1073 W. Shore Rd.; ✆ **519/724-2291;** www.peleeisland museum.ca) is a great place to start, with exhibits on the island's natural history as well as its human history. Projecting from the island's southwest corner into Lake Erie, **Fish Point** is Pelee's number-one birding site, with a lagoon full of black-crowned night herons and other waders, and shorebirds flocking all over its flat, woodland-bordered beach. If you're here in spring or fall, during the busy migration season, contact the **Pelee Island Bird Observatory**'s field station at Fish Point (✆ **519/724-2829;** www.pibo.ca) to join one of its education programs.

Head east from Fish Point to ramble around another rare ecosystem, **Stone Road Alvar** (Stone Rd.). *Alvar* is an Estonian word for this kind of limestone plain, covered with a patchy mosaic of thickets, oak and hickory trees, red cedar savanna, and prairie grass. That mixed vegetation harbors a number of rare snakes and butterflies, as well as threatened songbirds

Pelee Island lighthouse.

like the blue-gray gnatcatcher and yellow-breasted chat. The northeast headland of **Lighthouse Point** (East Shore Rd.) is another wonderful nature preserve; bring binoculars to spot aquatic birds in the wetlands behind its restored 19th-century lighthouse.

The island's conservation-minded authorities are expanding its network of bike and walking paths so that visitors can "go green" and leave their cars behind when they explore the island. You can bike around the island's rim in about 4 hours—if you don't stop to bird-watch. But hey, that's a big if. —*HH*

ⓘ www.pelee.org.

✈ Pelee Island airport (Griffing Air Service, ✆ **419/626-5161**).

🚢 **Pelee Island Transportation** (✆ **800/661-2220** or 519/724-2115; www.ontarioferries.com; Apr–Dec). From Leamington, Kingville, or Sandusky, 1½ hr.

🛏 $$ **Anchor and Wheel Inn,** 11 W. Shore Rd. (✆ **519/724-2195;** www.anchorwheelinn.com). $$$ **Wavecrest Bed and Breakfast,** 79 E. Shore Rd. (✆ **519/724-1111;** www.wavecrestpelee.com).

Birding Meccas 111

Sandy Island

Red Cockades in Gullah Land

South Carolina, U.S.

Once a rice plantation, now inhabited only by a few descendants of former plantation slaves, peaceful Sandy Island is less than an hour's drive from the frenetic attractions of Myrtle Beach; on its northeast border lies Brookfield Gardens, a popular historic-home attraction. It's scary to think that not so long ago, in 1993, developers planned to build a bridge to connect this isolated Gullah community to the mainland. The 3-year legal battle to block bridge construction turned on an environmental issue: protecting Sandy Island's most endangered species, the **red-cockaded woodpecker.** For once the environmentalists won.

These beautiful woodpeckers were once abundant; now they may be reduced to only 4,500 family groups, their preferred habitats eliminated by logging and agriculture. The red-cockaded woodpecker is a handsome bird, but *very* picky: It will nest only in live pines in large open stands. And how many of those are left these days? To make matters worse, in 1989 Hurricane Hugo destroyed many of the trees that give them shelter and sustenance. Fortunately for the birds, Sandy Island makes an ideal haven. This pristine freshwater island lies tucked between two rivers, a rich mix of cypress swamps, longleaf-pine and oak forests, salt marshes, and sand hills rising as high as 78 feet (24m). Those longleaf pines are perfect for red-cockaded woodpeckers, who feed on the beetles, ants, roaches, wood-boring insects, and spiders that live in pines. Pecking vigorously at the pine trunks, the birds also release sticky resin that flows down the trees, thus setting up a handy barrier to thwart predators like snakes. Other trees just don't offer that feature.

Once the red-cockaded woodpeckers find those perfect pines, they're real homebodies. They don't migrate, they keep the same mates for several years, and they live in communal groups of five to nine birds that all pitch in to help with sitting on nests and raising chicks. After fledging, the young commonly stay with the group—another generation of homebodies.

Thanks to that environmental battle, you still have to catch a boat to visit Sandy Island. When you get here, you won't find visitor facilities—just forest, wetlands, and wildlife. The 120 or so residents of the island live in their own tight-knit community, away from the nature preserve part of the island (although you can visit their community with local guide Rommy Pyatt, who organizes a **boat tour** to the island; contact him at ✆ **843/408-7187;** www.toursdesandyisland.com). You may, however, see other mainlanders boating over for a peaceful day of bird-watching and beach strolling, especially if it's a lovely weekend day. Bring your binoculars so you can pick out the red-cockaded woodpecker that saved this island: He'll be the one with the black-and-white barred back, large white eye patches, black cap, and small red streak on each side of the head, like an ornament on a hat. Chances are good he'll be in a pine tree. —*HH*

ⓘ **Sandy Island tourist info,** near Murrell's Inlet (no phone; www.nature.org).

✈ Myrtle Beach International Airport (42 miles/68km).

Private boat landings at Sandy Island, Wacca Wache, Samworth Wildlife Management Area, Yauhanna.

$$ **Hampton Inn,** 150 Willbrook Blvd., Pawley's Island (✆ **800/426-7866** or 843/235-2000; www.pawleysisland hamptoninn.com). $ **Holiday Inn Express,** 11445 Hwy. 17 S., Pawley's Island (✆ **888/465-4329** or 843/235-0808; www.ichotelsgroup.com).

112 Birding Meccas

Trinidad

The Birds of Eden

Every year, Trinidad's capital city, Port of Spain, is swept up in a famously festive Carnival celebration. Meanwhile, a short distance away in the Caroni Swamp, Trinidad's national bird, the scarlet ibis, flits about, decked out more brilliantly than any Carnival reveler.

The sixth-largest island in the Caribbean, lying just 11km (6¾ miles) off the Venezuelan coast, Trinidad has such a varied ecosystem—mountainous rainforests, plains, several major river systems, extensive wetlands—that it supports some 400 species of birds, more than 600 species of butterflies, and 97 native mammals, including exotics like the red howler monkey, the ocelot, and the collared peccary (a type of boar). The crown jewel of Trinidad's natural world is the **Asa Wright Nature Center** (www.asawright.org), a 607-hectare (1,500-acre) wildlife sanctuary located in a former coffee, citrus, and cacao plantation high in the lush rainforest of Trinidad's hilly Northern Range. Day visitors can hike around miles of forest trails, take a guided nature tour, or have a buffet-style luncheon of local cuisine; you can also stay overnight in the Asa Wright Center Lodge, occupying an old plantation house and surrounding cottages. The bird-watching at Asa Wright is unparalleled: The center's 150-plus species list includes such rarely spotted birds as the violaceous trogon, the channel-billed toucan, the copper-rumped hummingbird, purple and green honeycreepers, the silver-beaked tanager, bearded and golden-headed manakins, the bearded bellbird, and a nesting pair of ornate hawk eagles. Twenty-nine types of bats have also been spotted in the area, as have leaf-cutter and army ants, nine-banded armadillos, iguanas, and tegu lizards. Visitors staying for 3 or more nights are allowed to peek in on the world's most accessible colony of rare, nocturnal oilbirds, which nest by day in a cave on the property.

Trinidad's increasingly threatened wetlands are also favorite destinations for birders. A top site is the **Caroni Swamp** on the west coast, where the scarlet ibis feasts on a shellfish diet that turns its plumage bright red. During peak season (Oct–Mar), the ibis population can reach 15,000. A boat tour through the swamp's marshes, lagoons, mud flats, and mangrove forests may reveal 190 other bird species, including egrets and herons, as well as tree boas, caimans, silky anteaters, raccoons, oysters, crabs, and 24 varieties of fin-fish. The 1,538 hectare (3,800-acre) **Nariva Swamp** on Trinidad's southeast coast is the largest wetlands in the Caribbean, a varied mosaic that includes Moriche palms, wild rice, and scattered hardwood forests. Birders can find 171 species here, from the Amazonian parrot and whistling duck to the rarely spotted red-bellied macaw and the endangered seed-eating finch; boating through the swamp, you may spot everything from butterflies and giant snails to opossums, anteaters, porcupines, anacondas, and manatees.

You may also want to visit the **Pierre-Point Wildfowl Trust** bird sanctuary (Flagstaff Hill, Long Circular Rd.; ✆ **868/658-4230**)—located, oddly enough, beside an oil refinery—and, between March and August, make nighttime visits to the beaches along Trinidad's northeast coast to view leatherback turtles laying their eggs. —*AF*

ⓘ www.gotrinidadandtobago.com.

✈ Piarco International Airport, 30 min. east of Port-of-Spain.

🛏 $$$ **Asa Wright Nature Center & Lodge,** Spring Hill Estate, Arima (✆ **800/426-7781** in the U.S., or 868/667-4655; www.asawright.org). $$ **Kapok Hotel,** 16–18 Cotton Hill (✆ **868/622-5765;** www.kapokhotel.com).

TOUR Caribbean Discovery Tours (✆ **868/624-7281;** www.caribbeandiscoverytours.com). **Nanan's Tours** (✆ **868/645-1305;** www.nanecotours.com).

Birding Meccas **113**

Little Cayman Island

Booby Bonanza

The Cayman Islands

If this scene had a soundtrack, you'd hear ominous drumrolls and deep bassoons: Cue up a massed horde of red-footed boobies, thousands of them, hovering tensely at twilight above the Caribbean Sea. Now enter, stage left, a circling crew of magnificent frigate birds, marauders famous for stealing other birds' food, stretching their 2.4m-wide (7¾-ft.) pointed black wings. The boobies spiral upward in a column, wheel swiftly, and dive like torpedoes toward shore. The frigate birds dart in to attack. Who will win this battle for survival?

This drama is played out every evening in nesting season on Little Cayman Island, an isolated, sparsely inhabited scrap of coral and sand in the Caribbean Sea due south of Cuba 374. About 10,000 nesting pairs of red-footed boobies—the largest colony in the Western hemisphere—hatch their chicks each February in the landlocked saltwater lagoon of Little Cayman's 162-hectare (400-acre) **Booby Pond Nature Reserve** (✆ **345/948-1010**). Buff-colored or white, with a wingspan of nearly 1.5m (5 ft.), the boobies have dark wingtips, blue bills, and, of course, unmistakably bright red feet. By day, they roam long distances from Little Cayman, flying as far as Cuba or Jamaica 262, to fill their crops with squid and small fish to take back to their chicks—that is, if they can get past the frigate birds first.

Nowadays Little Cayman's chief tourism draw is snorkeling and scuba diving (Jacques Cousteau once declared it one of the world's top-three diving spots), with no fewer than 60 dive sites, including the spectacularly sheer coral wall of Bloody Bay. Fishing is also an attraction; the milky-looking mud flats of South Hole Sound offer world-class bonefishing, and loads of tarpon are waiting to be caught in a brackish inland pool aptly named Tarpon Lake.

But long before those sports became so popular, this former pirate haven (treasure may still be buried here) was known as a bird-watcher's paradise. Though you can't go into the wetlands where the birds nest, lookout platforms have been built around the edges of the pond where you can watch that nightly twilight battle; there are also telescopes on the veranda of the visitor center, a traditional Caymanian gingerbread bungalow. Besides the boobies and the frigate birds, you'll see other rare water birds around the pond, including the shy West Indian whistling duck, and a lot of

A booby on Little Cayman.

snowy egrets, pure-white long-necked birds with startling yellow feet and a distinctive shaggy plume at the back of their heads. For a peak birding experience, come here the first 2 weeks of November, when the migratory birds are passing through as well.

Little Cayman also has the largest population of rock iguanas in the entire Caribbean, outnumbering the island's human population by well more than 10 to 1—drive carefully, because they have the right of way on Little Cayman's roads. —*HH*

ⓘ **Cayman Islands tourist info,** Cricket Square, George Town, Grand Cayman (✆ **345/949-0623;** www.caymanislands.ky).

✈ Grand Cayman (charter from there to Little Cayman).

🛏 $$ **Pirates Point Resort,** Preston Bay, Little Cayman (✆ **345/948-1010;** www.piratespointresort.com).

Sea Life 114

Islas Ballestas

Peru's Pacific Playground

Peru

Red rock arches spanning a cobalt sea, cliffs riddled with caves and crevices—the capriciously formed Islas Ballestas are a haven for marine life that almost seems like a man-made playground. Humboldt penguins, Inca terns, boobies, cormorants, and flamingos can all be seen hopping about this group of three small rocky Pacific islands just west of the Peruvian coast, and the undersea wildlife is equally rich.

Tourists are not allowed to go ashore on the Islas Ballestas (whose name means "crossbow"), but excursion boats can get you close enough to smell the guano and snap some great photographs. The highlight for many visitors to the Islas Ballestas is the show put on by the resident **sea lions.** These pinnipeds love to ham it up for the tourist boats and routinely perform flips and leaps worthy of Sea World within inches of their human admirers. Occasionally, you can also catch sight of marine otters and even the odd condor, which swoop down from the Andes from time to time to go fishing in the Pacific. The white guano (bird droppings) covering much of the surface of the islands is actually necessary for the birds' nesting as it adds stability, but every 4 to 7 years, when it gets too thick, it's harvested and converted into fertilizer for farms on the mainland.

Boat excursions to the Ballestas depart from the town of Pisco, 25km (16 miles) away, from December to March, leaving in the morning and generally lasting a few hours. The tours also include a viewing of the famous **Candelabra of the Andes,** a mysterious 180m-long (590-ft.) hillside geoglyph (man-made carving in the earth) in a shape that various observers see as

Sea lions on Islas Ballestas.

either a candlestick or a trident; its ancient origins may go back as far as 3,000 years. The Candelabra is best seen from the sea, so this is a great opportunity to combine some South American archaeology with your nature observation. The other great wildlife viewing in the area is at **Paracas National Reserve,** often included on an Islas Ballestas excursion. A spectacular landscape where the desert meets the sea, Paracas is known as Peru's Galápagos (p. 100) for its variety of unique species, from the desert's condors and rare marine cats to the dolphins, octopuses, squid, and purple crabs of the sea.

Situated 260km (162 miles) south of Lima and a few kilometers west of the Pan-American Highway, **Pisco** itself is a lively fishing town worth at least a half-day's exploration, although much of the traditional adobe architecture still shows the effects of the devastating 8.0 earthquake that struck here in 2007. You may also recognize the name Pisco from the popular Peruvian cocktail called Pisco Sour, made with a grape brandy traditionally aged in a cone-shaped pottery vessel, also called a *pisco*. —*SM*

ⓘ www.peru.info.

✈ Lima (260km/162 miles), then bus to Pisco (3-4 hr.).

Day trips from Pisco with **Peru Adventure Tours** (✆ **51/54/221-658;** www.peruadventurestours.com).

$$$ **Hotel Paracas,** av. Paracas 173, within Paracas National Reserve (✆ **51/56/545-100;** www.hotelparacas.com). $ **Hotel Villa Manuelita,** San Francisco 227 (✆ **51/56/535-218;** www.villamanuelitahostal.com).

115 Sea Life

Fernando de Noronha

Bay of Dolphins

Brazil

"Here is paradise," wrote explorer Amerigo Vespucci upon his arrival on the island in 1504. The largest of 21 islands on the Brazilian archipelago of the same name, Fernando de Noronha is one place that lives up to its billing. It has some of Brazil's most beautiful beaches, diamond-clear waters bathed by warm African currents, and an undersea world populated with healthy numbers of large pelagics, billfish, sea turtles, and especially its large population of resident dolphins—**spinner dolphins,** to be exact, so named for the exuberant spin they do as they leap out of the water. The tidal pools and lagoons of the Baía dos Golfinhos are transformed at low tide into a natural aquarium, where some 600 spinner dolphins live and breed. No wonder Fernando de Noronha was awarded World Heritage Site status in 2002 as an "oasis of marine life."

Fernando de Noronha owes much of its eco-purity to its remote location, approximately 483km (300 miles) off Brazil's northeast coast. Fernando do Noronha has another invaluable asset: a highly responsible conservation ethos. Seventy percent of the island archipelago is national parkland, and development is rigidly controlled through the Brazilian Institute of Environment and Renewable Natural Resources (IBAMA). The government limits the coming and going of visitors, allowing only 460 nonresidents on the island at one time. The dolphins' bay is a perfectly lovely 2.3km (1½-mile) crescent of sand, but it's strictly off-limits to visitors—although you can watch the dolphins from a cliff overlooking

Pig Bay, Fernando de Noronha.

the beach (binoculars help). At the **Praia de Atalaia** beach, only 100 people are allowed to visit each day, and snorkeling is permitted in the shallow tidal pools for only 25 minutes—and no suntan lotion, please, if you plan to swim in the pools. Strict controls are also exercised during turtle-hatching season at **Praia do Leão** (named for the rock offshore that resembles a sea lion), a critical nesting site for turtles. Don't worry: You'll have no trouble finding accessible, white-sand beaches, including two of Brazil's finest: **Praia do Leão** (see above) and **Baía do Sancho,** both with excellent swimming and snorkeling opportunities.

The island is actually the tip of an undersea mountain range in the southern Atlantic Ocean. Beaches are rimmed in mossy volcanic hills and peppered with oddly shaped rock formations—seismic hiccups from long ago. The island's interior is largely scrub brush, with dune buggies (the preferred mode of transportation) kicking up dust on the dry red-dirt roads.

Fernando de Noronha is a surfing mecca, particularly in December and January when the winds change direction, kicking up frothy, voluminous swells that draw longboards from around the world. But it's in the diving world that Fernando de Noronha truly rocks, especially during the winter months (July–Oct), when visibility can extend to 50m (164 ft.). Experts attribute the low incidence of shark attacks on humans to a perfectly balanced marine ecosystem; sharks have plenty to eat here, thank you! —*AF*

ⓘ **Tourist office,** Palácio São Miguel, Vila Remédios, Fernando de Noronha (✆ **55/81/3619-1352;** www.noronha.pe.gov.br).

✈ Fernando de Noronha (1 hr., 40 min. from Recife; 1 hr., 10 min. from Natal).

🛏 $$$ **Pousada Maravilha** (✆ **55/81/3619-0028;** www.pousadamaravilha.com.br). $$ **Pousada Solar dos Ventos** (✆ **55/81/3619-1347;** www.pousadasolardosventos.com.br).

116 Sea Life

Seal Island

A Smorgasbord for Great White Sharks

South Africa

If you've ever tuned into *Shark Week* on the Discovery Channel, chances are you've already seen Seal Island. Sixty thousand **cape fur seals** inhabit this rocky outcrop near Cape Town, and that constant supply of fresh red meat is a honey pot for the ocean's most fearsome predator—**great white sharks.** Their spectacular hunting behaviors, which involve those aerial feats so often shown on sensationalist nature programs, are not found in any other white shark habitat in the world—bad news for the seals of Seal Island.

The great whites that feed in False Bay, which surrounds Seal Island, are especially famous for their surface breaching: The sharks launch their entire bodies out of the water in order to snatch an unlucky seal from the surface. Whales normally leap all the way out of the water like this, for reasons unrelated to killing prey, but breaching takes on a whole new terrifying dimension when it's a menacing 2,000kg shark doing the deed. *Air Jaws* became the most successful shark show in history when it introduced TV audiences to the unique shark breaching off Seal Island. What's also striking is how close to shore these shark-on-seal attacks take place—almost within sight of Simonstown harbor in some cases.

For those who care to witness this extremely violent link of the food chain in person, there are plenty of charter outfits along False Bay, near Cape Town, that operate boat excursions to Seal Island—though the boats seem alarmingly small and flimsy given the size and acrobatic capabilities of the sharks touted in their marketing materials. (If surface viewing is all a bit too tame for you, very adventurous types can also find outfitters that will put you face to face, through a shark cage, with *carcharidon carcharias*.)

Within a certain distance of Seal Island in each direction, there's a sweet spot called the **Ring of Death** where the sharks wait for unsavvy seals—usually, the young, old, or infirm ones—to make a mistake. If the seals cross the Ring of Death near the murky bottom of the bay, they'll pass under the sharks unnoticed and make it to the open sea safely. But if they swim too near the surface, it's only a matter of time until a great white attacks, and that's almost always a fatal encounter.

Though you can get close enough to hear and smell the teeming seal population there, Seal Island itself cannot be visited—and you probably wouldn't want to, anyway. The attraction here is undoubtedly the wildlife interaction offshore, not any sort of natural beauty onshore. The rocks are thick with seal guano, and there's no soil or vegetation on the island, which reaches a maximum "elevation" of just 6m (20 ft.). To lay eyes on Seal Island from the water, it doesn't look like land at all, just a heaving mass of intertwined seals that have survived another day inside the Ring of Death. —*SM*

(i) www.capetown.travel.

Cape Town (35km/22 miles).

Transport available via tour operator (see below).

$$ **Four Rosmead,** 4 Rosmead Ave. (✆ **27/21/480-3810;** www.fourrosmead.com). $$$ **Mount Nelson,** 76 Orange St. (✆ **27/21/483-1000;** www.mountnelson.co.za).

TOUR African Shark Eco Charters, Simonstown (✆ **27/21/785-1947;** www.ultimate-animals.com). **Boat Company Tours,** Simonstown (✆ **27/83/257-7760;** www.boatcompany.co.za).

Sea Life 117

Ile Sainte Marie

The Island of Humpback Whales

Madagascar

To the native Malagasy people who call Ile St. Marie home, humpback whales were known as "Zagnaharibe" or "Trozona"—which translates to the "Great Gods." All it takes is a boat excursion into the whale-rich waters off this tiny tropical Indian Ocean island and you'll start to understand why.

It's easy to think, in this hyperconnected world, that there are no undiscovered tropical isles left on the planet. Well, take a look at this sleepy little gem. Ile Sainte Marie—also known by its Malagasy name, Nosy Boroha—lies just 8km (5 miles) from Madagascar 470, off the southeast coast of Africa. This serene, under-the-radar paradise for beach bums, divers, and nature lovers is not your average tropical isle. It's got a luxuriant and biodiverse landscape of coco trees and rare orchids, along with world-class diving and snorkeling. It's got fine palm-fringed white-sand beaches studded with black rocks. It's got pirate shipwrecks and a pirate cemetery (with the official pirate logo—skull and crossed tibia bones—on a tombstone).

But most intriguingly, it has humpback whales. From July to September, the whales travel from Antarctica to the warm Indian Ocean to breed. (Good news for whale-watchers, who are likely to see young calves swimming alongside their mothers.) The playful long-finned humpback is remarkably acrobatic for its size—it can grow up to 15m (50 ft.) long and weigh 35 tons—tail-slapping and leaping out of the water. The humpback was almost driven to extinction by hunting, but bans on hunting have helped the population recover to about 20,000 worldwide. The waters surrounding Ile Sainte Marie are a designated **whale sanctuary.**

Whale-watching expeditions from Ile Sainte Marie can be arranged through **Il Balenottero Diving Center** (✆ **261/20-57-400-36;** www.ilbalenottero.com), which partners with Megaptera, the international whale association, to document humpback sightings. That means that whale-watching safaris become scientific expeditions on which passengers help catalog the sightings—making these trips both thrilling and rewarding. Who knew a laid-back trip to a tropical paradise could be so fulfilling? *—AF*

ⓘ www.madagascar-tourisme.com or www.madagascarconsulate.org.za.

✈ Ivato airport, Madagascar.

⛴ Fastest service is **Cap Sainte Marie** (✆ **261/20-57-404-06;** www.cap-sainte-marie.com), Ambodifotatra, 1–3 hr. from Soanierana-Ivongo.

🛏 $ **La Crique** (✆ **261/20-57-902-45;** www.lacrique.net). $ **Soanambo Hotel** (✆ **261/20-22-640-54;** www.hsm.mg).

118 Sea Life

Lizard Island

Creatures of the Great Barrier Reef

Australia

When Captain James Cook first landed here in 1770, the thing that most impressed him about this little coral island in the Great Barrier Reef was the number of goannas, the local monitor lizards, muscular scaly creatures as much as 1.8m (6 ft.) long. Well, the lizards are still there—you may run into one or two on the island's walking trails, their forked tongues darting in and out—but otherwise Captain Cook would hardly recognize the place today. This 10-sq.-km (3¾-sq.-mile) private island resort, with 24 luscious white-sand beaches ringed by fringing coral reefs, is the kind of special, exclusive, drop-dead-gorgeous place that is catnip to honeymooners, celebrities, and even royals. It's known as a world-class diving and snorkeling destination, and the 40-villa luxury resort (see below for info) consistently wins top honors as the number-one hotel on the continent.

This is the kind of blissed-out place where a simple float in a pale blue lagoon can be utterly transforming. The waters surrounding Lizard Island have been a protected marine national park since 1939; you can grab a snorkel and mask and step right off the beach into rainbow-hued coral gardens at **Watsons Bay, North Point,** or the **Blue Lagoon.** The offshore snorkeling and diving on the island's inner and outer reefs is equally spectacular (you can arrange half- and full-day dive expeditions through the resort).

While you're here, don't miss an expedition to the **Giant Clam Garden,** a short boat ride from the island. Five species of giant clams live off Lizard Island, and they can be quite beautiful, distinguished by

Hiking on Lizard Island.

colorful flesh in iridescent greens and blues or swirling patterns. Giant clams, the world's largest living bivalve mollusk, can weigh more than 400 pounds and measure 1.2m (4 ft.) across—quite a sight for those more familiar with littlenecks. The terrifying clam of yore, the one that clamps down on some poor soul and won't let go, is a bit of a myth. It will shut its shell only as a defensive move if, say, you accidentally step into one—so don't. The massive clamshells are crusted with algae and sea squirts like the hull of an old schooner.

Lizard Island's waters seem to specialize in megaspecies—there's also a dive site known as the **Cod Hole** where giant potato cods in the 200- to 300-pound range are thriving and friendly (they like to be fed by hand). Potato cods are not cods at all but groupers, apparent to anyone who knows groupers—these fellows have the classic grouper pout.

You can experience Lizard Island in one of two ways. You can be a guest at the resort, of course. Or you could do volunteer work at the **Lizard Island Research Station** (owned and operated by the Australia Museum), where scientists are studying coral reefs to best learn how to conserve this increasingly vulnerable resource. You'll need to get permission to arrange stays at the research station. Learn how by going to **www.lizardisland.net.au**. —*AF*

ⓘ Voyages Lizard Island Resort: See hotel info below.

✈ Lizard Island (60-min. flight from Cairns).

🛏 $$$ **Voyages Lizard Island Resort** (✆ **61/2/8296 8010;** www.lizardisland.com.au).

Sea Life 119

Dirk Hartog Island

Landfall at Shark Bay

Australia

Shark Bay—what a great bloodthirsty name for a vacation spot. Yet most visitors come here not to wrestle sharks but to ooh and aah over **bottlenose dolphins** as they cruise into the knee-deep waters of the Monkey Mia Resort every morning, gliding past dutiful rows of tourists standing stock-still.

Yet there's so much more adventure to Shark Bay. With its immense sea-grass beds and shallow sandbar-stippled waters, it's poised at the intersection of three climate zones, making it one of the world's most biodiverse marine sanctuaries. Among its 323 fish species are masses of dolphins and manta rays, the world's largest population of dugongs (manatees), and of course sharks. So why hang around the inner reaches of the bay, when you can breeze out to the very westernmost edge of Australia—Dirk Hartog Island.

This long crescent of barrier island, 19 nautical miles across the strait from the Peron Peninsula, was in fact the first Australian soil where Europeans set foot. Blown off course—*way* off course—en route from South Africa to Indonesia, Dutch sea captain Dirk Hartog landed here on October 25, 1616, an event he commemorated by tacking a pewter plate to a post. (Today a stout 1909 lighthouse marks the headland, now known as Cape Inscription.) But over the centuries, Western Australia remained a lonely frontier. In the 19th century, the island was a remote sheep-farming outpost—there are still a few sheep left—with a couple of guano-mining operations and pearling camps. In

1968, Sir Thomas Wardle bought it, after failing to convince the government that it should become a historic monument. Since 1994, his family has developed it as an ecotourism destination.

On the boat over, peer down into the clear blue waters to observe Shark Bay's rich marine life, especially the **dugongs** (Sept–May) and migrating **humpback whales** (June–Oct). Once on the island, visitors buzz around on four-wheel-drive vehicles, whipping around alabaster-white sand dunes topped with prickly saltbush on the Shark Bay coast, or gazing out over the Indian Ocean from the west coast's rugged limestone cliffs, where waves crash fiercely against rock while water gushes skyward through cliff-ledge blowholes. Recreational fishing is huge here—game fishing out to sea, sport fishing in the sheltered east coast inlets, and spectacular cliff fishing on the west coast. Scuba diving is extraordinary (bring your own gear), with a long checklist of tropical and subtropical species to look for; there's also fine snorkeling around the coral bommies off Surf Point and Sandy Point. Come here in March and you can even watch loggerhead and green sea turtles laying their eggs at night on Turtle Bay.

It's possible to make this a day trip from Denham, sailing over with **Jetwave Boat Charters** (✆ **61/8/9384 0449;** www.jetwaveboatcharters.com.au) or flying in with **Shark Bay Air** (✆ **61/8/9948 1773;** www.sharkbayair.com.au). But for the full experience, stay overnight in the renovated sheepshearer's quarters, now a sleek seven-room lodge, or rough it in one of six campsites set around the island. —*HH*

ⓘ ✆ **61/8/9948 1211;** www.dirkhartogisland.com.

✈ Shark Bay.

🛏 $$$ **Dirk Hartog Homestead,** Dirk Hartog Island (✆ **61/8/9948 1211;** www.dirkhartogisland.com). $$ **Monkey Mia Dolphin Resort,** Monkey Mia Rd. (✆ **61/8/9948 1320;** www.monkeymia.com.au).

Sea Life

Turtle Island

Night of the Living Hawksbills

Sabah, Borneo

In the dead of night, the mother turtle crawls onto the beach. She digs a huge pit, and then lays her eggs—anywhere from 50 to 200 eggs at a time, trying to overcome with sheer numbers the vast odds against any one egg's surviving. Then she covers the pit in sand and crawls back into the ocean, never to see these offspring again.

This magnificent drama is enacted every summer night on a tiny tropical island off the coast of exotic Borneo (94). Pulau Selingan—aka Turtle Island, for obvious reasons—is one of three islands in a state-run nature sanctuary in the Malaysian part of Borneo, that big island in the South China Sea. (Borneo itself is divvied up between Brunei, Malaysia, and Indonesia). Lying 40km (25 miles) offshore from the town of Sandakan, the sanctuary accepts only 50 tourists per night (book with a local tour company). Accommodations are extremely basic, and you have to stay overnight—because this show only plays nighttime performances.

After arriving by speedboat from Sandakan, you're free to laze around on the beach all afternoon, lulled by the tropical sun and the beautiful blue waters of the Sulu Sea. Here's the extent of your daytime entertainment options: Study turtle exhibits in the park headquarters (two species nest here, green turtles and hawksbills), visit **turtle hatchlings** being raised in an outdoor nursery, or snorkel on the shallow coral reef that surrounds the island, busy with tropical fish. On the soft white-sand beaches, you may notice some curious tracks, evidence of last night's turtle invasion—deep round flipper scoops on either side of a wide shallow groove where the shell drags along.

As darkness falls, all visitors are confined to the park headquarters, waiting for a signal from a ranger. Curtain time could be anywhere from dusk until dawn, and you can't wait on the beach—if the turtles detect humans when they crawl ashore, they turn right around and swim away. Once the signal comes, guests go with a guide down to the beach to watch the female turtles deposit their ping-pong ball-sized eggs into a hole they've scooped in the sand. The next act is even more memorable: the audience-participation part of the show. Rangers move the new-laid eggs to a nursery to incubate for the next 60 days—a measure that has dramatically increased the survival of these endangered creatures—and then a number of already-hatched baby turtles are brought down from the nursery for guests to release back into the sea. You actually get to hold a sturdy little hatchling, set it down on the beach, and watch it hustle back into the sea. It's completing the cycle of life—and you helped! —*HH*

(i) **Sabah Park headquarters,** Kota Kindalu (✆ **60/88/211 881;** www.sabahparks.org.my).

✈ Sandakan.

🚢 and **TOUR Nasalis Larvatus Tours,** Lot 226, 2nd Floor, Wisma Sabah, Jalan Tun Abdul Razak (✆ **60/88/230 534;** www.nasalislarvatustours.com).

Sea Life **121**

Schiermonnikoog

Wadlopen: A Walk on the Sea

The Netherlands

Low-lying Schiermonnikoog is like the pearl in a necklace of islands known as the West Frisian Islands on the Netherlands' northern shore. At 16km (10 miles) long and 4km (2½ miles) wide, Schier, as it's known to the locals, is the smallest of the inhabited islands in the Wadden Sea, and possibly the prettiest. But at low tide, something magical happens: The shallow sea actually disappears and you can walk all the way to the next island.

Mud flat hiking—*wadlopen*—is a wildly popular summer pastime around these parts. Hiking on these soggy surfaces lets you see up close and personal just how alive the mud flats can be, with worms, shrimp, crabs, and fish providing sustenance for a wide range of fauna. You can actually mud-walk from the village of Kloosterburen to Schiermonnikoog (8km/5 miles). If you're game for a *wadlopen,* however, don't even think about doing it alone—Dutch law prohibits self-guided mud-walking. Always go with a tour operator or outfitter (see below) and be sure to reserve a spot well in advance—fools sure do love company.

Since 1989, the whole island of Schiermonnikoog has been protected as a national park, a remarkable collection of habitats that range from birch forests to broad, white-sand beaches along the North Sea coast. In its salt marshes and wetlands you'll find thousands of migratory seabirds, with plenty of gulls, terns, and spoonbills. Ducks, herons, and reed birds gather around the freshwater Westerplas pond; seals sun themselves on sandbanks off the northwest coast. Rare plants like tiny orchids and Parnassus grass can be found around the moss- and lichen-covered dunes. Most vacationers visit between spring and fall; only a hardy few brave the winter gales.

Some privately owned property is not included in the park—notably the dairy farms on the reclaimed polder land on the south shore, and the island's one village, also called **Schiermonnikoog,** with picturesque 18th-century gabled houses and neat landscaping. As in much of the rest of this green nation, most people here get around on bicycle; visitors aren't even allowed to bring motor vehicles. Tourists can also take covered-wagon tours drawn by sturdy little draft horses. Bike paths are everywhere throughout the island; pick up a map with cycling and walking routes at the Schiermonnikoog visitor center. ***Tip:*** Buy a combined ticket from the tourist information office in the departure hall for the ferry and a bicycle rental—you'll avoid long lines. —*AF*

ⓘ **Visitor center,** Torenstreek 20 (✆ **31/519/531-641;** www.nationaalpark.nl/schiermonnikoog). **Tourist office,** Reeweg 5 (✆ **31/519/531-233;** www.vvvschiermonnikoog.nl).

✈ Amsterdam (2 hr. to Lauwersoog).

⛴ 45 min. from Lauwersoog.

🛏 $ **Hotel van der Werff,** Reeweg 2 (✆ **31/519/531-203;** www.hotelvanderwerff.nl). $ **Pension Westerburen,** Middenstreek 32 (✆ **31/65/221-2287;** www.westerburen.nl).

TOUR Stichting (✆ **31/59/552-8300;** www.wadlopen.com).

122 Run Wild, Run Free

Assateague Island

Do the Pony on the Eastern Shore

Maryland & Virginia, U.S.

Misty of Chincoteague was one of my favorite books as a child—it's practically required reading for any girl in her Horse Phase—and as every *Misty* lover knows, they may be called Chincoteague ponies but they are really from Assateague Island. Neighboring Chincoteague Island comes into the picture because every July, Chincoteague townsfolk row over to uninhabited Assateague, round up the tough feral ponies, make them swim across the narrow channel separating the two islands, and sell the foals to raise money for the local fire department.

Legend has it that the ponies swam ashore from a shipwrecked Spanish galleon centuries ago, washing up on this 37-mile-long (60km) barrier island off of Virginia's Eastern Shore. The truth may be a little more prosaic—more likely they were put there in the late 1600s by English settlers who found the island a natural corral—but at this point it hardly matters. They're shaggy, sturdy little wild horses, running free on this one narrow barrier island.

Assateague is also a prime Atlantic flyway habitat where peregrine falcons, snow geese, great blue heron, and snowy egrets have been sighted. Dolphins swim off shore; bald eagles soar overhead. Like most of the Eastern Shore, it's a tranquil, wind-ruffled shore land with a lot of wildlife refuges and weather-beaten charm. Every year, however, the island moves closer to the mainland, as its oceanward beaches erode and sediment fills in the landward shore.

Horses on Assateague Island.

You can drive via causeway from the mainland right onto Chincoteague, an old fishing village that was settled by the English in the late 1600s; from there, take another causeway to Assateague, which was settled by wild horses at about the same time. (Go early in the day, because a strict quota system controls the number of cars on Assateague at any one time.) The island lies partly in Maryland, partly in Virginia; half of the horses live in a state park on the Maryland side, while the other half live in Virginia's national wildlife refuge. It's the herd from this Virginia refuge that supplies ponies for the annual **Chincoteague roundup,** which sustains the herd at a manageable size; the Maryland herd, unculled, sometimes threaten to overrun their marshy grazing lands.

The paved 7.2km (4½-mile) **Wildlife Drive,** which runs through the marshes, is the best place to see the wild ponies. Ranger-narrated bus tours cruise along periodically, and pedestrians and cyclists can enjoy this flat, easy loop all day long; automobiles can't go onto Wildlife Road, however, until after 3pm. At the end of the main road, you come to the Assateague National Seashore, a pristine beach with bathhouses, lifeguards, and a visitor center. It's a great place to settle on the sand, feel the wind in your face—and imagine the ghost of a wrecked Spanish galleon. *—HH*

ⓘ **Chincoteague National Wildlife Refuge,** Assateague Island, Virginia (✆ **757/336-6162;** www.nps.gov/asis).

✈ Ocean City, Maryland.

20-mile/32km drive from Ocean City.

$$$ **Island Motor Inn Resort,** 4391 N. Main St., Chincoteague (✆ **757/336-3141;** www.islandmotorinn.com). $$ **Refuge Inn,** 7058 Maddox Blvd., Chincoteague (✆ **888/257-0038** or 757/336-5511; www.refugeinn.com).

123 Run Wild, Run Free

Antelope Island

Brigadoon for Buffaloes

Utah, U.S.

Stranded in the middle of the Great Salt Lake, it's pretty surprising to find pronghorn antelope grazing. In fact, the animals that Kit Carson and John Fremont so admired in 1843, when they first named Antelope Island, were soon hunted to extinction; vanished for over a century, the antelopes were finally reintroduced only in 1993. But while you're looking for the antelope, wham! You run into the real stars of this Rocky Mountain island, a huge herd of **American buffalo,** those shaggy big-shouldered icons of the Wild West. On an *island.* How cool is that?

Considering that 50 to 60 million bison once roamed North America, the willful decimation of this species in the 19th century—by 1900 there were fewer than a thousand left—is one of natural history's sadder chapters. That's why conservationists in 1893 introduced a small number to this island, a former ranch, to preserve and rebuild the species. Currently the free-ranging herd stands 600 strong, one of the largest publicly owned herds in the nation. In the spring, look for the new calves trotting after their mothers—you can spot them easily in the herd, with their light tan coats. Isolated for so many generations on this lake island, the bison haven't interbred with domestic cattle the way so many of America's other bison have; that genetic purity makes them especially sought-after for breeding into other herds to improve their stock. Every November, visitors can attend the annual roundup,

A bison on Antelope Island.

where cowboys (some of them in helicopters) drive the herd up to corrals on the island's north end, where they vaccinate and then cull the herd—some are sold for breeding stock, and a few are released for an annual bison hunt.

By far the largest of the Great Salt Lake's 10 islands, and the closest to Salt Lake City, Antelope Island is easily reached at the north end by a long, low causeway (it was actually submerged for most of the 1980s, when the lake was at record high levels) that attaches it to the town of Syracuse, only 11km (6¾ miles) west of I-15. Antelope Island's coruscated rocky ridges, snow-topped in winter, make it look barren and rugged from afar, but once you get here you discover a great sweep of tawny sagebrush grasslands that support plenty of wildlife besides the antelopes and bison—rangeland dwellers like mule deer, bobcats, coyotes, bighorn sheep, badgers, porcupines, and jack rabbits, as well as curlews, owls, and hawks. Meanwhile, the lake's unique swarms of brine flies and shoals of brine shrimp make its salt marshes an important stop for migrating birds, from avocets, sanderlings, and black-necked stilts to eared grebes, California gulls, and the Wilson's phalarope. The island has several sand beaches at the north end, a sailboat marina by the causeway, and hiking tracks crisscrossing the island; a 6-mile (9.7km) paved loop road and 20 miles (32km) of gravel trails make it a great place for cycling and horseback riding. —*HH*

ⓘ **Park visitor center,** 4528 W. 1700 S., Syracuse (✆ **801/773-2941;** www.stateparks.utah.gov).

✈ Salt Lake City.

35-mile (56km) drive from Salt Lake City.

$ **Antelope Island campgrounds** (✆ **800/322-3770**). $$ **North Salt Lake Best Western CottonTree Inn,** 1030 N. 400 E., North Salt Lake (✆ **800/662-6886** or 801/292-7666; www.cottontreeinns.com).

Run Wild, Run Free

124

Admiralty Island

Fortress of the Bear

Alaska, U.S.

The human world may be fast closing in on wildlife habitat, but one place stands out as an oasis for flora and fauna. On Alaska's Admiralty Island, **brown bears** and other wildlife live the good life, unencumbered by encroaching development or compromised environment. The natural habitat is so healthy here, in fact, that the island holds the country's highest density of brown bears in North America, a population that outnumbers Admiralty's human counterparts three to one.

And it looks like things will stay that way. Here on Admiralty, humans have wisely ensured that the wildlife will have plenty of room to run wild and free in perpetuity. Most of the island, which lies in the **Tongass National Forest** in Southeast Alaska, is federally protected wilderness. The **Admiralty Island National Monument Wilderness** (✆ **907/586-8800;** www.fs.fed.us) contains a whopping million acres of wilderness land, much of it old-growth rainforest, perfect habitat for brown bears. It's no wonder the native Tlingit people called this island *Kootznoowoo,* or "Fortress of the Bear."

The wilderness habitat is ideal for other wild things as well—fat salmon fill the island creeks; salmon runs from July to August bring out the bears in high numbers. The **Seymour Canal** has the greatest known concentration of nesting bald eagles in the world. Seals, sea lions, orcas, and whales can be seen in the canal, chasing the massive schools of Pacific herring that arrive here to spawn. (Fishing the island waters is one of Admiralty's top attractions.)

A great way to experience all this raw, wild beauty is to stay in one of the U.S. Forest Service cabins, a number of them sturdy, rough-hewn antiques built by the Civilian Conservation Corps (CCC) in the 1930s. Many are set directly on lakefronts, with views of shimmering forests and snow-capped mountains across the water. The CCC also built the **Cross Admiralty Canoe Route** (you can buy a detailed map of the route from the U.S. Forest Service), portages linking seven mountain lakes in the heart of Admiralty Island's Kootznoowoo Wilderness. (It's recommended that you have intermediate to advanced paddling skills to attempt this route.) You will see floatplanes above but few people along this route; if solitude amid pristine surrounds are what you're looking for, this is the route for you—you can even stop and stay in a forest cabin along the way.

About those brown bears: All of Admiralty is brown bear country, and you *will* see signs of bears throughout the island. According to the Forest Service, conflicts between bears and humans are extremely rare. Visitors are advised to use good "bear-country etiquette." Hang your food at least 12 feet (3.7m) above the ground or use bear-resistant food containers.

Of course, if sleeping within sight and sound of brown bears is not your idea of fun, you can take a 30-minute floatplane flight to northeast Admiralty to the **Pack Creek Brown Bear Viewing Area,** where you can watch bears and other wildlife from a comfortable distance. Pack Creek contains a 400-acre (162-hectare) mud flat brimming with bear treats like clams; in July the creek becomes a veritable brown-bear feeding trough when pink and chum salmon return to their natal creek to spawn. —*AF*

(i) **Admiralty Island National Monument** (✆ **907/586-8800;** www.fs.fed.us).

✈ Juneau, then 20- to 45-min. floatplane.

🛏 Public-use cabins and campgrounds on Admiralty Island (National Recreation Reservation System; ✆ **877/444-6777;** www.recreation.gov).

125 Run Wild, Run Free

Sable Island

Of Seals & Horses

Canada

Little more than a long, curving spit of sand in the north Atlantic sea, Sable Island is a monochromatic landscape of sand, salt marshes, tawny beach grass, and more sand. No trees, no rocky headland, just sand—hence the name "sable," French for sand. When the fog rolls in—and it does roll in; it's foggy here one-third of the year—the whiteout effect can be discombobulating.

Sable Island is a fairly inhospitable place, especially in winter. But it has a sweeping, elemental beauty, and in the summer months green grass and colorful heather blanket the dunes.

The island is perhaps most known as a home to a celebrated herd of **wild horses,** from 200 to 350 in number, in fact a relatively tame crew that are descendants of animals brought to the island in the 1700s.

The horses are protected by the Canada Shipping Act, which makes access to the island extremely limited. You can see the horses just about everywhere—on the beach, in the dunes dining on beach grass, or scratching their backs against a weather-beaten cottage.

Sable Island is also home to the largest colony of **grey seals** in the world; you can see them in the surf and on the beach. Grey seals can grow up to 800 pounds, but even the biggest ones are no match for a great white: These seals are a favorite meal of the sharks that cruise the waters surrounding Sable. The island is so close to the Gulf Stream that in summer the water is warm enough to swim in—a rather unappetizing thought, as one researcher noted, when you see chunks of seal remains floating in the waves.

It's not easy to get to—the weather can make flying in and out tricky. Oh, and forget about a sweet little scenic ferry chug-a-lugging into port: Sable Island lies more than 161km (100 miles) offshore. Today, only a handful of full-time residents live on Sable Island, most of them employees at a scientific research station that tracks weather and pollution. No one is allowed on the island without written permission from the Canadian Coast Guard (see below).

Much like its sister island to the west, Cape Sable Island 109, Sable is one of the most dangerous places in the world for ships to navigate. It's little more than an exposed sandbar in the path of major shipping lanes and prime fishing grounds—and it's constantly changing shape. It's believed that the *Andrea Gail*—the swordfishing boat described in *The Perfect Storm,* which was lost in violent storm-tossed waters in 1991—went down near Sable Island. —*AF*

Canadian Coast Guard (www.ccg-gcc.gc.ca).

Halifax, Nova Scotia (2–3 hr.).

Arrange with the Canadian Coast Guard.

$$$ **Delta Barrington,**1875 Barrington St., Halifax (**877/814-7706** or 902/429-7410; www.deltabarrington.com). $$ **Waverly Inn,** 1266 Barrington St., Halifax (**800/565-9346** or 902/423-9346; www.waverleyinn.com).

Island Reserves

Isla Magdalena

Penguin Island

Chile

A penguin is a penguin is a penguin, you might say, especially when you've seen a few hundred thousand milling around in one place. But oh, those webbed feet! Those eyes! That waddle! Admit it: You're a goner.

Well, you're not alone. Penguins are one of the rock stars of the ecotourism circuit. Folks will go out of their way to see these adorable birds—and they have to; penguins cleverly thrive in frigid, end-of-the-world, out-of-the-way places. Penguins are birds who, by the way, cannot fly: They lost their aerodynamic chops years ago as they put on heft and solid bone to become spectacular swimming machines. Birds gotta fly and penguins gotta swim—the better to catch their favorite food, fish.

Isla Magdalena, Chile, lies inside the Magellan Strait at the southern end of South America, at the tail end of Patagonia and just north of Antarctica 486. It is a small, uninhabited island that during the summer months (Oct–Mar) becomes a breeding colony for some 120,000 Magellanic penguins. The rawness of the landscape, the sweep of the sea, the softly undulating hills, and the thousands of penguins make it a spectacular sight.

The **Magellanic penguin**—named, like so much in this part of the world, after the 16th-century Portuguese explorer who circumnavigated the world—is found only in southern South America and the Falkland Islands 473. It's a medium-size penguin with a black back, a white stomach, and two distinctive black bands between the head and chest. Studies show that while the penguin population in the Falklands is declining—overfishing is the likely culprit, but oil spills have also played a part—the numbers in Chile have stayed robust. Even ecotourism, which is bringing more people to Isla Magdalena than ever before, has not diminished the vitality of the rookery. This is one thriving ecosystem.

Isla Magdalena has no tourist facilities: no stores, no lodging, no dining options. To get here, you take a scenic 50-minute ferry ride from Punta Arenas through the Strait of Magellan; it's also an area visited by small cruise lines, like Silversea. In 1983, the island was declared a protected national monument, Los Pingüinos Natural Monument, and its only occupants are park rangers there to protect and monitor the penguin population, as well as educate the human population who drop in. Visitors walk on marked trails from the beaches to the highest point on the island, where a lighthouse serves as the island's Environmental Interpretation Center. Penguins are virtually everywhere; you'll also see cormorants, sea wolfs, and sea lions—and great views from the cliffs above the sea. —*AF*

(i) www.islamagdalena.com.

Punta Arenas (35km/22 miles).

Turismo Comapa, Punta Arenas (✆ **56/61/200200;** www.comapa.com).

$$$ **Hotel Cabo de Hornos,** Plaza Muñoz Gamero 1039, Punta Arenas (✆ **56/61/715000;** www.hoteles-australis.com). $ **Hotel Plaza,** José Nogueira 1116, Punta Arenas (✆ **56/61/248613;** www.hotelplaza.cl).

Island Reserves

Gorgona

Welcome to the Jungle

Colombia

It hasn't taken long for nature to regain complete control of Gorgona island. From the 1950s to the 1980s, this 26-sq.-km (10-sq.-mile) landmass in the Pacific was a maximum security prison—Colombia's Alcatraz—but since the facility was closed and Gorgona declared a Parque Nacional Natural (Natural National Park) in 1985, the jail buildings are now evocatively overgrown with dense vegetation, complete with monkeys swinging from vine to vine.

Like its more remote cousin to the west, the shark-diving destination Malpelo 474, Gorgona is one of those places where the natural environment is almost comically inhospitable to humans. Poisonous snakes slither along the floor of the rainforest here, and menacing sharks patrol the waters just offshore. (No doubt, this state of affairs helped with inmate detainment during the island's prison years.) Visitors who come ashore at Gorgona today are strictly supervised, limited to groups of 80 at a time, and forbidden from wandering too far away from the coastline, for fear of encountering those deadly critters. Nature is nothing if not fierce on Gorgona.

A whale swimming by Gorgona island.

As with so many ecosystems that have been isolated from the mainland for thousands of years, Gorgona shelters a wealth of endemic plant and animal species in its rainforests, including the small (and endangered) **blue lizard** of Gorgona. It's said that a permanent cloud hangs over the top of Gorgona, as its mountain peaks are perpetually shrouded in mist. Of course, this moisture acts as a sort of steroid for the already aggressive tropical flora here.

There is only one place to spend the night on Gorgona, and only one place to eat: The handsome lodge and dining room are both run by the park service and look like something out of *Swiss Family Robinson.* With the interior of the island mostly off-limits to visitors, tours of the island are limited to its perimeter, which has plenty of well-marked **nature trails** (though going with a guide is highly recommended); there it's possible to get a good look at the unique marine birds, reptiles, and plant life that have grown up and evolved here. Snorkeling and diving among the coral reefs in the emerald waters off Gorgona is excellent (as long as sharks don't make you flinch), and **humpback whales** even pass by the island from August to October with their calves. Gorgona also has some of the finest sandy beaches in Colombia, backed by palm trees and a thick curtain of green, letting you know that the creepy-crawly jungle is never far away on this island. —*SM*

ⓘ www.parquesnacionales.gov.co.

✈ Charter flights from Guapi, 30 min.

⛴ Cargo ship (8–10 hr.) or chartered speedboat (4–6 hr.) from Buenaventura.

🛏 Book through park service (✆ **57/1/382-1616**) or tour agency.

TOUR Aviatur (✆ **57/1/382-1616;** www.concesionesparquesnaturales.com).

128 Island Reserves

Coiba Island

Take a Walk on the Wild Side

Panama

You're walking through an uninhabited tropical island. Overhead a flock of scarlet macaws takes flight, their distinctive squawks and screams filling the air. But don't spend too much time taking in the spectacle—you might miss the howler monkeys on the tree next to you.

After hiking for hours, you've seen more exotic birds and animals than you could ever imagine, and you are falling under the breathtaking spell of Coiba Island, an untamed mosaic of forests, beaches, mangroves, and the second-largest coral reef in the Eastern Pacific, far off the coast of Central America.

Coiba stayed in this wild state almost by accident: From 1919 to 2004, it was Panama's version of Devil's Island 355—a prison, and a very effective one too. Far from the mainland, covered with wild jungle, surrounded by shark-infested waters—who would even *try* to escape from such a place? As a result, settlers who might have harvested Coiba's magnificent hardwood forests or cleared the land for housing never moved here. The prison is now closed, and Panama's National Authority of the Environment (ANAM) has taken over Coiba and several neighboring islands, protecting this precious and rare rainforest biosphere. You must get permission from the park office to come onto the island; various tour companies in nearby Santa Catalina organize Coiba eco-tours. While many visitors remain offshore, diving around Coiba's pristine reefs and mangrove lagoons, the entire 495-sq.-km (191-sq.-mile) island is open to hikers, with trails that even amateurs can walk with ease, as well as so-called "machete" trails which require—well, you get the picture.

Along with the **scarlet macaw,** Coiba is a haven for the **crested eagle,** which can be seen soaring overhead looking for prey. Easily identified by the frill of upstanding feathers on top of its black head, the crested eagle loves to fish, but it also has a special fondness for snakes—and Coiba has many snakes, some of them extremely poisonous (another deterrent to prison escapes). There's plenty of prey on Coiba for the crested eagle, and it plays an important role in the habitat, keeping down the numbers of certain species that might overrun this little slice of Eden. With 147 species of birds, along with 36 species of mammals, it's incredibly biodiverse. Four whale and dolphin species can also be spotted in offshore waters, including killer whales (orcas), humpback whales, and the rare **pantropical spotted dolphin.** The flora is so lush and abundant, botanists have yet to finish categorizing it. —*HH*

(i) **Coiba National Park** (✆ **507/998-4271;** www.coibanationalpark.com).

✈ Santiago, Panama (1 hr. from Panama City).

⛴ 1½ hr. from Santa Catalina (1½-hr. drive from Santiago).

🛏 $ **ANAM ranger station,** Coiba Island (✆ **507/998-0615**). $ **Casa Dos Palmas,** Santa Catalina (✆ **507/6614-3868;** www.dospalmascatalina.com).

TOUR Fluid Adventures, Santa Catalina (✆ **647/282-8167** in the U.S. or 507/832-2368; www.fluidadventurespanama.com). **Santa Catalina Boat Tours,** Santa Catalina (www.santacatalinaboattours.com).

Island Reserves 129

Kapiti Island

The Bush That Came Back

New Zealand

Talk about romantic pasts—back in the 1830s, the famous Maori chieftain Te Rauparaha was making daring raids on the mainland from his base on Kapiti Island, while American and Australian whaling ships cruised in with loads of blubber, harvested from nearby whale nursery waters, to be processed into precious whale oil. (You can still see relic blubber pots around the island.) In the mid-1800s, things got a little more humdrum; farmers razed its forests and grazed sheep and goats on its steep hillsides. But in the late 1800s, naturalists cast this fertile island, only 5km (3 miles) off the North Island's southwest coast, in its most dramatic role ever: as a world-class bird sanctuary.

A kereru on Kapiti Island.

It took some doing, but a century later bush land has gradually replaced farmland, covering Kapiti's high-peaked interior with a dense green tangle of scrub and restored native forests of kohekohe, tawa, and kanuka trees. Sheep, goats, feral cats and dogs, opossums, and finally even rats were eradicated—one of the few habitats where this has been successfully accomplished—to make the habitat safer for native species. Beginning with the brown kiwi and little spotted kiwi, which were reintroduced around 1900, a long list of rare native birds have been returned here, with mellifluous names like piwakawaka, takahe, kokako, miromiro, and toutouwi. With so few predators about, these rare birds have become so trusting and fearless—with the exception of the still-elusive kiwis—that they're easy to spot.

Now that the island is finally back to its natural condition, conservation officials aren't taking any chances. Only 50 tourists per day can come ashore, and only with access permits from the Department of Conservation (see below). Once you have your permit, book a trip with one of two licensed boat operators (no private boats allowed). You can go either to Rangatira or to the North End, but not both—that is, unless you stay overnight at Kapiti Nature Lodge (see below), located in the north end in a small valley still belonging to native Maoris.

From Rangatira Point, midway along the landward coast, you can hike through forest to the island's peak, **Tuteremoana** (521m/1,709 ft.); along the way you'll see (and hear) woodland birds such as the tui, bellbird, weka, kaka, kereru, and North

Island robin. North End expeditions pass through a variety of habitats—grassland, shrub land, forest, freshwater lagoon, shoreline—where you can see not only forest birds but also water birds (grey and brown teal, black swans, scaup, royal spoonbills) and shorebirds (gulls, oystercatchers, herons, and white-fronted terns). The Kapiti Nature Lodge runs several guided tours, including a nighttime excursion to observe the **little spotted kiwis.**

But wait! There's more! The clear waters off Kapiti's coasts are now designated marine reserves, a rare intersection of three different undersea habitats: boulder bottom, sheltered reef, and sand bottom. Even from the ferry, you'll spot dolphins and New Zealand fur seals, but divers and snorkelers get the best view of these waters, from the natural rock arch of Hole in the Wall to intricate coral structures rich with vividly colored sponges and flitting reef fish. —*HH*

ⓘ **Department of Conservation:** Wellington (✆ **64/4/384-7770;** for online permits, http://booking.doc.govt.nz). **Paraparaumu tourist office:** Coastlands Parade (✆ **64/4/298-8195;** www.naturecoast.co.nz).

✈ Wellington (1-hr. drive from Paraparaumu dock).

⛴ **Kapiti Marine Charter** (✆ **64/4/297-2585;** www.kapitimarinecharter.co.nz). **Kapiti Tours** (✆ **64/4/237-7965;** www.kapititours.co.nz).

🛏 $ **Kapiti Nature Lodge** (✆ **64/6/362-6606;** www.kapitiislandalive.co.nz). $$ **Ocean Lodge Motel,** 42–44 Ocean Rd., Paraparaumu (✆ **64/4/902-6424;** www.oceanmotel.co.nz).

130 Island Reserves

Cousin Island Special Reserve

Where the Birds Watch You Back

Cousin Island, the Seychelles

Such a cheeky bird, the **magpie robin.** With bold black-and-white plumage similar to the European magpie, and a friendly, curious personality like the tame European robin, it's fearless toward humans—especially when the humans in question have food. They'll follow you as you walk down the beach, and even seek out dinner on your kitchen table, if you've been careless enough to leave an open window or door.

One of the few places in the world to see this big-personality bird is Cousin Island, a tiny granite speck of an island in the Indian Ocean. Small as it is, this former coconut plantation has been restored to its original cover of lush tropical forest, and it's become known as an amazing haven for birds. Cousin Island—the world's first internationally owned bird reserve, owned by Nature Seychelles and administrated by Birdlife International—was established in 1968 to protect the endangered **Seychelles warbler,** a melodious bird whose call is similar to the human whistle. Today, however, this island sanctuary preserves a wide range of habitats that support rare species, from forests to wetlands to seashore. In addition to the magpie robin and Seychelles warbler, it hosts the Seychelles fody, a small yellowish bird that was once hunted to the verge of extinction because it competed with humans for the eggs of seabirds. There's the Seychelles blue pigeon with its bright red cap, the Seychelles sunbird with its curved black beak, and a host of terns, noddies, and shearwaters hanging out along the shore.

It's not all birds, either: Cousin Island is also the area's most important nesting site for **hawksbill turtles.** Up to 100 turtles at a time come ashore to bask in the daylight, where you can easily observe them. On other beaches on the island, they nest and lay their eggs under cover of dark. Cousin Island has its own giant tortoises, which at one time were nearly eradicated from the Seychelles; a plethora of geckos, skinks, and other lizards also call it home.

More than 10,000 nature lovers visit Cousin Island each year, binoculars in tow, and many educational groups also make the trek. There is no lodging on the island—apart from bird nests, of course—and you must travel with an approved tour operator, but the boat ride takes only about 90 minutes from **Praslin** (174), an island well-stocked with hotels, fabulous beaches, and breathtaking mountain views. Plan your trip to coordinate with the sanctuary's hours, open Tuesday to Friday between 10am and midafternoon. *—HH*

ⓘ **Cousin Island Special Reserve** (✆ **248/718-816;** www.natureseychelles.org).

✈ Praslin Airport, Grand Anse, the Seychelles.

🛏 $$ **Indian Ocean Lodge,** Grand Anse Beach, Praslin (✆ **248/233-324;** www.indianoceanlodge.com). $$ **Villas de Mer,** L'Amitié, Praslin (✆ **248/233-972;** www.seychelles-holidays.com).

TOUR Creole Travel Services, Victoria, The Seychelles (✆ **248/297-000;** www.creoletravelservices.com). **Masons Travel,** Victoria, The Seychelles (✆ **248/288-888;** www.masonstravel.com).

Island Reserves **131**

Cypress Island Preserve

The "Island" in the "Lake"

Louisiana, U.S.

This here is Cajun country, darlin', and it looks just like you thought it would—all bayous and swamps and gnarled cypress trees dripping with Spanish moss. Technically, there isn't one single Cypress Island here—that's just what they've named this 9,500-acre (3,845-hectare) preserve, after the many dense stands of cypress trees—but then Lake Martin, the dark and shallow spread of water that surrounds it, doesn't look like much of a lake, either.

Water and land are so commingled here, it's hard to tell where one starts and the other stops. It's like a dense carpet of floating vegetation, and all the trees just complicate things further—ridges of old-growth live oak, the tangled roots of cypress and tupelo, and pockets of hardwood forest, the kind that thrives only in boggy bottomland. But that's just what the **water birds** like about it. Some 20,000 or more water birds nest here, including so many herons, egrets, and ibis that it's perhaps the largest wading bird rookery in North America.

February through July, the rookery waters are off-limits, when the birds are breeding, but you can see plenty from the walking trail, built along a levee that circles the western and northern shores of the lake. You can also see a fair amount from the road that completes the lake circuit. Boat tours of the swamp (see below) are the best option for getting close to the nesting birds. At the south end of the lake, where the trail begins, a thick stand of cypress and buttonwoods is home to little blue herons, night herons, great egrets, snowy egrets, cattle egrets, a blizzard of white ibis, and even a few gaudy roseate spoonbills. Peer up into the trees to glimpse owls (barred and great horned), woodpeckers (pileated, red-bellied, downy, and hairy), and yellow-throated warblers—even if you can't see them, wait silently for a few minutes and you'll hear them. Forge ahead and you may see green herons, Louisiana herons, and stately blue herons stalking through the shallows as you round the lake, as well as osprey, anhingas, and bald eagles scrutinizing the water from high boughs, and wood ducks paddling around the surface. Note that the trail is shut down June through October to protect nesting alligators (you really don't want to argue with nesting alligators).

The southern end of Lake Martin is managed by the **Nature Conservancy** (www.nature.org), which leases the land from an oil company—don't be surprised to see oil rigs in other swampland nearby. The birds don't seem to mind, though, so long as they can raid neighboring crawfish farms to feed themselves. (Needless to say, the birds aren't so popular with the local crawfisheries.) Although much of the lake is nature preserve, duck hunting and fishing are permitted here—it's a good place for catfish, bream, largemouth bass, and crappie, or as the Cajuns call them, sac-a-lait. —*HH*

ⓘ Rookery Rd., off Hwy. 353 from Lafayette or Hwy. 31 from Breaux Bridge. **Tourist office,** 1400 NW Evangeline Thruway, Lafayette (✆ **800/346-1958** in the U.S., 800/543-5340 in Canada, or 337/232-3808; www.lafayettetravel.com).

✈ Lafayette, Louisiana.

 and **TOUR Champagne's Swamp Tours** (✆ **337/845-5567;** www.champagnesswamptours.com). **De la Houssaye's Swamp Tours** (✆ **337/298-2630;** www.delahoussayes.com).

🛏 $$ **Aaah! T'Frere's Bed & Breakfast,** 1905 Verot School Rd., Lafayette (✆ **800/984-9347** or 337/984-9347; www.tfreres.com). $$ **La Maison de Belle,** 610 Girard Park Dr., Lafayette (✆ **337/235-2520**).

132 Island Reserves

Sandy Island

Those Dam Eagles

Missouri, U.S.

Just a few miles north from metropolitan St. Louis is an astonishing spectacle, better than any nature special on TV: nesting **American bald eagles,** roosting by the hundreds in the tall silver maples and cottonwood trees. It's like a cross between Alfred Hitchcock's *The Birds* and a Fourth of July patriotic film montage: You can almost hear "God Bless America" playing in the background.

It happens every January and February at the Sandy Island Bald Eagle Sanctuary, on the banks of the Mississippi River. Few other eagle wintering spots are quite as impressive—and as accessible—as Sandy Island. The sanctuary's location is no accident: It's just downstream from Lock and Dam No. 25, built in 1939 and listed on the National Register of Historic Places—in fact, Sandy Island hardly seems like an island anymore, with all these levees and causeways built around the dam. But that broad stretch of open water created by the dam is a godsend for fish-eating birds like bald eagles.

You reach the sanctuary by driving right over to the lock from Highway N, then walking from the parking lot along the dam's levee to view the eagles. The forested acreage of the sanctuary is technically closed

Island Hopping the Maldives: The Sunny Side

For those folks inclined to view global warming with a jaundiced eye, you can put off that dream trip to the Maldives for now. True believers, on the other hand, book your trip right away. Climate change may mean a discomfiting rise in temperatures for some people and volatile weather for others, but for the Maldivians, global warming is about sheer survival. Climatologists predict that unless the current warming trend is arrested, sea levels will rise .9m (3 ft.) by the end of the century. The Maldives, an archipelago of sun-splashed coral islands in the Indian Ocean, lies so low in the water that its highest point is—you guessed it—a mere 3 feet above sea level. Yikes.

The only thing protecting each of these islands from being devoured by rising waters is the coral reef surrounding it. That coral reef, not to mention the luminous seas, palm-fringed atolls, and milk-white sand, is what draws hundreds of thousands of visitors each year to this delicate island ecosystem. The Maldives is a collection of 1,190 coral islands grouped into 26 coral atolls lying 483km (300 miles) south-southwest of India. Of these, 198 islands are inhabited, and by the time you read this, 100 islands will have been developed as resorts. Stranded, as they are, out in the middle of the Indian Ocean, the Maldives are not easy to get to, but travelers make the extra effort; it's estimated that some 600,000 people visit annually, and tourism has supplanted fish and coconuts as the nation's top industry.

A pier in the Maldives.

The Maldives straddle the equator—with hot, humid, subtropical weather to prove it—and are incredibly beautiful—so beautiful, in fact, that the entire nation is one of the final nominees to make the "Seven New Wonders of the World" list. Visitors are allowed on only 11 of the 26 atolls, however: **North Malé, South Malé, Ari, Felidhu, Baa, Lhaviyani, Addu Atoll, Meemu, Faafu, Dhaalu,** and **Raa.** In trying to keep its citizenry separate from the impact of tourism, the government has placed restrictions on unauthorized visits to uninhabited and fishing islands—which makes independent island hopping here tough unless you're traveling in an officially sanctioned live-aboard boat (see below) or on a guided island-hopping tour aboard a local *dhoni* (handmade motorized sailboat) from your resort base.

Malé is the nation's capital, the point of entry, and the point from which flights go out to the other islands—no island is more than a 45-minute flight away. Malé (pronounced *Mah*-lee) is also the world's smallest capital city, a tidy 2.6 sq. km (1 sq. mile) where 100,000 people jostle for space. If you're looking for a place in Malé to drink to your good fortune, forget about it: This Muslim nation bans the consumption of alcohol except in the resorts, on live-aboards, or at the airport (of course, expats have a monthly alcohol allowance, and the black market for booze is thriving). Once you arrive in Malé, you will be transferred by seaplane or speedboat to your island resort or hop aboard a live-aboard boat. These floating "safari yachts" are popular and comfortable ways to see the Maldives and experience the island's world-class diving opportunities. The safari boats also offer **dolphin- and whale-watching expeditions,** where you're likely to see spinner dolphins and blue whales, maybe even a pod of orcas.

Maldives Scuba Tours (✆ **44/1284/748010;** www.scubascuba.com) offers live-aboard and diving/snorkeling cruises through the atolls to dive sites as well as excursions to fishing islands and a range of resort islands on the way. Among the island resorts Scuba Tours travels to are the house reef surrounding 133 **Angaga** (South Ari Atoll; www.angaga.com.mv); the surfing island of 134 **Chaaya** (North Ari Atoll; www.chaayamaldives.com); the sandbanks and beautiful lagoon at 135 **Komandoo** (Lhaviyani Atoll; www.komandoo.com); and the luxurious 136 **Kunfunadhoo Island,** home to the resort **Soneva Fushi** (Baa Atoll; www.sixsenses.com/Soneva-Fushi). Many visitors combine 7-night stays on the boat with a 7-night stay at an island resort.

Maldives Liveaboards (www.maldivesliveaboards.com) also offers live-aboard cruising and diving trips to some of their favorite dive spots, including the **HP Reef,** on the North Malé Atoll, featuring spectacular coral outcrops and lots of pelagics; 137 **Kandooma Thila,** in the South Malé Atoll, with its vibrant marine life (gray reef sharks, white tip sharks, eagle rays), corals, and reef formations; and 138 **Rasdhoo Madivaru,** just off Madivaru Island, famous for one of the most breathtaking reef formations in the Maldives, an underwater ridge that attracts hammerhead sharks (before dawn), gray reef sharks, white tip sharks, Napoleons, eagle rays, jacks, and tuna.

Another great way to appreciate the beauty of these islands is on a flight by seaplane. Seaplanes are used to spirit guests to the island resorts, giving visitors a keen sense of how low-lying—and vulnerable—these island atolls really are. The Maldives have already experienced the potential damage of rising waters: The island archipelago was severely damaged by the 2004 Indonesian tsunami. Although the loss of life was relatively small—83 people died—some 20,000 people were displaced and the country suffered damages totaling a half-billion dollars. The country has rebounded, resorts have been rebuilt, and the coral reef system is thriving. Maldivians are back to work—but with an eye on the future and, perhaps, the slowly rising tides. —*AF*

ⓘ www.visitmaldives.com or www.maldives.com.

✈ Hulhule International Airport, Malé (visitors from the U.S. need to go through Singapore or the U.K.).

🛏 $$$ **Angsana Ihiru,** North Malé Atoll (✆ **960/664-3502;** www.angsana.com). $$$ **Cocoa Island,** South Malé Atoll (✆ **960/664-1818;** www.cocoaisland.como.bz).

November through February to protect the eagles' nesting grounds, but you can still get a good view of these magnificent birds soaring over the water, casting wide shadows—some adult birds have wingspans of up to 8 feet (2.4m)—as they peer hungrily into the swirling currents of the Mississippi, churned up by the dam. During warmer months, you won't get the eagle display, but you can hike around 28 acres (11 hectares) of wilderness here, and pack in plenty of other prime bird-watching.

These majestic birds, who live an average of 25 years, are known for mating for life. The female lays one to three eggs per year, and chicks remain in the nest for 10 to 11 weeks. The term "bald" is of course a misnomer; they earned that name at a time when the word "bald" meant "white." (Eagle spotters, a special subset of bird-watchers, have nicknamed bald eagles "baseballs" because that's what their easily spied heads look like from a distance.) Bald eagles do have distinctive white heads, but they don't get those until they're adults—don't expect to see white-headed chicks peeping out of those nests. A couple of decades ago, the bald eagle was nearly extinct, due to DDT contamination of their prey and habitat. But the species has made such an impressive comeback, it's been promoted from "endangered" to merely "threatened" on the Endangered Species list. Currently, there are approximately 65,000 bald eagles in North America—and the Sandy Island sanctuary is doing all it can to keep those numbers growing. —*HH*

ⓘ **Sandy Island Bald Eagle Sanctuary,** Hwy. N, 3 miles (4.8km) east of Winfield (no phone; www.nature.org).

✈ St. Louis.

33-mile (53km) drive from St. Louis.

$$ **Drury Inn Union Station,** 201 S. 20th St., St. Louis (✆ **800/378-7946** or 314/231-3900; www.druryhotels.com). $$$ **Hyatt Regency St. Louis Riverfront,** 315 Chestnut St., St. Louis (✆ **800/233-1234** or 314/655-1234; www.stlouisriverfront.hyatt.com).

Island Reserves 139

Plum Island

Plum Beautiful

Massachusetts, U.S.

Come here in May and you'll know exactly where that name comes from: A riot of white shadbush and pink beach plum burst into blossom against the pale dunes of the island's long Atlantic beach, your first promise that summer is on its way. But the first time I ever saw Plum Island was in autumn, and that's still my favorite time of year here. When you drive across the causeway, leaving prim colonial-era Newburyport behind, a magical calm seems to descend. Goldenrod and other tiny fall wildflowers pepper the grasses along the dunes' edge, and dizzying numbers of shorebirds pass through on their journey south, not to mention swarms of monarch butterflies. So what if it's too cold to swim? You can still canoe or kayak around the creeks, ramble on walking trails through the scrubby thickets and silvery marshlands, or just stroll down that pristine beach under a sky that seems to go on forever.

North of all the rocky drama of Cape Ann, where seafaring towns like Gloucester and Rockport seem pitted against the wild Atlantic, the last stretch of Massachusetts's Atlantic coast has a more modest wind-swept charm. Since 1942, this fragile coastal terrain has been preserved as one of the most important links in the Atlantic Flyway's **bird migration route.** This 13km-long (8-mile) barrier island is barely separated from the mainland—by the Merrimac River on the north, the Parker River to the west, and Plum Island Sound to the south—and the residential northern end of the island is packed with a jumble of scruffy beach shacks and weekend show-places on tiny lots. But turn right after the causeway and you'll find that the southern three-quarters of Plum Island is all park—and what a park it is.

The **Parker River Wildlife Refuge** covers 4,662 acres (1,887 hectares) of Plum Island; the last 77 acres (31 hectares) at the island's farthest southern tip is **Sandy Point State Park** (✆ **978/462-4481**), but you'll hardly know you've passed from one to the other. West of the refuge road lies a crazy quilt of creeks, mud flats, thickets, grasslands, and marshes, both salt- and freshwater; here herons and egrets wade, redwing blackbirds sing, woodcocks and bobolinks dart through the grass, and hawks and kestrels circle overhead. Rangers have erected nesting boxes for purple martins and waterview platforms for ospreys. The eastern side is all beach, a stunning 6-mile (9.7km) stretch of white Atlantic sand; from April to June, however, you'll have to be content to view it only from observation platforms, because the shoreline has been surrendered to **nesting piping plovers,** those adorable endangered little brown-and-white shorebirds. Don't worry, there are plenty of better swimming beaches in the area, notably **Ipswich** to the south and **Salisbury** to the north. In August, Plum Island's beach is open for business again—just in time for mosquito and greenhead fly season. Hey, it's nature. *—HH*

ⓘ **Refuge headquarters,** 6 Plum Island Turnpike, Newburyport (✆ **978/465-5753;** www.fws.gov/northeast/parker river).

Boston Logan Airport (35 miles/56km).

Plum Island Turnpike (3½ miles/5.6km east of U.S. 1).

$$$ **Blue, The Inn on the Beach,** 20 Fordham Way, Plum Island (✆ **978/465-7171;** www.blueinn.com). $$ **Essex Street Inn,** 7 Essex St., Newburyport (✆ **978/465-3148;** www.essexstreetinn.com).

Island Reserves

Metompkin Island

Pit Stop on Delaware Bay

Virginia, U.S.

It's hard not to love the jaunty little **red knot.** Though it's only 10 inches (25cm) tall, weighing less than 5 ounces (142 grams), that's *big* for a sandpiper. Just watch this robust little shorebird strut along the tidal mud flats on short, stout black legs, poking its straight beak into the sand. All it wants is to gorge itself on horseshoe crab eggs, double its body weight in 2 weeks, and then fly on north. *Way* north.

Don't let its size fool you: The red knot is one of the world's most prodigious long-distance fliers, breeding every summer in northern Canada, Alaska, and Siberia, then heading some 10,000 to 15,000 miles (16,100–24,140km) south—as far as Tierra del Fuego 487 in South America—for the winter. That makes its springtime stop-off on the Delaware Bay all the more important: If it doesn't fatten up then, what will it live on when it gets to the tundra, where the ground's still too frozen to peck for insects?

As many as 90% of the American red knot subspecies arrive all at the same time on Delaware Bay every spring, and two of their prime landing places are the undeveloped barrier islands of Parramore and Metompkin—some 3,000 red knots were counted there during one recent May period. Once heavily hunted in North America, the red knot is now a protected species; its feeding grounds on Parramore and Metompkin islands are refuges. But if it's not one thing, it's another: A recent drastic decline of horseshoe crabs in the Chesapeake waters spells serious trouble for the red knot, which is so dependent on eating those crab eggs to gain strength for the last leg of its migration.

Parramore Island can be visited only for research purposes, but Metompkin is open to the public for hiking, bird-watching, and fishing (its north end is part of the **Chincoteague National Wildlife Refuge;** its south end is in the Nature Conservancy's **Virginia Coast Reserve**). You'll need a boat to get here—one nearby boat ramp is at Gargathy Neck in Accomac, Virginia. The channel between Metompkin Island and the beaches may be closed off to human visitors during migration, but on this flat marshy island it's easy to view the red knots when they descend en masse. Bring binoculars to zoom in on the details: Notice how, below their mottled gray backs, the red knots' dull-white underbelly is beginning to turn pink. By the time they get up to the tundra to breed, the breast and head will be robin-red, making them the most colorful sandpipers around. —*HH*

(i) **Chincoteague National Wildlife Refuge** (✆ **757/336-6122;** www.nps.gov/asis). **Virginia Coast Reserve** (✆ **757/442-3049;** www.nature.org).

✈ Ocean City, Maryland (59 miles/95km) or Norfolk, Virginia (80 miles/129km).

⛴ Private boat transfer from Accomac, Virginia.

🛏 $$$ **Island Motor Inn Resort,** 4391 N. Main St., Chincoteague (✆ **757/336-3141;** www.islandmotorinn.com). $$ **Refuge Inn,** 7058 Maddox Blvd., Chincoteague (✆ **888/257-0038** or 757/336-5511; www.refugeinn.com).

Island Reserves **141**

Otter Island

Loggerhead Getaway

South Carolina, U.S.

Tucked in between glitzy resort islands like Kiawah (73), Seabrook, and Hilton Head (281) lies a whole other world, primitive and mysterious. You'd never expect 135,000 acres (54,633 hectares) of undeveloped tidal marshes, upland forest, peat bogs, and alligator-rife creeks so close to Savannah and Charleston. The ACE Basin—so named because the **A**shepoo, **C**ombahee, and **E**disto rivers come together in St. Helena Sound—is officially a National Estuarine Research Reserve, a protected habitat for waterfowl and migratory birds along the Atlantic Flyway. Stop by the excellent education center at Edisto Beach State Park, at the south end of palmetto-fringed Edisto Island, and you'll soon become an expert on the ecology of this critical watershed.

There are no bridges or ferries to uninhabited Otter Island, a marshy 2,000-acre (809-hectare) barrier island at the mouth of the bay, just south of Edisto Island; to get here, you'll need a boat (see below for info). Bennett's Point, on Mosquito Creek at the end of Hwy. 26, is a good launching spot: Head south from the landing into the Ashepoo River, then east about 6 miles (9.7km) to Day Marker #2—Otter Island will be on your left.

Despite the name, otters aren't the star citizens here these days—it's **loggerhead sea turtles,** which swim in nightly to deposit their eggs on its protected beaches between May and September. With their big heads and powerful jaws, loggerheads may weigh up to 350 pounds (159kg), with reddish-brown shells that can measure 3 feet (.9m) long. The hatchlings, however, are only about 2 inches (5cm) long when they emerge from the sand (also at night) and, by the light of the moon, scurry instinctively back into the water.

That's precisely why overnight camping is allowed only from October to April (call the South Carolina **Department of Natural Resources,** ✆ **843/844-8822,** for permits)—after the loggerheads have all safely returned to sea. Day visitors are still welcome from May to September, however, when you may see the turtles basking in the sun on the narrow quartz-sand beaches. You can always witness the egg-laying activity over on Edisto Island, where the state park runs turtle-viewing nights in nesting season.

Still, it's thanks to the loggerhead that Otter Island has been left in such a primitive state, and that's good news for wildlife lovers. The shoreline is fronted by a ridge of old sand dunes, now covered with forest scrub. Anchor your boat here and hike into its pine forests, following trickling creeks or the trails left by white-tailed deer (there are no formal trails). Raccoons, deer, feral hogs, and songbirds live in these woods, and pairs of bald eagles often nest here—and watch out for rattlesnakes. Reach the edge of a wind-swept marsh and you can commune with wood storks, osprey, and other water birds. Ah, unspoiled wilderness—no wonder the loggerheads like it here. *—HH*

ⓘ **Edisto Beach State Park Interpretive Center,** Palmetto Rd. (✆ **843/869-4430;** www.southcarolinaparks.com), or www.nerrs.noaa.gov/ACEbasin.

✈ Charleston (60 miles/97km).

Rent a canoe or kayak, or set up a guided outing, from **ACE Basin Outpost** (✆ **800/785-2925;** www.southsport online.com).

$ **Edisto Beach State Park campground and cabins** (✆ **866/345-PARK** [345-7275] or 843/869-2756; www.south carolinaparks.reserveamerica.com). $$ **Wyndham Ocean Ridge Resort,** 1 King Cotton Rd., Edisto Beach (✆ **843/869-2561;** www.wyndham.com).

4 Island Escapes

142 City Getaways

Waiheke Island

Auckland's Offshore Jewel

Auckland, New Zealand

You could do it as a day trip, really; Waiheke Island is just a 35-minute ferry ride from downtown Auckland by ferry. Plenty of Waiheke islanders commute into the city each day, and plenty of Aucklanders buzz out here for an afternoon of fun and sun.

But once you're here, why not kick back and stay awhile? Though it's only 19km (12 miles) long, hilly Waiheke Island is New Zealand's third-most-populous island, after the North 318 and South 226 islands, which means it's a sophisticated retreat—no roughing-it required. Though most of the attractions are clustered on the more populous western end, the island's just big enough to present a challenge for those who didn't bring their cars over on the car ferry (and that's a lot of visitors, given how tough it is to get car-ferry reservations at peak travel times). The trick is to figure out what you're interested in, because there are many different sides to cultured Waiheke.

There's art, for example—several artists have made the island their home, giving it a distinctly Bohemian vibe; grab a copy of the *Waiheke Island Art Map* from the visitor center to find out which ones welcome visitors to their studios. Or check out some of the award-winning wineries that take advantage of Waiheke's Mediterranean-like climate—most of them also have excellent restaurants attached (get a comprehensive list at www.waihekewine.co.nz). Weekend

Previous page: Lewis Farm on Block Island. Above: The ferry to Waiheke Island.

winery tours at **Stonyridge** (80 Onetangi Rd.; ✆ **64/9/372-8822;** www.stonyridge.com), **Te Whau Vineyard & Restaurant** (218 Te Whau Dr.; ✆ **64/9/372-7191;** www.tewhau.com), and **Passage Rock Wines & Restaurant** (438 Orapiu Rd.; ✆ **64/9/372-7257;** www.passagerockwines.co.nz) come highly recommended. And where there's wine, there's bound to be olive oil—discover the superb extra-virgin stuff at **Rangihoua Estate** (1 Gordons Rd., Rocky Bay; ✆ **64/9/372-6214;** www.rangihoua.co.nz). If you're a history nut, you can explore all the layers of Waiheke's history, from the old Maori settlement site at the **Waiheke Island Historic Village & Museum** (165 Onetangi Rd.; ✆ **64/9/372-7143**) to the World War II gun emplacements and tunnels at **Stony Batter** (Man O' War Bay Rd.).

Almost half of Waiheke's 90km (56 miles) of coastline is beach, and we're talking fine white sand here. The longest, and probably the best, is stunning **Onetangi Bay,** where you can swim and surf in crystal-clear water with views as far as the eye can see. **Little Oneroa,** near the main shopping town of Oneroa, is another popular beach; for more of a wilderness setting, try the crescent-shaped beach of **Whakanewha Regional Park,** where the warm shallow waters are great for kids. (The nearby wetlands are great for bird-watching as well.) The rocky cove of **Blackpool** attracts kayakers, **Putiki Bay** gets the boating crowd, and **Surfdale** is a top location for, you guessed it, surfers. —*HH*

ⓘ **Tourist office,** Artworks Courtyard, Oneroa (✆ **64/9/372-2941;** www.waihekenz.com).

✈ Auckland.

⛴ Matiatia, 35 min. from Pier 2, Auckland; car ferry from Half Moon Bay to Kennedy Point on Waiheke.

🛏 $ **Midway Motel,** 1 Whakaite Rd., Ostend (✆ **64/9/372-8023;** www.waihekemotel.co.nz). $$$ **Te Whau Lodge,** 36 Vintage Lane, Te Whau Point (✆ **64/9/372-2288;** www.tewhaulodge.co.nz).

TOUR **Ananda Tours** (✆ **64/9/372-7530** or 64/27/233-4565; www.ananda.co.nz). **Fullers** (✆ **64/9/367-9111;** www.fullers.co.nz). **Jaguar Tours** (✆ **64/9/372-7312;** www.waihekejaguartours.co.nz).

City Getaways

Sandhamn

Yachters & Stockholm Day-Trippers

Stockholm, Sweden

A city of islands itself, Stockholm (402) is just the beginning of an archipelago that stretches eastward to the Baltic Sea, with thousands of skerries and islets; some are large and densely inhabited, some are developed for tourism, and many are just rocky outcroppings to sail around. But among the Swedish capital's extensive collection of islands, there is one summer resort that is beloved above all others: Sandhamn. "Sand Harbor," as the name translates in English, lies at the eastern edge of the archipelago, a 2-hour boat ride from Stockholm. For the boaters of the region, Sandhamn is synonymous with sailing, as many summer weekends see important and glamorous regattas take to the waters off the island. But for non-yachters simply looking for a day trip or weekend getaway from the city, little Sandhamn is also just an idyllic place with a slow pace and rustic nature.

Technically, this barely 3-sq.-km (1¼-sq.-mile) island is called Sandön, but everyone calls it by the name of the marina and village, Sandhamn. From June to September, the 350-boat harbor is often filled to capacity, the biggest weekend being the **Gotland Runt** (Round Gotland Race, the most prestigious in the Baltic) at the beginning of July. Typically Swedish clapboard architecture lines the harbor, where the charming hotels and cafes are always abuzz with summer residents or day-trippers waiting for the boat back to Stockholm. Among the village's restaurants, **Sandhamns Värdshus** is one of the most popular, with an alfresco wooden deck overlooking the port.

Head away from the water, and Sandhamn town quickly fades away to lovely pine groves crisscrossed by flat walking and biking paths. Here and there, set discreetly among the trees like set pieces in an Ikea country-living spread, are the summer cottages of those lucky enough to own property here. Though they were once affordable, even the most diminutive resort homes on Sandhamn now cost hundreds of thousands of euros. Still, Sandhamn is refreshingly not a glitzy or exclusive-feeling place. Everyone, from the Swedish super-rich to mere mortals, gets around on foot or bicycle, and every outing is invigorated by the fresh scent of pines.

The sand- and pine-fringed shores of Sandhamn have some of the best beaches in the Stockholm archipelago, but the favorite spot for sunbathing and swimming is a beach called **Trouville** on the southern side of the island, about a 15-minute walk from Sandhamn town. Even in the height of summer, however, the waters of the Baltic Sea remain cold; many Swedes brave the low temperature and swim anyway, while visitors from warmer climates may find the water too frigid to take the plunge. Locals have a jokingly disparaging term for them—*badkruka* ("bath pot")—and this epithet is to be avoided at all costs: I suggest you brace yourself and jump in. —*SM*

ⓘ www.sandhamn.se or www.sandhamn.com.

✈ Stockholm Arlanda.

⛴ From Stockholm (Strandvägen), Waxholmsbolaget, 2 hr. (✆ **46/8/6795830;** www.waxholmsbolaget.se).

🛏 $$$ **Sands Hotell,** 130 39 Sandhamn (✆ **46/8/57153020;** www.sandshotell.se).

144 City Getaways

Seurasaari

Museum Among the Woods

Helsinki, Finland

In 1890, this Helsinki island's woods, wetlands, and rocky slopes became a public park. It was at this immediately popular picnic and party spot that Finns got their first exposure to such summertime staples as fireworks and ice cream. But Seurasaari saw its most important development as a recreational area in 1909, with the inauguration of the **Seurasaaren Ulkomuseo (Seurasaari Open-Air Museum).** Based on the model of the Skansen open-air park in Stockholm (see Djurgården 418), Seurasaari's characteristic Scandinavian landscape became home to dozens of examples of historic Finnish architecture, folksy wooden structures that were moved here in their entirety from every region of Finland.

The capital of Finland is not an urban jungle to begin with: Even central Helsinki

Celebrants at a Seurasaari festival.

is sprinkled with plenty of parks and green areas. Seurasaari, then, removed from downtown by a mere 5km (3 miles) but never inhabited, feels positively rural. Before its incarnation as a park, in fact, the island was known as Fölisö (Foul Island, as it was a grounds for grazing animals whose stink could get pretty rank). The animals are long gone, and year-round—it's enchantingly deserted in winter—visitors can stroll beneath the bowers of pines and spruces and enjoy the quiet of peaceful Seurasaari. Summer, however, is the only time when it's possible to enter the 87 transplanted farmsteads, churches, and traditional houses of the Open-Air Museum. Seurasaari is at its most festive during the **Midsummer** celebration (dates vary, but in 2010, it's June 25), with traditional crafts displays, folk dancing, and music performances. Every year, one newlywed couple is chosen to light the huge bonfire along the coast of Seurasaari, igniting the main event of this island's Midsummer party.

The warm weather and long-light season is also when Helsinkiers take to Seurasaari with provisions in tow for lazy **picnics,** whether on the island's Baltic beaches or on the smooth rock slopes that seem tailor-made for lounging. Most beachgoers wear bathing suits on Seurasaari, but it may be worth knowing that the island has a **nudist beach**—one of only three in Finland—though the men's and women's areas are strictly separated. Finns are known for their daredevil **winter swims,** and on Seurasaari they can find a patch in the ice, equipped with a swimming platform and ladder, where they can make like polar bears and plunge into the frigid sea. Unfortunately, the "traditional sauna" building of the Open-Air Museum is not available to them afterward!

Until the construction of the wooden Seurasaari bridge in the 1890s (connecting the island to the Meilahti district of Helsinki), boats were the only means of transport here. In summer, ferries still run between central Helsinki's Market Square and Seurasaari. *—SM*

ⓘ www.hel.fi or www.nba.fi/en/seurasaari_openairmuseum.

✈ Helsinki (6km/3¾ miles).

⛴ From Market Square (Kauppatori), 15 min.

🛏 $$$ **Hotel Glo,** Kluuvikatu 4 (✆ **358/9/5840-9540;** www.palacekamp.fi).

145 City Getaways

Ponza

Roman Summer Holiday

Rome, Italy

Ask any hip Roman what's the best nearby island to escape to in summer, and you'll get the same answer over and over: Ponza. If you've never heard of it, you're not alone, even among seasoned Italy travelers. While the more famous islands of Capri 257 and Ischia 228, to the south, are well known to foreign tourists, Ponza has been the insider domain of Italians for decades, untainted by mass tourism. Surrounded by calm emerald waters, crescent-shaped Ponza is an island of striking natural beauty, from its lizard-like contours to its moonscape-y rock formations. All over the island, yellow broom and prickly pear flourish on verdant hillsides. And thanks to Ponza's ancient roots—it's believed to be the island where Circe detained Odysseus in the *Odyssey*—there are some fascinating archaeological remains here that you won't find, or be able to explore quite as casually, anywhere else in Italy.

While there's a definite upscale feel here, the island's style is resolutely simple and low-key. You won't find any ritzy hotels or glitzy nightclubs, no megayachts or high-end shopping, no ambitious gourmet restaurants, and not even much English spoken—and that's exactly the way regular visitors and year-round *ponzese* residents like it. Most accommodations are summer villas or apartments that vacationers either own or rent for weeks at a time, though for shorter stays, there are a few hotels and B&Bs. Restaurants are folksy and family-friendly, serving fresh seafood caught by local fishermen.

Spectacular **Chiaia di Luna** beach is the crown jewel of Ponza's natural attractions (accessed from the port via one of the many ancient Roman tunnels on the island). Its name, "half-moon," refers as much to the curve of the bay here as to the stunning and very lunar-looking wall of limestone that towers 200m (656 ft.) above the beach. Shaded by the rock wall in the morning and enjoying full sun all afternoon, Chiaia di Luna is Ponza's most popular beach and one of the few on the island with a broad stretch of sand.

A bus connects the port with the island's other inhabited areas, but the ideal way to experience Ponza is to rent a small rubber motorboat *(gommone):* There are dozens of rental outfits, and it's a hassle-free affair given the safe sea conditions and Italy's lax attitude toward liability. Rudder in hand, you can explore the enchanting coves and promontories of Ponza's squiggly coast at your own pace. Navigate your way around **Spaccapurpi** (a natural arch that looks uncannily like a pair of pants), and then drop anchor at **Cala Felce,** a tiny, secluded beach with shallow, crystalline waters perfect for swimming. When seas are calm, you can set your *gommone* on full throttle and zip over to the nearby island of **Palmarola,** whose virgin coves and sea grottoes make for beatific bobbing under the Mediterranean sun. Before bringing your boat back into port, don't miss Ponza's **Grotte di Pilato,** a series of arched caves where an ingenious Roman-era *murenario* (eel traps and tanks) is preserved.

Besides boating, swimming, and taking in the beauty of the island, the "action" on Ponza centers around the picturesque port, where people who all seem to know each other stop for a *caffè freddo* (iced espresso) or grab a seat on the orange stucco wall above the harbor to watch the comings and goings of ferries. For the younger crowd, the de rigueur social activity is hopping on a shuttle boat from the port to the beach at **Frontone** for loud music and cocktails at sunset. —*SM*

ⓘ www.ponza.com.

✈ Rome-Leonardo da Vinci (67km/42 miles to Anzio).

⛴ **Caremar** (✆ **39/081/3172999;** www.caremar.it) operates several boats June–Sept from Anzio. 2 hr.

🛏 $$$ **La Limonaia a Mare B&B,** Via Dragonara (✆ **39/077/180511;** www.ponza.com/limonaia).

City Getaways **146**

Isla Taboga

Away from the Masses

Panama City, Panama

Visitors to bustling Panama City have long drifted over to fragrant Isla Taboga, which is just a 19km (12-mile) ferry ride from the city. Known as the "Island of Flowers," for its abundance of bougainvillea, hibiscus, and jasmine, it's a great place to unwind and spend a day on the beach. The ferry ride over is a treat in itself: It offers great views of Panama City and ships waiting to transit the canal.

No cars are allowed on the island, but it's only 4km (2½ miles) long, so most of its 1,000 residents get around by foot or golf carts. It's a short walk from the beach to the fishing village of **San Pedro,** where you'll find a few restaurants and hotels. The most famous attraction here is the **Iglesia San Pedro,** the second-oldest church in the western hemisphere, located in the center of town. Throughout the town, you'll find shrines devoted to the Virgen del Carmen, the patron saint of fishermen throughout Latin America. There are a few other historic buildings and ruins nearby, but most of the island comprises the simple homes of the island's fishermen along with the weekend homes of Panama City residents. The west side of the island is devoted to the **Taboga Wildlife Refuge** that protects nesting brown pelicans, but it's mostly off-limits to visitors.

History buffs should find Isla Tobago's role in Panama's development fascinating. The island was established in 1524, and became the starting point for conquistador Francisco Pizarro on his way to conquering Peru. In the 17th century, the island was the haunt of treasure-seeking pirates, including famous Welsh buccaneer Henry Morgan. Evidence of pirate booty was found in 1998, when more than 1,000 silver coins dating to the 17th century were unearthed. In the 19th century, the island became a port for the Pacific Steamship Navigation Company, which attracted hundreds of Irish immigrants. It also played host to painter Paul Gauguin in 1887 and was a training ground for the U.S. military during World War II.

If you'd like to get into the water and explore, most of the hotels here will rent snorkel gear. The best beach is **Playa Restinga,** in front of the old Hotel Taboga (now closed), going past the pier after the end of town. Like all beaches on the island, this beach is free; the best time to visit is during the weekday since it gets more "crowded" during the weekend. Getting here is easy anytime, however: Just hop a ferry from Panama City and you'll be away from it all in less than an hour. —*JD*

ⓘ www.taboga.panamanow.com.

✈ Panama City.

⛴ **The Calypso Queen** and **The Calypso Princess** (✆ **507/314-1730**). 45 min. from the Isla Naos pier on the Amador Causeway.

🛏 $$ **Cerrito Tropical,** Tobago (✆ **507/6489-0074;** www.cerritotropicalpanama.com). $$ **Vereda Tropical Hotel,** Tobago (✆ **507/250-2154;** www.veredatropicalhotel.com).

147 City Getaways

Ile d'Orléans

The Market-Garden of Québec

Québec City, Canada

As urban centers go, Québec City is already remarkably quaint. Still, when its denizens want to trade its picturesque alleys, fortresses, and castles for a more rural storybook setting, where do they go? Downriver to Ile d'Orléans. Whether it's biking the island's perimeter and taking in majestic vistas of the St. Lawrence River, or stopping at family-run farms to pick fresh fruit, Ile d'Orléans offers day-trippers a real back-to-the-farm experience, with plenty of scenery and recreation thrown in for good measure.

Lying within easy striking distance (20km/12 miles east) of Québec City, the island sits in the middle of the St. Lawrence River like a giant pair of lips. Its surface, 34km (21 miles) long by 6km (3¾ miles) wide, is a patchwork of long, slatlike farm plots that make it the primary market source for Québec City's gourmet food shops and farm-to-table restaurants. Against the Technicolor blues of sky and river, the green and golden fields yield grains for bread and cereal, plus seasonal fruit like apples and strawberries, and maple trees for—what else?—all things maple, the official flavor of Québec. The island is circumscribed by the **Chemin Royal,** or "royal road" (Rte. 368), and the classic excursion involves driving or biking along the road, pulling over at any farm stand that looks tempting. Ile d'Orléans is divided into six villages, of which three—Saint-Jean, Saint-Laurent, and Sainte-Pétronille—are regularly listed among the Most Beautiful Villages of Québec. Near the westernmost village of Sainte-Pétronille, a **lookout point** affords marvelous views of the Québec City area's most celebrated natural attraction, **Montmorency Falls,** just across the river.

The Huron nation knew Ile d'Orléans as Minigo, and explorer Jacques Cartier, who set foot here in 1535, dubbed it Ile de Bacchus—after the Roman god of wine—for its abundance of wild grapes. Later it was renamed Ile d'Orléans in honor of the then king of France. The island was one of the first parts of Québec to be settled by the French, and an astonishing number of French Canadians today can trace their ancestry to the early western inhabitants of Ile d'Orléans.

Until 1935, the island was reachable only by ferry. Although ferries still run from the Québec City docks, nowadays drivers can easily reach the island by crossing over the **Pont de l'Ile** (also known as the Taschereau Bridge). Though the island is now less isolated, the stewards of the island's culture have done an outstanding job of preserving the long-standing traditions here—Ile d'Orléans really does feel like a step back in time. —*SM*

ⓘ **Tourist office:** 490, côte du Pont, Saint-Pierre-de-l'Ile-d'Orléans (✆ **418/828-9411;** www.iledOrleans.com).

✈ Québec City–Jean Lesage.

15km (9⅓ miles) west of Québec City.

$$ **B&B Dans les Bras de Morphée,** 225, chemin Royal, Saint-Jean-de-l'Ile-d'Orléans (✆ **418/829-3792;** www.danslesbrasdemorphee.com). $$$ **Dominion 1912,** 126 rue Saint-Pierre, Québec City (✆ **888/833-5253** in the U.S., or 418/692-2224; www.hoteldominion.com).

Island Hopping the Faroe Islands: Nordic Retreats

The Faroe Islands lie in the heart of the Gulf Stream about halfway between Scotland and Iceland. Its archipelago of 18 islands—an autonomous province of Denmark—covers over 1,295 sq. km (500 sq. miles), much of it coastline; so it's not surprising that the primary occupation of its inhabitants is fishing. These slow-paced, relaxing islands are rocky, with low peaks and cliffs dominating the coastline, and are home to wildlife like puffins and fulmars. Its original residents were believed to be Gaelic hermit monks who arrived in the 6th century, introducing sheep and oat cultivation. Norsemen followed about 100 years later and their mark is felt in the Faroese language, which is rooted in Old Norse and spoken here in addition to English.

148 **Vágar Island** is the first island you'll see upon arriving in the Faroes by plane, as it hosts the airport. Visitors are greeted by breathtaking vistas as they approach the island, including great views of the quaint village of **Sørvágur.** Vagar connects with many other Faroe islands through a tunnel under the Vestmanna sound, which makes it a great home base. (Islands not served by the tunnel have car-ferry connections, so it's easy to hop around all of them by car.) Vagar means "bays" and gets its name from three bays that surround its villages, the most famous being **Sandavágur,** the best preserved ancient village in the chain. The church of Sandavágur is home to a stone bearing 13th-century runes, an artifact of the island chain's Viking past.

149 **Eysturoy Island** is the second-largest island in the chain and is often referred to as the only bridge over the Atlantic, spanning the channel of Sundani to connect with the island of Streymoy (see below). The rugged landscape boasts over 60 mountain peaks, including Slaettaratindur, the highest peak in the archipelago. A road barrels under the mountain leading to the quaint village of **Eiôi,** which is situated on an isthmus granting fantastic views of Slaettaratindur. The village of **Oyndarfjørôur** here is primarily known as a hiking site but is also home to a beautiful church that features an altarpiece by Danish painter Eckersberg.

Tórshavn, Faroe Islands.

The largest island in this chain, 150 **Streymoy Island** is divided into southern and northern regions. The capital city of **Tórshavn** is located in the south, and began as a Viking settlement. A walk through the capital's narrow streets, dotted with tiny black-tarred houses, is like a trip back into the Middle Ages. A visit to the **Faroese Natural History Museum** (V. U. Hammershaimbs gøta 13; ✆ **298/31-23-06**) and the open-air museum **Føroya Fornminnissavn** (✆ **298/31-07-00;** www.natmus.fo) in the nearby village of **Hoyvík** are both great places to put what you're seeing into perspective. Northern Streymoy is broad and mountainous. It's known for **Fossa,** the highest waterfall in the Faroes, as well as the **Vestmanna Birdcliffs**—a prime spot to see puffins, guillemots, fulmars, and kittiwakes. A boat tour can take you through its grottos and narrow sounds; visit www.puffin.fo/en for info.

151 **Suðuroy Island** is on the southernmost tip of the archipelago, and its distance from the other islands has led to the development of a language and culture different from the rest of the Faroes. It is said that its people are more open and approachable than the other island inhabitants and its landscape is idyllic, with green hills and steep cliffs favored by birds. Like the other islands in the chain, its back faces the Atlantic, while the east opens onto fjords. It is home to many villages, notably **Tvøroyri,** which was at one time an important trading spot; its buildings have been rehabbed and now include a museum. You'll also find tranquil fishing villages, some with lovely old churches. The village of **Hov** is rumored to be where Viking chieftain Havgrimur ruled, and it takes its name from his pagan alter where sacrifices were made. His grave is the only chieftain burial site on the islands.

Visitors can reach the last major island in this chain, 152 **Kalsoy Island,** the traditional way, via a wooden mail boat that makes its way to the spectacular green mountains of this northern isle and small villages like picturesque **Mikladalur,** the home of several famous Faroese painters. —*JD*

(i) www.faroeislands.com.

✈ Vagar Airport.

⛴ Syðradalur or Kalsoy. www.aferry.co.uk/faroe-islands-ferries-uk.htm.

🛏 $ **Hotel Bolid,** Niels Finsensgota, 51, FO-100, Tórshavn, Streymoy (www.faroeislands hotels.com/hotelbolid.htm). $$ **Hotel Streym,** Yvirir vio Strond 19, FO-110, Tórshavn, Streymoy (✆ **298/35-55-00;** www.hotelstreym.com).

Wild Things 153

Grand Isle

The Cajun Bahamas

Louisiana, U.S.

A few things you'll notice as you swing off the causeway and onto the last stretch of Hwy. 1: seagulls circling and screeching overhead; brown pelicans perched on weathered pier posts; the pervasive odor of fish, from sport fishermen piling onto chartered boats at the crack of dawn to seafood restaurants frying and fricasseeing well into the night. Most of all, you'll notice how many of the houses are built on stilts—a haunting reminder that the Gulf Coast is also a hurricane coast, and these barrier islands are always the first hit.

A delicate filigree of islands, bays, lakes, and bayous, the southern coast of Louisiana looks like it's disintegrating into the Gulf of Mexico, and in fact Grand Isle is—it loses a serious amount of beach every season, though an aggressive beach replenishment scheme counters that loss. Like the rest of the Gulf Coast, Grand Isle took a battering in 2005 from Hurricane Katrina, but Grand Islers are stubborn folks, fiercely attached to this fragile strip of sand and marsh at the mouth of Barataria Bay; they rebuilt at once. Hurricane Gustav in 2008? Grand Isle took a licking and kept on ticking.

The only inhabited barrier island in Louisiana, with a current population of around 1,500, Grand Isle was first settled in the 1700s, with smugglers Jean and Pierre Lafitte among its early residents. In the 19th century it was a fashionable resort—the adulterous heroine of Kate Chopin's 1899 novel *The Awakening* first met her lover while summering on Grand Isle. Today, however, it's much more laid-back, a mecca for recreational and commercial fishermen, handily located only a couple of hours south of both New Orleans and Baton Rouge. Premier among its annual events is the **Tarpon Rodeo,** the nation's oldest fishing tournament, which has been held every July since 1928. The island itself is 8 miles (13km) long; marinas and motels line the highway until it ends in 100-acre (40-hectare) **Grand Isle State Park** (© **985/787-2559** or 888/787-2559; www.crt.state.la.us/Parks), with its fine yellow beaches, fishing piers, nature trail, and campgrounds, on the eastern tip of the island.

With more than 280 species of fish swimming in its warm clear waters, Grand Isle is often listed as one of America's top-10 fishing destinations. You can head out into the gulf for tarpon, sailfish, and marlins; surf-fish in the bay for speckled trout and redfish; or drop a line from the Old Fishin' Bridge for croaker and drum. Those oil rigs off the coast? They may spoil the view, but the legs of the rigs shelter so many fish, the anglers aren't complaining. Fishing is so popular that most local motels provide a fish-cleaning room, and have kitchenettes in the rooms as well as barbecue pits outdoors, so that guests can feast on the catch of the day. Even little kids get into the action, taking nets into the shallow waters to go crabbing. A fresh crab you just caught yourself makes a mighty fine dinner, after all. *—HH*

(i) **Tourist office,** GI Port Commission Building (© **985/787-2997;** www.grand-isle.com).

✈ New Orleans.

95-mile (153km) drive from New Orleans.

$$ **Cajun Tide Beach Resort,** 3032 Hwy. 1 (© **985/787-4726;** www.cajuntidebeachresort.com). $$ **Island Paradise Suites,** 140 Coulon Rigaud Lane (© **985/787-7800;** www.islandparadisesuite.com).

154 Wild Things

Kodiak Island

Bear Bonanza

Alaska, U.S.

Kodiak Island is sometimes referred to by Ireland's nickname, "the emerald isle," but that nickname doesn't do this Alaskan island's varied terrain justice. In reality, Kodiak is an island of contrasts where visitors can enjoy mountainous terrain in the north and east or travel the 100 miles (161km) to the southern end to find tundra, bushes, and grassland. As the second-largest island in the U.S. and home to one of the country's largest and most remote National Wildlife Refuges—it encompasses two-thirds of the island's available land—this is the perfect place to leave civilization behind and reconnect with nature.

The island was formed 20,000 years ago by shifting glaciers, which left jagged peaks and fjordlike valleys. Today, it is the busiest fishing port in the Gulf of Alaska, best known for its salmon and crab, and many of its 13,000 or so residents work in canneries. Some are members of the native Koniaga tribe, or descendents of Russian fur traders who appeared on the scene in the 18th century. Kodiak is also known for having the largest Coast Guard station in the U.S.

Kodiak's biggest claim to fame, however, has to be the **Kodiak bear,** the world's largest carnivore. One of these full-grown bears can grow up to 10 feet (3m) tall and weigh over 1,500 pounds. To count on seeing one of these big bears, you need to get out on a plane or boat and visit at the right time of year. The easiest way is on a Kodiak-based floatplane. Landing on the water, you don rubber boots and walk up to half an hour to get to where bears congregate. In early July to early

Bears on Kodiak Island.

August, depending on salmon runs, flights land on **Frazer Lake** for viewing at Frazer fish pass. A .75-mile (1.2km) walk on a dirt lane leads to the viewing area. The **Kodiak National Wildlife Refuge** (© **888/408-3514** or 907/487-2600; http://kodiak.fws.gov) controls the viewing area.

Once you're done ogling the island's bears, you'll find plenty of other activities on hand, from whale-watching to fishing to kayaking to simply lounging on one of Kodiak's beaches. Top off your visit with a trip to the city of **Kodiak** (on the northeast part of the island), where you'll find shops full of native art as well as Russian arts and crafts, and a couple of museums.

There are two ways to get to Kodiak: by air or ferry. It's a 1-hour flight from Anchorage, or 10 hours by ferry from Homer. The ferry ride is an adventure in itself, as the boats make their way through the Barren Islands, sometimes chartering choppy waters along the way. The U.S. Fish & Wildlife Service provides a naturalist on each ferry, so the trips are informative as well as scenic. Once on the island, most visitors opt to rent a car to get around. Driving through this beautiful wilderness is an experience you won't forget. But don't forget to get out of your car—it's the best way to take in sightings of the island's abundant wildlife. —*JD*

ⓘ **Kodiak Visitor Information Center,** 100 E. Marine Way (© **800/789-4782** or 907/486-4782; http://kodiak.org).

✈ Anchorage (251 miles/404km).

Tustumena and Kennicott, **Alaska Marine Highway System** (© **800/624-0066** or 907/486-3800; www.ferryalaska.com).

Best Western Kodiak Inn, 236 W. Rezanof Dr. (© **907/486-5712;** www.kodiakinn.com). $$ **A Smiling Bear Bed & Breakfast,** near Fort Abercrombie (© **907/481-6390**).

TOUR Helios Sea Tours (© **907/486-5310;** http://home.gci.net/~len/newhelios).

Wild Things **155**

Isla Holbox

Swimming with Whales

Mexico

It's only about an hour from the raucous beach party that is Cancun, but Holbox Island is everything Cancun is not. Pronounced "*Hole*-bush," Holbox is a return to a slower, more leisurely time. The island has the feel of an old-fashioned Caribbean destination, where the streets are dusted with sand and fishermen head out at sunrise to bring in the day's catch. Even though all that separates the island from mainland Mexico is a shallow lagoon, Holbox is a genuine escape from the long arms of civilization: The island has no banks, no ATMs, no high-rises, and no cars; the preferred mode of transportation is golf cart—head to a *rentadora* and pick out a shiny one for yourself. U.S. dollars and Mexican pesos rule; credit cards are taken only at the larger hotels and restaurants. The island's one beach bar is set down in the sands in front of the **Hotel Faro Viejo** (av. Juárez y Playa S/N; http://faroviejoholbox.com), where you can watch the sun melt into oranges and pinks on the milky horizon.

A sandy strip of coral island off the northeastern corner of the Yucatán Peninsula where the Gulf of Mexico meets the Caribbean Sea, Holbox Island has one village, also called **Holbox,** home to 1,600 residents. For years, this sleepy little backwater was an insular hideaway, home to a tight-knit population, descendants of pirates and Mayan Indians, and most of them fishermen. But all that may be changing. Tourists are coming to Holbox in increasing numbers not just for the laid-back lifestyle; they are coming to swim alongside the hundreds of migrating **whale sharks** that began showing up some six years ago. The largest fish in the ocean—it can grow to 15m (49 ft.) long and weigh 10 tons—whale sharks have found the warm waters of the Gulf of Mexico a hospitable summer feeding and mating ground. Swimming with these gentle giants is the undersea equivalent of a day on Holbox: quiet, dreamy, and positively reinvigorating.

The waters surrounding the island are a marine sanctuary, the **Yum Balam Ecological Reserve,** but to further protect the whale sharks, the Mexican government has decreed Isla Holbox to be the only port allowed to offer trips to swim with the whale sharks. A number of experienced operators and resorts run whale-shark excursions, including **Holbox Tours & Travel** (✆ **52/305/396-6987;** www.holboxwhalesharktours.com).

Holbox also has 11km (6¾ miles) of flat, white-sand beaches lapped by shallow, placid, bottle-green seas. You can dip into the water right off the beach or head for a swim in the cool, clear waters of the freshwater lagoon that separates Holbox from the mainland, **Yalahau Lagoon.** —*AF*

ⓘ www.holboxisland.com or www.travelyucatan.com.

✈ Cancun to Chiquila (1 hr.).

⛴ Chiquila (10–45 min., depending on ferry; www.holboxmonkeys.com.mx).

🛏 $$$ **Casa Sandra** (✆ **52/984/875-2171;** www.casasandra.com). $$ **VIlla Delfines** (✆ **52/984/875-2196;** www.villasdelfines.com).

156 Wild Things

French Island

Back to the Bush

Australia

The ferry ride over here from Phillip Island 103 takes only 30 minutes—but what a difference. Instead of smartly developed Wildlife Attractions, what you get on French Island is just . . . wildlife. And you'll have to bushwalk, kayak, or cycle to see even that.

For most of its existence, French Island seemed more of a place you want to escape *from* than a place you want to escape *to.* Aboriginal Bunarog hunters were massacred here by the Gippsland tribe; hardscrabble 19th-century settlers cut down all the big trees to fuel their chicory kilns and salt evaporators; ragtag prisoners labored in the fields of a dreary prison farm, from 1916 to 1975. One early explorer described it as "a useless mass of scrub, with scarcity of water and barren soil."

But as nearby Melbourne boomed and the mainland became more developed, an uninhabited backwater like French Island began to be a rare commodity. Those extensive mud flats, salt marshes, and mangrove lagoons may have been useless to farmers, but an incredible number of bird and fish species thrived there. As the tea tree scrub grew back with a vengeance, koalas and Sambur deer, not to mention rare potoroos (ratlike cousins of the kangaroo) multiplied in this predator-free environment.

In the 1960s, when it was still a prison, the government had big expansion plans for French Island—plans that included an airport, steel works, and other factories. Local environmentalists raised an outcry, believing that this isolated ecosystem was worth preserving. Thankfully, the government listened. Today the northern three-quarters of French Island, plus a swath of seagrass-rich waters off its north coast, is all national parkland; the wetlands in the northwest are designated RAMSAR sites, where 33 different species of wading birds live. The park is home to the largest colony of **koalas** in the state of Victoria, though you'll have to spot them in the wild for yourselves. Orchids bloom all over the island, more than 100 different kinds, many of them found only here. At high tide, the beaches at **Fairhaven** and **McLeod** are lovely, quiet, sandy stretches, though there's a muddy bottom at low tide. With a canoe or kayak, you can also explore stands of rare white mangroves, whose spreading roots harbor all sorts of shoreline species, as well as thick swarms of mosquitoes in summer.

Even today, only about 60 or 70 people live here, mostly sheep and cattle farmers, descendants of the original settlers. There's only one shop; there are no power lines or sewers. You can bring a bike over on the ferry, but not a car—the only cars here are owned by residents and local tour guides, and the few roads are unsealed. Close as it is to Melbourne, it's still a well-kept secret, with surprisingly few visitors. French Island may fall short of groomed perfection, but that's not the point. For tranquillity and rough-and-ready charm, French Island can't be beat. —*HH*

(i) **Tourist office** (✆ **61/3/9585 5730** or 61/3/5980 1209). **Park office,** by the Tankerton jetty (✆ **61/3/5980 1294;** www.parkweb.vic.gov.au).

✈ Melbourne (60km/37 miles).

⛴ From Stony Point, 15 min., or from Cowes (Phillip Island 103), 30 min.

🛏 $$ **McLeod Eco Farm,** Freeman's Point (✆ **61/3/5980 1224;** www.mcleodecofarm.com). $$ **Tortoise Head Lodge,** Tankerton (✆ **61/3/5980 1234;** www.tortoisehead.net).

TOUR French Island Eco Tours (✆ **61/1300/30-70-54** or 61/4/2917 7532; www.frenchislandecotours.com.au). **French Island Tours** (✆ **61/3/5980 1241;** www.frenchislandtours.com.au). **Wildlife Coast Cruises,** Cowes (✆ **61/3/5952 3501;** www.wildlifecoastcruises.com.au).

Great Outdoors 157

Fasta Åland

Rugged Slice of Sweden

Åland Islands, Finland

Though Fasta (or Mainland) island, the largest in an archipelago of nearly 6,500, is an autonomous province of Finland, its culture is decidedly more inspired by Sweden—even the official language is Swedish. Because it's situated between Finland and Sweden in the Baltic Sea, the island is popular with vacationing Swedes and Finns alike, who come for its beautiful scenery and nature trails. The rugged landscape encompasses fields, meadows, and dense woods—plus lots of red granite that lends a distinctive hue. This diversity of habitats provides a home for an equally diverse amount of wildlife, all of which are protected by the government.

This island's natural beauty comes most alive at its nature preserves. You can choose to visit these on short guided tours that focus on nature or ones that also offer

Fasta Åland.

background into local history and culture. Book a tour through **Getout Adventures,** Svinö Färjfäste c/o Café Ingela, 226 30 Lumparland (✆ **358/40-871637**).

Mariehamn, the capital city, is home to 40% of the island's population, and features two busy harbors, one at its eastern shore and another on its western shore. The town, a picturesque place that's filled with wooden houses and colorful gardens, bustles with Baltic ferries that stop principally because Åland is not a part of the E.U. customs zone—meaning duty-free goods may be sold abroad. Those who wish to explore the island's nautical history can visit the maritime museum **Sjöfartsmuseum** (Hamngatan 2; ✆ **358/18-19930;** www.sjofartsmuseum.aland.fi), or the **Museum Ship *Pommern*** (www.mariehamn.ax/pommern) here.

As a maritime center, Fasta island also offers many opportunities to get out on the water to ski, bodyboard, and fish. Although the island has a number of traditional hotels (see below), you can opt to stay in luxury campgrounds, with spacious tents complete with fireplaces, if you prefer to sleep in the great outdoors. Just don't leave this rugged wilderness behind without treating yourself to one of Finland's most relaxing experiences—a good, hot sauna. **Alandia Adventures,** Stornasvagen 5 22410, Godby (✆ **358/40-5417413**), can arrange outdoor activities, including camping, as well as spa treatments. *—JD*

ⓘ **Åland Tourist Information,** Storagatan 8, Mariehamn (www.visitaland.com/en).

✈ Mariehamn Airport.

⛴ Ålands Ferry, which is run by the **Viking line** (www.vikingline.fi/reservations); departs from Kappelskär and lands in Mariehamn.

🛏 $ **Park Alandia Hotel,** Norra Esplanadgatan 3, Mariehamn (✆ **358/18-14130**). $ **Pommern Hotel,** Norrgatan 8–10, Mariehamn (✆ **358/18-15555;** www.hotellpommern.aland.fi).

Great Outdoors 158

Ile au Haut

The High Island Lowdown

Maine, U.S.

Like its neighbor, Mount Desert Island 294, much of Ile au Haut—over half—is dedicated to **Acadia National Park.** Yet very few park visitors make it over to this other Penobscot Bay island, well south of the main park territory. Mount Desert has a nice solid causeway linking it to the Maine shore; Ile au Haut depends on a little mail boat, which chugs back and forth across 6 miles (9.7km) of water to the mainland. Only about 75 people, many of them lobstermen and their families, live here year-round; the population doubles (to a whopping 150 or so) in summer. There is a school on the island, but only about half a dozen kids go there, and for high school they have to commute by boat to the mainland.

That fancy French name—"high island"—came from explorer Samuel Champlain on his 1604 voyage up the Maine coast, and considering the mini–mountain range that cuts across this 6-mile-long (9.7km) island, it certainly fits. But fancy French names seem at odds with the laid-back small-town quality of Ile au Haut; say it like the islanders do, "Eye-la-Ho" (rhymes with "Idaho") and you're much more in tune with the place. The island was the last community in the U.S. to stop using crank telephones—that tells you all you need to know about the time warp quality of the place.

If you don't have your own bike, you can rent one on the boat, and that's a good idea, because you'll want to explore beyond the quaint fishing village—for a start, head south of town to check out the **Ile au Haut Lighthouse,** less than a mile south of town, on Robinson's Point. Built in 1907, this stout little brick lighthouse was the last traditional-style lighthouse built along this coast, and though it's now automated—the keeper's house has been turned into a bed-and-breakfast inn—it's still a working light.

A park ranger meets every mail boat run in summer to give hikers bound for the park all the maps and advice they need. There are 18 miles (29km) of walking trails roaming around the park's wooded hills, marshes, and rocky coves. The **Long Pond trail** loop heads to narrow mile-long Long Pond, a freshwater pond that's great for swimming. The **Goat trail** is rewarding for bird-watchers, leading from the salt marshes to Squeaker Cove, where harlequin ducks bob on the water. The **Western Head trail** loops around the south tip of the island, where seals flop around the granite boulders and gulls circle overhead. Outside of the park on the eastern shore, **Boom Beach** is more smooth rocks than sand, but it's a lovely place nonetheless; the **Thunder Gulch trail** is great on a hot summer day, shaded by spruce forest until it emerges on an ocean's-edge rock ledge continually spritzed with sea spray. The word "picturesque" doesn't even begin to cover it. *—HH*

(i) www.isleauhaut.com.

From Stonington Maine to the town landing (45 min.); summers only, from Acadia National Park to Duck Harbor (1 hr., 15 min.). **The Mail Boat** (✆ **207/367-5193**).

$ **Acadia National Park campground** (✆ **207/288-3338;** www.nps.gov/acad). $$$ **Inn at Ile au Haut** (✆ **207/335-5141;** www.innatileauhaut.com).

159 Great Outdoors

Shelter Island

Gimme Shelter

New York, U.S.

Like a prize clutched in the long pincer claw of Long Island, this quiet residential island nestles between the down-to-earth North Fork and glam-packed South Fork, protecting Peconic Bay from wide-open Gardiners Bay and the Atlantic Ocean beyond. Car ferries shuttle continuously back and forth, one north to Greenpoint, the other south to North Haven, near Sag Harbor; Route 114 connects the two ferry landings, cutting across the belly of this ragged triangular island, moth-holed with coves, ponds, and inlets. Yet accessible as Shelter Island is, once you're here you'll feel that it's a world unto itself.

Shelter Island was very much a shelter in its early years—its first settlers, in 1652, were royalist refugees from Cromwell's England, as well as prominent Quakers seeking religious freedom. At first Shelter Island was devoted to farming, but with the rise of the whaling era, islanders turned to the sea (both Sag Harbor and Greenpoint were big whaling ports). Then, in 1871, Shelter Island discovered a new source of income: summer vacationers. Hotels, bathing pavilions, and yacht clubs sprang up, and farmland turned to summer homes—from camp-meeting cottage communities (like Oak Bluffs on Martha's Vineyard 367) to elaborate beachview sprawls of Victorian gingerbread. Today Shelter Island's year-round population of 2,500—which includes several descendants of pre-Revolutionary settlers—swells to 8,000 in summer; many of the summer folk count as longtimers too, their families having summered here for four or five generations. There are four public beaches and a public golf course, but much of the island's social life revolves around the private golf, beach club, and yacht club.

All of which begs the question: Can you come here for just 1 or 2 days and not feel like an outsider? Of course you can. Don't expect a lot of culture and nightlife—there is minimal shopping, and no theaters, cinemas, or night clubs, for residents pride themselves on the island's lack of "buzz"; there are only a few fine restaurants, which book up quickly in season. For nature lovers, however, the island couldn't be better. Its southeastern third has been set aside as the 2,039-acre (825-hectare) **Mashomack Preserve** (off Rte. 114; ✆ **631/749-1001**), where several walking trails explore a rich mosaic of tidal creeks, salt marshes, and tranquil beaches where piping plovers nest in spring. With all those calm, protected bays, Shelter Island provides plenty of scenic kayaking; **Shelter Island Kayak Tours** (✆ **631/749-1990**) offers rentals and guided tours. Beaches here tend to be narrow strips of sand, but the protected waters are perfect for swimming; head to **Crescent Beach** or **Silver Beach,** both on the southwestern side of the island.

You can also walk around the **Heights Historic District,** the Victorian-era summer community southwest of Dering Harbor, or visit the Shelter Island Historical Society's restored **Havens House,** 16 S. Ferry Rd. (✆ **631/749-0025;** www.shelterislandhistorical.org). Sylvester Manor, the estate of the island's 17th-century English owners, isn't open for tours, but a new young Sylvester heir is converting it to an ambitious organic farm—a sure sign that Shelter Island is meeting the future in its own freethinking way. *—HH*

ⓘ www.shelter-island.org.

JFK Airport (98 miles/158km), LaGuardia Airport (96 miles/154km).

Greenport (2 hr., 50 min. from Manhattan).

Dering Harbor, 10 min. from Greenport; South Ferry, 10 min. from North Haven.

$$ **Candlelite Inn,** 3 S. Ferry Rd. (✆ **631/749-0676;** www.thecandleliteinn.com). $$ **Ram's Head Inn,** 108 Ram Island Dr. (✆ **631/749-0811;** www.shelterislandinns.com).

Great Outdoors 160

Campobello Island

FDR's Rugged Getaway

Canada

In the summer, when Franklin and Eleanor Roosevelt wanted to escape the pressures of political life, they took their family to the rustic island getaway of Campobello. FDR looked upon the island as his second home—his son Franklin, Jr., was born there and he fell ill with polio during one of his summer retreats on Campobello. (This incident was the inspiration for *Sunrise at Campobello,* a play and movie chronicling the story of FDR's stubborn refusal to let his affliction get in the way of his destiny.)

Over the years, this rocky New Brunswick island has held a place for both native fisherman and wealthy families. Today, you can still see the grand houses built as summer homes sharing space with the homes of residents. You can also see the 34-room Roosevelt home, nestled in **Roosevelt Campobello International Park.** The park is a symbol of the friendship between Canada and the United States, and draws thousands of visitors each year. They are greeted by a series of buildings that include quaint cottages, a visitor's center, and flower gardens. Outside, over 2,000 acres (809 hectares) of nature is on hand to explore, including walking trails, beaches, bogs, and oceanfront with fantastic rock formations.

The island is only about 20 miles (32km) long, located at the entrance of Passamaquoddy Bay. It is part of New Brunswick, Canada, but is also connected to Lubec, Maine, via the Franklin Delano Roosevelt Bridge. Besides the park, the island offers abundant opportunities to enjoy nature: It's an excellent site for birding, providing the opportunity to spot osprey and eagles in abundance. Unspoiled Herring Cove Provincial Park is located on the eastern coast. It features a mile-long sand and pebble beach and a 9-hole golf course. The adjacent campground offers shady or sheltered sites with niceties like showers, kitchen shelters, and playgrounds. Activities include guided nature walks and a whale-watching tour. For reservations, call **Herring Cove Provincial Park and Golf Course** (✆ **506/752-7010**).

The island's iconic **East Quoddy Lighthouse** is one of the most photographed lighthouses in the world, and a trip here wouldn't be complete without a stop at the **Bay of Fundy** to gaze at this picturesque structure. Although now automated, it keeps its 150-year vigil, signaling to boats on foggy nights. Intrepid souls can wade out at low tide for a better look, but it's also a striking sight for those who would rather stay on land. *—JD*

ⓘ **The Campobello Welcome Center,** 44 Rte. 774, Welshpool (✆ **506/752-7043;** www.campobello.com).

St. John, New Brunswick.

East Coast Ferries (✆ **506/747-2159**). Ferries run from Deer Island June–Sept (30 min).

23km (14-mile) drive from Whiting, Maine.

$ **Lupine Lodge,** 610 Rte. 774 (✆ **888/912-8880** or 506/752-2555; www.lupinelodge.com). $$ **Owen House, A Country Inn & Gallery,** 11 Welspool St. (✆ **506/752-2977;** www.owenhouse.ca).

161 Great Outdoors

Rota Island

Getting Your Feet Wet

Mariana Islands, Micronesia

Come on in, the water's fine. The tropical Island of Rota, part of a U.S. commonwealth within Micronesia, about 64km (40 miles) north of Guam 456, is a volcanic formation that rises some 488m (1,601 ft.), creating a spectacular backdrop for its unspoiled beaches. It draws people looking for a peaceful getaway, and is particularly popular with divers and snorkelers who come to explore its clear sparkling waters, coral reefs, and many shipwrecks—Rota and the 14 other islands of the Marianas played a significant role in World War II naval battles.

Most dives are just a 10- to 15-minute boat ride away from the island, and there are trips designed for divers of all skill levels. At **Coral Garden,** experienced divers can explore the remains of one of three World War II Japanese auxiliary submarine chasers scattered on the bottom of the ocean floor. Beginners can delight in dives where small, colorful fish swim along with them. It's also easy to get a good view of stingrays gliding along the sand flats. You can set up a dive with **Dive Rota** (www.diverota.com/index.htm).

The western side of the island is known for its **natural swimming hole,** where you can take a refreshing dip after a long day in the sun, or just float along watching an unforgettable sunset. Of course, there really are no bad views on the island, and you may find it tempting to just lounge on the beach, taking it in. The island is known for its unhurried pace and welcoming islanders; about 3,000 residents live here year-round, many of them descendents of the native Chamorro and Carolinian tribes.

Rota is also home to many species of exotic flora and fauna. Don't miss the chance to visit the **Sagua'gaga Seabird Sanctuary,** which features dozens of species, or **Taisacana's Botanical Gardens and Nature Trail,** a great place to learn about indigenous plants. Other natural draws are the **Tonga Cave,** a natural stalactite cavern that served as a hospital for Japanese soldiers during the war, located in Songsong village. Just a mile away is the **Rota Cave Museum,** a giant limestone cave, thought to be about 10 million years old and featuring artifacts from the native Chamorro tribe to the World War II era.

When you're ready to take some postcard-perfect shots, go to **Songsong village,** the island's largest, and aim your camera at Wedding Cake Mountain, a formation that looks like—you guessed it—an elaborately layered cake. Such sweet scenery is just one reason this island is a decadent natural wonder. —*JD*

ⓘ **Mariana Visitors Authority** (✆ **670/664-32001;** www.mymarianas.com).

Rota International Airport.

$ **BP Hotel and Restaurant** (✆ **670/532-0468**). $$ **Rota Resort and Country Club** (✆ **670/532-1155**).

Untouched Retreats 162

Block Island

The Word on the Block

Rhode Island, U.S.

Many a visitor has landed on this wind-whipped glacial outcrop, 12 miles (19km) off the Rhode Island coast, and thought immediately of Ireland—those dramatic clay cliffs, hundreds of sweet-water ponds nestling in the rolling green interior, dry-stone walls overgrown with moss, wild roses clambering over beach dunes. For centuries, since the first Europeans landed in 1661, Block Island was considered a desperate outpost, fit mostly for pirates, smugglers, and scavengers. Then the post–Civil War tourism boom hit, and Block Island found its calling. Today, most of its hotel rooms are still in those original rambling Victorian-style seaside inns; though there are only around 900 year-round residents, tens of thousands of visitors arrive every summer.

Somehow Block Island has been able to reap the benefits of tourism without letting it spoil the island's throwback charm. Development so far remains under control—you won't find any fast-food franchises or chain stores. Police officers tool around on bikes, and children tend lemonade stands in front of picket fences. There's not much point in bringing a car over on the ferry, since the island is a mere 7 miles long by 3 miles wide (11×4.8km); there's only one gas station, anyway. Most visitors make do with bicycles or mopeds, or call a taxi when they need to get somewhere faster.

Most of the action—and in summer it's active indeed—is in Old Harbor. After you've strolled through the **Block Island Historical Society Museum,** Old Town Road at Ocean Avenue (✆ **401/466-2481**), and pedaled out to tour the two 19th-century lighthouses—**Southeast Lighthouse,** on Mohegan Trail a couple miles south of Old Harbor, and **North Lighthouse,** on Corn Neck Road north of Crescent Beach—you're done with sightseeing and ready to hit the beach. Block Island has 17 miles (27km) of beach, so there's always a place to spread your towel. Only two beaches have lifeguards, food service, and rental facilities—**Pebbly Beach,** just south of the Old Harbor, and 3-mile-long (4.8km) **Crescent Beach,** north of Old Harbor. Other beaches, at the end of dirt roads off Corn Neck Road or West Side Road, may offer more solitude, if that's what you're after.

On Block Island's winding scenic roads, cycling isn't just transportation, it's a way to coast down hills, cool off in patches of shady woods, stop for a dip in a pond, or admire sweeping ocean panoramas from the south coast's 150-foot-high (46m) Mohegan Bluffs. You can also gallop on horseback along a beach (**Rustic Rides Farm,** W. Side Rd.; ✆ **401/466-5060**), tramp along 17 miles (27km) of walking trails laid out by the Nature Conservancy (nearly a quarter of the island is conservation land), go parasailing (**Block Island Parasail;** ✆ **401/864-2474;** www.blockislandparasail.com), or kayak around Great Salt Pond—rent a kayak from **Pond & Beyond** (New Harbor; ✆ **401/466-5105;** www.blockisland.com/kayakbi) or **Champlin's Resort,** on Great Salt Pond (✆ **401/466-2641;** www.champlinsresort.com). Sailboats bob in the marinas, and sunburned guests sip cold drinks on the long porches of those historic inns. Yes, Block Island does summer vacation right. —*HH*

ⓘ **Tourist office,** Old Harbor ferry landing (✆ **800/383-BIRI** [383-2474] or 401/466-2474; www.blockislandchamber.com).

✈ Block Island, 15-min. flight from Westerly, Rhode Island, on **New England Airlines** (✆ **800/243-2460;** www.blockisland.com/nea).

⛴ From Newport (2 hr.) or Point Judith (30-min. passenger ferry, 1-hr. car ferry; www.blockislandferry.com); New London, Connecticut (1 hr., 15 min.; Block Island Express; ✆ **860/444-4624**); Montauk, New York (1 hr., Viking Fleet; ✆ **888/358-7477**).

🛏 $$$ **Atlantic Inn,** High St. (✆ **800/224-7422** or 401/466-5883; www.atlanticinn.com). $$ **Spring House Hotel,** 902 Spring St. (✆ **800/234-9263** or 401/466-5844; www.springhousehotel.com).

163 Untouched Retreats

Smith Island

Where the Past Comes to Life

Maryland, U.S.

Imagine a lazy summer day spent nosing along in a kayak or fishing in the heart of Chesapeake Bay. Then imagine having the bay practically to yourself, and you're in Smith Island—the shallow waters around this Chesapeake Bay island lure herons, egrets, ibis, osprey, and pelicans in greater numbers than people. If it's peace you're looking for, Smith Island won't disappoint—it's still every bit as tranquil and untouched as Tom Horton described in his 1990s memoir *Island Out of Time*.

Smith Island is actually a cluster of islands making up Maryland's largest inhabited offshore community. Its population of fewer than 300 people are scattered among the villages of Ewell, Rhodes Point, and Tylerton—the last of which is separated from the other villages by water. All three are bound together by the island chain's seafood industry and strong Methodist roots. Change comes slowly to this remote part of Maryland, and both residents and visitors like it that way. Islanders even have their own distinctive brogue that's similar to the West Country of England, passed down from the settlers who arrived here in the 1600s from Cornwall and Wales.

Most visitors are drawn to these remote islands to kayak, bird-watch, fish, and enjoy some excellent fresh seafood and a famous dessert, the multilayered **Smith Island cake.** This sugary concoction made of crème, frosting, and sometimes crushed candy bars is as closely associated with the island as Key lime pie is to Key West. You won't find many shops, but the ones on hand often have the cake on offer, accompanied by fresh preserves. And you won't find any bars, period. The island is dry. If you are staying at a B&B, check with the owners to see if they'll allow you to bring your own liquor.

The boat that takes you here from the mainland will let you off in **Ewell,** where you can rent golf carts and bicycles (cars are not allowed) next to the Bayside Inn Restaurant. Before leaving Ewell, though, be sure to visit the **Smith Island Center** (✆ **410/425-3351**) on Smith Island Road to get a sense of the island's layout and history. On Ewell, you can also make a stop at the Middleton House on Caleb Road, the center for the **Martin National Wildlife Refuge,** which manages over 4,000 acres (1,619 hectares) of marshland. The refuge itself is not open to visitors, but it does host exhibits about area wildlife.

If fishing is your heart's desire, head to **Tylerton** and venture out with **Chesapeake Fishing Adventures,** 2997 Tylerton Rd. (✆ **410/968-0175;** www.cfadventures.com), which offers a variety of charter packages from a lazy afternoon of casting to multiday trips. Fishing season in Maryland is from mid- to late April to December and it's best to make reservations beforehand. Since Tylerton is separated from the island chain's other villages, you'll need to get there by boat. Try either the ***Captain Jason 11*** (✆ **410/425-4471** or 410/251-4954) or ***Captain Waverly Evans*** (✆ **410/968-1904**). The *Captain Jason 11* can also be charted for bird-watching excursions. —*JD*

ⓘ **The Crisfield Visitor Center,** 1003 W. Main St. (✆ **410/968-1543;** www.visitsmithisland.com).

✈ Crisfield Airport, then 12-mile (19km) boat ride.

Crisfield City Dock, **Captain Otis Ray Tyler** (✆ **410/968-1118**).

$ **Inn of Silent Music,** Tylerton (✆ **410/425-3541** or 970/724-3809; www.innofsilentmusic.com). $$ **Susan's on Smith Island Bed and Breakfast,** 20759 Caleb Jones Rd., Ewell (✆ **410/425-2403**).

Untouched Retreats

Pawleys Island

Shabby Chic

South Carolina, U.S.

It's fitting indeed that Pawleys Island's signature gift item should be a rope hammock—what better way is there to enjoy a summer afternoon than to sling yourself between two trees and let the ocean breeze rock you to sleep?

Anyone who's ever sweltered through a muggy, buggy Low Country August can sympathize with the 18th-century rice planters who packed up their households and moved to this breezy coastal strip every summer. Over the years, everyone from George Washington to Franklin Roosevelt to Winston Churchill followed suit. It's more of a peninsula than an island, really, divided from the mainland only by the Waccamaw River, which runs parallel to the beachfront for about 30 miles (48km), from Murell's Inlet to Wynah Bay. Technically, Pawleys Island is one 3-mile-long (4.8km) section between Pawleys Inlet and Midway Inlet, a narrow strip of houses along one road that's set apart from the rest of the peninsula by a swath of tidal creeks and marshes, great for kayaking, bird-watching, and crabbing. However, the adjoining communities of Litchfield and Murrell's Inlet also claim a Pawleys Island postal address, and although they are a little more built-up than historic Pawleys Island, development has still been kept at a minimum and the pace is laid-back.

What really matters is the Atlantic Ocean side of the peninsula, a nearly unbroken stretch of pale gleaming sand that's cleaner and better-kept than almost any other part of the Grand Strand. Public access to the beach on Pawleys is often complicated, though, for most of the oceanfront land was snapped up years ago by private owners. Don't be surprised by how ramshackle some of these century-old wooden beach houses look; that "arrogantly shabby" appearance is all part of the Pawleys Island vibe. For many visitors, coming to Pawleys means renting one of those houses near the beach, usually available on a weekly basis; local rental agencies to contact (months in advance) include **Pawleys Island Realty** (✆ **843/237-2000;** www.pawleysislandrealty.com), **Lachicotte Company** (✆ **800/422-4777** or 843/237-3366; www.lachicotte.com), or

Fishing on Pawleys Island.

the **Dieter Company** (✆ **800/950-6232** or 843/237-2813; www.dietercompany.com).

If you weren't lucky enough to rent a beachfront property for your stay here, there's still prime beach to be had nearby. Head north from Pawleys, past Litchfield Beach (also beautiful) to **Huntington Beach State Park,** along Hwy. 17, 3 miles (4.8km) south of Murrells Inlet (✆ **843/237-4440**), a 2,500-acre (1,012-hectare) park that features a wide, firm orangish beach. It's a great place for bird-watching, crabbing, and bicycling down the boardwalk, as well as camping, fishing, and swimming.

The golf courses aren't technically on Pawleys Island, either, but there are at least a dozen superb courses a few minutes' drive away, starting with the Jack Nicklaus–designed course at Pawley's Plantation; just across Hwy. 17, you'll find The Heritage Club, Caledonia Golf Club, and True Blue Golf Club. Contact the **Waccamaw Golf Trail** (✆ **888/293-7385;** www.waccamawgolftrail.com) for booking tee times at discounted rates. *—HH*

ⓘ **Tourist office,** Hwy. 17 at the Planter's Exchange (✆ **843/237-1921;** www.visitgeorgetowncountysc.com).

✈ Myrtle Beach International Airport.

20-mile (32km) drive from Myrtle Beach.

$$ **Pawleys Plantation Golf & Country Club,** 70 Tanglewood Dr. (✆ **800/367-9959** or 843/237-6100; www.pawleysplantation.com). $$ **Seaview Inn,** 414 Myrtle Ave. (✆ **843/237-4253;** www.seaviewinn.net).

Untouched Retreats 165

Molokai

The Hawaiian Outsider

Hawaii

Though it's separated from the well-groomed resorts of West Maui only by the 9-mile-wide (14km) Pailolo Channel, Molokai is a world away from the entrenched tourism of the more famous Hawaiian islands. Beyond the geographical sense of the word, long and narrow Molokai truly is an island—isolated and unique, with a strong local flavor that has developed in spite of (or perhaps because of) its well-trodden Hawaiian brethren. More ethnic Hawaiians live on Molokai than anywhere else in the archipelago, so if you're looking for what's left of the "real" Hawaii—the good and the bad—give this island a try. There's no glamour or luxury here; unlike its neighbor to the west, Lanai 295, Molokai has not emerged as a swank destination for the private jet set. However, for outdoor enthusiasts, the attractions of Molokai are unforgettable and intimate, and the north shore of the island has the highest sea cliffs in the world, at over 3,000 feet (914m) tall.

Molokai's slender, slightly undulating shape, accented by a few peninsular notches, has earned it comparisons to the shape of a fish (many locals say it's a shark), or, to less marine-inclined eyes, some sort of old-fashioned footwear. To get your bearings on Molokai, it helps to think of the island as a bedroom slipper. The heel is at the west, and the toe is at the east. Virtually all the western half of the slipper is a bare, red-dirt surface, while the eastern half of Molokai is mountainous and lush. Along the top of the slipper, from the instep to the

A mule tour down the Kalaupapa cliffs.

toe, is where Molokai's famous **sea cliffs** plunge dramatically toward the ocean. Molokai's de rigueur tour is the breathtaking mule ride down the sea-cliff trail to **Kalaupapa,** a former leper colony and National Historic Site.

There are no high-rise hotels or condos here—"no buildings taller than a coconut tree," as the marketing literature for the island proudly states. In the interest of preserving their island's *mana* (Hawaiian traditions and way of life), residents have staunchly resisted "selling out" and following the lucrative tourism model of Maui 263 and others. Their admirable stewardship, however, has caused them to have the highest unemployment rate of all the Hawaiian islands. Most attempts at resort-style developments—which would guarantee hundred of jobs—have failed on Molokai. In 2008, even the ecofriendly Molokai Ranch, the island's largest employer, shut down all its operations (leaving 120 jobless) after coming up against stubborn local resistance to its plans for expansion.

With its sleepy red-dirt towns and relatively few options for dining and accommodations, Molokai works well for many visitors as a day trip from Maui, whether by air from Kahului or boat from Lahaina. Several helicopter tours from Maui fly over the Pailolo Channel for panoramic views of Molokai, including a dazzling mid-air view of those towering cliffs on the island's northern coast. —*SM*

ⓘ **The Moore Center,** 2 Kamoi St., Ste. 200, Kaunakakai (✆ **800/800-6367;** www.molokai-hawaii.com), or www.gohawaii.com/molokai.

✈ Molokai airport (interisland flights from Honolulu and Maui).

⛴ From Lahaina, 90 min. **Molokai-Maui Ferry** (✆ **866/307-6524;** www.molokaiferry.com).

🛏 $$ **Dunbar Beachfront Cottages,** Kainalu (✆ **800/673-0520;** www.molokai-beachfront-cottages.com).

Untouched Retreats

Corn Islands

The Real Deal

Nicaragua

Imagine a lush and lovely tropical island (or two) with unspoiled beaches and vibrant coral reefs, a friendly, low-key paradise that's largely undiscovered by the globe-trotting hordes. A dreamy little place where there are no cruise ships, no malls, no celebs fleeing the paparazzi. For anyone who has a yen to live the laid-back *caribeña* lifestyle, this may be the spot for you.

The Corn Islands—Big and Little—are one of the best-kept secrets of the Caribbean. Just 81km (50 miles) off the coast of Nicaragua in the western Caribbean, the Corns are not luxe, by any means. Restaurants are open-air and topped by thatched roofs—and not of the Disney faux-thatched-roof variety, mind you. You will not be swathed in perfumed sheets or wrapped in cool minimalistic furnishings, but you can stay at charming and colorful little *posadas,* many run by European expats with style and panache. Looking to get somewhere fast? Golf carts are the preferred mode of rapid transit. And if it's a sizzling nightlife you're after, head to Aruba 261 or St. Maarten 216—although the restaurant/disco **Nico's,** located on Big Corn island's south end, is a rocking good time on Sunday nights.

For lovers of tropical heat, the weather is obliging, with average temps of 29°C (84°F) year-round and winds from the east—people staying on the windward side of the islands get a nice little breeze at night to rock them to sleep. And both islands are ringed by stunning azure seas and coral reefs teeming with marine life. You'll see huge staghorn coral formations, anemones, sea fans, sea stars, and all manner of fish, from sea devils to spotted drum. **Dive Nautilus** (✆ **505/575-5077;** www.divebigcorn.com), on Big Corn, offers dive, snorkeling, fishing, and glass-bottom-boat trips on both Big and Little Corn islands. **Dive Little Corn** (www.divelittlecorn.com), that island's only dive shop, offers dive and snorkeling trips as well as dive courses taught by PADI-certified instructors and kayak rentals.

One favorite dive spot is the rock/coral formation known as "**Blowing Rock.**" It rises 30m (98 ft.) from the sea floor, its craggy top visible above the ocean surface, with a colorful array of fish both small and large—including shark and barracuda. Fishing, in fact, is still the main industry here, and you will dine like a king on fresh fish and Caribbean lobster pulled from the sea—accompanied by home-baked *coco* (coconut) bread, of course.

Little Corn is even more primitive than Big Corn; it has no paved roads and no cars, which suits a growing number of travelers just fine. In fact, some prefer Little Corn's über-laid-back quality of life to the "fast" lanes of Big Corn. Just about a square mile in size (versus 6-sq.-km-long/2½-mile-long Big Corn), the island is little more than gorgeous white-sand beaches and tropical forest. To get from one place to the other, you bike or walk (or travel on horseback). When you're not biking or walking, you're paddling about in the clear emerald sea.

English is the main language on both islands; Nicaragua was a British colony until 1894, and its natives are descended from the original British settlers and freed slaves. The name "Corn Island" has nothing to do with corn, by the way. It's an English bastardization of the Spanish word for meat, *carne*. The islands were used to store supplies, including meat, back in the 16th and 17th centuries. —*AF*

ⓘ www.bigcornisland.com.

✈ Big Corn: Managua or Bluefields (La Costena airline; 3 hr.).

⛴ Little Corn (water taxi from Big Corn: 30 min.).

🛏 $$ **Casa Canada,** Big Corn Island (✆ **505/644-0925;** www.casa-canada.com). $ **Casa Iguana,** Little Corn Island (www.casaiguana.net).

Untouched Retreats **167**

Caye Caulker

The "Go Slow" Island

Belize

For anyone who's ever had the urge to flee the rat race and parachute onto a tropical island with velvety air and a breezy, barefoot lifestyle, Caye Caulker would likely fit the bill. It's the kind of laid-back, sun-saturated spot that's as inoculated to the rat race as a civilized place can be. It's Mayberry in the tropics.

Located 1.6km (1 mile) west of the Belize Barrier Reef, this funky fishing village is an 8km-long (5-mile) island that's situated a few miles south of Ambergris Caye **44**. The vegetation is lush and tropical, houses are wooden clapboard, the streets are soft sand, and shoes are optional. The island motto is "Go Slow," and the languid pace might drive Type A folks batty—especially when it comes to getting what they want when they want it—but others appreciate the leisurely, meditative vibe.

Belize is a flavorful stew of cultures, of Creole, Chinese, Mestizo, Indian, Maya, and more—and Caye Caulker has an authentic Belizean feel. Although tourism is now the island's major industry, big business has not intruded here; visitors are catered to in small, personal ways. Lodging largely consists of family-run inns, gaily painted guesthouses, and weather-beaten motels on stilts planted in the sand. Dining is local and home-cooked. Look for fish, rice and beans, and curries. In lobster season, which begins in June and ends 9 months later, you can eat local spiny lobster just about every night at modest prices.

In spite of its modest, no-frills demeanor, Caye Caulker has a fairly spectacular draw: the **Belize Barrier Reef,** the longest continuous barrier reef in the Western Hemisphere and one of the last unspoiled coral reefs in the world. It runs for 306km (190 miles) of rich and diverse marine habitat less than half a mile offshore. The diving and snorkeling along the reef is world-class. Just 16km (10 miles) north is the **Hol Chan Marine Reserve,** one of the most popular diving and snorkeling sites with a spectacular variety of marine life. Many people think the best diving in Belize lies on the outer atolls, just 20 minutes from Caye Caulker. **Turneffe,** the largest of the atolls, has a beautiful and varied underwater terrain. Recommended tour operators include **Belize Diving Services** (✆ **501/226-0143;** www.belizedivingservice.com), which has been operating full-service dive trips out of Caye Caulker since 1978, and **Frenchie's Diving** (✆ **501/226-0234;** www.frenchiesdivingbelize.com), whose divemasters and captains have a combined 70 years of dive experience.

You can enjoy sailing, diving, birding, jungle tours, fishing, and windsurfing in the clear azure waters of the Caribbean here. One thing Caye Caulker does not have is big, wide, white-sand beaches. Sand beaches tend to be squeezed between mangrove forests and ocean, and sea grass grows in the wading shallows. Most people

Caye Caulker.

swim off the public piers that extend beyond the sea grass or at the **Split,** a gathering place to sip the local Belikin beer and watch the sunset. Go slow indeed. —*AF*

ⓘ www.belizetourism.org or www.cayecaulker.org.

✈ Belize City to Caye Caulker (Tropic Air; 15 min.).

Water taxi (45 min.) between Belize City, Caye Caulker, and San Pedro (Ambergris Caye): **Caye Caulker Water Taxi Association** (✆ **501/223-5752;** www.cayecaulkerwatertaxi.com).

$$ **Iguana Reef Inn,** Back St. (✆ **501/226-0213;** www.iguanareefinn.com). $ **Seaside Cabanas,** Front St. (✆ **501/226-0498;** www.seasidecabanas.com).

Untouched Retreats 168

Guadeloupe

The Butterfly

Guadeloupe moves to its own gentle rhythms. This French Overseas Territory has no grand resorts to compete with upscale neighbors like Antigua (50) and St. Barts (260), and the shopping is certainly not as cosmopolitan as that on nearby Martinique (68). But then, a stay at an upscale hotel might hermetically seal you off from the soul of Guadeloupe, which lies in its small inns and B&B-style *gites,* rustic harborfront cafes, and beachside seafood shacks. The language and laws here are Gallic (the island has been a French administrative center since the 18th c.), but the flavor is pure Caribbean Creole, saucy and exuberant. If luxury linens and sleek minimalist surrounds mean a lot to you, head elsewhere—but if a quiet getaway to an authentic slice of the French West Indies sounds more to your liking, by all means come to Guadeloupe.

Physically, Guadeloupe is stunning. Its nickname, "The Butterfly Island," comes from the shape of its two main islands, which are separated by a narrow channel called the Rivière Salée. **Grand-Terre** is largely flat and dry, with fine-sand beaches and sugar plantations. **Basse-Terre** is wild, lush, and mountainous, with an active volcano in **Mount Soufriére,** Guadeloupe's highest peak. The **Guadeloupe National Park** is a real wonder: a 29,987-hectare (74,100-acre) park named a UNESCO Biosphere Reserve, with a protected tropical forest, dense stands of giant ferns, and tumbling waterfalls. The beaches are classic Caribbean: The seas surrounding the island are teal blue and shadowed by palm-fringed beaches. Some, like Grand Terre, have incredibly soft white sand; others, like the west end of Basse Terre, have strands of black volcanic sand.

Jacques Cousteau once described the waters off Guadeloupe's **Pigeon Island** as "one of the world's 10 best diving spots" and the whole island still offers excellent opportunities for scuba diving. The allure is the relatively calm seas and **La Réserve Cousteau,** a kind of French national park with a number of stellar dive sites, where the underwater environment is rigidly protected. For information, contact the **Centre International de la Plongée (C.I.P. Bouillante),** Lieu-Dit Poirier, Malendure Plage, Pigeon (✆ **590/98-81-72;** www.cip-guadeloupe.com).

Renting a car is the best way to get around and see the island. Keep in mind that many of the roads are winding and often the thoroughfare of choice for meandering goats, cows, and stray dogs. Life on Guadeloupe moves to a languorous, lilting beat, and music and food play important roles in the day-to-day culture. For music, you won't have to listen long to hear the irresistible double beat of **zouk,** the popular French West Indies music (by way of West Africa). For dining, the classic French food and wine in Guadeloupe are excellent, but the local Creole cuisine is divine; try land crab sautéed in coconut and hot pepper or fat freshwater crayfish *(quassous)* drenched in a spicy Creole sauce. Then toast to your good fortune with the island's famous Ti-Punch, a sassy mix of rum, cane sugar juice, and lime. —*AF*

(i) www.go2guadeloupe.com or www.guadeloupe-info.com.

✈ Pole Caraibes International Airport.

🛏 $$$ **Hôtel Fleur d'Épée** (✆ **590/90-40-00;** www.hotel-fleur-depee.com). $$ **Tainos Cottages** (✆ **590/28-44-42;** www.tainoscottages.com).

169 Untouched Retreats

Quirimbus Archipelago

Painted Faces & Pristine Beaches

Mozambique

All too often, the conservation of precious resources becomes a consideration only when said resources are on the brink of extinction. In Mozambique, the Quirimbus Archipelago is a brilliant example of a nation putting measures in place to protect its natural treasures while they're still in an unspoiled state. Even more amazing is that these bold and visionary steps were carried out by a government that coalesced only 10 years ago, following centuries of brutal colonial rule, civil wars, and natural disasters. By declaring both the Quirimbus Archipelago and the southern coast's Bazaruto Archipelago 52 protected national parks, Mozambique has, in the words of the World Wildlife Fund, become a "global leader in conservation." In the process, it has helped preserve two of the most exquisitely untouched regions in the world.

A 250km (155-mile) stretch of 27 coral islands that traces the country's northern coastline, the Quirimbus Archipelago has breathtaking Indian Ocean seas and pristine coral beaches where the sand is so white it almost burns your eyes. Some of these islands have never been developed; others, like historic Ibo Island, burned brightly as vital trading posts centuries ago but now exist in a suspended state of grand decay.

In contrast with the Bazaruto Archipelago, which has a slightly more sophisticated feel, these northern isles have a sleepy, spellbinding charm—it's like stepping back hundreds of years into an Africa of ancient mosques, natives with painted faces, and faded colonial architecture. The islands have some of the richest, most pristine coral reefs in the world, and the government is taking great pains to oversee any tourism initiatives (in fact, the handful of resort operators are not only employing locals but also providing needed aid in healthcare and schools).

A lovely slip of sand in a turquoise sea, the 1km-long (½-mile) **Medjumbe Island** has gentle surf and outstanding diving, snorkeling, deep-sea fishing, and windsurfing. New reefs are still being discovered. A stay in one of the resort's 13 chalets is like owning your own tropical isle. In the southern end of the archipelago, **Matemo Island** not only has a luxury resort but is also the home of several indigenous villages, where locals make a living on subsistence fishing and build traditional wooden dhows. The island turns into Little Italy in August, when beach-loving Italians come for month-long stays.

From Matemo, it's a 30-minute boat crossing to **Ibo Island,** next to the Ilha de Mozambique 344. This island was once East Africa's most important trading center. Some historians trace the island's origins back to 600 A.D., when it developed into a port for Arab traders, who dealt in gold, ivory, and slaves. The Portuguese took control of the archipelago around 1590, erecting a star-shaped fort, a cathedral, and beautiful public buildings—built on the burgeoning slave trade. Today, the once-elegant buildings are abandoned, left to rot when the Portuguese fled the country in 1975. Blanketed in mossy vines, the village is rich with the ghosts of the past: faded Portuguese tiles, rusted ironwork, old prison cells. Many of the Ibo Island native women wear white painted faces—a practice known as **Muciro painting,** a beauty regimen using a cream made from an indigenous plant. Be sure to look for the beautiful filigreed **silver jewelry** made locally, a native art that may be dying out.

The best time to visit the Quirimbus islands is from May to October; the region is hottest in December and January, and February and March mark the rainy season. —*AF*

(i) www.mozambiquetourism.co.za.

Flights from Johannesburg, South Africa; Dar es Salaam, Tanzania; and Nairobi, Kenya, to Pemba. Fly from Pemba to Quirimbus on charter flights arranged by lodges (20 min.–1 hr., depending on the island).

$$ **Ibo Island Lodge** (© **27/021/702-0285;** www.iboisland.com). $$$ **Matemo Resort** (© **27/011/658-0633;** www.matemoresort.com). $$$ **Medjumbe Resort** (© **27/011/658-0633;** www.medjumberesort.com).

Beautiful Beaches 170

Caladesi Island

Blue Ribbon Beach

Florida, U.S.

Every year, Florida geologist Stephen Leatherman—aka Dr. Beach—publishes a list of America's top beaches. Every year, Caladesi Island is right up there in the top 10—or at least it was until 2008, when Caladesi was named the number-one beach in America. After that, it's now officially retired from competition.

Considering how many fine beaches there are along this Tampa–St. Petersburg coast, what makes Caladesi so special? For one thing, it's uninhabited and undeveloped—a breath of fresh air among the densely built-up string of barrier islands fringing the St. Pete peninsula. Its calm, shallow waters are extraordinarily clear, much clearer than those of the next island to the south, the one actually named Clearwater. Its 4-mile-long (6.4km) gulfside beach is dazzling white sand that's remarkably pristine—and because it isn't raked daily like so many resort beaches are, you can find all sorts of unusual shells.

As for sun-worshiping hordes, you won't find them on Caladesi, despite all Dr. Beach's accolades—you can't get here except by boat, and the number of visitors is purposely kept low. Only 62 passengers at a time can come over on the small ferry from neighboring Honeymoon Island, and they are allowed to stay only 4 hours; if you arrive on your own boat, you can moor at the marina at the island's north end, but with only 108 slips, it tends to fill up in high season. There's no hotel or campground (although many boat owners sleep overnight on their boats). Come here at the right time and you may well feel as if you have the island to yourself.

Caladesi (Spanish for "beautiful bayou") once was the southern half of the unromantically named Hog Island, until a 1921 hurricane severed it in two. Honeymoon Island, the other half, is now connected to the mainland by the Dunedin Causeway, but Caladesi was left cut off by water. That isolation, however, turned out to be Caladesi's strongest asset. Now a state park, Caladesi has been provided with a few useful amenities, clustered near the marina—picnic tables, showers and restrooms, a playground, a cafe, and a beach concession, where you can rent kayaks and canoes for exploring the mangrove forest on the other side of the island. Walkways have been built through the dunes, preserving their fragile ecosystems of sea oats, wildflowers, and palm trees; there's also a marked nature trail through the pine flatwoods of the interior (keep your eyes peeled for ospreys, armadillos, and gopher tortoises).

But on the whole, it's a quiet, unpruned bit of beachy wilderness, which makes it extremely popular with birds, from the beach's shorebirds—American oystercatchers, black skimmers, royal and least terns, Wilson's and piping plovers—to the water birds that hang around the mangroves, including pelicans, egrets, roseate spoonbills, and herons. Loggerhead and green turtles nest on the beaches, too. It's the perfect antidote to the Tampa metro sprawl, so close and yet so totally different. *—HH*

ⓘ **Caladesi Island State Park** (✆ **727/469-5918;** www.floridastateparks.org/CaladesiIsland).

✈ Tampa International (20 miles/32km).

⛴ 20 min. from Honeymoon Island State Park (Caladesi Island Connection; ✆ **727/734-1501**).

🛏 $ **Barefoot Bay Resort & Marina,** 401 E. Shore Dr., Clearwater Beach (✆ **866/447-3316** or 727/447-3316; www.barefootbayresort.com). $$ **Sheraton Sand Key Resort,** 1160 Gulf Blvd., Clearwater Beach (✆ **800/325-3535** or 727/595-1611; www.sheratonsandkey.com).

171 Beautiful Beaches

Tinharé

Paradise Found

Brazil

No wonder so many honeymooners choose this tropical island as their getaway; it's as remote as you can get. Morro de São Paulo boasts four beaches facing the open sea, with turquoise waters, natural swimming pools, and coral reefs. Inland, you'll find lush vegetation along with exotic birds and monkeys. There are no cars and few street lights on the island. Once you land you'll be greeted by locals offering to take your bags by wheelbarrow up the steep uphill trail from the docks to the main village. On the winding path, you'll see small stores selling native wares, along with little restaurants and bars. After you are settled in your *pousada* (inn), you can get around like the natives do: by horse, donkey, tractor, or foot.

Morro de São Paulo is the largest town on the historic island of Tinharé, located in the region known as the Dende Coast. It suffered many attacks by French and Dutch ships during the 16th century and was considered an easy target by pirates. This legacy is evident by the presence of one of the island's main features: a

Island Hopping the Seychelles: Indian Ocean Castaways

A sprinkling of pearls in a sea of ethereal blue, the 115-island archipelago of the Seychelles is one of the world's most idyllic beach destinations. Set down in the West Indian Ocean some 1,800km (1,118 miles) from Africa's east coast and only 4 degrees south of the equator, these once-isolated tropical isles have become synonymous with castaway island luxury. Only 16 islands currently have accommodations, but a big part of the Seychelles' appeal is hopping from one stunning stretch of sand to another, snorkeling, diving, sailing, and soaking up the shimmering, sun-splashed atmosphere along the way.

A beach in the Seychelles.

The pristine beauty of these islands belies their fragility, and the Seychelles government is taking the high road in sustainable tourism—as in demanding small-scale, environmentally responsible development. What that means for the consumer are luxe, uncrowded accommodations, supremely personalized service, and correspondingly high rates. Fourteen islands are already protected marine reserves—in fact, 45% of this island nation is fully protected conservation land and nature reserves. Good thing, because these are the oldest living oceanic islands on earth, with 80 endemic species of flora and 2,000 endemic species of invertebrates.

The Seychelles are divided into two island clusters: the raised granite **Inner Islands** and the low-lying coral cays and atolls of the **Outer Islands.** Of the Inner Island group, **172** **Mahé** is the nation's largest island and the entry point for people flying into the Seychelles and the transportation hub for excursions to other islands in the archipelago, whether you go by air, ferry, or private or tour boat. It's also the site of the country's capital, **Victoria.** Mahé is the most populated island in the nation, by far: 90% of Seychelles citizens live on Mahé, some 72,000 people. Which goes to show how underpopulated these islands really are: The Seychelles has the smallest population of any nation in Africa.

Mahé may be the country's financial, cultural, and social heart, but in the tradition of its sister islands it also has fabulous beaches, including the secluded **Port Launay** and **Beau Vallon,** a popular beach lined with lodgings and restaurants. But if you've just arrived and are itching to find a remote and uninhabited desert island, head to the **173** **Sainte-Anne Marine Park,** a sea-and-sand sanctuary ringing six beautiful little islands: **Sainte-Anne, Moyenne, Longue, Cerf, Round,** and **Cachèe.** It's a stupendous place to snorkel and noodle about in sparkling-clear seas, with thousands of colorful fish under your flippers. You can arrange full- and half-day trips with the **Marine Charter Association** (✆ **248/22-46-79**).

The two other main islands of the Seychelles are **174** **Praslin** and **175** **La Digue.** In Praslin, the UNESCO World Heritage Site the **Vallée de Mai** (✆ **248/32-17-35;** www.

sif.sc) is a remnant of a prehistoric palm forest that some believe is the original Garden of Eden. It's a richly biodiverse ecosystem, home to 6,000 Coco de Mer palms; these trees can live up to 400 years and produce the world's largest seed. The forest is also the last refuge of the endangered black parrot, the national bird of Seychelles. Praslin may be the most touristed island in the archipelago; a number of excursions to neighboring islands leave from here.

Some travelers think that **La Digue** is the most beautiful island in the Seychelles, and there are countless magazine covers to prove it. The island has a leisurely, old-world pace and some of the nation's most stunning beaches, including **Anse Source d'Argent,** a white-sand beauty studded with large granite boulders.

(176) **Bird Island,** the northernmost island in the archipelago, is aptly named—from May to September, millions of sooty terns arrive here to nest. But it could just as well have been called Tortoise Island, for the giant land tortoises that make their home here. Bird Island is an eco-tourist's dream: Only 7% of the island is used for development, but the island's one 24-bungalow lodge lets you experience the wild island habitat in laid-back luxury. On (177) **North Island,** an 11-chalet luxury ecotourism lodge is run by one of the world's most respected outfitters, **Wilderness Safaris** (www.wilderness-safaris.com), which is truly going wild here: working to return the island habitats to their native state, weeding out invasive species, and reintroducing indigenous species. The entire island of **Cousin** (p. 135) is a nature sanctuary where some 250,000 birds nest.

Of the Outer Islands, only two have accommodations: (178) **Alphonse** and (179) **Descroches.** Each of these islands has one luxury lodge, lovely beaches, and opportunities for fly-fishing and diving. But for some, the Outer Island of (180) **St. François** is the Seychelles' most beautiful tropical isle, a palm-fringed reef surrounded by sand flats that offer superb bonefishing. A must-see in the Outer Islands is the country's second World Heritage Site, the (181) **Aldabra Atoll,** the largest raised coral atoll in the world; at its center is a massive lagoon with a vibrant marine environment. Aldabra is the home of the world's largest population of giant land tortoises: Some 150,000 tortoises—the largest of which grows to nearly 360kg—live and thrive on this truly idyllic spot. —*AF*

(i) www.seychelles.travel or www.sif.sc.

Seychelles International Airport (on **Air Seychelles;** www.airseychelles.com). Air Seychelles and **Helicopter Seychelles** (www.helicopterseychelles.com) provide charter flights to/from most of the Inner and Outer islands.

High-speed catamaran **Cat Cocos** (www.catcocos.com) operates round-trips between Mahe and Praslin (45 min.).

$$ **Clef de les Ilets,** Beau Vallon, Mahé Island (www.clefdesiles.com). $$$ **North Island Seychelles,** North Island (© **248/29-31-00;** www.north-island.com).

fort near the harbor built in the 17th century, close to the island's beautiful lighthouse. Both offer panoramic views of the beaches and provide great places for dolphin spotting.

The true attractions here, though, are the beaches, all beautiful, and each with its own personality—all are named in reference to their distance from the main settlement. **First Beach** attracts surfers during the winter months, when the waves are at their most challenging. During the summer, visitors enjoy this beach's crystal-clear waters and seaside restaurants, serving up spicy fare. **Second Beach** draws the young and young at heart with nightly luaus and music. Spirited parties are known to go on here until morning. **Third Beach** offers a more placid experience, drawing divers and snorkelers with its large barrier reef. Those who truly want to get away from it all can choose peaceful **Fourth Beach,** also known as the enchanted beach. If your ideal soundtrack is a light breeze stirring a palm tree, this is the island for you.

Although most *pousadas* and restaurants on the island accept credit cards, there's no bank and just one ATM—so it's best to bring some extra cash. If you're getting to the island by water, your best bet is to go by catamaran, leaving from behind the Mercado Modelo in downtown Salvador. As you approach, you'll see the remains of the fort that once protected this island paradise. *—JD*

ⓘ **CIT (Central de Informações Turisticas),** Praça Aureliano Lima s/n (✆ **55/75/3652-1083;** www.morrodesaopaulo.com.br).

✈ Tinharé from Salvador International Airport (30 min. on Addey or Aerostar).

Catamarans depart from downtown Salvador from the Terminal Maritimo do Mercado Modelo. **Lancha Ilhabela** (✆ **55/71/9118-2393** or 55/71/9132-8262); **Catamarã Farol do Morro** (✆ **55/71/3319-4570**); and **Catamarã Biotur** (✆ **55/75/3641-3327**). 2 hr.

$$ **Anima Hotel,** Fourth Beach (✆ **55/75/3652-2077;** www.animahotel.com). $$ **Pousada o Casarão,** Praca Aureliano, Lima s/n (✆ **55/75/3652-1022;** www.ocasarao.net).

Beautiful Beaches **182**

Barbuda

Pink Pearl

From above, Barbuda looks like nothing so much as a pink pearl dropped into a rippling green sea. It's small (just 176 sq. km/68 sq. miles), a mere dot in the ocean compared with its sister island, Antigua **50**, 48km (30 miles) due north. It's sparsely populated, with only 1,200 inhabitants, most of whom live in the island's only village, **Codrington.** It's sparsely visited: slightly off the beaten path and not easy to reach. The landscape is flat and scrubby, and most roads are unpaved. You can count the lodging options on one hand.

That's the iffy news. The good—no, great—news is that Barbuda has some of the most breathtaking beaches in the entire Caribbean. Blushing pink-sand beaches and sugary white-sand beaches, take your pick—all lapped by gentle, azure seas. And, even better: The island is the ideal getaway for those looking for peace, quiet, and a lovely beach to call their own. It's the kind of place where having nothing to do isn't a complaint; it's a blessing.

The island's 27km (17 miles) of soft-sand beaches are protected by barrier reefs. Beaches on the southwestern shore rimming the Caribbean Sea stretch to the horizon for 16km (10 miles) and are best for swimming. Among them, the picture-perfect sand of **Pink Sand Beach** owes its blushing pink hues to crushed coral. Beaches on the island's eastern shore fronting the Atlantic, such as **Hog Bay** and **Rubbish Bay,** are good for strolling and shell collecting.

If you want to see more of the island beyond the beaches, you can rent a four-wheel-drive or have a taxi driver give you a tour. In the 18th century, the island served as a breadbasket for the workers on Antigua's sugar plantations and also supplied slave labor to work the sugar cane fields (all slaves were freed in 1834). The Codringtons, the family who leased much of Barbuda back in high colonial days, remain a ghostly presence on the island. The ruins of the 1720 Codrington estate, **Highland House,** are located on the highest point on the island. Other places to visit include the **Frigate Bird Sanctuary,** located in the island's northwestern lagoon and accessible only by boat. The sanctuary contains more than 170 species of birds and is home to some 5,000 frigate birds. —*AF*

ⓘ www.antigua-barbuda.org.

✈ Antigua, V.C. Byrd International Airport (15 min.).

⛴ **Barbuda Express** (✆ **268/560-7989;** www.antiguaferries.com; 90 min.).

🛏 $$$ **Coco Point Lodge** (✆ **268/462-3816;** www.cocopoint.com). $$$ **Lighthouse Bay Resort** (✆ **888/214-8552;** www.lighthousebayresort.com).

183 Beautiful Beaches

Formentera

Cool Antidote to Crazy Ibiza

Spain

For the young and style-conscious *bella gente* (beautiful people) of Italy, there is no summer escape with more cachet than the Spanish island of Formentera. Trendy Romans and Milanese come here in droves every July and August to soak up the island's laid-back hippie vibe and pristine, sun-drenched, nudist-friendly beaches. The smallest of the Balearic islands, and only a 3km (1¾-mile) ferry ride from the legendary party isle of Ibiza 246, Formentera offers a different kind of hedonism for vacationers who prefer intimate bonfires over a raging club scene and Moroccan-motif boutique hotels to big, splashy resorts. And in certain circles, there is nothing like the smug satisfaction that comes from being able to tell people about your trip to insider-ish Formentera, province of gorgeous soccer players, their well-tanned showgirl flings, and the paparazzi who sell photos of them canoodling to the European tabloids.

Most who come to Formentera—it draws everyone from high-profile fashion designers wanting to keep a low profile to 25-year-old wannabe bohemians—choose the island because it's so diametrically opposed to the Ibiza experience; some just come as a day's detox trip from Ibiza when the wild revelry there gets to be too much. Though package tours are an increasingly popular way of getting to Formentera, there are still no high-rise condos, and no tacky all-inclusive "tourist villages." Accommodations are independently run, small, and low-key, and the same is true of the dining and entertainment options on Formentera. The price tag for almost everything on the island is still fairly low by Mediterranean island standards.

This 83-sq.-km (32-sq.-mile) island is stretched out along three axes like an upside-down *Y*, and the best way to get around is on a moped, available for rent near the ferry dock in **La Savina.** The shoreline of Formentera is mostly rugged, with rocky coves and cliffs, but there are some truly beautiful beaches, where the sugary sand is blindingly white, and the crystal-clear water is a sublime shade of stony light green and perfect for snorkeling. Just off the northern tip of Formentera is the islet of **Espalmador;** the two are connected by a sandbar that you can walk across when the tide is low.

The busiest and best-equipped beach is **Platja de ses Illetes,** near La Savina; it's a bathtub-like bay where yachts bob at anchor, their billionaire owners trolling the sands for younger babes. At Formentera's other beaches, you'll find none of that kind of atmosphere—just near-empty sands and idyllic spots for swimming. Almost all sunbathing here involves nudity of some kind—women tend to go without their bikini tops and men often sport "the full Monty."

Other than relaxing on the beach and swimming, however, there isn't a whole lot to do on Formentera: The island has no centralized "scene" to speak of, and anyone with an appetite for culture would actually do better wandering the old streets of Ibiza. For shoppers, Formentera's boutiques, proffering ethno-chic woven items, are concentrated in the hamlet of **Sant Ferran de Ses Roques.** But the island's slow pace and lack of drama (though there is a fair amount of posturing among the beautiful people who escape their stresses here, and among the yacht set at Platja Illetes) makes Formentera perfect if you need to catch up on sleep, or reading, or writing your own novel. And of course that blistering Mediterranean sun will send you home enviably bronzed. —*SM*

ⓘ www.illesbalears.es.

✈ Ibiza, then ferry.

⛴ From Ibiza (Eivissa) 30 min., Trasmapi (www.trasmapi.com) or Umafisa (www.umafisa.com).

🛏 $$$ **Sa Volta,** Miramar 94, Es Pujols (✆ **34/97/132-81-25;** www.savolta.com).

Beautiful Beaches **184**

Kefalonia Island

Wish Fulfillment

Greece

When people think of a Greek island, most conjure up an image that is tidily fulfilled by the beautiful island of Kefalonia. This place has it all, including breathtaking mountains, forests bejeweled with tropical flowers, beaches with sparkling blue water, historic landmarks juxtaposed with new architecture, and a lively nightlife. As a sailing and trading capital in the region, it also has a cosmopolitan gloss that many of the other Greek islands don't—but it's nicely tempered by the down-to-earth beauty of its many beaches.

Myrtos, the island's most famous beach, is located just north of **Argostoli,** its capital city, located on the southern part of the island. It is arguably one of the most beautiful beaches in the world, surrounded by striking vertical cliffs. Visitors flock to enjoy its crystal-clear waters, or lounge on the beach looking out on passing boats. You'll find other beautiful, but less crowded, beaches scattered throughout the island, many of them winners of The Blue Flag Award, Europe's gold standard for clean, environmentally sound beaches and marinas. It's easy to visit a different beach every day; just rent a car, moped, or motorcycle and be on your way.

Away from the beaches, the island boasts many attractions. **Assos Castle,** just outside of Argostoli, stands as an excellent example of a 16th-century Venetian fortress. The castle includes a domed building intended for convicts, and the prison yard and cells are still intact. You can drive part of the way there, but be prepared for a long walk up the hill to see the castle up close. Another popular spot for a day trip is **Spili Melissani,** a small enclosed lake known for its deep-blue color. You can take a guided rowboat and marvel at the sun playing off the brilliant hue of the water, creating a kaleidoscope of colors. Kefalonia is also known for its excellent wines, and a visit wouldn't be complete without your sipping one of its excellent vintages. A laid-back afternoon could include a trip to **Calliga Vineyard** or **Gentilini Vineyard,** both near Argostoli. You can arrange a tour through the tourist office (see below for info).

Although Kefalonia is not known as a party island, there are plenty of bars and clubs to enjoy after the sun goes down, many of them located in Argostoli or on private resorts. If you go during summer, you may also be able to find a party on the beach. When all is said and done, perhaps the greatest gift that the island has to offer is relaxation. However you choose to spend your day, you definitely won't need a watch to enjoy this island getaway. —*JD*

ⓘ **Argostoli Tourism Office,** Port Authority Building on Ioannis Metaxa (✆ **30/26710/22-248**).

✈ **Kefalonia Airport** (8km/5 miles outside Argostoli).

Strintzis Line (✆ **30/21082/36-011** in Athens, 4½ hr.).

$$ **Hotel Ionian Plaza,** Vallianou Square (✆ **30/26710/25-581**). $ **Mirabel Hotel,** Vallianou Square (✆ **30/26710/25-381;** www.mirabel.gr).

185 Beautiful Beaches

Usedom

The Singing Island

Germany and Poland

On the map, it looks like a curve of Baltic coast that somehow broke loose from Western Pomerania, with the Achterwasser and Stettiner Haff lakes rushing in to fill the gap. Though anchored to the German coast with bridges at both north and south ends (and a railway over the northern bridge), Usedom lies so far east that the eastern tip is actually part of Poland—you can walk down the beach from Ahlberg to the large commercial port of Świnoujście. But it's the German side that's the tourist magnet, a beloved getaway since the early 19th century. Only 250km (155 miles) from the German capital, Usedom has been nicknamed the "Bathtub of Berlin."

I prefer Usedom's other nickname, though—"the singing island," so called because the white sand of its 40km-long (25-mile) strand is so fine, it squeaks when you walk on it. The most popular section is southeast, from Bansin through Heringsdorf to Ahlberg—you can hardly tell when you're leaving one town and entering the next—known collectively as the **Dreikaiserbäder,** or "three imperial spas." (A fourth resort, Zinnowitz, lies up the coast to the northwest.) The architecture of these

Usedom beach.

towns is enchanting—elegant pale hotels and brightly painted villas, in the historicist or Art Nouveau styles of the late 19th century. A handful of "wellness hotels" and thermal baths preserve old-world spa traditions. Landscaped garden promenades, open-air concert pavilions, and tree-lined side streets hark back to genteel seaside holiday traditions; note the canopied chairs lined up for rent on the beaches. Each resort town also has a long pleasure pier extending into the Baltic, where you can still envision a parade of ladies with parasols and bustled dresses and gents in well-cut linen suits. (Upscale **Heringsdorf** has the longest pier, with a restaurant at the end.) Horse-and-carriage rides along the promenades, pleasure-boat excursions from the piers—it's the antithesis of spring-break beach-party madness.

For more rural atmosphere, try **Koelpinsee,** located on the narrow strip of land dividing Achterwasser from the Baltic shore; it's only a short walk from tree-covered dunes to serene panoramas of wooded lakeshore and gliding swans. Northwest of Koelpinsee, the old fishing village of **Koserow** is another relaxing resort, where you can hike up **Streckelsberg Hill** for horizon-wide vistas of island and sea. Several small towns along the waist of the island—Zempin, Trassenheide, Loddin—still look like old farming villages, with thatched cottages and weathered beachside huts for salting fish—though, never fear, they too have resort accommodations. For a break from the beach, investigate the hilly wooded interior—easily explored, with more than 400km (249 miles) of hiking trails and 100km (62 miles) of bike paths. To find picturesque sleepy villages with tiny medieval churches, check out the 16th-century castle in **Stolpe** and the medieval town gate in **Usedom,** the southern gateway to the island. Don't expect charm, though, at the infamous town of **Peenemünde,** on the northwestern tip—the top-secret World War II research center here produced the deadly V2 missile, a high-tech history now explored in several museums in town. —*HH*

ⓘ **Tourist office,** Waldstrasse 1, Bansin (✆ **49/38378/477110;** www.usedom.de).

✈ Heringsdorf.

⛴ Świnoujście, 11 hr. from Copenhagen, 6½ hr. from Ystad, Sweden. Contact **Polferries'** U.K. agents (✆ **44/871/222-33312;** www.directferries.co.uk).

🛏 $$ **Ringhotel Ostseehotel Ahlbeck,** Dünenstrasse 41, Ahlbeck (✆ **49/38378/600;** www.seetel.de). $$$ **Travel Charme Strandhotel Zinnowitz,** Dünenstrasse 11, Zinnowitz (✆ **49/30/42439/650** or 49/38377/38-000; www.travelcharme.com).

186 Beautiful Beaches

Koh Phi Phi

Loungin' Below Limestone Cliffs

Thailand

Endowed with the kind of preposterous natural beauty that tropical dreams are made of, Thailand's Phi Phi islands are a classic side trip from the larger resorts of Phuket 2, 48km (30 miles) away, and Krabi, 42km (26 miles) away. **Phi Phi Don** is the larger of the two islands, and the one where all the facilities are, while the nearby, uninhabited **Phi Phi Leh** is an excursion destination for snorkeling and one jaw-dropping sandy bay made famous by the film *The Beach*. Phi Phi Don's infrastructure was all but wiped out by the tsunami that swept across the Andaman Sea in December 2004; much has been rebuilt (if irresponsibly so), and the waves of day-trippers and backpackers continue to wash in as before.

Given its magazine-cover good looks, you might think Koh Phi Phi would be an exclusive, luxury destination—something along the lines of French Polynesia's Bora Bora 75. However, as with Thailand's other resort islands, development here has lacked stewardship, and the result has been a hodgepodge of hotels and services accessible to all budgets, but not the most careful protection of the environment.

A profusion of wallet-friendly guesthouses in **Tonsai Village,** along Phi Phi Don's iconic hair-thin isthmus, has made the island a haven for backpackers who don't seem to mind the maintenance issues of those accommodations. (The island's laid-back and permissive attitude, though it's not nearly as wild as Phuket, is another boon for the shoestring set.) A few luxury resorts—appreciably removed from the hubbub of the backpacker strip—provide the total escape package for families and couples looking to splurge a bit, with pampering facilities, spas, and private beaches in what is undeniably one of the most awesome natural locations in Southeast Asia.

Even if you've never read the book or seen the movie *The Beach*, you'll want to see **Maya Bay** (hire a longtail boat from Phi Phi Don to do so), a principal location for the film adaptation of Alex Garland's 2000 bestseller. Located on Koh Phi Phi Leh, this is a stunning bay of turquoise water surrounded on three sides by limestone cliffs; the fourth side is white sand. Keep in mind that this is the most famous single attraction in the Phi Phi islands and swarming with tourists and speedboats. Though it's a madhouse most of the time, you can try coming in the early morning or after 5pm for something a bit more like the postcard images.

The clear water and rich marine life around the Phi Phi islands attract **divers and snorkelers,** and there are plenty of operators on Phi Phi Don that will rent you equipment and shuttle you out to the area's coral wonderlands. For an up-close-and-personal encounter with the islands' trademark limestone cliffs, seek out **Cat's Climbing Shop** in Tonsai Bay for **rock-climbing** trips. Daredevils can also embark on exhilarating **cliff jumps** of up to 16m (52 ft.) over Tonsai Bay (book tours in Tonsai Village). —*SM*

(i) www.phiphi.phuket.com.

Seaplane landings from Krabi and Phuket, 30 min.

From Krabi, 90 min.; from Phuket, 2 hr.

$$$ **Phi Phi Island Village Beach Resort & Spa,** Lo Bah Gao Bay (✆ **66/2/54157-2224;** www.ppisland.com).

Islands to Get Stranded On

La Blanquilla

Castaway in the Caribbean

Venezuela

A fan-shaped island built of limestone and sand, 186-sq.-km (72-sq.-mile) La Blanquilla is a dream destination for wannabe castaways. With milky-white beaches and glassy tide pools, it's a favorite anchorage for certain discriminating Caribbean cruisers. Yet this "white island"—so named for its shimmering alabaster beaches—is one of Venezuela's most unspoiled federal dependencies (offshore islands) in the western Caribbean Sea. Other than those occasional tour groups on desert-island adventures, no one comes here but the Guardia Costera (Coast Guard) and day-tripping fishermen.

La Blanquilla offers wonderful **snorkeling and diving** opportunities: The undersea "wall" is only 20m (66 ft.) offshore, and because of the island's remoteness, marine life is abundant and healthy. The reefs around the island are known for their wealth of rare black coral. You can also spot blueheads, French angelfish, porcupine fish, balloon fish, red-lipped blenny, queen and princess parrotfish, and flying fish. On land, keep an eye peeled for colorful parrots, owls, iguanas, lizards, hermit crabs, and wild donkeys.

The best way to see La Blanquilla is by chartered boat. You'll see the odd sailboat or two bobbing in the coves north of Americano Bay (located north of **Playa El Yaque**), which has a spectacular and secluded white-sand beach of sparkling blue waters. But note that in Venezuelan waters you have to embark aboard a crewed boat licensed by the authorities and with a Venezuelan crew. **Explore Yacht Tours** (✆ **58/212-635-2166;** www.explore-yachts.com) is a Caracas, Venezuela–based company that charters full-service crewed powerboats and sailboats in Venezuela's southern Caribbean seas; it also offers dive, fishing, and cruising packages.

Lost World Adventures (✆ **800/999-0558** in the U.S. and Canada; www.lostworldadventures.com) can offer a customized trip to La Blanquilla by air from Porlamar on Isla Margarita 275 or on an all-inclusive chartered sailboat departing from Los Roques 27 or Juan Griego on Isla Margarita.

If you plan to explore the island beyond its white-sand beaches, be sure to wear shoes (even socks)—prickly-pear cactus is everywhere, and the barbs can be tenacious. Just follow the donkey paths, and you'll avoid most of it. If you come by boat, you can enjoy secluded anchorages north of Americano Bay. Though there are only a handful of palm trees, shade is at hand in caves along the shore. And it's never a bad idea to bring along a few small bottles of cheap rum to barter for fish fresh from the Caribbean, from tuna to red snapper to spiny lobster. —*AF*

ⓘ www.venezuelatuya.com or www.think-venezuela.net.

✈ Puerto La Cruz (mainland, 172km/107 miles); Porlamar (Isla Margarita, 81km/50 miles); Los Roques (161km/100 miles).

⛴ Los Roques; Juan Griego (97km/60 miles); Puerto La Cruz (mainland); Porlamar (Isla Margarita, 113km/70 miles).

🛏 $$ **LagunaMar,** Porlamar, Isla Margarita (✆ **58/295/400-4035;** www.lagunamar.com.ve).

188 Islands to Get Stranded On

Tobago

Robinson Crusoe's Paradise

When Daniel Defoe wrote his adventure classic castaway tale *Robinson Crusoe,* he couldn't have chosen to set it on a more stunning island than Tobago. (Although Isla Robinson Crusoe **371** in Chile disputes that Tobago was the setting, it's hard to quibble when you are enjoying such an inspiring setting.) Since Defoe's day, it has gone on to inspire nonfictional explorers, including Jacques Cousteau, who was enchanted by its turquoise waters and coral reefs. This island of pristine white sand is only 32km (20 miles) northeast of bustling Trinidad **112**, but the pace here is

Scarborough beach.

so relaxing that many Trinidadians come here for weekend escapes. It also draws travelers wishing to laze on the beaches or explore the green mountains of Tobago's rainforest with its glorious flora and fauna, including exotic birds and darting green iguanas.

Tobago is approximately 42km (26 miles) long and 9.7km (6 miles) wide, so you'll want to rent a car or hire a taxi to get around. Its capital, **Scarborough,** provides a beautiful view of the nearby mountains from its position on the southern coast. While on this part of the island, be sure to climb the hill to **Fort King George,** just above the town. It was built by the English in the late 18th century, but frequently changed hands as other countries invaded. The fort's old barracks serves as the **Tobago Museum** (✆ **868/639-3970**). Also on-site are the ruins of a military hospital.

Those who love marine life can follow in Cousteau's webbed footsteps and enjoy a day of snorkeling or diving in the clear, warm water that surrounds the island. You'll see a vast variety of colorful tropical fish, sponges, and nearly 300 varieties of coral. The cliffs and volcanic formations are home to large sea creatures like whales, dolphins, sharks, turtles, and squid. A variety of snorkeling tours can be arranged at www.mytobago.info/snorkelling05.php.

If you prefer to stay on dry land, consider a 5-hour naturalist-led tour to get a closer look at the incredible tropical birds and other wildlife on the island. You'll pass through the rainforest, coconut plantations, and dazzling waterfalls while on your tour. For details, contact **Newton George,** Speyside (✆ **868/660-5463** or 868/754-7881).

Although most people come to Tobago to enjoy the island's tranquillity, lively nightlife can be had. This is, after all, the region that produced calypso, soca, and steel drum music. Local hotels and bars play everything from karaoke music to the laid-back sounds of reggae, perfect soundtracks for a vacation away from it all. —*JD*

ⓘ **Tourism Division of the Tobago House of Assembly,** airport office (✆ **868/639-0509**), or I. B. Mall in Scarborough (✆ **868/639-2125**).

✈ Tobago.

🛏 $$$ **Arnos Vale Hotel,** Scarborough (✆ **868/639-2881;** www.arnosvalehotel.com). $$ **Blue Waters Inn,** Batteaux Bay, Speyside (✆ **800/448-8355** in the U.S., or 868/660-4314; www.bluewatersinn.com).

Islands to Get Stranded On **189**

Tangier Island

Getting Crabby in the Marshes

Virginia, U.S.

Perched proudly in the wide expanse of Chesapeake Bay, 12 miles (19km) from the Eastern Shore of Virginia, Tangier Island is defiantly remote—so remote that the natives haven't yet lost their ancestors' distinct Elizabethan brogue. The roads here, laid out in the 17th century, are so narrow you can barely drive a modern car along them, and so there are no cars; islanders get around instead on traditional flat-bottomed shove boats and sleek motorboats. Houses on Tangier are more likely to use their back doors, which face the creeks, than the front doors that face the lanes. Touristy it ain't—and that's just why you'll feel like going native within a few hours of arriving on Tangier.

Some countrysides have walking trails laid out; Tangier Island has water trails, five of them, lacing through the marshes, channels, and lagoons. The Orange Trail circles the main body of the island, ducking under bridges that link the island's various low-lying landmasses. It winds up in the harbor amid a working fleet of wooden-hulled Chesapeake Bay deadrise boats, used for crabbing and oystering (note the crab shanties set on pilings in the water, where peeler crabs are kept in tanks until they shed their shells to become soft-shell crabs). The Yellow Trail branches off across the southern lagoon to an outlying hook of white-sand beach where terns and black skimmers nest in tranquil solitude. The Green Trail zips across the channel to outlying **Port Isobel,** a nature preserve owned by the Chesapeake Bay Foundation, where a walking trail has been laid out through the marshes. The Blue Trail slips through the marshes of the island's southwest corner, gliding under the Hoistin' Bridge, the island's highest bridge, a traditional trysting spot for young couples. The Pink Trail circles a large northern lobe of the island, the **Uppards,** where you'll view haunting relics of the days when this was a thriving community, before it sank into marshland.

Visitors can rent golf carts or bicycles, or take buggy tours to see the sights. It's a good idea to start at the new **Tangier History Museum** (16215 Main Ridge Rd.; ✆ **302/234-1660;** www.tangierhistory museum.org), where you can learn about the island's war history, its unique isolated culture, and the natural forces that are gradually breaking up the island's landmass. The museum lends visitors kayaks and canoes for the water trails, and also has mapped out a fascinating walking tour of the main island, pointing out island landmarks that shed light on its quirky customs (such as why you'll see mossy gravestones of ancestors in so many front yards here).

Perhaps the best way to understand what Tangier Island is all about is to book an overnight stay that includes a "waterman's tour"—a visit to a crab shanty, followed next morning by an excursion on a working crab boat. Contact either the Bay View Inn (see below) or **Hilda Crockett's B&B** (✆ **757/891-2331**) for details. *—HH*

ⓘ www.tangierhistorymuseum.org or www.tangierisland-va.com.

✈ Norfolk International Airport (112 miles/ 180km).

⛴ From Reedville, Virginia (1½ hr.); Onancock, Maryland (1 hr.); or Crisfield, Maryland (45 min. or 1¼ hr.).

🛏 $$ **Bay View Inn,** 16408 W. Ridge Rd. (✆ **757/891-2396;** www.tangier island.net). $ **Sunset Inn,** 16650 W. Ridge Rd. (✆ **757/891-2535;** www.tangierisland sunset.com; open Apr–Oct).

Islands to Get Stranded On

Yap

Sorcerers & Stone Money

Micronesia

Occupying its own remote, isolated corner of the vast Pacific Ocean, the island of Yap has a native culture as fascinating and richly textured as any on the planet, one that encompasses sorcerers, stone money, and bawdy dances featuring men in colorful hibiscus skirts.

A reef-fringed tropical paradise where the seas are a cozy 28°C (82°F) year-round, Yap is indeed lush and lovely. But don't expect to run into anyone you know while you're here; Yap gets fewer than 5,000 visitors a year, and for good reason: It's a long, long way from anywhere. Yap lies in the northwestern Pacific just 9 degrees above the equator, 805km (500 miles) southwest of Guam 456 and 483km (300 miles) northeast of Palau 454.

Yap is actually one of a cluster of islands that stretch for some 966km (600 miles) across the Pacific and one of four states that make up the Federated States of Micronesia (FSM). The indigenous population can trace its roots back thousands of years and has maintained its customs through sometimes harrowing 20th-century occupations (during Japanese rule, islanders were forced into labor gangs). Following the Japanese surrender at the end of World War II, the American soldiers swept in, bringing with them modern schools and healthcare. But even those islanders who have had a thorough primary and secondary education and speak fluent English often opt to live out the local traditions and customs.

One of those entrenched customs is the continued use of gigantic stone discs as money, a tradition that experts suggest may go back as far as 125 A.D. These stones can reach up to 3.6m (12 ft.) in diameter—and even more remarkably, they come from the neighboring island of Palau, several hundred miles away. The Yapese, excellent navigators, quarried the stones in Palau and carried them back to the island by outrigger canoe—a rough journey made even more perilous by the sheer weight of the stones. Amazingly, each individual stone's value is different, determined by a number of factors, including size, shape, the quality and texture of the stone, and how arduous it was to haul it to the island. Most of the stones are now kept in Stone Money Banks in each village.

Yap is increasingly on the radar of tourists as a world-class dive spot, where underwater visibility often exceeds an impressive 45m (148 ft.). The marine scenery is superb, where table corals are reportedly the size of dinner tables, and divers may encounter huge mounds of blue staghorn, golden elkhorn, and giant brain corals. Yap has the largest concentration of **manta rays** in the world, fed by the rich plankton in the surrounding mangroves. With wingspans of 4.8 to 6m (16–20 ft.), manta rays can weigh up to 1,350kg (2,976 pounds), and unlike stingrays—which have spines or stingers on their tails—they pose no threat to divers.

The snorkeling is equally rewarding here, particularly in the area around **Manta Bay Channel** and along the inner reef; the seas are alive with clown fish and turquoise parrotfish. Most of the resorts offer **dive or snorkel packages,** as well as **cultural tours** to local villages. You can even sail on traditional outrigger canoes, the same seaworthy vessels the Yapese have been navigating for thousands of years. The canoes are beautifully hand-carved and decorated with geometric designs.

A visit to Yap is an immersion in a unique culture, and as such, respect for the islanders' traditions and lifestyle is paramount. The tourism bureau recommends that you always ask permission before photographing someone, and dress modestly—bathing suits should be worn for swimming and sunbathing poolside only. —*AF*

(i) www.visityap.com.

✈ Yap (connections from Guam or Palau).

🛏 $$ **Manta Ray Bay Resort** (✆ **691/350-2300;** www.mantaray.com). $$$ **Traders' Ridge Resort** (✆ **691/350-6000;** www.tradersridge.com).

191 Places of Worship

Ojima Island

The Red Bridges of Matsushima

Japan

Why would anybody need a getaway from Matsushima? This beautiful bay, dotted with hundreds of pine-covered islets, has for centuries been classed as one of Japan's top-three scenic wonders (the other two are Miyajima in Hiroshima Bay and Amanohashidate on the north coast of Honshu). Gazing across the sweep of the bay from Matsushima town is like looking at a gigantic version of a pond in a Japanese bonsai garden: Gnarled pine trees writhe picturesquely upward from the islands, most of them little more than humps of volcanic tuff and white sandstone. Even the great 17th-century haiku poet Basho was so overwhelmed when he finally beheld its beauty, he could only write, "Matsushima, Ah! Matsushima! Matsushima!"

And yet for Buddhist monks from Matsushima's powerful Zuiganji temple, seeking a place for spiritual retreat, gazing upon that panorama wasn't enough. That's why they took over tiny wooded Ojima Island, literally a stone's throw from the mainland (it's connected to the town by the gentle arch of red Togetsu Bridge). Here, as part of their

Ojima Island.

ascetic discipline, young monks-in-training patiently carved out 108 shallow caves—108 being a significant number in Buddhist thought—and decorated them with scriptures, Buddhist images, and sutras that would help focus their prayers and meditations. As befits a monkish refuge, women were strictly forbidden to set foot here, at least until after the reforms of the Meiji Restoration in 1868.

Only about half of the caves have survived, and nowadays the island has a distinct air of neglect; the stone images are crumbling and worn, moss-covered and water-stained. Yet somehow, that gentle sense of decay makes this tranquil island seem even more otherworldly. There's no entrance fee, there's no gate, and the bridge never closes. You can walk around the entire island in about 20 minutes, tallying up how many images of the Buddha you spot. Along the graveled paths, look for the monument to Basho, inscribed with a haiku by his traveling companion Sora. You can almost picture the island as it was when Basho and Sora arrived in 1689 to view the meditation rock of a renowned Buddhist hermit, the Venerable Ungo.

You can't miss the monks' other island, **Godaido,** set right by the ferry pier in the center of town; it's one of Matsushima's most iconic postcard images. Built in 809—it's completely man-made—Godaido is just big enough to hold one pagoda, which shelters five holy statues that are displayed to the public only every 33 years (their next scheduled appearance is 2039). It too is connected to land by a bright red bridge. Farther out in the bay an even longer red bridge skims over the water, leading to **Fukuurajima,** a rather overgrown botanical garden island. It'll take an hour or so to walk around it, reading the labels on various shrubs, flowers, and trees. It's not quite as much of a spiritual experience as Ojima—but then, very few things are. —*HH*

(i) **Tourist office,** Kaigan station (✆ **81/22/354-2263**) or Kaigan Pier (✆ **81/22/354-2618**); also www.pref.miyagi.jp.

Matsushima-Kaigan.

Matsushima-Kaigan pier, 50 min. from Hon-Shiogama.

$$ **Matsushima Century Hotel,** 8 Senzui, Matsushima (✆ **81/22/354-4111;** www.centuryhotel.co.jp). $$ **Taikanso,** 10–17 Inuta, Matsushima (✆ **81/22/354-5214;** www.taikanso.co.jp).

Places of Worship

Putuo Shan

Sacred Peak

China

Just an hour's flight from Shanghai, Putuo Shan is worlds away from the bustling Chinese metropolis. This tiny, 12-sq.-km (4⅔-sq.-mile) island, 32km (20 miles) off the China coast in the East China Sea, is an oasis of calm, with little vehicular traffic, no chain stores, and no flashing billboards. It is filled with temples and green gardens and ringed by scenic beaches with soft, smooth sand. Most important, it is a holy place for Buddhists from all over the world, who make pilgrimages to the peak in the center of the island known as Mount Putuo, one of the four most sacred mountains in Buddhism. A trip to this "garden in the ocean" is a serene, rejuvenating escape from urban China.

The ancients called this small island the "Number One Buddhist Paradise in China." An imperial order in the 13th century decreed Putuo Shan and its temples sacred to the Bodhisattva Avalokitesvara, a goddess of mercy and compassion (known in its female form as Guanyin). Much of the island was destroyed during the Cultural Revolution in 1949, but with the atheist Chinese government apparently opening its arms to Buddhism lately, Mount Putuo and its remaining monasteries and temples have undergone a renaissance: The island now has some 33 temples, and of the 3,000 permanent residents, 1,000 are monks.

Climbing Mount Putuo is not for the faint-hearted; although it rises only 300m (984 ft.), it has more than a thousand steps to ascend. You can take a cable car instead up the mountain. The island's main temple is also its largest, **Fuji,** which traces its origins back a thousand years; its golden glazed roofs signify that it was designated a royal temple, with its buildings tucked into 1.6 hectares (4 acres) of manicured gardens. The most prestigious, however, is the royal temple **Fayu,** originally built in the 16th century and surrounded by ancient trees; inside the temple is a 1,000-year-old gingko—the leaves still turn a golden yellow in the autumn. The Fayu temple is known for its fantastic dragon ornamentation and sculpted stone slates, as well as a pure gold statue of Guanyin that survived the Cultural Revolution purge. … major temple on Putuo Shan is … known as the "garden temple," which … pillowed in trees and the creases of Fodsin… Shan ("Folding Mountain").

Tourism is booming on this and the other islands in the Zhoushan (or Zhejiang) province; a million people visit Mount Putuo annually, many taking the ferry across the small inlet from nearby **Zhoushan Island.** Many come to Putuo Shan simply to enjoy its lovely beaches, including the **Hundred Step Beach** and the **Thousand Step Beach,** where sunbathing, sand sculpting, and "sandbathing" are the main activities—although you'll see some people in the water, reports are that the fetid East China Sea may not be fit for swimming. Be sure to ask around before you take the plunge. —*AF*

(i) **Putuoshan Scenic Area Management Committee** (✆ **86/580/319-1919;** www.mtputuo.com).

✈ Shanghai to Zhoushan Island (1 hr.).

⛴ From Shanghai (4–12 hr.) or Zhoushan Island (15 min.).

🛏 $$ **Xilie Villa,** 1 Xiang Hua St., Putuo Shan (✆ **86/580/609-1505;** www.xlxzhotel.com).

193 Places of Worship

Majuli Island

The Sacred in the Everyday

India

Majuli is one of the largest freshwater-river islands in the world, with abundant bird life and long-standing cultural traditions. But it is best known for its importance in Vaishnavism, a simpler form of traditional Hinduism, initiated in the early 15th century by the religious reformer Srimanta Sankardev, whose approach toward faith was steeped in prayer and the love of one god rather than idol worship. Sankardev believed that Vishnu-Narayana is the one supreme God and all other gods and creatures are subservient to him.

Sankardev focused on the importance of faith in everyday life through dance, theater, and art, and established 65 *satras* (monasteries) on Majuli, some of which still stand and are used to train young disciples. They are also open to visitors for overnight stays. Outside of the *satras,* people gather at the *namghar,* or temple, to sing and pray. In keeping with the philosophy of union between the sacred and mundane, temples are also used as gathering places to discuss village concerns.

Although Vishnu-Narayana is looked upon as the supreme god, other Hindu deities are also celebrated at festivals on the island. Because Krishna was thought to have played with his consorts on Majuli, nearly every islander takes part in the 3-day song, dance, and theater festival of **Ras Purnima,** in the month of Kartik (Oct–Nov). It's a great time to visit and participate in a joyous demonstration of faith.

Majuli sits in the enormous, and often rough, Brahmaputra River. It has about 20 villages, home to nearly 150 residents, most of whom come from the Deori and Sonowal Kacharis tribes. Most residents work in agriculture, tending to rice fields, or make their living fishing or dairy farming. The women of the island are expert weavers, creating beautiful textiles of cotton and silk. Many types of rice are grown, including *bora,* a sticky brown rice used to make the traditional dessert *peetha,* produced especially for the spring festival. Some native crafts are also linked to festivals; local pottery is made during the Ali-ao-Ivignag festival in February and March, and mask making is done at the end of winter for the Paal Naam festival.

As a study in contrasts, you may want to include a visit to the cosmopolitan city of **Jorhat,** about 20km (12 miles) away on the mainland, in your trip. The city is known for its traditional tea gardens as well as its cultural vigor. It's produced historians, journalists, and writers, including Birendra Kumar Bhattacharya, a recipient of India's most prestigious prize for literature, the Jnanpith Award.

The ecosystem here is host to an abundance of flora and fauna, including many rare and endangered species. The **Gibbon Wildlife Sanctuary** is a popular attraction, notable for its fine collection of primates. Visiting birders will get a chance to spot the greater adjutant stork, pelican, Siberian crane, and whistling teal. Before visiting, though, bear in mind that rainfall is frequent and often heavy here. The best time to visit is during the dry season from November to March when most of the music, dance, and theater is performed, providing prime opportunities for spiritual renewal and escape. —*JD*

(i) **Assam Tourism,** Station Road, Guwahati, Assam (✆ **91/361/2547102**).

✈ Jorhat from Guwahati. (From Jorhat take a boat to the island.)

⛴ Government ferry services to Majuli run from Nimatighat. Private boats may also be rented.

🛏 $$ **Hotel Brahmaputraashok Ashok,** M.G. Road, Guwahati (✆ **91/361-2602281;** www.hotelbrahmaputraashok.com).

194 Places of Worship

Simi Island

Isle of Churches

Simi, Greece

The tiny island of Simi boasts one of the most beautiful harbors in Greece. Visitors arriving by ferry are rewarded with views of pastel-colored mansions scattered on the steep hillsides—a reminder of its prosperous past as a center for shipbuilding, trading, and sponge diving. But the island's biggest claim to fame is its many churches and monasteries. Natives like to say that you can worship in a different church every day of the year, making this island retreat a perfect place for spiritual renewal.

The most famous holy landmark of all is located in the village of **Panormitis.** The Venetian-style **Monastery of the Archangel Michael,** dedicated to the patron saint of the island and the protector of sailors, was founded in 450 A.D., and renovated in the 18th century. Through the years, it has provided a home for Greek Orthodox monks, and today it has become a destination spot for those who appreciate sacred art. It boasts many stunning artifacts, including a silver icon of Michael and paintings from the Byzantine period. The monastery still functions as a home for monks, who live in cells within the building. It's even possible to rent one of these cells for an overnight stay. Call the guest office (✆ **30/22410/72-414**) for more information. If you are taking a day trip, be sure to reserve at least an hour to visit the cells and the two museums onsite, where you'll see thousands of offerings from pilgrims seeking favors.

Simi is made up of four areas: **Yialos,** the main harbor; **Chorio,** its uppermost town; **Pedi Bay,** the valley below Chorio; and **Nimborios,** the community to the north of Yialos. The island has only about six taxis—all leaving from the stand at the center of the harbor. You can also rent mopeds, but, since there are few roads, you are better off walking or using public transportation.

Most visitors arrive by boat from Rhodes 330 on a day trip. Just don't be surprised if you fall in love with this laid-back island and decide to stay here longer—many visitors make return pilgrimages to Simi's sandy beaches and rites like the Simi Festival, offering an international roster of music, theater, and film performances each June through September. —*JD*

ⓘ **Symi Visitor center** (www.symivisitor.com).

✈ Rhodes Airport (11km/6¾ miles).

Three boats connect Rhodes to Simi: the car ferries *Proteus* and *Simi* (1 hr., 40 min.), and the hydrofoil *Aegli* (about 1 hr.).

$$ **Aliki Hotel,** Akti Gennimata (✆ **30/22410/71-665**). $$ **Hotel Nireus,** Akti Gennimata (✆ **30/22410/72-400**).

5 Treasure Islands

195 American Classics

Balboa Island

Taffy Town

California, U.S.

It's not much bigger than a postage stamp, 3 blocks deep and a mile long, but Balboa crams a lot of old-fashioned seaside charm into its small space. It's got quaint Cape Cod–style architecture; fine, sandy beaches; and a vintage-Americana feel. In June, the **Balboa Island Parade** marries small-town celebration (costumed dogs and decorated golf carts figure prominently) with big-time bonhomie. The parade was begun in 1993 to celebrate the restoration of the 1927 Balboa Fire Station, for years the only government building on the island, home to the fire department, public offices, and a drunk tank during the boisterous days of Prohibition.

Now a proud part of the city of Newport Beach, Balboa Island at the turn of the 20th century was more or less swampland. At low tide it would appear as a mud flat locals referred to as Snipe Island. An enterprising fellow named W. S. Collins dredged up some of the swamp and filled in the land to form Balboa, where he carved up neat little lots (he sold the ones with prime harbor views for a whopping $600). The charm—and the selling point—was a sunny, laid-back holiday-by-the-seaside. The reality, in those early days, was a little more rough-hewn, with no electricity or gas until around 1920.

But as the infrastructure grew, so did the island populace, including Hollywood celebrities. Balboa's proximity to the harbor was catnip to recreational boaters, including such famous yachtsmen as James Cagney and John Wayne. Originally parceled out for as little as $250 a lot, Balboa Island now holds some of the priciest real estate in California.

Today Balboa looks pretty much like it did nearly a century ago, but its honky-tonk heart is now strictly G-rated. A boardwalk is lined with shops, art galleries, and the old-fashioned pleasures of a seashore town. Saltwater taffy is sold in big barrels in candy stores. Walking is the favored mode of transportation, and the evening stroll is a nightly ritual. You can take a cruise from one of the many **yacht charters** (see the Balboa Island website, below). A small **amusement park** with timeless carnival rides—including a carousel and Ferris wheel—is a foolproof draw for younger children. Picturesque bungalows, white picket fences, puppies, kids, and blue California skies: Balboa Island is a little slice of all-American apple pie. —*AF*

ⓘ www.balboa-island.net.

✈ John Wayne Airport or Long Beach Airport.

15-min. drive from John Wayne airport or 25-min. drive from Long Beach.

$$ **Balboa Inn,** 105 Main St., Newport Beach (✆ **877/BALBOA9** [225-2629]; www.balboainn.com).

Previous page: Newport.

American Classics 196

Nantucket Island

Scrimshaw Gem

Massachusetts, U.S.

The old whaling captains knew a good thing when they saw it. Walk around tiny Nantucket—the only town on the island—and you'll gape at stately Greek Revival sea captains' mansions, one after the other, lining the brick sidewalks. Though the whaling trade died in the 1870s, out-of-the-way Nantucket—30 miles (48km) off the Massachusetts coast—escaped redevelopment, and the town still exudes a prim New England-y charm. Modern-day captains of industry have built showplace beach "cottages" around the island's 110-mile (177km) coast, attracting designer boutiques and chichi restaurants; ferries from Cape Cod and Martha's Vineyard 367 regularly disgorge crowds of day-trippers to wander the brick sidewalks and gape at the mansions, ice-cream cones in hand. But it's easy to get out of town and discover Nantucket's sandy, wind-scrubbed natural beauty.

Like any summer resort, Nantucket gets overrun in July and August—try to get a last-minute reservation to bring your car over on one of the six daily car ferries from Hyannis. It's far better to take a high-speed passenger ferry and get around on foot and by bicycle. Get the historic low-down at the state-of-the-art **Whaling Museum,** 13 Broad St. (✆ **508/228-1894;** www.nha.org), where you can also hook

Nantucket lighthouse.

up with a Historical Society walking tour of town. But there's so much more to Nantucket than just the historic district. Flat, sandy, treeless Nantucket is heaven for bicyclists, with paved bikeways leading in all directions and rental shops right by the wharf. My favorite route is the 17-mile (27km) loop out to **Siasconset Beach** ('Sconset to locals). At 'Sconset, you can ramble along panoramic bluffs, and then head north along coastal Polpis Road, stopping off for the classic Nantucket photo op in front of the red-and-white-striped 1850 **Sankaty Head lighthouse** (moved from its eroding cliff to a safe spot beside the Sankaty Head golf course). Also along Polpis Road, explore the fringes of sea and land on nature trails at **Windswept Cranberry Bog** or the **Coskata-Coatue Wildlife Refuge.**

Getting out on the water is an essential Nantucket pastime, whether you join a deep-sea fishing excursion (several boats depart from Straight Wharf), rent a kayak or sailboard at **Jetties Beach** (North Beach St., just west of town), or just splash around in the surf at popular **Surfside Beach** south of town. For sunset beach strolls, the place to be is **Madaket Beach,** at the western end of Madaket Road.

Stay overnight and you'll discover a different island, once the ferries have left port. On clear summer evenings, it's a super place for stargazing, far from big-city light pollution. Just south of town, the hilltop **Loines Observatory,** 59 Milk St. Extension (✆ **508/228-9273**), is open to the public Monday, Wednesday, and Friday nights; if there's an interesting sky event, like the close orbit of Mars the summer I visited, there's bound to be a line out the door. Standing in line with the locals, listening to how everyone spent their day—that's a pretty fine way to get in tune with Nantucket. —*HH*

ⓘ **Nantucket Visitor Services,** 25 Federal St. (✆ **508/228-0925;** www.nantucket-ma.gov).

✈ Nantucket Airport.

⛴ Nantucket town, service from Hyannis, Harwich Port, or Martha's Vineyard.

🛏 $$$ **Beachside at Nantucket,** 30 N. Beach St. (✆ **800/322-4433** or 508/228-2241; www.thebeachside.com). $$ **Jared Coffin House,** 29 Broad St. (✆ **800/248-2405** or 508/228-2400; www.jaredcoffinhouse.com).

197 American Classics

Mackinac Island

Car-Free, Carefree

Michigan, U.S.

First of all, you pronounce it "*Mack*-i-naw," like the raincoat—the nearest mainland town is spelled Mackinaw City, so out-of-towners will get it right. Cropping out of the narrow Straits of Mackinac, which divide the Upper and Lower Peninsulas of Michigan, this summer resort island is a Victorian period piece of white frame houses and trim gardens. Nowadays, the great green Mackinac Bridge spans the Straits, connecting the peninsulas. But at the height of summer, when getting from here to there becomes less important than getting away from it all, that bridge is beside the point. What you want instead is the passenger ferry from Mackinaw City, heading away from the bridge to the time warp of Mackinac Island.

Long before the bridge was built in 1957, Mackinac was one of the Midwest's

Mackinac Island.

favorite summer resorts, and it's still a cherished holiday destination—and still blissfully car-free, which means you have three options for getting around: on foot, by horse-drawn carriage, or on a bike. Pedaling happily along the limestone cliffs overlooking the straits, you may wonder why the automobile was ever invented. A complete circuit of the island on traffic-free Lake Shore Road is only 8 miles (13km); you can rent bikes in town.

You'll have to stop along the way, of course, to drink in the views—don't miss Arch Rock on the east coast, a boulder pierced with a gaping 30×40-foot (9×12m) hole gouged by waves and glaciers, or Sunset Rock on the west bluff above town. Most of the island is covered by **Mackinac Island State Park** (✆ **906/436-4100;** www.mackinacparks.com), with 70 miles (113km) of paved roads and trails where cyclists can explore the cedar- and birch-forested interior. Above the town, you can also cycle up to **Fort Mackinac,** 7127 Huron Rd. (✆ **906/436-4100;** www.mackinacparks.com), built by British soldiers during the American Revolution to keep the Straits open for the lucrative fur trade. Costumed interpreters are on hand to shoot off rifles and cannons and perform military band music. The cliff-top site was chosen specifically for sentries to watch over the lakes, so you can just imagine how fantastic the views are.

Of course, if you'd rather take in the scenery from a rocking chair, you can always plunk yourself down on the white colonnaded veranda—the world's longest front porch—of the landmark **Grand Hotel** (see below), built in 1887. Even if you're not staying here, you can tour the historic premises. Or shop your way along downtown's Main and Market streets, lined with flower-bedecked balconies; be sure to pick up some of the island's trademark rich fudge. Mackinac has three golf courses, but it also has two butterfly conservatories (the **Butterfly House,** downtown at 296 McGulpin St., and **Wings of Mackinac,** up past the carriage tour barns on Surrey Hill). That's the sort of vintage charm that summer memories of Mackinac Island are made of. —*HH*

ⓘ **Mackinac Island Chamber of Commerce** (✆ **877/847-0086;** www.mackinacisland.org).

✈ Mackinaw City, 12 miles (19km) from ferry docks.

⛴ Depart from Mackinaw City or St. Ignace. **Arnold Transit,** 15–45 min. (✆ **800/542-8528;** www.arnoldline.com). **Shepler's Ferry,** 16 min. (✆ **800/828-6157** or 231/436-5023; www.sheplersferry.com). **Star Line,** 16–18 min. (✆ **800/638-9892** or 906/643-7635; www.mackinacferry.com).

🛏 $$$ **Grand Hotel,** W. Bluff Rd. (✆ **800/33-GRAND** [334-7263] or 906/847-3331; www.grandhotel.com). $$ **Mission Point,** 6633 Main St. (✆ **800/833-7711** or 906/847-3312; www.missionpoint.com).

198 American Classics

Ocean City

Family Fun on the Jersey Shore

New Jersey, U.S.

It doesn't get much more old-time American than summer on New Jersey's "OC." With a real wood-planked boardwalk lined with carnival rides and funnel-cake vendors, plus long stretches of sandy beach and activities galore for kids, Ocean City is a uniquely family-friendly seaside resort. And because it's a dry community—no booze is sold here or consumed in public places—Ocean City is a world away from other, raucous, party-focused Jersey Shore locales. So much of Ocean City hearkens back to a simpler, sunnier era, readily apparent in its appealingly retro (though some are downright tacky) lineup of motels and vacation rentals, most within a few blocks of the beach if not right on the water. It may not be a destination for aesthetes, but for many families in the Northeast and mid-Atlantic who vacation here every year, Ocean City is an island paradise.

From the "mainland," you can drive over one of four bridges or take the ferry from Cape May to reach Ocean City. The island itself is a narrow strip covering an area of just 7 sq. miles (18 sq. km); it's much longer north-south than it is east-west, with clean beaches of fine sand fronting the Atlantic Ocean on the east and the bay on the west. Once you're here, Ocean City's simple grid layout of numbered streets makes it easy to get around on foot or by bike.

Setting the tone for Ocean City's particular brand of old-fashioned summertime fun is its **classic boardwalk.** The 2½-mile (4km) promenade is filled with kids of all ages playing arcade games or miniature golf, fighting losing battles with melting ice-cream cones, or squealing down a waterslide. The smells from food stalls here—saltwater taffy, fudge, and french fries—really do transport you to another time. Best of all, the boardwalk is safe at all hours.

Away from the boardwalk, Ocean City teems with ways to stay active under the sun, almost all of which are kid-focused or kid-friendly. There are sports camps and leagues, sailing schools, and summer programs of all kinds here, but for less structured fun, you can also take to the water with a kayak or WaveRunner (available for rent at many outfitters), or go on parasailing, tubing, water-skiing, and even fishing excursions. Of course, for the most basic summer pleasure of all—being a beach bum—Ocean City has 8 miles (13km) of silky oceanside or bayside shore.

In the evenings, summertime residents—many of whom rent houses or apartments here by the week, month, or season—congregate at the **Music Pier,** off the boardwalk, for nightly concerts. For nightlife with a little more pizazz, adults can turn to the bright lights and casinos of Atlantic City, only a 30-minute drive away. Also within easy striking distance, for day trips of the nonwatery variety, are the Cape May County Park and Zoo, the Atlantic City Aquarium, and historic villages, homes, and lighthouses. —*SM*

ⓘ **Ocean City Regional Chamber of Commerce,** 16 E. 9th St. (✆ **609/399-1412;** www.oceancitychamber.com).

Atlantic City or Philadelphia International.

Three Forts Ferry from Delaware City, 5 min. **Cape May-Lewes Ferry** (✆ **800/64-FERRY** [643-3779]; www.capemaylewesferry.com).

19-mile (31km) drive from Atlantic City or 71-mile (114km) drive from Philadelphia.

$$$ **Flanders Hotel,** 719 E. 11th St. (✆ **609/399-1000;** www.theflandershotel.com). For vacation rentals, consult www.oceancitynj.com.

Jewels of the South Seas

199

Raiatea & Tahaa

Secret Slices of Paradise

Bora Bora 75 and Moorea 86 may be the current darlings of French Polynesia, but for those who like to stay ahead of the curve, the Society Islands of Raiatea and Tahaa offer some less-touristed slices of paradise. Raiatea is the most sacred island in the South Seas, with the best-preserved archaeological site in Polynesia. Separated from Raiatea by a thin lagoon, the "vanilla island" of Tahaa is even more traditional, and is home to one of the most luxurious resorts in the region, Le Taha'a Private Island & Spa (see below). Caressed by omnipresent trade winds, both islands are dripping with enchanting lore and remain (unlike some of their Tahitian sisters) blessedly untouched by modern life.

Most people who visit Raiatea and Tahaa do so as a day trip or short excursion from nearby Bora Bora or Moorea (both of which are a 45-min. flight away). Though they're technically two separate islands, a shared lagoon makes Raiatea and Tahaa function as a single destination with diverse and complementary attractions; their proximity has made their history and cultures inextricably linked.

One of the reasons Raiatea isn't as well-known as its more famous neighbors in French Polynesia is that its lush and rocky coastline, however picturesque, has no sandy beaches. But don't let this deter you—the waters around Raiatea and Tahaa are dotted with ***motus,*** tiny uninhabited islets that are the definition of tropical fantasy. (Seen on countless PC screensavers, your basic *motu* is a strip of sand, backed by a mound of green, punctuated by perfect palm trees, and surrounded by crystalline turquoise water.) Rent a *motu* for a few hours or the day, have a picnic, and act out your own episode of *Lost,* comfortable in the knowledge that someone will pick you up well before sundown.

But the highlights of visiting Raiatea and Tahaa aren't limited to the sea and watersports. The stone temple, or *marae,* at **Taputapuatea** is Raiatea's spiritual treasure and the most extensive archaeological

A *marae* on Raiatea.

site in the South Seas, second in importance only to Easter Island 375. Set in a coconut grove on the shore of the lagoon, Taputapuatea is marvelously evocative of the pre-European era here. Raiatea's **Mount Temehani** is not the island's tallest peak (it's 792m/2.598 ft. high) but its most sacred one. As the place where ancient Polynesians believe their souls ascended after death, the mountain is inextricably linked with Polynesian mythology. Mount Temehani is also the only place in the world where the fragrant *tiare apetahi* flower grows, its petals opening each morning with a crackling sound. Also on Raiatea, the **Faaroa River** is the only navigable waterway in French Polynesia, and trips along the river in powered outrigger canoes give you a glimpse of the island's lush and mountainous interior.

To the immediate north of Raiatea lies Tahaa. According to legend, Tahaa was detached from Raiatea by a sacred eel, and in the lagoon that separates the two islands are shipwrecks that divers and snorkelers can explore. Tahaa is commonly known as the "Vanilla Island" because of its many vanilla plantations—80% of Tahiti's vanilla is grown here, and you can smell the richly aromatic bean being harvested all over the island. As on Raiatea, four-wheel-drive vehicles are the best way to discover all the hidden corners of the island and are easily rented in town. Ferries, informal charters, and water taxis operate shuttle services between Raiatea and Tahaa.

The deep-water harbors of Raiatea and Tahaa make both islands popular hubs for sailing—whether you bring your own vessel or begin a South Seas charter from here—as well as larger cruise ships, which dock periodically at the Gare Maritime in Utaroa, on Raiatea. When cruise ships are in port, thousands of passengers spill onto shore, inundating the islands. Try to plan your organized activities for days when cruise ships are not expected. —*SM*

(i) www.raiatea.com.

✈ Raiatea airport (served by interisland flights from Papeete, Tahiti; Bora Bora; Moorea; and Huahine).

🛏 $$$ **Le Taha'a Private Island & Spa,** Motu Tautau, Tahaa (✆ **800/657-3275;** www.letahaa.com). $$ **Raiatea Lodge Hotel,** Uturoa (✆ **689/600-100;** www.raiateahotel.com).

Jewels of the South Seas

Fiji

Bula Bula

For many travelers, Fiji is *the* quintessential South Pacific island. It's the tropical paradise you imagine hitching a steamer trunk to escape to. The place you daydream about during long winter workdays. The island whose images of waving palm trees, beautiful beaches, and grass-skirted dancers are practically tattooed into the wanderlusting globe-trotter's brain.

Well, guess what? Fiji lives up to its billing. Its coral reefs are rebounding after decades of rising ocean temperatures. Its beaches are as spectacular as ever. Fiji is safe, clean, and incredibly hospitable to visitors, and its tourism infrastructure is sophisticated and designed for ease of travel. The Fijian culture remains strong, built on family, ritual, and a sunny outlook. Everywhere you go, you'll be greeted with a warm Fijian *"Bula,"* which can mean "cheers" or "welcome" or even a hearty "hello."

This South Pacific island archipelago comprises some 333 islands, some of which are home only to traditional Fiji villages. Its two main islands are **Viti Levu** and **Vanua Levu.** Viti Levu is where **Nadi,** the gateway to Fiji (and the main airport) is located; here is where you'll find hotels, restaurants, and shopping. On the northwest coast of Viti Levu is **Yasawa,** home to many of Fiji's best beaches and resorts as well as transfers, by seaplane or boat, to other islands. The **Mamanuca Islands** are a beach and watersports paradise of coral reefs and shimmering blue seas. The **Coral Coast** is situated on Viti Levu's western coast and contains many of the nation's top resorts. It's a colorful stretch of coastline, with blue lagoons and breathtaking beaches. **Suva,** Fiji's capital, has a stately, vintage appeal, with Victorian architecture from its days as a colonial outpost. The **Outer Islands** are perfect specks of palm-fringed white beach dropped into the South Pacific waters (much of the movie *Castaway* was filmed on one of the Outer Islands). A day trip from Suva to **Levuka,** the country's original capital, always highlights a visit to Fiji. The old town has retained its 19th-century appearance, and the backdrop of sheer cliffs makes it one of the South Pacific's most beautiful places.

A visit to Fiji is as much about experiencing colorful Fijian culture as it is about perfect beaches and world-class watersports. Don't leave without being entertained during a *meke,* where islanders wearing costumes of printed bark cloth *(tapa)* perform traditional songs and dance. Watching a Fijian fire-walking performance (actually a Hindu religious observance) is thrilling. And definitely attend a *lovo,* a traditional Fijian feast featuring a whole roast pig and food wrapped in banana leaves and cooked in an earth oven over hot stones. It's the perfect example of South Seas hospitality. *Bula! —AF*

ⓘ www.fijime.com.

✈ Nadi.

🛏 $$ **Rydges Hideaway Resort Fiji,** Viti Levu (✆ **679/650-0177;** www.hideawayfiji.com). $$$ **Turtle Island** (✆ **800/255-4347** in the U.S., or 679/672-2921; www.turtlefiji.com).

201 Jewels of the South Seas

Bali

Island of the Gods

Indonesia

Bali is one of those enchanting island paradises that doesn't seem diminished by modernity or rising tourism numbers. This Indonesian island, tucked between Java to the east and Lombok to the west, has even rebounded from the horrific bombings that shook it in 2002 and 2005. Today, some two million people visit Bali annually—it's the country's top tourist attraction, by far. But no matter how many people flock to Bali, it has managed to retain its peace-loving nature, deeply engrained culture, sanguine outlook, and enduring spirituality.

Bali's distinctive civilization may have something to do with its isolation as a Hindu majority in a country that is the largest Muslim country on the planet. Of its population of three million people, more than 90% are Hindu. Ancient and modern temples dot the countryside (some 10,000 in all), and life in Bali revolves around *Tri Hita Karana,* a spiritual principle espousing the wisdom of maintaining a harmonious three-way balance between man and God and the environment.

But Bali is blessed with much more than a rich culture and benevolent spirituality. Simply put, Bali is one of the most beautiful places on earth. It has breathtaking beaches and steep mountain slopes, terraces embroidered with green rice paddies and lush vegetation. If you're looking for a beautiful swimming beach with gentle surf, tawny sand, cinematic sunsets, and a mystical vibe, head to **Sanur,** on Bali's south coast. If you're looking for a little more wave action, head to **Uluwatu,** on Bali's southern tip—it's one of the world's most famous surf spots, with awesome breaks in Temples, The Peak, and Race Track. On Bali's western tip is **Labuan Lalang,** an uninhabited island with some of the best diving on Bali. Nearly 7,000 hectares (17,297 acres) of marine waters and pristine coral reef are protected as part of the **Bali Barat National Park,** including **Menjangan Island. Ubud** is a charming central town away from the coasts; it's the island's center of arts. Balinese arts are justly celebrated around the world; be sure to take in a Balinese dance performance, featuring beautifully costumed dancers.

Bali is a big island (5,633 sq. km/2,175 sq. miles), so if you want to explore as much as possible, you may want to rent a car. Many visitors hire a **private taxi** (car and driver/tour guide)—an inexpensive and enlightening way to experience the island through the eyes of an insider. **Bike tours** of rural Bali are popular; you pass villages, fields of rice, and coffee plantations, and sample Bali cuisine; a number of operators are based in Ubud. Try **Happy Bike Cycling Tours** (✆ **62/81/999-260-262;** www.happybiketour.com) or **Banyan Tree Cycling Tours** (✆ **62/81/338-798-516;** http://banyantree.wikispaces.com). —*AF*

ⓘ www.balitourismboard.org or www.indo.com.

✈ Denpasar's Ngurah Rai international airport (48km/30 miles).

🛏 $$$ **Chedi Club at Tanah Gajah,** Jalan Goa Gajah, Tengkulak Kaja (✆ **62/361/975-685;** www.ghmhotels.com). $$ **Poppies Cottages,** Poppies Lane I (✆ **62/361/751-059;** www.poppiesbali.com).

Jewels of the South Seas 202

Sumatra

Where History & Beauty Meet

Indonesia

Sumatra was once known as Swarnadwipa, the Sanskrit term meaning "Island of Gold," for gold deposits found by the island's first settlers, members of the Hindu empire of Srivijaya, who arrived in the 7th century. Over the centuries, other groups would try to claim this tropical paradise for their own, beguiled by its striking volcanic **Barisan mountain chain,** with peaks averaging over 610m (2,000 ft.). The highest peak rises over 3,658m (12,000 ft.) in the middle of the range. The mountains make a majestic backdrop for its lush rainforests, home to exotic animal species like tigers, elephants, and rhinoceros. Sumatra has the distinction of being both the largest island in Indonesia and the sixth-largest island in the world. Despite its geographical significance, it is less touristy than better known islands like Bali 201 and Java 346, making it more of a bona fide getaway.

Although Hinduism dominated its early history, Islam began making inroads here during the 13th century. The first Europeans to settle were the Portuguese, who staked their claim in the 1500s. They were followed by the Dutch and English about a century later, and the Dutch influence can be seen in the architecture in the capital city of **Medan.** The Dutch struggled with the native Atjehnese, a Muslim tribe, in sometimes bloody battles. Another chapter opened during World War II, when Japanese forces commanded the island from 1942 to the end of the war. The island won its freedom from the Dutch in 1950, and was officially declared part of the Republic of Indonesia, but that did not spell an end to conflict; the Atjehnese led a rebellion in 1958, and tensions still sometimes flare up. Another factor to consider is the devastating earthquake that hit the island in October 2009. At press time, thousands were believed dead or missing and many buildings were leveled. It's best to check on the current situation before planning a trip.

Once on the island, you could do worse than spend a day or two discovering the city of Medan and its environs. Medan is in North Sumatra, a province resplendent with rainforests, jungles, volcanic lakes, and lovely beaches. The town is notably home to the **Museum of North Sumatra,** which houses prehistoric artifacts that reflect the island's changing leadership: Buddhist statues share space with weaponry and Arabic gravestones. Nearby **Maimoon Palace** is another example of the island's history. It was built in 1886 by an architect blending Asian, Western, and Middle Eastern influences. **Gang Bangkok Mosque**—the oldest mosque on the island—is also worth a visit while you're in the Medan area.

Be aware that Medan is a major port, home to more than two million people. If you want to get away from the crowds, I recommend renting a motorcycle or car and taking in the island's natural glories beyond this port. Sumatra's flora and fauna outside this hub make for breathtaking sights. The island is home to 10 national parks, including 3 that are listed as World Heritage Sites. You can climb smoking volcano craters in the town of **Berastagi,** or see an orangutan in the rainforest canopy of **Bukit Lawang.** The rainforests host unique species including the Rafflesia arnoldii, the world's largest flower—just one of this island's rare treasures. *—JD*

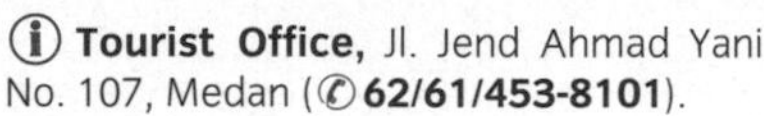

ⓘ **Tourist Office,** Jl. Jend Ahmad Yani No. 107, Medan (✆**62/61/453-8101**).

✈ Polonia International Airport.

🛏 $$ **Grand Angkasa Hotel** (✆ **62/61/455-5888;** www.grand-angkasa.com). $ **Tiara Medan Hotel** (✆**62/61/457/4000;** www.tiarahotel.com/).

203 Priceless Places

The World

A Global Archipelago

Dubai

Leave it to the Las Vegas of the Middle East to come up with the idea to build an artificial archipelago in the shape of the world map—but hey, if you've got the financial resources of Dubai, why not? The concept—to create from scratch some 300 islands that, pieced together and viewed from above, resemble the landmasses of planet Earth, and to give it the grandiose name "The World"—was dreamed up in 2003. The contract, with overall development costs estimated at $14 billion, was awarded to Dubai's premier developer, Nakheel (the same group behind Dubai's Palm Islands, man-made islands just off the mainland that form the shape of a palm tree trunk and fronds), and assembly of the islands of The World was completed in early 2008. At press time, construction was underway (but temporarily stalled) on the dozens of islands that have already been sold to investors worldwide for reclamation as glitzy shopping districts, resorts, and residential complexes.

The engineering behind the project, located just 4km (2½ miles) off Dubai's Jumeirah Beach, has been an enormous and ingenious undertaking (made somewhat easier by the relatively calm and shallow waters of the Persian Gulf—known in the Arab world as the Arabian Gulf). To form the ersatz archipelago, sand was dredged from the ocean floor and deposited in piles of appropriate size and shape. To create a stronger foundation for each island, and to promote the kind of lush vegetation that would attract investors, organic materials like plants and soil were mixed in with the sand that forms each island.

Including the wispy, man-made sandbars that are The World islands' oval-shaped breakwater, the entire development occupies 9×6km (5½×3¾ miles). The individual islands range in size from 2 to 8 hectares (5–20 acres), with anywhere from 50 to 100m (164–328 ft.) of seawater between them. To handle the flow of water traffic between The World and Dubai (a boat ride of under 10 min.), four transportation hubs have been set up within the archipelago and dubbed North (somewhere near London), South (Antarctica), East (Tokyo), and West (Los Angeles). For interisland transit, dozens of waterways and intricate right-of-way regulations have been established. There are no bridges to The World; it can be accessed only by sea or helicopter.

Unconfirmed reports hint at several celebrities buying into the development: Tommy Lee apparently expressed interest in purchasing Greece as a getaway for his ex-wife, Pamela Anderson. Brad Pitt and Angelina Jolie have denied rumors that they put down a deposit on Ethiopia. With Dubai's economy currently on the rocks, and much of the ambitious archipelago still for sale, now may be the time for you, too, to own a piece of The World—still priced out of most people's budgets, they're going for a mere $10 million and $45 million apiece.

Island Hopping the Lofoten Islands: Midnight Magic

Imagine, if you will, a string of northerly isles where colorful fishing shacks stand against a backdrop of craggy granite cliffs, where red-cheeked children play in the shadow of rugged gray pinnacles. Beautiful and awe-inspiring, the Lofoten Islands are a Grimms' fairy tale come to life.

The Lofotens are a remote island archipelago in the north Atlantic and a district in the county of Nordland, Norway. The landscape is breathtakingly cinematic, with ice-tipped peaks fringed by deep blue seas and a rocky shoreline fronted by sandy beaches. The Lofoten Islands stretch 250km (155 miles) south-southwest from the fjord of Ofoten to the outer Røst islands. Although the islands lie north of the Arctic Circle, the passing Gulf Stream keeps temperatures relatively mild. The air is fresh and clean, kissed by sea spray and Arctic breezes.

Hamnøy.

The main islands are 204 **Austvågøy,** 205 **Gimsøy,** 206 **Vestvågøy,** 207 **Flakstadadøy,** 208 **Moskenesøy,** 209 **Varøy,** and 210 **Røst.** On the eastern coast of Austvågøy, **Svolvær** is the largest town in the archipelago. A Norwegian fjord, the **Vestfjorden,** separates the islands from the mainland. This body of water is the heart of the Norwegian cod fisheries. The world's largest cod-fishing event, **Lofotfiske** (www.lofotfiske.net), takes place between January and March. You can even stay in old traditional fishing cabins, here known as *rorbuer.* Many of these cabins hug the shoreline, built on stilts above the water's edge. If fishing for monster cod is on your agenda, head to the old fishing camp of **Henningsvar,** with its quaint waterfront, *rorbu* cabins (www.henningsvar-rorbuer.no), and fish-drying racks—nicknamed "Lofoten's cathedrals."

In late autumn, when the herring return to the Vestfjorden for the winter, they are chased by between 500 and 700 hungry orcas, also known as killer whales. Orcas can grow up to 4 to 5 tons, live to be 60 years old, and hang out with their family their entire lives. (Well-mannered, too; they eat only one herring at a time.) You can take a "killer whale safari" to see these amazing animals up close with one of several outfitters, including **Orca Tysford** (✆ **47/75-77-53-70;** http://tysfjord-turistsenter.no/safari), which takes visitors out on the sea by large boat or inflatable dinghy and—if you're really crazy—lets you snorkel as a pod of killer whales passes by. **GoArctic/Orca Lofoten** (✆ **47/45-83-27-10;** www.goarctic.no) offers "Nature, Seabird & Orca Excursions" from October to mid-January.

Perhaps the most dramatic experience in Lofoten is a tour over turbulent waters—the "Lofoten Maelstrom" (called the Moskestraumen by local fishermen), one of the world's strongest tidal currents in open waters. The treacherous strait separating Moskenesøy from the offshore island of Varøy to the south has been called "the world's most dangerous waters." Take a ride on the Maelstrom—or just go fishing—with **Moskstraumen Adventure** (✆ **47/97-75-6021;** www.lofoten-info.no/moskstraumen-adventure) in the town of Å.

A fishing boat in the Lofotens.

There's a lot of history in these stone mountains; human settlement traces back 6,000 years to Stone Age hunters. The Vikings built 10 to 15 chiefdoms in northern Norway during the Iron Age, one of them in the town of Borg on the island of Vestvågøy. Excavations in the 1980s uncovered the 6th-century remains of the largest building ever found in Europe from the Viking era; experts believe it was the home and farm of a rich and prosperous chieftain. Among the artifacts uncovered were goblets and pitchers, dinnerware, no doubt, for he-man Viking banquets. You can see these and the remains of the farm at the **Lofotr Viking Museum** (✆ **47/76-08-49-00;** www.lofotr.no).

All of the inhabited islands are linked by ferry. You can rent a car and cruise one of the great drives in the north of Norway: the **E10,** from Hamnøy in the extreme northeast of Austvågøy island to the southwestern tip of Moskenesøy; the region's first ferry-free road connection with the mainland was completed along this route in 2007. But walking or cycling Lofoten's beautiful little fishing villages is a fine way to appreciate the dramatic juxtaposition of gaily painted fishing shacks and sheer mountain cliffs—a scene reflected, for extra drama, in the glassy seas. Begin in the north at little **Hamnøy** and stroll south through **Sakrisøy, Reine, Moskenes,** and **Sørvågen.**

Dramatic scenery is not the region's only natural draw. Here, in northern Norway, the skies give the mountains and the sea a run for their money. The aurora borealis (northern lights) paint the evening skies from September to April, and in the summer the Lofotens become the light-filled Land of the Midnight Sun. —*AF*

ⓘ www.lofoten-info.no or www.visitnorway.com.

✈ Bodø to Svolvær.

⛴ From Skutvik, take the 2-hr. ferry to Svolvær. Ferry information and reservations: Lofotens og Vesterålens Dampskibsselskab A/S (aka **DDF;** ✆ **47/94-89-73-34** or 47/81-03-00-00; www.ovds.no for reservations and information).

🛏 $$$ **Anker Brygge,** Lamholmen, Svolvær (✆ **47/76-06-64-80;** www.anker-brygge.no). $$ **Nusfjord Rorbu,** Flakstadoy (✆ **47/76-09-30-20;** http://nusfjord.no).

To suit the project's needs, the architects of The World have taken some liberties with the Earth's geography. For instance, South America isn't one big landform but rather a collection of more than 20 islands laid out next to each other. The channels that run between the islands allow for some nifty shortcuts that would actually work well in the real world, such as the waterway running straight from the Persian Gulf to the North Sea. Some further geological nit-picking: There are no towering sand dunes to replicate the Alps and the Himalayas, and no mechanism is in place beneath The World to re-create plate tectonics. Of course, climate can't quite be reproduced on The World islands, either, and that means it's all global warming, all the time: The temperature on the glittering sand beaches of Antarctica reaches an iceberg-scorching 40°C (104°F) in the summer.

Note: As of press time, the World Islands project was stalled—proving that even high-rolling Dubai could be affected by the global credit crunch. Though much of the land reclamation for the islands' creation has been completed, construction on the islands has been halted for the time being. Developers still plan to carry out the project, though it may take a few more years. —*SM*

(i) www.theworld.ae.

Dubai International Airport (15km/9⅓ miles).

From Jumeirah Harbor or Umm Suqeim Harbor, about 10 min.

$$$ **Emirates Towers,** Sheikh Zayed Rd., Dubai (✆ **971/4/330-0000;** www.jumeirahemiratestowers.com). $$ **Novotel,** 2nd Zaabeel Rd., Sheikh Zayed Rd., Dubai (✆ **971/4/318-7000;** www.novotel.com).

Priceless Places

Sea Island

The 24-Carat Golden Isle

Georgia, U.S.

How much does it cost to vacation on Sea Island? If you have to ask, you probably can't afford it—the island's only hotel, The Cloister, is the poshest resort on the Georgia coast, with the rest of the island occupied by the vacation homes of some very serious movers and shakers.

Anybody can drive over to Sea Island, however, following the Sea Island Causeway from St. Simons Island, itself accessible by causeway from the mainland. Soon after you've reached the island, a left-hand turn will lead you up the Cloister's main drive; continue along Sea Island Drive as it doglegs left and you can cruise along the beachfront, following Sea Island Drive, aka Millionaire's Row. The wide-open view out over the Atlantic is breathtaking, and the lavish homes lining the road are pretty gape-worthy too.

While all of the nearby barrier islands—collectively known as the Golden Isles, for very good reason—boast exclusive resorts, The Cloister outdoes them all. Developed in the late 1920s, soon after causeways were built to connect the mainland to this flat, wind-swept spit of marsh and sand, the Cloister was always conceived of as a haven for the elite. The original hotel building, a stunning Addison Mizner structure in a jazzy Spanish-Moorish style, was replaced in 2006 by a new 175-room building that replicates the white stucco towers and red-tile roofs of

Sea Island.

the original. But that's just the centerpiece of this sprawling palm-shaded resort, a vast landscaped compound with three 18-hole golf courses, three curvaceous outdoor pools, 10 tennis courts, riding stables, a shooting range, a yacht club, a full-service spa, extensive children's programs, four restaurants, and a beach club presiding over a 5-mile-long (8km) strip of pristine sand. All rooms are exquisitely appointed, and the service is legendary; in 2009 four different components of the complex each won a Mobil Five-Star award. Book a meal at one of the restaurants (the Georgian is the resort's haute cuisine star), even if you're not staying here, to sample Cloister-style luxury.

With the renovation, The Cloister developed more options for prospective guests—you can also stay at the Cloister Beach Club, set near the pools and beach, or The Lodge at Sea Island Golf Club, a faux–English manor perched on the edge of the Plantation golf course. Around a third of the island's 600-some private homes—quaintly referred to as "cottages"—are also available for guests, with rental including access to all of the hotel's considerable amenities. Though The Cloister has a devoted clientele, many of whom return year after year, the increased number of rooms has given the Cloister a little more negotiability on room rates than it once had. Scout around, and you just may find a vacation at Sea Island more affordable than you think. *—HH*

(i) www.seaisland.com.

✈ Savannah, Jacksonville, Brunswick Glynco Jetport, or McKinnon Airport on St. Simon's Island (private jets only).

84-mile (135km) drive from Savannah or 18-mile (29km) drive from Brunswick.

$$$ **The Cloister,** 100 First St. (✆ **800/SEA-ISLAND** [732-4752] or 912/638-3611; www.cloister.com).

Priceless Places 212

Jekyll Island

Welcome to the Club

Georgia, U.S.

Back in the late 19th century, only folks like the Vanderbilts and the Rockefellers—*la crème de la crème*—got to visit Jekyll Island. From 1886 to 1942, it was the private domain of the exclusive **Jekyll Island Club,** a society of such wealth and privilege that at one time its members represented *one-sixth* of the world's wealth.

The rambling verandas and cream-colored stucco turrets of the Jekyll Island Club still stand—as the Jekyll Island Club resort—but nowadays the island is owned by the state of Georgia and open to all. In fact, Jekyll Island proudly refers to itself as a "public golf resort," because its three championship golf courses (plus the club's original 9-hole Great Dunes Course, a pitch-perfect imitation of a Scottish links) are available to anyone, not just resort guests, unlike on other coastal islands. (The three courses share a clubhouse at 322 Captain Wylly Dr.; ✆ **912/635-2368**). The same is true of the 13 superb clay courts at the **Jekyll Island Tennis Center,** 400 Captain Wylly Dr. (✆ **912/635-3154**). Once you've paid the $3 "parking fee" to cross the soaring causeway to the island, you're as good as a member.

Set off the mainland just south of St. Simons Island and Sea Island 211, Jekyll Island also has 10 miles (16km) of beautiful white-sand Atlantic beaches, including three public beaches. It's a typical Low Country landscape, full of gnarled oaks and towering palmettos and wetlands (nearly two-thirds of this little island is

Jekyll Island Club.

marshland), and a significant Audubon birding site on the Atlantic flyway (call ✆ 877-4JEKYLL [453-5955] or 912/635-3636 for details). The topography is flat, making it a great place to tour on secluded bicycle trails or on horseback gallops along the beach. And on a sweltering Georgia summer afternoon, what could be better than the waterpark **Summer Waves,** 210 S. Riverview Dr. (✆ **912/635-2074**).

Once you're here, of course, it's hard to resist gawking at the Gilded Age splendors that would have excluded you in another era. The Jekyll Island Club National Historic Landmark District covers 240 acres (97 hectares) of the island's western side, where you can visit several of the showplace shingled "cottages" those tycoons of yore erected. Guided tours depart hourly from the **Jekyll Island Museum** on Stable Road (✆ **912/635-4036**), including stops at the Rockefeller family's **Indian Mound Cottage** and the **du Bignon Cottage.** Other cottages have been converted to art museums, including the **Goodyear Cottage** (✆ **912/635-3920**) and **Mistletoe Cottage** (✆ **912/635-4092**). Or check out the two-story ruin of **Horton's Brewery,** founded on the northwest end of the island in 1742 by Georgia founding father General Oglethorpe. Its walls were built of colonial Georgia's most typical building material, tabby, made of—what else?—the crushed shells of Low Country oysters. *—HH*

ⓘ **Tourist office,** 901 Jekyll Island Causeway (✆ **912/635-3636**). **Jekyll Island Authority** (✆ **877/4JEKYLL** [453-5955]; www.jekyllisland.com).

✈ Savannah, Jacksonville, or Brunswick Glynco Jetport.

90-mile (145km) drive from Savannah, 65-mile (105km) drive from Jacksonville, or 21-mile (34km) drive from Brunswick.

$$ **Jekyll Island Club Hotel,** 371 Riverview Dr. (✆ **800/535-9547** or 912/635-2600; www.jekyllclub.com). $$ **Jekyll Oceanfront Resort,** 975 N. Beachview Dr. (✆ **800/736-1046** or 912/635-2531; www.jekyllinn.com).

213 Priceless Places

Newport

Money Talks

Rhode Island, U.S.

Driving around Newport, I can't help but gawp at the century-old mansions—Italianate *palazzi,* Tudor-style manors, faux French châteaux, all set in elegant formal landscaping, with imposing gates to keep out the hoi polloi (for example, you and me). It's incredible to imagine the sort of wealth that built these homes, even more incredible to realize that these were just these families' summer houses (offhandedly referred to as mere "cottages").

Poised at the southern promontory of Aquidneck Island, set coolly adrift in Narragansett Bay, Newport has a quirky, independent history. Founded in 1639, it was an early haven for religious freedom; it has the nation's oldest **Jewish synagogue** (85 Touro St.) and a **Quaker meetinghouse** founded in 1699 (Broadway and Marlborough sts.). But Newport was also at various times a pirate hide-out, the epicenter of the New England slave trade, and a major manufacturing spot for whale oil. The tony Newport we see took off only in the mid–19th century, when wealthy Southern planters began to build summer refuges on these breezy New England shores. Northern industrialists soon followed, and for several years the socialites vied to see who could build the grandest villas.

Many homes are still private property, but several are open to the public for guided tours. I'm partial to **The Breakers** (Ochre Point Ave.), a 70-room 1895 mansion designed for Commodore Vanderbilt by Richard Morris Hunt and patterned after Italian Renaissance *palazzi*. Hunt also designed the classically porticoed **Marble House** (596 Bellevue Ave.), modeled after Versailles' Petit Trianon. The French chateau look is carried on at **The Elms** (567 Bellevue), an imposing golden-stone mansion with wonderful gardens. Rounding out the Bellevue Avenue lineup, **Beechwood,** 580 Bellevue Ave. (✆ **401/846-3772**), was built for the famous Mrs. Astor, who personally maintained a list of who counted and who didn't in New York and Newport society.

In the Gilded Age spirit of one-upmanship, *New York Herald* publisher James Gordon Bennett, Jr., in 1880 hired McKim Mead & White to design a club to outdo the reigning Newport Reading Club. His upstart Newport Casino—a rambling shingle-style edifice with dark-green turrets and verandas—provided a grass court for a novelty sport called lawn tennis; as the sport's popularity skyrocketed, its national championship, first held here in 1881, eventually became the U.S. Open. The Horseshoe Court is still a working grass court (there's also a walled court for court tennis, the nearly extinct ancestor of lawn tennis), and the elegant wood-paneled club rooms now hold the **International Tennis Hall of Fame,** 194 Bellevue Ave. (✆ **800/457-1144** or 401/849-3990; www.tennisfame.org).

Though in the 1960s it became connected to the mainland by the soaring Newport Bridge, Newport still gives off a country-clubbish summertime vibe, with sailboats and yachts bobbing in the harbor, and a string of arts festivals including the notable Newport Folk Festival and the JVC Jazz Festival. In the end, I always wind up driving or cycling along the coastal loop of Ocean Road, where the wide-open skies, empty sweeps of marshland, and salty breezes remind me why the wealthy came here in the first place. *—HH*

ⓘ **Tourist office,** 23 America's Cup Ave. (✆ **800/326-6030** or 401/849-8048 www.gonewport.com).

✈ T.F. Green Airport, Providence (28 miles/45km).

🛏 $$$ **Hyatt Regency Newport,** 1 Goat Island (✆ **800/233-1234** or 401/851-1234; www.hyatt.com). $$ **Mill Street Inn,** 75 Mill St. (✆ **800/392-1316** or 401/849-9500; www.millstreetinn.com).

TOUR Preservation Society of Newport County, 424 Bellevue Ave. (✆ **401/847-1000;** www.newportmansions.org).

Priceless Places **214**

St. John

The Rockefeller Gift

U.S. Virgin Islands

Sleepy, laid-back, unspoiled St. John is the gem of the U.S. Virgin Islands, and intentionally so. The impetus originally came from Laurance Rockefeller, who bought up nearly half the island and in 1956 donated all the land to the United States; today two-thirds of the island and most of its offshore waters are protected as **Virgin Islands National Park** (✆ **340/776-6201;** www.nps.gov/viis). Tropical greenery, dense with orchids, vines, and more than 140 species of birds, has grown over what was once a series of Danish-owned sugar plantations; expect to stumble upon charming ruins along its roughly 20 miles (32km) of hiking trails (the **Annaberg Trail** is a prime place to explore). You'll come out suddenly upon panoramic views of turquoise waters so sparkling you'll catch your breath.

Too small to have its own airport (something I consider a good thing), St. John is an easy 20-minute ferry ride from St. Thomas. You'll arrive in its chief port and largest town, cruise ship–free **Cruz Bay,** a pastel-painted village so laid-back that the streets don't even need names. Though the island's resorts have some excellent high-end restaurants, eating in one of Cruz Bay's casual open-air restaurants is a much more authentic West Indian experience. The island's relative prosperity means that locals are invariably friendly and welcoming, with none of that uneasy haves/have-nots dynamic that can so easily sour an island paradise.

Those inviting turquoise waters inevitably make watersports some of the island's chief attractions. One of my first snorkeling experiences ever was at Trunk Bay, where the National Park Service has set up the 675-foot (206m) **Underwater Trail** along a reef where undersea features are labeled with signs 5 to 15 feet (1.5–4.5m) beneath the water's surface. For a novice like me, it was a fantastic way to learn various coral structures or the difference between a sea fan and an anemone. Bright parrotfish flit by, and if you're lucky you may even spot hawksbill or leatherback sea turtles. More adept snorkelers can head for remote places like **Waterlemon Cay, Salt Pond Bay,** or **Haulover Bay,** where the snorkeling is a lot more challenging. Scuba diving, windsurfing, kayaking, deep-sea fishing, and sailing are also popular; equipment rentals are available from suppliers in Cruz Bay, in the Trunk Bay park visitor center, or in the higher-end resorts.

The full spectrum of accommodations is available on the island, from top-class resorts like refined Caneel Bay down to some of the Caribbean's most comfortable and well-run campgrounds at Cinnamon

St. John.

Bay and Maho Bay, with several handy condos and charming bed-and-breakfasts in between. Reserve well in advance, however, for—by design—there's a limited stock of rooms. Once you're here, you'll be oh so glad of it. —*HH*

ⓘ **Tourist information,** near the Battery in Cruz Bay (✆ **340/776-6450**).

Cruz Bay, 20 min. from St. Thomas.

$$ **Cinnamon Bay Campground,** Cruz Bay (✆ **340/776-6330;** www.cinnamonbay.com). $$$ **Westin St. John Resort,** Great Cruz Bay (✆ **888/627-7206** or 340/693-8000; www.westinresortstjohn.com).

Priceless Places 215

Pantelleria

An Exotic Black Rock Between Continents

Italy

As a warm-weather destination, it is, at first blush, a peculiar choice: Pantelleria's black-lava coastline has zero sandy beaches (though the waters that surround it are calm and clean, and smooth volcanic rocks double as lounge chairs or diving boards) and little "scene" to speak of. Yet there's no denying the quiet chicness and subtle exoticism of Pantelleria, and for much of Italy's fashion set and intelligentsia, summering here, in a restored *dammuso,* is the epitome of the Mediterranean good life. Giorgio Armani was one of the first celebrities to buy property here, and he still comes back every year to Pantelleria, a place that, in many parts, looks like one of his magazine ads.

It may fly the flag of Italy, but Arab-inflected Pantelleria is cultural cross-pollination personified, one of those wonderful Mediterranean oddities that's just remote, small, and strange enough to have stayed under the radar of mass tourism. Situated just 48km (30 miles) from the continent of Africa between Sicily 331 and Tunisia, the island has been ruled by the Romans, the Arabs, the French, and the Turks over the centuries. Many villages of Pantelleria—Khamma, Rekhale, Bukkuram, Bugeber—still bear the names given them in the 9th century, when Arabs conquered this part of the Mediterranean and named the island Bent el Rhia (Daughter of the Wind). The island's architectural hallmark, the *dammuso,* are dry masonry buildings (with a special domed roof for capturing rain on an island where fresh water is scarce) dating back at least a millennium. All in all, the man-made structures of Pantelleria have much more in common with the Middle Eastern desert than anything in Rome or Florence.

As for what to do on Pantelleria, the first thing is to rent a moped. The island's rural 83 sq. km (32 sq. miles) are easily explored with two wheels and 125 cubic centimeters. While the coastal terrain is rocky and chiseled, it's gloriously green and fertile farther in, with loamy volcanic soil ripe for both prized capers and the Zibibbo grape, from which the island's famous *passito* dessert wine is made. A picturesque lake, the **Specchio di Venere** (Venus's Mirror) is inland Pantelleria's most popular attraction. Here, in waters given otherworldly shades of blue by the underlying volcanic sand, bathing in the purportedly therapeutic mud is a time-honored activity. On the southern part of the island, a lovely pine wood ends in a spectacular line of cliffs, known as **Salto la Vecchia** (the old jump), rising 300m (984 ft.) above the sea. Wine buffs shouldn't miss a visit to the vineyards where *passito* and *moscato* are made. I like **Donnafugata,** on the northern coast (✆ **39/0923/915649;** www.donnafugata.it).

After exploring Pantelleria from the land, take a boat tour around the island. Whether you rent your own small craft or hire a charter (both options are available at the village of Scauri), this is the best way to sample the island's alluring coves and bathing spots. Pantelleria's signature geological formation is called the **Arco dell'Elefante,** a natural arch of lava that resembles an elephant's trunk, dipping into the sea. Island tradition has it that in times of drought, the good-natured elephant would use this trunk to procure water for the islanders. —*SM*

ⓘ www.italiantourism.com.

✈ Pantelleria.

From Trapani, ferries (7 hr.) operated by **Siremar** (✆ **39/0923/545455;** www.siremar.it); hydrofoils (2½ hr.) operated by **Ustica Lines** (✆ **39/0923/22200;** www.usticalines.it).

$$$ **Il Monastero** (✆ **39/02/581861;** www.monasteropantelleria.com).

216 Colonial Outposts

St. Martin/St. Maarten

Two Nations on One Island

French St. Martin and Dutch St. Maarten share an island, an arrangement that's worked out nicely for more than 300 years. In fact, this little 96-sq.-km (37-sq.-mile) island is the world's smallest landmass shared by two sovereign states. Many colorful yarns have been spun about how the island was divvied up, but as with many places in the Caribbean that were fought over and traded and coin-tossed during the years of European colonization, the reality is probably too dull for legend. Today, if you're not paying attention, you won't even know you've crossed over from one side to the next—there's no sign or gate or Customs to announce it for you. It's that neighborly.

The differences are there, however. St. Maarten is much more Americanized, with comfortingly familiar fast-food restaurants and well-known hotel chains. English is spoken everywhere. As someone once said, St. Maarten is Caribbean 101 for those who prefer to ease into exotic locales. St. Maarten is more developed than St. Martin (some say *too* developed), and your first glimpse of the island (if you've arrived by plane) is a visual cacophony of casinos, high-rise hotels, and that irritating bugaboo of too much crammed into too small a space: traffic gridlock. **Philipsburg,** St. Maarten's capital, is the cruise ship capital of the Caribbean and a duty-free paradise for shoppers looking for deals on jewelry, watches, and electronics. Philipsburg itself is much improved with its new boardwalk, which faces the sandy beach and the sea and the ruins of **Fort Amsterdam,** a 1631 garrison that was the Dutch's first bastion of defense in the New World.

St. Martin is, on the other hand, determinedly French, from its French cafes and bistros to the quaint, innlike lodgings tucked up into hillsides that look out, French Riviera style, onto the sparkling Caribbean. People speak French (and English, *bien sur*), and the grocery stores sell French cheeses and wines and even French toiletries. St. Martin has in the little village of **Grand-Case** one of the top culinary towns in the region, with one restaurant after another perched beachside serving some of the best food on the island. The main town of **Marigot** has wonderful outdoor cafes around the waterfront and some serious shopping.

Of course, both sections of the island have beautiful beaches and wonderful spots to go swimming, snorkeling, sailing, or sunbathing. But perhaps my favorite spot on either island is another little island that lies in the French cul-de-sac just off Orient Beach, on St. Martin. It's a 10-minute boat ride to the **Ilet Pinel,** a tiny, uninhabited isle that allows visitors during the day. It has a perfect lagoon, fringed with coconut palms, set on a crescent of beach with mist-shrouded hills in the distance. Sink into the clear, warm waters, and listen: no jet skis, no motorboats, no worries. It's the Caribbean of your dreams. —*AF*

(i) www.st-maarten.com or www.st-martin.org.

✈ St. Maarten (Queen Juliana International Airport).

🛏 $$$ **Hotel L'Esplanade,** Grand-Case, St. Martin (✆ **866/596-8365** in the U.S.; www.lesplanade.com). $ **Mary's Boon Beach Plantation,** Simpson Bay, St. Maarten (✆ **599/545-7000;** www.marysboon.com).

Colonial Outposts

Montserrat

The Emerald Isle

Drinking green beer and tucking into corned beef and cabbage on St. Patrick's Day makes perfect sense if you're in Dublin, say, or Manhattan (411). But celebrating St. Paddy's on a Caribbean vacation? That's blarney. A tropical island with more than a little Irish in its bloodlines, Montserrat is the only spot in the Caribbean where St. Patrick's Day is a full-fledged public holiday. That's because in the 17th century the island became a refuge for Irish Catholics who were forced to leave other Caribbean countries under the British flag. The culture that developed on Montserrat was largely informed by the Irish colonists who made their home here. Today, however, that culture is shot through with the singular sizzle of the West Indies—from reggae to pepperpot soup to calypso. It makes for an intoxicating stew.

This British Overseas Territory is one of the Leeward Islands, and on a clear day the folks in Antigua (50) have a good view of the island's undulating terrain. Ireland's nickname, the Emerald Isle, easily applies here: Montserrat is lush and green, with emerald hills that rise seductively above the sea.

Most of the islands surrounding Montserrat are built on foundations of coral, accumulated slowly and methodically over time. Montserrat came into the world in a shudder of violence, when an undersea volcano split the sea bottom. In 1995, the Soufrière Hills volcano erupted, sending out a blinding ash cloud, raining lava onto the streets, and literally burying the island's 2-centuries-old capital town, Plymouth.

Two-thirds of the island's inhabitants were forced to flee, and Plymouth became a modern-day Pompeii, its buildings half-buried under volcanic debris and the town abandoned. The tourist industry was devastated (it had already been hard hit by Hurricane Hugo in 1989). Today Montserrat is still rebounding, which means that

Soufrière Hills volcano.

tourist facilities are not as developed as those of neighboring islands (the island has only one hotel but numerous guesthouses and villas), the pace is not nearly as frenetic, and the vibe is a lot more casual. All that makes this a lovely, laid-back, almost pastoral place to fully enjoy all that the Caribbean has to offer without the crowds and the big-ticket prices. You want beaches? Montserrat's are made of soft gray volcanic sand and lapped by luscious aquamarine seas. Crave some serious diving or snorkeling? Surrounding coral reefs provide prime opportunities to see exotic sponges and corals, reef fish, and hefty sea turtles. Plan an underwater outing with the **Green Monkey Inn & Dive Shop** (✆ **664/491-2960;** www.divemontserrat.com).

You can even do some volcano viewing. The **Soufrière Hills volcano** still sends out little spurts of steam; but it's set well away from civilization, and the island has several prime vantage points from which to watch the action. If you've got weather-mad kids, be sure to visit the new interpretation center at the **Montserrat Volcano Observatory** (✆ **664/491-5647;** www.mvo.com), which has actual volcanic artifacts on display.

When you're in Montserrat, be sure to try the national dish, goat water. It's a local version of traditional Irish stew. And just so you don't forget where the island's roots are firmly planted, the folks at Customs stamp passports with a nice green shamrock. May the roads rise up to meet you when you come! *—AF*

ⓘ www.visitmontserrat.com.

✈ Antigua.

⛴ The sailboat **Ondeck** (✆ **268/562-6696;** www.ondeckoceanracing.com) leaves from Antigua; 4 hr.

🛏 $ **Bunkum Beach Guest House** (✆ **664/491-5348;** www.bunkumbeachguesthouse.com). $$ **Tropical Mansion Suites** (✆ **664/491-8767;** www.tropicalmansion.com).

Colonial Outposts 218

St. Kitts

Sweet Stuff

Sugar cane is the engine that drove the world economy in the 18th century, and this little Caribbean island was a sugar-production workhorse for its British overseers for many decades. At one time there were 68 sugar plantations chugging along on this 28-hectare (69-acre) island—built, of course, on the backs of slaves who were imported here to do the heavy lifting.

Today, the now-independent two-island nation of St. Kitts and Nevis (28) has a rich sugar cane heritage that it has turned to its advantage. Many of the visitors who come to this island stay in captivating inns set in vintage plantation houses. The island has some 200 historic sites that date from the British settlement. The island's capital, **Basseterre,** is a living-history tableau of British colonial architecture; the town square, known as the **Circus,** was a favorite post-dinner promenade spot for plantation owners. At the square's center is the **Victorian Berkeley Memorial Clock.** And believe it or not, St. Kitts shut down its last sugar cane factory only in 2005. Fields of sugar cane still flourish next to crumbling stone windmills; some of that sweet stuff now goes into making rum—whether at the **St. Kitts Rum Company** or in moonshine stills—as well as the national drink, Cane Spirits Rothschild (CSR).

St. Kitts is twice the size of its sister island, Nevis, and has three times as many inhabitants, many of them descendants of the slaves brought to the island in the 18th century. But in comparison with other popular Caribbean islands, little St. Kitts is still at heart a sleepy tropical backwater—that's part of its charm. It's also one of the region's friendliest spots; Kittitians are known for their laid-back geniality. Tourism is fast becoming the island's number one industry, however: St. Kitts sees an increasing amount of cruise ship traffic into Basseterre harbor; it has one of only two ports in the Caribbean large enough to berth a ship the size of the *Queen Mary II.*

Like Nevis, St. Kitts has a surfeit of natural beauty: green volcanic hills rising from turquoise seas; lush vegetation and a profusion of colorful tropical blooms; and, of course, lovely beaches—some of the best for swimming and sunbathing are **Cockleshell Bay, Banana Bay, South Friar's Bay,** and **Frigate Bay.** Scuba diving and snorkeling are popular activities; **Pro Divers,** in Basseterre (✆ **869/466-DIVE** [466-3483]; www.prodiversstkitts.com), offers PADI diver training and fun dives. **Bluewater Safaris,** in Bassetere (✆ **869/466-4933;** www.bluewatersafaris.com), does day sails, snorkel trips, sunset cruises, and fishing trips in customized catamarans.

A good way to get around the island is by rental car or taxi. Taxi drivers double as guides and are happy to give you the lay of the land; just be sure to settle on a flat fee before you head out on a 2-hour tour with the meter ticking. But perhaps the most fun way to see St. Kitts is a 3-hour scenic tour on the **St. Kitts Scenic Railway** (Basseterre; ✆ **869/465-7263;** www.stkittsscenicrailway.com), where railroad cars wind around mountain slopes, cruise past secluded black-sand beaches, and time-travel through fields of sugar cane, back 300 years to the days when sugar was king. —*AF*

(i) www.stkittstourism.kn.

✈ Robert L. Bradshaw International Airport.

🛏 $$$ **Ottley's Plantation Inn** (✆ **800/772-3039** in the U.S. or 869/465-7234; www.ottleys.com). $$$ **Rawlins Plantation Inn** (✆ **800/346-5358** in the U.S. or 869/465-6221; www.rawlinsplantation.com).

219 Colonial Outposts

Paquetá

Colonial Brazil

Brazil

Join the boatloads of *cariocas* (cityfolk) who live and work in Rio de Janeiro for a relaxing day trip to Paquetá. You won't hear car horns blaring on this 1-sq.-km (⅓-sq.-mile) island—cars are not allowed—but you will get a taste of 19th-century Brazil. Paquetá has changed little from its days as a pleasant retreat for the Portuguese aristocracy. The streets are filled not with the exhaust of car engines but the melodious clip-clop of horse-drawn carriages and parades of cyclists. Charming **colonial buildings** and **historic homes** are framed in cascades of bougainvillea. The island, once a plantation breadbasket for Rio, is lush with royal palm and coconut trees, breadfruit and mango groves, and the African tree baobab, an import known here as Maria Gorda (Fat Mary).

Paquetá is one of 130 islands in Guanabara Bay in the Brazilian state of Rio de Janeiro. The lovely beaches are the main draw—the island has 11 small stretches of sand. Although you may see locals swimming in the bay, you might want to reconsider joining them. Industrialization has polluted the waters, not only making swimming risky but also effectively ending a fishing trade that thrived for centuries. Still, sunbathing remains a popular activity, and the views of the bay and surrounding mountains are worth the trip alone.

In the early 19th century, the king of Portugal (and then Brazil), **Dom João VI,** had a summer home on Paquetá. He and his family had been exiled to Rio in 1807 in the wake of France's invasion of Portugal. In an odd twist, his own sons would help lead the rebellion in Brazil that won the country's independence from Portugal in 1825; his eldest son, Pedro, became Brazil's first emperor.

The quietest and nicest times to visit Paquetá are from April to November, which is winter in Brazil. Weekends are the busiest times on the island, when families fill the ferries that leave from Rio's Praca XV; both 80-minute ferries and fast ferries (hydrofoils) make daily runs to and from the island. Cars are not allowed on the island, so you get around on foot, by renting a bike at one of the many suppliers on the island, or by hiring a horse and buggy for an old-fashioned tour. Paquetá's big event is **St. Peter's Festivity,** honoring the patron saint of fishermen; St. Peter's remains a major celebration despite the decimation of the fishing industry. —*AF*

ⓘ www.ilhadepaqueta.com.br/paqueta.htm.

✈ Rio de Janeiro.

Barcas S/A (✆ **800/704-4113** [Brazil]; regular ferry [1 hr.], 55/21/2533-7524; fast ferry, 55/21/2533-4343; www.barcas-sa.com.br).

$$ **Hotel Farol** (✆ **55/21/3397-0402;** www.hotelfaroldepaqueta.com.br). $$ **Hotel Lido** (✆ **55/21/3397-0182;** www.hotellido.portalpaqueta.com.br).

Colonial Outposts 220

Gorée Island

House of Slaves

Senegal

Tourism has its darker, more contemplative sides. There's grief tourism, where people make pilgrimages to scenes of unimaginable tragedy. War tourism encompasses a range of destinations, from battlefields to concentration camps. Here on Gorée Island another sort of pilgrimage is played out daily, when travelers come to honor the millions of West Africans who were forced into slavery hundreds of years ago.

Now a World Heritage Site, Ile de Gorée lies just 3.2km (2 miles) from the west coast of Dakar, the capital of Senegal. It's the country's top tourist destination, and its playful charm is drawn from the saucy mix of Senegalese and French colonial cultures. It's a tiny, picturesque place with sun-dappled palms and fading colonial architecture. For many Senegalese, it's a tranquil respite from the urban jungle of Dakar.

But Gorée Island is best known for its place in history: as a port of call for the slave trade during its heyday in the 18th century, when 10 to 15 million African slaves were shipped out of West Africa to the Americas. The island's most famous historic attraction is the **Maison des Esclaves (House of Slaves),** the first thing you see when you ferry in to the island harbor. This reconstructed late-18th-century structure is billed as a holding place where slaves were imprisoned before their journey overseas. It has a fortresslike exterior; you cross through a "Door of No Return" to an interior with twin stone stairs, thick walls, forbidding basement cells, and an aura of gloom.

It turns out, however, that Gorée's role in the Atlantic slave trade may be much less significant than earlier believed, and the story behind the "House of Slaves" may be nothing but a fanciful tale. Historian Philip Curtin contends that the island was too small and too inconveniently located to have played a major role in the slave trade, exporting no more than 200 to 300 slaves a year in important years and none at all in others. This is in contrast to nearby Saint-Louis 221, where the lucrative business of slave trading was conducted briskly, with some 10,000 slaves processed annually. Scholars also debate whether the House of Slaves—actually a wealthy traders' home—was ever a holding cell for slaves in transit. No matter: Some 200,000 people visit Gorée and the House of Slaves every year, including heads of state (George Bush, Pope John Paul II, Bill Clinton) and dignitaries from around the globe. Its importance as a pilgrimage site for the descendants of slaves and as a symbol of the brutal slave trade remains undiminished.

First settled in 1444 by the Portuguese (whose explorers conceived of the slave trade), Gorée was later held by the Dutch and the British before the French—who had settled on nearby Saint-Louis—wrested control in the late 1600s. The island would remain under French control for nearly 300 years until Senegal achieved independence in 1960.

Connected to the mainland by a 20-minute ferry, Gorée Island is an easy day trip destination from Dakar. Pick up a self-guided walking-tour map from the dockside Syndicat d'Initiative (see below) and stroll the narrow streets of gaily painted brick houses with wooden shutters and roofs of red clay tile. It's quiet and peaceful—the island has no cars or trucks—a fitting memorial to a tumultuous time. —*AF*

ⓘ **Syndicat d'Initiative** (✆ **221/823-91-77**).

✈ Dakar.

⛴ Dakar (20 min., pedestrian only).

🛏 $ **Hostellerie du Chevalier de Boufflers** (✆ **221/822-53-64**).

221 Colonial Outposts

Saint-Louis

French Kiss

Senegal

Saint-Louis is one of those exotic and quixotic places that can seem a tangle of contradictions. This French colonial city is set down on the sandblasted plains of the West African sub-Sahara. Here, bougainvillea spills over pastel walls with peeling French lettering; goats scratch in the dirt for food. Colorful houses with wrought-iron balconies seem plucked straight out of New Orleans's French Quarter; other architectural relics crumble with decay. Under palm trees and feathery ferns, vendors sell fruit from wooden carts; a block away you can buy pastries at a storefront patisserie. Locally caught prawns and crawfish are served in an elegant sauté of butter and pastis.

Saint-Louis's faded grandeur belies its heritage as one of the most important and powerful cities in West Africa, the first French settlement in Africa and a vital trading center, through which flowed gold from Ngalam, gum arabic from the Sahelian steppes, and ivory from the Sudan. It was the center of French culture in Africa, but it was also a major crossroads for slave traffic. It's believed that as many as 10,000 slaves a year passed through the island in the 18th century, many of them routed from the African interior to the Americas.

Founded by French colonists in 1659, the island was baptized Saint-Louis-du-Fort to honor the French king Louis XIV. By the late 1700s, the city was inhabited by 10,000 people. Intermarriages between French traders and freed slaves produced a class of Creoles known as the Métis. The Métis women, known as *signares,* were famously beautiful and famously industrious. Saint-Louis was named the capital of Senegal in 1872, but its decline began soon after; Dakar replaced it as capital in 1958. Today this remarkable collection of original colonial architecture has been granted UNESCO World Heritage Site status.

The geography of the island is just as remarkable as its history. Saint-Louis is ringed by the Senegal River, but the Atlantic Ocean is only a narrow spit of land away. Little more than a dune bordered on either side by tawny beaches, the **Langue de Barbarie**—some 25km (16 miles) long—is all that separates the river Senegal and the roaring Atlantic. As a result, Saint-Louis is very much a seafaring and fishing center. (The city itself sprawls beyond the island, where its center lies, to the mainland.) This proximity to so much water also means that this low-lying area—including the old city—is under serious threat from rising sea levels.

The island lies in the Sahel, a desert zone that separates the dry Sahara from the wet savanna. In the dry season, the island is swept by sandstorms; in the wet season, tidal pools become fertile feeding grounds for flamingos and other birds (in fact, the world's third-largest ornithological park, the **National Park of the Birds of Djoudj,** lies 60km/37 miles north of Saint-Louis). When the pools dry up, the salt that remains is raked and sold at market.

You reach the city of Saint-Louis from mainland Senegal by walking or driving over the **Pont Faidherbe,** a 19th-century cast-iron bridge said to have been built to drape over the Danube but shipped here instead. The best way to see the town and such historic buildings as the **Cathedral**—a handsome 1828 neoclassical building that was the first church in West Africa—is on foot. You can pick up a walking-tour map of the town at the Initiative Syndicate of Saint-Louis (see below). —*AF*

ⓘ **Syndicat d'Initiative Office de Tourisme de Saint-Louis BP,** 364 Saint-Louis du Sénégal (✆ **221/339-61-24-55;** www.saintlouisdusenegal.com).

✈ Dakar.

5-hr. drive from Dakar.

$ **Hotel de la Residence** (✆ **221/339-61-12-60;** www.hoteldelaresidence.com). **Hotel du Palais** (✆ **221/339-61-17-72;** www.hoteldupalais.net).

Colonial Outposts **222**

Lamu

Exotic Enclave

Kenya

If it's your first time traveling to Africa, do the obvious: Go on a safari. And if, after you've seen the lions, rhinos, and elephants, the special history and culture of the continent gets under your skin, consider a different, nonzoological type of African destination the next time around. For many, mostly European habitués, that destination is the island of Lamu. Just 2 degrees south of the Equator, off the east coast of Kenya, Lamu is a place that seems stuck in time. For centuries, it was a bustling Indian Ocean port of call and an important link in the spice trade, and that atmosphere is totally palpable here today. Lamu is like an exotic stage set that also happens to have amazing beaches.

The streets of Lamu are quiet, cool, and car-free, lined with thick-walled white stone buildings, their arches and decorative cutouts evoking the centuries of Muslim influence here: Lamu was founded by Arab traders in the 1400s. Virtually every house has a roofed veranda on the top floor. The entire island has one proper town—the busy **Lamu Town,** which, as the oldest and best-preserved Swahili settlement in East Africa, is a UNESCO World Heritage Site. Monuments here include the turreted **Lamu Fort** and **Riyadha Mosque** (both from the 19th c.), but the most interesting sights are the much more ancient, nameless traditional houses, some of which date back to Lamu Town's 14th-century foundations. Elsewhere on the island, there are a handful of lesser villages; one of the most well known for visitors is **Shela.** Here, guesthouses line gorgeous golden sandy beaches where traditional dhows and brightly colored fishing boats with names like *Beyonce* loll in the surf. Dolphins swim in the waters offshore, and you'll probably meet a few when you're out for a dip. There isn't a single automobile on the island; instead, you're shuttled around by boat, donkey, or scooter when you aren't using your own two feet.

There may be donkey droppings in the streets and Swahili spoken in the markets, but Lamu tourism is an exclusive affair. Some of the most famous families in the world have holiday property here, and for all the island's African authenticity, the cuisine on Lamu is surprisingly inflected by haute-European culinary trends. With its beautiful, simple architecture (most is Swahili, from the 19th c.), gorgeous people (a mix of African and Arab ethnicities), and rich heritage, relaxing Lamu is a magnet for well-heeled travelers looking for something with more cultural cache than the been-there, done-that south of France.

What makes Lamu so attractive—that it's completely exotic and romantic, without the blight of extreme poverty that plagues so much of Africa—is also what makes vacationing here a surreal and perhaps even guilt-ridden experience. Going for drinks at the friendly and fabulous colonial-style **Peponi Hotel** (where everybody meets at some point while on Lamu), you might well rub elbows with princes (or Prince himself), and revel in the absurdity of finding such glamour here, a place whose economy hinged for centuries on the slave trade, while just across the water is an entire continent struggling to meet basic human needs.

Getting to Lamu involves flying first to Nairobi, and from Nairobi, catching a small plane to Manda Island. (For a lot more money, you can also fly to Lamu itself, where there's an airstrip served by small charter planes from Nairobi.) Because Lamu isn't easy to reach, and because its rhythms take some time to get to know, it's the kind of place you should plan to visit for at least a week. —*SM*

(i) www.magicalkenya.com.

Lamu airport (all international flights connect through Nairobi).

25-min ride from Manda Island.

$$$ **Peponi Hotel,** P.O. Box 24 (✆ **254/020/8023655;** www.peponi-lamu.com).

A mosque on Lamu.

Civilization Unplugged

223

Isla Contadora

The Pearl of Panama

The Pearl Islands, Panama

For some U.S. audiences, the name "Pearl Islands" conjures one image: that of CBS reality show *Survivor,* which was shot here in 2003. Although development is still minimal in this archipelago sprinkled throughout the gulf of Panama, it's also a place where comfortable hotels and tourist services have grown up amid the jungle vines, and where you can have a slightly less tribal experience than what the contestants of Season 7 had to deal with. The "resort island" of Contadora has the most amenities of the 200-plus Pearl Islands, though it's by no means luxurious or sophisticated. Anyone seeking a truly cushy getaway would do well to seek out another Central American destination. The advent of the resort business has not diminished the local spirit of Isla Contadora, and it's still the Pearl Islands' top destination for an authentic Panamanian experience.

Contadora's principal attractions are its beaches, a dozen public stretches of sand where sunbathers laze and snorkelers strap on gear to explore the offshore reefs. High tide and low tide can vary by up to 5m (16 ft.) of water depth off Contadora, so the snorkeling is decidedly better during low tide. Close to the beaches of **Playa Larga** and **Playa Sueca** (the only nude beach in Panama), you can often spot sea turtles and sharks—some startlingly large, up to 4m (13 ft.) long. A number of species wiggling in the reef here are venomous, so before you set out, it's essential to familiarize yourself with anything that could be harmful.

Besides its sand and sea, Contadora has a palm-treed **golf course** where you can play under the steamy Panamanian sun. Beyond that, don't expect too much culture here: Contadora has no ruins or historical sites, and bugs are omnipresent. But its people are warm and welcoming, and it's a great place to unplug from civilization for a few days or a week. As you wander around the island, which can be traversed on foot in about an hour, you'll pass the ritzy vacation homes of wealthy Panamanians who come here to escape their daily rigors. And, of course, if you're inclined to relive a slice of *Survivor: Pearl Islands,* you can always grow out your hair and invent an "immunity challenge" for your traveling companions. Contadora has plenty of rustic landscapes that look the part.

On the flight into Contadora from Panama City (which is how most foreign visitors arrive), be sure to get a window seat: The flight takes you right over the Panama Canal, where you can get a fascinating aerial view of ships negotiating the passage and the elegant mechanics of the canal locks. You'll also get a sweeping panorama of the hundreds of other, as yet uninhabited, Islas de las Perlas. —*SM*

ⓘ www.visitpanama.com or www.thinkpanama.com.

✈ Contadora airport (20-min. flight from Panama City).

🛏 $$ **Punta Galeon** (✆ **888/790-5264** in the U.S. or 507/250-4220; www.puntagaleonhotel.com).

224 Civilization Unplugged

Andaman Islands

Escape from the Modern World

India

For a vacation that blends tropical relaxation and edifying colonial history all at a very affordable price, the Andaman Islands in the Indian Ocean's Bay of Bengal are a very attractive spot. They also have the added cachet of being a far-flung, authentic destination where Western-style tourism has yet to arrive.

The Andaman Islands—around 550 in the archipelago, of which 26 are inhabited—are historically and politically part of India, though ethnically, they do not belong to the subcontinent. Until recently, the population consisted of mostly aboriginals. Geographically, the islands are much closer to Thailand and Myanmar than to India, with a similar landscape of long, sandy beaches backed by dense rows of palm trees, mangroves, and, in the interior, lush rainforests exploding with tropical flora and fauna.

The city of **Port Blair** is the Andamans' capital, located on the 1,536-sq.-km (593-sq.-mile) **Middle Andaman Island.** Though the historic urban core of Port Blair is busy and dirty, there are plenty of worthwhile tourist attractions within a short drive or boat ride. Just 9km (5⅔ miles) from the city, **Corbyn's Cove** is a classic palm-fringed beach ideal for swimming and sunning in the balmy waters of the Bay of Bengal. The best nature trail in the vicinity is on **Mount Harriet,** where you can trek for 5km (3 miles) among lush tropical vegetation, butterflies, and birds. Offshore, divers and snorkelers will find one of the richest coral ecosystems in the world, where a vast array of tropical fish swim along the colorful reefs. A bit farther out, the waters teem with sharks, including hammerheads, nurse sharks, and leopard sharks. Sport-fishing excursions allow tourists to try their hand at reeling in a big-game prize like tuna or marlin.

Though most vacationers prefer to spend their time on the beaches and wildlife areas of the island, Port Blair city offers several historical sights that should not be missed, including the infamous **Cellular Jail,** where British authorities imprisoned and executed freedom fighters during the Indian struggle for independence, when the Andamans were used as a penal colony. A steamer cruise along the harbor is one of the best ways to take in the panorama of the old port town.

Port Blair is often visited in conjunction with **Havelock Island** (57km/35 miles away by ferry), a smaller island where ecotourism is being heavily promoted. Havelock's "Beach No. 7," also known as **Radhanagar Beach,** is one of Asia's most stunning. Another island that's a short hop from Port Blair is **Ross Island,** which was the British headquarters in the Andaman Islands prior to Indian independence. The island is now a wildlife lover's dream, with wooded nature walks and resident species of exotic birds. **Chidiya Tapu** (31 km/19 miles from Port Blair), also known as "Bird Island," is covered in mangroves and has a lovely west-facing beach with spectacular sunsets.

Part of the Andamans' appeal is how untouched by modern life they remain. Western tourists do not come to the Andaman Islands in large numbers, so expect that some facilities may be a bit more primitive than those found in more developed parts of the world. —*SM*

ⓘ www.andamanisland.com.

✈ Port Blair airport (via domestic Indian airlines from mainland cities Chennai and Kolkata).

🛏 $$ **Megapode Nest,** Haddo, Port Blair. $$$ **Sinclairs Hotel Bayview,** South Point, Port Blair (✆ **91/3192/227824;** www.sinclairshotels.com).

TOUR Andaman Holidays (✆ **91/3192/234924;** www.andamanholidays.com).

Civilization Unplugged

225

Koh Tonsay

Sandy Retreat from Culture

Cambodia

For a well-rounded Cambodian holiday, first go the temples at Angkor Wat, then tour the city of Phnom Penh, and then kiss the cultural overload goodbye with some deserved beach time on the country's southern coast. The tiny, practically deserted island of Koh Tonsay, just south of the resort town of Kep, is Cambodia's best-kept secret for seaside relaxation among the natural splendor of the Gulf of Siam.

Koh Tonsay, which means "Rabbit Island" in Khmer, though the etymology is disputed, is most commonly visited as a day trip from Kep, but if you're looking for a real back-to-basics getaway, consider spending several days here. The island covers barely 2 sq. km (¾ sq. miles) and remains blessedly primitive. There are no cars or motorbikes on Koh Tonsay, and a generator provides electricity from 6 to 9pm only. The only residents of the island are seven families who make their living from fishing and coconut farming. So why come here? For the beaches. Koh Tonsay's two main stretches of white sand are absolutely pristine and usually empty, and the shallow, calm waters are a shade of turquoise that makes for some glorious, I'm-in-paradise swimming. All in all, this couldn't be farther from the overwhelming sense of cultural obligation at Angkor Wat.

If you do decide to extend that day trip from Kep, bamboo huts on stilts near the beach are the only overnight option on Koh Tonsay. Your shower and toilet might be outside on the sand, but the units are a bargain at about $7 per night. In the evening, don't miss a chance to go swimming in the bioluminescent waters off the island, where plankton emit glowing phosphorous, creating a twinkle on the water that perfectly reflects the millions of stars in the unpolluted sky overhead. Simple restaurants on the island are run by local fishermen and their families, who literally pluck your seafood out of the water minutes after you order.

Kep, the base for travel to Koh Tonsay, is notable in its own right for its history as a retreat for wealthy French-Cambodians in the 1920s—though many of the Art Deco villas there still bear the scars of Khmer Rouge destruction, it's a charming base for exploring southern Cambodia. The 20-minute longboat hop from Kep to Koh Tonsay covers only 5km (3 miles), but once you reach those coconut-lined island shores, you're a world away from civilization, eastern or otherwise. Enjoy it while you can, because some southeast Asian travel mavens warn that it's only a matter of time before Koh Tonsay becomes another overdeveloped resort like Thailand's Phuket. —*SM*

ⓘ www.thaigov.go.th or www.tat.org.

✈ Phnom Penh (148 km/92 miles), then bus (4 hr.) and private boat.

🛏 $ **Bamboo Huts,** Koh Tonsay (no phone or website; inquire in Kep). $$ **Champey Inn,** 25 av. de la Plage, Kep (✆ **855/12/501-742**).

226 One of a Kind

The South Island

The Kiwi Playground

New Zealand

Cloven in half by narrow Queen Charlotte Sound, New Zealand has something of a split personality. Though the South Island is larger by far than the North Island 318, it only has one-fourth of North's population—which gives it a lot more room for natural beauty and invigorating sports adventures. On successive days you can surf off a golden-sand beach, sail up a misty fiord, and ski down the face of a glacier; and you can backpack through green misty wilderness for days, then sip sauvignon blanc at posh wineries.

Most visitors fly into **Christchurch,** known for its formal gardens and graceful Victorian architecture. If you're an oenophile, however, take the ferry from Wellington right into the quaint waterfront village of **Picton,** a handy jumping-off point for the Marlborough wine region, where more than a hundred wineries produce easily half of New Zealand's wine output, and the top-end half at that. Contact **Marlborough Wine Tours** (✆ **64/3/578-9515;** www.marlboroughwinetours.co.nz) to arrange a tour. North of wine country, one of the jewels in the national park system, **Abel Tasman National Park,** hugs a dramatic stretch of balmy coast, a great place for sea kayaking and hiking. **Abel Tasman Wilson's Experiences** (✆ **64/3/528-2027;** www.abeltasman.co.nz) can arrange journeys there.

Fly into **Queenstown,** in the island's midsection, if you have a yen for adrenaline sports—bungee jumping, hang gliding, sky diving, rock climbing, hot-air ballooning, white-water rafting, the whole shebang. Skiers flock here from around the world in winter, that is, June through September, when the northern hemisphere's snows have disappeared (check out www.nzski.com for the skiing lowdown). Unfortunately, the word is out about **Milford Sound,** that stunning narrow 22km-long (14-mile) fiord off the Tasman Sea that's now jampacked with daylong bus tours from Queenstown. Base yourself instead in the charming lakeside resort of **Te Anau,** where your drive to Milford Sound is a dramatic 2-hour adventure through the primeval landscape that director Peter Jackson captured in *Lord of the Rings*—vertiginous waterfalls, pristine lakes, virgin forest, and steep peaks surrounding deep-gouged fiords. Vast **Fiordlands National Park** has several breathtaking long-distance hiking trails: the Milford, the Hollyford, the Kepler, and the Routeburn tracks. The classic 53km (33-mile) Milford Track walk takes 4 days, but **Trips 'n' Tramps** (✆ **64/3/249-7081;** www.milfordtourswalks.co.nz) offers guided 1-day samples.

The entire west coast, in fact, seems like one huge parkland. North of the Fiordlands, the Franz Josef and Fox glaciers in

Fiordlands National Park.

Westland National Park, State Hwy. 6 (✆ **64/3/751-0807;** www.glaciercountry.co.nz), plunge spectacularly to the sea, and make this a superb place for guided walks and heli-hikes. Inland, New Zealand's highest mountain, snowcapped **Mount Cook,** is a magnet for skiers and mountaineers (Sir Edmund Hillary trained here before climbing Mount Everest). Try a half-day hike on the Hooker Valley trail in **Mount Cook/Aoraki National Park** (✆ **64/3/435-1186;** www.doc.govt.nz): You'll cross two swinging bridges over gorges, pass two pristine lakes and alpine meadows full of wildflowers, cross a boardwalk over boggy tussocks, and wind up right at the frosty face of a glacier. That's South Island in a nutshell for you. *—HH*

ⓘ www.purenz.com.

✈ Christchurch or Queenstown.

🛏 $$ **Glencoe Lodge,** Terrace Rd., Mount Cook Village (✆ **64/3/435-1809;** www.mount-cook.com). $$ **Milford Sound Lodge,** Hwy. 94, Te Anau (✆ **64/3/249-8071;** www.milfordlodge.com).

TOUR Canterbury Trails (✆ **64/3/337-1185;** www.canterburytrails.co.nz). **Real Journeys** (✆ **64/3/249-7416;** www.realjourneys.co.nz).

227 One of a Kind

Taiwan

Unexpected Splendors Beyond Taipei

Let's face it: Taiwan doesn't generally leap out as a vacation destination. Chances are your notion of Taiwan (which is technically part of China) is that of a densely urban island, its streets clogged with traffic and garish neon lights, leading to a sprawl of semiconductor factories. Well, there's that, but there's also the other 95% of Taiwan, which holds some eye-popping surprises for visitors.

Dubbed Ilha Formosa ("the beautiful island") by Portuguese sailors in the 16th century, Taiwan is striking and steep, with hills and mountains accounting for two-thirds of its area. Those dramatic landscapes are traversed by scenic highways that can be traveled with your own car, or for far less hassle, by coach bus (ask for a *kuokuang* ticket when booking, as this will ensure a more comfortable ride and timely schedule). By far the most popular natural attraction is **Taroko Gorge,** an out-of-this-world mix of marble and red-rock canyons, crystalline water, and lush vegetation.

Trains are a romantic way to get around, since the country has many original 19th-century depots. Taiwan's premier train experience is the **Alishan Forest Line,** a narrow-gauge alpine railway that chugs to the top of Alishan National Scenic Area with spectacular vistas of the sunrise, the sunset, or the sea-of-clouds phenomenon hanging over the dense trees below. Taiwan Railway Administration offers special tourist trains that include accommodations; you'll ride in fancy salon and dining cars, where guests can even sing karaoke.

The ancient city of **Tainan** is Taiwan's cultural capital, with hundreds of temples and almost constant festivals. Within easy day trip distance of Taipei, mountainous **Wulai** has stunning waterfalls and breathtaking panoramas from its cable car. For the Taiwanese version of a gold rush town, visit the old mining town of **Chiufen,** whose traditional architecture and teahouses feel like a time warp. Hot springs are abundant in the geological hot spot of Taiwan, and you'll find no shortage of hotel-resorts where you can soak in the therapeutic waters: Two of my favorite areas are **Chihpen** and **Taian. Kenting National Park** at the southern tip of Taiwan and the **Penghu archipelago** (to the west) are Taiwan's no-brainer choices for beaches and watersports. Parts of the island were hard hit by Typhoon Morakot in 2009 and, at press time, several villages in southern Taiwan were still recovering from the devastating floods and landslides.

The throbbing capital of **Taipei** may not inspire love at first sight, but there's still good reason to give this dynamic metropolis some of your time. The food, for one, is irresistible, whether at proper restaurants or (even better) at roadside vendors, from dumplings to crab cakes to seafood stews. Without a doubt, the cultural trove of Taipei is the **National Palace Museum** (✆ **886/2/2881-2021;** www.npm.gov.tw), where in 1949 the Kuomintang installed the 10th-century treasures from Beijing's Forbidden City. The collections here—600,000 artifacts, estimated to be 10% of China's artistic wealth—are so vast that only 1% are on display at a time. Another highlight in the capital is the ascent to the top of **Taipei 101 Tower** (✆ **886/2/8101-8899;** www.taipei-101.com.tw), currently the tallest skyscraper in the world (though another contender in Dubai will surpass it in late 2009). Taipei 101's segmented shape recalls telescoping pagodas, or a bamboo stalk, or stacked Chinese takeout boxes of glass and steel. —*SM*

ⓘ www.go2taiwan.net.

✈ Taiwan Taoyuan International Airport, Taipei.

🛏 $$$ **Landis Taipei,** 41 Min Chuan E. Rd., Section 2, Taipei (✆ **886/2/2597-1234;** http://taipei.landishotelsresorts.com).

One of a Kind 228

Ischia

The Green Island

Italy

Capri 257 may have the fame and notoriety, but beautiful Ischia is bigger, less crowded, and more reasonably priced than its swanky neighbor to the southeast. Pronounced *Ish*-kee-ah, this rocky volcanic island is 10km (6¼ miles) long and 7km (4⅓ miles) wide. Its long and sometimes turbulent history owes much to a strategic location in the Gulf of Naples along the Amalfi Coast as well as the presence of healing thermal springs, which have drawn visitors for centuries. Over the years, Ischia has been ruled by the Greeks, the Romans, the Byzantines, barbarians, and various pirates and privateers.

Ischia is known as the "Emerald Island" for its moss-backed volcanic curves, hillside vineyards, and groves of scented pines. Flowers bloom spectacularly in the rich volcanic soil. Whereas Capri is jet set (Jackie O bought her first set of capri pants here), Ischia is laid-back and bucolic. It was not really a tourist destination until the 1950s, when folks escaping the hordes on Capri were casting about for another beautiful island to conquer. Even now, with tourism the main industry, the island is not nearly as crowded as Capri in the height of summer.

Some people like to hit Capri, just 30km (19 miles) away, for a couple of days and then settle in on Ischia for the rest of the week. Many Western Europeans come to Ischia specifically for its health spas, the centerpiece of which are the hot springs and volcanic mud warmed by volcanic gases rising up from deep below the island's long-dormant volcano, **Monte Epomeo,** which last erupted in the 14th century.

The island also has lovely sandy beaches, including a few where seawater and hot springs commingle for a double-tonic effect. Most of the activity is concentrated in Ischia Porto, around the main harbor (porto means harbor), and Ischia Ponte (ponte means bridge), by the bridge to the island promontory that flanks a small natural harbor. The promontory was the site of the original settlement, fortified by a castle erected as far back as the 5th century B.C. The castle, **Piazzale Aragonese,** Ischia Ponte (✆ **39/081/992834;** www.castellodischia.it) you see today was built by the Aragonese over the ruins of the earlier fortifications. You can climb up for panoramic views of the stunning coastal landscape, with glittering blue seas guarded by rugged volcanic cliffs.

The public bus system **SEPSA** (✆ **39/081/991808** or 39/081/991828) is very reliable and a good way to see the sights. Or you can do like the locals do and rent a scooter and zoom around on the curving roadways. Either way, Ischia provides a way to experience *la bella vita,* island-style, without the crowds and the high price tags. —*AF*

ⓘ **AACST tourist office of Ischia,** Corso Vittoria Colonna 116 (✆ **39/081/5074231;** www.infoischiaprocida.it).

✈ Naples.

Medmar (✆ 39/081/5513352; www.medmargroup.it) runs ferries from Napoli to Ischia Porto and from Pozzuoli to both Ischia Porto and Casamicciola. **Caremar** (✆ **39/081/0171998** from abroad, or 892123 from anywhere in Italy; www.caremar.it) runs ferries to Ischia Porto and Casamicciola from Pozzuoli, Procida, and Naples.

$$ **Albergo Il Monastero** (✆ **39/081/992436;** www.albergoilmonastero.it). $$$ **Hotel Regina Isabella** (✆ **39/081/994332;** www.reginaisabella.it).

229 One of a Kind

Naxos

Substantial in the Cyclades

Greece

Santorini 238 and its spectacular crater apart, the Cyclades islands aren't generally known for their intrinsic natural beauty. There are other attractions—whether nightlife, archaeology, or beaches—that draw visitors to this mostly scrubby Greek archipelago set amid the wine-dark seas of the central Aegean. But green and fertile, hilly Naxos is the exception. It's the largest island in the Cyclades—about three times the size of nearby Mykonos 245—and still a place where tourism hasn't ruined the local flavor.

From the moment you land at the ferry port below Naxos town (also known as Chora), it's clear that this isn't just another vacationer-swamped Greek island. The development here far predates tourism, and though visitors will certainly find warm Greek hospitality, the island doesn't depend on summer traffic for its livelihood. Naxos is self-sufficient—agricultural income from olives and fruit pays most of the bills—and you really get the sense that the rhythms of life here are for and by the locals. To get into the swing of things on this island, it's recommended that you stay at least a few days.

Naxos has been continuously inhabited for about 6,000 years, and there are remarkable vestiges of its long and storied past just about everywhere. Architecturally, the island is perhaps best known for its **Venetian castles and towers** dotting the landscape. These were built from the 13th to the 16th century, when Venice's maritime republic ruled the island. In those days, the wealthy lived in a walled citadel above Chora town called the **Kastro.** Today, this area is Naxos's main tourist

A church facade on Naxos.

attraction, where visitors can wander among evocative arched alleyways and gaze up at the impressive residences of the powerful Venetian families who lived here 800 years ago. One of the palaces has been converted into the excellent **Domus Venetian Museum** (✆ **30/22850/22-387**), with exhibits and tours that bring the bygone aristocratic era to life. Earlier art-historical treasures on Naxos include many **Byzantine chapels,** which have fine frescoes from the 9th to 13th century. In the island's interior, don't miss a trip to the upcountry village of **Apiranthos,** with its handsome architecture, laid-back pace, and shady *plateas* (squares) filled with men playing backgammon.

Of course, who plans a trip to the Greek islands without at least some sunbathing on the agenda? Fortunately, Naxos also has some of the Cyclades' best beaches, like **Agios Prokopios, Plaka,** and **Agios Georgios,** whose long strip of golden sand comes as a shock after you've seen what passes for a "beach" on most Greek islands. The water offshore is a blissful turquoise, and the seafront is lined with atmospheric tavernas where you can break up the sunning and swimming with some fresh grilled seafood, or a hand-picked salad of local veggies, and a glass of crisp white wine.

Naxos's central location in the Cyclades, a new airport, and frequent ferry connections from north and south make it very easy to incorporate into any Greek islands itinerary. Accommodations tend to be small, independent affairs with quirks (there are no real resort hotels here), so don't come expecting five-star luxury and amenities. —*SM*

ⓘ www.gnto.gr.

✈ Naxos (served by domestic flights from Athens on Olympic Airways).

From Piraeus, daily ferry (6 hr.) and high-speed ferry (4 hr.); www.gnto.gr.

$$ **Hotel Glaros,** Agios Georgios (✆ **30/22850/23-101;** www.hotelglaros.com).

One of a Kind **230**

Dominican Republic

Colorful Caribbean Tapestry

Thanks to a profusion of affordable vacation packages, the sugary beaches of the Dominican Republic have lately emerged as one of the most popular Caribbean destinations for sun-seeking North Americans and Brits. Most make a beeline to the so-called "Coconut Coast," the eastern tip of the island, which is home to the well-known resort of **Punta Cana.** But the D.R., which shares the island of Hispaniola with Haiti 400, to the west, is more than just the all-inclusive hotels of Punta Cana. The Dominican Republic is a lively amalgam of cultures, with a rich history that runs from Taino Indians to Christopher Columbus to Major League baseball.

In travel circles, the name Punta Cana has become shorthand for "inexpensive warm-weather getaway." With nonstop flights from much of the U.S. to Santo Domingo lasting only a few hours, it's even conceivable to go for a long weekend from North America. Miles of brilliant white-sand beach lined with leaning palms and a festive assortment of watersports, beach bars, and boutiques make Punta Cana a great place to unplug and still enjoy lots of amenities. It would be a shame, however, to limit yourself to the resort bubble while so many sights, and the real pulse of the D.R., lie so close by.

A baseball game in the Dominican Republic.

On arrival in or departure from the D.R., be sure to carve out at least a few hours to tour old **Santo Domingo.** The colors and vibrant spirit here are infectious, and the crumbling colonial architecture is wonderfully evocative of the capital's history as a crossroads for all—French, Spanish, Africans—who fought for control of Hispaniola. Columbus landed here on his famous voyage in 1492, and the **cathedral** of Santo Domingo houses a funerary monument that may indeed be Columbus's final resting place (though this is disputed by Seville, Spain, which claims to have the explorer's bones).

Not far from the resorts of the Coconut Coast, the cultural pride and joy of the Dominican Republic is, curiously enough, a replica of a Mediterranean village, called **Altos de Chavon** (www.altosdechavon.com). Complete with Renaissance plazas, churches, and shops that look like something out of the Italian or Spanish countryside, Altos de Chavon is de rigueur as a day trip. The village also hosts a music festival, with open-air concerts taking place in its Greek-style amphitheater.

For die-hard sports fans, of course, a mention of the Dominican Republic calls to mind baseball greats. *Beisbol* is a way of life here, and as a result, the D.R. has been a reliable producer of Major League star players over the decades, from Manny Mota to Manny Ramirez and David Ortiz. One of the most fun ways a visitor and sports enthusiast can get into the local passion for baseball is to catch a game in the sugar-factory town of **La Romana** (near Punta Cana). Here, at Michelin Baseball Stadium, the home team is called the *Azucareros* ("Sugar Bowls"), a nod to the Dominican Republic's deep roots as a sugar cane plantation island. —*SM*

(i) www.godominicanrepublic.com.

✈ Santo Domingo, connections from North, Central, and South America.

🛏 $$$ **Hotel Santo Domingo,** av. Independencia (✆ **800/877-3643** in the U.S., or 809/221-1511; www.hotelsantodomingo.com.do). $$ **Iberostar Bavaro,** Punta Cana (www.iberostar.com).

Island Hopping the Shetland Islands: The Furthest Isles

"Breathtaking" doesn't begin to describe them. The Shetland Islands simply stun visitors with their unconventional beauty—stark, wind-swept, and treeless, with ruffled bogs, wildflower-spangled heath, and jaw-dropping sea cliffs. Shaggy native ponies graze the moors, seals and sea otters slither around rocky coves, and a full 10% of all of Britain's seabirds nest here in midsummer, when the sun barely sets (Shetlanders call it "the Simmer Dim"). Three oceans—the Atlantic, the Arctic, and the North Sea—collide around this string of 100 islands, only 17 of them inhabited. Lying at Scotland's northern extremity, they are so ragged in shape, so deeply indented, they have a combined 4,860km (3,020 miles) of coastline. Wherever you stand on the Shetland Islands, you're never farther than 5km (3 miles) from the sea.

Though the ancient Romans called them Ultima Thule—"the furthest isle"—the Shetlands aren't nearly as remote as they used to be, since the oil industry has come to town. North Sea oil has been a mixed blessing, bringing economic prosperity and up-to-date facilities but also introducing a flood of short-term residents with little connection to local customs. And Shetlanders fiercely prize their heritage, which is more Viking than Celtic—the Vikings ruled here from A.D. 800 until 1469, when the islands became a Scottish possession, often ruled harshly by its feudal lords. Shetlanders still resist identifying themselves as Scots.

By far the largest island is southernmost 231 **Mainland,** where the capital, **Lerwick,** sits halfway down the eastern coast. An old smuggler's haven, later the center of Northern Europe's herring trade, Lerwick has long been surprisingly cosmopolitan. The **Shetland Museum** (on the waterfront at Hay's dock) is packed with artifacts and exhibits explicating Shetland's unique culture and history. Drive north of Lerwick and you'll enter a landscape that must have reminded early Norse settlers of the fjord lands (check out the tiny village of **Voe,** with its little wooden houses). At the narrow isthmus of Mavis Grind, you can throw a rock to the right into the North Sea and another to the left into the Atlantic Ocean. Head west to **Esha Ness** to hike along the west coast's spectacular jagged cliffs. South of Lerwick, check out the **Crofthouse Museum** in Boddam, set in an old thatched croft house that demonstrates traditional Shetland rural life. Farther south, near Sumburgh airport, **Jarlshof** is an amazing archaeological museum where excavations have uncovered relics of seven distinct civilizations, from the Bronze Age up to a 15th-century manor house and an entire Viking village.

Puttering around Mainland is fun, but the true Shetland spirit lives on outlying islands—for example, 232 **Papa Stour,** off the west coast of Mainland (catch the ferry in West Burrafirth). Sparsely populated Papa Stour (the name is Old Norse for "island of priests") was the site of a 6th-century Celtic monastery, but Viking chieftains prized its strategically sheltered harbor—the Norse lords didn't surrender this island until the 1600s. An ancient stone circle sits above the beach at Housa Voe, and an excavated Norse house at Da Biggins. Legend has it that the wildflowers grow so profusely on the heathy uplands of Papa Stour, fishermen could use the scent to guide them in from many miles out to sea.

Even farther west lies far-flung 233 **Foula,** a tiny island only 5km (3 miles) wide by 8km (5 miles) long, one of the world's most extraordinary birding sites. Its towering sea cliffs are home to about 3,000 pairs of the world's great skuas, known in the local dialect as "bonxie," among many other rare species. With a population of only 400, there are more sheep than humans on Foula; until the early 1800s, Old Norse was the main language spoken. The once-a-week mail boat to Foula takes 2½ hours, but in summer you can also fly here, making it a doable day trip from Mainland.

A 20-minute ferry ride from the town of Toft on Mainland, peaceful 234 **Yell** is the second-largest island in the Shetlands, but the peat lies so thick on its soil that farming is a challenge. Only about 1,000 people live here, mostly on traditional croft farms hugging the coast. Take a bracing coastal hike, and don't forget to look down at the water's edge, where hundreds of otters burrow in the peaty shoreline. As you drive north, stop off in **Burravoe** at The Old Haa Visitor Centre, a museum of local crafts and history set in a merchants' house dating to 1672. From Yell, the outermost Shetland island, 235 **Unst** is a 5-minute ferry ride from Gutcher. Unst is loaded with historical sites—a short drive east from the ferry landing at Belmont, there's **Muness Castle,** a fine rubble-cast tower house built for Scottish lord Laurence Bruce in 1598; on the southwest coast at Underhoull there's an excavated 9th-century Old Norse longhouse; nearby Lund offers the ruins of a medieval church. On the northern tip of Unst, the **Hermaness Bird Reserve** is one of Britain's most important ornithological refuges, its 182m-high (600-ft.) cliffs loaded with kittiwakes, razorbills, guillemots, and the inevitable puffins. On your way back south, stop off at **Baltasound** and mail your friends a postcard from the northernmost post office in the British Isles—oh, that'll make them jealous. *—HH*

(i) Tourist office, Market Cross, Lerwick, Mainland (✆ **44/1595/693-434;** www.visitshetland.com).

✈ Sumburgh Airport, Mainland, 1 hr. from Aberdeen via **Flybe** (✆ **44/871/700-2000;** www.flybe.com). Tingwall airport near Lerwick flies to Fair Isle, Foula, Papa Stour, and Out Skerries via **Directflight** airways (✆ **44/1234/757-766;** www.directflight.co.uk).

Overnight car ferry from Aberdeen to Lerwick, 14 hr., via **NorthLink** (✆ **44/845/600-0449;** www.northlinkferries.co.uk). Interisland ferries from Mainland to Yell, Unst, Whalsay, Fetlar, Bressay, Papa Stour, Out Skerries, and Fair Isle: **Shetland Islands Council** (✆ **44/1595/743-970;** www.shetland.gov.uk/ferries).

$$ **Baltasound Hotel,** Baltasound, Unst (✆ **44/1957/711-334;** www.baltasound-hotel.shetland.co.uk). $$$ **Grand Hotel,** 149 Commercial St., Lerwick, Mainland (✆ **44/1595/692-826;** www.kgqhotels.co.uk).

Natural Wonders 236

Tasmania

Classy Tassie

Australia

Like the dot under an exclamation point, Tasmania punctuates the Australian continent. Island isolation gave Australia a menagerie of unique species, but Tasmania kicks it up another notch. While Australia's climate is mostly tropical, Tasmania lies in the temperate zone, which puts an entirely different spin on its ecosystem. Tasmania's got wallabies, bandicoots, wombats, and opossums, but it's got *different* wallabies, bandicoots, wombats, and opossums. It's also a land of unique tree frogs and parrots, a place of such ecological rarity that its wilderness (some 20% of the island) has won World Heritage status.

Named after Abel Tasman, the Dutch explorer who first mapped this part of the world in the 17th century, Tasmania wasn't really settled until the early 19th century, when the English government needed a far-flung spot to stash convicts; the sobering remains of a famously harsh penal colony have been preserved on the southeast coast at **Port Arthur.** Take a 2-hour drive on the state-of-the-art **Heritage Highway** the convicts built between the island's capital, **Hobart,** and the next largest city, inland **Launceston;** you'll be continually tempted to stop by the splendid assortment of Georgian and Victorian architecture en route.

In order to properly appreciate Tasmania, however, you have to get into the wilderness. Visitors are often surprised by Tasmania's size—it's the 26th-largest island in the world—yet its dense rainforests, mountain peaks, alpine meadows, great lakes, eucalyptus stands, and fertile farmland are all easily accessible. Nearly a third of the island is protected within 14 national parks; only a couple hours' drive from Hobart, you'll find yourself in a rugged terrain of incredible beauty.

Cradle Mountain.

Running through it like a spine is the 85km (53-mile) **Overland Track** (www.overlandtrack.com.au), the best-known hiking trail in all of Australia. At one end the trail is anchored by **Cradle Mountain,** a spectacular jagged gray ridge face with four craggy peaks; at the other lies the long narrow glacier-carved **Lake St. Clair,** Australia's deepest freshwater lake. The trek between them traverses high alpine plateaus, marshy plains of rare button grass, springy heathland, fragrant eucalypt forest, dusky woods of myrtle beech (one of the few Australian native trees that isn't an evergreen), and one of the planet's last temperate rainforests. The path is well marked and improved, including stretches of boardwalk and a series of public sleeping huts. Tour companies run 5-to-10-day guided treks along its length; plenty of shorter hikes are available as well.

Along the way, you'll run into quolls, red-bellied pademelons (the kangaroo's Tasmanian cousins), and hordes of other scampering marsupials. As for the Tasmanian devil—well, despite their cartoon image, there's nothing cuddly about those stocky, sharp-snouted little black scavengers. But Tasmanians are perversely fond of these ornery little mascots; they rallied to protect them when news came out of a rare facial cancer ravaging the species. Perhaps that's because Tasmanian devils are part of what sets Tasmania apart from the rest of Australia, a wondrous land unto itself. —*HH*

(i) **Tourist office,** 20 Davey St., Hobart (✆ **61/3/6230 8233;** www.hobarttravelcentre.com.au); also www.discovertasmania.com.au.

✈ Hobart.

⛴ Devonport (10 hr. from Melbourne).

🛏 $$$ **Cradle Mountain Lodge,** Cradle Mountain Park (✆ **61/2/8296 8010;** www.cradlemountainlodge.com.au). $$ **Macquarie Manor,** 172 Macquarie St., Hobart (✆ **61/3/6224 4999;** www.macmanor.com.au).

TOUR Tasmanian Expeditions (✆ **1300/666 856** in Australia, or 61/3/6339 3999; www.tas-ex.com).

Natural Wonders

Langkawi

Colorful Legends & Ancient Nature

Malaysia

Its undulating terrain, studded by the "rival" mountains of Gunung Macinchang and Gunung Raya, is covered in a blanket of lush rainforest. Where it meets the warm waters of the Andaman Sea, the squiggly coast of Langkawi is fringed with long stretches of soft sandy beach, coconut palms, and casuarina trees. But what sets Langkawi apart from other tropical paradises is its heart: Centuries-old folklore permeates the local culture, and just steps away from the five-star waterfront resorts and golf courses there are still real Malaysian villages where life happily drawls along at a slow pace.

Langkawi is the largest and most inhabited of the Langkawi archipelago, a group of 99 islands off the northwestern coast of peninsular Malaysia. Its name is said to mean "island of the reddish-brown eagle" in Malay, and though there are other legends surrounding the etymology of Langkawi, the eagle one has a passionate following, and a huge 12m tall (39 ft.) statue of an eagle greets arrivals at Dataran Lang (Eagle Square) in the main port of

Kuah. (***Folklore alert:*** Kuah ["gravy"] gets its name because gravy was spilled during a fight that broke out during a wedding between the two families of the mountain's Gunung Macinchang and Gunung Raya.) Kuah is the only real town on the island, while the rest of Langkawi consists of *kampungs* (villages), rice fields where buffalo wallow, and flourishing tropical flora.

With an impressive array of natural attractions, Langkawi has been designated a UNESCO World Geopark. The island was part of the primordial landmass of Gondwanaland, and many of the forests and mineral deposits here are more than 500 million years old. A ride on the **Langkawi Cable Car** up to the peak of 710m (2,329-ft.) **Gunung Macinchang** provides breathtaking views over the canopy of a Cambrian rainforest. Throughout the island, more than a dozen intriguing **caves** exhibit elaborate limestone stalactites and stalagmites. Among the island's several waterfalls, **Telaga Tujuh** in the northwest corner of Langkawi is the most visited. Its name means "seven wells" for the seven pools of water that are created by the cascade, which flows gently and picturesquely over smooth rock framed by verdant vegetation.

Of course, beaches are the initial draw for most who book a trip here. For gorgeous sand and the best action, tourists and locals alike congregate at **Pantai Cenang.** Sunbathe or swim along 2km (1¼ miles) of palm-backed beach, and then grab your sari and hit the food stalls, markets, and bars of this lively strip. **Tanjung Rhu** is Langkawi's "Casuarina Beach" and notable for the striking black rock formation standing in the calm, clear, chalky-blue water just offshore. Secluded **Teluk Datai** is where the island's most exclusive and expensive resorts have been developed, and its relative isolation makes it most suitable for romance or anyone seeking a real escape. From any of these beaches, you can arrange watersports and excursions, like island-hopping snorkeling trips or kayaking out in the archipelago.

Though Langkawi has always had many attractions to lure vacationers, tourism didn't really begin to take off until the past decade. As locals will tell you, this is no coincidence. The most prominent story in Langkawi folklore is that of Mahsuri, a beautiful young maiden who was wrongly accused of adultery. When, as the Islamic tradition dictated, she was put to death by stabbing, white blood ran from her wounds, thus proving her innocence. As she gasped her last breaths, Mahsuri cursed Langkawi to have seven generations of bad luck. Mahsuri died in 1819, and only now—after seven generations—has Langkawi begun to see prosperity. *—SM*

ⓘ **Langkawi Tourist Information Centre** (✆ **60/4/966-7789;** www.langkawigeopark.com.my).

✈ Langkawi International, connections to Kuala Lumpur, Penang, and Singapore.

🛏 $$$ **Casa del Mar,** Jalan Pantai Cenang, Mukim Kedawang (✆ **60/4/955-2388;** www.casadelmar-langkawi.com).

Natural Wonders **238**

Santorini

Island of Epics

Greece

It's the poster child of Greek Island tourism, with whitewashed towns precariously balanced atop the red rim of an ancient volcanic crater that towers over the cobalt waters of the Aegean. The romantic image of Santorini (known as *Thira* to Greeks) has single-handedly sold countless vacations to Greece. Once a volcanic cone, Thira blew its top sometime around 1600 B.C., and everything but the outline of the crater fell into the sea. This episode gave rise to the myth of the lost city of Atlantis, the existence of which archaeologists have been able to neither prove nor refute. But whether it was the legendary Atlantis or not, no other island—in Greece or anywhere else—possesses quite the same brand of epic natural splendor as Santorini.

When you arrive by ferry at the larger port of **Athinios** or the smaller **Skala,** the full drama of Santorini's spectacular topography comes into focus: The island is steeper and taller than you'd imagined, and you have to crane your neck to see the towns perched on top. Another reality of visiting Santorini—one that's downplayed in the marketing brochures—reveals itself when you disembark at the dock; that is, you're not the only one who made the journey here. Especially in summer, expect to share the 13-sq.-km (5-sq.-mile) island with thousands of tourists, honeymooners, and cruise passengers.

The island's principal town, **Fira,** has a prime location on the edge of the caldera, looking west over the wine-dark sea and the island's densest concentration of hotels, restaurants, and accompanying mass-tourism junk. The aerielike hamlet of **Oia,** on the highest part of the crater rim, is romance central and where you'll find those impossibly gorgeous vistas—blue church dome in foreground, glittering sea beyond—captured in so many photographs of Santorini. As sublime as the views are from these two towns, the key to experiencing Santorini's authenticity is to spend time away from Fira and Oia once you've had your sunset cocktails and snapped your photos—or to time your strolls through the villages for the early morning or early evening, avoiding the day-tripper crush. Or just come in the off season (Sept–May).

Sunning and swimming in the Aegean are valid pursuits here, though you have to head down from the caldera rim and its hypnotic views, of course, to reach the water. Santorini's beaches are concentrated on the southern and eastern coasts of the island (not on the inner curve of the crater, but along its slightly less impressive outer edge). Most shorelines consist of black or red sand, which absorb the sun and get brutally hot and crowded in summer—another good reason to schedule your trip for months other than July and August. Ancient-history buffs shouldn't miss Santorini's two small but fascinating archaeological sites, **Akrotiri** and ancient **Thira.** The former is a mesmerizing time capsule of life during the height of Minoan civilization, just before the catastrophic eruption of 1600 B.C. wiped it out. You can also take boat tours across Santorini's "lagoon" to another speck of the caldera, the island of **Thirassia.** On the way, you'll pass the smoldering **Nea Kameni,** which emerged from the sea only 300 years ago as a sober reminder of Thira's violent natural history. —*SM*

(i) www.santorini.net.

Santorini (Thira) Island International Airport (served by Aegean Airlines and Olympic Airways via Athens).

Blue Star Ferries (www.bluestarferries.com) and **Hellenic Seaways** (www.hellenicseaways.gr) from Athens-Piraeus, other islands in the Cyclades, and Crete.

$$$ **Astra Apartments,** Imerovigli (✆ **30/22860/23641;** www.astra-apartments.com).

Natural Wonders 239

Lampedusa

Italian Traditions in an African Landscape

Italy

Named for the *lampa* (light) that guided sailors safely around its perimeter, Lampedusa hovers in a sort of Mediterranean limbo south of Sicily 331 and northeast of Africa. Here, in a desertlike landscape where agave, prickly pear, and golden-white limestone bake in the sun, you'll find one of the most exotic places you can travel to and technically still be in the European Union. And because it's not easy to access from mainland Italy, Lampedusa is one of the few surviving Italian islands with a real sense of local culture, undiluted by mass tourism.

Lampedusa has never been terribly fashionable, and it probably never will be. You won't find glamorous resorts or nightlife (though the breezy luxury at Il Gattopardo di Lampedusa hotel, carved out of traditional stone structures called *dammusi,* will impress the style-conscious). Yet there's something oddly appealing about this scrubby, sometimes derelict island that makes first-time visitors want to become regulars season after season. The island has no historical sights—a nice change of pace for those who feel overwhelmed by the wealth of heritage on display everywhere else in Italy. Even the buildings in town, most of which were built in the 1950s and 1960s, lack architectural character—although the main drag, **Via Roma,** is lined with elegant bars and bakeries that could have been plucked out of Rome or Florence. Here you can cool down with an espresso *granita,* sugar up with a fresh *cannolo,* and toast the simplicity of life on this working Italian island.

The time-honored traditions of Italian community life are alive and well on Lampedusa, and more authentic here than in other more obvious Italian seaside destinations like Capri 257 or Portofino. In the evening, everyone comes together for a collective *passeggiata* (stroll). Cleaned up from a day's work, fishermen hold their children's hands while teenage boys on *motorini* show off for the opposite sex. The film *Respiro,* which was shot entirely on Lampedusa, perfectly captures this daily rite and the rhythms, sights, and sounds of Lampedusa in general.

For beach lovers, Lampedusa has a real treasure. On the south side of the island, about 5km (3 miles) west of town, is one of the most beautiful beaches in Italy, called **Isola dei Conigli,** which refers to the "Island of Rabbits" just offshore. The beach itself is on the Lampedusa side, and is a crescent of sand with waters as close to Caribbean turquoise as you'll find in the Mediterranean. The bay is so shallow and calm that even kids can wade the 50m (164 ft.) from the mainland to Isola dei Conigli. In summer, *caretta caretta* sea turtles lay their eggs here, at which time naturalists close off part of the beach. —*SM*

ⓘ www.italiantourism.com.

✈ Lampedusa airport (flights from Palermo).

⛴ From Palermo, 9 hr.

🛏 $$$ **Il Gattopardo di Lampedusa,** Cala Creta (✆ **39/011/8185270;** www.gattopardodilampedusa.it).

240 Natural Wonders

Aero Island

Fairy-Tale Island

Denmark

There are places that work hard to create magic. Then there are those real-life spots that feel truly touched by fairy dust. Aero Island is one such place. It's a small island in the Danish Baltic Sea, 30km (19 miles) long and 8km (5 miles) wide, lined with villages with cobblestone streets and 17th-century cottages, medieval churches, farms built on patchwork hills, and quiet, idyllic beaches. It's a warm, happy place, not least because Aero gets more sunshine than any other spot in Denmark—summers may be short, but the sun doesn't go down until 11pm.

Some 7,000 people live on Aero Island, where locked doors are a rarity. There are no bridges to the island; the only way to get here is to take a 1-hour car ferry. Biking is a favored mode of transportation. But for all its old-fashioned charm, Aero is a 21st-century pioneer at the vanguard of sustainable energy. The island has the world's largest solar power plants and the world's largest solar collector system for heating. Its goal is to be 100% self-sufficient in renewable energy, and it's almost there. In 2008, Aero achieved 80% self-sufficiency in electric and heating usage. It's a remarkable achievement for such a small, off-the-beaten-track place.

You have to really want to get to Aero Island—it's not an easy place to access. Once you're there, you can get around by bike, car, or bus (Fynbus; www.fynbus.dk), which links the villages including the island's largest town and main port, **Marstal.** Of the island's 14 communities, little **Aeroskobing** looks like something straight out of Hans Christian Andersen, a Lilliputian jewel box of remarkably preserved half-timbered cottages hugging neat, one-lane streets—you almost expect to see dolls in 17th-century garb emerging from the gabled facades. But people live and work in these structures, many in thoroughly modern interiors set behind storybook exteriors.

The countryside is no less magical. The rural landscape is one of wheat fields and dairy farms punctuated by the occasional old windmill. Three massive modern windmills were added in 2002; today they are responsible for providing 50% of the island with its electricity. —*AF*

(i) www.aeroeisland.com. Aeroskobing Turistbureau, Vestergade 1 (✆ **45/62/52-13-00**).

✈ Copenhagen.

🚆 Copenhagen, Odense, or Svendborg.

⛴ Svendborg: Aerofaergerne A/S (✆ **45/62/52-40-00;** www.aeroe-ferry.dk).

🛏 $$ **Hotel Aeroehus,** Aeroskobing (✆ **45/62/52-10-03;** www.aeroehus.dk). $$ **Pension Vestergade on Aero,** Aeroskobing (✆ **45/62/52-22-98;** www.vestergade44.com).

Natural Wonders 241

Bimini

Hemingway Fished Here

The Bahamas

Ernest Hemingway put Bimini on the map when he came here to fish and write (but mostly fish) in the 1930s. In fact, it was a 230kg marlin caught off the waters of Bimini that inspired Papa Hemingway to write *The Old Man and the Sea*. When he wasn't fishing and he wasn't writing, Papa was hanging out at the Compleat Angler bar, built—appropriately enough—out of abandoned liquor boats.

With a prime position in the Gulf Stream, whose warm waters favor big game fish like marlin, Bimini is considered by many to be the sport-fishing capital of the world. Despite the tourism industry that's grown up around Bimini's extraordinary fishing, the islands—there are actually two, North and South Bimini—have retained a certain tropical rumrunner mystique. It may have something to do with Bimini's roguish beginnings. Settled in the 1920s by freed slaves from Nassau, the island prospered as a rumrunning port during Prohibition in the United States. (Unfortunately, the same strategic location that favored Bimini during Prohibition has made it a popular station in the drug trade between South America and the U.S.)

Fishing in Bimini.

The most developed part of Bimini is the north island, which measures 12km (7½ miles) long and, in places, just 200m (656 ft.) wide. Here, in crowded **Alice Town,** the trappings of tourism are inescapable. But it's also in Alice Town where you find Bimini's nightlife. Sadly, one of the town's most famous structures, the historic Compleat Angler hotel and bar, which was filled with Papa Hemingway memorabilia, burned to the ground in 2006. **South Bimini** and its main town of **Port Royale** are quieter and more laid-back, with family-friendly condos. The two islands are connected by an easy, 2-minute ferry ride.

Whether you're an avid fisher or a beach bum, Bimini has plenty to offer the watersports enthusiast. The island has a wealth of scuba- and snorkel-friendly **dive spots,** from half-submerged shipwrecks like the **SS *Sapona,*** which ran aground during a 1926 hurricane, to the mysterious Bimini Road. This intriguing "pavement" of flagstones, lining the sea floor under 5 to 10m (16–33 ft.) of water off the north end of North Bimini, looks uncannily man-made, though there are also convincing geological explanations for its neat rectangular layout.

For the simple pleasures of sun and sand, the beach that runs along much of the western side of North Bimini is lovely—and all yours midweek in winter. Contrary to other Bahamas destinations, Bimini's high season is the summer. Even though the weather and sea conditions from December to March are ideal for a relaxing vacation, calmer waters mean better fishing. And few sportsmen would want to miss the chance to go on a **fishing charter** here. Charters can be easily arranged from any of the marinas on North or South Bimini, or from south Florida, just 81km (50 miles) to the west.

Ponce de León came to South Bimini in the 16th century in search of the **Fountain of Youth,** and though historians say he never found it, the mere fact that he even sought the miraculous waters here has spawned a tourist attraction. Less far-fetched is a saltwater pool called the **Healing Hole,** whose lithium- and sulfur-rich waters are said to have curative properties. Not surprisingly, local guides are happy to profit from tours to the places associated with these myths. —*SM*

(i) www.bahamas.com.

✈ Bimini North Seaplane Base and South Bimini Airport (served by charter and scheduled flights from Ft. Lauderdale, Florida, and Nassau).

🛏 $$ **Bimini Big Game Resort & Yacht Club,** King's Hwy. (✆ **800/737-1007** in the U.S., or 242/347-3391; www.biminibiggame.com). $$$ **Bimini Sands Condominiums,** South Bimini (✆ **242/347-3500;** www.biminisands.com).

242 Natural Wonders

The Big Island

Feel the Mana

Hawaii, U.S.

They don't call it the Big Island for nothing: The largest island in the Hawaiian chain, Hawaii is big in many other ways as well. It has the world's tallest mountain, **Mauna Kea,** and the world's largest, **Mauna Loa.** It has not one but several natural microclimates, from misty rainforest around **Hilo** on the east coast to rolling upcountry hills to blasted lava-rock shelves on the northwest **Kohala Coast.** Endemic island species abound, from tropical *ohia* and *koa* trees to rare lobelias, from elusive little honey-catchers to majestic Hawaiian hawks. Yet for all its outsize attributes, it's the least populated island in the chain, a place where you can get away from the crowds and really relax into island life. The Big Island's economy isn't dominated by tourism either, thanks to cattle ranching and farming; some of the world's best coffee and macadamia nut crops thrive along the Kona Coast.

With not one but five volcanoes brooding over the island, it's easy to sense that connection to essential life forces that native Hawaiians call *mana.* To see Kilauea's red-hot lava still bubbling through the earth's crust, take a helicopter ride over **Hawaii Volcanoes National Park** (Hawaii Belt Rd. [Hwy. 11]; ✆ **808/985-6000;** www.nps.gov/havo); you can also drive the park's Crater Rim Road to really experience the sulfuric smells and hot steam of this turbulent landscape. On snowcapped Mauna Kea you'll feel you can almost touch the sky, 13,255 ft. (4,040m) above sea level, at one of the world's great astronomical observatories. Take an excursion to the summit to view its

Hawaii Volcanoes National Park.

13 powerful infrared telescopes, and then join nighttime **stargazing sessions** at the visitor center, halfway up Summit Road, off Hwy. 200 (✆ **808/961-2180;** www.ifa.hawaii.edu/info/vis).

The northwest Kohala coast is still encased in hardened black lava flow, where—paradoxically, perhaps—the island's cushiest resorts have been cultivated in oases of manicured greenery. Many of these coastal enclaves were originally the estates of Hawaiian kings; check out the vestiges of the royal preserves at the **Mauna Lani resort** (68-1400 Mauna Mani Dr., off Hwy. 19; ✆ **808/885-6622**), including a set of ingenious fishponds and, alongside the Fairmont Orchid golf course, the Pacific's largest rock-art site, the spectacular **Puako Petroglyphs** (Holoholokai Beach Park, N. Kaniku Dr.; ✆ **808/885-1064**).

While the resorts provide plenty of top-class golf and tennis, watersports are the Big Island's ace in the hole—including fantastic diving and kayaking in the calm east-side waters and big game fishing off the west coast. If eating local is your passion, you've chosen the right island, too. On the southwest **Kona Coast,** some 600 small **coffee plantations** line 32km (20 miles) of the Mamalahoa Highway, many of which welcome drop-in visitors (check out www.bigisland.org for a list). Mid-island, around Waimea, prime beef cattle graze on impossibly green slopes; several stables offer horseback riding around those sprawling ranches. **Merriman's,** perhaps the island's best restaurant (65-1227 Opelo Rd. [Hwy. 19], Waimea; ✆ **808/885-6822;** www.merrimanshawaii.com), showcases local produce and meats in its creative Hawaiian regional cuisine. *—HH*

ⓘ **Big Island Visitors Bureau** (✆ **808/961-5797** or 808/886-1655; www.bigisland.org).

✈ Kona (west coast) or Hilo (east coast).

🛏 $$$ **The Fairmont Orchid,** 1 N. Kaniku Dr. (✆ **866/540-4474** or 808/885-2000; www.fairmont.com/orchid). $ **Volcano House,** inside Hawaii Volcanoes National Park (✆ **808/967-7321;** www.volcanohousehotel.com).

6 Pleasure Islands

Party Animals 243

Koh Pha Ngan

Full Moon Frenzy

Thailand

Before booking your trip to this beach-party isle in the Gulf of Thailand, consult the lunar calendar. Just how wild your stay on Koh Pha Ngan will be depends on whether you time your visit to coincide with the infamous Full Moon Party. Then again, with other lunar-ruled bashes like the Half-Moon Festival and Black Moon Party going on the rest of the month, the chance to get loose and let it all hang out under the tropical night sky is never more than a week away.

Traveler-revelers in the know go to Koh Pha Ngan for one reason only: the **Full Moon Party** (http://fullmoonparty-thailand.com) at crescent-shaped Haad Rin beach. Each month, these enormous beach extravaganzas draw upwards of 25,000 people from all over the globe for 1 night of pure, unadulterated, check-your-inhibitions-at-the-shore transgression. Multiple stages and sound systems, blaring music spun by the hottest DJs on the international club scene, ensure something to suit everyone's party style. Somewhere between the techno beats, the sideshow fire-eaters and jugglers, and impromptu displays of pyrotechnics, partygoers go for a dip in the moonlit bay off Haad Rin. The twice-monthly **Half-Moon Festival** (www.halfmoonfestival.com) at Baan Tai village is almost as crazy.

While those moon-centric parties are without a doubt the headlining act on Koh Pha Ngan, there is also a wide range of perfectly relaxing activities to pursue here, from bumming it on a quiet beach like **Chaloklam Bay** to snorkeling off the **Mae Haad** sandbars and diving at **Koh Ma** (a deserted island connected to Koh Pha Ngan by a sandbar, with colorful fish and coral). Local guides can take you on **jungle treks** into the island's interior, where you're likely to spot monkeys, wild pigs, and all manner of native birds. **Than Sadet** is a national historic site with idyllic green pools and a waterfall, once frequented by the kings of Siam. Yoga facilities, meditation centers, and massage treatments also abound on the island.

Koh Pha Ngan figured prominently in Alex Garland's 2006 novel *The Beach,* about backpacker hedonism in Thailand. Since then, the island's tourism infrastructure has matured considerably, and with it, so has the age bracket of the average visitor. Whereas the island was once the sole province of the blotto backpacker set, who crashed in hostels or huts or just somewhere on the beach, Koh Pha Ngan now also caters to couples and families with fully equipped resorts, many quite secluded and exclusive. In many ways, Koh Pha Ngan seems to be following the pattern of neighboring island Koh Samui 302, but with a more careful eye on conservation. Recent growth aside, don't expect a lot of glitz and glam here: Koh Pha Ngan is still a place that's ruled by the laid-back rhythms of beach life, coconut palms swaying in the breeze. —*SM*

Previous page: A celebrant on Paradise Island.

ⓘ www.kohphangan.com.

✈ Koh Samui (15km/9⅓ miles), then boat.

⛴ From Koh Samui, about 30 min.

🛏 $$$ **The Diamond Cliff Resort & Spa,** 284 Prabaramee Rd. (✆ **66/76/340-501;** www.diamondcliff.com). $$ **Drop In Club Resort,** 157/1-10 Haad Rin, Baan Tai (✆ **66/77/375-444;** www.dropinclubresortandspa.com).

244 Party Animals

Hvar

Lavender Fields & Trendy Nightlife

Croatia

With its attractive mix of historical sites, gorgeous nature, and affordability compared with the rest of the Mediterranean, Croatia has been a top insider pick of travel experts for some years. In summer, Croatia's hottest destination is the long and skinny island of Hvar, in the Dalmatian archipelago (p. 331). By day, hit the beach and catch some rays, safe in the knowledge that you've come to the sunniest destination in the eastern Adriatic. By night, glam it up for one of the trendiest summer nightlife scenes in Europe.

Thanks to its size, geological diversity, and history, Hvar offers vacationers a variety of ways to enjoy the island, from daytime outdoor adventures to all-night revelry. It would be just as valid to spend your time on Hvar exploring the island's dramatic coastal coves by sea kayak as sleeping in until 3pm and then heading down to an **après-beach party,** where the dance music gets turned up and the drinks start flowing before sunset. Hvar has some excellent beaches, but the best are actually just offshore, at the **Pakleni islands,** which are a short hop by boat from Hvar town.

Like an open-air potpourri sachet, Hvar is filled with the soothing and luxurious scents of rosemary, lavender, heather, and sage—walk down any path or road of the island's interior and you can't miss the heady fragrance. The lavender fields may look wild, but the flowers are carefully cultivated for use in the lucrative production of essential oils and perfumed soaps. Hvar is also one of Croatia's most venerable wine regions, and most of the vineyards are concentrated in the western half of the island. A tip for anyone wishing to do the winery circuit: Rent a bike and pedal your way around, as the territory is mostly flat and distances are manageable; the handy cycling website www.pedala.hr outlines some different routes. (If instead you choose to drive your own car and are stopped by local authorities after you've had a few glasses, even a low blood alcohol reading is enough to get you a stiff fine.)

Hvar has recently become one of the Med's "it" destinations for yachtsetters and hip young things, and their ground zero for nightlife is **Hvar Town.** The harbor is lined with floodlit palm trees and chockablock with outdoor bars like **Carpe Diem** (✆ **385/21/742369;** www.carpe-diem-hvar.com), where it's de rigueur to show up with a fashionable outfit and golden tan to match. If that sounds like too much effort (or just a bit obnoxious), skip Hvar Town and head for the quieter hamlets of **Jelsa** and **Stari Grad** instead for a mellow night out. —*SM*

Hvar.

ⓘ www.tzhvar.hr.

✈ Split (75km/47 miles), then ferry.

From Split and Dubrovnik (via Split) in Croatia (1–1½ hr.); from Pescara and Ancona in Italy (8–10 hr.).

$$$ **Hotel Podstine,** Pod Stine (✆ **385/21/740400;** www.podstine.com). $$$ **Sun ani Hvar Hotels Group,** various locations (✆ **385/21/750750;** www.sun canihvar.com).

Party Animals 245

Mykonos

Chic Greek

Greece

The most cosmopolitan island in Greece may lack Santorini's 238 showstopping crater, but it's one of the best places in the Aegean to visit if you're in search of a good time. Mykonos greets you with its agreeable vibe as soon as you step off the ferry. The energy here is palpable, and after stopping off at other, sleepier Cycladic islands like Paros 32 and Naxos 229 on your way to Mykonos, you finally have the sense that you've called at a port with a little action.

In fact, the "action" on Mykonos can be as little or as much as you want, depending chiefly on what time of year you go and how late you stay up. In July and August, the 85-sq.-km (33-sq.-mile) island is filled to capacity with hedonistic 20-somethings, who party all night in Mykonos's tavernas and clubs. Boutiques stay open until 2am, enabling much shopping under the influence, and the next day, while everyone sleeps off those hangovers, the beaches are quiet until well after lunchtime. If that's not your rhythm or age group, just avoid those peak summer months and you'll enjoy Mykonos in all its Mediterranean sophistication. The island is often called a Greek St. Tropez, and for good reason.

Mykonos town, also known as **Chora,** is a bewitching maze of whitewashed, cubic houses and everyone's introduction to the island, and where you're sure to get hopelessly lost at one time or another. The most picturesque quarter of Chora is **Little Venice,** with its stylish waterfront bars that are packed from late afternoon to sunset. Up on a hill behind town are the signature **windmills** emblazoned on so many Mykonos postcards. Chora and its port are also the departure point for ferries to the island of Delos 401, one of the most popular day trips in the Aegean for its important archaeological site.

Mykonos is mostly flat, with little vegetation, so don't expect any jaw-dropping nature; but it does have its share of excellent beaches. Two of the most famous beaches, **Paradise** and **Super Paradise,** are places where nudist sunbathing is allowed and where dance music blares all day long. For a more relaxing day of sun and surf, try **Ornos** or **Kalo Livadi.** If you're seeking respite from the action, book a hotel on the "back," or north and east, sides of the island, which are much quieter than the highly developed west coast. —*SM*

ⓘ www.gnto.co.uk.

✈ Mykonos, connections to Athens.

From Piraeus (4 hr.) and other Cyclades islands (45 min.–2 hr.), **Hellenic Seaways** (www.hellenicseaways.gr) and **Blue Star Ferries** (www.bluestarferries.com). Schedules and bookings at www.ferries.gr.

$$ **Argo Hotel Mykonos,** Platys Gialos 84 (✆ **30/22890/23405;** www.argo-mykonos.gr). $$$ **Belvedere Hotel,** School of Fine Arts District (✆ **30/22890/25122;** www.belvederehotel.com).

Party Animals

Ibiza

Fiesta Capital of Europe

Spain

Survey any fun-loving Italian, Brit, or German, and you're sure to uncover some wild tales involving a vacation on the Spanish island of Ibiza—the rental car that ended up in the surf, the missed flights, the inexplicably lost pieces of clothing. . . . In the western Mediterranean, there is no place whose name is more synonymous with extreme partying.

As the little sister of the larger and more popular Majorca 4, Ibiza was fairly unknown until the middle of the 20th century, when it became a favorite sun-drenched destination for hippies and artists. Nowadays, this second largest of the Balearic islands has evolved—or devolved—a long way from its flower-child-tourism roots and become one of the most legendary destinations in Europe for summer revelry. Most visitors here, who come in droves during the sweltering months of July and August, are middle-class Europeans on air-and-hotel package tours, but the island is also a mecca for glamour girls like Kate Moss and Jade Jagger (both firm fixtures here in summer) and gays, which ensures a certain amount of chic amid the mass-market, alcohol- and drug-fueled madness.

The main towns on Ibiza are **Ciudad de Ibiza** (often referred to as Ibiza Town or Eivissa in local Catalan dialect) and **San Antonio,** which are also the island's biggest nightlife destinations with legendary clubs and bars like **Pacha** (✆ **34/97-131-36-00;** www.pacha.com) in Ibiza, and **Café del Mar** (✆ **34/97-180-49-46;** www.cafedelmarmusic.com) in "San An." Hotels in San Antonio traditionally draw heavily on the British soccer-hooligan demographic, especially in San Antonio's notorious **West End,** so for something slightly more relaxing between rounds of clubbing, it's worth spending a bit more for a private villa on or near the beach somewhere. Whatever you do, don't show up on Ibiza in high summer without accommodations already booked.

Ibiza, for all its focus on hard-partying, does offer more than all-night strobe lights and pounding bass: The beaches are quite beautiful—and because most people on vacation here spend much of the day sleeping off the previous night's excesses, you can have them largely to yourself for the entire morning and early afternoon. Broad and brilliant white **Es Pujols** is the most popular beach, while horseshoe-shaped **Es Cana** is another good choice with plenty of watersports and beach bars. The beach of **Playa des Cavallet** is clothing-optional and very gay-friendly. For a break from the sun and sand, Ibiza's dramatic coastline even hides away some wonderful caves like **Cova de Can Marçá,** near Puerto de San Miguel.

Ibiza is also an island with historic roots, and wandering around the charming old architecture of Ibiza town is a great antidote to all the craziness. The island's interior contains some lovely countryside—between omnipresent billboards touting this nightclub or that. The writers and artists who pioneered tourism to Ibiza from the 1950s to 1970s used to frequent **Bar Anita** (✆ **34/97-133-50-90**) in San Carlos, a sort of community center that still retains a bit of that bohemian atmosphere. You can also visit the two famed "hippie markets" of **El Canar** (at Es Cana beach) and **Las Dalias** (in Eivissa) for more tastes of this heritage.

It's worth noting that the authorities on Ibiza are not as permissive as their island's free-wheeling reputation would lead you to believe: Heavy fines and deportation are not uncommon for drunk and disorderly conduct. —*SM*

ⓘ **Passeig Vara de Rey,** 1, Ibiza Town (✆ **34/97-130-19-00;** www.illesbalears.es).

✈ Es Codolar International Airport, Ciudad de Ibiza.

🛏 $$$ **Cas Gasi,** Cami Vell a Sant Mateau, Apartado 117 (✆ **34/97-119-77-00;** www.casgasi.com). $$ **El Hotel Pacha,** Paseo Marítimo, Ibiza Town (✆ **34/97-131-59-63;** www.elhotelpacha.com).

Party Animals 247

Tenerife

Canary-a-Go-Go

Canary Islands, Spain

The "land of eternal spring," this colorful, fizzy island has a reputation as a party place—and really, you'd have to be a Scrooge-size grump to not enjoy yourself amid so much sun-splashed beauty. The largest of Spain's Canary Islands, Tenerife is a celebration, all right, of buttery yellow sun, blue sky, flowering hillsides, golden beaches, and swooping volcanic slopes. It has in the historic village of La Laguna a UNESCO World Heritage Site and in its melting-pot culture a world of flavors.

Tenerife owes much of its sunny exoticism to its location, 100km (62 miles) off the coast of continental West Africa, and to its ancestral people, the aboriginal Guanche tribe, the Canaries' earliest and now extinct inhabitants, having been conquered (and largely decimated) by the Spanish 500 years ago. But even though Tenerife enjoys a tropical climate and is closer to Africa than it is to Spain, the island's infrastructure is thoroughly modern and über-European—little wonder it's such a popular holiday spot for travelers from Europe and the U.K.

Although Tenerife gets knocked for its "concrete coastline"—that would be the raft of megaresorts and tourist traps along the island's popular southwest shore—it shouldn't stop anyone from missing the island's plentiful charms. Tenerife is a multidimensional vacation spot. If you want to bring the family, it has plenty for kids to do (great swimming, snorkeling, sailing). Ecotourists thrill to the mountainous interior and botanical gardens. **Pico del Teide** (rhymes with "lady") is the tallest mountain in Spain, a snow-dusted peak that rises to 3,718m (12,198 ft.) amid soft green shoulders; it's actually a dormant volcano. Scuba divers thrill to the island's underwater volcanic rocks and rich marine life; the **Dive Center Corralejo,** on the northeast coast (✆ **34/92-853-59-06;** www.divecentercorralejo.com), offers PADI-certified training courses and recreational dives to offshore reefs and islets. Beach bums can luxuriate on the island's natural black-sand beaches (the golden-sand beaches are imports from the Saharan desert). History lovers can hit the cobblestoned streets of charming old-world villages like **La Laguna** and **La Orotava.** The main town on the north coast, **Puerto de la Cruz,** has a 17th-century fort, **Castillo de San Felipe** and **Botanical Gardens** (✆ **34/92-238-35-72**) that date from 1788. And throughout the island, the pleasing and colorful architecture—houses with plant-filled interior courtyards, woodwork of beautifully carved Canary Island pines, gingerbread frills—makes everyone happy. Of course, Tenerife has its party-animal side, with discos and nightclubs that go-go till the wee hours—the concrete coast being the nerve center for the island's nightlife. But this stretch of shore represents just a tiny fraction of island real estate—so get out into the beauteous countryside and experience the real Tenerife.

The Canary Island archipelago, composed of seven large and six small islands, lies in the east Atlantic Ocean, but the excellent transportation system (including airports and ports on every island) makes it easy to get to and hop from island to island. The best way to explore the island is by car; Tenerife has more than 100 car rental locations. —*AF*

ⓘ www.webtenerifeuk.co.uk, www.abouttenerife.com, or www.turismodecanarias.com.

✈ Tenerife Sur airport (Reina Sofía), about 20km (12 miles) from Playa de las Américas.

🛏 $$$ **Hotel Botanicao & the Oriental Spa Gardens,** Puerto de la Cruz (✆ **34/92-238-14-00** or 902/080-000 in Spain; www.hotelbotanico.com). $$$ **Hotel San Roques,** Garachio, Isla Baja (✆ **34/92-213-34-35;** www.hotelsanroque.com).

248 Party Animals

Key West

Last Mango in Paradise

Florida, U.S.

Key West is an anything-goes, party-hearty destination that seems the complete antithesis of the nature-oriented, family-friendly Florida Keys (p. 62). And for many visitors, that's exactly *why* they choose Key West.

Old-time "conchs" (pronounced *conks*), as the locals call themselves, habitually gripe that their island paradise has been ruined. What was once a slow-paced, slightly scruffy port of call for sport fishermen and social dropouts has become a commercialized cruise ship stop, with boisterous restaurants, bars, and T-shirt shops lining the heart of Old Town, Duval Street. Every evening, revelers grab a go-cup and crowd the docks behind Mallory Square for the traditional Sunset Celebration, a rowdy carnival of sketch artists, acrobats, food vendors, and other buskers (not to mention pickpockets) trading on the island's bohemian image. The revelry kicks up yet another notch during Fantasy Fest (around Halloween) and Hemingway Days (in July).

But others defend Key West's live-and-let-live mentality as its greatest asset. Over the years, writers as diverse as Robert Frost, Ernest Hemingway, Tennessee Williams, and S. J. Perelman have found inspiration in its palm-shaded precincts. No one has defined the genial Key West spirit better than musician Jimmy Buffet, whose Parrothead acolytes still launch into choruses of "Margaritaville" at bars like **Sloppy Joe's** (201 Duval St.) and **Captain Tony's Saloon** (428 Green St.). Key West's gay social scene is legendary, with rainbow flags fluttering outside gay hangouts, nonstop dance clubs and drag performances, and a stream of same-sex couples happily strolling hand in hand. You can't deny the refreshing sense of freedom at gay-magnet **Higgs Beach** or around the swimming pools at the many guesthouses with a predominantly gay clientele.

Laid-back Key West still exists, but you have to seek it out: in tropical backyard gardens, side streets lined with the verandas and gingerbread trim of Victorian-era homes, the coral beaches and calm Atlantic waters on the island's south side, or funky **Bahama Village,** where pet

Island Hopping St. Vincent & the Grenadines: Trim the Sails

The largest island of the 32-island independent nation known as the Grenadines, 249 **St. Vincent** may not be the tourist magnet of some of its sister islands, but it does have a storied history that may help explain why. St. Vincent was one of the last holdouts of native resistance against European settlers in the region. The Caribs (Kal-linagoes) fought off both the British and the French through two fiercely fought Carib wars until 1796, when the warrior natives waved the white flag and were unceremo-niously shipped off to Honduras. In fact, the first permanent settlers of St. Vincent were not Europeans at all but black slaves who were shipwrecked on the island in 1635 and gradually absorbed into the tribe; their progeny was known as the Yellow Caribs. Today most of the people who live on St. Vincent are descendants of black slaves (brought to the island in later years by European colonists to work the sugar plantations) and the sprinkling of Black Caribs who remained on the island after the Carib surrender.

St. Vincent may lack large-scale tourism, but it is a scenic wonder, with lush vegeta-tion and dramatic topography. It's also a pleasure capital, with a lively music scene—the sweet night air is filled with the sounds of calypso, soca, and steel drums. The region's administrative center, St. Vincent is also the breadbasket of the Grenadines. The island's volatile volcano, **Mount Soufriére,** has been both a blessing and a curse. Major eruptions in 1812 and 1902 took the lives of thousands of islanders and did untold damage, but volcanic ash is nature's primo fertilizer. The rich St. Vincent soil grows a prodigious supply of mangoes, papayas, bananas, breadfruit, and coco-nuts—a bounty on full display daily at the **Kingstown Market,** in the capital city, Kingstown. The volcanic activity has also produced dazzling gold- and black-sand beaches on the western coastline, while the east is rugged and mountainous.

The island's largely undeveloped terrain is also encouraging a burgeoning ecotourism industry. **Sea Breeze Nature Tours** (✆ **784/4584969;** www.seabreezenaturetours.com) offers dolphin- and whale-watching tours, snorkeling trips, and tours of loca-tions featured in the film *Pirates of the Caribbean.*

The Grenadines archipelago extends 72km (45 miles) southwest of St. Vincent and includes **Bequia, Mustique, Canouan, Union Island, Palm Island, Petit St. Vin-cent,** and the **Tobago Cays.** These are some of the world's finest sailing waters, where you can opt for bareboat or charter, sail or power cruise—and just let the gentle trade winds carry you from one delicious (and uninhabited) sugary-sand cay to another. You can also snorkel off the boat along fringing reefs, home to rich marine life, or anchor on one of the Grenadines islands for lunch or dinner—radio ahead to reserve a spot.

250 **Bequia** may be one of the Caribbean's best-kept secrets; it's the largest of the Grenadines and just 14km (8⅔ miles) south of St. Vincent. The island has secluded

beaches and a laid-back ambience—and an excellent anchorage for visiting yachts in Port Elizabeth. You can rent watersports equipment on the white sands of **Friendship Bay. Industry Bay** and **Lower Bay** are both beautiful beaches shaded by palms, with good swimming and snorkeling. **Dive Bequia,** at the Gingerbread House in Admiralty Bay (✆ **784/458-3504;** http://bequiadive.com), specializes in diving and snorkeling trips where you might spot tarpon, damselfish, and chain morays. Note that you can also get to Bequia via **ferry** from St. Vincent (✆**784/458-3348;** www.admiralty-transport.com).

The elite mystique of little 251 **Mustique** has much to do with its reputation as an exclusive luxury hideaway for the rich and famous. The privately owned island has been a favorite of Princess Margaret, Mick Jagger, and other boldfaced names. Mustique enjoys the requisite tropical-island attributes: velvety beaches lapped by turquoise seas, lissome palms, and a necklace of coral reef. It also has an architectural look that has become synonymous with Mustique style: the neo-Palladian mansions designed by stage designer Oliver Messel. So far, 18 of Messel's 30 house plans have been realized. You can stay here in a Messel-style villa (www.mustique-island.com) or reserve a room in the island's only hotel, the **Cotton House** (www.cottonhouse.net), or the one guesthouse, the **Firefly** (www.mustique-island.com).

Another privately owned island is one of the world's top honeymoon destinations. 252 **Petit St. Vincent** (pronounced *Pet*-ty St. Vincent). Four yellow Labrador retrievers have the run of the place, and you will too, if you get to stay in one of only 22 stone cottages on the 46-hectare (114-acre) island. The cottages have no phones or televisions, but if you've got a craving for a rum punch, just put a note in your mailbox, run up the attached flag, and your wish will be granted. The Atlantic Ocean side of the island is great for snorkeling; the gentle Caribbean side, perfect for lazing about.

Finally, you wouldn't want to visit the Grenadines and miss the 253 **Tobago Cays** (www.tobagocays.com), an archipelago of five uninhabited islets and a 567-hectare (1,400-acre) lagoon encircled by coral reef. It's one of the top spots to snorkel in the Caribbean. This protected national marine park can be reached only by water. You can take day charters or boat excursions from nearby island resorts or other islands; the closest islands are Union, Mayreau, and Canouan. Tread lightly when you're there, if you will; degradation of the reef from overuse by visiting yachts, cruise ships, and fishermen has become cause for concern. —*AF*

ⓘ www.svgtourism.com.

✈ St. Vincent via Barbados (35 min.), Grenada (30 min.), Martinique (45 min.), St. Lucia (20 min.), Puerto Rico (2 hr., 20 min.), and Trinidad (1 hr.); charters to most islands via St. Vincent.

$$ **The Frangipani,** Bequia (✆**784/458-3255;** www.frangipanibequia.com). $$$ **Petit St. Vincent,** Petit St. Vincent (✆**800/654-9326** in the U.S. or 954/963-7401; www.psvresort.com).

chickens and stray cats roam the streets outside trendy cafes and B&Bs. To rediscover the charms of vintage Key West, tour some of the vacation retreats of its past visitors: **Key West Heritage House Museum,** 410 Caroline St. (✆ **305/296-3573;** www.heritagehousemuseum.org); **Audubon House,** 205 Whitehead St. (✆ **305/294-2116;** www.audubonhouse.com); the **Ernest Hemingway Home,** 907 Whitehead St. (✆ **305/294-1136;** www.hemingwayhome.com); and the **Harry S Truman Little White House,** 111 Front St. (✆ **305/294-9911;** www.trumanlittlewhitehouse.com). Some folks never left at all—read the wacky epitaphs on their gravestones at the quirky Key West Cemetery (701 Passover Lane).

Ease into the mood by taking one of the town's ubiquitous sightseeing tours, whether by trolley, train, bike, or on foot (several are listed at www.historictours.com/keywest). Forget about bringing a car; the best way to get around Key West—which, after all, is only 2×4 miles (3.2×6.4km) and flat as a pancake—is by bicycle or moped. *—HH*

ⓘ **Tourist office,** 402 Wall St. (✆ **800/527-8539** or 305/294-2587; www.keywestchamber.com).

✈ Key West or Miami International Airport (159 miles/256km).

🛏 $$ **Ambrosia Key West,** 622 Fleming St. (✆ **305/296-9838;** www.ambrosiakeywest.com). $$ **Oasis,** 822 Fleming St. (✆ **800/362-7477** or 305/296-2131; www.keywest-allmale.com).

Party Animals **254**

Paradise Island

Activities Abound at Atlantis

The Bahamas

There is probably only one island in the world where you can swim with dolphins, see the Jonas Brothers in concert, and shop at designer boutiques all in the space of a few hours: that place is The Bahamas' Paradise Island, a 3.2km-long (2-mile) strip just across from The Bahamian capital of Nassau on New Providence Island 349. If you're looking for authentic island charm, choose another Bahamian destination, but if all you want is hassle-free fun in the sun and nonstop entertainment, within a few hours' flight of most of North America, then waste no time booking a trip to Paradise Island—and, specifically, to the **Atlantis resort** (see below for contact info).

Leaf through any travel publication and you'll no doubt see advertisements for the megaresort that is virtually synonymous with Paradise Island. The astounding Atlantis conglomeration counts a staggering 3,769 guest units between hotel rooms, suites, cottages, and oceanfront villas. There are other resorts and hotels on Paradise Island, but even guests of the tony One and Only Club here confess that Atlantis is where all the action is, and where everyone who comes to Paradise Island ends up spending most of their time. With more than 35 restaurants, helmed by the hottest chefs on the global dining scene, and a huge water park with rides and wildlife encounters, Atlantis is the most unabashedly over-the-top vacation destination in the Caribbean.

The savvy marketing folks at Atlantis have made sure that the resort appeals to the broadest possible base. Billions of dollars have been poured into state-of-the-art facilities that exist nowhere else in the Americas. For animal lovers of all ages, the resort's **Dolphin Cay** offers visitors a chance to swim with the Atlantis's resident dolphins (a few of which are rescues from aquariums forced to evacuate during Hurricane Katrina) in a 5.6-hectare (14-acre) lagoon and beach area. Kids also love Atlantis's **Aquaventure,** a 57-hectare (141-acre) water park with innovative slides, rides, wave pools, rapids, and a mile-long lazy river. And for when, if ever, you feel overstimulated by Atlantis's packaged attractions, there are long stretches of beautiful beach nearby, like **Paradise Beach,** with its *chikees* (thatched huts) providing relief from the baking sun. Paradise Island also has a gorgeous 18-hole, Tom Weiskopf–designed golf course, whose greens abut the turquoise sea.

Sundown is when the grown-up entertainment at Atlantis really comes alive. **Celebrity chefs** Nobu Matsuhisa, Bobby Flay, and Jean-Georges Vongerichten have all loaned their names to restaurants in the Atlantis sprawl, and there's a happening **casino** here as well. Big-name concerts—pop sensations like the Jonas Brothers, or adult-contemporary mainstays like Gloria Estefan—also come to Atlantis throughout the year. Between all that and the onsite bars and nightclubs, the partying goes on into the wee hours. Recover the next day, perhaps, with a treatment at the resort's luxurious **Mandara Spa.**

Atlantis has thought of everything, though none of it comes cheap: Rack rates start at $300 per night, which doesn't include any meals or dolphin encounters. You can save a good deal of money by booking a room at one of Paradise Island's more proletarian accommodations, then wandering over to Atlantis and paying for its attractions a la carte—the prices are the same whether or not you're a resort guest. —*SM*

(i) www.nassauparadiseisland.com.

✈ Nassau-Lynden Pindling International (14km/8⅔ miles).

🛏 $$$ **Atlantis,** Casino Dr. (✆ **888/877-7525;** www.atlantis.com). $$ **Comfort Suites Paradise Island,** Paradise Island Dr. (✆ **242/363-3680;** www.comfortsuitespi.com).

255 The Aristocrats

Isle of Wight

Victoriana by the Sea

Channel Islands, U.K.

Blame it on Queen Victoria. In 1845 the young Queen made this Channel island all the rage when she began coming here for seaside holidays with her beloved consort Prince Albert; you can still tour their Italianate mansion, **Osbourne House** (outside Whippingham, south of East Cowes; ✆ **44/1983/200022**), its cozy clutter of personal objects perfectly preserved, including the bed where 81-year-old Victoria died in her sleep in 1901. Following the queen's example, 19th-century celebrities from Tennyson to Julia Margaret Cameron to Charles Dickens flocked here to enjoy Wight's mild climate, sandy beaches, and panoramic walks over dramatic chalk downs. By the turn of the 19th century, there were 10 pleasure piers dotted around the island, of which three—at Ryde, Sandown, and Yarmouth—still stand. The U.K.'s oldest theme park, **Blackgang Chine** (✆ **44/1983/730052;** www.blackgangchine.com), opened in 1843 on the southwest side of the island; it's still in operation, with many of its old-fashioned attractions intact.

Yachtsmen, too, favored the Isle of Wight, especially the port of Cowes, which

Isle of Wight.

lies directly south of Southampton across a 4.8km-wide (3-mile) channel, the Solent, known for its treacherous tidal currents—where better to hone one's sailing skills? The annual Cowes Week regatta was launched in 1826; in 1851 the first **America's Cup** race took place around the island; and in 1854 the Royal Yacht Squadron moved into an old Tudor castle overlooking Cowes harbor.

Unlike many 19th-century resorts, however, the Isle of Wight is still going strong. Yachts still fill the harbor at Cowes, with the Cowes Week regatta returning every August. The twin towns of Sandown and Shanklin still share a 9.7km-long (6-mile) sweep of golden beach on the east coast, where shallow waters and abundant sunshine (Sandown holds Britain's record for most days of sunshine per year) draw holiday-making families to a well-preserved Victorian-era esplanade. Ryde, on the northeast coast, and steeply terraced Ventnor on the south have also preserved their Victorian-era beachfronts. The restored **Isle of Wight Steam Railway** (Havenstreet; ✆ **44/1983/882204;** www.iwsteamrailway.co.uk) is another step-back-in-time experience. Walking remains an Isle of Wight specialty, with the 106km (65-mile) **Coastal Path** circling the island, taking in stunning views of its chalk cliffs. Every May the 2-week Isle of Wight Walking Festival kick-starts the tourist season, with more than 300 themed walks scheduled for visitors.

Amid all this prim Victoriana, imagine the impact of 600,000 rock fans in 1970 for the third annual **Isle of Wight Rock Festival,** where among other acts Jimi Hendrix blew fans' minds. Revived in 2002 (www.isleofwightfestival.com), that festival books many of the U.K.'s top acts for a long weekend in June (the 2009 lineup included everyone from the Zombies and Neil Young to Razorlight and the Ting Tings). Held in Seaclose Park in mid-island **Newport,** the island's capital and largest town, the festival includes a huge campground where many concertgoers hang out for 3 days, rain or shine. Even Queen Victoria might have been amused. *—HH*

ⓘ **Tourist office,** 67 High St., Shanklin (✆ **44/1983/862942;** www.iwight.com).

✈ London Heathrow (145km/90 miles).

⛴ Ryde (20 min. from Portsmouth), West Cowes (22 min. from Southampton), East Cowes (55 min. car ferry from Southampton).

🛏 $$ **Bourne Hall Country Hotel,** Luccombe St., Shanklin (✆ **44/1983/862820;** www.bournehallhotel.co.uk). $$$ **The George Hotel,** Quay St., Ryde (✆ **44/1983/760331;** www.thegeorge.co.uk).

256 The Aristocrats

Isle of Islay

Queen of the Hebrides

Inner Hebrides, Scotland

Only 26km (16 miles) of cold grey sea lie between the Kintyre peninsula, on Scotland's west coast, and the Isle of Islay. Still, that's more than enough distance to keep Islay (pronounced Eye-la) isolated and unspoiled. That romantic remoteness long ago gave Islay its greatest claim to fame: Far from the mainland's tax officers, Islay's distillers did quite a business in freebooting whisky in the 18th century. Once the excise tax was lifted, the island swiftly became a whisky powerhouse.

Islay whisky isn't for everyone, but its fans consider it the finest and truest expression of malt whisky. Islay's brown peaty water infuses the local malts with an earthy tang, adding hints of briny salt air and even a little mossy seaweed. It's a strong flavor, further concentrated by the antiquated pot-still methods that Islay's distillers proudly preserve. Nearly all these distilleries run weekday tours year-round (call ahead for appointments).

Begin down south in the island's main resort town, **Port Ellen,** where three famous distilleries are strung along the coast east of town (note the sheer coastal cliffs, riddled with caves where illegal stills and smuggling rings once operated). **Laphroaig** (1.6km/1mile east of Port Ellen; ✆ **44/1496/302-418;** www.laphroaig.com) was officially founded in 1815, though illegal stills had operated here for years. Since 1994, sweet smoky Laphroaig has held a prestigious royal warrant from Prince Charles. Laphroaig's longtime rival, **Lagavulin** (3km/1¾ miles east of Port Ellen; ✆ **44/1496/302-730;** www.malts.com), uses unique pear-shaped stills and a distilling process that adds extra time at every stage—distilling, fermenting, aging—to give this dark, peaty whisky an especially deep, rounded flavor. Up the coast another mile or so, 19th-century **Ardbeg** (✆ **44/1496/302-244;** www.ardbeg.com) closed down in the 1980s but was revived in 1997 by Glenmorangie, which restored its old stills, copper-topped kilns, and mash tuns to produce a classic peaty Islay malt. Fortified with a few drams, you may commune with the Celtic past at the mossy ruins of **Dunyvaig Castle,** above Lagavulin, and up the coast at **Kidalton** (12km/7½ miles from Port Ellen), where a superb 9th-century stone cross stands in the roofless church.

Along Loch Indaal, which deeply notches Islay's west coast, you'll find two more fine distilleries. In Bowmore, Islay's capital, **Bowmore Distillery** (School St.; ✆ **44/1496/810-671;** www.morrisonbowmore.com) is the island's oldest, founded in 1779; here you'll see one of the country's last old-fashioned malting floors, where a maltman gently hand-turns the malting barley with a wooden shovel. (Don't miss Bowmore's round church, craftily built with no corners where the devil might hide.) Then head around the loch, stopping in Bridgend to buy heathery tweeds at the **Islay Woollen Mill** (✆ **44/1496/810-563**), which wove all the cloaks and kilts worn in the movie *Braveheart.* Continue around the loch to small privately owned **Bruichladdich** (✆ **44/1496/850-190;** www.bruichladdich.com), which produces small batches of an especially delicate malt, using unpeated barley and clear spring water, in another revived 19th-century distillery. Ah, so many single malts, so little time! —*HH*

ⓘ www.discoverislay.com.

Islay Airport, Glenegedale.

Port Ellen or Port Askaig (2 hr. from West Tarbert, Kintyre, via MacBrayne steamers; ✆ **44/1475/635-235;** www.calmac.co.uk).

$$ **Bridgend Hotel,** Bridgend (✆ **44/1496/810-212;** www.bridgend-hotel.com). $$$ **Harbour Inn,** The Square, Bowmore (✆ **44/1496/810-330;** www.harbour-inn.com).

The Aristocrats 257

Capri

The Mediterranean Jewel That's Always in Style

Italy

First of all, get the pronunciation right: It's *Cah*-pree, not Ca-*pree*. What many call the most beautiful island in the Mediterranean, and whose iconic name has been co-opted for everything from 1950s automobiles to cropped pants, may have had its heyday several decades ago, but the captivating idea of Capri remains. The marina is frequently filled to capacity with billion-dollar yachts (the moorage fee here is sky-high), and international celebrities party at venerable nightclubs like Anema e Core. Capri's secluded bathing spots are filled with glamazons right out of a Dolce & Gabbana ad, and nearly every backdrop on the island oozes a quiet sense of privilege. And if the allure of hobnobbing with modern-day Jackie O's isn't enough, Capri is one of the most naturally splendid places in Europe: Marvel at the island's rock formations and grottoes, its wild forests and manicured lemon groves, and the ultracivilized lifestyle that's been carved out here over the past 2,000 years.

A jagged monolith of sheer limestone cliffs studded with tenacious pine trees, Capri presents a rugged profile to anyone arriving by sea, and no matter how many times you've been here, that arresting appearance takes your breath away each time you sail into port. The island's stunning landscape and its convenient location in the Bay of Naples made it a popular retreat as early as ancient Roman times. The emperor Tiberius built no fewer than a dozen villas here—the **Villa Jovis,** on the impossibly tall northeast tip of the island, is the best preserved of them. In more recent history, Capri was a darling of the international jet set, whose heyday on the island peaked in the 1960s. Though most hotels and restaurants in Capri remain deliberately priced out of most travelers' budgets, and the harbor is still filled with astounding yachts in high season, its luxury status is somewhat undermined by omnipresent day-trippers from Sorrento and Naples.

The key to enjoying Capri is to avoid the most congested tourist areas, **Capri Town** and the port of **Marina Grande,** between 10am and 5pm. Get out on the water with an **island circumnavigation tour** (✆ **39/081/8377714;** www.motoscafisticapri.com), or use your own two feet to explore the quieter, wilder sides of the island, which is a hiker's paradise. Whether it's the gentle trek to the top of **Monte Solaro** (also accessible by chairlift) or the **Pizzolungo** trail that skirts the most dramatic part of the island, between the **Faraglioni** rock formations and the **Arco Naturale,** you're never far from vistas that'll give you vertigo and glamorous backdrops for vacation photos. The **Blue Grotto** (or *Grotta Azzurra*) is Capri's single main "attraction" and an unabashed tourist trap that will cost you an arm and a leg.

Capri.

Yet the giddy experience of being in the tiny dinghies that go through the 1m-tall (3¼-ft.) cave entrance—and seeing the electric blue water once you're inside—is worth all the hype.

Whereas Capri Town is where all the glitzy storefronts and cafes are to be found, the island's other inhabited center, **Anacapri,** represents a mellower, more authentic alternative with its own warren of labyrinthine lanes and whitewashed houses. A hair-raising, ribbon-thin "highway," where orange municipal buses seem poised to careen off the precipice at every turn, connects the two towns. *—SM*

ⓘ **Capri Tourist Board,** Piazza Umberto I, Capri Town (✆ **39/081/8370686;** www.capritourism.com).

✈ Naples, then hydrofoil or ferry.

⛴ From Naples or Sorrento, hydrofoil or ferry (20 min.–1 hr.).

🛏 $ **Hotel Tosca,** Via Birago 5, Capri Town (✆ **39/081/8370989;** h.tosca@capri.it). $$$ **Punta Tragara,** Via Tragara 57, Capri Town (✆ **39/081/8370844;** www.hoteltragara.com).

The Aristocrats

258

Büyükada

Car Free in the Sea of Marmara

Princes Islands, Turkey

When the warm weather arrives, Istanbulites leave their cars behind and board a ferry to the elegant retreat of Büyükada. Historic architecture, clean air, pine trees, and a slow pace reign at this largest and most beloved island in the Sea of Marmara's Princes archipelago (*büyük* means "big" and *ada* means "island"). One of the most appealing aspects of Büyükada—and what makes it such a welcome contrast to chaotic Istanbul—is that no motor vehicles are permitted on the 5.4-sq.-km (2-sq.-mile) island; instead, public transportation is by horse-drawn carriages. Princes and empresses of old (and one exiled Leon Trotsky) made this island their favorite retreat, and anyone visiting Istanbul in the summer should try to fit in at least a day trip: The relaxing and scenic ferry ride alone, not to mention an abundance of creature comforts, is enough to recharge any traveler's batteries.

Life on Büyükada centers around the *fin de siècle* **Iskele Meydani (Dock Square),** where lively cafes, bakeries, ice-cream shops, and stands selling *lahmujun* (Turkish pizza) perfume the air around the landmark clock tower. **Phaetons** (the local term for Büyükada's signature horse-drawn carriages) depart from here for tours of the island, whether you want a quick overview of the seaside near the port or a more in-depth look at historical sites of the interior and the magnificent garden villas of the **Nizam district.** Prices are fixed by the local government—no haggling necessary. Bicycles, the other chief means of getting around the mostly flat island, can also be rented in the square. Farther inland, a donkey terminus serves those who wish to make the ascent up 202m-high (663-ft.) Yüce Tepe hill to **Hagia Yorgi** church, much revered for its supposed wish-granting and healing properties. And although the water in the Sea of Marmara never really gets all that warm, there are a few good—if crowded—beaches, like **Prenses Plajı,** where you can go for a swim.

In the evenings, as during the day, the island population congregates at **Dock Square,** perhaps for calamari and the divine chocolate soufflé at **Milto** (✆ **90/216-382-53-12**), or for ice cream and a waterfront stroll in the moonlight. For those seeking a bit more action, Büyükada has several energetic **casinos and clubs** where you can dance the night away with Istanbul's hot young things. Despite the nightlife, however, Büyükada is a wonderfully safe getaway, and you'll see children playing in town at all hours. (You'll also see well-groomed phaeton horses wandering loose in the streets after their workday is finished.)

Though most who overnight on Büyükada are the well-to-do Turks who own homes here, there are a few hotels in town. (For weekend stays in summer, it is essential to book months in advance.) For period atmosphere, the top address is the **Splendid Palace Hotel** (see below), which was built in a subtly Orientalized Art Nouveau style in 1906, on the model of the Hotel Negresco in Nice, France, and hasn't been updated much since. —*SM*

(i) www.tourismturkey.com.

✈ Istanbul Ataturk (16km/10 miles to Kabatas port, then ferry).

⛴ **IDO ferry** (www.ido.com.tr) from Istanbul's Kabatas port (90 min.).

🛏 $$$ **Splendid Palace Hotel,** 23 Nisan Caddesi (✆ **90/216-382-69-50;** www.splendidhotel.net).

259 The Aristocrats

Santa Catalina

Double Your Pleasure

California, U.S.

When chewing-gum magnate William Wrigley, Jr., fell in love with Catalina Island in 1915, he did what any self-respecting tycoon would do: He built an exclusive resort town and invited A-list friends like Laurel and Hardy, Cecil B. DeMille, John Wayne, and even Winston Churchill to enjoy it with him. But luckily, Wrigley was also a nature lover. Determined to preserve his own private Eden, he kept 88% of the island off-limits to development.

Wrigley's forethought ensured that this little island, only 22 miles (35km) off the Southern California coast, would remain a world unto itself, a haven of clean air, untrafficked roads, and crystal-clear water. In 1975 Wrigley's estate deeded most of the rugged, hilly interior outright to the Catalina Island Conservancy, which has vigorously protected his legacy. Arriving in Avalon, the island's port and only town, you'll notice swarms of varicolored golf carts—this is the only city in California authorized to limit the numbers of cars on city streets, so locals use golf carts or even Segways (rent your own near the dock). Avalon still bears the Art Deco look of Catalina's heyday, most prominently at the round white **Casino,** overlooking the bobbing yachts in the harbor. Posh boutiques line Crescent Avenue, and the town features an immaculately groomed vintage golf course, built in 1892 for those early Wrigley guests; on a knoll above town, visitors can dine at the California Revival landmark **Catalina Country Club.** While you're in town, be sure to visit the **Wrigley Botanical Garden** (✆ **310/510-2288**), designed by Mrs. Wrigley to showcase the unique botany of California's coastal islands.

Casino at Santa Catalina.

Lush stands of giant kelp offshore make this one of the West Coast's most fascinating snorkeling and scuba sites, with underwater visibility of 40 to 100 ft. (12–30m) on a good day. At several marine reserves—**Lover's Cove, Casino Point, Toyon Bay,** and **Blue Cavern Point**—artificial reefs have been built to protect fish from the industrial chemicals that still contaminate the waters closer to Los Angeles. Contact **Diving Catalina Island** (✆ **877/SNORKEL** [766-7535]; www.divingcatalina.com) or **Catalina Divers Supply** (✆ **800/353-0330** or 310/510-0330; www.catalinadiverssupply.com) to rent gear or set up dive tours.

To explore the unspoiled interior, there are plenty of trails for hiking or mountain biking; you can also book a naturalist-led Jeep tour with the **Conservancy** (✆ **310/510-2595;** www.catalinaconservancy.org), or take **Santa Catalina Island Company**'s 4-hour bus tour (✆ **310/510-8687;** www.visitcatalinaisland.com), which includes a visit to the Wrigleys' famous Arabian horse ranch (SCICo also offers 45-min. underwater tours of the kelp forest and nighttime trips to observe flying fish). Don't be surprised if you see buffalo roaming the range, the offspring of a few movie-prop bison imported in 1929—just another of the quirks that make Catalina so special. —*HH*

ⓘ **Catalina Island Visitors Bureau,** Green Pleasure Pier, Avalon (✆ **310/510-1520;** www.catalina.com).

✈ Los Angeles International (45 miles/72km).

⛴ **Catalina Express** (✆ **800/481-3470;** www.catalinaexpress.com) from San Pedro or Long Beach; **Marina Flyer** (✆ **310/305-7250;** www.catalinaferries.com) from Marina del Rey; **Catalina Flyer** (✆ **800/830-7744;** www.catalinainfo.com) from Newport Beach.

🛏 $ **Hotel Catalina,** 129 Whittley Ave. (✆ **800/540-0184** or 310/510-0027; www.hotelcatalina.com). $$ **Hotel Vista Del Mar,** 417 Crescent Ave. (✆ **800/601-3836** or 310/510-1452; www.hotel-vistadelmar.com).

The Aristocrats 260

St. Barts
St. Tropez of the Caribbean

In spite of its reputation as a ritzy, sun-blazed stopover for celebrities, the St. Barts I know is a place of quiet pleasures: magical villas tucked away on flower-filled cliffs; wave-lapped, light-dappled cul-de-sacs; a sunny disposition and a distinctly French sensibility. Most of the islanders, in fact, are of French or Swedish descent. And the beaches—considered by many to be the most beautiful in the Caribbean—are rarely crowded, never cluttered.

Yes, there are European-style discos and bars that go-go all night and flashy yachts elbowing their way into the little seaport of **Gustavia,** the island's enchanting capital. Old and new money also feed a vibrant luxury-goods market. But the island has no clanging casinos or giant cruise ships blocking harbor views. And a number of factors ensure that things will stay that way.

For one thing, the island is quite small, just 21 sq. km (8 sq. miles); you can get from one end to the other in under 30 minutes. Plus the terrain is vastly different from that of its neighbor, St. Maarten 216, where flat, sandy scrubland is the prevailing landscape. St. Barts is a volcanic island, where the creases and folds of the landscape translate to roads with Monte Carlo–style hairpin curves and roller coaster dips and rises.

Another reason St. Barts (which is officially called St. Barthélemy) has retained its quaint character is the simple fact of getting there. The flight from St. Maarten is just 10 minutes long, but for many people, landing a tiny plane on a tiny airstrip lined up between two volcanic hills and braking mere feet from sunbathers on the beach is 10 minutes of white-knuckle terror. Those who go by boat or high-speed ferry have the unpredictable, sometimes stomach-churning seas to contend with.

Local authorities, keenly sensitive to the perils of overdevelopment, have placed style and size restrictions on new resorts, which cannot have more than 12 rooms (the largest resort has 68 rooms); most are tastefully tucked into the glorious landscape. And by and large, St. Barts can be prohibitively pricey, from the luxury resorts and upscale restaurants to the ultrachic designer boutiques. But it doesn't have to cost a fortune to stay here: You can rent a villa or private home (half the visitors who come here do), cook your own meals, and beach-hop with the rest of the islanders—all the beaches are public and free.

So what do you do on St. Barts? You arrive at the airport (or the ferry landing) and rent a car so you can do as the locals do: beach-hop from one glorious strand of sand to the next. (The best known beach is **St-Jean Beach,** which is actually two beaches divided by the Eden Rock promontory.) First stop in at Match, the grocery store across from the airport, for supplies. (Check out the French canned goods and household items—even the toothpastes have more than a soupçon of style.) You can then take advantage of the myriad water activities—**parasailing, snorkeling, scuba diving**—and world-class **spa treatments.** You let your hair get tousled and sun-bleached, and you dine alfresco amid flickering candlelight. And, yes, you may spot a celebrity living it up, but then again, you may be too busy living it up yourself to care. —*AF*

ⓘ **Office du Tourisme,** quai du Général-de-Gaulle (✆ **590/27-87-27;** www.st-barths.com).

✈ Flights connect through St. Maarten (10 min.).

⛴ ***Voyager*** vessels (✆ **590/87-10-68;** www.voyager-st-barths.com); 45 min. from St. Maarten.

🛏 $$$ **Hotel Guanahani,** Grand Cul-de-Sac, 97133 St. Barthélemy, F.W.I. (✆ **800/223-6800** in the U.S., or 590/27-66-60; www.leguanahani.com). $$ **Les Ilets de la Plage,** Plage de St. Jean, 97133 St. Barthélemy, F.W.I. (✆ **590/27-88-57;** www.lesilets.com).

261 Beach Bums with Culture

Aruba

One Happy Island

This little island packs a lot into its small, 181-sq.-km (70-sq.-mile) frame. On its southern coast are quintessentially beautiful Caribbean beaches and gentle, sparkling seas; on its windward northern shores are beaches rimmed by rugged cliffs and boulders. Its most populated coastlines are filled with high-rise resorts, timeshares, budget motels, casinos, nightclubs, and supersize cruise ships—there to meet the needs of the 600,000 visitors who arrive annually.

And why wouldn't they come? Aruba is sunny and dry most all the time, with average temps hovering around 28°C (82°F) and an average of 51cm (20 in.) of rain a year. It's not called "One Happy Island" for nothing: This is fun in the sun on a near-daily basis.

A golf course on Aruba.

Aruba is one of the southernmost islands in the Caribbean, a mere 24km (15 miles) from the South American coastland. In fact, the first Arubans boated over from Venezuela about 4,500 years ago. Since the mid–17th century, Aruba has been largely a Dutch protectorate, and today its official language is still Dutch, although its polyglot population comprises some 60 nationalities. But most everyone speaks English, just one factor that makes Aruba extremely popular among North Americans. In fact, the island is one of the most Americanized in the Caribbean (70% of its visitors come from the United States), with most prices given in dollars and lots of American-style eateries and chains. But the Dutch influence is evident everywhere, from the fanciful and colorful Dutch colonial architecture in its capital, **Oranjestad,** to such relics from the Dutch settlement as the 1796 **Fort Zoutman,** the island's oldest surviving historical structure.

But it's the sunny island pastimes that most define Aruba. Every watersport under the sun is available here, from snorkeling to kayaking to deep-sea fishing to sailing. The calm surf and sandy bottom make **Arashi Beach,** near the California Lighthouse at the island's northwestern tip, one of Aruba's best swimming sites. The island's mecca of windsurfing is just minutes south at **Hadicurari,** or Fishermen's Huts; the shallow water is also excellent for swimming. Home of high-rises, **Palm Beach** is Aruba's best spot for people-watching. **Boca Grandi,** a virtually deserted expanse of dramatic sand dunes and sea grasses, is reminiscent of Cape Cod, but the aqua, azure, and sapphire waters are unmistakably Caribbean. For sheer tranquillity and open space, **Manchebo Beach,** also known as Punto Brabo, is top-notch; the sand here stretches 110m (361 ft.) from the shore to the hotels.

The island also has four golf courses and a world-class tennis center. But most of all it has those gorgeous, sugary-sand beaches, lapped by turquoise seas and framed by impossibly blue skies some 345 days a year—give or take an odd rainy day. —*AF*

ⓘ **Aruba Tourism Authority** (✆ **800/TO-ARUBA** [862-7822]; www.aruba.com).

✈ Queen Beatrix International Airport.

🛏 $$ **Amsterdam Manor Aruba Beach Resort,** Eagle & Manchebo Beaches, J. E. Irausquin Blvd. 252 (✆ **800/932-6509** in the U.S. and Canada, or 297/527-1100; www.amsterdammanor.com). $$$ **Radisson Aruba Resort & Casino,** Palm Beach/Noord, J.E. Irausquin Blvd. 81 (✆ **800/333-3333** in the U.S. and Canada, or 297/586-6555; www.radisson.com/palmbeachaw).

262 Beach Bums with Culture

Jamaica

The Caribbean's Most Distinct Flavor

From Bob Marley and the unmistakable sounds of reggae to headline-making Olympians—the 1988 bobsled team and, more recently, Beijing games sprinting star Usain Bolt—Jamaica has earned more publicity for the Caribbean than any other island. For anyone seeking some real living culture along with their tropical beach getaway, Jamaica should be high on the list. The superlatively turquoise waters of the Caribbean may be elsewhere, at Turks and Caicos (p. 12) or the Caymans 18 and 113, but the seas and sand here are plenty clean for beach bums. Without a doubt, Jamaica has the most interesting and robust local flavor—complete with all the hang-loose, dreadlocked Rastafarians you're imagining—of any island in this fabled sea.

For the majority of visitors, especially first-timers, a trip to Jamaica means **Montego Bay,** which is fully equipped with glitzy hotels, clubs, and restaurants and even has its own airport, eliminating the need to fly to Kingston (130km/81 miles away by car). The megasize cruise ships spill out thousands of passengers here daily, encouraging touts to roam the beaches with pitches for watersports, reggae clubs, and pub crawls. With all that action, however, comes a citylike vibe: Mo' Bay can feel a little hectic—not what everyone expects from a Caribbean beach holiday. But no trip to Jamaica is complete without a stop at **Time N' Place** (✆ **876/954-4371;** www.mytimenplace.com) in Falmouth (just east of Montego Bay) for a daiquiri. Sure, it's touristy, but the laid-back beach hut, where you can sip daiquiris and Red Stripes in hammocks, is an unforgettable, "I'm in Jamaica, mon!" experience.

Honeymooners and families often prefer the newer resort area of **Negril,** on Jamaica's far western tip, for its romantic **7-Mile Beach** and pampering all-inclusive resorts. **Ocho Rios,** almost due north of Kingston, is another significant resort area that offers a lot of natural beauty; "Ochie" is where you'll find the famous **Dunn's River Falls,** which cascades some 212m (696 ft.) to the sea. Near the eastern end of Jamaica, **Port Antonio** is more of an elite enclave and a still-untouched part of the island. Rafting trips on the island's **Rio Grande** depart from here. For wildlife enthusiasts, boat "safaris" on the **Black River** (east of Negril, on the south coast) put you face to face with American crocodiles and one of the richest swamp ecosystems in the Caribbean.

Jamaica is a big island (11,396 sq. km/4,400 sq miles), and getting around it takes some time; so pick your base wisely depending on what sort of vibe you're after. But no matter which area you choose, you'll be surrounded by mellow Jamaican music and smiling locals bedecked in the green, red, and yellow of

Zip-lining in Jamaica.

the country's flag, and have no trouble finding fantastic little places to eat the delicious island cuisine. Jamaica's well-established tourist infrastructure also means activities galore, from horseback riding on the beach to zip-lining in the forest to swimming with dolphins. Coffee beans are grown in the mist-shrouded mountains of eastern Jamaica; the famous brand **Blue Mountain** (www.bluemountaincoffee.com) welcomes the public at its Mavis Bank facility for plantation visits and factory tours.

Venture away from the established resort spots, and you'll discover Jamaica's more authentic nooks and crannies, not all of which are savory: Poverty and crime are a problem on many parts of the island, and it pays to be a savvy traveler when visiting these areas. **Kingston,** for instance, on the southern coast and toward the eastern end of Jamaica, several hours from Montego Bay and Negril, is a vibrant city of 750,000 that may tempt you with its cultural offerings, but it's best to keep your touring there to daytime hours and to go in a group. The **South Coast** of Jamaica remains largely undeveloped for tourism and offers plenty in the way of hidden treasures, but don't expect it all to be well-scrubbed and hospitable. For better or worse, going off the beaten track is always going to involve some sketchiness, and that's part of why you come—to see the real Jamaica, away from the resort bubble. —*SM*

ⓘ ✆ **800/233-4582** in the U.S., or 876/952-4425; www.visitjamaica.com.

✈ Montego Bay-Sangster International (for Montego Bay, Negril, and Ocho Rios) and Kingston-Norman Manley International (for Kingston and Port Antonio).

🛏 $$$ **The Caves,** Negril (✆ **876/957-0270;** www.thecavesresort.com). $$ **Royal Decameron Montego Beach,** Montego Bay (✆ **876/952-4340;** www.decameron.com).

Beach Bums with Culture **263**

Maui

Hawaii's Irresistible All-Arounder

Hawaii, U.S.

You could travel halfway around the globe, to more exclusive and exotic island locales, and still not find the sort of stunning terrain, world-class recreation, and sunny relaxation that Maui offers. It's no wonder this Polynesian paradise has been voted

"Best Island" in the world numerous times by the glossy travel press. Locals have a saying for their island: *Maui No Ka Oi* ("Maui is the best"), and on many, many counts, I'd have to agree.

Hawaii neophytes often pick Maui for their first foray into the archipelago and find such bliss here that they never bother to check out Kauai 88, the Big Island 242, or Oahu 51. While those other Hawaiian islands have their unique appeal and attractions, there's something about Maui that screams "vacation," and it lures you back again and again when all you want from your trip is to unplug and have a good time. Maui is without a doubt the most pampering of the Hawaiian islands, with the greatest variety and number of amenities and opportunities when it comes to rest and relaxation, cultural exploration, or adventure travel.

On maps, Maui is shaped roughly like a human head and shoulders (the head's at the west end, with the popular beach resort area of Kaanapali along the "forehead"). With seemingly endless sandy beaches, gentle salty breezes, and spectacular sunsets, Maui's west-facing resort developments are popular for good reason. Along that coast, the historic, pedestrian-friendly town of **Lahaina** is full of shops, restaurants, and galleries. In the evening, make your way to the **Old Lahaina Luau** (✆ **800/248-5828;** www.oldlahainaluau.com) for some traditional Polynesian culture—hula dancing, pigs roasting on a spit, and classic island dishes like *po* (mashed taro root).

At busy **Black Rock Beach** in Kaanapali, you'll find some of the best snorkeling in this part of the Pacific. All beaches on Maui, even those in front of the ritzy resorts, are public. In winter, don't miss a chance to go on a **whale-watching** excursion: Humpbacks migrate to the waters off Maui every year to mate or birth their calves. Another highly recommended day trip is a **Trilogy** (✆ **888/225-MAUI** [225-6284]; www.sailtrilogy.com) sailing and snorkeling outing to Lanai 295.

The rural interior of the island offers the Hawaiian version of cowboy country, in towns like **Makawao,** and the formidable volcanic crater of **Haleakala** (3,055m/10,023 ft.). When you need a break from the sun and sand, take a trip back in time to the untouched earthly paradise of **Hana,** along the southeast coast.

Haleakala National Park.

Maui's five-star resorts (concentrated mostly at **Wailea** and **Kapalua**) are legendary, but for a less cocooned atmosphere, I recommend booking a condo somewhere near **Kaanapali:** The location is perfect for exploring everything on the island, and you'll be well-positioned for any and all watersports and excursions you choose. —*SM*

ⓘ ✆ **800/525-MAUI** (525-6284); www.visitmaui.com or www.gohawaii.com.

✈ Kahului International and Kapalua-West Maui.

🛏 $$$ **Four Seasons Resort Maui at Wailea,** 3900 Wailea Alanui (✆ **808/874-8000;** www.fourseasons.com/maui). $$ **Kaanapali Beach Rentals** (✆ **800/887-7654;** www.kaanapalibeachrentals.com).

Beach Bums with Culture

264

Penang

British Trading Post Turned Playground

Malaysia

Golden sands and shimmering blue seas, along with a rich history and delicious local cuisine, have earned this popular Malaysian getaway the marketing nickname of "Pearl of the Orient." Certainly, Penang has everything you could ask for from an island holiday: fun beaches, beautiful resorts, cultural attractions, and scrumptious food—its namesake curry is a staple on Southeast Asian menus worldwide. If you have only a short time to visit Malaysia but want to take in as wide an experience as you can *and* catch some rays, Penang is a great choice.

While Penang is largely a tourist destination these days, it didn't start out that way. Originally called "Pulau Pinang" (Isle of the Betel Nut), Penang was ceded to the British East India Company in the 18th century and became a vibrant trading center where merchants of many ethnicities and cultures met and melded. Much of that heritage is still plenty evident today, especially in the historic city of **Georgetown.** Spending a few hours touring the sights in this UNESCO World Heritage Site, on foot or by trishaw, is a must for any visitor to Penang. Georgetown also has the best bars and clubs on the island.

Hands down, the prime beach destination on Penang is along the northern shore, on the sandy, resort-filled strip called **Batu Feringgi.** The beachfront here is backed by hotels of every kind, and you can just stroll down the sand until you find a spot you like. **Tanjung Bungah** and **Teluk Bahang** are the other major beach areas on the island. Owing to Penang's rich and varied pan-Asian history, street food is also a big part of the island experience. Head for the tantalizing stands along **Gurney Drive,** or just stop anywhere you see hawkers and smell something good. For a great panorama of the island, take the **funicular** up to the top of Penang Hill. From here, beyond the green slope, you can spot the colorful spires and rooftops of places of worship from every religion that's ever come to the island—Buddhist, Hindu, Christian. The intrepid can check out the **Snake Temple** in Sungai Kluong, a Buddhist shrine where live pit vipers are still kept.

Shopping is also an important pursuit on the island, whether you choose to browse the western-style plazas of **Gurney Plaza** and **Queensbay,** or traditional flea markets like **Rope Walk.** Famous products include wood carvings and silver jewelry, as well as a wondrous array of nutmeg-based oils and food items—no surprise, considering Penang's history in the spice trade. Bargaining is expected, and a fun skill to hone among the island's amiable merchants. —*SM*

ⓘ www.tourismpenang.gov.my.

✈ Penang International.

🛏 $ **Lone Pine,** Batu Feringgi 97 (✆ **60/4/881-1511;** www.lonepinehotel.com). $$$ **Shangri-La's Rasa Sayang Resort & Spa,** Batu Feringgi (✆**60/4/888-8888;** www.shangri-la.com).

265 Laid-Back Rhythms

Madeira

Captured Sunlight

Portugal

This sun-dappled tropical isle is an exotic mix of old-world Europe and West African sizzle. The "pearl of the Atlantic," Madeira is an autonomous region of Portugal but is actually closer to Africa than it is to the motherland. The island is lush and mountainous, its deep folds and creases swathed in green vegetation, blue jacaranda and birds of paradise, and fruit gardens. Beautiful terraced vineyards and fields of sugar cane are carved out of steep slopes, surrounded by a bright blue sea. The island's capital, picturesque **Funchal,** sits on a hillside overlooking a wide bay, with high sea cliffs looming in the distance.

Only 57km (35 miles) long and about 21km (13 miles) across at its widest point, the island is a favorite holiday destination for Europeans (although for good beaches, you'll need to go to sister island **Porto Santo**). Madeira is ambrosia for wine lovers, home to perhaps the most famous wine in the world, the eponymous Madeira. Grapes don't normally take hold in tropical climates—the humidity and rich soil usually mean poor quality and disease. Yet Madeira is blessed with a singular *terroir*. Its volcanic soil is perfect for hardy, exotic, strangely named grapes like Bastardo and Strangled Dog. Over the years, the island's inventive winemakers discovered that if they fortified the local wine with alcohol they could produce a rich port that would last for literally centuries. Geographic location also blessed Madeira, for it could handily supply the New World with wine; the heat it endured on such journeys only improved its taste. (That heat is now simulated in ovenlike lofts on the island.)

Madeira has long had a legendary following among wine connoisseurs. In 1478, when the Duke of Clarence faced execution for treason in the Tower of London, he chose to drown himself in a tub of Madeira rather than face the axe. Shakespeare referred to it in his plays (in Henry II, the Prince of Wales is accused of selling his soul for a glass of Madeira and a chicken leg), and Madeira was the wine used to toast the American Declaration of Independence (George Washington reputedly could not get by without a pint a day).

Madeira wine is currently going through a quality renaissance, led by innovative island winemakers. The prizewinning wines of **Henriques & Henriques** (✆ **351/29/194-15-51;** www.henriquesehenriques.pt) consistently garner top spots in international blind tasting competitions; you can tour the headquarters in the town of Càmara de Lobos. The quaint white town house of the **Madeira Wine Company** (✆ **351/29/174-01-10;** www.madeirawinecompany.com), in Funchal, features creaky lofts piled high with oak, mahogany, and satinwood casks, as well as a wood-raftered tasting room where shelves hold

100-year-old wine—captured sunlight from Victorian times.

Madeira is about much more than just wine, however. The beautiful countryside is ripe for exploring on foot; in fact, 2,500km (1,553 miles) of walking trails trace the old *levadas,* or irrigation aqueducts, over mountains, into rural countryside, and past rock pools, waterfalls, and breathtaking seascapes. Guided tours along the *levadas* are offered by **Madeira Explorers** (✆ **351/29/176-37-02;** www.madeira-levada-walks.com). —*AF*

ⓘ www.madeira-island.com, www.madeirarural.com, or www.visitportugal.com.

✈ Madeira International Airport (flight from Lisbon: 1 hr., 25 min.).

🛏 $$$ **Estalagem Quinta da Casa Branca,** Rua da Casa Branca 7, Funchal (✆ **351/29/170-07-70;** www.quintacasabranca.pt). $$ **Hotel Quinta da Penha de França,** Rua da Penha de França 2, Funchal (✆ **351/29/120-46-50;** www.hotelquintapenhafranca.com).

Laid-Back Rhythms

Cozumel

Carefree Recreation off the Yucatán

Mexico

The idea of going down to coastal Mexico on vacation is enticing enough, but in a country known for its relaxing rhythms and warm weather, Cozumel ups the ante by being an island with all the advantages of a Mexican beach holiday, yet little of the mass-market feel and spring-break craziness that plague such tourist-magnet places as Cancún.

Since 1996, Cozumel's marine habitats have been a national park, and well before then, they've been recognized—since Jacques Cousteau started filming his documentaries here in the 1960s—as one of the best **dive spots** in the entire world. There's no need to show up already an expert: The island's many friendly diving outfitters, along with the protected conditions of the coral reefs, make this a great place to get scuba-certified. **Palancar, Santa Rosa,** and **El Cedral** reefs are some of the island's most famous sites, along with the tunnels of **Devil's Throat.** You can also explore the undersea world of **Chankanaab Lagoon park** (www.cozumelparks.com) on the **Atlantis Submarine** (✆ **866/546-7820** from the U.S. and Canada; www.atlantisadventures.com), which dives to depths of 30m (100 ft.) among awesome coral towers and Technicolor schools of tropical fish.

As for beaches, Cozumel's unique geographical position means that gentle breakers lap at the western shore of the island, where the waters are aquarium-calm, while the eastern side gets lashed with strong waves. Cocktail-hour **catamaran excursions** are ideal for romantics eager to explore these waters, while snorkeling with rays at **Stingray Beach** or swimming with dolphins at **Dolphin Discovery** (✆ **52/998/193-3360;** www.dolphindiscovery.com) are great activities for the young and adventurous.

For those who wish to spend more time above the water's surface than below it, there's plenty to keep you busy on Cozumel. **ATV and Jeep tours** are a fun way to explore the island's junglelike interior and evocative Mayan ruins. All island travel agencies can arrange these, but for something really memorable, try the horseback tours at **Rancho Palmita** (no phone) on the Costera Sur highway, across from the Occidental Cozumel resort.

Snorkeling in Cozumel.

Of course, what would a trip to any part of Mexico be without the local cantina culture? **San Miguel** is the island's only real town and where all the action is. While the party-loving crowd will be relieved to find the full complement of Señor Frog's–type bars and clubs in San Miguel, the scene tends to be more mature than at similar establishments in, say, Cancún.

For visitors seeking something a bit more authentic, plenty of restaurants in town specialize in traditional Mayan recipes. Every Sunday evening, locals congregate around the main plaza of San Miguel with their families for live music and socializing in the balmy air.

The best and most commonly used accommodations on Cozumel are vacation rentals; whether you opt for a large beach house or a smaller condo, the units generally come with staff that will do all your cleaning and cooking, if you wish. Any agency you book accommodations with can also arrange every imaginable excursion and tour. —*SM*

(i) www.islacozumel.com.

✈ Cozumel Airport or Cancun Airport (45 min. to Playa del Carmen, then 30-min. ferry).

⛴ From Playa del Carmen, 30 min.

🛏 $$ **El Cantil Oceanfront Condominiums,** av. Rafael Melgar, San Miguel (✆ **52/987/869-1517;** www.elcantilcondos.com). $$$ **Presidente Intercontinental Cozumel,** Costera Sur Km 6.5 (✆ **800/327-0200** in the U.S., or 52/987/872-9500; www.intercontinentalcozumel.com).

Island Hopping the Whitsunday Islands: Turquoise Bliss

Off the coast of Queensland, forming a pleasure- and relaxation-oriented way halfway between the mainland and the Great Barrier Reef, the Whitsunday Islands are many an Australian's idea of the perfect holiday. This chain of 74 islands (8 are inhabited) is an idyllic palette of gorgeous light aqua, sugary-white sand, and swathes of unspoiled green. There's a common theme to many of the Whitsundays: Often, there's only one resort on the island, and the rest is protected parkland veined with hiking trails. The beaches and reefs tend to offer the same spectrum of recreational opportunities from island to island—snorkeling, sea kayaking, and wind- and motor-powered watersports—yet each of the Whitsundays has its own special character and appeal. Most foreign travelers who visit the Whitsundays do so as part of a Great Barrier Reef trip; Australians are more likely to use the islands as a destination in and of themselves.

Airlie Beach, Queensland, is the jumping-off point for the Whitsundays, and though it's not an island itself, its broad array of excursions and outfitters makes it a valid base for exploring the archipelago. Island-hopping around the Whitsundays is perfectly doable on your own with regularly scheduled ferries and shuttles; otherwise, there are cruise outfitters that will give you a comprehensive tour. Even better, charter a sailboat, as these can access smaller and more secluded coves, where you can drop anchor and spend unforgettable nights under the Austral sky.

Whitehaven Beach on Whitsunday Island.

267 **Whitsunday Island** is the largest in the group; though it's uninhabited parkland, it receives more traffic than any other part of the archipelago because it lays claim to the Whitsundays' iconic postcard attraction: **Whitehaven Beach** is a stunning vision, unique in the world, of white silica sand swirled with light turquoise over the shallows of pristine Hill Inlet. It's among the most photographed sites in Australia and inundated with day-trippers all day, every day, but you simply can't come to the Whitsundays and miss Whitehaven Beach. Excursions are offered from anywhere in the archipelago, and when booking, be sure that your tour includes Hill Inlet (the bigger boats don't).

Any holiday in the Whitsundays will include at least a brief stop on 268 **Hamilton Island,** the largest and best-equipped, services-wise, and a major gateway to Great Barrier Reef. Most all Whitsundays interisland boats stop at Hamilton, and it has the islands' main airport; the constant comings and goings of vacationers make for a lively energy. When it comes to entertainment and activities, Hamilton has it all, as well as accommodations for all tastes and budgets. This was also the island featured in Tourism Queensland's "Best Job in the World" promotional contest: In 2009, a Brit named Ben Southall was chosen from a field of international applicants to be the Whitsunday Islands caretaker; he was based on Hamilton and blogged about his experiences at www.islandreefjob.com.au.

Daydream Island Resort and Spa is the only game on the eponymous 269 **Daydream Island.** This is one of the Whitsundays' most family-friendly options, with its man-made outdoor aquarium (reef lagoons with controlled habitats of fish and coral), miniature golf course, swimming pools, and kids' programs like outdoor movie nights.

The swankiest place in the Whitsundays by far is 270 **Hayman Island,** home to the one-name luxury boutique resort, Hayman. Discerning and deep-pocketed travelers come from far and wide for the pampering atmosphere and hip modern aesthetics of Hayman, and for the wide range of well-organized, hassle-free watersports offered from the beach in front of the resort, from catamaran sailing and windsurfing to sea kayaking and water-skiing. Hayman is the ultracivilized antidote to some of the more rough-and-tumble islands in the group.

Nature lovers will want to plan a day or two on 271 **Brampton Island,** which is almost entirely National Park. Paths and trails afford hikers easy access to the island's wooded interior, which includes an ancient forest of melaleuca (paperbark) trees. All manner of excursions and entertainment are organized from the island's single resort, Voyages Brampton Island, which offers great value and an escape from Whitsundays day-trippers. Brampton is fringed by coral reef where you can snorkel and dive practically alone—just you and your mask and fins and teeming marine life all around.

Abundant jellyfish rule out ocean swimming off 272 **Long Island,** but there are beautiful views from this island with three secluded resorts on quiet bays. Couples-oriented Long Island is very tropical-feeling, and any of the bars here will make up potent Long Island Iced Teas for you to sip while watching the sunset. Students and backpackers in the Whitsundays have long preferred 273 **South Molle,** where the no-frills Koala Adventure Resort has an appealing summer-camp feel, with shared bunks, tons of outdoor fun by day, and rollicking Aussie revelry by night. Party-loving singles—and not many others—will love 274 **Lindeman Island,** home to the Whitsundays' only Club Med resort. The rest of Lindeman is an undeveloped 670 hectares (1,656 acres) of world heritage park. —*SM*

ⓘ ✆ **61/7/4945-3711;** www.tourismwhitsundays.com.au or www.whitsundaytourism.com.

✈ Great Barrier Reef Airport, Hamilton Island.

⛴ Cruise Whitsundays and Fantasea Adventure Cruising operate ferries from Airlie Beach to Hamilton Island, and from there to the smaller island resorts.

🛏 $$$ **Hayman,** Hayman Island (✆ **61/7/4940 1234;** www.hayman.com.au). $$ **Water's Edge Resort,** Airlie Beach (✆ **61/7/4948 2655;** www.watersedgewhitsundays.com.au).

Laid-Back Rhythms

Isla de Margarita

The Caribbean, Venezuela-Style

Venezuela

If you're looking for a slightly raffish Caribbean island that's a little off the beaten path, but with plenty of shopping, nightlife, and restaurant options—and decidedly un-Caribbean-like prices—it's hard to beat Isla de Margarita, 40km (25 miles) off Venezuela's northeastern coast. It's got all the physical attributes of the quintessential Caribbean island: gorgeous beaches, warm breezes, and turquoise seas. Strands of sugary sand are fringed in green, with volcanic hills rising up in the tropical haze. Best of all, it exudes an earthy, laid-back charm that's a refreshing break from the cool, ultraluxe homogeneity that has pervaded the hospitality business of late.

Mainlanders head to this biggest island in Venezuela's Nueva Esparta state to play on and off the beaches and stock up on duty-free goods. Isla de Margarita has two large towns, **Porlamar** (with a population of 85,000) and **Pampatar** (with a population of 50,000), both on the island's more populous eastern coast, and here is where the nonbeach action is—and there's plenty of it. It's a jumble of shopping malls, casinos, and restaurants. Porlamar, home to a third of the island population, is also the island's nightlife center. Prettier Pampatar, 10km/6 miles northeast of Porlamar, has upscale restaurants and shops; it's also the site of the **Castillo de San Carlos Borromeo,** a 17th-century stone fortress. The rest of the island is composed of sleepy little fishing villages and lovely beaches, some chock-full of tourist facilities, others just sand and sea. Jeep tours give you a good sense of the range of sights and island habitats; try **Walter's Tours** (✆ **58/0295/274-1265** or 58/0416/696-2212; www.margaritaislandguide.com).

Margarita is a little rough around the edges—stray dogs and cats roam small towns, upkeep can be dodgy, and hawkers work the beaches with an impressive vigor. Yet the island's growing presence on the tourism radar screen means that prices are going up. The island has no mega-luxury resorts, but a few international chains have muscled in to compete with a handful of big, sprawling hotels and palm-fringed inns. Many beachside lodgings, however, are composed of a smattering of apartments around a pool, with clean, basic rooms; don't expect 400-thread-count linens, and you won't be disappointed. Do, however, expect to pay less than you'd spend on holiday on most other Caribbean islands—and getting around is certainly a bargain in oil-rich Venezuela.

Christopher Columbus landed here in 1498, greeted by the native Guaiqueries, who were later enslaved by the Spanish. It wasn't until 1814 that the island won its independence from Spain and became the country's first free territory. Margarita was once known as the "Pearl of the Caribbean" for the pearl-rich oyster beds Columbus discovered nearby. The beds, and the pearls, are long gone, plundered by the treasure-mad conquistadors.

These days, the biggest treasures left to claim are the fine beaches, the perfect tropical climate—hot, hot, hot (average temp: 31°C/88°F), with little rain and low humidity—and the opportunity to play in the warm seas and pounding surf. Not only is Margarita a paradise for heat-seeking beach bums, but **Playa El Yaque,** on the south side of the island, is also one of the world's top kite-surfing and windsurfing locations, where the waters are smooth and the winds average 18 to 22 knots year-round (best time to go: Dec–May). For boards and lessons, try **El Yaque Paradise** (✆ **58/0295/263-9418;** www.hotelyaqueparadise.com) and **El Yaque Motion** ([tel/fax] **58/0295/263-9742;** www.elyaquemotion.com). A boat tour in the **Laguna La Restinga** national park cruises a natural lagoon through mangrove forests filled with bird life (including the blue-crowned parakeet) and the occasional ocelot. Although it looks peaceful and vibrant, the park is currently classified as "critically endangered" in large part because of illegal commerce and human encroachment—another reason to see Margarita Island now. *—AF*

ⓘ www.margarita-island-venezuela.com.

✈ Porlamar or Caracas, 40-min. flight to Margarita.

⛴ **Conferry** (✆ **58/0212/782-8544**), Punta de Piedras, on the southern end of Margarita. La Guaira (30 min. from Caracas, on the coast), and Puerto La Cruz and Cumaná (a few hours east of Caracas, on the northern coast), 2–4 hours, depending on the ferryboat.

🛏 $$$ **Hesperia Isla Margarita,** Playa Bonita (✆ **58/0295/400-7111;** www.hesperia.com). $$ **Hotel Costa Linda Beach,** Playa El Agua (✆ **58/0295/249-1303;** www.hotelcostalinda.com).

276 Laid-Back Rhythms

Fire Island

New York's Small-Town Secret

New York, U.S.

Everyone's heard about the Hamptons, of course—that chichi beach enclave at the far eastern end of Long Island, where wealthy New Yorkers gravitate in packs every summer. But plenty of folks who wouldn't be caught dead in the *Gossip Girl*–ish Hamptons have their own summer getaway: Fire Island. Sure, the houses are smaller and more closely packed together; and you can't roll in by car, but have to take a ferry, then get around on foot and by bicycle. But what Fire Island lacks in social cachet, it more than makes up for in friendliness and small-town feeling.

Much of this long, skinny barrier island—it's only a half mile wide but 32 miles (51km) long—is national seashore and parkland, separating clusters of houses in several distinct cozy hamlets. About halfway along, **Ocean Beach** is the hub of island activity, with most of the island's hotels and restaurants, accompanied by a lively weekend singles scene. Singles also gravitate to the beach-house shares of (from west to east) Kismet, Fair Harbor, Corneille Estates, Ocean Bay Park, and Davis Park. Other towns are definitely family-oriented, prizing quiet and a 1950s-era vibe—from west to east, Saltaire, Dunewood, Atlantique, Seaview, and Point O'Woods.

For other visitors, Fire Island is synonymous with a vibrant gay social scene, centered on two adjacent towns to the east of Ocean Bay Park, **Cherry Grove** and **Fire Island Pines.** The quieter community of the Pines attracts gay men, while party-central Cherry Grove draws a crowd of women and men; the woods between Cherry Grove and The Pines, affectionately known as the "Meat Rack," hosts some extraordinary scenes of its own.

With the exception of the private Fire Island Summer Club, Fire Island's beaches are open to all, free of charge. There are beaches on both the north shore, fronting the Great South Bay, and the south shore, fronting the Atlantic; each town has its own beach, sometimes two, and often a marina as well. At the far ends—near the east-end wildlife preserve of **Watch Hill,** and around the west end's historic **lighthouse**—beaches are clothing-optional, though going topless is tolerated everywhere. The wide, dune-edged beaches of **Smith Point,** at the far eastern tip, are a magnet for surfers. If you're coming over on the ferry for only a day, the most convenient beach is the broad white strand of **Sailor's Haven,** between Ocean Bay Park and Cherry Grove; here you can also wander around the stunning **Sunken Forest,** a marshy 40-acre (16-hectare) maritime forest with its trees twisted and bleached by salt air and sea wind.

Fire Island is very much a summer destination; when Memorial Day hits, the hamlets fill with warm-weather revelers, but after September, almost everything shuts down. The biggest day of the year out here is July 4th, but not for the usual patriotic reasons—that's the date of the annual **Invasion of the Pines,** when boatloads of drag queens from Cherry Grove come and "terrorize" the posh Pines. *—HH*

ⓘ www.fireisland.com or www.nps.gov/fis.

✈ John F. Kennedy International (39 miles/63km); LaGuardia (48 miles/77km).

⛴ From Bay Shore to Ocean Beach/Kismet/Ocean Bay Park, **Fire Island Ferries** (✆ **631/665-3600;** www.fireislandferries.com). From Sayville to Cherry Grove/The Pines/Sunken Forest, **Sayville Ferry** (✆ **631/589-0810;** www.sayvilleferry.com). From Patchogue to Watch Hill, **Davis Park Ferry** (✆ **631/475-1665;** www.pagelinx.com/dpferry/index.shtml).

🛏 $$ **Clegg's Hotel,** 478 Bayberry Walk, Ocean Beach (✆ **631/583-5399;** www.cleggshotel.com). $$ **Grove Hotel,** Cherry Grove (✆ **631/597-6600;** www.grovehotel.com).

7 Leisure Islands

Take a Hike 277

Wizard Island

Wizard of OR

Oregon, U.S.

Crater Lake is such a piercing color of blue that it looks like a digitally enhanced ad for something bracing and pure, like after-shave or mountain spring water. The lake, which is the caldera that formed when the ancient volcano **Mount Mazama** erupted 7,700 years ago, is the deepest in the United States (almost 2,000 ft./610m). Its basin is bare volcanic rock, and its waters are only rain and snowfall; there are no streams or rivers to dump sediment into the lake, which explains its penetrating, practically silvery hue. The only relief to the mirrorlike surface of Crater Lake is Wizard Island, a cinder cone that rises like a sorcerer's hat, studded with hemlocks and pines, near the western shore of the lake.

A hike to the summit of Wizard Island—which is 6,933 feet (2,113m) above sea level but only 755 feet (230m) above the surface of the lake—provides an unforgettable panorama of American Northwestern natural beauty, with 360-degree views of that sublimely glassy water and the pristine slopes of the ancient crater rim all around you. Based on tree-ring dating alone, Wizard Island could be as young as 800 years, though it's likely been around since a subsequent eruption of Mount Mazama 6,000 years ago. The island is a significant (dormant) volcano in its own right, rising over 2,700 feet (823m) above the floor of the lake.

Access to Wizard Island is by park-concessioned tour boats only, which run for just a few months in the summer. Be aware that it takes planning and the best part of a day to do the Wizard Island excursion; it's not something you're likely to experience on a visit passing through to see Crater Lake National Park. From early July to mid-September only, **Volcano Boat Tours** (✆ **888/774-CRATER** [774-2728]; www.xanterra.com) will take you to Wizard Island as part of a lake circumnavigation and fascinating natural history lecture. Boats depart from Cleetwood Cove on the north shore of the lake twice daily, at 9:55am and 1pm, and advance purchase of the $37 round-trip tickets is recommended. To reach the Cleetwood Cove boat landing, you'll need to park at the **Cleetwood Cove Trailhead** and hike (a steep 1-mile/1.6km downhill) to the dock. Once on Wizard Island, you can choose to stay either 3 hours or 6 hours (return boats come by at 1 and 4pm and sometimes even later to pick up stragglers, as overnight camping is prohibited). Bring a picnic and plenty of water.

The summit hike is 1.75 miles (2.8km) round-trip, with a moderate elevation to cover (you start at 6,176 ft./1,882m and climb to 6,940 ft./2,115m). Near the base of Wizard Island, you'll walk along a path shaded by hemlocks and Shasta red firs that have rooted in the hard volcanic rock. As you follow the switchbacks toward the top of the cinder cone, the trees thin out, the path steepens as loose pumice crunches underfoot, and the lake views, through tenacious stands of Whitebark pines, get even more sublime. At the very top, you're rewarded with the crater known as the **Witches' Cauldron,** 500 feet wide and 100 feet deep (152×30m). Hardly a belching pit of nefarious volcanic gases, the crater is the quiet home to pioneer grasses, wildflowers, and pines.

Before heading back on the tour boat, extreme types can even go for a swim in Crater Lake, but beware, those glittering waters are bracing indeed, at an average summer temperature of 55°F (13°C). —*SM*

Previous page: Wizard Island.

ⓘ www.nps.gov/crla.

✈ Klamath Falls, Oregon (60 miles/97km), and Medford, Oregon (80 miles/129km), connections to western U.S. airports.

⛴ Cleetwood Cove, on the north shore of Crater Lake (3 miles/4.8km).

🛏 $$$ **Crater Lake Lodge,** 565 Rim Dr., Crater Lake National Park (✆ **888/774-2728;** www.craterlakelodges.com).

278 Take a Hike

Manitou Islands

Outdoor Fun Atop Mishe Mokwa's Cubs

Michigan, U.S.

Geologists will tell you that the Lake Michigan islands of North and South Manitou, part of the **Sleeping Bear Dunes National Lakeshore,** were formed by glacial activity thousands of years ago, but the Native American explanation for their existence is far more endearing. Chippewa legend relates that long ago, a mother bear named Mishe Mokwa and her two cubs fled the Wisconsin shore of the lake when a forest fire broke out. The bears took to the lake waters and swam east, toward the Michigan shore, but only the mother bear survived the journey. Her cubs, exhausted by the rough waters, drowned within sight of land. North and South Manitou islands, it's said, were raised by the Great Spirit over the places where they perished, and the mainland stretch of Sleeping Bear Dunes is where mama kept a vigil for her little ones.

North Manitou shoal light.

Located within easy striking distance of the Traverse City area (the ferry leaves from Leland, Michigan), the uninhabited Manitou islands are a wonderful recreation destination with leisurely hikes, bird-watching, hunting and fishing opportunities, and a smattering of homesteads and other abandoned buildings from the island's 19th-century settlements. North Manitou is more than twice the size of its southern sister, with 22 sq. miles (57 sq. km) to South Manitou's 3 sq. miles (7.8 sq. km).

Generally speaking, **North Manitou** is more of a DIY wilderness experience than the south island, with fewer facilities and sights. Shaped like a bulbous isthmus that's broken off from the mainland, North Manitou is traversed by well-maintained trails that make for satisfying day- or overnight hikes. The island's policy of "free camping" means you can choose your own site (though you'll still have to pay a fee). On the southwestern tip of North Manitou, near Dimmick's Point, is a nesting area for the endangered **piping plover.** Elsewhere on the island, birders regularly sight bald eagles and raptors such as hawks. **Lake Manitou,** practically in the dead center of the island, has decent fishing.

South Manitou is dominated by a wide, round bay on its eastern side, where the ranger station and dock are located; over the years, the bay has saved a lot of cargo and human lives, as it was used by ships plying the waters between Chicago and the Straits of Mackinac as a safe harbor in times of rough weather on Lake Michigan. Accessible by a moderate round-trip, 7-mile (11km) hike from the dock, the **Valley of the Giants** is a magnificent grove of centuries-old cedars, the most ancient of which may be over 500 years old, with a trunk circumference of 18 feet (5.5m). En route to the cedars, you'll see the shipwreck of the *Francisco Morazan,* a package freighter that didn't make it to the protected bay of South Manitou in time and foundered in 1960 off the southern shore of the island. Sitting atop high limestone bluffs that overlook Lake Michigan, the **Perched Sand Dunes** take up most of the western coast of South Manitou. Throughout the island, which is equipped with campsites and trails, you'll come across schoolhouses, barns, and lighthouses—ghosts from South Manitou's period as a rest and refueling station for ships on Lake Michigan and as a (failed, due to sandy soil) agricultural settlement.

Don't care to embark on either island's hiking trails? Take one of **Lake Manitou Transit's sunset cruises** (round-trip from Leland and offered most evenings in summer; see ferries below for contact info), which take in the island highlights that are visible from shore. —*SM*

ⓘ **Sleeping Bear Dunes National Seashore,** U.S. National Park Service (✆ **231/326-5134;** www.nps.gov/slbe).

✈ **Traverse City–Cherry Capital Airport** (30 miles/48km to Leland), connections to the upper Midwest.

From Leland, Michigan, 1 hr. to North Manitou, 1½ hr. to South Manitou. **Manitou Island Transit** (✆ **231/256-9061;** www.leelanau.com/manitou).

$ Camping (✆ **877/444-6777;** www.nps.gov/slbe).

279 Take a Hike

Cape Breton Island

North America's Highland Wilds

Canada

A superstar in the environmental world, an outdoor adventurer's playground, and a beauty with a litany of accolades to prove it—the island was named one of the top island destinations in the world by *Travel + Leisure* magazine—Cape Breton is the northernmost island in Nova Scotia and linked to the province's mainland by the Canso Causeway. The island's distinctly Scottish culture—Gaelic is still spoken in certain areas here—is rooted in the migration of thousands of Scots settlers here in the 18th and 19th centuries. Cape Breton also has a vivid Arcadian presence; French colonists settled the region in the 18th century. It's an intensely flavorful cultural stew, and music is the common language. There's some serious fiddlin' going on around here: Cape Breton is one of the few places in North America where Celtic *céilidhs* (traditional dances) are common.

The Scots who settled this part of Canada were generally Highlanders who'd rebelled against the English Crown. The Scottish Highlands don't have a scenic coastal highway, but the North American version does: the **Cabot Trail** (www.cabottrail.com), a 300km (186-mile) loop built in 1939 to take advantage of the island's astounding sea views. Along the way, you pass through the **Cape Breton Island National Park** (www.pc.gc.ca), a starkly beautiful wilderness with a split personality: In the interior rises a melancholy plateau of wind-stunted evergreens, bogs, and barrens, a fitting home for druids or trolls; around the edges, the

Cape Breton Island.

mountains tumble to the sea suddenly in a dramatic landscape of ravines and ragged, rust-colored cliffs. The gateway to Cape Breton park is the Acadian town of **Chéticamp,** the most French-speaking part of the island.

The Cabot Trail circuit takes around 6 to 8 hours to drive and has literally dozens of hikes, from short hops of under an hour to half-day treks of varying difficulty. For detailed hiking information, go to www.cabottrail.com. The road has lots of brake-testing steep climbs and whooshing descents, and drivers will want to stop at many pullouts. The most gorgeous stretch is the 44km (27 miles) from Chéticamp to Pleasant Bay along the western coast. You'll lose the water views for a time after Pleasant Bay, as you cut across the headlands to Cape North, where it's believed English explorer John Cabot first set foot on the North American continent. Going down the eastern coast, you'll pass through a series of towns with Scottish names—Ingonish Centre, Ingonish Ferry, South Ingonish Harbour—and then make a precipitous climb to the promontory of Cape Smokey, where panoramic views explode on every side.

Stop and stretch your legs on some of the hiking trails that head inland from the road. The best ones are the .8km-long (.5-mile) **Bog Trail,** which follows a boardwalk into the gnarled bogs of the tableland, and the .8km (.5-mile) **Lone Shieling loop,** which enters a verdant hardwood forest that includes 350-year-old sugar maples; a re-creation of a Scottish crofter's hut is a highlight of the trail. An 11km (6.8-mile) trail leads along the bluffs of Cape Smokey; even if you don't go all the way to the tip, it's worth walking partway just to feel the headland winds and taste the salt air. —*AF*

ⓘ http://novascotia.com, http://cbisland.com, or www.pc.gc.ca.

✈ Halifax (282km/175 miles); some connections into Sydney Airport.

⛴ **Bay Ferries** (✆ **888/249-7245;** www.catferry.com) operates ferries on the Bar Harbor–Yarmouth and Portland-Yarmouth routes.

🛏 $ **Cape Breton Highlands Bungalows,** Cabot Trail, Ingonish Beach (✆ **902/285-2000**). $$ **Inverary Resort,** Shore Rd., Baddeck (✆ **800/565-5660** or 902/295-3500; www.capebretonresorts.com).

Take a Hike **280**

Great Barrier Island

Tramping It Up on the Barrier

New Zealand

In a country already overflowing with outdoor adventures, it might seem like overkill to set your sights on a remote island. But then again, why not? Separated from the North Island 318 by the Hauraki Bay (100km/62miles from Auckland), "the Barrier" is an unspoiled playground for hikers, boaters, surfers, divers, and bikers. Its diverse, hilly terrain is veined with more than 100km (62 miles) of well-maintained paths, and its meandering coastline is a virgin setting for exhilarating water activities. All of this, and it's still considered a "suburb" of Auckland.

The Maori called the island *Motu Aotea* (island of the white cloud), but its dry, matter-of-fact English name came when Captain Cook observed that the 285-sq.-km (110-sq.-mile) island formed a barrier between the open waters of the Pacific Ocean and the protected Hauraki Bay. The contrast between the ocean-facing east coast and the bay-fronting west coast is striking. On the east coast, wind-swept dunes give way to beach sand worn to a fine, white grain from thousands of years of erosion by the Pacific surf. Surfing, in fact, is the principal activity on the east coast, at the reliably good breaks of **Medlands Beach, Whangapoua Beach, Awana Beach,** and **Kaitoke Beach.** The sheltered west coast is blessed with a seemingly endless supply of picturesque bays and islets ideal for sailing and kayaking. (For either activity, you can rent equipment or, even better, join a tour with one of the seasoned outfitters in Port Fitzroy or Tryphena.) Paddling around these clear and shallow waters, you're likely to see dolphins, rays, penguins, and even whales from time to time.

Down under, hiking is called **tramping,** and paths are called tracks; you'll hear both terms frequently on The Barrier. The **New Zealand Department of Conservation** (www.doc.govt.nz) maintains Great Barrier's extensive network of tracks, though for the best tramping experience, it's often better to go with a guide; **Discover Great Barrier** is the only DOC-licensed outfitter for walks. The most rewarding excursion for many is the relatively short hike to the top of **Windy Canyon.** From here to Kaiaraara, a full-day walk takes you to the summit of Great Barrier's highest point, **Mount Hobson** (Hirakimata in Maori, 621m/2,037 ft.), with tremendous only-in-New-Zealand views down verdant slopes, spiked with crags, to the azure sea.

The contrasting sea conditions around the island have, on two notorious occasions, been tragic for ships negotiating the extreme north and south points of Great Barrier. Off the remote northern tip of the island, the SS *Wairarapa* sank in 1894, killing the 140 men onboard. 1922 saw the foundering of the SS *Wiltshire* off the southeast edge of Great Barrier. Both wrecks are now dive sites.

Great Barrier doesn't have any centralized electricity, and even some of the posher-looking guesthouses are little more than glorified cabins. Facilities islandwide are mostly primitive, and there's a great small-community feel to the villages (total native pop. 852). Luxurious post-hike pampering is not what Great Barrier is about, which is great news to the relatively small number of outdoor enthusiasts who visit every year. —*SM*

ⓘ www.greatbarriernz.com.

✈ Great Barrier Island Airport, service from Auckland (30 min.).

⛴ From Auckland, **SeaLink** (www.sealink.co.nz; year-round, 4½ hr.) and **Fullers** (www.fullers.co.nz; Oct–Mar, 2½ hr.).

🛏 $$ **FitzRoy House,** Glenfern Rd., Port FitzRoy (✆ **64/9/429-0091;** www.fitzroyhouse.co.nz).

281 The Sporting Life

Hilton Head

Ace in the Hole

South Carolina, U.S.

Ever since a cadre of transplanted Scotsmen founded America's first golf club in Charleston in 1786, South Carolina has been a golfing mecca. But few spots are as devoted to the game as this 12-mile-long (19km) barrier island, which boasts no fewer than 24 fastidiously manicured golf courses—that's more than 400 holes, artfully designed over the past 50 years by just about every major golf course architect,

Hilton Head.

from Robert Trent Jones to Pete Dye to George and Tom Fazio.

Connected to the mainland by two bridges, Hilton Head is hardly an isolated outpost, but development has been carefully monitored to preserve the natural beauty of its broad Atlantic beaches, the gentle sea marshes on the sound, and stands of live and water oak, pine, bay, and palmetto trees. A surprising amount of the island has been set aside as nature reserves, where everything from osprey and egrets to alligators, bobcats, and white-tailed deer live undisturbed; loggerhead turtles lay their eggs on the beaches, and bottlenose dolphins cavort just offshore. The resorts here—or "plantations" as they are traditionally called—strive more for low-key elegance than for glitz or bright lights; even the lower-priced lodgings—and there are plenty—seem rustically toned down. Everything seems to be designed to get visitors outdoors, cycling along tucked-away bike paths, kayaking through salt marsh creeks, galloping through maritime forest preserves, or taking an early-morning jog along the firm-packed broad beaches.

Still, golf is the jewel in Hilton Head's crown. Among the island's most fascinating courses are the island's oldest, the **Ocean Course** at Sea Pines (see below), where the landscape of live oak, pines, and tidal marshes has been so well preserved that it is not only a golf course but also an Audubon bird sanctuary. Another classic course at Sea Pines, the **Harbour Town Golf Links** challenges golfers to bring their best shot-making finesse. At Port Royal, the marsh-edged **Robber's Row** course was laid out on a Civil War battleground and is thickly strewn with historic markers. And if there's a single course in the area you "must" play, it's the public **Hilton Head National** course just over the causeway in Bluffton (Hwy. 278; ✆ **843/842-5900;** www.golfhiltonheadnational.com), a Gary Player 18-holer with gorgeous scenery that evokes Scotland, complemented by an additional 9-hole Bobby Weed layout.

The challenge is in figuring out how to hit as many different courses as possible while you're here. The obvious first step is to book into one of the island's top golf resorts, such as **Palmetto Dunes** or **Sea Pines** (see below), each of which has three top 18-hole courses to sample. Another four golf clubs on the island cooperate under the umbrella **Heritage Golf Group** (www.heritagegolf group.com): the **Port Royal Golf Club, Palmetto Hall Plantation, Oyster Reef Golf Club,** and the **Shipyard Golf Club.** Another strategy is to book a golf vacation that will line up rounds for you on several different courses, such as the packages offered by **Golf Island** (✆ **888/465-3475;** www.golfisland.com). *—HH*

ⓘ **Tourist office,** 100 William Hilton Pkwy. (✆ **843/785-3673;** www.hiltonhead island.org).

✈ Savannah (65 miles/105km).

🛏 $$ **Palmetto Dunes Resort,** 4 Queens Folly Rd. (✆ **800/827-3006** or 843/785-1161; www.palmettodunes.com). $$$ **Sea Pines Resort,** 32 Greenwood Dr. (✆ **866/561-8802;** www.seapines.com).

282 The Sporting Life

Isle of Anglesey

Coasting to Glory

Wales

To many travelers, the Isle of Anglesey is just a blur from the train window as they speed from London to the western port of Holyhead, to catch a ferry to Ireland. Others stop off briefly for the novelty value of having a photo snapped beside a signpost for the world's longest town name, Llanfairpwllgwyngyllgogerychwyrndrobwllllantysiliogogogoch (known for convenience's sake as Llanfair PG). But Anglesey is well worth a longer stay, especially if you're interested in sports and the outdoors. Isolated from the Welsh mainland by the narrow Menai Strait, low-lying Anglesey offers a startling contrast to the mountainous drama of neighboring North Wales. Instead of plunging cascades, stark gray cliffs, and terraced slate-mining towns, it's a mellow rural backwater, a land of whitewashed cottages dotting flat farmland.

Kissed by the Gulf Stream, Anglesey has a surprisingly mild climate, and as soon as you cross the famous 19th-century cast-iron suspension bridge across the Menai Strait—a groundbreaking engineering feat in its day—you may well feel inspired to get out of the car and stretch your legs. Nearly all of Anglesey's remarkably unspoiled coastline has been designated a national Area of Outstanding Natural Beauty; it's a snap to pick up any section of the 201km (125-mile) **Anglesey Coastal Path,** which circles nearly the entire island, passing seaside cliffs where puffins nest and a proliferation of wide flat golden beaches (among the best are Trearddur Bay, Porthdafarch, Benllech, Llandona, and Llanddwyn).

Gone are the strenuous Methodist dictates of North Wales; on Anglesey, relaxing and enjoying yourself are positively encouraged. The town of **Beaumaris,** just north of the Menai Strait, is a popular yachting center, with an almost Mediterranean atmosphere, while surfers gravitate to the beaches around **Rhosneigr** on the southern coast. East of Rhosneigr, the 750-hectare (1,853-acre) **Newborough Forest Preserve** is a great place for hiking through dusky stands of Corsican pines, planted to protect the wide beaches and coastal dunes of adjacent Llanddwyn Island; nearby **Maltraeth Marsh** is a notable wetland site for bird-watching.

Golf and tennis are played year-round—buy an **Isle of Anglesey Golf Pass** (✆ **44/845/450-5885,** golf@nwt.co.uk) and you can try out five of the island's nine excellent golf courses. **Pony trekking** is perennially popular, with riding stables in Dwyran, Trearddur Bay, and Llanddona, and several bridleways around the countryside. The island also makes the most of its flat topography by offering four signposted **cycling routes** along back lanes, taking in ruined medieval churches, Roman relics, and Neolithic burial chambers, as well as shops, villages, and nature preserves. —*HH*

ⓘ **Wales Tourist Board visitor centers,** Railway Station Site, Llanfair PG (✆ **44/1248/713-177**), or Holyhead, Port Terminal (✆ **44/1407/762-622**); also www.islandofchoice.com.

✈ Anglesey (connect through Cardiff).

⛴ Holyhead, ferries to Dublin and Dun Laoghaire, Ireland (1 hr, 45 min. to 3 hr., 30 min.).

🛏 $$ **Cleifiog Uchaf,** off Spencer Rd., Valley (✆ **44/1407/741-888;** www.cleifioguchaf.co.uk). $$$ **Tre-Ysgawen Hall,** Capel Coch, Llanfegni (✆ **44/1248/750-750;** www.treysgawen-hall.co.uk).

TOUR **Anglesey Adventures** (✆ **44/1407/761-777;** www.angleseyadventures.co.uk). **Anglesey Outdoors** (✆ **44/1407/769-351;** www.angleseyoutdoors.com).

283

Isle of Arran

Scotland in Miniature

Scotland

Set at the mouth of the Firth of Clyde on Scotland's west coast, Arran seems almost like a greatest-hits version of Scotland. Its northern end is a rugged Highlands landscape of mountains and glens, perfect for **paragliding, rock climbing, gorge hiking,** and **mountain biking;** in the gentle green hills of the south, you can stroll through formal gardens, relax on a beach, or kayak around the ragged coast and offshore islands. Golf? There are no fewer than seven courses here, laid out variously on parkland, heath, or seaside links. As for history, the island has its share of ruined castles and standing stones, as well as any number of sites associated with 14th-century rebel hero Robert the Bruce—you can't get any more classically Scottish than that.

Best of all, you can easily do an entire circuit of the island by **bicycle,** following the main coast road (A841), which makes a neat 97km (60-mile) circuit. While it's possible to do it in 1 day, I recommend booking a hotel on the west coast so you can cycle for 2 days—that way you'll have time for all sorts of delightful detours en route.

Heading clockwise around the island from Brodick, you'll pass through **Lamlash,** a pleasant seaside resort, then **King's Cross Point,** where Robert the Bruce is said to have sailed for the mainland after hiding out on Arran for months. The road climbs to **Dippin Head,** then swings around the southern shore, with great views of the **Ailsa Crag lighthouse.** Coast downhill toward **Sliddery,** with its overgrown old Norse keep; at **Tormore,** north of Blackwaterfoot, detour a mile inland to visit some standing stones. **Drumadoon Point** on the west coast has basalt columns and the remains of an old fort, and **King's Hill** has caves where Robert the Bruce hid out from his enemies for months.

Climb to the craggy northern end of the island, where you can check out the castle ruins at **Lochranza,** reputedly Robert the Bruce's hunting seat. Back on the east cost, you'll pass dramatic **Glen Sannox** and the **Fallen Rocks,** huge sandstone boulders that have tumbled off the cliffs. On your right looms the island's highest mountain, **Goat Fell** ("mountain of the winds"); at its foot you'll find red sandstone **Brodick Castle,** ancestral home of the dukes of Hamilton (check out its extraordinary gardens), and the **Isle of Arran Heritage Museum,** a series of restored buildings tracing life on Arran from prehistoric times to the present. It's like a condensed version of this compact mini-Scotland—a wee wonder indeed. —*HH*

ⓘ **Tourist information,** The Pier, Brodick (✆ **44/1770/303-774;** www.visitarran.com).

Brodick, 55 min. from Ardrossan. **Caledonian MacBrayne Ferries** (✆ **44/9705/650-0000;** www.calmac.co.uk).

$$$ **Auchrannie Country House Hotel,** Auchrannie Rd., Brodick (✆ **44/1770/302-234;** www.auchrannie.co.uk). $$ **Best Western Kinloch Hotel,** Blackwaterfoot (✆ **44/1770/860-444;** www.bw-kinlochhotel.co.uk).

TOUR Arran Adventure, Auchrannie Rd. (✆ **44/1770/302-244;** www.arranadventure.com).

284 Amphibious Attractions

Great Keppel Island

Bushwalking & Beaches

Australia

Who says the Great Barrier Reef region is all about diving and underwater pleasures? Great Keppel Island offers a very strong argument that this part of Australia is a landlubber's adventure paradise, too: There's not a high-rise resort—yet (see below)—in sight on Great Keppel, but there's still plenty to keep active types entertained, whether it's watching seabirds or bush walking in the interior. And at only 13km (8 miles) from the mainland city of Yeppoon, this is an easy getaway even for a weekend.

The island's small size, just 14 sq. km (5½ sq. miles), makes it easy to get to know the place well in a short period of time. One of the most rewarding activities is exploring its natural side—90% of Great Keppel is designated bush land of the **Keppel Bay Islands National Park.** Locals can point you in the right direction for bush walks of varying length and difficulty, but it's best to pick up a copy of Allan Briggs's *A Concise Guide to the Walking Tracks of Great Keppel Island* if you'd rather set off on self-designed adventures.

Walking is also the way to reach the best swimming on Great Keppel, which boasts 27km (17 miles) of gorgeous beaches. Whereas some other islands off the Queensland coast are prone to tides that sometimes wash away the beaches for hours at a time, Great Keppel's beaches have sugary shores and turquoise water all day long. The ocean here is crystal clear, and yes, there's great **snorkeling** in the undersea coral gardens offshore.

Accommodations on the island tend to be guesthouses or self-contained holiday rental units, all of which are affordable and attractive to nature-loving backpackers or families seeking serenity. For something a bit more social, the **Great Keppel Island Holiday Village** (see below) organizes activities like kayaking and motorized canoe excursions. Development on Great Keppel,

Island Hopping Around the Champlain Islands: Vermont's West Coast

Whether you're coming east out of New York's stately Adirondack Mountains, or west out of the gentler Green Mountains of Vermont, there's a wonderful *Ahhh!* moment when you crest the last hill and see vast Lake Champlain glittering before you. The sixth-largest freshwater lake in the United States, Champlain's strategic location on the border of Canada made this inland sea a hotly contested prize in the Seven Years' War, the American Revolution, and even the War of 1812. Today, Champlain's chain of islands are one of New England's choicest vacation secrets, an unspoiled wonderland for fishing, hiking, canoeing, kayaking, and biking (contact **Lake Champlain Bike Trails,** www.champlainbikeways.org, for a map of scenic cycling routes), as well as swimming off landlocked Vermont's only sand beaches.

Biking by Lake Champlain.

Connected by bridges, causeways, and roads, these islands are easy to get around, but they offer few amenities for tourists—a handful of accommodations and only slightly more restaurants. The main road, U.S. Hwy. 2, takes 30 miles (48km) to run the length of the islands from the Vermont shore back to the Alburg peninsula, the last bit of Vermont before you reach the Canadian border. It's a straight, quick shoot, and if you're tempted to gawk at the scenery, locals in pickup trucks will impatiently whiz past you or hug your tail. When the opportunity arises, veer off on one of the side roads and take it slowly, or pull over at one of the many parks to enjoy the scenery.

One thing you'll notice as you're tooling around these parts: The odd place name "Hero." That's because the central string of islands—originally called North Hero, Middle Hero, and South Hero—was deeded to a group of Revolutionary War heroes, most notably Ethan Allen and Samuel Herrick of the Green Mountain Boys. In 1783, Ethan Allen's cousin Ebenezer Allen was the first of those war vets to settle on South Hero, later opening a tavern on the southernmost tip of the island, now called Allen's Point. The largest island, Middle Hero, was later renamed 285 **Grand Isle.** (South Hero is still there, but it's a separate town on the same island.) On the side roads of South Hero, look around for a scattered handful of quirky miniature stone castles erected in the early 20th century by Swiss immigrant Harry Barber, a local gardener who erected them to remind himself of the Alps. Along U.S. 2 on Grand Isle, you can visit a relic of the early settlers, the Hyde Log Cabin, built of cedar logs in 1793—the oldest log cabin in New England—with a log schoolhouse dating to 1814 next door. **Grand Isle State Park,** east of U.S. 2 halfway up Grand Isle's east coast, is a popular spot with a beach, plenty of campsites, and superb lake views from its steep shoreline—a good place to try to sight Champ, a cousin of the Loch Ness monster that locals claim inhabits the depth of Lake Champlain.

Farther north, cross a drawbridge to charmingly rural 286 **North Hero,** which is mostly quiet farmland with a couple of unspoiled villages. At its southern tip, Knight Point State Park is a lovely spot to gaze over the channel—aka "The Gut"—at Grand Isle, from the vantage point of the historic Knight Tavern, built here in the 1790s when interisland ferries (the only way to get around the islands) docked here.

The earliest European visitors to the islands, of course, were the French—Samuel Champlain, for whom the lake is named, first set foot on the islands 4 centuries ago, in 1609. Follow Route 129 west from Alburg, Vermont, to the other large island in the group, 287 **Isle La Mott,** where the French built a fort in 1666 to protect settlers from Indian attack. Though the fort was torn down long ago, a shrine to St. Anne where the troops worshiped is still there, although the current buildings are more modern. While the shrine is Isle La Mott's most popular tourist attraction, an even more remarkable feature of this remote, lightly populated island lies all around its southern end—the ancient coral fossils and rock formations of the Chazy Reef, the world's oldest coral reef (480 million years old), its dark limestone thrusting from the earth's crust. Head for the Fisk Quarry on West Shore Road to see parts of the fossil reef; the quarry itself is famous for its black marble, prominently used in buildings all over the islands.

If your interests are more water-based, check out the smaller islands lying in the protected waters of the lake between Grand Isle and the Vermont shore. Of these, the most popular is 288 **Burton Island,** reachable via a 10-minute ferry ride from Kill Kare State Park, south of St. Albans, Vermont. With its overnight campsites, a 100-slip marina, a swimming beach, and a number of marked nature trails, this low island dotted with ancient hemlocks, stout cedars, and slender birch trees makes a great getaway. With your own boat, you can also visit neighboring Knight Island and Woods Island, also state parks. —*HH*

ⓘ **Lake Champlain Islands Chamber of Commerce,** North Hero, Vermont (✆ **800/262-5226** or 802/372-8400; www.champlainislands.com).

✈ Burlington, Vermont, or Plattsburgh, New York.

⛴ **Lake Champlain Ferries** (✆ **802/864-9804;** www.ferries.com) makes the 12-min. run to Grand Isle from Plattsburg, New York.

🛏 $$$ **Shore Acres,** 237 Shore Acres Dr., North Hero Island (✆ **802/372-8722;** www.shoreacres.com). $$ **Thomas Mott Homestead,** 63 Blue Rock Rd., Alburg (✆ **800/348-0843** or 802/378-4270; www.thomas-mott-bb.com).

despite its popularity as a tourist destination, has been minimal so far, but there are plans afoot to build a megaresort on the western side of the island, with 300 hotel rooms, 500 villas, a large marina, and a golf course. The resort's backers say it will be ecofriendly despite its large footprint (and infringement on the surrounding reef), but most Great Keppel regulars are opposed to the prospective newcomer. —*SM*

ⓘ www.greatkeppelisland.org.

✈ Great Keppel Airport (connections to Queensland airports).

 From Rosslyn Bay, Queensland. Keppel Tourist Services or Freedom Fast Cats (30 min.).

🛏 $$$ **Great Keppel Island Holiday Village,** off Rockhampton (✆ **61/7/4939 8655;** www.gkiholidayvillage.com.au).

Amphibious Attractions **289**

Achill Island

Wet Suits & Hiking Boots

Ireland

Mention West Coast surfing, and most people picture the broad golden sands of Southern California. Yet this craggy Atlantic island off Ireland's wild west coast has lately become its own magnet for kayakers, surfer dudes, scuba divers, and other wet-suited types. Hugging close to the less-traveled coast of County Mayo, north of Galway—you can drive right onto the island on a road bridge from the Currane Peninsula—Achill is Ireland's largest island, and it may not be quite as unspoiled as tiny **Clare Island** to the south, which travel writers tend to rave about. But Achill offers a lot more action, while maintaining the atmospheric Irish backdrop of humble cottages, rambling drystone walls, native Gaelic speakers, machair grasslands spangled with wildflowers, and turfy upland tracks.

To begin with, Achill has no fewer than five beaches granted Blue Flag status for their water quality, natural beauty, and services. Going clockwise around the island, they are picturesque **Dooega,** in a protected cove off spectacular Atlantic Drive on the south coast; near Keel, photogenic **Trawmore Strand,** a 3km-long (1¾-mile) beach that challenges surfers, windsurfers, and sea kayakers with its tricky rollers and riptides; horseshoe-shaped **Keem Bay** on the western promontory; and on the north coast near Dugort, sprawling **Silver Strand** and **Golden Strand.** Farther inland, you'll find freshwater **Keel Lake,** cupped dramatically in the highlands, a superb spot for trout fishing and for a somewhat calmer windsurfing experience. Shore fishing and surf-casting are popular all around Achill, and anglers also venture out into the Atlantic in charter boats for catches that may include cod, ling, conger, pollock, wrasse, mackerel, skate, dogfish, ray, blue shark, thresher, and porbeagle sharks. Most of these charter boats are also available for scuba diving and sightseeing excursions.

Lest you get too waterlogged, reserve some time while you're in Achill for **hillwalking,** which some visitors end up enjoying even more than the watersports. The rugged island has two sizable peaks, **Slievemore** and **Croaghaun,** the latter of which falls off dramatically into the sea on the northeast coast, forming the highest sea cliffs in Europe. With most of the island's interior held as common land, almost everything is accessible along public walking trails, with a number of designated routes taking you from sea cliffs to sandy beaches to peat bogs, past ancient lichen-crusted megaliths, ruined stone towers, and deserted villages left behind when the mid-19th-century Great Famine so radically depopulated Achill. Of course, if you'd rather explore on horseback, upland pony trekking and wind-stirred gallops along Keel Beach are available as well (contact **Calvey's Equestrian Centre; ✆ 353/87/988-1093;** www.calveysofachill.com).

Drop-dead views, invigorating rocky climbs, and the evocative scent of peat smoke and heather—what other surfing mecca could add all this to the mix? *—HH*

ⓘ **Tourist office,** Cashel (✆ **353/98/47353;** www.achilltourism.com/index.html).

✈ Knock International Airport, Charlestown.

96km (60-mile) drive from Charlestown.

$$ **Achill Cliff House Hotel,** Keel (✆ **353/98/43400;** www.achillcliff.com). $$ **Lavelle's Seaside House,** Dooega (✆ **353/98/45116;** www.lavellesseaside house.com).

TOUR Achill Adventures, Slievemore Rd., Dugort (✆ **353/98/43148;** www.achill adventures.com); ***Colm Ciara*** charter boat (✆ **353/86/3603057**); ***Cuna Na Cuime*** charter boat (✆ **353/98/47257**).

290 Amphibious Attractions

Isle of Great Cumbrae

Making the Circuit

Scotland

On a clear day, you may find yourself at the highest point on Great Cumbrae, 127m (417 ft.) above sea level, beside a hulking rock known as "The Glaidstone." The triangulation pillar points out all the far-flung places you can see: Ben Lomond to the north, the Isle of Arran 283 and the Kintyre peninsula to the southwest, Ailsa Craig to the south, and even—if you're lucky—Northern Ireland in the misty distance. It's a wind-whipped panorama indeed, exciting enough to make you forget how your calves ache from pumping your bicycle up that hill.

Despite that impressive name, Great Cumbrae is a tiny island, no more than 6.4km long and 3.2km wide (4×2 miles). The B896 road that circles its coast is only 18km (11 miles) long with very light traffic, a classic **cycling route;** to reach the Glaidstone, cut over to the inner circle road (B899), which climbs to the summit of this hilly island. (Rent your bike in the main town, Millport, from **Mapes & Son,** 3–5 Guildford St.; ✆ **44/1475/530444.**) It's an intriguing island to explore, punctuated with unusual rock formations, thanks to the island's location on a geological fault line; the islanders have given the rocks fanciful names like Crocodile Rock, Indian Rock, Lion's Rock, and Queen Victoria's Face (they've even given Crocodile Rock and Indian Rock corny paint jobs, so you can't miss their garish features). On the quiet west coast, waterfalls plunge over old sea cliffs and you'll find a number of raised beaches, especially around Bell Bay. Seals flop around the coves, and seabirds nest in the cliffs.

Of course, some watersports enthusiasts never get farther than Sportscotland's **National Centre Cumbrae** (✆ **44/1475/530757**), conveniently by the ferry slip on the northeast coast, where you can take sailing, windsurfing, powerboating, and sea-kayaking lessons. Just south of the ferry slip, scuba divers can explore the wreck of a Catalina flying boat from World War II.

Though the summer crowds have lessened somewhat, Cumbrae is a time-honored day trip destination from Glasgow (the ferry ride from Largs, on the western Ayrshire coast, takes only 10 min.), especially for families headed for Millport's soft sandy beach and old-fashioned seaside amusements. I have to admit to a soft spot for this sort of faded Victorian-era seafront, with its tearooms and ice-cream parlors; come here out of season and you'll feel like you've got the place to yourself. Appropriately, tidy little Millport boasts the world's narrowest housefront (The Wedge, only as wide as its front door) and one of the world's smallest cathedrals, the lovely 19th-century Gothic Revival **Cathedral of the Isles** (College St.; ✆ **44/1475/530353**). On a rainy weekday, you can amuse yourself at the University of Glasgow's **Robertson Marine Life Museum & Aquarium** (Marine Parade; ✆ **44/1475/530581;** www.gla.ac.uk/centres/marinestation). *—HH*

ⓘ **Tourist office,** 28a Stuart St., Millport (✆ **44/1292/678100**).

✈ Glasgow/Prestwick (1 hr.).

⛴ 10 min. from Largs. **Caledonian MacBrayne** ferries (✆ **44/9705/650-0000;** www.calmac.co.uk).

🛏 $ **College of the Holy Spirit,** College St., Millport (✆ **44/1475/530353;** www.island-retreats.org). $ **Westbourne House,** Westbay Rd. (✆ **44/1475/530000;** www.westbourne-house.com).

Amphibious Attractions

Zitny Ostrov

Europe's Largest River Island

Slovakia

A trip through Eastern Europe usually means traipsing from one fairy-tale village or city to the next. When you've had your fill of Hungarian hamlets and Czech charm, hop off the train in Bratislava, and then venture east to explore the Danube River isle of Zitny Ostrov. Also known as "Rye Island," this is the biggest river island in Europe, at nearly 1,900 sq. km (734 sq. miles), and Slovakia's most fertile agricultural region.

Zitny Ostrov stretches the definition of island just a tad: Its southern boundary is the formidable Danube; its northern boundary is the meandering Little Danube, a gentle tributary that separates Zitny Ostrov from "mainland" Slovakia by little more than 50m (164 ft.) in places. The calm flow of the Little Danube, however, is a small-boater's dream: **Rowing and kayaking** are both favorite activities here, providing Disney-esque scenery of farms and alluvial forests along the way. Zitny Ostrov is also wonderful for **cycling,** and one of the most popular bike routes on the island is the round-trip circuit (92km/57 miles total, mostly flat) from Bratislava to the **Gabcikovo Water Works,** where boats negotiate fascinating navigation chambers to overcome the 20m (66-ft.) altitude difference between the bottom and the top of the dam.

Water, and the exploitation of it, has always been the lifeblood of Zitny Ostrov, and today it has Central Europe's largest supply of high-quality drinking water. In the north-central part of the island, you can drive or bike to the **ancient water mills** of Jahodná, Tomásikova, Jelka, and Dunajska Klátov. These intriguing constructions, with wooden paddle wheels, are all set impossibly picturesquely along the shady green banks of the Little Danube.

As is common throughout Slovakia, resorts have been built around Zitny Ostrov's several reservoirs, so if you don't feel like boating or biking anywhere, you can go for a swim in any number of freshwater public swimming pools or manmake lakes, many of which have therapeutic thermal waters. Try the well-equipped and family-friendly (it has a water slide) **Thermal Park Dunajská Streda** (in the eponymous main town of Zitny Ostrov; ✆ **421/31/552-40-91;** www.thermalpark.sk) or **Termalpark Vel'ky Meder** (✆ **421/31/555-21-04;** www.termalsro.sk).

Round out your tour with a day or two seeing the highlights of **Bratislava,** the Slovakian capital that lies just north, across the Little Danube, from Zitny Ostrov. Have coffee on the historic square of Hlavné Námestie, tour the Primate's Palace, take a Danube cruise, and climb up to Bratislava Castle, the 16th-century landmark that dominates the city. —*SM*

ⓘ www.slovakia.travel.

✈ Bratislava, connections throughout Europe.

40km (25 miles) from Bratislava.

$$$ **Hotel Bonbón,** Alžbetínske nám. 1202/2 (✆ **421/31/557-52-22;** www.bonbon.sk).

292 Amphibious Attractions

Valdes Island

Kayaking the Sandstone Coast

Canada

As one of the top destinations for kayaking in British Columbia's Gulf Islands, Valdes is most definitely a place to be seen from the water. The knife-shaped island's perimeter is a series of dramatic sandstone cliffs, atop which sit weathered firs, oaks, and pines. A few broad and sandy beaches offer idyllic shore rest as well as front-row seats for some of the most spectacular sunsets in British Columbia. On Valdes, it's all about the coastal adventure, but kayakers can also leave their boats on the northern tip of Valdes and stretch their legs along one of the forested trails in Wakes Cove Provincial Park.

Once out on the water, paddle toward the north shore of Valdes and the island's magnificent **sandstone galleries.** Carved by thousands of years of winter storms, these towering tawny cliffs feature one amazing, supremely photogenic feature after another—from honeycombed caves to bulbous rock protrusions, to umbrella-type overhangs where kayakers can pull over and get out of the rain (this is the Pacific Northwest, after all; precipitation is part and parcel of the experience). Just be aware that the same powerful forces of nature that sculpted the sandstone could also pummel you—pay attention to tides and incoming weather.

The best place on Valdes to go ashore and take a break from the paddling is at **Blackberry Point,** on the western shore of the island, toward the southern tip. This is a lengthy stretch of beach (about 120m/394 ft.) where big, gnarled pieces of driftwood lie strewn as if by an artist. With its western exposure and views across the Trincomali Channel to other islets and Vancouver Island 296, sunsets here are phenomenal: The whole scene is a Northwest watercolor in the making. Overnight camping is possible at Blackberry Point;

the only other campground is at **Wakes Cove Provincial Park** (see below) on the northeast side of Valdes. The 205-hectare (507-acre) park was opened in 2002 and has **hiking trails,** picnic areas nestled among old-growth Douglas firs, and a protected anchorage for kayakers.

While in the area, most kayakers also visit the neighboring Gulf Islands of **Gabriola** (north of Valdes, known as Petroglyph Island for its ancient and mysterious stone carvings), **Galiano** (across Porlier Pass to the south, with a great campground at Dionisio Point), and on the way back to Vancouver Island, **Thetis,** which is most notable for its warm and welcoming **pub** (✆ **250/246-3464;** www.thetisisland.com), where paddlers reward themselves with hot food and cold beer. Going ashore on any of these islands, you'll find quiet, hiker-friendly roads and trails that invariably lead to stunning lookouts.

Valdes has no public boat docks, restaurants, hotels, or electricity. (The vacation homes here are powered by solar energy.) A third of the island is a First Nations Reserve for the Lyacksun First Nation. Much of the rest of the island is now owned by the Weyerhaeuser logging and paper corporation, which maintains the small campground at Blackberry Point.

To reach Valdes, you'll need to put in somewhere along the northeastern coast of Vancouver Island; the town of Ladysmith, which is a 45-minute drive south of Nanaimo, is the most popular jumping-off point for kayaking in the Gulf Islands. If you don't have your own equipment, **Sealegs Kayaking** (✆ **877/KAYAK-BC [529-2522]** or 250/245-4096; www.sealegskayaking.com), in Ladysmith, is a full-service outfitter that rents boats, provides lessons, and offers multiday tours of the Gulf Islands. —*SM*

ⓘ www.vancouverisland.com.

✈ Floatplane to Valdes, or commercial flights to Nanaimo (40km/25 miles from Valdes).

🛏 $$ **Hawley Place Bed & Breakfast,** 302 Hawley Place, Ladysmith (✆ **250/245-4431;** www.bbcanada.com/9973.html). $ **Wakes Cove Provincial Park camping** (✆ **250/539-2115;** www.env.gov.bc.ca).

Amphibious Attractions **293**

Wellesley Island

Water Under the Bridge

Thousand Islands, New York, U.S.

In a way, the Thousand Islands region is the inverse of the nearby Adirondacks: The 'Dacks is a mass of thick forest dotted with specks of blue water, while the Thousand Islands is a span of blue water dotted with specks of thick forest. The name is a bit misleading, though—how many granite outcrops actually pepper these 35 miles (56km) of the St. Lawrence River is anybody's guess. Threading around its labyrinthine channels, you can easily lose count, you'll be so busy camping, picnicking, bird-watching, and hauling in record catches of muskie, walleye, pike, perch, and king salmon.

The point of visiting here is to sample many islands, but a good place to start is Wellesley Island, in the shadow of the Thousand Islands Bridge, spanning the St. Lawrence. (On adjacent Hill Island, a stone's throw across the border into Canada, the **1000 Islands Skydeck** [✆ **613/659-2335;** www.1000islandsskydeck.com] offers sweeping 360-degree views of the region.)

Wellesley Island's Boldt Yacht house.

Wellesley Island State Park covers almost a third of this large island; the rustic park contains the area's largest camping complex, a 600-acre (243-hectare) nature center laced with miles of **hiking trails,** a sandy beach, a 9-hole golf course, and a marina with **canoe and fishing boat rentals** (✆ **315/482-2722**). Many of the park's wilderness campsites are so secluded, you can reach them only by foot or boat, but there are also some waterside cabins and a set of fully outfitted two- and three-bedroom cottages, rentable by the week. Outside of the park, don't miss the **Thousand Island Park historic district** on the southwest tip of the island, a beautifully preserved community of gingerbread cottages, relics of a Victorian-era "camp meeting" religious retreat.

While the fishing around the island is excellent, to widen your options head for nearby **Alexandria Bay,** on the New York shore of the St. Lawrence, where several charter boats are based (check out www.alexbayfishingguides.com for a list of local operators). Alex Bay is also the jumping-off point for boat tours to two enormous summer "cottages" built by Gilded Age industrialists in the Thousand Islands' resort heyday: **Boldt Castle** on Heart Island (✆ **800/847-5263**) and the dramatic medieval-style **Singer Castle** on Dark Island (✆ **315/324-3275**); contact **Uncle Sam Boat Tours** (✆ **315/482-2611**).

More and more visitors to the Thousand Islands choose to explore by kayak, following the **Thousand Islands Water Trail** (www.paddle1000.com) from Kingston to Brockville, Ontario. Outfitters near Wellesley Island include **1000 Islands Kayaking Company,** 58 River Rd., Lansdowne, Ontario (✆ **613/329-6265;** www.1000islandskayakingco.com), and **Misty Isles,** 25 River Rd., Lansdowne (✆ **613/382-4232;** www.mistyisles.ca). If wildlife is your interest, kayak over to Grass Point Marsh; it's also fun to check out the "cottages" on Rock Island or challenge yourself by circumnavigating large Grindstone Island, just downriver from Wellesley.

If boating is your passion—and why else have you come here?—don't miss the **Antique Boat Museum** downriver at

Clayton, New York (750 Mary St.; ✆ **315/686-4104**), which has a truly stupendous collection of some 250 vintage wooden boats. —*HH*

ⓘ **Wellesley Island State Park,** 44927 Cross Island Rd., Fineview, NY (✆ **315/482-2722;** www.nysparks.state.ny.us/parks/info.asp?parkID=164).

✈ Syracuse, New York.

90-mile (145km) drive from Syracuse.

$$$ **Hart House,** 21979 Club Rd., Wellesley Island (✆ **888/481-LOVE** [481-5683] or 315/482-5683; www.harthouseinn.com). $ **Wellesley Island State Park campground** (✆ **800/456-2267**).

Amphibious Attractions 294

Mount Desert Island

Acadian Idyll

Maine, U.S.

It's fitting indeed that the name of this famous Maine island is pronounced like "dessert," not like "desert"—it's definitely a special treat, rather than a barren wasteland. Dominated by splendid **Acadia National Park,** this glacier-chiseled mound of rugged cliffs, sheltered bays, and quiet woods lies conveniently connected by causeway to the coast of Maine. Most visitors crowd onto 32km (20-mile) Park Loop Road, a spectacular drive that starts near the Hulls Cove Visitor Center and follows the rocky coast, loops back inland along Jordan Pond and Eagle Lake, and adds a detour to Cadillac Mountain—a sort of greatest-hits tour of the island. But why spend your time poking along in traffic, staring out at the ocean, when you could be skimming along the water's surface, skirting the coast, and exploring the coves in your own light and agile sea kayak?

Mount Desert's ragged silhouette makes it perfect for kayaking, surrounded as it is by small bays and coast-hugging islands and nearly knifed in half by narrow, 7-mile-long (11km) Somes Sound, the only true fjord in the continental United States. You may want to begin in the island's main town, **Bar Harbor,** set on Frenchman's Bay, where you can rent your kayaks from outfitters including **Coastal Kayaking Tours,** 48 Cottage St., Bar Harbor (✆ **800/526-8615** or 207/288-9605; www.acadiafun.com); **Loon Bay Kayaks,** Barcadia Campground, junction of Routes 3 and 102 (✆ **888/786-0676** or 207/677-2963); or **Aquaterra Adventures,** 1 West St., Bar Harbor (✆ **877/386-4124** or 207/288-0007; www.aquaterra-adventures.com). Frenchman's Bay is populated by seals, osprey, and other wildlife; summer boasts even more spectacular wildlife: humpback, finback, minke, and (occasionally) right whales, which migrate to cool summer waters offshore to feast on krill and plankton. Head south from the bay and you'll reach Atlantic waters, where popular park sights include **Thunder Hole,** a shallow cavern where the surf surges boisterously in and out, and Otter Cliffs, a set of 100-foot-high (30m) granite precipices capped with dense spruce that plummet down into roiling seas. From your kayak you can also enjoy open views of waterside villages and the great shingled "cottages" of the wealthy elite—Carnegies, Rockefellers, Astors, Vanderbilts—who summered here in the island's late-19th-century heyday as a resort.

Kayaking is insanely popular here, but it's certainly not the only way to explore Mount Desert. **Bike** around the forested interior on crushed-rock carriageways laid out for Gilded Age tycoons; visit a series of geological formations using a GPS system to track down EarthCache clues; or take a catamaran cruise (contact **Bar Harbor Whale Watch Company;** 1 West St., Bar Harbor; ✆ **888/533-WALE** [533-9253] or 207/288-9800; www.barharborwhales.com), to see more whales in their offshore feeding grounds. Or hike the **Precipice Trail,** where you can get prime viewing of rare peregrine falcons, nesting in a cliff on **Champlain Mountain** (daily mid-May to mid-Aug, rangers lead a program describing peregrine activity). *—HH*

ⓘ **Acadia National Park visitor center,** State Hwy. 3 north of Bar Harbor (✆ **207/288-3338;** www.nps.gov/acad).

✈ Trenton, Maine.

10-min. drive from Trenton.

$ **Bar Harbor Campground,** 409 State Hwy. 3, Salisbury Cove (✆ **207/288-5185**). $$$ **Harborside Hotel & Marina,** 55 West St., Bar Harbor (✆ **800/328-5033** or 207/288-5033; www.theharborsidehotel.com).

---

295 Amphibious Attractions

Lanai

The Archipelago's Exclusive Enclave

Hawaii

The most recently developed island for tourism in the Hawaiian archipelago may be the smallest, but with that petite size comes exclusivity. In the past few decades, the former pineapple plantation island of Lanai, just 9 miles (14km) across the channel from Maui 263, has become a luxury playground that still has much of its precious local flavor intact. When you stay on Lanai, you get the sublime feeling that this Hawaiian island belongs to you—at least for a week or so.

The state tourism board has given Lanai the sobriquet of "Hawaii's Most Enticing Island," because Lanai (140 sq. miles/363 sq. km, with 18 miles/29km of unspoiled sandy beaches) is basically the private province of the guests who can pony up the cash to stay at its two five-star resorts—there aren't many other accommodations options here. (Many say that Lanai really "arrived" as Hawaii's enclave for the rich when Bill Gates rented out the Manele Bay resort for his 1994 nuptials.) In exchange for the hefty price tag of your hotel room, you'll have free rein of the island's outdoor activities (hiking and four-wheeling to the heights of Lanai are de rigueur, along with swimming and exploring along the 47-mile/76km coast) and an intimate window on local life in the island's one and only town, Lanai City. **Lanai City** was originally the village that supported the workers of the Dole Pineapple Plantation (closed in 1992), and some institutions there, like the **Lanai Plantation Store** (aka Lanai City Service), which is ground zero for island gossip and groceries, feel like a time warp.

On the southern side of Lanai, **Hulopoe Bay** has one of Hawaii's best all-around beaches, a stunning crescent of golden sand backed by palms, picnic facilities, and clear, cobalt blue water great for snorkeling in summer. Nearby is one of the island's two luxury resorts, the **Four Seasons at Manele Bay** (information below); the other property is also a Four Seasons, the inland, plantation-style **Lodge at Koele** (✆ **808/565-4000;** www.fourseasons.com/koele).

Jumping into Hulopoe Bay.

Beachcombers should head to **Shipwreck Beach,** on the northeast coast, a windswept stretch of sand unsuitable for swimming but with evocative remains of the many vessels that have foundered offshore over the years.

Running for 7 miles (11km) up and over the top of Lanai's highest point, Mount Lanaihale (3,368 ft./1,027m), the **Munro Trail** is a must for hikers or off-road vehicles, and provides wonderful views of neighboring Maui. Perhaps Lanai's most unique and unusual sight is the so-called **Garden of the Gods** at Keahiakawelo, a garden of strange rock stacks set amid a barren landscape; come at sunset for the best color and light effects. Lanai also has two championship golf courses, attached to the two resorts; the oceanfront **Challenge at Manele** course was designed by Jack Nicklaus, while the upcountry **Experience at Koele** course is a Greg Norman masterpiece incorporating tropical geography and lofty views.

If you don't care to spend Four Seasons levels of money for the privilege of overnighting on Lanai, you can also visit the island as a **day trip from Maui** with the 45-minute passenger ferry from Lahaina (much easier than flying from Maui). Unless you're going with an organized tour group, it's best to get a rental car with four-wheel-drive upon arrival in Lanai and a good map or set of directions from a local: Most of Lanai's best attractions are at the end of unmarked or dirt roads. *—SM*

ⓘ **Tourist information,** 431 Seventh St., Ste. A, Lanai City (✆ **800/947-4774;** www.gohawaii.com/lanai); also www.visitlanai.net.

✈ Lanai Airport (interisland flights only).

⛴ Lahaina Marina, Maui (45 min.), **Expeditions Lahaina** (✆ **800/695-2624;** www.go-lanai.com).

🛏 $$$ **Four Seasons Resort at Manele Bay,** One Manele Bay Rd. (✆ **808/565-2000;** www.fourseasons.com/manele). $$ **Hotel Lanai,** 828 Lanai Ave. (✆ **800/795-7211,** or 808/565-7211; www.hotellanai.com).

296 Out & About

Vancouver Island

Canada's Great Pacific Adventure

Canada

From kayaking among orcas to watching grizzly bears feast on salmon, the wildlife encounters that await on Vancouver Island are stupendous. The scenery—from rocky fjords to impenetrable old-growth evergreen forests—is the Pacific Northwest at its most spectacular. And the postcard-perfect city of **Victoria** awaits when you want a dose of urban sophistication along with your natural splendors. Vancouver Island is too big, and its highlights are too diverse and numerous, to cover on a single visit, but no matter what itinerary you carve out, you won't be disappointed.

At over 32,000 sq. km (12,355 sq. miles), "Van Isle" is the largest island in Western North America—it's about the same shape as New York's Long Island, but 10 times the size. Most people's point of entry is Victoria, one of the loveliest port cities in the Pacific, and which a smitten Rudyard Kipling once compared to "a little bit of old England," set against something akin to the natural beauty of Italy's Bay of Naples combined with the Himalayas. The city's enchanting **Inner Harbour** is lined with such landmark buildings as the **Fairmont Empress Hotel** (721 Government St.; ✆ **250/384-8111**); stop for a drink in the hotel's Bengal Lounge, but skip the overpriced guest rooms. Victoria's top attraction is the marvelous **Butchart Gardens** (✆ **866/652-4422;** www.butchartgardens.com), whose 20 hectares (49 acres) of painstakingly maintained, gorgeously arranged plants and flowers leave even non-garden-types agape. From Victoria, the only way to go on Vancouver Island is west: It takes about 5 hours to drive from end to end, though many remote areas are accessible only by floatplane.

Killer whales are the big cheese of Vancouver's wildlife offerings, and **Telegraph Cove,** near the northwestern tip of the island, is one of the best places in the world for **orca watching.** Here, **Johnstone Strait** is home to more than 100 orcas, so sightings are practically guaranteed. For boat trips, I recommend **Stubbs Island Whale Watching** (✆ **250/928-3185;** www.stubbs-island.com). To see the whales from land, head 17km (11 miles) south of Telegraph Cove to **Robson Bight Ecological Reserve,** where the orcas scratch their bellies on so-called "rubbing stones" along the shore. **Sea kayaking** is also possible along Vancouver's protected waterways—with such majestic surroundings, this is always an unforgettable experience. Whether you see a pod of orcas or just a few playful porpoises, you can't help but come away humbled by nature.

The town of **Campbell River,** along Vancouver's northern coast, is known as the "salmon-fishing capital of the world," but there are plenty of spots all over Vancouver for **freshwater and saltwater fishing** (for steelhead, trout, halibut, rock cod and ling cod, shellfish, and five species of salmon). **Grizzly watching** has also become quite popular here, and the best way to see these formidable bears is with **Knight Inlet Lodge**'s grizzly tours (✆ **250/337-1953;** www.grizzlytours.com). Viewing is from the safety of a boat cruise along shores where grizzlies are known to fish, though depending on the season, you may be able to climb tree stands to observe the bears from land.

The rough and rugged west side of Vancouver is famously pounded by Pacific gales and waves in fall and winter. **Storm watching** is an activity in its own right here and most awesome at **Long Beach** in **Pacific Rim National Park** (near the resort towns of Tofino and Ucluelet). Gaze in amazement at the sheer power of nature lashing the shore, and then tuck in somewhere cozy and dry for a hot chocolate.

When the city of Vancouver (across the Strait of Georgia) hosts the Winter Olympics in 2010, visitor numbers—and prices—are likely to go up all over the region as soon as Bob Costas and crew show TV audiences worldwide just how breathtaking, and jampacked with outdoor activities, this part of the world is. —*SM*

ⓘ www.hellobc.com or www.vancouverisland.com.

✈ Victoria International Airport, Comox Valley Airport, and Nanaimo Airport, connections to Vancouver, Calgary, and Seattle. For more remote destinations, floatplanes and seaplanes are widely available.

⛴ Many routes to Victoria and Nanaimo from mainland British Columbia and Washington State (1–5 hr.). June–Sept, make reservations if you're driving a car aboard.

🛏 $$ **Hidden Cove Lodge,** 1 Hidden Cove Rd., Telegraph Cove (✆ **250/956-3916;** www.bcbbonly.com/1263.php). $$$ **Sidney Pier Hotel & Spa,** 9805 Seaport Place, Sidney (✆ **250/655-9445;** www.sidneypier.com).

Out & About 297

Gran Canaria

From Sand Dunes to Majestic Mountains

Canary Islands, Spain

Venture up to the green ravines and forests of Gran Canaria's interior, and you might be reminded of the mountain ranges of the American West, while just 25km (16 miles) away, there are coastal dunes, complete with camels, that look perfectly Saharan. The dramatic, diverse terrain of this Canary Island has earned it a hackneyed but ever-apt nickname: "Miniature Continent." Don't think of the "Gran" in the island's name as referring to its size—it's only the third largest in this Spanish archipelago, behind Tenerife 247 and Fuerteventura—but to the cinematic effect of its stupendous scenery.

The reality, however, is that most tourism on Gran Canaria is funneled toward the reliably hot and dry southern coast, a mecca for northern European sun seekers and party animals. Booking package trips to Gran Canaria as a holiday weekend break from their cold and damp hometowns, many visitors stick to the eyesore resort developments of the south and completely miss the hidden wonders of the interior. Of course, for the thousands of 20-somethings who flock here annually, the beach scene and manic nightlife of the south coast are enough. The oldest and principal resort town here is **Maspalomas,** the uncontested highlight of which is its 6km (3¾-mile) stretch of rolling dunes that slope, terraced by the wind, to gorgeous Atlantic waters. (***Tip:*** Spare yourself the leg cramps and make the trek across the shifting sands by camel.) All over the southern coast, the usual array of watersports and excursions—jet-skiing, paragliding, dolphin watching, booze cruises—are in plentiful supply and well patronized by fun-loving vacationers.

If and when you do fancy a break from the south coast's manufactured entertainment, the natural treasures of Gran Canaria are only a short car or bus ride away. Go for a tour of the island's amazing rock formations, like the 80m (262-ft.) monolith of **Roque Nublo** (a stunning photo op, especially at sunset), or to **Pico de las Nieves** (at 1,950m/6,398 ft., the highest point on the island), overlooking majestic valleys and ridges of pine forest. Each of these naturalistic highlights has numerous paths for hiking, and outdoors enthusiasts can also avail themselves of the newly restored *caminos reales* ("royal roads," or ancient pedestrian paths) that radiate from Cruz de Tejeda, in the center of the island, and provide opportunities for challenging hikes and leisurely walks of all kinds.

On the northern part of Gran Canaria, **Cenobio de Valerón** is an archaeological site where hundreds of grain silos are carved into the mountains. The **Museo y Parque Arqueólogico Cueva Pintada** (www.cuevapintada.org), near Gáldar, is the island's most important archaeological area, with painted caves dating back to the pre-Hispanic era.

Gran Canaria is also one of the few Canaries with a robust living culture beyond the cookie-cutter beach hotels. The bustling capital of **Las Palmas de Gran Canaria** is the largest town in the archipelago and offers historic architectural sights as well as vibrant local color. Over on the east coast, **Agüimes** is a wonderfully evocative Canarian village, and the nearby area of **Guayadeque Ravine** is famous for its cave dwellings (and fun, if kitschy, cave restaurants). Scuba divers will find the island's best dive spot at **El Cabrón Marine Reserve,** just southeast of Agüimes, with an incredibly diverse undersea life and great visibility. —*SM*

(i) **Centro Insular de Turismo,** av. España, Centro Comercial Yumbo, Playa del Ingles (✆ **34/92-877-15-50;** www.grancanaria.com).

✈ Gando Airport,16km (10 miles) south of Las Palmas, with connections to mainland Europe.

🛏 $$ **Riu Palace Maspalomas,** Playa del Ingles (✆ **888/748-4990** in the U.S.; www.riu.com). $$$ **Seaside Hotel Palm Beach,** av. del Oasis, Maspalomas (✆ **34/92-872-10-32;** www.seaside-hotels.de).

Out & About

Menorca

Family-Friendly in the Balearics

Spain

Smaller than Majorca 4 and more, ahem, wholesome than Ibiza 246, Menorca (also spelled Minorca) has steered clear of mass tourism and kept its island traditions intact. Yet its beaches are some of the best in Spain, with an abundance of watersports and (mostly) uncrowded expanses of sand on which to play and bronze. So if you've outgrown the flash of the other Balearic Islands but are still attracted to this part of the Mediterranean, Menorca is an ideal choice for a relaxed getaway with just enough action.

The southern coast of the island is relatively smooth, and it's here you'll find Menorca's longest stretch of sandy beach, **Son Bou. Cala Galdana,** in the township of Ferreries, is known as the Queen of the Calas (coves) for its stunning setting amid the pines. The curvy northern coast is rockier and home to Menorca's most dramatic coves and inlets, where deeper water affords snorkelers and divers a good view of the local fish and crustaceans. Most every cove or patch of sand has free or inexpensive parking nearby,

A lookout in Menorca.

some kind of beach bar, and opportunities to go out on the water, whether for a parasailing session or windsurfing lessons.

Hiking in the island's nature reserves is also rewarding, as the trails offer wonderful panoramas and the fresh scent of pine trees all around: Try **Cap de Favaritx, Cap de Cavalleria,** and **S'Albufera.** Many of the same trails can also be explored by bike, and you'll find numerous rental outfits all over the island.

Menorca's relative lack of traffic and manageable distances—50km (31 miles) from east to west, and 20km (12 miles) from north to south—make it easy to pursue a variety of activities while being based in one hotel or rental property. Lying at the eastern extremity of crescent-shaped Menorca, Mahón is the main city on the island, with a lively and picturesque harbor filled with impressive British colonial architecture. A leisurely walk along the **Mahón waterfront** at sunset, camera at the ready, is one of the must-do's while on Menorca. The smaller city of Ciutadella, at the western end of Menorca, is a gem, with Moorish and baroque architecture. Don't miss the **Ciutadella cathedral,** a fantastically embellished church built on top of an ancient mosque.

Menorca was a British possession from 1708 to 1802; the popularity of gin on the island is undoubtedly a vestige of that history. Tours of the island's **Xoriguer Distillery** are a fun way to sample several different Menorca-made liquors. From July to August, be sure to catch a balmy evening performance of the **Festival de Música d'Estiu** (summer music festival) in Ciutadella, when classical concerts are held in evocative churches and historic places. —*SM*

ⓘ www.illesbalears.es.

✈ Menorca-Mahón, connections through Spanish and European hubs.

🛏 $$ **Hotel Port Mahón,** av. Fort de L'Eau, Mahón (✆ **34/97-13-626-00;** www.sethotels.com). $$ **Visit Menorca** rental villas and apartments (✆ **34/90-21-101-11;** www.visitmenorca.com).

299 Out & About

São Miguel

Volcanic Vitality

The Azores, Portugal

Of the nine islands that make up the Atlantic castaway archipelago of the Azores, São Miguel is the largest (760 sq. km/293 sq. miles) and most populated (150,000) with the most action on offer for leisure-seeking travelers, whether it's whale-watching or soaking in hot springs or simply hiking and driving around its striking landscape. While describing São Miguel's diverse scenery—which ranges from lakes and mountains to green plains and blue ocean—promotional materials for São Miguel liken the island to a love child of Switzerland and Hawaii. It's an awfully poetic comparison, alright, but not an exaggeration. São Miguel is known as the "Green Island" of the Azores, and sure enough, the first thing you'll probably notice is that just about everything seems to be covered in a carpet of lush foliage.

Arriving by air or by sea, most visitors' introduction to São Miguel is its cosmopolitan capital, **Ponta Delgada.** Here, lovely architectural squares and cobblestoned streets are full of historic charm as well as contemporary flair: It would be easy to spend several days just sampling all the restaurants, bars, and oceanfront cafes in town. Ponta Delgada's lively marina is also the departure point for **swim-with-the-dolphins, whale-watching, sport fishing,** and other waterborne excursions (see www.azores.com for a full listing of outfitters). But the real splendor of the island, and what makes it such an original getaway, is the countryside. With an average width of 10km (6¼ miles) and an overall length of 64km (40 miles), São Miguel is refreshingly manageable in size, with good roads, though it's essential to have your own wheels to reach the island's many natural attractions.

Many of São Miguel's most interesting sites have to do with its natural history as a volcanic island—there are four stratovolcano calderas here. In the center of São Miguel, the **Lagoa do Fogo** (Fire Lake) is a dream for day hikers: After completing the well-marked trail through velvet-green hills, you arrive at the water-filled (with beach!) caldera of an extinct volcano. Farther to the east, the caldera of **Furnas** is still very much alive, with geysers emitting spouts of boiling water. Locals use the natural environment around Furnas (which means "ovens") as a place to cook traditional meals, burying pots of meats and vegetables right in the hot ground. Or you can go for a soak in the **natural thermal pool** at the **Terra Nostra Garden Hotel and Botanical Park** (see information below). Near the western end of São Miguel, the twin lakes atop **Sete Cidades** crater are another sublimely tranquil hiking spot. The toughest hike on the island, however, is to the summit of **Pico da Vara** (1,103m/3,619 ft. and São Miguel's highest point).

São Miguel's rugged mountain scenery can make you forget you're on an island that also has some terrific beaches for swimming, though with such dramatic coastal features, you do have to know where to go to find the sandy strips. The standout for swimmers and sunbathers is the accessible-by-boat-only **Ilheu,** off the resort town Vila Franca do Campo. The tiny triangular landform is blessed with a perfectly circular natural swimming pool in the center. In Vila Franca do Campo itself, the best beach is **Vinha d'Areia,** where there's also a small water-slide park. **Praia dos Moinhos,** In Porto Formoso, is an isolated beach that is home to the ruins of an old fortress. *—SM*

ⓘ www.azores.com.

✈ Ponta Delgada, connections to Lisbon (2 hr.).

🛏 $$$ **Terra Nostra Garden Hotel,** Rua Padre Jose Jacinto Botelho 5, Furnas (✆ **351/296/549-090;** www.terranostra hotelazores.com).

Out & About **300**

Samos

A Walk in the Woods

Greece

According to Epicurus, the ancient philosopher born on Samos in 341 B.C., life is supposed to be about happiness and tranquillity. Several millennia later, his native island is still a pretty good place to achieve that goal. Mountainous and densely forested Samos (picture the landscape in the movie version of *Mamma Mia*!) is a world away from the scrubby, mostly flat topography of so many other, more popular Greek islands, though it still boasts some superbly inviting beaches.

On a map, the shape of Samos recalls a vertically squashed, miniature Australia. Most visitors arrive at **Vathi,** a deep natural harbor near the eastern tip of the island. If there's one blight on gorgeous Samos, it's some of the recent development along the eastern coast, where generic resort towns have become magnets for European package tours—the kind of fly-me-anywhere-there's-sun travel that begets soulless beachfront hotels and often obnoxious group behavior. Pythagoras, the Samian native mathematician who devised one very famous theorem, would probably turn over in his grave if he could see the circus of sunburned hordes that one of those port towns, his namesake **Pithagorio,** has become.

While the masses crowd the rocky beaches of eastern Samos, you should head inland, to the island's most interesting villages and wonderful **hiking and cycling paths,** or to the northern coast, with its fabulous sandy beaches of **Megalo Seitani** and **Micro Seitani,** accessible only by boat or a 45-minute scenic hike from Karlovassi. The interior region of **Platanakia** is Samos at its most picturesque: Here, the charming hill towns of **Manolates, Vourliotes,** and **Stavrinides** are hidden among woods and streams that foiled the pirates who repeatedly invaded the island. Leisurely walks along the shaded roads between those villages are some of the most rewarding pursuits on Samos and provide a much-needed respite from the Aegean sun.

The eastern tip of Samos is barely 1km (⅔ mile) from Turkey, and the most popular day trip from Samos is the excursion to the archaeological site of **Ephesus,** truly one of the best collections of ancient ruins in the Eastern Mediterranean, with splendors from both the Greek and the Roman eras. From Vathi, there are a few boats per day to Kusadasi, Turkey, from which it's a short trip to Ephesus. Samos also has its own archaeological attractions, the most noteworthy being the **Efpalinion aqueduct** (access from Pithagorio), a 1,000m-long (3,281-ft.) tunnel that connected coastal Vathi to the mountain streams of the interior. Much of the aqueduct is walkable, but claustrophobes should beware. —*SM*

The Samos waterfront.

(i) www.samosguide.com.

Samos-Aristarchos International, connections to Athens, Thessaloniki, Mykonos, and Santorini.

Samos's Vathi port is served by ferry from many other Greek islands and Piraeus, but the fastest and most frequent connections are to Kusadasi, Turkey (1½ hr.).

$$ **Daphne Hotel,** Platanakia, Agios Konstantinos (**30/22730/94493;** www.daphne-hotel.gr).

301 Out & About

Skyros

Unspoiled Getaway in the Sporades

Greece

Tourism hasn't arrived in a major way on this southernmost island of the Sporades archipelago, and that's a very good thing—and probably a temporary one in a country whose islands have almost all become magnets for sun-seeking summer crowds. For now, Skyros is very much ruled by a calm and relaxing vibe, whether you're exploring the island's wild landscape, swimming at its secluded sandy beaches, or soaking up the local rhythms of its traditional villages.

Linaria is the port of entry for all boats to Skyros (which don't call nearly as frequently as on other islands, part of why Skyros remains relatively untrodden).

From here it's a short ride (your own car or moped is recommended for getting around the island—public transportation is limited) to the Skyrian capital of **Chora** (aka Skyros town), with its characteristic Greek isle architecture of whitewashed cubes. This is a traditional village where local men still wear Greek fishermen's caps and sandals, but you'll find plenty of lively, traveler-friendly spots for eating and drinking on Chora's main drag. Climb the narrow streets that lead from the market to the **Byzantine kastro,** which includes the monastery of **Agios Georgios,** Skyros's big-deal historical-religious site—famous for its 10th-century black-faced icon of St. George, brought from Constantinople. The citadel has magnificent views over town and off a sheer cliff that drops to the sea.

The topography on Skyros is divided between the dense pine forests of the northwest (ideal for hiking) and the more barren and rugged terrain of the northeastern and southern parts of the island. The best beaches are in the north, including **Molos beach** (3km/1¾ miles from Chora), which is the largest and sandiest on the island; accordingly, it's also Skyros's most heavily developed and well used. **Windsurfing** is popular here, and a bit away from the main beach stretch there are sections of sand suitable for nude sunbathing. A number of midrange hotels line the beachfront of Molos, and there are many casual **tavernas** perfect for sunset cocktails. About 10km (6¼ miles) west of Chora, take your pick between the neighboring beaches of **Pefkos** and **Agios Fokas:** The former is a narrow crescent of golden sand backed by lush Mediterranean greenery; the latter, even more beautiful, feels more secluded and is reminiscent of a perfect lake beach, with pebbly shores and a calm bay.

Skyros is also home to a rare breed of especially small ponies that were introduced to the island as far back as the 8th century B.C. Though the armies of Alexander the Great are said to have ridden these sturdy animals in battle, and they're believed to be the short horses depicted on the Parthenon friezes, most Skyrian ponies are now under the protection of nonprofit agencies (in other words, don't expect any pony rides, unless you spot one in someone's pasture and can convince the owner to let you hop on for a minute). Otherwise, you can see the animals at the **Skyrian Pony Center** on the way to Atsitsa Bay. —*SM*

ⓘ www.gnto.gr.

✈ Skyros Airport, 4km (2½ miles) from Chora; connections to Athens and Thessaloniki.

⛴ From Kymi (2 hr.). **Skyros Shipping Company** (✆ **30/22220/91790;** www.sne.gr).

🛏 $$ **Skiros Palace Hotel,** Yirismata (✆ **30/22220/91994;** www.skiros-palace.gr).

Out & About **302**

Koh Samui

Beach Bliss in Thailand

Thailand

Not so long ago a laid-back and slightly scruffy bohemian beach hangout, with thatched bungalows on the beach and dusty red-dirt roads, Koh Samui has made the leap into the big time. It's now neck and neck with rival Koh Phuket ❷ in the competition for most popular beach destination in Thailand. Boutique resorts on beautiful beaches sell increasingly higher standards of pampered luxury. What Koh Samui lacks are high-rise hotels and disco-thumping nightlife—reason enough, for some folks, to choose Koh Samui over Phuket.

Thailand's third-largest island, Koh Samui has all the attributes of a tropical island dream getaway: blissfully warm seas, velvety air, and crescents of pristine white-sand beaches fanned by coconut palms. Samui's most beautiful (and popular) beaches are **Hat Chaweng** and **Hat Lamai,** both fronting the Gulf of Thailand on the island's east coast. At 7km (4⅓ miles), Chaweng is a long drink of sand and water, and plenty crowded in high season. The smaller Lamai is quieter and just as pretty. **Ngam** beach is the west coast's top spot, with powdery white sand and superb sunset viewing.

Renting a car is a good way to see all that Koh Samui offers; you can do a loop along the island's coastline in about 2½ hours (but don't miss the island's lush and mountainous interior). The hairpin turns on the hilly roads should keep you on your toes. Perhaps the most efficient way to get around is by "the poor man's taxi" or *songtaew,* covered pickup trucks that follow Route 4169, the ring road, around the island. Hail one anywhere along the highway and beach roads—and be sure to barter the fare; it's acceptable and even expected, especially at night, when prices go up.

Like Phuket, Koh Samui has exceptional diving and snorkeling opportunities. The **Samui International Diving School** (at the Malibu Resort, Chaweng Beach; ✆ **66/7742-2386;** www.planet-scuba.net) is a full-service dive center, with PADI courses and daily dives. Some of the better snorkeling off Koh Samui is found along the rocky coast between Chaweng Noi and Lamai bays.

Koh Samui is not the first place you'd go to see important Buddhist *wats* (temples) in Thailand, but it does have a few worthwhile sites. The most important landmark for local islanders is the 11m-tall (36-ft.) **Big Buddha,** in **Wat Phra Yai.** It's located on Koh Faan, a small islet connected to the shore by a causeway, with shops and restaurants at the base. Two temples in Samui hold the bodies of mummified monks; most people visit **Wat Khunaram,** on Route 4169 south of Lamai, where the mummified body of monk Loung Pordaeng is in the same meditation position as when he died nearly 40 years ago. And, curiously, he wears sunglasses.

If you simply can't get enough of the sun and sea, take a boat trip 30km (19 miles) offshore to the **Angthong National Marine Park,** composed of 42 limestone islets rimmed by coral reefs. It's a spectacularly scenic area, with white-sand beaches kissed by cerulean seas. On the park's largest island, **Koh Wua Talab,** take a hike to the central peak and bring your camera—the views of the surrounding islets and seas are killer. —*AF*

ⓘ **Tourism Authority of Thailand (TAT),** Thawi Ratchaphakti Rd. just north of the main ferry terminal, Nathon (✆ **66/7742-0504;** www.tourismthailand.org); also www.kohsamui.org.

✈ Bangkok to Koh Samui airport (1 hr.).

⛴ **Songserm** (✆ **66/7728-7124** in Surat Thani; www.songserm-expressboat.com) runs a loop from Surat Thani pier to Samui in 2 hr.

🛏 $ **Milky Bay Resort,** Koh Pha Ngan (✆ **66/7723-8566;** www.milkybay.com). $$$ **Saboey Resort & Villas,** Big Buddha Beach (✆ **66/7743-0456;** www.saboey.com).

The Caribbean Unplugged

303

Isla Mujeres

Escape from Cancún

Mexico

Never mind that there are other islands in the area—like the larger and more established resort destination of Cozumel 266. Thanks to its informal, laid-back vibe, Isla Mujeres is known to one and all in the Yucatan by its one-word nickname, *Isla*. Though it's only 8km (5 miles) from and easily visible from the mainland, tiny Isla Mujeres is a tantalizing 180-degree personality shift from crazy Cancún and a boon for anyone whose definition of a Mexican vacation involves not only beachy fun in turquoise waters and a steady supply of *cerveza* but also the actual possibility of relaxing. If you need to chill out, hop on that 20-minute ferry to Isla, and feel your muscles start to unwind.

The knobby, triangular spit at the northern end of the island is where the port and only town are located. The town is a walkable grid of fewer than a dozen streets with small, independent lodging and dining—no international chains here. If you opt for accommodations in town, you can grab your beach towel and walk less than 5 minutes to reach **Playa Norte.** This excellent stretch of fine, sugary sand is all the beach you need on Isla; it's equipped with watersports and friendly bars where you can sip tropical drinks from shady hammocks. Playa Norte is angled slightly to the west, making it one of few beaches in this part of Mexico that gets a great view of the sunset. (The sun sets over

Isla Mujeres beach.

Cancún, and while vacationers in the high-rises there primp and prep for a wild night of partying, you'll still be rubbing your feet through the sand, no big evening plans afoot, and happy as a clam about it.)

Southeast from town, Isla Mujeres extends, like a skinny barracuda, for about 6.4km (4 miles) before disappearing into the Caribbean; for any exploration of Isla beyond the confines of town, a golf cart is practically obligatory (rent one at the ferry dock). Puttering around on a golf cart is in fact integral to the Isla Mujeres experience: Distances are short and, in keeping with the island's sleepy tempo, you'll never need to go faster than about 20 mph. Though most get around Isla with the help of a motor, you can also rent pedal bikes for next to nothing; **mountain bikes** are recommended as some of the island's best hiking and biking paths aren't paved.

The main leisure attraction on the southern end of the island is **Garrafón National Park** (✆ **52/998/193-3360;** www.garrafon.com), a full-service reef-side "eco-park" run by Dolphin Discovery. Water activities on offer here run the gamut from snorkeling to transparent canoes to an overwater zip line. (The **swim-with-the-dolphins** programs cost extra; see www.dolphindiscovery.com.)

Back in the golf cart, visit the **Turtle Sanctuary** (✆ **52/998/877-0595**), a successful and privately funded facility where guests can even take part in the turtle-hatching releases (usually scheduled May–Oct). Rounding out Isla's roster of quick and easy sites are the **Mayan temple of Ixchel,** a ruin on a bluff near the lighthouse at the southern tip of the island, and the **Hacienda Mundaca** (Carr. Garrafón, Km 6), a former pirate's fortress turned zoo—with reptiles, monkeys, and a jaguar—in the middle of the island.

By late afternoon, day-tripping hordes from Cancún have been loaded back onto their tour boats to the mainland, and Isla Mujeres town returns to its chilled-out self. Maybe you cap off the day with a **yoga class**—an increasingly popular activity on the island, and available in poolside *palapas* at hotels like the **Na Balam** (✆ **52/998/877-0279;** www.nabalam.com)—or maybe you just walk back to Playa Norte, crack open that guilty-pleasure paperback and a cold *cerveza,* and bask in the glow of sunset. —*SM*

ⓘ Av. Rueda Medina 130 (✆ **52/998/877-0307;** www.isla-mujeres.net).

✈ Cancún.

From Puerto Juarez (Cancún), Ultramar (✆ **52/998/877-0307;** www.granpuerto.com.mx).

$$$ **Casa de los Sueños,** Carretera a Garrafón 9a/b, Fracc. Turquesa (✆ **52/998/877-0651;** www.casadelossuenosresort.com). $$ **Hotel Belmar,** av. Hidalgo 110 (✆ **52/998/877-0430;** www.rolandi.com).

The Caribbean Unplugged

Utila

Hangin' with Whale Sharks

Bay Islands, Honduras

Like Roátan 43, its sister Bay Island to the east, Utila lies along the Mesoamerican barrier reef system (number two in the world after Australia's Great Barrier), and most who have even heard of the island are divers who know that it offers one of the best chances on the planet to spot the elusive **whale shark.** These gentle giants, which can measure up to 12m (39 ft.) in length, are the world's largest fish and are present in the waters around Utila year-round (though they're most typically seen Feb–May and Aug–Sept). In fact, this animal is so central to the Utila tourism economy that the spotted silhouette of the whale shark—emblazoned on shop signs, restaurant menus, and charter boats—has practically become the official logo of the island.

Of course, nothing is guaranteed when it comes to wildlife sightings, and even if you aren't lucky enough to spy a whale shark through your mask, the rest of the diving scene on Utila is still plenty satisfying. This little island (11×4km/6¾×2½ miles) is a true unspoiled tropical paradise, with 60 never-crowded dive sites. Under the water, enjoy a kaleidoscopic and encyclopedic array of Caribbean marine creatures, from octopus to sea turtles to eagle rays to reef fish of every stripe. Shipwrecks like the 30m (98-ft.) transport vessel ***Halliburton,*** just off Eastern Harbor, are great fun to explore, with all kinds of hatches to swim through and portholes to stick your head through. There are about a half dozen dive resorts on the island that include scuba equipment and excursions as part of a package rate, or you can stay in simpler accommodations—dorm-style beds can cost as little as $2 per night—and independently arrange your own equipment rentals and boat dives with a PADI-certified operator like **Underwater Vision** (✆ **504/425-3103;** www.underwatervision.net).

Nondivers can visit the ***caylitos*** (little cays), off the southwest end of the island. The quintessential private island of **Water Cay** has absolutely no facilities, but you can take the 30-minute ride from Eastern Harbor for a blissful day of sunbathing and picnicking on a picture-perfect, palm-fringed sandy shore. The pristine islets of **Sandy Cay** and **Little Cay** are also available to rent out for as little as $100 per night—that's for a totally charming bungalow that sleeps up to 14. Back on Utila, nature lovers can visit the **Iguana Breeding and Research Station** (www.utila-iguana.de), which also runs informative guided **hiking tours** that take in the varied island landscape.

Granted, Utila doesn't offer a full range of watersports, and there isn't much action here: The slow pace of the island seems to mimic that of the lumbering whale shark. **Eastern Harbor** is the only real town on the island, with one hotel, restaurant, and shop-lined main street that takes 20 minutes to walk end to end. All the dive operators have a presence at Eastern Harbor's **Municipal Dock,** and **Chepes Beach,** at the far end of town, is good for swimming and lazing on the sand.

So while the Honduran Bay Island of Roátan sits poised to become the Caribbean's Next Big Thing, with all the cruise ship tourists, upscale development, and direct flights that go along with it, Utila looks to remain fairly unchanged—remote and authentic—for the foreseeable future. With lodging and food so affordable on Utila, the island is especially appealing as a longer-term stay for backpacker types or for those taking a dive master course. —*SM*

ⓘ www.aboututila.com.

✈ Utila Municipal Airport, connections to mainland Honduras.

⛴ From La Ceiba (1 hr.). **Utila Princess** (✆ **504/425-3390;** www.utilaprincess.com).

🛏 $$ **Private islands of Sandy Cay and Little Cay** (✆ **504/425-2005;** www.aboututila.com). $$$ **Utopia Dive Village** (✆ **504/3/344-9387;** www.utopiadivevillage.com).

305 The Caribbean Unplugged

Saba

Tiny Haven with Transportation Thrills

As far as sheer geographical extent goes, Saba is the "least" of the Lesser Antilles islands. In spite of its mere 8 sq. km (3 sq. miles), however, this Dutch West Indies isle manages to contain the highest point in the entire Kingdom of the Netherlands: Its volcanic summit is 873m (2,864 ft.) tall. Tiny, sleepy Saba is a haven for nature lovers and relaxation seekers—the absolute flip side of bigger and busier Caribbean destinations. For one thing, there are no beaches here, though the coastal waters teem with marine life and excellent dive spots. No-drama Saba is best suited to avid divers, hikers, or those who want to unplug from "real life" and aren't looking for the typical Caribbean formula of lolling on the sand.

Saba is a gorgeously eroded extinct volcanic cone, and the dramatic topography you see on land continues as a mountainous slope below the surface. It bears repeating that the island's steep shoreline is completely devoid of palm trees and sand. One of the biggest activities here is simply taking in the glorious scenery from a hotel terrace or other vista point. Hiking on Saba is satisfying, and relatively easy, given the short distances. The **Saba Conservation Foundation** (© **599/416-3295;** www.sabapark.org) maintains the trails and can provide information about the flora and fauna along the way.

The island's dive sites are under the aegis of the **Saba Marine Park** (see Saba Conservation Foundation, above) and include four underwater mountains (2km/1¼ miles offshore) and coral reefs. There's also a (difficult) snorkeling trail marked by buoys. Due to the depths and sea conditions here, it's best to set out for any undersea exploration with a reputable outfitter. A good bet is **Sea Saba Dive Center** (© **599/416-2246;** www.seasaba.com), which offers 4-hour day-boat dives and experienced guides/instructors.

Because of Saba's small size and lack of beaches, many who visit the island do so as a day trip from St. Maarten 216. From that island's Queen Juliana Airport, it's a 12-minute hop to Saba. Whether you come for the day or stay a bit longer, you will experience one of the Caribbean's most hair-raising airplane landings: Occupying the sort-of-flat northeast edge of the island, **Juancho Yrausquin Airport** has the shortest commercial airstrip in the world, only 394m/1,293 ft. (the length of five Airbus 380s, which do not fly here). Takeoffs are even more thrilling: Within a few seconds of the engines propelling you down the runway, Saba disappears below you and you're somehow aloft over the deep blue sea. Flight buffs should book the jaunt from St. Maarten for this adventure alone.

The other unmissable component of any trip to Saba is also transportation-related: The island is traversed by an adrenaline-pumping mountain highway, known to one and all as **The Road.** The work of visionary Saba local Josephus Lambert Hassell (foreign engineers said it couldn't be built), the 31km (19-mile) motorway climbs like a corkscrew from the airport to the lofty settlement of **Windwardside** (elev. 541m/1,775 ft.) before descending to a Dutch village called, appropriately enough, **The Bottom.** The Road is frequently and fittingly compared to a roller coaster for its flying curves, heart-in-your-throat vistas, and the fact that for every uphill stretch, Hassell added a significant dip, possibly just for the fun of it. Alas, there's no loop-de-loop. —*SM*

ⓘ www.sabatourism.com.

✈ Juancho E. Yrausquin Airport; all flights are through St. Maarten (connections to North America, South America, and Europe).

🛏 $$ **The Gate House,** Hell's Gate, Zion's Hill (✆ **599/416-2416;** www.sabagatehouse.com). **Willard's of Saba,** Booby Hill (✆ **800/504-9861** in the U.S., or 599/416-2498; www.willardsofsaba.com).

The Caribbean Unplugged **306**

St. Eustatius

Dive into the 1700s

To visit this unspoiled and diminutive West Indies island today, you'd never know that St. Eustatius—"Statia" to habitués—was once a bustling hub of Caribbean trade, its main port of Oranjestad filled with hundred of ships loading and unloading cargo, salty types streaming in and out of harbor taverns and places of ill repute throughout the day. During the Revolutionary War, Dutch-held Statia supplied the American colonies with guns and ammo, and when the war was over, Statia was one of the first places to recognize the United States of America as a new and separate nation. What irony, then, that so few North Americans know anything about Statia.

Like its Antilles neighbor Saba 305 (30km/19 miles northwest), Statia is not a beach bum's island, but divers take heart: At sites like **Crack in the Wall,** you'll find astounding pinnacles of coral shooting up from the ocean floor and can swim among barracudas, black-tip sharks, and rays. Snorkelers can also get into the action on the Caribbean side of St. Eustatius. The underwater scene at **Crooks Castle Beach,** near Oranjestad, is a fascinating marine archaeological site with remnants of an 18th-century man-of-war and the walls of warehouses, taverns, and ships that sank below the surface more than 200 years ago. Full-service **Dive Statia** can arrange any sort of diving or snorkeling excursion (✆ **599/318-2435;** www.divestatia.com).

The prettiest beaches on Statia, though they're few, face the Atlantic, where rough waves and undertows are a turnoff for swimmers. Still, beachcombing on the island can be quite rewarding if you're lucky enough to uncover one of Statia's fabled treasures—**blue-glass beads,** manufactured by the Dutch East India company and used as currency for such products as rum, tobacco, and even slaves. The beads tend to appear on shore after storms, and the beach that yields them most frequently is **Crooks Castle.**

Statia consists of two extinct volcanic summits, the Quill and Little Mountain, joined by a valley so narrow that the St. Eustatius airport runway cuts across half of it. **Hiking on the Quill** is a marvelous journey through a primeval rainforest filled with brilliant tropical flowers and lush greens. To get a primer in Statian flora all in one spot, visit the **Miriam C. Schmidt Botanical Garden,** on the Atlantic side of the Quill. This sprawling and panoramic spot is an excellent place to bring a picnic.

The one and only town on Statia is historic **Oranjestad,** whose anchorage once saw the comings and goings of all those merchant ships centuries ago. The 1636 bastions of Fort Oranje were painstakingly restored for the U.S. centennial in 1976, and the ramparts are still lined with old cannons. Oranjestad today is a quaint but quiet town, with no nightlife to speak of. In fact, what passes for a big night out on Statia is crab catching on top of the Quill. The 610m (2,001-ft.) crater is a breeding ground for the crustaceans, which come out after dark only to be snatched up by Statians who take them home and turn them into the local delicacy, stuffed crab.

Of course, if that doesn't sound like enough excitement for you, you can always pop over to Statia as a day trip from St. Maarten 216, 17 minutes away by air. —*SM*

(i) www.statiatourism.com.

✈ Franklin D. Roosevelt Airport; all flights are through St. Maarten (connections to North America, South America, and Europe).

🛏 $$ **King's Well Resort,** Oranje Bay Rd.-1 (✆ **599/318-2538;** www.kingswellstatia.com). $$ **The Old Gin House,** Oranjebaai 1, Oranjestad (✆ **599/318-2319;** www.oldginhouse.com).

307 The Caribbean Unplugged

Virgin Gorda

Marine Playground

British Virgin Islands

Oh, for the days of the age of exploration, when you could discover a new place and name it any old thing that popped into your head. In 1493, on his second voyage to the New World, Christopher Columbus was running out of names; the ocean was littered with dots grandiosely titled "Columbus." When the explorer came upon an island whose mountain looked like nothing so much as a reclining woman with a big belly, he pronounced it Virgin Gorda, or "Fat Virgin," and sailed on.

Tortola 31 may be the biggest and most populous island in the B.V.I., but many people consider Virgin Gorda—in spite of its inelegant name—the crown jewel of the 60-island chain. It has softly undulating volcanic hills with excellent hiking trails, azure seas, and pristine, secluded beaches. At its center is the pregnant belly of Columbus's imagination: **Gorda Peak,** at 408m (1,360 ft.) the island's highest point and a great summit to climb. The most photographed beach in the B.V.I. is **The Baths,** on the island's southwest shore, where immense granite rocks are strewn along the powdery white-sand beach, forming lovely grottoes and hidden pools. Most scientists believe these granite boulders exploded onto the scene eons ago by undersea volcanic fireworks.

Virgin Gorda is the third largest of the British Virgin Islands, but at 22 sq. km (8½ sq. miles), it's not a big place by any means. Even so, the island is uncrowded and unpretentious, with goats and cows scratching in the dry scrub and a genuinely congenial populace. If you're looking for quiet, pampered seclusion, Virgin Gorda neatly fits the bill—the lodging model here is one of boutique resorts of impeccable taste and understated luxury. Laurance Rockefeller established the tone in the 1960s, when he built an ultraprivate "wilderness beach" resort on Little Dix Bay. Other major resorts followed, much in the same vein. You might even say the island is undercommercialized, certainly when it comes to nightlife and shopping. And that's just fine with the visitors who keep coming back year after year.

Like Tortola, Virgin Gorda is a sailor's paradise, with sublime anchorages in protected waters. A trip to Virgin Gorda is as much about getting out on the water as it is about pampered privacy. Boat and tour operators, too numerous to list here, offer crewed or bareboat charters, day sails, and cruises; an extensive list of operators is available on the B.V.I. official tourism website (see below). Spend a day exploring the sparkling coves and islets of the **North Sound** (also called Gorda Sound), on the northeast coast of the island. The North Sound is the largest noncommercial deep-water harbor in the Caribbean, with sheltered anchorages, gentle trade winds, and excellent snorkeling; it's one big marine playground. Some of Virgin Gorda's best beaches are found on the surrounding small islands. Unspoiled **Prickly Pear Island** is a 98-hectare (242-acre) national park; head to Vixen Point for a memorable swim and snorkel. Plan your visit around lunchtime, when you can join the peripatetic sailors and yachties at the supremely casual **Sand Box Bar and Restaurant** (✆ **284/495-9122**), at Vixen Point, for conch fritters and fresh lobster salad. —*AF*

ⓘ www.bviwelcome.com.

✈ Tortola (Beef Island International Airport; 19km/12 miles).

Ferry from Tortola (several companies including **Speedy's:** ✆ **284/495-5235;** www.speedysbvi.com; 30 min.) or private resort boat pickup.

$$$ **Biras Creek Resort** (✆ **877/883-0756** in the U.S. or 310/440-4225; www.biras.com). $$ **Nail Bay Resort,** Nail Bay (✆ **800/871-3551** in the U.S., or 284/494-8000; www.nailbay.com).

Remote Adventures **308**

Cumberland Island

Just You & the Birds

Georgia, U.S.

It takes some effort to reach this barrier isle and national seashore at the southern end of the Georgia coast, practically into Florida—unless you've got your own boat, you'll have to take a 45-minute ferry ride from St. Mary's. Once you get there, you may be surprised to find its gleaming sands deserted. What kind of a national seashore is this?

But that's all part of Cumberland Island's subtle charm. Originally a cotton plantation and then a summer retreat for the Carnegies, Cumberland Island has been mostly uninhabited since 1972, with only a few private owners remaining in clustered compounds. Over the years, the wilderness has gradually closed in, until the main road through the interior seems a mere tunnel through a vine-draped canopy of live oaks, cabbage palms, magnolia, holly, red cedar, and pine. Only 300 people are allowed on the island at any given time, many of them overnight guests at the island's only lodging, the stately turn-of-the-century **Greyfield Inn** (see below). (There are also two bare-bones campgrounds for visitors who prefer roughing it.) Although the island has a few historic sites—a restored Carnegie mansion, a tiny African-American meetinghouse—most visitors tend to be nature lovers, fond of **hiking** (there are over 50 miles/81km of hiking trails), **bicycling** along the old carriage roads (rent bikes at the Sea Camp Dock), and **kayaking** through the silent salt marshes.

Cumberland's sloping 16-mile-long (26km) beach isn't just a bland strip of

Cumberland Island beach.

powdery sand, like some manicured oceanfront resort. Little meadows nestle among the dunes, creeks cut their way to the sea from freshwater ponds, and tidal mud flats glisten. The beach runs the entire length of the island, affording plenty of space for beachgoers to find their own patch of secluded sand. It's not a place to come for high-octane watersports, but the shell hunting is superb, especially early in the morning after a storm. The waters are relatively shallow and calm for swimming, although there are no lifeguards. Nor are there snack bars, showers, or changing rooms—it's just you, the sand, and a wide-open sky.

In late spring and summer, in fact, birds far outnumber humans on Cumberland Island. Bring your binoculars, because this is a major destination on the Atlantic flyway, with more than 335 species showing up throughout the year to nest on the tidal flats or build their nests behind the dunes. (Please respect cordoned-off beach areas in season.) Inland you'll also find alligators, armadillos, raccoons, deer, wild turkeys, and loggerhead turtles, as well as a herd of nearly 300 wild horses that graze on the marsh grasses.

Those who return to Cumberland Island year after year do so for its unhurried pace, a lifestyle attuned to the rhythms of nature. It's not a place to visit in a hurry, barging in and then charging out. Give yourself a day or two to slow down, breathe the salt air, and get sand between your toes—you'll be glad you did. *—HH*

ⓘ **Cumberland Island National Seashore,** St. Mary's, Georgia (✆ **912/882-4336,** ext. 254; www.nps.gov/cuis); also www.cumberlandisland.org.

✈ Jacksonville, Florida (30 miles/48km to St. Mary's).

⛴ 45 min. from St. Mary's (reservations recommended; ✆ **912/882-4335** or 877/860-6787).

🛏 $$$ **Greyfield Inn,** Cumberland Island (✆ **866/401-8581** or 904/261-6408; www.greyfieldinn.com). $ **Sea Camp** or **Stafford campgrounds** (reservations: ✆ **912/882-4335** or 877/860-6787).

Island Hopping the San Juan Islands: Orcas & Evergreens

Mist hovers over the dark water. The perfect silence is broken only by the black dorsal fins of killer whales knifing through the surface. At continent's edge, in the upper-left-hand corner of the United States, lies an unspoiled landscape of deep blue waterways, evergreen forests, mountain vistas, and every opportunity for active types to get out and explore it. Washington State's San Juan Islands are a Pacific Northwest paradise for boating, kayaking, and hiking. Orcas, which swim in large pods here much of the year, are an emblem and major attraction of the San Juan Islands, and whale-watching opportunities abound in the archipelago. Microsoft execs have built vacation homes here, but development remains unobtrusive and the local character down-to-earth. Man has just enough of a presence here for recreation to be easy, but the San Juans are still very much a place where the water and the trees are in charge.

Just a 2-hour drive north of Seattle, the town of Anacortes, on 309 **Fidalgo island,** is most people's jumping-off point for the San Juans. Anacortes is a real working town with loads of marine charm—get a taste for it at 100-year-old **Marine Supply & Hardware Co.** (202 Commercial Ave.; ✆ **360/293-3014;** www.marinesupplyandhardware.com), or simply wander around **Cap Sante Marina,** where boat charters of all kinds are available (**Skyline** is the island's other full-service marina, on the western end of Fidalgo, and close to stunning **Deception Pass,** which leads to nearby Whidbey Island). Before heading to the **Anacortes Ferry Terminal** (for Washington State Ferries to the San Juan Islands), spend an hour or two wandering the shops and restaurants of **Commercial Avenue,** Anacortes's main strip.

The first island you'll reach on the ferry from Anacortes is 310 **Lopez,** the most rural of the three major San Juans, and the friendliest: Locals wave as they drive by (and you're expected to do the same), and you can get a taste of this close-knit, eccentric community by spending time at the shops and cafes of Lopez Village, the heart of island life. Be sure to pick up a jar or two of locally made Lopez Larry's specialty mustards. Low-key Lopez is great for biking and kayaking and has several public stretches of beach that are perfect for lazy beachcombing as well as wooded trails that make for invigorating hikes.

Fisherman Bay and Lopez Village.

The largest of the San Juans is 311 **Orcas island.** On a map, it looks like a cloak draped around a central fjord called the East Sound. (A note on the pronunciation of Orcas: the *s* is soft.) At the isthmus that connects the two halves of the island, the town of **Eastsound** is the hub of local culture and commerce on Orcas. On the eastern half of the island, don't miss a drive to the top of 2,409-foot-tall (734m) **Mount Constitution;** it's the highest point in the San Juans, with breathtaking views of the entire archipelago. **Moran State Park,** which leads up to the summit, is also home to two lakes suitable for swimming and fishing, as well as miles of hiking trails for all levels. A thriving artist community makes up a sizable chunk of the year-round population on Orcas, and the island is especially well known for its pottery.

Most visitors with limited time in the archipelago head straight to 312 **San Juan Island,** and for good reason: It has the most services and the best whale-watching. The lively port town of **Friday Harbor** has plenty of restaurants, galleries, shops, and the **Whale Museum** (62 1st St.; ✆ **360/378-4710;** www.whale-museum.org). On the west side of the island, **Lime Kiln Point State Park** is one of the best shore vantage points for watching killer whales, which frequently swim along the channel between San Juan and Vancouver Island (p. 299). From much of the western and southern coasts of San Juan Island, there are also majestic views of the Olympic Mountains. Well-rounded San Juan also has oyster and alpaca farms, as well as a winery, that welcome visitors. **Roche Harbor,** on the west coast of the island, is the toniest resort in the archipelago. Ferries from Anacortes to Lopez, Orcas, and San Juan islands also stop at the very private, 8-sq.-mile (21-sq.-km) **Shaw Island** along the way. For nearly 3 decades, Franciscan nuns who lived on the island greeted visitors—in full habits and reflective orange safety vests—at the ferry dock and sold them wares from their small general store; an encounter with these women of the cloth was the island's major draw, but in 2004, the sisters left. Now, Shaw is occupied only by about 200 residents, who have passed several measures barring lodging, restaurants, and retail stores, making it clear that tourists aren't particularly welcome here.

The San Juans are a perfect destination for nature lovers who like a slow pace. They're not a place for sun seekers and swimmers. Even in summer, it's often cool and damp, and the water stays at a temperature the orcas like—nice and cold. Accommodations range from campgrounds to upscale resorts, but in the summer it's always essential to book your stay well in advance and, if you're planning on taking a car on the ferry (recommended), to be in line at the ferry terminal at least 2 hours before your scheduled sailing time. —*SM*

ⓘ ✆ **888/468-3701;** www.visitsanjuans.com.

By small plane or seaplane from Seattle or Sea-Tac International (65 miles/105km to Anacortes, then ferry).

From Anacortes (Fidalgo Island), **Washington State Ferries** (1–2 hr. for interisland trips; ✆ **206/464-6400;** www.wsdot.wa.gov/ferries).

$$ **Anaco Bay Inn,** 916 33rd St., Anacortes (✆ **360/299-3320;** www.anacobayinn.com). $$$ **Roche Harbor Resort,** San Juan Island (✆ **800/451-9810;** www.rocheharbor.com).

Remote Adventures 313

Isle Royale

Serenity Among Moose & Wolves

Michigan, U.S.

As its promotional materials like to point out, Isle Royale National Park gets as many visitors in a year as Yellowstone gets in a day. Remote and untouched, Isle Royale is a narrow strip of wilderness in the northwest part of Lake Superior, 2 hours by boat from the nearest mainland port. Extensive **hiking trails** (165 miles/266km total) and myriad inland waterways for canoeing and kayaking make this an ideal north-woods getaway for rugged, adventurous types.

No cars, nor wheeled vehicles of any kind, are allowed on Isle Royale, so any getting around on the 45-mile-long, 9-mile-wide (72×14km) island is under the power of your own two (hiking) feet or (paddling) arms. Isle Royale's two towns, with park service information centers, groceries, and boat rentals, lie at opposite ends of the island: **Rock Harbor,** where the island's one hotel is located and where ferries from Copper Harbor and Houghton, Michigan, land, is at the eastern tip; smaller **Windigo,** where boats from Grand Portage, Minnesota, arrive, is at the western edge. Between the two is a vast wilderness of ridges covered with spruce and fir trees where you'll enjoy backcountry solitude and perhaps spot a **moose** or two. Isle Royale's ecosystem supports both eastern timber wolves and moose in a delicate predator-prey relationship: When the population of one thrives, so does the other.

The Isle Royale coast.

Traversing the interior can be done solely on foot (you'll often see troops of Boy Scouts here to earn their 50-Mile Hike merit badges) or as a sort of biathlon of hiking and boating. Isle Royale's center is peppered with lakes, each with their own rocky islets, and portage routes for canoers and kayakers are clearly marked. **Ryan Island,** in skinny **Siskiwit Lake,** along the island's southern shore, holds the odd distinction of being the largest island on the largest lake on the largest island on the largest freshwater lake (Superior) in the world. Throughout Isle Royale, there are basic campgrounds, many with Adirondack shelters, available on a first-come, first-served basis. For adventures involving less commitment, you can also embark on any number of day hikes from either Rock Harbor or Windigo, with the possibility of ranger-guided interpretive walks.

Lake Superior's weather can be notoriously harsh and unpredictable, even on what appears to be a mild summer day. Boats are strongly discouraged from venturing out to the open lake waters, where even close to shore, random squalls pose a serious threat to small craft like canoes and kayaks. As testimony of nature's wrath in this part of the country, a number of larger **shipwrecks** can be seen (by scuba divers willing to brave the chilly waters of Superior) in the shoals off the western edge of Isle Royale.

To really unplug from civilization, you'll want to spend a few days on Isle Royale. Camping at one of the island's 36 campsites is certainly an economical and invigorating option, but considering the potentially inclement weather of Lake Superior, I highly recommend booking accommodations at **Rock Harbor Lodge.** After a windy or rainy day in the outdoors, you can at least retire to the lodge's cozy dining room, be warmed by the fireplace, and enjoy the camaraderie of fellow islandgoers.

Note that due to severe winter weather, Isle Royale is open only from mid-April to late October. —*SM*

ⓘ **National Park Service** (✆ **906/482-0984;** www.nps.gov/isro).

✈ Seaplane (30 min.) from Houghton County Memorial Airport, Michigan.

⛴ From Houghton, Michigan (6½ hr.), and Copper Harbor, Michigan (4½ hr.), and Grand Portage, Minnesota (2–3 hr.).

🛏 $ Camping contact info is the same as for the National Park, above. $$$ **Rock Harbor Lodge** (✆ **906/337-4993** in summer or 866/644-2003 in winter; rockharborlodge.com); open only May–Sept.

314 Remote Adventures

Isla Bastimentos

Jungle Fever

Panama

The word is out on Panama, spread by savvy globe-trotters, nature lovers, surfers and divers, eco-tourists, and beach bums. If you're looking for an unspoiled tropical paradise, packed with rainforest jungles, palm-shaded, sugary-sand beaches, sparkling turquoise seas, and nature at its ripest, head here. Panama, they say, is the Costa Rica of 30 years ago—which is to say that its extraordinary natural treasures remain relatively undiscovered.

And fortunately for one lush and biologically diverse region of the country, it's going to stay that way. The **Bocas del Toro** archipelago, a ribbon of seven meltingly lovely tropical islands and hundreds of islets off the northern coast of Panama, is largely a nature reserve, thanks to the foresight of the Panamanian government. **Bastimentos Marine National Park (Parque Nacional Marino Isla Bastimentos),** designated national parkland in 1988, comprises 13,233 hectares (32,700 acres) of island, barrier reef, and sea. The park takes up about a third of Isla Bastimentos, one of the largest islands in the archipelago, and dense jungle takes up most of the island. Bastimentos also has secluded lagoons, coral gardens, caves, and stunning beaches with names like **Red Frog Beach** (named for the strawberry-colored frogs that dart about in the surf). You can hike into the jungle past waterfalls and tropical blooms, or along beaches under shady palm trees and over cool creeks.

Keep in mind when you visit that this part of the world is wild in the purest sense—it's nature unplugged and unbridled. You can stay in one of several pioneering ecolodges where blue butterflies alight on your bedpost. Right outside your door, monkeys fly through the trees; lizards slink along the floors. Birds come in a paint box of electric colors, filling the jungle with bone-rattling cries and shrieks. The multitude of frogs alone is worth a trip; how about frogs with polka dots? Bromeliads in pastel hues climb the jungle canopy. The beaches have no umbrellas or vendors hawking their wares—just nesting sites for sea turtles. And much of civilization is far away—the island has no roads or cars and is accessible only by boat. In fact, this region is called the "Venice of the Caribbean" for its ease in getting from place to place by boat. Much of the island's offshore marine sanctuary has yet to be explored—it's that unspoiled.

But the hammer and nail of civilization may not be that far away. A luxury resort, with villas, a boutique hotel, a 100-slip marina, and a spa, is back on track after a long strike and financial restructuring. The **Red Frog Beach Resort** (www.redfrogbeach.com) will enjoy a prime location just outside the park boundaries on Red Frog Beach. Whether the strawberry frogs stick around to frolic in the surf when the construction crews arrive remains to be seen. —*AF*

(i) www.islabastimentos.com or www.bocasdeltoropanama.info.

Isla Colón (transfer from Panama City or San Jose, Costa Rica).

Water taxis leave the mainland from Almirante (35 min.) and Changuinola (45 min.). You can also take a 10-min. boat ride from Bocas del Toro.

$$ **La Loma Butterfly Farm and Jungle Lodge** (© **507/6619-5364;** www.thejunglelodge.com). $$$ **Tranquilo Bay Eco Adventure Lodge** (© **713/589-6952** in the U.S., or 507/380-0721; www.tranquilobay.com).

Remote Adventures

Hokkaido

Japan's Last Frontier

Japan

Think of it as Japan's version of the Wild West. The most northern island in the Japanese archipelago, Hokkaido is a land of sparsely settled mountains and forests that still feel like frontier territory. Unlike the rest of overpopulated Japan, Hokkaido, with its large number of huge wilderness parks, actually offers solitude and room to breathe. Though few foreigners make it this far north, despite the 1988 opening of the Seikan railway tunnel, outdoorsy young Japanese flock here in droves for backpacking, skiing, backcountry camping, and long-distance cycling.

Skiing and winter sports are Hokkaido's biggest claim to fame—after all, it was the 1972 Winter Olympics in Sapporo that first put this region on the international radar. Sapporo is not only Hokkaido's main city but Japan's largest town north of Tokyo (and, yes, it's the home of Sapporo Beer—enjoy an evening at the **Sapporo Bier Garten** on the grounds of its original red-brick brewery: N7 E9; © **81/11/742-1531;** www.sapporo-bier-garten.jp). From Sapporo, skiers generally head west to the **Teine Highland** and **Olympic** ski area (© **81/11/681-3191;** www.sapporo-teine.com), site of Olympic alpine, bobsled, and toboggan events, which is easily reachable by train; or, even better, travel west to **Niseko** (www.niseko.ne.jp), a 3½-hour bus ride from Sapporo, which has three interconnected ski areas blessed with fine powder, off-piste skiing, and extensive night-lit runs.

Those oh-so-skiable mountains, of course, were heaved up by the same volcanic forces that created all of Japan, so there's something quintessentially Japanese about basking in hot springs on any

Snowboarding in Niseko.

Hokkaido vacation. An hour or so south of Sapporo, one of the highlights of popular **Shikotsu-Toya National Park** is the coastal resort **Noboribetsu Onsen,** known for its curative hot springs. Pre- or post-soak, you can hike through nearby **Hell Valley** for a view of the bubbling hot water that made Noboribetsu famous.

In contrast to the rest of Japan, Hokkaido's summers are not muggy but bright and clear, which makes it an ideal time to brave far-flung **Shiretoko National Park** (the name means "end of the earth" in ancient Ainu), a ruggedly remote peninsula at the island's northeastern tip. Cut off for centuries by jagged volcanic ridges, its virgin forests are still home to endangered Yezo sika deer and Hokkaido brown bears. Seals and seal lions flop around the rocky coves on its dramatic waterfall-laced western coast, which you can view on a boat tour from the gateway town of Utoro. Hiking and camping are the main draw for Shiretoko—its northern quarter has no roads at all, offering a real into-the-wild experience. If all you want is a gentle taste, only 15km (9⅓ miles) from Utoro you can tramp on easy trails around the peaceful forested Five Lakes area, or wade up a warm mountain stream to **Kamuikukka Falls,** where you can loll around the hot springs at its base. Think of it as the Wild West with a spa experience built right in. *—HH*

ⓘ **Hokkaido-Sapporo Tourist Information Center,** Sapporo Station (✆ **81/11/213-5088**). Also www.visit-hokkaido.jp/en or www.snowjapan.com.

✈ New Chitose Airport, Sapporo (1½ hr. from Tokyo).

🚆 Hakodate (6 hr. from Tokyo), Sapporo (9 hr. from Tokyo).

🛏 $$$ **Hotel Shiretoko,** 37 Utorokagawa, Shari Cho, Utoro (✆ **81/152/24-2131**). $ **Nakamuraya Ryokan,** N3 W7, Chuo-ku, Sapporo (✆ **81/11/241-2111;** www.nakamura-ya.com). $$ **Oyado Kiyomizu-ya,** 173 Noboribetsu Onsen-machi, Noboribetsu (✆ **81/143/84-2145**).

Remote Adventures 316

Réunion Island

The Extreme Island

If you've ever traveled to the Big Island of Hawaii 242, Réunion may seem oddly familiar, like a French cousin on the other side of the globe. Dwarfed by Madagascar 470, 805km (500 miles) to the west, and overshadowed by high-profile Mauritius 459, its nearest neighbor to the east, this volcanic blip in the Indian Ocean is a dramatically beautiful gem that savvy French tourists have been keeping to themselves. With its rugged mountains and offshore coral reefs, it's a natural hot spot for those addicted to high-adrenaline sports.

Réunion's most distinctive feature is the three *cirques,* or natural amphitheaters created by collapsed volcanoes in the island's interior. The wildest and most remote, **Cirque de Mafate** in the northwest, is completely sealed off by mountains—it can be reached only by a strenuous hike or a stunning helicopter flyover. The largest cirque, **Cirque de Salazies,** is tops for picturesque scenery, from its emerald-green vegetation, waterfalls, and dramatic mists, to the charming mountain village Hell-Bourg, once voted the prettiest village in France (never mind how far away from the rest of France it is). A heart-stoppingly tortuous mountain road makes a dramatic entrance into **Cirque de Cilaos,** in the heart of the island, a world-famous canyoning destination where you can also "take the waters" at the historic hot springs in the town of Cilaos.

Nearly a thousand kilometers of hiking trails crisscross the cirques, as well as steep tracks that challenge mountain bikers. While the Piton des Neiges that formed the island is extinct, Réunion also has one of the world's most active volcanoes, **Piton de Fournaise** (Furnace Mountain) on the southeast coast, and most visitors feel compelled to view the bubbling yellow-and-red lava of its caldera, by either hiking to the rim or flying over in a helicopter (some hardy souls even dare to camp there overnight). Given how strong the thermal drafts are throughout these plunging valleys, it's no surprise that Réunion has become known as a great place for hang gliding, parasailing, and sky diving, as well as for whitewater rafting on the rapids coursing through the cirques.

A coastal road circles the island, connecting the various towns that have sprung up on its flat, gentle coastal areas (there's also a cross-island road from St-Benoit to St-Pierre). But even on the coast, thrill seekers can get their kicks, with fine scuba diving and deep-sea fishing off the west coast near **St-Gilles-les-Bains,** and surfing around the black-sand beach of **St-Leu.**

Settled by French traders in 1642, Réunion has a wonderful polyglot culture; most of its 700,000 inhabitants speak French or Creole, but their ancestors come from Africa, China, India, and Malaysia, as well as France. That variety is reflected in the local cuisine as well—good news for those who like a fabulous meal after a day of extreme sports. —*HH*

ⓘ **Tourist office,** 2 place Etienne Regnault, St-Denis (✆ **262/262/418300**). Also www.reunionisland.net or http://reunion.runweb.com.

✈ Roland Garros Airport, Réunion (connections to Paris, Singapore, Madagascar, and Mauritius).

🛏 $$ **Iloha Seaview Hotel,** Pointe des Chateaux, St-Leu (✆ **262/262/348989**). $$$ **Le Saint Alexis,** 44 route de Boucan Canot, St-Gilles-les-Bains (✆ **262/262/244204;** www.hotelsaintalexis.com).

8 Islands of History

Myth & Legend

Crete
Goin' Minoan
Greece

Traveling around mainland Greece, it's easy to feel awed by the glories of classical Greece. But take an overnight boat trip south to Crete, and classical Greece suddenly seems like yesterday's news. On this austere cypress-dotted island—Greece's largest, and the fifth largest in the Mediterranean—you'll stroll around landmarks dating back to the Bronze Age, and hunt down traces of the ancient gods themselves.

Get your first taste in **Iraklion,** Crete's largest city, at the **Archeological Museum** (1 Xanthoudidou; ✆ **30/2810/226-092**), its galleries chock-full of Minoan art and artifacts, decorated with distinctively Minoan motifs of bulls and dolphins. (Though under renovation until 2010, the museum still displays its chief treasures in an annex.) While Iraklion itself is a gritty modern seaport, you can still see relics of its centuries-long glory as a Venetian trading center (1204–1669)—two impressive city gates, defensive walls, a stout harborside fort, and an arsenal (don't miss the grave of native son Nikos Kazantzakis, author of *Zorba the Greek* and *The Last Temptation of Christ,* in the southwestern corner of the walls).

You'll want to devote an entire day to Crete's greatest tourist attraction, just 5km (3 miles) south of Iraklion: the **Palace of Knossos** (Knossos Rd.; ✆ **30/2810/231-940**). Historians believe this was the original labyrinth of King Minos, designed by the architect Dedalos—as legend claims, to imprison the Minotaur, a grotesque bull-man monster who fed on human sacrifices. As I wandered around its walkways, I did feel distinctly as if I were in a maze—some 1,300 interconnected rooms sprawl over 2.4 hectares (6 acres), encompassing not only a royal residence but also a ceremonial center, administrative headquarters, and endless storerooms and workshops, grouped around a vast central courtyard. The British archaeologist Arthur Evans, who excavated Knossos in the early 1900s, made a controversial decision to rebuild several portions, replacing walls, floors, and stairs, and hired artists to repaint the gaudy frescoes and tapering red columns. Archaeologists may see it as sacrilege, but I have to admit, it sure made it easier for me to imagine ancient Minoans actually living here.

Take another day to cross the scrubby Messara Plain, nearly to the southern coast, to the **palace of Phaestos** (✆ **30/2892/091-315**), said to be the domain of Minos's brother Radamanthis. Set on a dramatic jutting prow of land, Phaestos stands as an evocative sun-bleached ruin, though you can get a fair idea of its original splendor from the ceremonial staircase and the great stone-paved court with its breathtaking panorama.

A longer day trip south from Mallia into the Lasithi Plain, in the craggy center of the island, takes you even further back in time: to the **Diktaion Cave** (outside the village of Psychro), regarded since ancient times as the birthplace of Zeus, where he hid from his father Cronus. Descend a slippery path into the narrow cavern, where guides can explain the mythological significance of various pools and rocky chambers. Entering this rift in the earth is a spooky primal experience—no wonder the ancient Cretans felt their gods speaking to them here. —*HH*

Previous page: Mont-St.-Michel.

ⓘ **Tourist office:** 1 Xanthoudidou (✆ **30/2810/246-299**).

✈ Iraklion or Chania.

⛴ Iraklion or Chania, 6–10 hr. from Piraeus/Athens. www.ferries.gr.

🛏 $$ **Lato Boutique Hotel,** 15 Epimenidou, Iraklion (✆ **30/2810/228-103;** www.lato.gr). $$$ **Megaron Hotel,** 9 Beaufort, Iraklion (✆ **30/2810/305-300;** www.gdmmegaron.gr).

318 Myth & Legend

The North Island

A Maori Old Time

New Zealand

Scenic, sophisticated, sports-loving New Zealand is a vacation mecca for many reasons. But lots of other countries have beaches, ski resorts, wine regions, and historic cities; nowhere else on earth has Maoris. New Zealand's aboriginal peoples are still a force to be reckoned with here, proudly preserving their ancient myths and customs against a uniquely New Zealand backdrop of sulphur springs, geysers, and volcanoes.

The tried-and-true place to start any visit to the North Island is the hot-spring valley of **Rotorua,** set a few miles inland from the curve of the island's north coast. With a population that's about one-third Maori, exhibits of Maori culture are one of the bigger tourism draws here. There are several replica Maori villages open to the public, including **Te Puia,** Hemo Road (✆ **64/7/348-9047;** www.nzmaori.co.nz); the **Tamaki Maori Village,** 1220 Hinemaru St.

A geyser in Rotorua.

(✆ **64/7/349-2999;** www.maoriculture.co.nz); and **Mitai Village,** 196 Fairy Springs Rd. (✆ **64/7/343-9133;** www.mitai.co.nz). All of these offer a nighttime *hangi,* or traditional Maori feast with cultural performances, sort of a Maori version of a luau. (Several of the big hotels in town host *hangis* as well.) To get into the Maori spirit, you can paddle your own *wara* (Maori canoe) on Lake Rotorua (contact **Mana Adventures,** Memorial Dr.; ✆ **64/7/348-4186;** www.manaadventures.co.nz).

South of town, the small village of **Te Wairoa,** or Buried Village, on Tarawera Road (✆ **64/7/362-8287;** www.buriedvillage.co.nz), is Rotorua's version of Pompeii, an excavated townscape dug out of the lava that destroyed it when Mount Tarawera erupted in 1886. For a glimpse of a modern, real-life Maori village, visit **Whakarewarewa Thermal Village,** 9a Tukiterangi St. (✆ **64/7/349-3463;** www.whakarewarewa.com), on the south edge of town.

Most New Zealand visitors make it to Rotorua; many fewer get over to explore the island's northeast corner, where nearly half the population is Maori. Begin in **Gisborne,** site of Captain James Cook's first 1769 landing. Towering over the city, Mount Hikurangi—the first place in New Zealand where the sun alights each morning—is sacred to the Maori, with nine carved figures at its peak; to climb to the top, get permission from the Ngati Porou tribal authorities in Ruatoria (✆ **64/6/864-8660;** www.ngatiporou.com). At the foot of Gisborne's Kaiti Hill, you can marvel over the finely crafted wall panels and rafters at the large **Te Poho-o-Rawiri Marae** meetinghouse (✆ **64/06/868-5364**). Then head north out of town on Hwy. 35, a panoramic 334km (208-mile) coastal drive that rolls through several memorable Maori attractions, including **Whangara,** the setting for the film *Whalerider* (contact Whalerider Tours; ✆ **64/6/868-6139**); four *marae,* or traditional meetinghouses, around sweeping **Tokomaru Bay;** the wonderfully ornate St. Mary's Church at **Tikitiki,** commemorating Ngati Porou soldiers who died in World War I; **Te Araroa,** with its landmark 600-year-old pohutukawa tree; on Hicks Bay, the richly carved **Tuwhakairiora meetinghouse;** and around east on Cape Runaway, **Whangaparaoa,** where legend says the great migration canoe *Tainui* first landed, some 800 years ago. —*HH*

ⓘ **Rotorua tourist information,** 1167 Fenton St. (✆ **64/7/348-5179;** www.rotorua.co.nz). **Gisborne tourist information,** 209 Grey St. (✆ **64/6/868-6139;** www.gisbornenz.com).

✈ Rotorua or Gisborne.

🛏 $$$ **Peppers on the Point,** 214 Kawaha Point Rd., Rotorua (✆ **64/7/348-4868;** www.peppers.co.nz). $ **Te Kura Bed & Breakfast,** 14 Cheeseman Rd., Gisborne (✆ **64/6/863-3497;** www.tekura.co.nz).

Myth & Legend **319**

Tahiti

Quintessential Polynesia

The idea of Tahiti—an exotic, tropical paradise with an especially gracious local culture—grabbed hold of the world's imagination early in the age of exploration. European explorers returned enraptured from their South Seas voyages with tales of Tahiti's natural beauty and the contentment of the natives. This image of Tahiti has stuck to this day: The island has one of those poetic names that's more than a travel destination; it's become synonymous with a certain lifestyle, used to market luxurious home scents and bath products around the globe.

Tahiti and its neighboring islands, now known collectively as the Society Islands of French Polynesia, were settled during eastward migration of south Asian peoples several millennia ago, a time when gods and mortals coexisted on the island, to hear the oral histories still recounted today. The history of Tahiti is interwoven with its colorful mythology: One such story relates that the shape of Tahiti—it's composed of the volcanic mountains **Tahiti Nui** and **Tahiti Iti,** separated by a narrow isthmus—looks like a fish because once upon a time, Tahiti "swam away" from the waters of Havai'i, the lagoon between nearby Raiatea and Tahaa 199. The ancestral Tahitians, the Maohi (ethnically and linguistically related to the Maori of New Zealand and to native Hawaiians), made their living off the fertile soil of the island and from fishing in their hand-carved wooden outrigger canoes.

The first Europeans—in their odd "ships without outriggers"—sailed by Tahiti in the 16th century, but surprisingly enough, it took another hundred years before any westerners actually landed in Tahiti and attempted to trade with the locals. The British were the first to do so, in the 1760s, and the legendary Captain Cook brought home with him thousands of illustrations of the amazing flora and fauna he found there, which must have looked positively psychedelic back in dreary England. The European influence, however, did much to corrupt the traditional Tahitian way of life. Western visitors introduced such vices as prostitution and alcohol, as well as foreign diseases like smallpox, typhus, and influenza, which decimated the local population by the end of the 18th century. Perhaps the most famous single European to become an expatriate on Tahiti was the late-19th-century artist Paul Gauguin, who painted local women and landscapes with rich colors evocative of the strange, faraway, and most serene island life.

Tahiti has been a French overseas territory since 1946. International tourism came to the island in the mid–20th century, but tourism to Tahiti proper is now a bit past its prime: Travelers to French Polynesia today favor the "easier" and more pristine islands of Bora Bora 75 and Moorea 86, with their overwater bungalows that cater to the honeymoon set. On Tahiti itself, parts of the island, especially around the capital city of **Papeete,** can feel too busy and developed for someone who has flown halfway around the world to find an unspoiled South Seas paradise, but look deeper within Tahiti, and there's plenty of authentic culture to be found—and plenty of full-service resorts, too.

A great place to go for an overview of Tahiti's history, from the geological to the cultural, is at the **Musée de Tahiti et Ses Isles** (Punaaiua; ✆ **689/583476**), west of Papeete. Displays on everything from handicrafts to religion are wonderfully easy to digest and accompanied by placards in English. Visit the **Musée Gauguin** (Mataiea, 51km/32 miles west of Papeete; ✆ **689/571058**) for interesting exhibits about French artist Paul Gauguin's time in Tahiti (after which he "defected" to the Marquesas; see p. 408).

Modern-day Tahitians work hard to keep their ancient ways alive, and there's no better time to visit than in July, when the annual **Heiva I Tahiti** festival is held. During the festival, which is based in Papeete, there are abundant crafts displays, ancient sports competitions, and traditional dance performances. —*SM*

ⓘ www.tahiti-tourisme.com.

✈ Tahiti-Faa'a, Papeete.

🛏 $$ **Hotel Le Royal Tahitian,** 4km (2½ miles) east of downtown (✆ **689/504040;** www.hotelroyaltahitien.com). $$$ **Intercontinental Resort Tahiti,** Faa'a, Papeete (✆ **689/865110;** www.tahiti.interconti.com).

Myth & Legend 320

Gotland

Reliving the Middle Ages

Sweden

In some other parts of hip and cutting-edge Sweden, the country's medieval attractions are relegated to a touristy strip filled with shops selling kitschy Viking souvenirs. On the island of Gotland, however, the Middle Ages are treated much more reverentially: Gotland is rightly proud of its history, and throughout the island, cultural programs actively perpetuate the time warp aspects of its impressive millennial heritage.

Ground zero for Gotland's historical offerings is **Visby,** which offers an intimate encounter with the daily life of an important medieval city and one-time Viking seaport. The atmospheric old town, a UNESCO World Heritage Site since 1995, greets visitors with an imposing ring of 13th-century limestone walls. Along the fortifications, 50 original watchtowers still stand, and the entire circuit is bordered by a moat. Inside the 4km (2½-mile) circuit lies a pristine skyline straight out of a children's fable: Visby is a lovingly preserved medieval townscape of shops, churches, and suggestive old alleys. All the architectural elements you'd expect—vaulted stone cellars, steep gabled timber roofs, and Gothic churches—are represented here. There's even a restaurant, **Clematis,** occupying a 13th-century warehouse, where you eat off wooden plates, drink out of jars, and eat your food with one utensil only—a knife.

But Visby is much more than a manicured museum: Throughout the year, but

A Gotland Medieval tournament.

especially in the summer, Visby is the stage for all kinds of historical reenactments that bring the Middle Ages to life for all ages and all senses. **Medieval Week** (usually the first week in Aug; www.medeltidsveckan.se) is the absolute culmination of these events, when jousting tournaments are held in the grassy common, ceremonial parades file down the streets, and a central market offers sideshows and traditional food stalls and crafts displays. Visitors who really want to get into the spirit can even rent period dress from the event's costume warehouse.

Although the medieval period is the main era promoted on Gotland, the island has a history that goes back over 10,000 years and is thought to be the original homeland of the "barbarian" Goths. Rich archaeological finds include embellished coins and medals and intriguing rune stones. All over the island, some 94 churches in the Gothic and Romanesque styles still stand as evocative witnesses of Gotland's illustrious past. A visit to the **Gotland Historical Museums** in Visby helps tie all the centuries of heritage together. And—this being Sweden—you can be assured that even as you relive the Middle Ages on Gotland, you never have to forgo design hotels, cool museum shops, and trendy cafes. —*SM*

ⓘ **Tourist office,** Skeppsbron 4–6, Visby (✆ **46/498/201700;** www.gotland.info).

✈ Gotland (connect through Stockholm).

🛏 $$$ **Medeltids Hotellet,** Norra Kyrkogatan 3–7, Visby (✆ **46/498/291230;** www.medeltidshotellet.se). $ **Villa Alskog,** Alskog (✆ **46/498/491188;** www.villa-alskog.se).

321 Myth & Legend

Daufuskie Island

The Spirits of the Gullahs

South Carolina, U.S.

Like its fellow Low Country sea islands, Daufuskie has a picturesque landscape that borders on steamy Southern Gothic. Live oaks wreathed in silvery Spanish moss frame dense woods, where unseen critters croak and twitter. Thick, salty air hangs in beams of sunlight, its perfume pungent and primeval. Tidal flats stretch long, bony fingers into the sea. It seems only natural that the island is rife with ghosts.

Daufuskie's rich black loam once grew cotton so silky it had its own name—Sea Island cotton—and in the years leading up to the Civil War, the island was the site of 12 prosperous cotton plantations. West African slaves were brought to this isolated place to work the cotton fields, and over the years they developed a unique culture that married African traditions with the customs of the New World. In the postwar period, after the slaves were freed and white plantation owners fled the island, its isolated position—with no causeways to the mainland—kept the old traditions alive. "Gullah" refers to the descendants of those slaves, their culture, and their language, a musical hybrid of English and West African.

Most of the old places on the island are haunted, it's said, including the 1883 lighthouse at Bloody Point, where Daufuskie legend Arthur Ashley "Papy" Burn once lived. Papy had four wives; he made wine from sweet scuppernong grapes, elderberries, and pears, and stored it in the Lamp Room that once housed the lighthouse's back range light. He called the little

A house on Daufuskie Island.

brick structure **Silver Dew Winery,** and it's still here. Other historic structures on the island include the white-frame **First Union Baptist Church,** built in 1864, and the two-room schoolhouse, the **Mary Fields Elementary School,** where a young Pat Conroy taught for a remarkable year, later immortalized in his autobiographical novel *The Water Is Wide* (made into a movie with Jon Voight called *Conrack*). As you travel around the island (golf carts are the favored mode of transportation), check out the old Gullah homes: You'll spot a peeling blue windowsill here, a faded blue roof there, even a whole house done up in brilliant sky blue, for the Gullahs believed that painting the window trim blue kept the evil spirits away.

Success seemed forever to elude Daufuskie. The boll weevil wiped out the cotton crop in 1921; another local treasure, the Daufuskie oyster, was doomed by environmental pollution, the oyster beds shut down in 1959. Mid-20th-century Daufuskie had a dwindling but tight-knit populace of Gullah-speaking African Americans eking out a meager island existence in peaceful isolation. But today, as old-timers die out and real-estate development creeps in (though at nowhere near the pace of Hilton Head), Gullah heritage tours have become a popular tourist activity. Big oaks that withstood hurricanes and bulldozers stand guard over sprawling "Low Country–style" homes and golf courses. The Daufuskie oyster is back, growing plump and creamy in newly pristine waters; the waters brim with fish, shrimp, crabs, and the occasional gator. The spirit of the Gullahs resides on Daufuskie still. —*AF*

ⓘ www.daufuskievacation.com.

✈ Hilton Head, South Carolina (½ hr. away).

⛴ 40 min. from Hilton Head: **Calibogue Cruises** (✆ **843/342-8687;** www.daufuskiefreeport.com; departing Broad Creek Marina); or **Palmetto Ferry Company** (✆ **843/684-7819;** departing Salty Fair Marina).

🛏 Villas and condos (✆ **800/445-8664;** www.daufuskievacation.com).

TOUR Guided bus tours: **Calibogue Cruises** (✆ **843/342-8687;** www.daufuskiefreeport.com).

Island Hopping the Dalmatian Coast Islands: Nature & History on Display

The Croatian coast has more than 1,000 islands, all of them temperate jewels along the Adriatic Sea, luring celebrities and ordinary visitors alike who come to enjoy relaxing beach getaways and to explore some of the beautiful historical towns that cling to the region's rocky terrain. But perhaps the country's most enticing islands are off its southern coast, known as lower Dalmatia. Island hopping is one of the chief delights here; each lower Dalmatian island has its own vibe and attractions, and no trip would be complete without touring at least one or two—all are well connected by ferries (visit www.korculainfo.com/croatia/jadrolinija for info) and not too spread out. Given their long history, it's easy to feel like you are walking through the centuries on these islands, taking in castles, palaces, and battlefields spanning over 10,000 years. Whichever islands you choose to visit, you will find most delightfully free of tourist traps and modern developments. (The Dalmatian island of Hvar is covered separately because it's more built up and has a decidedly trendy nightlife scene.)

Korčula.

The largest island in lower Dalmatia, 322 **Brač** is a study in contrasts: Beautiful beaches lie next to sparkling azure waters and dusty quarries of sandstone and dolomite, once mined by the Romans for its cities, amphitheaters, and temples. The island's largest town and landing point, **Supetar,** comes to life in summer with free concerts and festivals. Farther south, the town of **Bol** is home to what may be Croatia's most publicized beach **Zlatni Rat** (Golden Cape). 323 **Korčula,** which is just a little over a mile from the mainland across the Peljesac Channel and south of Brač, once was covered with so many pine trees that the sight led the Greeks who settled here around 400 B.C. to dub the island Black Corfu. Today, tourists are drawn by **Korčula Town's** well-preserved walled city and its medieval attractions, plus the city's claim that it is the birthplace of legendary explorer Marco Polo. 324 **Mljet Island,** south of Korcula, is legendary as the holiday island of Ulysses. **National Park Miljet** takes up one-third of this lush island, and boasts two salt lakes surrounded by dense pine forests. To the west of Mljet, 325 **Lastovo** is home to many vineyards and more than 30 churches and chapels, some dating all the way to the 5th century; many of the island's buildings are dotted with emblematic chimneys that mimic the minarets of mosques. The main church is Saint Cosmas and Damian, known to islanders as the **Lastovo cathedral.** Northwest of Lastovo, 326 **Vis** offers a winning blend of nature and history. A wharf, a castle built by the Venetians, a 17th-century church, and several beaches are the main attractions in its town of **Komiža.** Tiny **Biševo**, a piece of land southwest of Vis, is the site of the **Blue Cave,** a sea cave that "lights up" in shades of blue and silver for an hour each day. *—JD*

For hotel and visitor information in Hvar, see p. 247.

War & Intrigue 327

Magna Carta Island

Checkmate by the Thames

England

Dateline: June 15, 1215. As dawn rose over the Thames, King John of England was encamped with his retinue at Wraysbury; south of the river, several of his feudal barons gathered on the silvery water-meadows of Runnymede. When the river mists parted, the despised king and his disaffected barons met midway, where John averted civil war by signing the Great Charter, or Magna Carta—a revolutionary document that officially limited royal power and guaranteed inalienable rights to his subjects.

But where was that halfway meeting point? Historians are still debating. Was it in the buttercup-spangled meadows of Runnymede, an ancient place of council named after the magical charms, or runes, consulted there? Was it on the north bank, under the sacred yew tree of Ankerwycke, near the 12th-century Benedictine priory of St. Mary? Or did King John and the barons meet in a neutral spot in between, on the wooded slip of island just off the north bank?

The Magna Carta specifically attests that it was signed in Runnymede, but considering how the marshy course of the Thames shifts, back in 1215 this island could well have been part of Runnymede. Victorian author Jerome K. Jerome in *Three Men in a Boat* wrote, "Certainly, had I been one of the Barons, at the time, I should have strongly urged upon my comrades the advisability of our getting such a slippery customer as King John on to the island, where there was less chance of surprises and tricks." In 1834, the Harcourt family, lords of the manor at Ankerwycke, promoted Magna Carta Island as the site, digging out the channel between it and the riverbank and erecting a Gothic-style stone cottage, decorated inside with the coats of arms of all 25 Magna Carta barons. Nearby lies a large flat stone—popularly called the Charter Stone—where, tradition claims, the barons laid the document for King John to sign.

The National Trust nowadays owns both Ankerwycke (amazingly enough, that 2000-year-old yew tree still stands in the park, beside the priory's ruins) and the meadows of Runnymede. Magna Carta Island, however, is privately owned, though you can see the Charter Stone and the cottage clearly from the upstream end of Runnymede park. You can easily spend an afternoon strolling around the broad green fields of **Runnymede** (✆ **44/1784/432891**), which is dotted with memorial oak trees and monuments, including the marble plinth of the John F. Kennedy Memorial, a classical pagoda erected by the American Bar Association honoring the Magna Carta, and, commanding the crest of Cooper's Hill, the marble cloister of the Air Forces Memorial. You can hike to Runnymede on the Thames towpath; you can drive there on the A308; or—the best way to appreciate the site—you can take a boat ride up the Thames (contact **French Brothers;** ✆ **44/1753/581900;** www.boat-trips.co.uk), which will bring you even closer to Magna Carta Island. It's a perfect add-on to a tour of Windsor Castle, only 5km (3 miles) to the north—for if King John hadn't signed that paper, there might not even be a Windsor Castle today. —*HH*

ⓘ **Runnymede Estate,** Windsor Rd. (✆ **44/1784/432891;** www.nationaltrust.org.uk).

✈ Heathrow.

🚆 Wraysbury or Egham.

🛏 $$ **Royal Adelaide Hotel,** 46 King's Rd., Windsor (✆ **44/1753/863916;** www.theroyaladelaide.com). $$$ **Runnymede Hotel & Spa,** Windsor Rd., Egham (✆ **44/1784/436171;** www.runnymedehotel.com).

328 War & Intrigue

Guernsey

Where the Nazis Dug In

Channel Islands, U.K.

Though it's been officially part of the English kingdom ever since William the Conqueror, Guernsey—along with its neighboring island Jersey 102—lies tantalizingly close to France, nestled in the Gulf of St. Malo only 48km (30 miles) from the Normandy coast. Guernsey has always had an ambiguous relationship to Britain; during the Hundred Years War it passed back and forth from French to English possession, and its rocky inlets made natural hideouts for French pirates from nearby St-Malo 348. Nowadays Guernsey's beautiful beaches and cliff-top walks recommend it as a quick getaway for English holidaymakers, but it's even more popular as a tax haven for corporations and equity funds, which take advantage of Guernsey's offshore tax status (it's legally an independent Crown possession, with its own currency, and not part of the European Union).

On my last visit to the island, I stumbled upon relics of one of the most fascinating periods in Guernsey's history—from 1940 to 1945, when German soldiers occupied the Channel Islands as part of Hitler's Atlantic Wall defense. Guns, casemates, and observation towers are dotted all around the Guernsey coast, though, not having planned ahead, I missed going inside—the relics are maintained by local history buffs, and are open only limited hours, usually on weekends April through October. Just south of the airport, however, in a whitewashed farmhouse just inland from the island's spectacular southern cliffs, **The German Occupation Museum** (rue de Les Houards; ✆ **44/1481/238205;** www.festungguernsey.supanet.com) keeps

German Occupation tower and corn fields on Guernsey Island.

more regular hours and evocatively recreates day-to-day life during those Occupation years with several striking dioramas, from a humble kitchen scene to a full streetscape.

Once I started looking for them, I noticed defensive tunnels honeycombing the hills around picturesque **St. Peter Port,** the island's largest town (St. Peter Port's streets are so steep, it became known for its nimble cart-pulling donkeys). **The La Vallette Underground Military Museum** (✆ **44/1481/722300**) displays artifacts from the Occupation years in air-conditioned tunnels originally built to store fuel for U-boats, in the headland just south of the harbor; another section of tunnels nearby now houses **The Guernsey Aquarium** (✆ **44/1481/723301**). Just west of town, a meticulously restored **communications bunker** (✆ **44/1481/700418**) sits in the extensive gardens behind the **La Collinette Hotel** (see below), which was a gracious private villa when the German Naval Signal Corps commandeered it in 1942, taking advantage of its panoramic hilltop position.

Perhaps the spookiest site lies in the heart of the island, in St. Andrews parish: the **German Military Underground Hospital** (La Vassalerie Rd.; ✆ **44/1481/239100**). All you can see of it aboveground are the entrances and the square holes of escape shafts, but underground lies an immense labyrinth of tunnels, hewn out of solid rock by Nazi prisoners of war from France, Spain, Morocco, Algeria, Belgium, Holland, Poland, and Russia. *—HH*

ⓘ ✆ **44/1481/723552;** www.visitguernsey.com.

✈ La Planque airport, Guernsey.

⛴ St. Peter Port. **Condor Ferries** (✆ **44/845/6091024;** www.condorferries.com).

🛏 $$ **The Clubhouse at La Collinette,** rue St. Jacques, St. Peter Port (✆ **44/1481/710331;** www.lacollinette.com). $$ **Le Friquet Country Hotel,** rue de Friquet, Castel (✆ **44/1481/256509;** www.lefriquethotel.com).

War & Intrigue

329

The Isle of Skye

Lair of the McDonalds

Inner Hebrides, Scotland

In Gaelic, it's called Eilean a' Cheò, or "the misty isle"—a fitting name for this rugged beauty, the largest island of the Inner Hebrides, its coastline sliced deep by fiordlike lochs, the jagged black Cuillan Hills bristling across its Highland interior. The first time I visited Skye, you had to take a ferry over the narrows from Lochalsh, but in 1995 a bridge finally opened to link Skye to the west coast of Scotland. Islanders still aren't sure this was a good thing.

Skye has always treasured its island independence. For nearly 4 centuries in the Dark Ages, the Norse Vikings who settled here (those fiords must have made them feel at home) became increasingly estranged from Norway. Their Norse-Gaelic descendants became the Lords of the Isle, ruling the Western Isles almost as a separate nation until the 15th century. The last Lords, the powerful McDonald clan, were also involved in one of the most romantic chapters in Scots history, when gallant 24-year-old Flora MacDonald in 1746 helped Bonnie Prince Charlie flee his captors after his defeat at Culloden.

Soon after you cross the bridge from Kyle of Localsh to the island, head about a half-hour's drive south on A851 to Armadale (there's also a direct ferry from Mallaig), where you can learn all about Clan Donald at **Armadale Castle** (✆ **44/1471/844-305;** www.clandonald.com). Flora was married here in 1750, though the castellated gray stone manor you see today was built later. On your way back north on A851 through the green and gentle Sleat peninsula, check out the picturesque remains of the McDonalds' ancient **Knock Castle** (Teangue, near Kilbeg, off A851) and **Dunsgiath Castle** (over on Sleat's west coast at Tokavaig). From Broadford, you can also detour south on B8083 to **Elgol,** where a 4km (2.5-mile) walking trail from the jetty leads to a tiny cave where Prince Charlie hid out his last night on Skye.

From Broadford, pick up A87 and head north through an increasingly craggy landscape, past **Portree,** Skye's largest town, to Uig (departure point for ferries to the Outer Hebrides). A mile and half north of Uig sits restored **Monkstadt House,** the slate-roofed farmhouse where Flora first brought Prince Charlie, who was disguised as her maidservant. Continue 8km/5 miles north on A855 to Kilmuir, where Flora is buried under a tall stone cross in **Kilmuir churchyard;** also in Kilmuir, the **Skye Museum of Island Life** (✆ **44/1470/552-206;** www.skyemuseum.co.uk) illuminates Skye's traditional crofter lifestyle in a series of restored thatched cottages. An additional 3.2km (2 miles) north on A855, there's another mossy ruined McDonald castle at **Duntulm.**

The McDonalds weren't Skye's only clan—follow A850 west from A87 to the village of Dunvegan, where the chiefs of Clan MacLeod have lived for 800 years at glorious **Dunvegan Castle** (✆ **44/1470/521-206**), said to be Britain's oldest inhabited castle, perched on a rocky promontory once accessible only by boat. Nearby, check out one of Britain's finest restaurants, The Three Chimneys (see The House Over-By, below) up the western shore of Loch Dunvegan in Colbost.

It's only fitting that this rebel Highland island should also boast one of the country's finest whiskys. Complete your Skye circuit by continuing south from Dunvegan on A863; swing a couple of miles west on B8009 to tiny Carbost, on the shore of Loch Harport, where the **Talisker Distillery** (✆ **44/1478/614-308;** www.malts.com) has been making award-winning single-malt whisky since 1830. *—HH*

ⓘ **Tourist office,** Bayfield House, Portree (✆ **44/1478/612-137;** www.skye.co.uk).

✈ Inverness (128km/80 miles).

⛴ Armadale (30 min. from Mallaig; ✆ **44/1475/635-235;** www.calmac.co.uk). Kylerhea (from Glenelg; www.skyeferry.com).

🌉 From Kyle of Localsh via A87.

🛏 $$$ **The House Over-By,** Hwy. B884, Colbost (✆ **44/1470/511-258;** www.threechimneys.co.uk). $$ **Sligachan Hotel,** Sligachan (✆ **44/1478/650-204;** www.sligachan.co.uk).

330 War & Intrigue

Rhodes

Greek Colossus

Greece

Imagine an island so powerful, so mighty, that astride its harbor entrance stood a colossal statue fashioned from iron, bronze, and marble. No, I speak not of Manhattan 411, whose massive Statue of Liberty welcomes visitors to modern-day America, but of its progenitor, the legendary Colossus of Rhodes. This 36m (118-ft.)

statue announced entry to the Greek island of Rhodes when it was a burgeoning center of trade and power in the Aegean. The Colossus was built sometime around 280 B.C. to honor Helios, the Sun God. The statue's fall—it literally tumbled over during an earthquake around 226 B.C.—presaged the fall of the Greek empire.

The largest island in the Dodecanese island chain, Rhodes remains a vital regional center and it's easily one of the most popular holiday destinations in the Dodecanese. It's the quintessential Greek island, encapsulating all that Greece is famous for, including superb beaches, dazzling whitewashed villages, vineyards climbing undulating hills, and world-class antiquities. Its obeisance to the sun god has its rewards—the sun shines on the island some 320 days of the year.

Just 24km (15 miles) from the coast of Turkey, Rhodes has long been the prize of conquerors from both East and West. The **Old Town** of the capital (also called Rhodes) is a World Heritage Site, where the architectural gumbo includes Gothic, Byzantine, Arab, and Venetian styles. Leap into the 21st century in **New Town,** which offers Versace and a McDonald's for the current occupation of shoppers and tourists. That, in a nutshell, is modern Greece.

Luckily, the countryside is littered not with fast-food wrappers but with antiquities, including the **Acropolis of Rhodes** (✆ **30/22410/27674**), ruins from the Hellenistic period. It's perched on a rocky plateau above the village of Lindos, with splendid views of the blue Aegean. The mountainous interior is great for mountain biking and hiking. And the **Valley of the Butterflies,** a national park in Lindos filled with thousands of beautiful butterflies, is a must-visit.

The beautiful village of **Lindos,** on the island's east coast, has charmingly crooked alleyways and whitewashed houses. The beaches here are justifiably popular, crescents of sugary white sand lapped by turquoise seas. Like many other beaches on the island's eastern coast, these sheltered sands offer gentle waves, perfect for families with young children. The *meltemi* wind kicks up the surf on west coast beaches (like Ixia), making them ideal spots for windsurfing. You can get expert instruction and windsurfing rentals at **Planet Windsurf** (www.planetwindsurf.com/destinations/rhodes/windsurfing.asp).

Before leaving, don't miss a taste of Rhodes wine—wine has been cultivated in the island's fertile soil since the Phoenician occupation, nearly 7,000 years ago. In Rhodes, past and present commingle as naturally as the sea and sky. Why, there's even talk of rebuilding that glorious monument to the once-great Greek empire and the gods who watched over it—albeit with a 21st-century twist: the Colossus of Rhodes reborn as a light sculpture. —*AF*

ⓘ **Hellenistic Tourism Organization** (South Aegean Tourist Office, at the intersection of Makariou and Papagou; ✆ **30/22410/23255;** www.ando.gr/eot); also www.rhodes.ws.

✈ Diagoras International Airport (14km/8⅔ miles from Rhodes Town).

⛴ Kos (2–7 hr.), Piraeus (11 hr.), Athens (12–17 hr.), Santorini (7–14 hr.), Marmaris, Turkey (1 hr.). www.ferries.gr.

🛏 $$$ **Atrium Palace Lindos,** Kalathos Beach (✆ **30/22440/31601;** www.atrium.gr). $$ **Spirit of the Knights Boutique Hotel,** 14 Alexandridou, Old Town (✆ **30/22410/39765;** http://rhodesluxuryhotel.com).

331 War & Intrigue

Sicily

Crossroads of Mediterranean Culture

Italy

As the largest and most strategically located island in the Mediterranean Sea, it's no wonder that Sicily has a pedigree on par with the most illustrious civilizations in world history. In the past century, Sicily has made headlines mostly for its organized crime operations and Godfather-type mob bosses, but long before there were Mafia dons, there were Phoenicians, Greeks, Arabs, and Normans here. From east, west, north, and south, they conquered and inhabited this sun-soaked triangle off the toe of Italy, endowed the island with fascinating monuments and works of art, and enriched the cultural patchwork that is still so magnificently evident in Sicily today. The key factor in shaping the particular character of *bella Sicilia* is that the island has been a crossroads of diverse populations for millennia.

Suspended between the continents of Europe and Africa, Sicily has an exotic air all its own that's difficult to pin down—the scenery and wealth of cultural attractions vary dramatically over the 25,000-sq.-km (9,653-sq.-mile) island. In the capital city of **Palermo** alone, you can walk down Parisian-inspired boulevards that empty into bazaars with a decidedly Middle Eastern feel. Wherever you go in Sicily, whether it's to the chaotic cities of Palermo and **Catania,** or to laid-back seaside towns like Siracusa, or to destinations in the island's rugged interior, you're never lacking for things to see and do. Sicily is very easy to get around, whether by rental car or by the island's extensive bus and train networks, and it's also more affordable than "mainland" Italy.

The earliest, most important group to settle on Sicily were the Greeks, who came in the 8th century B.C. and made the island part of Magna Graecia. The Greeks flourished for more than 500 years on Sicily, but wars with Carthage eventually left them vulnerable to Rome, which expanded here in the 3rd century B.C. Nevertheless, some of the greatest landmarks of all Greek civilization, rivaling even the masterpieces of ancient Athens, are in Sicily. The most glorious are at Agrigento's **Valley of the Temples,** where seven Doric temples stand in various stages of preservation along a dramatic rocky ridge. In the western part of Sicily, the archaeological sites of **Segesta** and

Sicilian ruins.

Selinunte also have impressive Greek remains, and on the island's southeastern tip, Siracusa's **Parco Archeologico della Neapolis** (✆ **39/0931/66206**) is a fine place to explore a broad range of Greek and Roman ruins in one setting. Evidence of the Romans' occupation of Sicily is scattered all over the island, though the most notable site is the **Villa Romana del Casale** in **Piazza Armerina.** Here, in mountainous central Sicily, a wealthy Roman built a villa in the 3rd century A.D., and adorned the floor of the entire complex with polychrome marble mosaics that depict everything from bikini-clad babes lifting weights to ferocious animal hunts.

In the Middle Ages, it was Islam's turn to reign in Sicily. Muslims from North Africa, Spain, and Persia all settled here, though eventually their infighting left them vulnerable to invasion by Norman forces, who conquered Sicily in the 11th century under Roger I. The castles and cathedrals that were built during the Norman period in Sicily are some of the island's most unique and fascinating architecture, as they are a clear result of the artistic cross-pollination between Muslim and Christian traditions. Visit the **Palazzo dei Normanni** (✆ **39/091/7051111**) in Palermo and the **Cathedral of Monreale** to see the dazzling mosaics that were commissioned during this time. And while the Renaissance, which transformed cities like Florence and Rome in the 15th and 16th centuries, largely skipped over Sicily, the island got its fair share of the next period—the Baroque—whose delightful artistic flourishes can be seen in the southeastern cities of **Noto, Modica,** and **Siracusa.**

Of course, if and when you tire of the relentless history and culture that Sicily tosses your way, you can turn your attention to other pursuits. **Mount Etna** is the largest active volcano in Europe, and going to the summit is an unforgettable encounter with the forces of nature. The coast of Sicily offers plenty of **beaches** for sunning and swimming, particularly on the east coast, near Taormina, and along much of the southern coast, where the sand is sugary and the sea placid. —*SM*

ⓘ www.regione.sicilia.it/turismo.

✈ Palermo and Catania airports.

⛴ From Naples or Civitavecchia (near Rome), Snav sails overnight to Palermo (✆ **39/091/6014211;** www.snav.it).

🛏 **Grand Hotel Timeo,** Taormina (✆ **39/0942/23801;** www.framon-hotels.com). $$ **Villa Fabbiano,** Taormina (✆ **39/0942/626058;** www.villafabbiano.com).

War & Intrigue

332

Qeshm

The Persian Gulf's Long Island

Iran

To look at the rocky and mostly barren coastline of Iran's Qeshm island, it's not immediately obvious how Cassell's Bible could consider Qeshm a possible site of the Garden of Eden. Yet the interior of this sandy strip in the Strait of Hormuz holds sites so historic and naturalistic as to make the designation a bit more convincing. In addition to being an island that has seen epic battles and cultural commingling for thousands of years, Qeshm is also notable for its ecotourism attractions, from unique caves and rock formations to forests growing in its salty coastal waters.

Though Iran is heavily associated with Islam today, Qeshm's roots predate that religion by at least a millennium. Historians assert that two ancient sources, Ptolemy and the Roman writer Ammianus Marcellinus, knew of this island and referred to it as "Alexandria." Countless wars between Arabs and Europeans alike have been waged over Qeshm for its geopolitically important location near the mouth of the Persian Gulf—trade routes between China, Africa, and India all passed through here. The battle led by the Portuguese for control of Qeshm was among the island's most ruthless, and evidence of their destructive occupation can still be seen. During an Anglo-Persian attack on Qeshm in 1622, English explorer William Baffin was mortally wounded on Qeshm. There has even been carnage here as recently as 1988: At the end of the Iran-Iraq war, the U.S. Navy guided missile cruiser *Vincennes* mistakenly shot down Iran Air flight 655—official reports state that the Navy thought the aircraft was an F-14 military fighter jet—resulting in 290 civilian fatalities.

Qeshm, whose Arabic name, Jazirat At-Tawilah, means "long island," is 135km (84 miles) long by 40km (25 miles) at its widest point. At 1,200 sq. km (463 sq. miles), it's the largest island in the Persian Gulf, and getting around to the sights takes some time; allow a few days to see it all and consider visiting with a tour operator (that's the most common way for westerners to travel here). The evocative **Portuguese castle,** a striking amalgam of European fortress design and unmistakably Middle Eastern tawny stone and desert vegetation, is among the most visited man-made attractions on the island. The interior of Qeshm has some truly arresting natural features, like the **Kharbas caves,** which were formed 3,000 years ago by water erosion, and are believed to be sites of pre-Islamic worship places—perhaps by adherents of the cults of Mithras or Zoroaster. The otherworldly rock formations in **Chahkouh Valley** and **Stars Valley** have wind-swept escarpments that look like something out of *Star Wars.* The **Hara sea forest** is a protected area where the native hara tree grows in dense mangrove clusters in the coastal saltwater.

In 1991, Qeshm was made a free trade zone. At the same time, the island's tourism infrastructure was built up, making this a more congenial place to visit than you might expect. In the future, a bridge connecting Qeshm to Bandar Abbas, on Iran's southern coast, will make connections even easier. —*SM*

(i) www.qeshm.ir.

✈ Qeshm-Dayrestan (served by Iran Air, via Tehran).

⛴ From Bandar Abbas, fast ferry (25 min.) and regular car ferry (40 min.).

🛏 $$$ **Qeshm International Hotel,** Qeshm City (✆ **98/763/522-4906**).

TOUR **Iran Guided Tours** (www.iranguidedtours.com).

333 War & Intrigue

Kotlin Island

Headquarters of the Baltic Fleet

Russia

For most of us, the words "Russia" and "navy" call to mind images of the type propagated in such films and books as *The Hunt for Red October.* Stern commanders barking orders from spiritless control centers while wind and rain whip up fierce seas outside—that kind of thing. But the history of **Kronshtadt,** on Kotlin island, Russia's most venerable naval port, goes much further back than the Cold War. From its position in the narrowest part in the Gulf of Finland, Kronshtadt and its forts have been guarding St. Petersburg (Leningrad in the Soviet era; 404) for 300 years. The sea fortress at Kronshtadt is among the most formidable in world history, and it has never been taken by foreign military force.

Peter the Great founded Kronshtadt in 1704, after confiscating Kotlin island from Sweden. The body of water—the Gulf of Finland—where Kronshtadt sits is rather shallow and stays frozen for at least 4 months of the year. This allowed for some ingenious engineering and beefing-up of protection for the harbor of St. Petersburg: Workers hauled great wooden frames across the frozen sea, drilled holes in the ice, and constructed several entire islands on either side of Kronshtadt to completely block off the approaches to St. Petersburg. In the 19th century, Kronshtadt was fortified even further with 11 new batteries, armed with heavy turret guns.

Kronshtadt's most notorious chapter came in the early 20th century, when, on February 28, 1921, sailors from the battleship Petropavlovsk issued a resolution against the standing Bolshevik government and called for a return of political freedoms. Political leaders—Lenin and Trotsky chief among them—did not receive the rebellion well, of course, and in the aftermath of the Kronshtadt uprising, 8,000 people—civilians and sailors—left Kronshtadt to live in Finland, 527 people were killed, and 4,127 were wounded.

Opened to visitors in the mid-1990s, the Kronshtadt of today has a slightly different look than it did in its heyday as headquarters of the Russian Baltic Fleet. For one, the church of St. Andrew, once the artistic pride and joy of the island, was demolished under the Communist regime in 1932. The early-19th-century **Naval Cathedral**—a striking monument in the neo-Byzantine style—is now the main architectural sight on Kronshtadt. Furthermore, sweeping changes in Russian political history over the past century, combined with engineering works, have physically changed the topography of the island. Several forts disappeared with the construction of the St. Petersburg Dam, and some of the forts can now be reached from the mainland without a boat. Among the most important surviving, visitable forts are Fort Konstantin, Fort Rif, Fort Chumnoy, and Fort Totleben. Even on a modern map, however, the slender shape of Kronshtadt and Kotlin Island is uncannily reminiscent of a warship, its bow patrolling the Baltic Sea. —*SM*

ⓘ www.russia-travel.com.

✈ St. Petersburg (30km/19 miles).

From St. Petersburg, 1 hr.

$$$ **Kempinski Moika** 22, Moika river embankment 22, St. Petersburg (✆ **7/812/335-9111;** www.kempinski.com).

War & Intrigue **334**

Puerto Rico

Really Old Old San Juan

The United States

On so many Caribbean islands, the past seems wiped away, eradicated in favor of palm-fringed beaches, cruise ship ports, and luxe resorts. Puerto Rico has beaches and resorts too, but I soon get bored with too much beach time—that's why I was so happy to prowl around the narrow cobbled streets and courtyards of **Old San Juan,** the Caribbean's biggest historic district.

In 1540, long before any English settlers set up in North America, the staunch old fort of **El Morro** (the name means

San Juan fortress.

"headland") was built by Spanish colonists to guard the entrance to San Juan Bay. This massive battlement of sand-colored stone withstood many onslaughts over the centuries, from the first attack from Sir Francis Drake in 1595 down to the 1898 Spanish-American War bombardment that finally made Puerto Rico a U.S. possession. Over the years it grew from one stout round tower into a labyrinth of dungeons, barracks, vaults, lookouts, iron grates, and bulwarks that my kids scampered around with delight. Even more impregnable, the newer (1634) and larger **Fort San Cristóbal** was designed to protect the city from land-based attack while El Morro protected it from the sea. Connected to El Morro by tunnels and bastion walls, it's a marvel of strategic design, with 150-foot-high (46m) stone walls and overlapping fortifications that cover 27 acres (11 hectares). Check out the Devil's Sentry Box, a lonely little round tower on a triangular point, from which sentries often mysteriously went AWOL. Combined as the **San Juan Historic Site,** the two forts sit a mile apart along Calle Norzagaray (✆ **787/729-6960;** www.nps.gov/saju).

Where else in the Western Hemisphere can you find so many 16th- and 17th-century buildings? On Plaza de San Jose (look for the statue of Ponce de León in the center), the tidy white colonial **church of San Jose** was founded by Dominican friars in 1523; the settlement's first governor, Ponce, was buried here until 1913, when his remains were moved 2 blocks south to a marble tomb in the grand cream-colored **Cathedral of San Juan,** founded in 1521. The sprawling governor's palace, **La Fortaleza** (Calle Fortaleza; ✆ **787/721-7000**), was begun in 1533, and the arcaded city hall, **Alcaldía** (Calle San Francisco; ✆ **787/724-7171**), dates from 1604. But the grand prize belongs to the castellated white **Casa Blanca** (Calle San Sebastian; ✆ **787/725-1454**), the oldest extant house in the Western Hemisphere, which was built in 1521 for the de León family.

To envision what Columbus saw when he first sighted the island back in 1493, you'll need to head 25 miles (40km) east of San Juan to visit **El Yunque,** Route 191 (✆ **787/724-8774;** www.fs.fed.us/r8/caribbean), a 28,000-acre (11,331-hectare) patch of virgin forest that encompasses four separate rainforest microclimates. On its walking trails, you can spot orchids blooming in the treetops and incredibly tall ferns swaying among the tree trunks, and hear the trademark soundtrack of any Puerto Rico visit—the peep of millions of tiny *coqui* tree frogs. —*HH*

ⓘ ✆ **800/866-7827;** www.gotopuerto rico.com.

✈ San Juan International.

🛏 $$ **Comfort Inn,** Calle Clemenceau 6, Condado (✆ **877/424-6423** or 787/721-0170; www.comfortinn.com). $$$ **Ritz-Carlton San Juan,** av. de los Gobernadores 6961, Isla Verde (✆ **800/542-8680** or 787/253-1700; www.ritzcarlton.com).

War & Intrigue **335**

Beaver Island

The Island Kingdom

Michigan, U.S.

Remote and inaccessible, this pastoral island on Lake Michigan's northern shore doesn't seem like much—a sparsely populated (with only around 500 year-round inhabitants) land of hushed forests and serene natural beauty. It's hard to fathom the high drama that enfolded Beaver Island back in the mid–19th century, when a "king" ruled here, and his followers were forced to take drastic action against a power-mad tyrant.

The first human occupants of Beaver Island were Native Americans, who used it as hunting and fishing grounds. White settlers arrived in the early 1800s, fishing, trapping animals for fur, and trading for goods from passing ships. By midcentury, however, a little community of Mormons had settled here, led by charismatic James Strang. A few years earlier, Strang was one of many who had claimed the leadership position of the Mormon movement when its head, Joseph Smith, was killed. Brigham Young eventually won that position, and Strang and a band of followers decided to strike out and find a place to build their own colony, settling on Beaver Island. As the colony grew, it clashed with resident non-Mormons, who were ultimately driven off the island.

With the "gentiles" gone, Strang grew increasingly power-mad. He crowned himself "king" of the island he called "the Kingdom of St. James," and embraced polygamy, which he had opposed for years. During their 8 years on the island, the Mormons were extremely productive, building infrastructure and turning profits, but growing more and more unhappy with their leader. Defectors tried to oust Strang through legal channels. When that failed, two followers took the law into their own hands and shot King James in the back at the water's edge; he lived for 3 weeks before succumbing at age 43. (No one served time for the shooting.) Soon after, the 2,600-person Mormon colony on Beaver Island was forced off the island by a mob from nearby Mackinac Island 197. Fishermen from Ireland became the next wave of settlers.

Today little obvious evidence of the "Kingdom of St. James" remains. The **Old Mormon Print Shop Museum** (✆ **231/448-2476;** www.beaverisland.net), built in 1850, is one of the few structures left of the Mormon settlement; it now holds the **Beaver Island Historical Society** and has a room devoted to Strang and his island brethren. But the Mormons are still here in other, more subtle ways. If you decide to rent a bike to explore the 54-square-mile (140-sq.-km) island—a popular activity for seasonal visitors—keep in mind that the roads you'll travel along were likely built by the Mormons, and the open fields where deer and snowshoe hare frolic were first cleared by the Mormons. Hardworking and industrious, the Mormons who settled this little slice of earthly paradise were eventually undone by a man who would be king of Beaver Island. *—AF*

(i) www.beaverisland.org or www.beaverisland.net.

Charlevoix Michigan (14 miles/23km).

2 hr. from Charlevoix: **Beaver Island Boat Company** (© **888/446-4095;** www.beaverislandboatcompany.com).

$ **Beaver Island Lodge,** 38210 Beaver Lodge Rd. (© **231/448-2396;** www.beaverislandlodge.com). $ **Shanoule B&B,** 27715 Paid Een Og Rd. (© **231/448-2092;** http://beaverisland.org/shanoule).

336 War & Intrigue

Washington Island

Refuge at Death's Door

Wisconsin, U.S.

Thrusting into Lake Michigan like the thumb on Wisconsin's mitten, the resort region of Door County is like a mellow Midwestern version of Cape Cod, a summer getaway spot full of dunes and rambling beaches, panoramic sea cliffs, tiny fishing villages (now tiny resort towns), and charming B&Bs. But what if you need to get away from Door County? Seven miles away, across a swirling channel, perches Washington Island, a welcoming haven throughout centuries of storm-tossed history.

First it was the Potawatomi Indians, who camped out here when the warlike Winnebagos drove them from the peninsula. Unfortunately, when the Potawatomis paddled 300 war canoes back over to attack their enemies, they drowned in the treacherous strait, forever after known as the Door of Death. In 1617, the island provided refuge for Huron Indians hiding out from the armed rampage of Iroquois Indians from New York. The French called the strait Port des Morts; in 1679, it apparently claimed the fur-laden ship of famed French explorer Robert LaSalle. In 1816, the yet-unsettled island got its modern name from the crew of an American ship, the *Washington,* who were stranded here for days after getting separated from their fleet.

Eventually, Death's Door became safer to navigate, after lighthouses were built around the strait—you'll see two on Pilot and Plum islands as you steam across on the car ferry from Door County. While most visitors today come to Washington Island each June to August for beaches, nature walks, and fishing, in earlier generations it offered safe haven to all sorts of refugees—a pre–Civil War settlement of runaway Negro slaves, Irish immigrants fleeing the Great Famine, and a sizable population of Scandinavian fishermen, hoping for a new start in the Great Lakes. An overwhelming number were Icelanders, who first came here in 1870 (it's America's second-oldest Icelandic community). On Main Road, look for an assemblage of traditional Norwegian carved log buildings called Den Norske Grenda; there's a wonderful handcrafted **Norwegian Stave Church** across from the Trinity Lutheran Church on Town Line Road; and the **Norse Horse Park** (1391 Main Rd.; © **920/847-2373;** www.norsehorsepark.com) raises several heritage breeds of Scandinavian horses, sheep, and poultry.

Then what if you need to get away from Washington Island? On the island's east end, in Jackson Harbor, a pedestrian-only ferry will take you on a 15-minute journey to tiny **Rock Island.** Though it's now a state park, for many years Rock Island was the private retreat of C. H. Thorardsen, an Icelandic immigrant who made a fortune in electrical manufacturing in Chicago, and his wife, a daughter of Washington Island's Icelandic community. Their summer home here is now open to the public, a traditional Scandinavian stone boathouse decorated with Icelandic-style runic carvings. Rock Island's other attraction is the oldest lighthouse in northern Lake Michigan, now restored to its 1910 appearance, and aptly named after—who else?—the Potawatomi Indians, those first refugees to brave Death's Door. —*HH*

ⓘ www.washingtonisland.com.

✈ Austin Straubel Airport in Green Bay, Wisconsin (85 miles/137km).

⛴ **Washington Island Ferry** (30 min. from Northport Pier; ✆ **800/223-2094** or 920/847-2546; www.wisferry.com). **Island Clipper** (30 min. from Gill's Rock; ✆ **920/854-2972;** www.islandclipper.com).

🛏 $$ **Findlay's Holiday Inn,** 1 Main Rd. (✆ **800/522-5469** or 920/847-2526; www.holidayinn.net). $$ **The Washington Hotel,** 354 Range Line Rd. (✆ **920/847-2169;** www.thewashingtonhotel.net).

War & Intrigue **337**

Ship Island

The Original Six Flags

Mississippi, U.S.

It doesn't look like much on the map—a skinny crescent of land 11 miles (18km) from shore, across the shallow Mississippi Sound from Gulfport and Biloxi. But there's a very good reason it was named Ship Island: It has the only deep-water harbor between Mobile Bay and the Mississippi River. And in the checkered history of the Gulf Coast, that was a critical asset indeed.

Today Ship Island's pillowy white beaches are part of the **Gulf Islands National Seashore,** which stretches from Pensacola, Florida, to Gulfport, Mississippi. While Florida's close-to-shore barrier islands are reachable via causeway, most of Mississippi's are so far out, you need a private boat to get there. Ship Island is the big exception, with half- and full-day boat trips run out of Gulfport (see below). Before hitting the beach, look for park rangers waiting at the dock so that you can tour the park's top historic site: **Fort Massachusetts.**

There's a lot of history for those ranger tours to cover. Over the years, six different flags have flown over this flat, scrubby little island—French (it was discovered in 1699 by explorer Pierre d'Iberville), British (acquired at the end of the Seven Years' War), Spanish (ceded by Britain after the Revolutionary War), and then American (acquired in 1810 with the Louisiana Purchase). The British took it over again during the War of 1812 and used it as their base for a failed attack on New Orleans.

Though it reverted to the U.S. after that war, when Mississippi seceded from the Union in 1861, the stars-and-bars of the Confederate flag were hoisted over the half-built circular fort on the western tip of Ship Island. Then the Union ship USS *Massachusetts* anchored offshore and bombarded the ragtag fort; eventually the Confederate soldiers abandoned the island, and Union troops moved in. Giving it the geographically confusing name of Fort Massachusetts (in honor of their ship), they built the brick casements you'll see today, though the fort was never fully completed. For a few months things were really jumping—that precious harbor provided a vital base for Admiral Farragut's fleet, which attacked New Orleans in April 1862 and Mobile in 1864. In later years of the war, however, this increasingly desolate outpost became a prison for Confederate POWs and a lonely home base for one segregated regiment, the all-black 2nd Regiment of Louisiana Guards.

Remote and undeveloped, Ship Island lies at the beautiful mercies of the Gulf of Mexico. In 1969 Hurricane Camille sliced the island in two, creating East and West Ship Islands; there used to be a lighthouse here, too, but Hurricane Katrina knocked it down in 2005. In 2008, Hurricane Ike nearly submerged both East and West Ship Island. But repairs continue, and after all, that wind-swept drama is part of the Ship Island mystique. —*HH*

ⓘ ✆ **850/934-2600** or 228/875-9057, ext. 100; www.nps.gov/guis.

✈ Gulfport-Biloxi International Airport.

⛴ Apr–Oct half-day tours run by **Ship Island Excursions** (✆ **866/466-7386** or 228/864-1014; www.msshipisland.com).

🛏 $$$ **Courtyard by Marriott Gulfport Beachfront,** 1600 E. Beach Blvd., Gulfport (✆ **800/442-0887** or 228-864-4310; www.marriott.com). $$ **Holiday Inn Gulfport/Airport,** 9515 Hwy. 49, Gulfport (✆ **888/465-4329** or 228/679-1700; www.ichotelsgroup.com).

338 War & Intrigue

Tybee Island

The Lighthouse Keeper

Georgia, U.S.

Heading east on U.S. 80 out of the romantic port town of Savannah, you drive across a mass of barrier islands, separated by mazy narrow channels and nested inside each other like Russian dolls. Whitemarsh, Wilmington, Talihi, McQueens, Cockspur—often you don't know when you've passed from one to the other. When you finally run into the crashing waves of the Atlantic, you're on Tybee Island, a land's-end sort of site that just cries out for a lighthouse.

Today Tybee Island is the Savannah area's top beach getaway, known for its wide 3-mile-long (4.8km) strand of soft white sand, where sea turtles nest and dolphins cavort just offshore. Way back in 1732, however, Georgia's founding father, General James Oglethorpe, shrewdly sited the colony's first lighthouse here. The **Tybee Island Light Station** (30 Meddin Dr.; ✆ **912/786-5801;** www.tybeelighthouse.org) survives as one of the country's few complete light-station complexes—a towering lighthouse (Georgia's tallest) and two spick-and-span white-frame cottages, one for the assistant lightkeeper, a larger one for the head lightkeeper and his family, recently restored and furnished in keeping with the historical period.

Actually, the slim tapering black-and-white masonry tower you see today is the fourth lighthouse on this site. The first two were set too close to the water and had to be replaced, but the third time seemed to be the charm—completed in 1773, that lighthouse survived the American

Tybee Island lighthouse.

Revolution, when Savannah fell into British hands, and was still shining its beacon when the Civil War started. But being so close to Fort Pulaski, on neighboring McQueens Island, the Tybee light was in a risky position. In April 1862, Union forces under General Sherman landed on Tybee Island, set up artillery on the beach, and poured a relentless cannon fusillade at the fort, eventually breaching its masonry walls. Before fleeing, Confederate troops—determined not to let the enemy have a working lighthouse to guide its ships into the captured harbor—burned it down. After the war, a new lighthouse was erected on the 60-foot-high (18m) base remaining from the 1773 lighthouse; its state-of-the-art Fresnel lens, 9 feet (2.7m) tall, was installed in 1867. (Climb 178 steps to the top to see it up close.) After it was converted to electricity, the last lighthouse keeper retired in 1948, though the U.S. Coast Guard still maintains the light.

Just a couple miles west across the channel, you can also visit **Fort Pulaski,** named after the Polish general who died defending Savannah in the Revolutionary War. Nowadays it's open to the public as the **Fort Pulaski National Monument** (off Hwy. 80, McQueens Island; ✆ **912/786-5787;** www.nps.gov/fopu). Built in 1847, it has the era's typical pentagonal layout with brick walls 7½ feet (2.3m) thick; artillery shells from 1862 are still embedded in the walls. On a rocky islet just off the eastern tip of Cockspur Island, notice the stumpy little white **Cockspur Lighthouse,** which somehow survived Fort Pulaski's bombardment—it's so short, the cannon shells miraculously arced right overhead. —*HH*

ⓘ **Tourist office,** 802 First St., Tybee Island (✆ **800/868-2322** or 912/786-5444; www.tybeevisit.com or www.tybeeisland.com).

✈ Savannah.

🌉 18-mile/29km drive from Savannah.

🛏 $$ **DeSoto Beach Hotel,** 212 Butler Ave., Tybee Island (✆ **877/786-4542** or 912/786-4542; http://desotobeachhotel.com). $$$ **The River Street Inn,** 124 E. Bay St., Savannah (✆ **800/253-4229** or 912/234-6400; www.riverstreetinn.com).

339 War & Intrigue

Pea Patch Island

Reenactments at Fort Delaware

Delaware, U.S.

It's 1864 all day, every day, at this Civil War island fort. Staff, decked out in period costumes and armed with a wealth of colorful lore, play the roles of laundresses, blacksmiths, ammunition sergeants, and even Confederate prisoners to help the heyday of Fort Delaware—the main event on Pea Patch island—come alive for visitors.

Constructed between 1849 and 1859 in a strategic position in the Delaware River, **Fort Delaware** (✆ **302/834-7941;** www.destateparks.com/park/fort-delaware) became an important Union fortress that protected the cities of Wilmington and Philadelphia when the Civil War broke out. The main fort building, a pentagon of cold, grey stone with mere slits for windows, is appropriately austere. The corners of the fort are imposing battlements, and the entire structure is surrounded by a forbidding moat. Once you're within the fortress precinct, it's a much less intimidating place, where you can easily imagine the everyday goings-on here in the 19th century, when Pea Patch was on active military duty.

Tours of the fortress are a must, if a bit hokey, as guides are exceptionally well trained and entertaining and can relate fascinating tales of what went on here, such as how many soldiers and prisoners alike left detailed letters about life and conditions at Fort Delaware, including how badly the moat stank in the warm weather, or how POW patients were cared for at the fort's hospital. For younger visitors, the fort offers all kinds of interactive, educational programs that really help bring the "dry" subject of Civil War history alive.

As a day trip spot, Pea Patch is a great option for families who want a mix of activities. After filling up on history at the fort, which occupies only a fraction of the 300-acre (121-hectare) island, visitors can enjoy a picnic in one of the island's **nature areas.** Throughout Pea Patch, there are trails that take you past the habitats of marsh birds that call the island home, including herons, egrets, and ibis.

Pea Patch owes its folksy name to an old legend: At some unspecified "once upon a time," a ship carrying peas ran aground at this island, spilling its cargo in the vicinity and giving rise to a new crop of peas on the land here—hence the name, Pea Patch. —*SM*

ⓘ www.visitthefort.com.

✈ Philadelphia (35 miles/56km).

⛴ Three Forts Ferry from Delaware City or Fort Mott, New Jersey (5–10 min.; ✆ **877/98-PARKS** [987-2757]).

🛏 $$$ **Hotel du Pont,** 11th and Market sts., Wilmington, Delaware (✆ **800/441-9019;** www.hoteldupont.com).

Otherworldly Landscapes

Ternate Island

Scaling Heights & History

Maluku Islands, Indonesia

Ternate has been known for centuries as "Spice Island," a nod to the time when it was the world's only source of cloves, a commodity so prized that multiple nations fought to claim the island as their own. It's located at the gateway to the north Maluku Islands, west of New Guinea 469, and is visually dominated by 1,721m-high (5,646-ft.) **Mount Gamalama,** an active volcano with three enormous peaks. In 1999 and 2000, Ternate made headlines when it was plagued with religious violence between Muslims and Christians that affected many parts of Maluku; it's best to check into current political conditions before visiting this fascinating island.

Most tourists today come here mainly to glimpse the volcano and its ash-scattered beaches, bordering surprisingly clear waters. Though Ternate's 56,000 residents now raise corn, sage, coffee, pepper, and fruit along with cloves and do so in an awfully competitive market, the island's history as a spice capital is still very much a draw for visitors. From the 12th to the 17th centuries, Ternate was dominated by various powerful sultans in the region. The island's status as a trading mecca resulted in its being the first Maluku island to accept Islam, which is thought to have been introduced as a faith by traders from Java 346 in the 15th century. In the capital town of **Ternate,** you can visit an old **Sultan's palace,** which is now a museum. After the Portuguese arrived in the 15th century, a number of power struggles ensued until the 17th century, at which point the sultanates granted a spice monopoly to the Dutch. Evidence of the many forces that struggled for control here can be seen in the presence of **Spanish, Portuguese, and Dutch forts** scattered around the island. Ternate changed hands again during World War II when it was occupied by the Japanese, after which it became part of the republic of Indonesia, which it remains today.

In addition to its historic sites, Ternate boasts a number of natural attractions. **Toiler Besar Lake,** on the north side of the island, is a crater so deep that the water is far out of reach; that's for the best perhaps, considering that it is thought to be populated with crocodiles. The lake is surrounded by forests, and is popular with birders who enjoy sighting many of the island's exotic species, including cockatoos. A more modest site is also the most emblematic of the island: an enormous clove tree located on the middle of the island. Legend has it that it is the ancestor of clove trees the world over. It stands as a reminder of a time when the island was a trading heavyweight.

Of course, many visitors will want to set their sights not on history but on hiking up Mount Gamalama. The views from the volcano are stunning, but there is risk involved: The volcano erupts frequently. The largest recent eruption was in 1980, when 30,000 people were forced to flee to the nearby island of Tidore. Guided tours can be arranged through **Indonesia Volcano Trekking** (✆ **65/370/692-225;** www.indonesiavolcanoes.com). If you plan to hike, it's best to go during the island's dry season, which falls between May and September. *—JD*

ⓘ http://indonesia-tourism.com/north-maluku/accom.html.

✈ Babullah Airport.

🛏 $ **Hotel Indah,** Basoiri No. 3 (✆ **62/921/312-1334**). $ **Hotel Sejahtera,** Jl Salim Fabanyo No. 21 (✆ **62/921/312-1139**).

341 Exploration

St. Croix

Columbus's American Landing

U.S. Virgin Islands

It must have looked inviting when Christopher Columbus discovered it—the lush north coast of this 45km-long (28-mile) Antilles Caribbean island is the largest of its neighbors. Columbus promptly christened it Santa Cruz (Holy Cross), anchored his fleet of 17 ships, and sent some men ashore to the village to find fresh water. Naturally, along the way the crewmen decided to pick up a couple of the native Tainos for slaves. But they didn't expect the Carib Indians—themselves aggressive invaders who'd only recently taken over the island—to come at them with spears and arrows. By the time the Europeans sailed away, one Carib and one Spaniard lay dead. And so began the history of European settlement in the United States.

Columbus's first landing on what is now U.S. territory was recorded as November 14, 1493, in the logbook from his second New World expedition; on the 500th anniversary of that landing, this coastal area was renamed the **Salt River Bay National Historical Park** (Rte. 75 to Rte. 80, Christiansted; ✆ **340/773-1460;** www.nps.gov/sari). All the layers of St. Croix's history are found here—vestiges of a prehistoric settlement, the remains of a ceremonial Taino ball court, the ruins of a 17th-century Dutch colonial fort—although you'll have to hunt for them along hiking trails meandering around the tangled forest surrounding the bay. From 1880 on, the site's original excavators were little better than plunderers, selling artifacts to museums around the world; current park managers hope to recover them to display in the new visitor center, a hilltop white estate house from St. Croix's plantation era. In the meantime, Salt River Bay also boasts the largest remaining mangrove forest in the Virgin Islands and a submarine coral canyon; it's fun to visit by kayak from Salt River Marina (try **Caribbean Adventure Tours;** ✆ **340/778-1522;** www.stcroixkayak.com).

After Columbus left, St. Croix had many different rulers over the years—the Spanish, the Dutch, the English, the French, even the Knights of Malta—but after the Danish took over in 1733, St. Croix really boomed. Sugar cane was its claim to fame—only Barbados 467 produced more sugar—not to mention potent liquors distilled from the dregs of the sugar cane refining process. At one point, some 150 St. Croix plantations had factories for making molasses and rum. The sole survivor today is the **Cruzan Rum Factory** (pronounced like "Crucian," the nickname for St. Croix residents), on the island's lush western end (Estate Diamond 3; ✆ **340/692-2280;** www.cruzanrum.com/). Exploring the property on a half-hour guided tour, you'll see many original plantation features, such as a green wooden greathouse, a 19th-century square stone chimney, and the ruined base of an old windmill (St. Croix was once thickly dotted with windmills). The sugary aroma throughout the plant is intoxicating, and it's not hard to imagine that the laid-back islanders impart some of their own mellowness to the drink. *—HH*

ⓘ **St. Croix Chamber of Commerce** (✆ **340/733-1435**).

✈ Henry E. Rohlsen Airport, Estate Mannings Bay.

🛏 $$$ **The Buccaneer,** Gallows Bay, North Shore (✆ **800/255-3881** or 340/773-2100; www.thebuccaneer.com). $$ **Chenay Bay Beach Resort,** 5000 Estate Chenay Bay Rte. 82, East End (✆ **800/548-4457** or 340/773-2918; www.chenaybay.com).

Exploration 342

Curaçao

Tropical Holland

Most people's idea of a Caribbean island getaway involves unadulterated lazing on the beach and swimming in turquoise waters, but on Curaçao, those pursuits are decidedly secondary to cultural experiences. The largest of the Dutch Antilles, Curaçao is by far the most European island in the Caribbean, with Dutch-influenced architecture in the capital city of Willemstad. All over the island, forts from the colonial era still stand, giving Curaçao the feel of a Dutch Gibraltar. Curaçao is also well known for its warm people and distinctive local traditions. So if you're one of those people who get bored after about an hour on the beach, but you still want a dose of Caribbean culture, then Curaçao may be the perfect island for you.

In 1499, on an exploration voyage for Spain, Amerigo Vespucci spotted Curaçao, which had been previously inhabited only by the Arawak natives. Never the most peaceful colonists, the Spaniards proceeded to exterminate all but 75 of the Arawaks. The Spanish, however, would be ousted in turn by the Dutch, who occupied Curaçao from 1634. The island became an important outpost for the Dutch—even bigwig Peter Stuyvesant was sent to rule here in 1644—who endowed Curaçao with its most significant monuments and characteristic Caribbean-meets-the-Continent flavor.

Thanks to its striking Dutch architecture and dramatic harbor, **Willemstad** was inducted into the UNESCO roster of World Heritage Sites in 1997. Parts of the city indeed have the uncanny feel of a tropical Amsterdam, with perfect rows of houses with steep gabled roofs lining cobblestoned streets. The pastel paint and the orange Spanish roof tiles are the only architectural reminders that you're in the Caribbean, not northern Europe. A central

Houses on Curaçao waterfront.

canal divides Willemstad into two halves—old-world **Punda** and contemporary **Otrabanda** ("the other side"). The **Queen Emma Pontoon Bridge,** a sight in its own right, as it swings open throughout the day to let ships pass, connects the two districts. While in Willemstad, don't miss the **Waterfort Arches,** an evocative stretch of 9m-high (30-ft.) barrel-vaulted stone built in the 17th century. This is one of the nicer parts of the city and has lots of restaurants on a breezy terrace facing the sea.

Lively casinos and excellent duty-free shopping (concentrated in Punda) have given tourism a presence on Curaçao, and there are certainly water activities enough to satisfy swimmers and divers. A tour on the **Seaworld Explorer** submarine is a highly recommended way to check out the offshore treasures of Curaçao, including submerged shipwrecks and coral reefs teeming with sea life, while staying completely dry. Yet unlike some other Caribbean islands, which count on their high-rise resorts and sparkling beaches to bring revenue, Curaçao owes most of its current prosperity and multicultural atmosphere to the enormous refinery built here, by the Shell company in the early 20th century, to process crude oil from Venezuela, which lies just 56km (35 miles) to the south. Willemstad is also a big baseball town that has produced such MLB stars as Andruw Jones and whose Little League team has made it all the way to the World Series for the past decade.

And what about that blue liqueur that's named after the island? Blue Curaçao was in fact invented here, though the eerie color isn't natural: The potion is actually a colorless spirit made from *laraha* (a type of orange), then dyed blue to make it look more festive on bar shelves around the world. —*SM*

ⓘ **Tourist office:** On the Punda side of Queen Emma Bridge (✆ **599/9/434-8200;** www.curacao.com).

✈ Curaçao International (7km/4⅓ miles from Willemstad).

🛏 $$$ **Floris Suite Hotel,** John F. Kennedy Blvd., Piscadera Bay (✆ **599/9/462-6111;** www.florissuitehotel.com). $$$ **Hilton Curaçao Resort,** John F. Kennedy Blvd, Piscadera B (✆ **800/774-1500** in the U.S. and Canada, or 599/9/462-5000; www.hilton.com).

343 Exploration

Newfoundland

Land of Cod

Canada

It's a chilly, harsh environment, prone to fog and long winters and leaden gray skies. The land is cursed with few natural resources save a raw, wind-swept beauty. In the early days of European exploration, this inhospitable landscape, known as Newfoundland—literally, *new founde lande*—was a favored landfall but slow to develop permanent settlements: Countries staking claims in the New World erected temporary fishing camps here and sailed home with their bounty.

It's believed that Newfoundland was the first place in the New World discovered by European explorers. Archaeological digs have uncovered evidence of a Norse settlement (perhaps Leif Ericsson's Vinland) from around 1000 A.D., and Italian navigator John Cabot, working for the British, arrived in 1497—with such an

Newfoundland.

inhospitable landscape, it was among the last places in North America to develop permanent settlements. **L'Anse aux Meadows National Historic Site** (© **709/623-2608;** www.pc.gc.ca/eng/lhn-nhs/nl/meadows/index.x) was discovered by an international team of archaeologists in 1960 and declared a UNESCO World Heritage Site in 1978. Visitors can see three reconstructed Norse structures here as well as Viking artifacts. When the navigator Cabot made landfall in 1497, he exclaimed, "O, buena vista!" Today, on the docks of the town that grew up around Cabot's landfall, Bonavista, there is a replica of Cabot's 20m (66-ft.) caravel, ***The Matthew,*** which is open for tours from mid-May to late September (© **709/468-1493;** www.matthewlegacy.com).

But Newfoundland was more than a strategic pit stop for sailing ships arriving from northern Europe. It held a treasure that would prove as invaluable as gold or silver: In the Grand Banks island off the shores of the island was an immense fishing ground. The waters were so dense with codfish, goes the legend, that you could leave your boat and walk on their backs to shore. For centuries the Atlantic cod was, as one writer put it, "the engine of the Newfoundland economy." Cod caught on the Grand Banks during the age of exploration was salted and stored on ships destined for European tables. By the 1950s, the industrial world got in on the act, sending out supertrawlers to bring home tons of fish—a move that would prove disastrous. By the 1970s, the cod stock had dropped precipitously. Quotas were set, and fishermen found themselves having to travel farther out into more dangerous seas to make a living. But even quotas could not save the cod fishery from collapse. In 2004 a complete moratorium on cod fishing was imposed by the Canadian Department of Fisheries & Oceans.

The cod may be gone, but Newfoundland—still sparsely populated, with only 480,000 people in a 108,003-sq.-km (41,700-sq.-mile) territory—has numerous other attractions, including spectacular whale-watching opportunities (some 20 species come through annually) and a thriving ecotourism trade, in which kayaking, boating, and hiking the water's edge are bringing new generations to Newfoundland's bounteous shoreline.

Newfoundland's capital, **St. John's,** was founded in 1605, which gives it claim to being the oldest English-founded town in North America (1605), and it has a number of historic sites remaining from colonial times. Be sure to visit **Signal Hill** (✆ **709/772-5367**), the city landmark, which rises up above the entrance to the harbor and is topped with a craggy "castle" complete with flag fluttering overhead. Flags have flown atop this hill since 1704, and over the centuries a succession of military fortifications have occupied these strategic slopes. —*AF*

ⓘ http://visitnewfoundland.ca.

✈ St. John's.

🛏 $$ **At Wit's End,** 3 Gower St., St. John's (✆ **877/739-7420;** www.atwitsinn.ca). $$$ **Winterholme Heritage Inn,** 79 Rennies Mill Rd., St. John's (✆ **800/599-7829;** www.winterholme.com).

344 Exploration

Mozambique Island

Trading Post to the World

Mozambique

The name Mozambique conjures up images of steamy tropical nights, foreign intrigue, and exotic glamour. But in reality, this tropical nation on Africa's southeast coast is far less glamorous—the long-exploited Portuguese colony declared its independence in 1975, only to become entangled in a brutal 16-year civil war, complicated by drought and famine in 1982. Though it emerged from the shadows with a democratically elected government in the mid-1990s, much of old Mozambique was ravaged by the war; its future as a tourist destination depends mostly on its beautiful sun-kissed offshore islands like Bazaruto 52.

Yet there's one place where Mozambique's colonial Portuguese past has been preserved: on the tiny Ilha de Moçambique (Mozambique Island), just 4km (2½ miles) off the country's northeast coast. Originally a thriving Arab port, the island was taken over by the Portuguese in the late 15th century, who saw its potential as an important trading post for the flow of spices and exotica from the East. Vasco da Gama even sailed here around 1498, pretending to be a Muslim to curry favor with the local sultan, until his ruse was uncovered. His parting shot to the angry mob that chased him to his ship was just that—a cannon shot onto the island. The Portuguese built the **Fort of San Sebastian** around 1558 to protect their precious new port, which soon became the colony's most important settlement—and, indeed, the capital of Portuguese East Africa.

In the late 19th century, however, the island's fortunes plummeted. First the slave trade, one of its chief sources of wealth, was abolished. Then, in 1898, the capital was shifted to the mainland city of Maputo. By the time the Portuguese abruptly pulled out in 1975, the glittering former gateway to the country was abandoned and left to decay. That abandonment, however, helped to preserve not only the 16th-century fortress but an entire town filled with grand and richly ornamented 400-year-old architecture. Its wondrous mélange of Portuguese, Arab, Indian, and even Italian styles reflects the island's cosmopolitan place in the 16th- and 17th-century world. As the oldest

European settlement in Africa, the site is of such historic significance that the entire island was named a UNESCO World Heritage Site in 1991.

Today, Mozambique Island feels frozen in a time when the trade winds blew in from faraway lands. To get onto the island, you cross over a narrow one-lane causeway that's 3.5km (2¼ miles) long; the bus or *chapa* (minibus) from the mainland city Nampula drops you off on the island's southern tip. You can easily walk from one end of this tiny island to the other within a half-hour. Many of the historic buildings lie on narrow streets in "Stone Town," on the island's northern end; the majority of the island's residents live in remarkable reed houses on the southern end. You can't miss impressive **Fort San Sebastiano,** with its ingenious underground system of rainwater collection developed 400 years ago to compensate for the island's lack of fresh water. Other fascinating structures include the grand and newly restored 1674 **Palace of Sao Paolo,** in Stone Town's main square, and a **1522 chapel** built in the Manueline architectural style from the Portuguese Middle Ages. A major restoration and rehabilitation project is currently underway to protect the buildings from further deterioration. —*AF*

ⓘ **Mozambique Island tourist office** (✆ **258/26/610081;** www.mozambiquetourism.co.za).

✈ Nampula.

180km (112 miles) from the island by bus or car.

$$ **Omuhi'piti** (✆ **258/6/526351**).

Exploration **345**

Zanzibar

Spices, Ivory & Slaves

Tanzania

Cardamom, cloves, cinnamon, cumin, ginger, and pepper, which thrived in the tropical climate and fertile soils of Zanzibar, gave it and Pemba, the other main island that makes up the semiautonomous nation of Zanzibar, the nickname of "Spice Islands." Yet Zanzibar hardly needs a tag line: Its name, with those double *z*'s and exotic "bar" at the end, has got to be one of the most evocative in the world of a bygone era of trade and exploration. The reality of Zanzibar's history, however, hasn't always been so romantic. Along with its sultry beaches and suggestive bazaars, Zanzibar has had a turbulent past that it's still grappling with.

Capitalizing on Zanzibar's convenient location for trade—off the eastern coast of Africa and easy to defend—the first settlers, Arabs, came to the island in the 8th century. In fact, the first known mosque to be built in the southern hemisphere still stands here in the village of **Kizimkazi,** at the southern tip of the island. In the 15th century, Portuguese colonists arrived on Zanzibar and occupied the island for about 200 years, building up the port of **Stone Town** as their headquarters. But other European and Arab powers also vied for control of Zanzibar: The Portuguese were eventually ousted by the sultanate of Oman in 1729.

Without a doubt, it was during the sultanate's occupation, which lasted until the late 19th century, that Zanzibar experienced its most luxurious era—for the sultan and his court, who built opulent residences like the **House of Wonders** in Stone Town and kept numerous wives and concubines—as well as its darkest depths, for the slaves who became one of the principal trade commodities of these new Arab settlers. Zanzibar effectively became a major "processing center," operated by and profiting the sultans, for slaves from East Africa who would go on to work in European plantations in the Indian Ocean region as well as the Americas. It's estimated that some 50,000 slaves passed through Zanzibar in an average year in the 1700s and 1800s. Following military threats from and diplomatic relations with Britain, the Zanzibar slave market finally ended in 1873.

Zanzibar's favorable agricultural conditions made it an important growing and export center for the spice trade. Cloves were introduced in the early 19th century and exploded as a cash crop for the sultans who owned all the slave-staffed plantations. The heady aroma of the spices grown here would become synonymous with the romantic notion of Zanzibar. The island was also a chief exporter of ivory for many years.

Several notable explorers also made their way through Zanzibar in the 19th century: Burton and Speke, on their quest to find the source of the Nile, made "cosmopolitan" Zanzibar their base camp. The first European to see Mount Kilimanjaro, John Rebmann, set off on his expedition from Zanzibar. Dr. David Livingstone also spent time here, and several of his personal effects are kept in the **National Museum** (Creek Rd., Stone Town).

Owing to its long period of Arab influence, Zanzibar is predominantly Muslim and Swahili is the main language spoken, though there are other ethnic groups and religions here. The island has been independent of Britain since 1963 and is now a part of Tanzania. Although the "Spice Islands" atmosphere still lingers in its carved-wood doorways and vestiges of the sultanate's tenure, Zanzibar is decidedly less prosperous today and has significant social and infrastructure problems. Still, historic Stone Town and the island's excellent beaches draw plenty of tourists each year, who also provide Zanzibar with its main source of income. —*SM*

(i) www.zanzibar.net.

✈ Zanzibar-Kisauni International, 10km (6¼ miles) from Stone Town.

⛴ Azam Marine Ferry from Dar Es Salaam, 2 hr.

🛏 $$ **Zanzibar Palace,** 831 Kiponda St., Stone Town (✆ **255/24/2232230;** www.zanzibarpalacehotel.com).

TOUR **Zanzibar Travel** (✆ **44/1242/222027;** www.zanzibartravel.co.uk).

346 Exploration

Java

Historic Heart of Indonesia

Indonesia

Stepping off the airplane at Jakarta's Soekarno-Hatta airport, you inhale it immediately: the heady olfactory cocktail of clove, island hardwoods, and steamy tropical air. And when you get out and explore the island, you find that there are sensory stimuli of every kind to make Java a truly transporting travel experience. The richness of the land, combined with its key position along trade routes between the Far East and India, have given Java quite a diverse existence over the millennia. Go to Bali 201, Java's Buddhist neighbor to the east, for a beach holiday with touches of the exotic, but to be immersed in the real, fascinating culture of Indonesia, past and present, your best bet is Java all the way.

Java started out as a series of discrete kingdoms, the most powerful and prosperous of which left such indelible monuments as the Buddhist temple of Borobudur. In the 8th and 9th centuries, Muslim traders from India spread Islam to the islands of Indonesia, and to this day it remains the dominant religion on Java and in the rest of Indonesia. Europeans eventually got word of the island's ideal growing conditions for such moneymaking crops as sugar and coffee, and in the 17th century, the Dutch East India Company colonized Java to exploit its rich agricultural possibilities. By the 19th century, three-quarters of the world's coffee supply came from Java. The colonial period was not to last forever, and following a nationalist guerrilla war against the Dutch—coupled with international diplomacy—Indonesia gained its independence in 1945. The largest city on Java, Jakarta (Dutch Batavia) is now the capital of the Republic of Indonesia.

Java today is home to some 130 million people (occupying just 139,860 sq. km/54,000 sq. miles), making it the world's most populous island. The national motto of Indonesia is "Unity in Diversity," and Java is certainly the best exponent in the Indonesian archipelago of this creed. Along with the "native" Indonesians (of Sundanese or Javanese descent), there is a sizable population of Chinese Indonesians on the island, and there are large groups of people on Java, which is mostly Muslim, practicing Buddhism, Hinduism, and Catholicism.

Java is a vast territory that would take a lifetime to explore fully, but for a first visit, don't miss **Jakarta** and the "art city" of Yogyakarta in the southeast, with its 9th-century Buddhist treasures. In Jakarta, the best place to get an introduction to the culture and history of Indonesia—of which Java is a significant part—is **Taman Mini Indonesia Indah.** It's a slightly hokey theme park but an educational one, with reproductions of architectural types found throughout Indonesia, pavilions where you can learn about regional handicrafts, such as gong making, and agriculture, and even commune with spitting komodo dragons in the park's native fauna exhibit. Elsewhere in Jakarta, today a throbbing nexus of Asia-Pacific commerce, you can learn about Dutch colonial history, when Jakarta was called Batavia, at the **Jakarta History Museum** (Jalan Taman Fatahillah) and at several restored **historical residences,** or about Indonesia's battle for independence at the **National Monument** (Jalan Medang Merdeka Barat). With flashy commercial districts and high-rise hotels existing right alongside cramped and chaotic residential quarters, it seems there is something interesting happening on every street corner in Jakarta. There are bright colors and bright smiles all around, but it can be exhausting trying to take it all in.

When you hit the point of sensory overload, take the 1-hour flight to **Yogyakarta** in southeastern Java, where Java's most splendid cultural treasures lie. The main attraction in this area, the Buddhist temple of **Borobudur** (www.borobudurpark.co.id/en-index.html), was built in the 9th century A.D. and is without a doubt one of the most awesome artistic achievements anywhere in the world. The monumental complex of telescoping black-stone stupas and intricate storytelling reliefs—there are 2,672 decorative panels and 504 Buddha statues—rises to a height of 42m (138 ft.) from a ponderous solid masonry base. The effect is especially sublime if you go at sunrise, when the quintessential Javanese landscape of rice fields and the volcanic cone of Mount Merapi in the distance seem most mystical.

Don't leave Java without taking in its traditional performance arts. Spellbinding ***wayang Kulit*** shows use shadow puppets to relate tales from old Indonesian court life. **Gamelan** is an orchestra in which soft bamboo flutes, xylophones, and drums play a gentle rhythm—often in an open-air pavilion, caressed by warm island breezes that carry exotic scents—that is more soothing than any nature-sounds CD. Like Java itself, gamelan is the result of several cultural influences, and this hypnotic music may become the indelible soundtrack of your Javanese experience. —*SM*

ⓘ www.indonesia-tourism.com or www.javatourism.

✈ Jakarta Soekarno-Hatta, served by many international carriers; or Yogyakarta, served by Indonesian carrier Garuda.

🛏 $$$ **Amanjiwo,** Magelang (near Yogyakarta; ✆ **62/293/788333;** www.amanresorts.com). $$ **Grand Hyatt Jakarta,** Jalan M. H. Thamrin Kav. 28–30 (✆ **62/213/901234;** www.jakarta.grand.hyatt.com).

347 Exploration

Magnetic Island

World War II History Amid Splendid Nature

Australia

It owes its name to a fluke in the navigational instrumentation of one of the most famous sea voyagers in history. When Captain Cook sailed up the eastern side of Australia in 1770, he reported a mysterious malfunctioning of his compasses whenever he passed this island off the coast of Queensland. Unable to explain the bizarre behavior of his equipment any other way, Cook decided that there must have been some "magnetic" quality of the terrain on the island that was throwing his needles out of whack. Research has never proven Cook's claim, but the name he gave to this 52-sq.-km (20-sq.-mile) outcrop of land—the straightforward if geologically erroneous "Magnetic Island"—stuck. Easy to reach from the mainland and home to some interesting World War II sites as well as nature trails galore, the island today is a haven for Queenslanders.

As early as the 1800s, "Maggie Isle" (as it's fondly called by locals) was a popular outing spot for Europeans from mainland Australia, which, with the port of Townsville only 8km (5 miles) away, made for an easy day trip by sailboat or steamer. An inlet on the southern coast of the triangle-shaped island is still called **Picnic Bay,** recalling the purpose of the vessels that frequently docked here in that era. The island's natural resources, including hoop pine timber and granite for construction projects in Queensland, were also exploited during the 19th century. Tourism arrived on the island by the 1890s, when the first resorts were built.

During World War II, Cleveland Bay (between Townsville, on the mainland, and Magnetic Island) became an important staging area for military supply boats. To protect that waterway, and the base at Townsville, from potential sea assault, a complex of military structures—powerful searchlights, radar facilities, and gun emplacements—was built on the northeastern tip of Magnetic Island. The remains of these facilities are known collectively as "the Forts" and are today one of the biggest tourist attractions on the island. The guns have since been removed, having only ever fired one shot—at a U.S. Navy boat that arrived in the area without any warning. The **Forts Walk** is one of the highlights of visiting Magnetic Island. Along the way, you're likely to encounter one of the members of the local **koala colony** hanging out in the eucalyptus trees that line the easy, 2km-long (1¼-mile) path.

More than half of Magnetic Island is designated as National Park land, with Mount Cook dominating the hilly and densely wooded interior. On this very laid-back island, there are 24km (15 miles) of walking trails, many with spectacular views. In addition to the koalas that visitors frequently spot while hiking, there are also rock wallabies and possums running free and kookaburras (large Australian kingfishers) "laughing" in the trees. Offshore, cool blue ocean waters teem with sport-fishing opportunities and excellent diving spots typical of the Great Barrier Reef region. —*SM*

ⓘ www.magnetic-island.com.au.

✈ Townsville (8km/5 miles, connections through major eastern Australian airports).

⛴ From Townsville, **Sunferries,** 20 min. (✆ **61/7/4726 0800;** www.sunferries.com.au).

🛏 $$$ **Mantra One Bright Point,** 146 Sooning St. (✆ **61/7/4758 2100;** www.mantraonebrightpoint.com.au).

Pirates 348

St-Malo

Corsairs Gone Wild

France

Like Mont-St-Michel 364 up the Normandy coast, St-Malo thrusts out of the Channel on an outcrop of granite, a medieval walled city that almost seems to sprout organically from the rock. In season, swarms of tour buses and their passengers engulf the narrow cobbled streets, making St-Malo the most-visited destination in Brittany. But St-Malo has a dirty little secret: Connected to the mainland by multiple bulwarks and bridges, it's not really an island anymore, and much of that medieval charm is a Disneylandish fake, smartly rebuilt after the town was shattered by bombardments in World War II.

Somehow, though, such larceny is just what you'd expect of St-Malo. Despite its humble 6th-century origins as a monastery (evident in the Gothic **Cathédrale St-Vincent** at 12 rue St-Benoit), what really made St-Malo famous over the centuries was one thing: pirates. The town's outlaw nature dates back to 1144, when Bishop Jean de Chatillon made St-Malo an official place of asylum, thus attracting all sorts of miscreants to move there; for a few years in the 1490s, the renegade city even declared itself an independent nation. Throughout the Middle Ages, all the way until 1856, French kings licensed St-Malo ship captains to attack enemy ships heading up the English Channel, aka the "course" (hence the pirates' name, Corsairs). The Corsairs didn't limit themselves to the Channel, either, often venturing as far as the Caribbean. It was such a lucrative trade—a fair share of the booty flowed into the royal treasury as well—that in 1689, Louis XIV ordered the construction of stout **Fort National** (✆ **33/6/72-46-66-26;** www.fortnational.com) on its own rocky islet north of town (it's still accessible only at low tide) to protect St-Malo from reprisal strikes from the hated English, who bore the brunt of the privateers' activity.

A walk around St-Malo's ramparted **city walls** is an essential introduction to the historic core of the city; sweeping views of the bay underscore St-Malo's inevitable connection to the sea. At the town's chief museum, **Musée de l'Histoire de St-Malo** (Porte St-Vincent; ✆ **33/2/99-40-71-57**), located in the bristling gray towers of the walled town hall, exhibits explain the history of the Corsairs, including such dashing figures as 14th-century female pirate Jeanne de Clisson; René Duguay-Trouin, who captured more than 300 ships in the late 17th and early 18th centuries; and 19th-century Robert Surcouf, nicknamed the King of Corsairs. Other famous St-Malo natives—such as navigator Jacques Cartier and the French writer Chateaubriand—get their due here as well.

You can also arrange in advance for a guided tour of the secret cellars, hidden staircases, and pirate artifacts at the **Privateer's House,** or La Demeure de Corsaire (5 rue d'Asfeld; ✆ **33/2/99-56-06-40;** www.demeure-de-corsaire.com), an imposing gray-granite town house built in 1725 by François-Auguste Magon, a privateer who rose to such respectable heights that he became a director of the French East India Company—just another St-Malo success story. —*HH*

ⓘ Tourist office, Esplanade Saint-Vincent ✆ **33/825/13-52-00;** www.saint-malo.fr).

St-Malo, 3 hr. from Paris.

Weymouth, Poole, Guernsey, and Jersey (www.condorferries.co.uk).

$ **Hôtel de la Cité,** 77 Place Vauban ✆ **33/2/99-40-55-40;** www.hotel-cite-st-malo-bretagne.com). $$ **Hôtel Elizabeth,** 2 rue des Cordiers ✆ **33/2/99-56-24-98;** www.st-malo-hotel-elizabeth.com).

349 Pirates

New Providence Island

Historic Harbor

The Bahamas

New Providence may not be the biggest of the Bahamian islands, but it's the historic heart of this island nation, largely thanks to its superb natural anchorage, a protected harbor deep and wide and camouflaged in a veil of brush. Over centuries, that harbor has been a refuge for native Lucayan Indians, explorers, and freed slaves—and the stomping ground for a rogues' gallery of pirates, smugglers, and privateers.

Salvagers did well on the islands' shallow shoals: Shipwrecked vessels provided these marine "wreckers" with a livelihood. In slow times, legend has it that a few unscrupulous types even placed lights on nearby reefs to encourage impromptu shipwrecks. Today you can climb the crumbling remains of a watchtower on Yamacraw Hill Road, reputed to have belonged to the notorious 17th-century pirate Edward Teach, aka Blackbeard. The dioramas and displays of the **Pirates of Nassau,** an "interactive museum" in downtown Nassau (King & George St.; ✆ **242/356-3759;** www.piratesofnassau.com), gives you a vivid, if somewhat hokey, taste of that swashbuckling era; the attraction also offers pirate-themed tours of Nassau.

Another, darker chapter of New Providence's past is told at the **Vendue House,** built sometime before 1796. Originally it

Government House.

was a lively marketplace where, among other 18th-century "commodities," African slaves were bought and sold. This restored neoclassical structure was reborn in 1992 as the **Pompey Museum of Slavery & Emancipation** (Bay St.; ✆ **242/326-2568**), which tells the story of slavery and its aftermath in The Bahamas. Today, most of the island's population is of West African descent, whose ancestors were the slaves brought to the island by British Loyalists fleeing the American Revolution in the late 1700s, or those left here when the British banned the slave trade in 1807.

The Bahamas, now an independent sovereign nation, was a British crown colony for some 250 years; Nassau is virtually a living museum of British colonial architecture and artifacts, including the early-19th-century government buildings like **Parliament Square** and the neoclassical **Government House,** both painted a distinctive pink. If you have any doubts about the importance of the harbor, just look at how many forts were constructed to defend it from the Spanish and the French: the oldest fort still standing on the island, **Fort Montagu,** built in 1741 of local limestone; **Fort Fincastle,** built in 1793, with its 60m (200-ft.) tower with commanding views of the harbor; and the largest, **Fort Charlotte,** built by the British in 1787, with 42 cannons lined up impressively on its ramparts, none of which ever fired a shot.

In the 1920s, Nassau's harbor played host to a more modern breed of pirates: the vessels of bootleggers, supplying illegal liquor to the United States during Prohibition. Today, Prince George Wharf, which was built to accommodate the rum-runners' vessels, provides anchorage for massive cruise ships, whose passengers often overrun Nassau town with the same giddy abandon as the pirates of yore. —*AF*

ⓘ www.bahamas.com.

✈ Nassau, New Providence Island.

🛏 $$ **A Stone's Throw Away B&B,** Tropical Garden Rd. and West Bay St. (✆ **242/327-7030;** www.astonesthrowaway.com). $$$ **British Colonial Hilton,** 1 Bay St., Nassau (✆ **800/HILTONS** [445-8667] in the U.S. and Canada, or 242/322-3301; www.hilton.com).

Pirates **350**

Norman Island

Ahoy, Long John Silver

British Virgin Islands

Seen from the air, it looks like a splat of seaweed, intensely green against the blue waters of the Caribbean. But back in the old days, no one saw Norman Island from the air. You saw it from the deck of a pirate ship, and that ragged profile meant one thing: lots of coves and caves to hide booty in.

When Robert Louis Stevenson wrote *Treasure Island* in the early 1880s, his imagination had been fired by tales told to him by a seafaring uncle of his expedition to the British Virgin Islands, and specifically Norman Island. Over the years, many stories floated about of local people discovering mysterious caches of gold and silver coins, squirreled away in caves on such islands. As Stevenson fashioned his gripping yarn of hidden riches and bloodthirsty buccaneers, he drew upon his uncle's descriptions, as well as childhood memories of vacationing on Uist 476, in the Shetland Islands.

Today, the treasures of Norman Island are more for snorkelers and bareboaters, who find its caves and sheltered anchorages make a wonderful Virgin Islands getaway. Nearby Tortola 31—the gateway to the British Virgin Islands and one of the premier sailing centers of the entire Caribbean—is the jumping-off point for private boat excursions over the Drake Channel, 11km (6¾ miles) south to Norman Island. Contact **Travel Plan Tours** (✆ **284/494-2872;** www.aroundthebvi.com) to join one of their full-day sailing tours aboard a motor launch from Tortola to Norman Island; or rent a catamaran from **Moorings Limited** (✆ **888/952-8420** in the U.S. or 284/494-2331; www.moorings.com). Usually they require a 3-day minimum, but there are enough other places to explore around Tortola to make the stay worth your while.

Once here, you can row, kayak, or snorkel into the caves, located in Treasure Point, the rocky headland at the southern end of the wide sheltered cove of **The Bight.** At the base of Treasure Point's cliffs are three caves, where bats nest and algae on the cave walls glows in the darkness—almost like a bioluminescent night dive. You can also explore the 4km-long (2½-mile) island on foot, climbing through its scrubby vegetation to the top of **Spy Glass Hill**—to give it the name Stevenson used in his book—a perfect pirate lookout if there ever was one. Divers will also want to explore the island's reefs (contact **Blue Water Divers,** ✆ **284/494-2847;** www.bluewaterdiversbvi.com), visiting among other dive sites the wreck of the HMS *Rhone* off nearby Salt Island.

Though privately owned Norman Island is uninhabited, it's not really deserted—there are two lively bar/restaurants in the Bight: **Pirates,** located on the beach (look for its red tin roof), and just offshore an old moored lumber barge named the ***William Thornton*** ("Willie T" to locals). There are no accommodations on the island, but Norman Island's coves are so calm and sheltered that it's a prime place for sailors to anchor their boats overnight. *—HH*

ⓘ **Tortola tourist office,** near the ferry dock, Road Town (✆ **284/494-3134**); also www.normanisland.com.

✈ Beef Island Airport, connected by bridge to Tortola.

🛏 $ **Ole Works Inn,** Cane Garden Bay (✆ **284/495-4837;** www.quitorymer.com). $$$ **The Sugar Mill,** Apple Bay (✆ **800/462-8834** in the U.S., or 284/495-4355; www.sugarmillhotel.com).

351 Pirates

Ocracoke Island

Old Salt

North Carolina, U.S.

An isolated outpost for centuries, Ocracoke Island has a small-town, seafaring charm. Only about 750 residents live here year-round, a population that was once largely fishermen and sailors. You can tell the old-timers by their distinctive dialect, peppered with Cockney inflections—instead of "high tide," they say "hoi toide"—tracing a direct line from the Elizabethans who settled here 400 years ago.

In fact, the very first settlers from England, the doomed Lost Colony, sailed into the New World through the Ocracoke Inlet. When Ocracoke Village was established in 1715, it functioned as a base for boat pilots whose job it was to guide ships through the often-treacherous waters of the inlet. Adding to the danger, the **pirate Blackbeard** (aka Edward Teach) cruised these waters; he was killed in a bloody sea battle here in 1718 in a place now referred to as **Teach's Hole.** Navigation got a little easier after the squat, whitewashed **Ocracoke Lighthouse** was built in 1823—it's the second-oldest operating lighthouse in the country; you can see it from most any vantage point in the village, but the interior is not open to the public.

Those treacherous waters gave Ocracoke another of its distinctive historic features: the wild ponies that once ranged the island, descended from Spanish mustangs shipwrecked here in the 17th century. Now safely ensconced in pony pens (kept well away from the busy summer traffic) and cared for by the national park service, these "ponies" are actually full-grown horses, small but powerful. Isolation has ensured that their distinctive breed characteristics have remained pure.

In the summer, ferries chug in from either Cape Hatteras (30) or across the wide, shallow Pamlico Sound from the mainland, loaded with visitors arriving to swim and play on some of the East Coast's most beautiful beaches. Part of the **Cape Hatteras National Seashore,** Ocracoke's beaches are pristine, undeveloped stretches of tawny sand; **Ocracoke Beach** is consistently named one of the nation's finest, and it's a beauty, with frothy white surf rolling up in near-perfect precision. The visitors crowd Ocracoke Village's Silver Lake harborside, dining on briny Hatteras clam chowder in weathered wooden cafes and biking around the island's sand-dusted streets. For an isolated backwater, Ocracoke is surprisingly sophisticated, with some of the best grub on the Outer Banks, predominantly fresh seafood, a bounty of fish, crabs, shrimp, and clams. The ambience, like that along the rest of the Outer Banks, is sand-in-shoes casual.

A sturdy, self-sufficient lot, Ocracokers have lived through hurricanes and rough seas, carving out a rigorous, do-it-yourself kind of existence on the edge of nature. Despite (or maybe because of) the rigors of living on in splendid isolation, these islanders appreciate a good time: Any event is an excuse for a party, even hurricanes, which this part of the world experiences on a regular basis. For an old salt with feet of sand and a spine of steel, Ocracoke offers a rollicking good time. —*AF*

(i) **Cape Hatteras Seashore National Park** (✆ **252/473-2111;** www.nps.gov/caha); also www.ocracokevillage.com.

✈ Norfolk, Virginia (120 miles/193km).

⛴ 30 min. from Hatteras (north) or 2½ hr. from Cedar Island (south); reservations: www.ncdot.org/transit/ferry or ✆ **800/BY-FERRY** (293-3779).

🛏 $ **The Castle Bed & Breakfast,** Ocracoke Island (✆ **800/471-8848** or 252/928-3505; www.thecastlebb.com).

Pirates 352

Galveston Island

The Comeback Queen

Texas, U.S.

What other American city can claim such a rogue for a founding father? In 1817 debonair privateer Jean Lafitte, evading New Orleans's customs officers, launched a "pirate kingdom" on this 32-mile-long (51km) barrier island in then-Spanish Texas. Sitting at the mouth of a fine natural harbor, Galveston was perfect for his privateering operations, not to mention his sideline as a Spanish spy. U.S. authorities drove Lafitte from the island in 1821—he defiantly burned his settlement to the

Galveston.

ground as he fled—but more respectable citizens followed, developing that harbor into Texas's leading port and Galveston into its biggest city.

But that same harbor-mouth location that made Galveston so prized also made it fatally hurricane prone, and on September 8, 1900, the inevitable disaster struck. In the middle of the night, 6m-high (20-ft.) waves crashed over the long, low island, smashing houses into matchwood and hurling residents from their beds. By morning more than 6,000 islanders—one out of every six—were drowned, one-third of its buildings wrecked. It still ranks as the deadliest natural disaster in U.S. history (get the full story in the film *The Great Storm* at Galveston's **Pier 21 Theater** [✆ **409/763-8808**], which also screens a Jean Lafitte documentary).

Although Galveston valiantly rebuilt, erecting a stout 16km-long (10-mile) seawall and raising the entire island with landfill, most businesses relocated to inland Houston. As Houston boomed, Galveston dwindled—so much so that during Prohibition, residents turned to bootlegging and gambling (surely Jean Lafitte would have approved). In 1957 the Texas Rangers charged in to clean up the town, but afterward Galveston languished.

Ironically, that long decline had a silver lining. With real estate development at a standstill, nobody knocked down the gracious Victorian mansions of the East End (north of Broadway, 9th–19th sts.) or the ornate cast-iron facades of the old **Strand District** (19th–25th sts. between Church St. and the harbor), once dubbed the "Wall Street of the Southwest." In the 1960s and 1970s, a historic restoration movement rescued hundreds of dilapidated gems; walking around these districts today is a time warp experience. Three magnificent East End houses, known as the Broadway Beauties, were opened to the public: the castlelike stone **Bishop's Palace,** 1402 Broadway (✆ **409/762-2475**), built in 1892; the Italianate red-brick **Ashton Villa,** 2328 Broadway (✆ **409/762-3933**), from 1859; and the opulent brick-and-limestone 1895 **Moody Mansion,** 2618 Broadway (✆ **409/762-7668;** www.moodymansion.org). The jewel box **1894 Grand Opera House** (2020 Postoffice St.; ✆ **409/763-7173;** www.thegrand.com) once again hosts live theater. Every May, the **Galveston Historical Foundation** (✆ **409/765-7834;** www.galvestonhistory.org) organizes weekend tours of several Victorian mansions; every December, the

Dickens on the Strand festival (✆ **409/765-7834;** www.dickensonthestrand.org) packs the streets with merrymaking Galvestonians in crinolines and cutaway coats.

And then—déjà vu all over again—in September 2008 Hurricane Ike swept over that seawall and flooded Galveston anew. Several damaged sites, including Ashton Villa, took months to reopen; downtown's flaking, rusting cast-iron facades landed on the National Trust for Historic Preservation's 2009 America's Most Endangered Places list. Galveston's next comeback is still a work in progress, but I'm betting on Lafitte's old pirate kingdom to succeed in style. —*HH*

ⓘ **Tourist office,** 2328 Broadway (✆ **888/425-4753;** www.galveston.com).

Bush International, Houston.

67-mile/108km drive from Houston.

$$ **Harbor House,** #8 Pier 21 (✆ **800/874-3721** or 409/763-3321; www.harborhousepier21.com). $$$ **Hotel Galvez,** 2024 Seawall Blvd. (✆ **877/999-3223** or 409/765-7721; www.wyndham.com).

Prisons

353

Ile Ste-Marguerite

The Man in the Iron Mask

France

It's so easy to fall into sybaritic routines in the chic Riviera resort of Cannes—bronzing on the beach, browsing the designer boutiques of promenade de la Croisette, gambling and nightclub hopping at night. But if you want to jolt yourself out of that self-indulgent rut, hop on a ferry to the Ile Ste-Marguerite, the largest of the Iles des Lérins that pepper the Bay of Cannes. It's literally the sister island to nearby Ile St. Honorat, named after a 5th-century nun whose brother founded the still-thriving Cistercian monastery of St. Honorat. Marguerite's island convent is long gone, but what's here today is even more fascinating: the austere cell of a 17th-century prisoner whose identity is still shrouded in mystery.

Alexandre Dumas romanticized his story in the 1850 novel *The Man in the Iron Mask,* the title referring to the heavy iron casque that concealed the prisoner's face (in reality the mask was probably black velvet). Historians now believe he was one Eustache Dauger, described as a mere valet, but over the years nearly 100 different identities have been proposed—the son of Oliver Cromwell, perhaps, the real father of king Louis XIV, or (in Dumas's version) the king's twin brother. It was also rumored that while in prison he fathered a son, who was taken to Corsica 368 and later founded the Bonaparte family. Whoever the masked prisoner was, he lived here from 1687 to 1698, then was transferred to the Bastille, where he died in 1703, his name—and his exact crime—forever unknown.

Disembarking from the ferry, you'll be struck right away by the fragrance of Aleppo pines, eucalyptus, holly oaks, myrtle, honeysuckle, and clematis. Much of the island is a forest preserve; leave time to hike around and enjoy the breathtaking sea views from various observation points. It's only a short walk, however, on a well-marked path from the dock to the stout ramparts of the **Fort de l'Ile,** built of sun-bleached stone on this promontory by Spanish troops in 1635. After the French took over the fort in 1637, it served as a prison until it was decommissioned in 1944. Among its other prisoners were Huguenot pastors imprisoned after the revoked Edict of Nantes; Algerian hero Abd-El-Qader; and the exiled Marechal Bazaine, who daringly escaped in 1874.

In the main fort building, the **Musée de la Mer** (✆ **33/4/93-38-55-26**) occupies the old cisterns of the island's original Roman settlement. Its exhibits trace the history of the island, displaying artifacts of Ligurian, Roman, and Arab eras, plus the remains of ancient shipwrecks and other undersea excavations. But the main attraction is definitely the cell of the Man in the Iron Mask, where it seems that every visitor has scrawled his or her name on the walls. Standing in this grim stone cell, listening to the sea pounding the ramparts without, you'll feel a frisson of pity for that masked convict—whoever he was. *—HH*

ⓘ **Cannes tourist office,** 1 bd. De La Croisette (✆ **33/4/92-99-84-22;** www.cannes.com).

✈ Nice, then train to Cannes.

⛴ 1 hr. from Cannes: **Trans-Côte d'Azur** (✆ **33/4/92-00-42-30;** www.trans-cote-azur.com).

🛏 $$ **Hotel Moliere,** 5–7 rue Molière (✆ **33/4/93-38-16-16;** www.hotel-moliere.com). $$ **La Villa Cannes Croisette,** 8 Traverse Alexandre III (✆ **33/4/93-94-12-21;** www.hotel-villa-cannes.com).

354 Prisons

Chateau d'If

The Count of Monte Cristo

France

Of all the forbidding island prisons in the world, Chateau d'If may be the only one made famous by an imaginary character. Built in 1529 on an island of rock in the middle of the Marseilles harbor, the Chateau d'If—originally built for protection against aggressors—became a prison 10 years later. It was ideally suited for the role: Rough currents and its isolation from the mainland proved a formidable combination. In fact, Chateau d'If was so impregnable that only one prisoner ever escaped—and he was a work of fiction. With Edmond Dantes, the troubled protagonist in Alexandre Dumas's 1844 novel, *The Count of Monte Cristo,* Chateau d'If became part of literary history.

In Dumas's classic tale of jealousy, greed, and, ultimately, revenge, Edmond Dantes is wrongly accused of a crime and sent to Chateau d'If for the rest of his life. In a daring escape, he places himself in the body bag of a deceased prisoner, which is then thrown into the waters surrounding the island. Thus begins Dante's methodical march to destroy the people who made him a prisoner at Chateau d'If.

In truth, plenty of big-time prisoners were incarcerated at Chateau d'If, including Gaston Crémieux, one of the leaders of the Paris Commune—he was executed at the prison in 1871. A number of political prisoners and religious dissenters also served their prison terms in Chateau d'If, including more than 3,500 French Huguenots. It was a miserable place for anyone to live, but particularly for the poor, who were imprisoned in the windowless dungeon while their richer counterparts lived upstairs amid windows and fireplaces.

After the Chateau d'If ceased to function as a prison, it was opened to the public in 1890. Thanks to the tale of the Count of Monte Cristo, thousands of visitors per year pour into this historic site. The island's keepers feed the Monte Cristo frenzy, showing a running loop in the visitor center of the numerous films made from the Dumas novel. They also perpetuate the misconception that the Man in the Iron Mask—a different Dumas hero, from an 1848 novel—was also imprisoned at the Chateau d'If, although if that character ever existed, he was held in the Bastille and the island prison of Sainte Marguerite 353.

As a building, Chateau d'If is fairly unremarkable, with its blank round towers of pale stone. In fact, in various film versions of *The Count of Monte Cristo,* the filmmakers used a stand-in—the Chateau d'If just wasn't impressive enough for the big screen. From the island, however, visitors do get to see spectacular views of the port of Marseilles and the surrounding sparkling seas. Those same views must have haunted the island's prisoners and made them long for freedom—or, in the case of one immortal character, spin elaborate plans for the ultimate revenge. —*AF*

ⓘ **Chateau d'If** (✆ **33/4/91-59-02-30;** http://if.monuments-nationaux.fr).

✈ Marseilles.

⛴ 20 min., from the Quai de la Fraternité, Vieux Port. **Frioul If Express** (✆ **33/4/91-46-54-65;** www.frioul-if-express.com).

🛏 $$$ **Le Petit Nice,** Corniche Président-J.-F.-Kennedy/Anse-de-Maldormé, Marseilles (✆ **33/4/91-59-25-92;** www.petitnice-passedat.com). $$ **New Hotel Vieux Port,** 3 bis rue Reine-Elisabeth (✆ **33/4/91-99-23-23;** www.new-hotel.com).

Prisons **355**

Devil's Island

Island of Misery

French Guiana

A lush tropical isle isn't the kind of setting where you'd expect deprivation and despair, but that's just how Devil's Island earned its name. Devil's Island is actually the smallest of three islands collectively called the Iles du Salut (Islands of Salvation), lying a half-dozen miles off the coast of French Guiana in northeastern South America. But its name has become synonymous with the notorious French penal colony that occupied all three islands from 1852 to 1947.

Immortalized in the book and movie *Papillon* as well as the more historically accurate book *Dry Guillotine,* this tropical prison housed about 650 prisoners and 50 guards at a time; some 80,000 French criminals and political prisoners passed through over the years. Its best-known inhabitant was French general Albert Dreyfuss, who was falsely convicted of treason in 1895 and incarcerated here for 5 years.

All told, only about a quarter of the prisoners ever made it back to France. Tens of thousands died here, succumbing to a combination of tropical disease (malaria and yellow fever were common on these low-lying jungle islands) and harsh living conditions—stone cells, meager rations, forced labor, and solitary confinement. In an attempt to boost the colony's population, after their release prisoners were required to reside in Guiana for a period equal to their sentence (those sentenced to more than 8 years had to live there permanently). Many tried escaping, but the shark-filled ocean and piranha-infested rivers made this next to impossible; *Papillon* author Henri Charrière was one of the few who succeeded.

Today, the Iles du Salut—so named because in the 1760s they provided refuge for French settlers fleeing malaria on the mainland—are owned by the European Space Center, based 24km (15 miles) away in the mainland city of Kourou, once the administrative hub of the penal colony.

About 50,000 tourists a year visit the prison site, many as part of a cruise ship itinerary. Most tour **Ile Royale,** the largest of the islands, which housed the main prison buildings. In addition to a restaurant and hotel, the island exhibits plenty of abandoned prison cells and other artifacts of its dark past. (A particular favorite is the stone-filled swimming hole, built by convicts so that the warden and his family could enjoy shark-free bathing.)

A few hundred yards south of Ile Royale, 20-hectare (49-acre) **Ile de Saint-Joseph** displays rows of dreaded solitary confinement cells (20 guards were specifically assigned to convicts who went insane). Today it's reachable only by small craft. Just north of Ile Royale, the even smaller **Ile du Diable,** the true Devil's Island, was set aside for political prisoners, including the unlucky Dreyfuss. It's so difficult to approach, with its rocky coasts and treacherous surf, that prison authorities constructed a cable car from Ile Royale; the cables are long gone, and at last report the island is off-limits to tourists. Most likely you'll have to be content viewing it through binoculars. Just don't be surprised if you glimpse the brooding ghost of Albert Dreyfuss at the ocean's edge, staring back at you across the equatorial seas. —*AF*

(i) **Iles de Salut tourist office** (✆ **594/34-41-54;** infoslm@wanadoo.fr; www.ilesdusalut.com). **French Guiana tourism** (www.guyane.pref.gouv.fr or www.cr-guyane.fr).

✈ Cayenne (1 hr. from Kourou).

⛴ From Kourou (15km/9⅓ miles north of the island; 1–2 hr. by boat). **Sa Sotel** (✆ **594/32-09-95**); **La Hulotte** catamarans (✆ **594/32-33-81**); **Royal Ti'Punch** catamaran (✆ **594/32-09-95**); **Tropic Alizés** catamaran (✆ **594/25-10-10**).

🛏 $$ **Auberge des Iles du Salut,** Ile Royale (✆ **594/32-11-00;** www.destination.fr/guyane/aubergedesislesd.html).

356 Prisons

Robben Island

Island of Tears

South Africa

The sun shines just about all the time here, and the air is gin-clear, swept clean by the "Cape Doctor" winds that blow in from the southeast. Across the bay, Table Mountain towers over the city of Cape Town. The brightness of the sparkling sea, the vast robin's-egg sky, and the breathtaking panoramas are in jarring contrast to the island's main attraction. Off and on for nearly 300 years, Robben Island, 7km (4⅓ miles) from Cape Town, South Africa, served ably as a maximum-security prison, a miserable cage for thousands of prisoners. Most notoriously, it is where Nelson Mandela, the country's antiapartheid leader—and future president of a united South Africa—spent 18 years of his life in captivity.

Robben Island has been a place of exile for criminals, undesirables, and political prisoners ever since the Dutch arrived here in the late 17th century. It is a landscape ideally situated for impregnable confinement: The wind-whipped waves and rock-strewn reefs of Table Bay have snagged many a seafaring vessel—some 68 ships have run aground on Robben alone. The waters have a terrible beauty: In 1820, Makhanda, a Xhosa prophet imprisoned by British colonials on the island, escaped from the prison after a jailbreak only to drown in the turbulent seas.

The end of South African apartheid in 1994 effectively ended Robben Island's tenure as a political prison, but it wasn't until

1996 that the last prisoner was set free. In 1997, the government turned the facility into a museum, and in 1999 the island was designated a World Heritage Site as a symbol of "the triumph of the human spirit of freedom and of democracy over oppression."

Since then Robben Island has become one of the county's most popular attractions. Getting here couldn't be easier: You'll need to set aside a good half-day for the standard 3½-hour tour (see below for ferry details), which includes the boat ride there and back, a bus ride around the island, and tours of the facilities led by former prisoners. The prison itself has a grim banality, but the 2×2.4m (6½×8-ft.) cement cell where the prison's most famous occupant lived is a moving reminder of Mandela's long, arduous "walk to freedom."

Today the bright, sunny surrounds are a striking contrast to the prison facility. On Robben Island, the natural world is alive and thriving: Look for African penguins parading on the beach; springbok and eland gamboling in flower-filled meadows; and tortoises clambering over rocks. An 1864 lighthouse is still active, flashing a welcoming beam of light every 7 seconds to offshore mariners. —*AF*

(i) **Robben Island** (✆ **27/21/413-4220;** www.robben-island.org.za).

✈ Cape Town.

⛴ From the Nelson Mandela Gateway at the Victoria & Albert Waterfront, Cape Town, 25 min. (✆ **27/21/413-4220;** www.robben-island.org.za).

🛏 $$ **The Cape Cadogan,** 5 Upper Union St., Gardens, Cape Town (✆ **27/11/484-9911** or 27/21/480-8080; www.capecadogan.com). $$$ **Cape Grace Hotel,** West Quay Rd., Victoria & Albert Waterfront, Cape Town (✆ **27/21/413-4220;** www.capegrace.com).

TOUR Prebook well in advance, at www.robben-island.org.za.

Prisons

357

Alcatraz

The Rock

California, U.S.

This legendary island prison in San Francisco Bay occupies some of the most prized real estate in the world. Spectacular views across the water from Alcatraz take in one of the most iconic skylines in America, from the Transamerica Pyramid to the glorious span of the Golden Gate Bridge. But "The Rock"—surrounded by unforgiving waters, whipped at by perpetual winds, a heavy, damp chill hanging in its century-old Spanish-Revival buildings—couldn't feel more bleak or isolated. A visit to this formidable site, where some of America's most notorious criminals did hard time, is a transporting experience and one of the highlights of California sightseeing.

Originally named Isla de los Alcatraces ("Island of Pelicans"), Alcatraz was fortified as an army battery in the 19th century and became a military prison soon after, but it's the island's incarnation as a maximum-security federal prison (1934–63) that draws millions of visitors today. The fact that Alcatraz's stint as a prison came during one of the most sensational periods in the history of American crime—the days of prohibition and gangsters—only adds to the mystique. Thugs of a bygone era, like Al Capone and Machine Gun Kelly, did time on The Rock, and visitors seeking a slice of that history are not disappointed.

The prison closed in 1963 due to the high cost of operations and was designated a National Historic Site in 1976. Whether for a lack of funds or deliberate preservation, Alcatraz has never been gussied up. Maintenance around the island has been minimal, and so much the better for fans of authenticity: The sense of history that pervades the island is palpable. No sooner do you step off the ferry than you realize you've landed in a time warp: An official penitentiary sign stating NO ONE ALLOWED ASHORE WITHOUT A PASS (and framed by graffiti left over from the 1969–71 Native American occupation of Alcatraz) greets you at the tourist staging area. Along the path to the cell building, the warden's house—site of elegant cocktail parties during the prison years—is now just a shell, gutted by fire in 1970. The **prison control room,** with its midcentury radio equipment and typewriters, looks like the set of *Dragnet.* In the cellblocks, institutional mint-green and beige paint on the walls and cell bars flaked off long ago and hasn't been touched up.

What's perhaps most striking (and forbidding) about Alcatraz is the extreme physical reality of being here. This is a place where pelicans and seagulls, not humans, are meant to be, and the dreary loneliness of the island seems accentuated by the solitary **1854 lighthouse** that dominates the profile of Alcatraz. Strong winds make even walking around the island a laborious affair—it's hard to imagine how inmates playing basketball in the outdoor court ever made a shot—and the dampness is inescapable. Of course, the cold and unpredictable waters surrounding Alcatraz served as a better retaining device than any barbed-wire fence. Many inmates believed the waters were shark-infested, and wardens didn't dispel the rumor. In Alcatraz's 29 years as a prison, only 36 men tried to escape. The 1962 film *Escape from Alcatraz,* starring Clint Eastwood, recounts the most daring attempt ever conceived. But whether they were caught by guards or drowned in the Bay, not a single fugitive in the history of Alcatraz ever made it to freedom. (These days, fitness freaks can make the 1½-mile (2.4km) swim during the annual Escape from Alcatraz Triathlon.)

The cell of Robert Stroud, aka the "Birdman of Alcatraz."

Alcatraz Cruises (see below) is the only company authorized by the National Park Service to operate tourist visits to The Rock. Boats depart several times an hour from Pier 33, and one all-inclusive ticket (reservations are highly recommended) covers the round-trip boat ride, the cost of admission to Alcatraz, and the excellent audio tour, which is narrated by real former inmates and wardens and set to evocative sound effects like clanging bars and shouting in the mess hall. —*SM*

ⓘ www.nps.gov/alca.

✈ San Francisco International (11 miles/18km) and Oakland International (24 miles/39km).

⛴ **Alcatraz Cruises,** Pier 33, The Embarcadero, San Francisco (✆ **415/981-ROCK** [981-7625]; www.alcatrazcruises.com).

🛏 $$ **Argonaut Hotel,** 495 Jefferson St., San Francisco (✆ **415/563-0800;** www.argonauthotel.com). $$$ **The Fairmont San Francisco,** 950 Mason St. (✆ **415/772-5000;** www.fairmont.com).

Island Hopping the Orkney Islands: 1,000 Years of History

You've got to go north—way north, past John O' Groats, the Scottish mainland's northernmost tip—to get to this sparsely populated archipelago. The heather-clad hills and moors of the Orkneys support a small community of some 20,000 rugged souls, mostly fishermen and crofters, their lives fitted to the rhythms of its dark winters and long summer days (in June and July the sun stays over the horizon for as many as 18 hr. a day). The land's-end isolation of the Orkneys has one great virtue: With so little intervening settlement, the islands have preserved 1,000 years of history surprisingly intact, making it a virtual archaeological garden of megalithic chambered tombs, stone chambers, and fortified Pict brochs (round stone towers built by Orkney chiefs). Don't expect slickly developed tourist sites—often you'll have to ask at a farmhouse for the key to a crumbling cairn, where you can poke around the eerie chambers by yourselves.

On the island called 358 **Mainland** (that name alone tells you how insular Orkney society remains), the capital is still the Old Norse town of Kirkwall, with its narrow stone streets. The best archaeological finds, however, lie around the old Viking port of Stromness, on the island's southwest corner. Just north of town, off A965, you'll find the chambered cairn of **Maes Howe** (2700 B.C.), a superb achievement of prehistoric architecture, constructed from single rock slabs 5.4m (18 ft.) long and 1.2m (4 ft.) wide. Don't miss the passageway that the sun shines through only at the winter solstice. Maes Howe also contains the world's largest collection of Viking rune inscriptions, a sort of prehistoric graffiti left by marauding Norsemen who broke in hunting for buried treasure. Also along A965, 3.2km (2 miles) northeast of Stromness, the remarkable **Unstan Chambered Tomb** is a burial mound dating from 2500 B.C.; it's 35m (115 ft.) across, with a chamber over 2m (6½ ft.) high. Farther north, between the Loch of Stenness and the Loch of Harray, the Stonehenge-like **Ring of Brodgar** (1560 B.C.) is a circle of some 36 stones—nearly half of its original 60 stones surrounded by a deep ditch carved out of solid bedrock. Nearby stand the haunting remnants of an even more ancient stone circle, the four upright **Stenness Standing Stones.** Continue north to Skara Brae, a Neolithic village last occupied about 2500 B.C. Walking around its succession of stone-walled houses, joined by covered passages, you can almost imagine

The Ring of Brodgar.

the Neolithic people who lived here, because their homes are so amazingly preserved after having been buried in the sands for 4,500 years.

A handy causeway leading south from Kirkwall links Mainland to the next two islands to the south, 359 **Burray** and 360 **South Ronaldsay.** At the southern tip of South Ronaldsay, the closest Orkney land to the mainland, on Liddle Farm you'll find the Tomb of the Eagles, a fine chambered tomb dating from 3000 B.C. Farther west, at Old St. Mary's Church, lies an ancient church stone carved with the shape of two feet, thought to be a coronation stone for tribal chiefs. Scenic beach-edged Burray is mostly known as the major dive center of the Orkneys, but even here, history comes into play—in the Scapa Flow dive site you can prowl underwater around the wrecks of seven German warships, scuttled at the end of World War I.

You'll need to take a ferry to reach 361 **Rousay Island,** off the northeast coast of Mainland, which has a glorious cache of nearly 200 prehistoric monuments, the best of them clustered on its southwest corner. On a stark promontory broods the **Midhowe Broch and Tombs,** a 23m-long (75-ft.) Iron Age cairn divided into a dozen compartments. When it was excavated in the 1930s, the graves of some two dozen settlers, along with their cattle, were found inside. The other major sight, the nearby **Blackhammer Cairn,** is a megalithic burial chamber from the 3rd millennium B.C. Between them is an old Norse grave site, **Westness;** from here there's a marked 1.6km-long (1-mile) archaeological trail past dusty-looking excavations on either side.

On southeast 362 **Sanday Island,** reachable by plane or ferry, lies one of the most spectacular chambered cairns in the Orkneys: the **Quoyness Chambered Tomb** (ask for the key at the Lady Village post office), dating from around 2900 B.C., its 4m-high (13-ft.) chamber twice as high as the Unstan tomb on Mainland.

Warmed by the Gulf Stream, the Orkneys have a much milder climate than you'd expect; wildlife lovers can expect to see gray seals and an astounding number of bird species. Stay overnight to appreciate the awesome sunsets. —*HH*

ⓘ **Kirkwall Tourist Office,** 6 Broad St. (✆ **44/1856/872856**). **Stromness Tourist Office,** Ferry Terminal (✆ **44/1856/850716**); also www.visitorkney.com.

✈ Kirkwall Airport, Mainland Orkney. Small airstrip on Sanday.

⛴ **Orkney Ferries Ltd.,** Shore St., Kirkwall (✆ **44/1856/872044;** www.orkneyferries.co.uk).

🛏 $$ **The Ayre Hotel,** Ayre Rd., Kirkwall (✆ **44/1856/873001;** www.ayrehotel.co.uk). $$ **Stromness Hotel,** The Pierhead, Stromness (✆ **44/1856/850298;** www.stromnesshotel.com).

Pilgrims 363

Rameshwaram

A Spectacular Shrine to Shiva

India

If there were a Guinness Book of World Records entry for longest and most spectacular hallway in the world, the temple of Ramanathaswamy on Rameshwaram island would probably take the prize. At this Hindu pilgrimage site, one of the holiest in southern India, the 1,220m-long (4,003-ft.) corridor is just one of many architectural and artistic splendors adorning the monumental 12th-century temple complex, which owes its high religious status to one of the most important stories in Hindu mythology.

According to the Hindu epic *Ramayana,* Lord Rama (an incarnation of Vishnu) built a bridge across the sea from Rameshwaram to rescue his wife, Sita, from her abductor, the demon king Ravana, in what is now Sri Lanka (only 24km/15 miles away). Rameshwaram is also the supposed site where Rama worshiped Shiva in thanks for his support in defeating Ravana. For this reason, Rameshwaram is incredibly sacred to both Shaivites (devotees of Shiva) and Vaishnavites (devotees of Vishnu). And because Hinduism is always so wonderfully complicated, the main "deity" worshiped at Rameshwaram is the Linga of Sri Ranganatha, one of the 12 *jyotirlingas* of India. (A *jyotirlinga* is a shrine where Shiva is worshiped in the form of light shining through the earth; this light can be seen only by those who have reached spiritual enlightenment.)

Nowadays, Rameshwaram island—a landmass of some 62 sq. km (24 sq. miles) in the Gulf of Mannar and connected to the mainland by the 2.3km-long (1½-mile) Pamban bridge—is home to several temples associated with the Ramayana, but the main event is without a doubt the **Ramanathaswamy temple,** begun in the 12th century and embellished by subsequent dynasties. The star feature of the temple is the aforementioned hallway, a masterpiece of architecture that stretches for more than a kilometer and is lined with intricate columns that create a mesmerizing sense of perspective. Another oft-photographed element of the temple is its 54m-tall (177-ft.) *gopuram* (monumental entrance tower). Throughout the Ramanathaswamy temple, there are 22 wells, each with water that tastes totally different—and visitors are encouraged to try them all.

Rameshwaram is considered one of the principal pilgrimage sites in India. Hindu believers must make a pilgrimage here, as well as to Varanasi (aka Kashi or Benaras), in Uttar Pradesh, to attain *moksha,* or liberation from the cycle of death and rebirth *(samsara)* and an end to all the suffering and shackles of worldly existence. —*SM*

(i) www.tamilnadu-tourism.com.

✈ Madurai, 167km (104 miles; connections to major Indian cities).

Pamban Bridge connects Rameshwaram to mainland India (167km/104 miles. to Madurai).

$ **Hotel Royal Park,** Semma Madam, Ramnad Hwy. (✆ **91/4573/221680;** www.hotelroyalpark.in).

364 Pilgrims

Mont-St-Michel

Walking Up Abbey Road

France

Approaching across the coastal flatlands, you see its Gothic splendor erupt toward the sky, usually cloaked in dramatic fog. Set upon a massive rock just off the Normandy coast, the great Gothic abbey church of Mont-St-Michel rises dramatically from its rampart walls to an ethereal spire topped with a gilded statue of the archangel Michael, the abbey's guardian spirit. Just think of the engineering required to build this immense church on this tide-scoured outcrop—it's a marvel it has stood this long.

In the Middle Ages, this was a popular pilgrimage site, founded in the 8th century by St. Aubert; medieval pilgrims could get here only at low tide, walking across treacherous tidal sands, a challenge that increased the spiritual value of the journey. Enhanced over the next few centuries, however, as the abbey's monks grew richer and more powerful, the abbey came to look more like a fortress than a holy retreat—a fact that served it well in the Hundred Years' War (1337–1451), when it almost miraculously resisted capture by the English. The rampart walls also made it easy to convert to a prison after the monks were disbanded, in the days of the French Revolution. Since the late 19th century, it's been a national monument, not a church, although recently some new monks have settled in as well.

It's a steep walk to the abbey up Grande Rue, lined with half-timbered 15th- and 16th-century houses. Inside the **Abbey of Mont-St-Michel** (✆ **33/2/33-89-80-00;** www.mont-saint-michel.monuments-nationaux.fr), there are more staircases to climb. But it's worth it to investigate these stunning Gothic interiors, most notably the **Salle des Chevaliers** (Hall of the Knights) and graceful cloisters with rosy pink granite columns. Crowning the summit is the splendid abbey church, a rare example of one structure that displays the whole spectrum of Gothic architectural styles—note the round Romanesque arches in the 11th-century nave and transept, transitioning to the pointy flamboyant Gothic arches of the 15th-century choir area. I highly recommend staying overnight on the mount, especially if you come here in summer, so you can visit the church at night—not a bad idea for avoiding hordes of day-trippers.

The narrow land bridge that once connected Mont-St-Michel to the mainland, exposed only at low tide, was beefed up in 1879 into a permanent causeway, accessible at all hours, despite the fact that this bay has the highest tides in Europe. But the causeway blocked off the natural tidal processes, and as nearby coastal land was also reclaimed for agriculture, the bay gradually began to silt up. Around the bay you'll see work being done on an ambitious hydraulic dam project, to be completed by 2015 if all goes well—it will ensure that magical, mystical Mont-St-Michel remains a true island forever. —*HH*

ⓘ **Tourist office,** in the Old Guard Room to the left of the town gates (✆ **33/2/33-60-14-30;** www.ot-montsaintmichel.com).

Rennes (2½ hr. from Paris).

75 min. by bus from Rennes.

$ **Hôtel du Mouton-Blanc,** Grande Rue 28 (✆ **33/2/33-60-14-08;** www.lemoutonblanc.com). $$ **Les Terrasses Poulard,** Grande Rue 18 (✆ **33/2/33-89-02-02;** www.terrasses-poulard.fr).

Pilgrims 365

Grande Ile

Charming Canals & Rhineland Architecture

France

The most prominent landmark in the Alsatian skyline, **Strasbourg Cathedral,** rises from an elliptical-shaped island in the Ill river called Grande Ile. With Gothic spires that reach 142m (466 ft.) in height, the 15th-century cathedral took more than 400 years to complete and was the world's tallest building until 1874. The church and the remarkably well-preserved medieval surroundings that make up Strasbourg's historic core have earned the whole island designation as a UNESCO World Heritage Site. Whether you're taking in the soaring vaults of the cathedral or shopping along the manicured avenues of old Strasbourg, Grande Ile is one of the most magical places in Europe. However, the magic truly comes to life during the traditional Marché de Nöel, the most celebrated **Christmas Market** in France. Vendors' stalls, which look like real-life gingerbread houses and sell everything from *vin chaud* to handmade wooden toys, are bedecked with icicles and greenery, and twinkling lights crisscross the streets in the heart of the island—the whole effect is like looking inside a holiday snow globe and is enough to soften the most hardened Scrooge.

The storybook charm of Grand Ile is present well beyond the Christmas season, however. The most picturesque part of the island is **La Petite France,** often called la Venise du Nord ("Venice of the North") for its charming canals. La Petite occupies the western end of Grande Ile, where the Ill splits up into a series of short man-made canals. The bridge of Pont St-Martin marks the beginning of the district. The waterside buildings here were where medieval guilds were based, including those of the mill workers, fishermen, and leather tanners—crafts and trades that benefited from a nearby supply of water and drainage. Well-kept streets like Rue des Moulins ("street of the mills") and landmarks like Maison des Tanneurs ("house of the tanners") vividly recall that heritage.

All throughout the district, every corner offers a postcard view: Black and white timber-framed houses typical of the fairytale Rhineland line the streets, and window boxes are filled with colorful flowers. Perhaps the best street to stroll along is **Rue du Bain aux Plantes,** with its elaborately carved woodwork. If there's one iconic image of La Petite France, however, it is the **Ponts Couverts.** These were a series of "covered bridges," spanning four canals, built in the 14th century as part of the city's fortifications. Though four original stone watchtowers still punctuate each stretch of the linked span, the bridges are in fact no longer *couverts.* Just beyond the Ponts Couverts is the **Barrage Vauban,** a weir built in the 17th century to protect the city from river attack; it's now a lovely and panoramic spot, open to the public, from which to admire La Petite France.

As you might expect, an island this small and picture-perfect has most certainly been discovered by tourism. While shops and restaurants in the area do cater to day-trippers, Grande Ile remains beloved and frequented by the permanent residents of Strasbourg, who often visit the island on the weekends for family outings. —*SM*

(i) www.strasbourg.info.

✈ Strasbourg International, or Karlsruhe-Baden (40km/25 miles).

🛏 $$ **Hotel du Dragon,** 2 Rue Écarlate (✆ **33/3/88-35-79-80;** www.dragon.fr). $$$ **Regent Petite France,** 5 Rue des Moulins (✆ **33/3/88-76-43-43;** www.regent-petite-france.com).

366 Pilgrims

Reichenau

Keepers of the Flame

Germany

The name means "rich island," but that hardly does justice to this garden isle in the southern arm of the Bodensee (or, as the Swiss on the far shore call it, Lake Constance). Today it's a wonderfully peaceful retreat, with arching skies, a mild climate, and a quilted landscape of flower and vegetable gardens. But back in the days of the Holy Roman Empire, Bodensee commanded a key location on a major north-south route between Germany and Italy. It's no surprise that not one but three monasteries sprang up here, nursing the flame of civilization through the darkest days of the Dark Ages.

Soon after you cross onto the island, via a charming tree-lined 19th-century causeway, the first hamlet you come to is Oberzell, where the stout red-roofed tower of the austere **Stiftskirche St. George** (Seestrasse; no phone) rises abruptly from a cabbage field. Go inside to view its delicately faded naive frescoes, dating from the 10th century. But it's the next village, Mittelzell, where you'll find Reichenau's star attraction, the main reason for the island's World Heritage Site status: the triple-naved Romanesque **Münster St. Maria und Markus** (Burgstrasse; ✆ **49/7534/249**). Founded in 724 by the itinerant bishop St. Pirmin, a protégé of the great Frankish king Charles "the Hammer" Martel, over the years this imposing Benedictine abbey used its royal connections well. Nearly 700 monks lived here at its peak in the year 1000, in an abbey complex far more extensive than what you see today. It became known for its precious

A church on Reichenau.

relics, one of Europe's most extensive libraries, and a fabled scriptorium, where hundreds of skilled monks labored patiently over illuminated manuscripts. The monastery's treasures were dispersed all over Europe when the abbey lands were secularized in 1757 and the monks disbanded by Napoleon in 1803, but there are still several fine sacred objects in the basilica's 15th-century Gothic treasure room. The monastery's history is covered in detail at the **Reichenau Museum** (Ergat 1; no phone), in Mittelzell's 14th-century half-timbered town hall, originally the house of the abbey's bailiff. Also check out the **Krautergarten (Herb Garden),** in the shadow of the cathedral on Hermann Contractus Strasse, a replica of a typical medieval monks' herb and vegetable garden.

Farther west in the hamlet of Niederzell, the third of the island's Romanesque churches raises its twin towers over the fields: the **Stiftskirche St. Peter and St. Paul** (Egino-Strasse; no phone), well worth visiting for its rococo decorations and the Romanesque frescoes in its apse. A new Benedictine community was founded here in 2001, a wonderful sign that Reichenau's monastic traditions will live on. —*HH*

ⓘ **Tourist office,** Pirmimstrasse 145 (✆ **49/7534/92070;** www.reichenau.de).

Reichenau (on mainland, 10-min. bus ride from historic center), 15 min. from Konstanz, 12 min. from Radolfzell.

From Konstanz, 55 min.; from Radolfzell, 35 min. Apr–Oct only. **BSB Ferries** (✆ **49/7531/3640-389;** www.bsb-online.com).

$$ **Seehotel Seeschau,** An der Schiffslände (✆ **49/7534/257;** www.seeschau.mdo.de). $$ **Strandhotel Löchnerhaus,** Schiffslände 12 (✆ **49/7534/8030;** www.strandhotel-reichenau.de).

Pilgrims 367

Martha's Vineyard

Illumination Night

Massachusetts, U.S.

On my first visit to Martha's Vineyard—that salt-weathered island off Cape Cod, a summertime magnet for celebrities from musicians James Taylor and Paul McCartney to the late newsman Walter Cronkite and former President Bill Clinton—I followed everyone's advice and headed straight for postcard-pretty Edgartown, with its white picket fences and colonnaded Greek Revival sea captains' mansions. I rode the tiny On-Time ferry to the nature preserves of Chappaquiddick Island, where a notorious midnight car wreck ended the presidential ambitions of the late Senator Ted Kennedy. I even drove west to the end of State Road to marvel at the spectacular clay cliffs of Aquinnah (back then called Gay Head), its landmark lighthouse standing tall on tribal lands still belonging to the island's original residents, the Wampanoag Indians.

But after spending a few summers on the Vineyard with my family, my favorite historic area has definitely become **Oak Bluffs**—or, more precisely, the 34-acre (14-hectare) Wesleyan Grove, aka the **Campgrounds** (✆ **508/693-0525;** www.mvcma.org). In 1889, there were as many as 140 such "cottage camps" built for summer prayer retreats, a phenomenon of the late-19th-century religious revival in the United States. Most have since been razed, but Oak Bluffs' campground is a glorious survivor, an assemblage of doll-like gingerbread cottages packed closely on narrow streets surrounding the open-sided Tabernacle, where

A porch on Martha's Vineyard.

Methodist preachers once declaimed. Walking around here on a summer afternoon comforts me with a 19th-century vision of small-town community. I'm not lucky enough to know any residents, but you can get an insider's glimpse at the **Cottage Museum** (1 Trinity Park; ✆ **508/693-7784**). Someday I hope we'll hit Oak Bluffs on whatever mid-August weeknight is chosen (the date is a closely guarded secret) as **Illumination Night,** when the cottagers light up their homes with Japanese lanterns.

One day, driving past the Campground, I discovered another deeply knit community—the small beach known as the **Ink Well** (on Beach Rd. below Vaban Park), a traditional gathering point for the elite African-American families who summer in Oak Bluffs. Other African-American landmarks in town include the barn-red **Shearer Cottage** (4 Morgan Ave., East Chop; ✆ **508/693-4735;** www.shearercottage.com), the first guesthouse for people of color, and the **Adam Clayton Powell Cottage** on Dorothy West Street.

My kids, however, vote for Oak Bluffs' other historic landmark: the **Flying Horses carousel** (33 Circuit Ave.; ✆ **508/693-9481;** www.mvpreservation.org/carousel.html), set in an old-fashioned seaside cluster of refreshment stands and arcades. Built in 1876 at Coney Island, and brought to Martha's Vineyard in 1884, this is the United States' oldest working platform carousel. Though it's enclosed in a shed, the joyful strains of calliope music leak out like a pied piper's call to entrance children. Before you ride, take time to admire the craftsmanship of the handcarved vintage horses, with their real horsehair manes; look deep into their glass eyes and you'll spot tiny animal charms glinting within. God is in the details, they say. *—HH*

ⓘ ✆ **800/505-4815;** www.mvol.com/guides/visitors.

✈ Martha's Vineyard Airport.

Oak Bluffs, Vineyard Haven, or Edgartown; ferries run from Woods Hole (✆ **508/477-8600;** www.steamshipauthority.com), Falmouth (✆ **508/548-9400;** www.falmouthferry.com; or ✆ **508/548-4800;** www.islandqueen.com), or Hyannis (✆ **800/492-8082;** www.hy-linecruises.com).

$$ **The Dockside Inn,** 9 Circuit Ave. Extension, Oak Bluffs (✆ **800/245-5979** or 508/693-2966; www.vineyardinns.com). $$ **The Wesley Hotel,** 70 Lake Ave., Oak Bluffs (✆ **800/638-9027** or 508/693-6611; www.wesleyhotel.com).

Famous Islanders 368

Corsica

The Napoleon Complex

France

Lying just off the Italian coast—so close to Sardinia 387 you could almost swim there—Corsica by all rights should be Italian. Over the centuries it came under the sway of the Etruscans, then the Romans; the Genoese ruled for nearly 4 centuries, beginning in 1347. But the feisty Corsican people never bowed easily to any foreign yoke, and in 1729 Corsica declared itself a sovereign republic—not a good move, as it turned out, because the Genoese refused to leave and years of struggle ensued. In 1764 Genoa secretly sold the pesky rebel island to France, and once subdued, Corsica officially became a French possession in 1768. The very next year, when the second son of Carlo and Maria Buonaparte was born in the Corsican capital of Ajaccio, he was by birthright a French citizen—talk about flukes of history.

Halfway up the west coast of the island in modern-day **Ajaccio,** a Riviera-like town with palm trees and promenades, you can tour Napoleon Bonaparte's ancestral home, **Casa Buonaparte** (rue St-Charles; ✆ **33/4/95-21-43-89**), a four-story mustard-colored house with green shutters that the family owned from 1682 to 1923. Inside, fussy 18th-century salons display artifacts and furnishings—you'll see the bedroom where Napoleon was born, his death mask, and the trapdoor through which he reportedly escaped on his last visit to Corsica in 1799, en route from Egypt to Paris to seize power. Though he never returned, in the minds of the French people the future empire-maker would always be "the Corsican," and therefore not *really* French.

Corsican nationalism encouraged young Napoleon's anti-French sympathies, which landed him on the winning side of the French Revolution and paved the way for his meteoric rise to power. But in other ways as well, Napoleon's mercurial character seems totally a product of the untamable spirit of Corsica. Most holidaymakers come here for beaches and watersports, but beyond the gardenlike coastal areas you'll find a wild, mountainous interior. Several challenging multiday hiking trails—most notably the famous **Grande Randommé 20—**crisscross the rugged, oak-forested center, almost 40% of which is protected as the **Parc Naturel Regional du Corse** (✆ **33/4/95-46-26-70;** www.parc-naturel-corse.com). Here you can spot several one-of-a-kind species—the rare mouflon mountain sheep, the dainty Corsican nuthatch, and the nearly extinct Corsican red deer. Drive along the twisting coastal road D81 between Piana and Porto and you'll be startled by **Les Calanches,** an otherworldly landscape of savagely crumpled red-granite spires, accented with mad sprouts of green pine, gnarled gray thorn, and brilliant red-and-yellow blossoms. (From Porto, take a **boat tour** past the spiky red rocks with **Nave Va** (✆ **33/4/95-21-83-97;** www.naveva.com).

And yet Corsica is nicknamed *l'ile de beauté*, or "island of beauty," most likely because of the distinctive maquis that mantles the landscape—a low shrubby ground cover of juniper, gorse, myrtle, and oleander profusely mixed with sweet-smelling rosemary, thyme, lavender, and marjoram. Its heady aroma perfumes the air of Corsica, an intoxicating scent which native Corsicans, like Napoleon, never forget. —*HH*

ⓘ www.corsica.net.

✈ Ajaccio.

NGV from Nice, regular ferries from Marseilles, Nice, Toulon, Genoa, and Sardinia (www.corsica-ferries.co.uk, www.sncm.fr, www.lameridionale.fr, www.mobylines.com).

$$ **Hotel Le Porto,** Route de Calvi, Porto (✆ **33/4/95-26-11-20;** www.hotelleporto.com). $$$ **Les Roches Rouges,** Piana (✆ **33/4/95-27-81-81;** www.lesrochesrouges.com).

Famous Islanders

Elba

Rich Minerals & One Very Famous Exile

Italy

For most people, the Mediterranean island of Elba is best known as the place where Napoleon Bonaparte was exiled. However, after only 9 months on the island, Napoleon grew restless and returned to France to seek power again. (With his definitive defeat at Waterloo in 1815, the rest of Napoleon's life would be spent in exile on a much farther-flung island, St. Helena, in the southern Atlantic.) The 300 days that Napoleon spent here may be Elba's most famous era internationally, but they were a mere drop in the bucket for an island whose illustrious history goes back several millennia, largely due to its exceptional mineral wealth.

Elba, first of all, is naturally spectacular—its terrain surely does not have a Napoleon complex. Arriving into the main town of **Portoferraio** by ferry, you'll notice the rugged, densely forested coastline, dramatic rock walls, sandy bays, and beautiful natural harbors. The interior is lush and mountainous. The mineral foundations of Elba, especially on the southeastern tip of the island, are what drew the first major civilization, the Etruscans, to the island, then called "Ilva." Elba's rich deposits of iron and copper were exploited by the Etruscans, who built so many foundries on the island as to earn it the nickname "Fume" from Greek navigators who sailed in the vicinity.

When the Romans subsumed the entire Mediterranean basin in the 2nd century B.C., they occupied Elba, which had briefly fallen into Carthagian control, and continued the metallurgic industry that the Etruscans had established. Ruins like the elaborate **Villa delle Grotte** stand as testimony to the prosperity on Elba in the Roman period. To this day, even, mining is a major activity on Elba. In fact, the island is so loaded with iron and copper that aircraft flying overhead, or vessels sailing offshore, often have trouble with their navigational equipment.

Following the Roman period, barbarians and Saracen pirates occupied Elba, and in the Middle Ages, the island became a sort of hot potato territory that was

Elba.

tossed back and forth between various powers of mainland Europe, including Pisa, Spain, and, eventually, France in 1802. Each of those periods brought its respective rulers and building programs, evidence of which remains all over the island, like the 12th-century Pisan castle of **Volterraio** and the 18th-century Spanish fortress of **Forte San Giacomo.**

Elba's celebrated Napoleonic chapter began with his forced abdication as emperor of France in 1814. On May 13 of that year, Napoleon arrived at Portoferraio to begin his exile. Although Napoleon was nominally in charge of the island, and given a guard of 600 men, his actions were monitored by British naval patrols. While in residence on Elba, Napoleon found it necessary to build two sumptuous palaces on the island—the inland **Villa San Martino** (today rather unkempt) and the more impressive **Palazzina dei Mulini** in Portoferraio. He also sponsored a number of important public works projects that greatly benefited transportation and industry on the island.

Today, Elba's laid-back pace and gorgeous natural scenery make it a popular vacation destination for Italians and northern Europeans, though other nationalities have yet to discover its charms. Elba's size (224 sq. km/86 sq. miles), good roads, and a plethora of beaches make it an all-around good bet for a relaxing Mediterranean getaway. Recently, Elba has also become an important Tuscan wine region, producing unique varietals like the white Ansonica and the red Aleatico. —*SM*

ⓘ **Tourist info,** Via Carducci 150, Portoferraio (✆ **39/0565/930727;** www.aptelba.it).

✈ Marina di Campo, connections to Milan, Pisa, Bern, Zurich, Munich, and Friedrichshafen.

⛴ From Piombino, Toremar or Moby Lines, 1 hr.

🛏 $$ **Hotel Ilio,** Capo Sant'Andrea (✆ **39/0565/908018;** www.hotelilio.com). $$$ **Villa Ottone,** Loc. Ottone (✆ **39/0565/933042;** www.villaottone.com).

370 Famous Islanders

Upolu

Stevenson's Treasure Island

Samoa

Robert Louis Stevenson may have been born in gloomy Scotland, but he was always a globe-trotter at heart. During his invalid childhood (poignantly described in his *Child's Garden of Verses*), he developed the vivid imagination that later produced adventure classics like *Kidnapped* and *Treasure Island*. Haunted by illness for most of his adult life—he once described himself as "a mere complication of cough and bones"—he led a peripatetic life, constantly searching for a healthful climate. When tuberculosis threatened to end his life at the age of 39, Stevenson countered by moving to one of the most exotic spots on earth, amid the waterfalls and orchid-draped rainforest of the Polynesian islands of Samoa.

In 1890 Stevenson and his wife, Fanny, bought 127 hectares (314 acres) of virgin land on the slopes of Mount Vaea above **Apia,** the main coastal town where mid-19th-century European missionaries built their clapboard houses and churches when they first settled on Upolu, one of Samoa's two large main islands. (The other is Savaii 377.) You can still see traces of that colonial past along Beach Road in Apia, which—despite a string of high-rise waterfront hotels—still has a relaxed small-town atmosphere. In the Courthouse on Ifi-ifi Street in Apia, the small **Museum of Samoa** (✆ **685/63-444**) offers exhibits devoted to Samoan history.

The Stevensons named their estate on Apia **Vailima** (Cross Island Rd., 5km/3 miles south of Apia; ✆ **685/20-798**), or "Five Waters," because five streams crossed the property. At first they lived in a tiny shack, but by 1891 they had begun the sprawling veranda-laden mansion you can visit today. It astounded the islanders with its opulence—five airy bedrooms, a book-lined library, a ballroom large enough to accommodate 100 dancers, and the only fireplace in Samoa. (The rooms often filled with smoke, however—the native builders had no idea how to make chimney flues.) Notice the Samoan textiles on the walls of Stevenson's downstairs smoking room, and the piano in the redwood-paneled great hall, encased in glass to protect it from Samoa's humidity. Already a wealthy, world-famous author, Stevenson had food and wine shipped in from around the world, and the family dressed formally for dinner every evening—except for bare feet—served by Samoans dressed in tartan-patterned lava-lavas. After Stevenson's death in 1894, Vailima became the home of Samoa's head of state, until severe hurricane damage in 1990 and 1991 prompted a total renovation, to restore its appearance to how it was when Stevenson lived here.

The Samoans revered Stevenson because he excelled at something they valued highly: storytelling. They honored him with the name Tusitala, or "storyteller," and when he died, they ceremonially bore his corpse along a trail called the "Road of the Loving Hearts" to his grave on Mount Vaea. There are two trails, a steep one that takes half an hour and a more leisurely climb that takes about an hour. Along the walk, look for the lovely cascade that Stevenson made his swimming pool. His simple white marble tomb on the hilltop, overlooking the sea, is inscribed with his own verse: "Home is the sailor, home from the sea / And the hunter home from the hill." —*HH*

ⓘ **Tourist office,** Beach Rd., Apia (✆ **685/63-500;** www.samoa.travel).

✈ Faleolo International Airport.

🛏 $$$ **Aggie Grey's Hotel,** Beach Rd., Apia (✆ **800/448-8355** in the U.S. or 685/22-880; www.aggiegreys.com). $$ **Coconuts Beach Club,** Si'umu (✆ **866/726-6268** in the U.S. or 685/24-849; www.coconutsbeachclubsamoa.com).

Famous Islanders

Isla Robinson Crusoe

Castaway Classic

Juan Fernández Islands, Chile

All he had was a knife, a musket and gunpowder, carpenter's tools, and a Bible. Yet Scottish sailor Alexander Selkirk was convinced that the ship he'd been sailing on, the privateer *Cinque Ports,* was in such bad condition, it was bound to sink. He begged the captain to let him stay behind on this tiny volcanic island in the South Pacific rather than die a watery death on the open seas.

The *Cinque Ports* did indeed soon founder, while Selkirk managed to survive on the island for 4 years, living mostly on native fruit and the wild goats abandoned by previous Spanish explorations. Rescued in 1709—a visiting ship found him clad in goatskins, hairy as an ape, his bare feet leather-hard—he returned to Scotland a celebrity. Whether or not he actually met writer Daniel Defoe, Defoe's enormously popular 1719 novel *The Adventures of Robinson Crusoe* immortalized Selkirk's story.

The remoteness of Isla Más a Tierra (renamed Robinson Crusoe Island in 1966) did not recommend it to settlers. For the next century and a half, most visitors were pirates or fur trappers (the Juan Fernández fur seals were nearly hunted to extinction, though their numbers are now rebounding). In 1814, the Spanish government exiled several Chilean *criollo* patriots to the island—you can still visit the dank **Patriot's Caves** where they lived, above the island's one town, **San Juan Bautista,** on a steep hill overlooking Cumberland Bay on the northeast coast. (It's an hour by ferry from the airstrip.) Though Chile established more permanent settlers on this offshore territory in the late 19th century, even today only about 600 people live here, most of them trappers of the local spiny lobsters.

Between September and March, however, there is always a smattering of tourists, come to retrace Selkirk's footsteps, to scuba dive (a sunken World War I warship makes a great diving site), or to view the amazing wildlife. Agriculture never thrived on the jagged ridges and valleys of its mountainous interior, so most of the land is still virgin wilderness, with huge ferns, eucalyptus and guayaba trees, and dense undergrowth. Its island isolation gives it a high rate of endemic species; since 1977 it has been a World Biosphere Reserve. Rare birds include the Magellanic penguin and the critically endangered Juan Fernández Firecrown, an exquisite red hummingbird. Visit **Rebaje de la Piña,** a nature reserve in the southeast, near Puerto Francés, for extraordinary wildlife spotting.

A walking trail leads up to **Mirador de Selkirk,** a peak where Alexander Selkirk used to scan the horizon for ships; local guides can take you by boat to **Puerto Ingles,** site of a cave reported to be Selkirk's. Recent archaeological digs have discovered old nautical instruments and hut foundations left from Selkirk's sojourn. Whatever you do on this mist-hung, wind-whipped Pacific isle, the spirit of Robinson Crusoe will haunt you. —*HH*

ⓘ www.comunajuanfernandez.cl.

✈ Robinson Crusoe Island, 3 hr. from Santiago, **TAIRC airlines** (✆ **56/2/531-4343;** www.tairc.cl) and **LASSA Aeroservicios** (✆ **56/2/273-5209**).

🛏 $$ **Refugio Nautica,** av. El Palillo, San Juan Bautista (✆ **56/32/275-1077;** www.islarobinsoncrusoe.cl).

TOUR Endemica Expediciones (✆ **56/32/275-1003;** www.endemica.com).

372 Famous Islanders

Isle of Shoals

The Loneliest, Lovely Rock

New Hampshire & Maine, U.S.

In 1839, when Thomas Laighton moved into the lighthouse onto tiny, barren **White Island** with his young family, the Isle of Shoals had a sort of Wild West reputation. Native "Shoalers" were the descendants of 15th-century fishermen who profited from the almost freakish abundance of fish in the cold, deep Atlantic waters around this tiny archipelago, 6 miles (9.7km) off the New Hampshire coast. Hardworking, hard-drinking, and cussedly independent, they had become so isolated, they spoke a dialect that mainlanders could barely understand.

But for Laighton's daughter Celia, her childhood on White Island—"that loneliest, lovely rock" as she later described it—was magical, a romance embroidered with legends of ghosts, shipwrecks, murders, and pirates (Blackbeard's treasure was said to be buried around here, although who could bury anything in such solid rock?). In 1847, when Celia was 12, the family moved from the lighthouse to nearby Hog Island (now called **Appledore Island**), where Laighton built the grand Appledore Hotel resort. Celia married at 16 and moved to the mainland, but, an islander at heart, after 10 years she returned to Appledore, where she became the hostess at her father's hotel. By then Celia Thaxter was a much-admired poet, and her presence drew an impressive roster of writers and artists to summer at the Appledore—Ralph Waldo Emerson, Nathaniel Hawthorne, Henry Wadsworth Longfellow, Harriet Beecher Stowe, Sarah Orne Jewett, William Morris Hunt, Childe Hassam—creating what was in essence the country's first writers colony.

Sightseeing cruises from the New Hampshire mainland circle around the various islands that make up the Isle of Shoals, viewing the battered 1859 lighthouse on White Island (currently being restored, thanks to a campaign by local school kids), as well as Gosport Village, a replica of Star Island's original fishing hamlet. If you can, book a cruise that includes a **Star Island** guided walking tour—you can get off the boat and browse through the Celia Thaxton artifacts at the **Vaughn Cottage Museum** (Gosport; ✆ **603/430-6272**) and see a gull-spattered stone pedestal commemorating Captain John Smith (yes, Pocahontas's John Smith) who first mapped these islands in 1614. Star Island's rambling white Victorian-era Oceanic Hotel, built in 1873 to try to cash in on Appledore's success, gives you a fair idea of what the now-vanished Appledore was like in its heyday. Celia's brothers eventually ran the Oceanic too; from 1897 on, the Oceanic has specialized in religious conferences and retreats.

With a little planning, you can also visit Appledore Island, a short distance north of Star Island. Today it is mostly occupied by the **Shoals Marine Laboratory** (✆ **607/255-3717** or 603/964-9011; www.sml.cornell.edu), which brings visitors

Cruising by the Isle of Shoals.

over on a research vessel from Star Island. Next to the ruins of Celia's cottage, which burned down in 1914 with the hotel, occasional tours are led through her stunning garden, which Childe Hassam immortalized on canvas; Thaxter's book *An Island Garden* is a horticultural classic. She lies buried in the Laighton family graveyard nearby. —*HH*

ⓘ www.seacoastnh.com.

✈ Portsmouth, New Hampshire.

From Portsmouth: **Isle of Shoals Steamship Company** (✆ **800/441-4620** or 603/431-5500) or **Portsmouth Harbor Cruises** (✆ **800/776-0915** or 603/436-8084; www.portsmouthharbor.com). From Rye Harbor: **Island Cruises** (✆ **603/964-6446;** www.uncleoscar.com) or **Granite State Whale Watch** (✆ **800/964-5545** or 603/964-5545; www.whales-rye.com).

$$ **Oceanic Hotel,** Star Island (✆ **603/430-6272** or 603/601-0832; www.starisland.org).

Famous Islanders **373**

Avery Island

Hot Sauce & a Nature Reserve

Louisiana, U.S.

Just about every kitchen in the United States has a connection to Avery Island, Louisiana. You know that little bottle of Tabasco sauce in your refrigerator or your pantry? It was made right here, in the heart of Louisiana bayou country, on a salt dome that has belonged to the same hot-sauce-making family since the 19th century. Granted, Avery's classification as an "island" is somewhat tenuous: Only some narrow and muddy, moatlike bayous isolate it from the rest of the firmament. Owing to the solid dome of rock salt that makes up the island's foundation, Avery's perimeter is a nearly perfect circle, and it rises to a surprisingly high elevation—163 feet (50m)—for landforms in the swamps of Louisiana's Gulf Coast.

Though the island had been long known to native Americans for its precious natural resource—salt—Avery was named for the family that inhabited it from the 1830s. The island's history as a hot-sauce hot spot got underway just before the Civil War, when a certain E. A. McIlhenny and Mary Eliza Avery were betrothed. Soon after their wedding, McIlhenny—known as Mr. Ned—began making Tabasco-brand pepper sauce on the island. The original recipe and manufacturing process, which was given a U.S. patent in 1870, remains largely unchanged today. The peppers used for the sauce are native to Avery, and the salt "bedrock" of the island is the only salt allowed in Tabasco.

Tabasco sauce may be Mr. McIlhenny's legacy in the world, but his greatest gifts for visitors to Avery Island are the **Jungle Gardens** and **Bird City.** McIlhenny had a great affinity for nature and saw to it that flora and fauna from Louisiana and beyond could flourish here. The Jungle Gardens feature a striking assortment of exotic plants like Japanese camellias and Egyptian papyrus. Bird City was begun as a colony of 10 egrets in 1890, when those birds were being slaughtered by the thousands for ladies' feathered caps. Today the egret population here is in the thousands, and there are several other species of water bird that migrate through Avery Island every spring. Throughout the island, tufts of Spanish moss cling to gnarled oaks, creating a romantic and haunted Old South atmosphere.

Tabasco factory visits include a video on the history of the sauce and its roots on the island, as well as a guided tour of the bottling and packaging plants. Hurricane Rita significantly interrupted Tabasco production on Avery Island when it struck the Gulf Coast in 2005; the McIlhenny family has since poured millions of dollars into reinforcing the island's levees and emergency pump systems. —*SM*

ⓘ ✆ **337/365-8173;** www.tabasco.com.

✈ New Orleans (140 miles/225km) or Baton Rouge (89 miles/143km).

From New Orleans, take Rte. 90 west to New Iberia, and then follow signs.

$$ **Holiday Inn New Iberia,** 380 W. Hwy. 90 Frontage Rd., New Iberia, Louisiana (✆ **800/315-2621;** www.holidayinn.com).

374 Famous Islanders

Cuba

From Spanish Sugar Colony to Castro & Communism

Even the most seasoned globe-trotters will tell you that the most fascinating and bizarre travel experience they've had wasn't in some remote African village, but 90 miles (145km) off the coast of Florida—in Cuba. What makes Cuba so captivating and puzzling is this sense of "so close, but so far away" that encompasses almost everything about life on this island, which has been carefully manipulated by the Communist Castro regime since 1959. Although its tumultuous and variegated history, which has shaped the island's remarkable stature on the world stage, far precedes his ascension to power, there's no doubt that one person—Fidel Castro—now comes to mind when you think of Cuba.

Little is known about the earliest history of Cuba—when, like so many precolonial Caribbean islands, it was inhabited by Arawak, or Taino, natives. Columbus landed on Cuba in 1492, and within a decade, extensive Spanish settlements were present on the island. The generally mild climate and the fine natural harbor of the capital of **Havana** made Cuba a natural stopping point for seaborne traffic sailing between Europe and central and South America; during the days of Spanish occupation, sugar cane was Cuba's chief agricultural product. To this day, more than half of Cubans are black or mulatto, descendants of the black African slaves who were brought to work on the island's sugar plantations in the 19th century.

By the late 1800s, the Cuban independence movement began to stir, and in an uprising led by a poet named José Martí, the island cast off Spanish rule in the 1890s. In 1898, the sinking of the USS *Maine* by a Spanish mine in Havana harbor, which resulted in 274 crew deaths, precipitated the Spanish-American War and bolstered U.S. support of Cuba, which would continue through the early 20th century. By the 1950s, however, relations with the U.S. rapidly deteriorated when a young lawyer named Fidel Castro fomented opposition to then-president Batista's corrupt police state, which finally resulted in Castro assuming the flailing reins of the Cuban state in 1959. It quickly became clear to the U.S. that Castro was adopting Marxist principles and suppressing political freedoms, and soon the Communist Soviet Union stepped in as a Cuban ally. It was at this time that thousands of Cubans fled the island to start a new life in America; most of them went to the nearby shores of Florida.

Political opinions aside, Fidel Castro's staying power and global influence throughout the second half of the 20th century and beyond has been remarkable. Though Fidel is officially in retirement now due to poor health, he continues to wield some authority through his brother and current Cuban president, Raul Castro. Cubans are well educated but living in poverty, and almost everything Cuban nationals or visitors do is subject to scrutiny by the secret police; the barter system is used to acquire just about everything. Recently, however, the government has passed a series of civil liberties for Cuban citizens, perhaps signaling a new era for the country as the 21st century progresses. Though the U.S. still stands alone in the world in prohibiting open travel to the island (via a trade embargo that stemmed from the Cuban Missile Crisis of 1962), relations between the U.S. and Cuba also appear to be thawing. In 2009, Cuban-Americans were granted permission to travel freely to the island.

Visiting Cuba today is truly like going to another place in time, like stepping into the pages of a dark comic book. The streets are filled with cars from the Eisenhower era, salsa music, and men playing dominoes in tailored straw hats. For a real throwback, go for a drink at the rooftop bar of the **Hotel Nacional** in Havana—you'll swear you time-warped back to the 1950s. Havana may be the focus of political headlines, but there's also much more to Cuba for the traveler than the capital. With golden beaches that meet gentle turquoise water for miles on end, diving sites in the coral islets offshore, and nightlife, **Varadero** (on the north coast, east of Havana) is the principal destination in Cuba for sun-and-sand tourism. Remote **Baracoa,** on the mountainous far-eastern tip of the island, is the place to go for an exotic feel: Here, in a lush tropical landscape of banana and palm trees, is where Christopher Columbus landed in Cuba on his first voyage to the Americas. Baracoa is part of Guantánamo province, which has numerous natural attractions, like the 305m-high (1,000-ft.) **Salto Fino waterfall,** as well as one very famous United States–run prison.

Whatever the island has been subjected to under Castro, what strikes you most about the people you'll encounter here is their incredible warmth and soul: Cubans are underdogs, and their rich culture thrives regardless of economic or political realities on the island. —*SM*

ⓘ U.S. travelers should check http://travel.state.gov for updates on travel to Cuba. All others can visit www.cubancan.cu.

✈ José Martí International (Havana).

🛏 $$ **Hotel El Castillo,** Calle Calixto García, Baracoa (✆ **537/214-5195**). $$$ **Hotel Nacional de Cuba,** Calle 21 y O, Vedado, Havana (✆ **537/836-3564;** www.hotelnacionaldecuba.com).

9 Islands of Mystery

Ancient Marvels 

Easter Island

Mute Witnesses

Chile

Though it may be the most remote inhabited place on earth—4,000km (2,485 miles) off the coast of Chile—Easter Island lives on tourism. And just about every visitor comes here to see the same thing: an enigmatic horde of some 600 immense stone figures hewn from dark volcanic tufa rock.

You can't deny the power of these sculptures. The faces are huge, with jutting brows and square jaws and startling white coral eyeballs. Every statue is strikingly individual, which suggests that they represented specific ancestors rather than gods. They were designed to be mounted grandly on ceremonial stone platforms, ringed around the edge of the island.

But these big statues are shrouded in mystery. Fossil evidence suggests that **Rapa Nui** (the native name, which means "Navel of the World") was once covered with palm trees, which the original islanders may have razed during a frenzy of statue building—an act that spelled environmental doom for this isolated population. (Trees are being replanted, but it's still a shadeless place.) Because that first population died out, no oral tradition has been passed down to explain why the statues, or **moais,** were built; many were found lying half-finished in an inland quarry, tumbled carelessly on their sides, or abandoned midroute to their pedestals. When the first Europeans visited the islands in 1722, the moais were upright; 50 years later, the next visitors found them knocked over, whether by desperate islanders or by hostile neighbors we'll never know.

Even more baffling, how were such massive sculptures built by such primitive people? Experts assume that the moais were hauled from the quarry to the coast on a wooden sledge atop log rollers—hence the need for cutting down trees. Apparently the eyes weren't added until they were levered upright onto the platforms. Perhaps the islanders thought the eyes gave the moais spiritual power—when the statues were knocked from their platforms, most were toppled face forward, as if to hide the eyes in shame.

Some statues have been reerected; they stand in an inscrutable row, staring wordlessly over this volcanic blip in the middle of the Pacific. Tourism is now Easter Island's main economic base; there are a handful of basic hotels and restaurants, along with tour guides (besides the moais, there are a few ancient temples, cave paintings, and petroglyphs to see), watersports operators (the island has some lovely white-sand beaches), and stables for horse trekking. From November to March, a stream of planes from Santiago, full of package tourists, land on the island's tiny airstrip; cruise ships pull up, disgorging 800 to 900 passengers at a time; private island-hopping charter planes pop in, letting privileged travelers snap a few shots of the moais, then jet off somewhere else. Dependent on tourist dollars, modern-day Easter Islanders are exploiting their last precious resource as carelessly as their ancestors exploited those now-vanished forests. Will they be able to safeguard these mysterious sites before it's too late? —*HH*

ⓘ www.chile.travel.

✈ Mataveri (on Easter Island) 5½ hr. from Santiago.

Previous page: Moais on Easter Island.

$$ **Hotel Taura'a,** Atamu Tekema, Hanga Roa (✆ **56/32/210-0463;** www.tauraahotel.cl). $$$ **Posada de Mike Rapu,** Te Miro Oone (✆ **866/750-6699** in the U.S., or 56/2/206-6060 in Santiago; www.explora.com).

TOUR **Wilderness Travel** (✆ **800/368-2794** in the U.S. or 510/558-2488; www.wildernesstravel.com).

376 Ancient Marvels

Huahine

Acropolis of the South Seas

Blame the Protestant missionaries. In their zeal to save the souls of the natives living on this paradisiacal South Pacific archipelago, they had to knock down the old temples. Christianity was a natural fit for the Polynesians, who, although they worshiped many gods, regarded one as the supreme being. But in their stone temples, or maraes, idols were lined up on altars, and live offerings were sacrificed on another stone. That simply *would not do.*

And so, throughout Polynesia, the maraes were systematically destroyed—or most of them were. But not on the Society island of Huahine (pronounced *Who*-a-hee-nay). Ruled by a single powerful chieftain, Huahine remained fiercely independent for a long time—it did not become a French possession until 1897, more than 50 years after Tahiti 319. And with less missionary interference, an extraordinary number of maraes survived. Around the

Huahine Nui and Huahine Iti.

village of **Maeva,** on the shores of Lake Fauna Nui, the remains of some 40 maraes have been restored, making it one of the world's most important archaeological sites. They may not have the same eerie power as the giant moais on Easter Island 375, but in their own way they present a more complete window into the ancient mysteries of this once nearly obliterated culture.

Like so many of its sister islands, Huahine—which is actually two islands, **Huahine Nui** and **Huahine Iti,** enclosed by the same unspoiled coral reef—offers the whole checklist of Polynesian amenities: splendid beaches, turquoise lagoons, jagged peaks of dark volcanic rock, reed-thatched huts, and lush tropical groves of breadfruit, mango, banana, and papaya trees, along with some of the friendliest islanders in all of the Society Island chain. It's almost impossible to believe that it's real and not some Disneylandish movie set. South of the airport, at the north end on Huahine Nui, the main town of **Fare** still preserves the atmosphere of a plantation-era South Seas trading port.

But in precolonial times the island's power center was across the island at Maeva, where the chieftain's families lived. West of Maeva village, by the lake you'll see **Fare Potee,** a reconstruction of a traditional reed-sided meetinghouse that stood here in 1925. Historical markers here give you great background on the maraes. Lying at the heart of a tribal community, a marae was the site of all important ceremonies. Only priests and chiefs could enter the *tapu,* or sacred terrace, often encircled by a dry-stone wall; upon the *tapu* stood an *ahu,* or great altar, along with smaller stones for offerings. Smaller stone shelters outside the *tapu* were used as tombs or shrines. A few maraes surround the meetinghouse, with six more located up a steep path on Matairea Hill. Follow the lakeshore east across the bridge to see the large **Manunu Marae;** in the water nearby you'll also see several restored stone fish traps, built to catch fish as the tides flow in and out to sea. It's easy here to imagine life as the ancient Polynesians lived it—a paradise that was never lost. —*HH*

ⓘ www.tahititourisme.com/islands/huahine/huahine.asp.

✈ Huahine (35 min. from Papeete, Tahiti).

🛏 $$ **Pension Mauarii,** Avea Beach (✆ **689/68-86-49;** www.mauarii.com). $$$ **Te Tiare Beach,** Fiiti (✆ **888/600-8455** in the U.S., or 689/60-60-50; www.tetiarebeach.com).

TOUR Island Eco Tours (✆ **689/68-79-67;** pauljatallah@mail.pf).

Ancient Marvels

Savai'i

The Puzzle of Pulemelei

Samoa

The stepped pyramid of **Pulemelei** was clearly a Very Big Deal when it was first built—it's the biggest ancient structure in Polynesia, 65×60m (213×197 ft.) at its base, and 12m (39 ft.) high. Sitting silently, overgrown and crumbling, in the middle of the jungle, it still has an undeniable aura of power.

But when archaeologists dug Pulemelei—or Tia Seu, as some call it—out of the Samoan jungle in the 1950s, they had to admit they were stumped. They could date its stones and guess that the mound was built about A.D. 1100 to 1400, but the settlement that surrounded it was apparently mysteriously abandoned around 1700 to 1800, leaving no clues as to the mound's purpose. Was it a chieftain's residence, a ritual site for pigeon snaring, a sentry tower, a celestial observatory, or a place of worship? Were those stone pedestals at the corners of its leveled-off top ceremonial thrones for worthies, or receptacles for conch-shell trumpets, which were blown every night to call holy spirits back to this resting place?

Even Polynesian oral traditions don't agree—some claim that Pulemelei was built by the great god Togaloa; others say it was the launching point for the great West Polynesian Diaspora, which makes this place equally significant to Tahitians, Hawaiians, and New Zealand Maoris. Some even believe Pulemelei is the gateway to the afterlife, which explains the neatly aligned entryways scooped out of the earthen slopes on its east and west side, a feature found on no other such mound.

Pulemelei's island, Savai'i, is the largest in the volcanic South Sea archipelago of Samoa, but it's much more rugged than its neighbors. As South Pacific hideaways go, this is it: lush inland jungles and waterfalls, desolate-looking lava fields, and beach-edged lagoons that offer superb snorkeling. Amazingly, you'll find very few other tourists here, though it's only an hour's ferry ride or a 10-minute flight from the Samoan capital of Apia on Upolu Island 370.

Many historians consider Savai'i the cradle of Polynesian civilization—it was a major political capital, and any chieftain who lived here would have been powerful indeed.

Left alone, Pulemelei's pile of packed earth and basalt stones would soon be swallowed by jungle again. But that's another thing no one can agree on—what is to be done with Pulemelei. Located on an old copra plantation, Lesolo, it's still privately owned, and although the landowners would like to develop the site for tourism, local villagers have taken them to court to stop excavations, which they believe desecrate the holy site. When Thor Heyerdahl brought a team of archaeologists here in 2003, ritual fires were lit to purify the area, in case human remains were disturbed (Heyerdahl's people discovered none), but it's still a politically sensitive issue. Hire a local guide to lead you through the jungle to Pulemelei, and imagine what this site could look like, when—and if—it's ever done justice to. —*HH*

ⓘ **Tourist office,** Beach Rd., Apia (✆ **685/63-500;** www.samoa.travel).

✈ Savai'i.

⛴ Savai'i (1 hr. from Apia).

🛏 $$ **Kitano Hotel Tusitala,** Beach Walk St., Apia (✆ **685/21-122;** www.kitano.ws). $ **Tanu Beach Fales,** Tanu Beach, Savai'i (✆ **685/540-50;** www.samoa-hotel-accommodation.com).

378 Ancient Marvels

Pohnpei

Mysteries in Paradise

Senyavin Islands, Micronesia

One of the lushest islands in the Pacific is Pohnpei, the largest of the four states in the Federated States of Micronesia (FSM). Its jungly atmosphere is due to its rainfall—it gets more rain than any other island in the world besides Kauai 88. As a result, this island is rightfully famous for its breathtaking waterfalls, and many visitors choose to

Island Hopping on Lake Titicaca: Jewels in the Crown

It's the jewel of the Andes: a huge deep-blue freshwater lake sitting in its cup of mountain peaks, an awesome 3,800m (12,467 ft.) above sea level. To locals, however, measuring the altitude is irrelevant: Lake Titicaca is a mysterious and sacred place. According to myth, Viracocha, the creator deity, called up the sun, moon, and stars to rise from icy Lake Titicaca to lighten the dark world. Powerful spirits still live in this amazing sky-high lake, they say. Gliding over the calm blue surface, you may find yourself staring down into the water's cold depths to connect with them.

Set in the Andean *altiplano,* or high plateau, on the border between Peru and Bolivia, Lake Titicaca requires some advance planning. For one thing, will you arrive on the Bolivian side, through the picturesque lakeside town of Copacabana—a 3-hour bus ride from Bolivia's capital, La Paz—or will you arrive on the Peruvian side, through Puno, a 1-hour flight or 10-hour train ride from Cusco? Although it's possible to see the entire lake in one trip, it's a large body of water—176km (109 miles) long and 50km (31 miles) wide—and boat excursions out to its islands visit only one side or the other.

While the Bolivian tour boats take you to two islands that figure largely in local mythology—the Isla del Sol (Island of the Sun) and the Isla del Luna (Island of the Moon)—the Peruvian side offers the most intriguing option: a tour to the 379 **Uros islands,** or Los Islas Flotantes, perhaps the most unique islands in this book. Centuries ago, in order to escape Inca oppression, the Uros Indians began to live literally on the lake, in the reedy shallows just off the lakeshore, on tiny floating islands woven of the local totora reeds. Continually repairing and replenishing these dense pads is part of their daily routine; the islets—there are around 40 of them at any given time—last roughly 30 years before the base rots away in the lake depths. Tour boats visit a few of the larger islands, whose residents wait intently for the tourists, ready to hawk their handmade textiles and reed-crafted items—a blatant commercialism that spoils the anthropological experience for some travelers. Other Uros, however, keep to their own smaller thatched islands, far from the snapping cameras, where they quietly fish and catch birds. When you get out of the tour boats, the strange sensation of walking on the springy islets—almost like being on a mattress—may make you giggle at first. Several hundred people live on this string of islands; besides the residents' huts, various islands have schools, a post office, a public telephone, a small hotel, and souvenir shops—the largest island, Huacavacani, even has a Seventh-Day Adventist church. Though their houses are modest, the canoes that they pole around the lake—also made of reeds—are works of art, often with fancy prows shaped like animal heads. For a small fee (of course), locals may offer to give you a short ride in the boats.

Isla Suasi.

While you can visit the Uros islands on a half-day tour—many operators run excursions from Puno, at quite reasonable prices—the full-day excursions are a better option, because once you've seen the novelty of the floating islands, you'll continue on to the natural beauty of 380 **Taquile island,** out in the middle of the lake about 35km (22 miles) east of Puno. Long and narrow Taquile rises steeply in the middle, its hillsides stepped with terraces in the traditional Inca fashion; it's a steep climb from the docks to the main village, but when you turn around, the views of the lake are breathtaking. Residents still follow a traditional lifestyle, farming and weaving extraordinary fine textiles; although they welcome outsiders—some even offer meals or overnight accommodation in their simple homes—they still speak native Quechua and have no electricity. They do, however, have a few solar panels, which somehow feels apt, considering how close to the sun their high-altitude village is.

Overnight tours allow you also to visit 381 **Amantani** island, 2 hours north of Taquile. Rockier and more barren than Taquile, it is nonetheless beautiful, with fragments of Inca and pre-Inca ruins and a handful of farming villages. Two peaks dominate the round island—Pachatata (Father Earth) and Pachamama (Mother Earth)—and hiking up their slopes gives you an incredible panorama of fields, terraces, grazing cows and alpacas, and the sparking blue lake surrounding it all. The islanders' communal lifestyle welcomes visitors to stay in local homes or eat with families, or even join in village celebrations, where intricate folkloric dances are accompanied by Andean flutes and panpipes. As on Taquile, the handcrafted clothing items sold in the village shop are extraordinary.

View of Lake Titicaca.

For the ultimate Titicaca experience, however, you may want to splurge on a visit to private 382 **Isla Suasi,** home to a few llamas and vicuñas and one solar-powered luxury resort hotel (built of traditional adobe and stone with a thatched roof). It can take up to 6 hours to get to this tiny, isolated island by boat from Puno (generally visiting the Uros and Taquile islands en route), but the payoff is gorgeous 360-degree Titicaca vistas, mind-blowing high-altitude sunsets, and total peace and quiet. There's not much to do except read in a hammock, enjoy a traditional eucalyptus sauna, canoe around the island (you circumnavigate it in an hour), dine on locally grown Andean specialties, and stargaze at night, so close to heavens you almost feel you can touch the stars. *—HH*

(i) **Tourist office,** Plaza de Armas, Puno (✆ **51/1/574-8000** or 51/51/365-088; www.peru.info).

✈ Manco Capac, Juliaca, Peru (45km/28 miles from Puno).

🛏 $$$ **Isla Suasi Eco-Lodge,** Isla Suasi (✆ **866/447-3270** in the U.S. or 51/1/213-9739; www.casa-andina.com). $ **Kantuta Lodge,** Isla Amantani (✆ **51/9/636-172** or 51/9/812-664; www.punored.com/titicaca/amantani/img/lodge.html). $$ **Sonesta Posada del Inca,** Sesquicentenario 610, Sector Huaje, Puno (✆ **800/766-3782** in the U.S. or 51/51/364-111; www.sonesta.com laketiticaca).

camp near one of them, letting the water lull them to sleep. And why not totally immerse yourself in this gorgeous island of rivers and high, mountainous peaks? Its tropical splendor is a luxury not to be missed.

Pohnpei has the largest population in the FSM, with approximately 34,000 inhabitants, known for their hospitality. Many visitors come here to enjoy world-class surfing or to explore the island's jungly terrain, looking for rare bird species and other wildlife. It isn't uncommon to find that the room in your hotel has a visitor: Colorful geckos abound here.

But there is another compelling reason to visit this paradise: The ruins of the ancient city of **Nan Madol** are just off the eastern coast of the island. The city—known as the "Venice of the Pacific"—is actually a series of small artificial islands linked by canals, begun in the 8th or 9th century. It is believed that some of the islets were used for specific purposes, such as food preparation on **Usenamw,** and canoe making on **Dapahu.** Many others are thought to have been used specifically as homes for the priests. It's a spot that poses many more questions than it answers, making this historic landmark one of our modern marvels. I recommend arranging a tour through the Pohnpei Visitor's Bureau—a good guide can help explain the mysteries surrounding you.

Nan Madol's impressively tall, and, in some cases, large stone structures were built as homes for nobility and the priests who tended the mortuaries, although common people lived there as well. The royal mortuaries feature columnar basalt walls surrounding its tombs; the most impressive are located on the islet of **Nandauwas,** where a wondrously high 7.5m (25-ft.) wall stands around a tomb site. The homes of royalty and magicians were surrounded by pillars as well—these columns were definitely an indication of status.

The city was the heart of political and religious activities for the Saudeleur dynasty, which lasted for about 500 years, from 1100 to 1600 A.D., and it's thought that the island could have been part of the lost continent of Lemuria. The stones that made up the city are presumed to have been brought to the site from Pohnpei. The question of how these heavy stones were transported remains unknown, and to this day some natives of Pohnpei believe that magic was used. —*JD*

ⓘ **Pohnpei Visitor's Bureau,** Kolonia, Pohnpei (✆ **691/320-4851;** www.visit-fsm.org).

✈ Pohnpei International Airport.

🛏 $ **Cliff Rainbow Hotel,** Pohn Rakied St, Pohnpei (✆ **691/320-2415**). $ **Harbor View Hotel,** Kolonia, Pohnpei (✆ **691/320-5244**).

Ancient Marvels **383**

Yonaguni Island

Underwater Monument

Japan

At Japan's western point, just off the coast of Taiwan 227, lies tiny Yonaguni, a quiet island of about 2,000 people who live simple, traditional lives. Over the years it has attracted divers, drawn by its large population of hammerhead sharks. In 1987, a diver named Kihachiro Artake made a discovery that would lure even more tourists to this tiny island: a massive pyramid-shaped underwater rock formation off its southern coast. It's now known as the **Yonaguni Monument** and consists of sandstone and mudstones thought to be deposited 20 million years ago.

There is some debate over whether the formation is natural or man-made: Some scholars believe its flat parallel angles and right angles suggest that humans may have had a hand in constructing the monument, when the sea level was lower and the rock was above water, which would have been about 6,000 years ago. It's questionable whether humans had the tools then to modify it at all, making a facelike formation on its side even more mysterious.

Those who favor the theory that it occurred naturally cite that there are similar, smaller formations on other parts of the island and assert that what look to be drawings are actually just scratches on the rock. Either way, the monument makes for great viewing and plenty of divers are willing to brave the strong currents to get a close look. You can check it out for yourself with a guided tour through **Yonaguni Diving Service,** Kubura (✆ **81/9/8087-2658;** www.yonaguniyds.com).

Although known primarily for its underwater attractions, Yonaguni also boasts many aboveground rock formations, the most famous being **Tatigamiiwa,** or "standing god rock," which is near the underwater ruins. Islanders who practice the island's religion use this spot as a place of worship.

The best way to view Tatigamiiwa and to get around the island in general is by rental car; you'll find many photo ops (uncrowded beaches and wild ponies, to name just two) along the way. The island also offers a real chance to experience a traditional Japanese village—the sort of place where people leave their sliding doors open to catch the ocean breezes. These inhabitants even speak a unique dialect that developed over centuries of isolation—not to worry, though, the island culture is laid-back and very welcoming to visitors. It's not uncommon to be invited to share a cup of its famous sake—some of the strongest made in the world—with the hosts of your hotel. **Open Coast** (www.opencoastravel.com) runs a tour around Yonaguni that visits some sake factories and includes samples.

The main village, **Sonai,** in the north, has the most to offer visitors in terms of hotels and restaurants, but don't miss a trip to **Kuburba** and, just north of that village, to **Kuburabaria,** a cliff offering dazzling views of the sunset and to the mysterious depths below. —*JD*

ⓘ www.city.ishigaki.okinawa.jp/International/yonaguniisland.html.

✈ Yonaguni Airport.

🛏 $ **Irifuku Ryokan,** Sonai, 907-1801 (✆ **81/9/8087-2017**). $ **Minshuku Sakihara,** Sonai (✆ **81/9/8087-2976**).

Ancient Marvels

Inishmore (Inis Mór)

A Gaelic Riddle

Aran Islands, Ireland

On a clear day you can see the offshore Aran Islands from both the Cliffs of Moher and the coastline of Connemara; tour guides are fond of pointing them out to busloads of tourists who'll never make it over the water. Yet with just a little effort—it's an easy day trip from Galway City—you'll discover a place where the mossy Celtic past seems tantalizingly close at hand. Many hardy locals still live in stone cottages, cast out to sea every day in small round *currachs* made of tarred canvas, and

Pony ride to Dun Aengus.

speak only Gaelic among themselves. Those bulky patterned sweaters of pale raw wool you'll see for sale in all the shops? Walk along Inishmore's rocky coves, or along its wind-swept cliff tops, and you'll realize why Aran Islanders *need* to wear sweaters like that.

As soon as you get off the ferry in Kilronan, take the path to the **Aran Heritage Center/Ionad Arann** (✆ **353/99/61355;** www.visitaranislands.com), where you can get a crash course in island history. If Kilronan's shops and pubs seem overwhelmed with ferry trippers—and sometimes in summer they are—rent a bike, hail a minivan, or, even better, hire an old-fashioned jaunting cart to get out and about the island.

It's only 7km (4⅓ miles) west to the island's chief attraction, the Iron Age fort of **Dún Aengus** (✆ **353/99/61008**), set broodingly at the eroding edge of a 90m-high (295-ft.) western sea cliff. Historians still haven't solved the mystery of who built Dún Aengus (or, in Gaelic, Dún Aonghasa)—it could have been an ancient Celtic tribe called the Fir Bolgs, who lived here a few centuries B.C., or it could have been 8th- or 9th-century Danes. Nor can scholars agree on what the fort was used for. When you walk up the hill (a 20-min. hike from the visitor center), you pass a chevaux-de-frise zone, where sharp stones jut defensively out of the ground, and its walls are certainly defensive—6m (20 ft.) high in some places, and the thickest 4.3m (14 ft.) thick. Yet the design of the structure—three concentric semicircles opening to the sea—looks more like a theater than a fortress. If it was a fort, why are there no dwellings inside, or any provision for bringing in water in case of siege? And within the centermost horseshoe, what is the purpose of that large table rock, almost like a sacrificial altar?

Whoever built it also felt the need to build several such structures nearby—leave the other tourists behind and visit the unexcavated **Dún Dubhchathair,** or Black Fort, 2km (1¼ miles) southwest; the circular terraced **Dún Eochla,** set inland at the island's crowning summit; and **Dún Eoghanacht,** commanding the island's western headlands, 7km (4⅓ miles) northwest. Though smaller than Dún Aengus, they have the same primitive power and the same sense of mystery. If only these stones could speak! —*HH*

ⓘ **Tourist office,** Kilronan waterfront (✆ **353/99/61263**).

✈ Inis Mór, **Aer Arann** (✆ **353/81/821-0210;** www.aerarann.com). Galway City (37km/23 miles from Rossaveal).

⛴ Kilronan (40 min. from Rossaveal).

🛏 $$ **Aran Islands Hotel,** Kilronan (✆ **353/99/61104;** www.aranislandshotel.com). $$ **Galway Harbour Hotel,** New Dock Rd., Galway City (✆ **353/91/569-466;** www.galwayharbourhotel.com).

385 Otherworldly Landscapes

Sylt

The Shape-Shifting Island

Germany

Beautiful people flock to the island of Sylt—one of Germany's most chic and expensive resort spots—to browse the upscale boutiques of **Kampen,** lounge on the white-sand beaches of **Rantum,** and "take the cure" at the spas of **Wenningstedt,** from mud baths to sunshine therapy (a fancy name for nude sunbathing). But there's a distinct fiddling-while-Rome-burns quality to it all. This long, skinny West Frisian island—the northernmost place in Germany—is practically nothing but beach, and that beach is disappearing every day.

In fact, Sylt (pronounced *Zoolt*) has existed only since 1362, when the Great Mandrenke flood deposited so much sediment in the sea that it built up into a long T-shaped sand spit running parallel to the coast of Denmark. The island is still only about 550m (1,800 ft.) wide at its narrowest point, depending on which day you measure it. Reminders of Sylt's exposure lie everywhere—in the iodine tang of the air, the constant whipping winds, the rain-soaked climate that Germans call *Reizklima;* even the most fashion-conscious visitors regularly go about in yellow slickers, nicknamed Sylt "mink."

This remarkably fragile ecosystem is constantly pummeled by North Sea surf on the west; in contrast, the tranquil Wadden Sea on the east is so shallow, it turns to marshy mud flats at low tide (attracting hordes of migratory water birds, it has become a bird sanctuary). Sylt's sand dunes shift by as much as 3 to 4m (10–13 ft.) a year, despite the islanders' ongoing efforts to stabilize them by planting marram grass and hardy wild Siberian roses. Sheep are grazed on man-made sea dikes, in hopes they'll pack down the soil with their hooves; some islanders have even built homes atop the dikes. But storm surges continue to gnaw away at the land; on some mornings after violent storms, vast areas of beach simply disappear, sucked out into the North Sea. For centuries, the citizens of Sylt desperately built groins and breakwaters to stave off destruction, but nothing seems to work. While sunbathing on Sylt's soft white strands, in the distance you'll see barges pumping sand from offshore depths, which will later be dumped by bulldozers back onto the fugitive beaches.

Despite the jet set invaders, Sylt preserves its traditional Frisian culture, especially on the eastern peninsula known as **Sylter Friesendörfer,** or Sylt's Frisian Villages—Tinnum, Keitum, Munkmarsch, Archsum, and Morsum. Here you'll find villages full of reed-thatched cottages (visit the restored **Old Frisian House** in Keitum), and people who still speak the local dialect Söl'ring, a quirky blend of Danish, Dutch, and English. Every year on the night of February 21, the islanders celebrate **Biikebrennen,** an ancient pagan rite in which towering stacks of wood on the beaches are set ablaze, lighting the night sky. Afterward, everyone adjourns to local restaurants for a traditional dinner featuring savory kale (distinctly seaweedy in appearance), while those bonfires flicker on through the long northern night, driving away winter, appeasing the ravenous gods of the sea. —*HH*

ⓘ **Tourist office,** Strandstrasse 35, Westerland (✆ **49/4651/82020;** http://en.sylt.de or www.westerland.de).

✈ Sylt.

Westerland (around 3 hr. from Hamburg, via railroad causeway from Niebüll).

Rømø-Sylt Line (✆ **49/180/3103-030;** www.syltfaehre.de). List (from Havneby, Denmark), 40 min.

$$ **Hotel Wünschmann,** Andreas-Dirks-Strasse 4 (✆ **49/4651/5025;** www.hotel-wuenschmann.de). $$$ **Stadt Hamburg,** Strandstrasse 2 (✆ **49/4651/8580;** www.hotelstadthamburg.com).

Otherworldly Landscapes 386

Staffa

Where the Sea Sings

Inner Hebrides, Scotland

Barely one kilometer long and half a kilometer wide, Staffa's so small, it makes neighboring Iona 390 look gigantic. Nobody lives on this sparse little island in the Inner Hebrides; nobody has in the past century and a half. Even the sheep that used to browse on the scanty grass of its single upland plateau have been moved to other summer pastures. The forbidding black basalt cliffs of its headlands are a rigid row of distinctive hexagonal columns, which looked so much like a stockaded fort that early Viking visitors named it Staffa, or "pillar island" in old Norse.

But where there are sea cliffs there are often sea caves, gouged out of the rock by pelting rain and dashing sea, and Staffa's got a treasure-trove of them—Clamshell Cave and Goat Cave on the east; MacKinnon's Cave, Cormorant Cave, and Boat Cave on the southwest; and the biggest of them all, **Fingal's Cave** on the island's southern tip. Standing an imposing 20m (66 ft.) high and 75m (245 ft.) long, Fingal's Cave's vertical columns look eerily like the ribbed pillars of a Gothic church nave, inspiring many 19th-century admirers to describe it as a "cathedral of the sea." It's a romantic spot indeed, with swirling waters echoing and resounding inside—hence the Gaelic name, *An Uamh Ehinn,* which means "musical cave."

The melodic effects of this cave are its claim to fame, and indeed the main reason anybody visits Staffa. In the late 18th century, English artist Sir Joseph Banks came here and wrote glowingly of this picturesque cave, which he renamed Fingal's Cave, in tribute to the Irish hero Finn MacCool (after all, the Hebrides islands are not that far from Northern Ireland, where you'll see similar basalt columns in the Giant's

Causeway). Banks did such a good PR job for the cave that a stream of famous visitors arrived over the next several years, drawn by the early 19th-century Romantic movement's passion for grand, rugged, "sublime" natural landscapes. These travelers included, naturally, a raft of poets—Wordsworth, Keats, Tennyson, Sir Walter Scott, Robert Louis Stevenson—and even Queen Victoria herself. Felix Mendelssohn wrote a haunting air titled "Fingal's Cave" as one of the centerpieces of his Hebridean Symphony. J. M. W. Turner painted a renowned depiction of Fingal's Cave, a dramatic canvas full of boiling seas and lowering skies, in which the cave itself is almost totally hidden in a dazzling patch of fog.

Now owned and protected by the National Trust for Scotland, Staffa can be visited on tour boats from either Iona or Mull, which land on the rocky shallows; metal stairs and a walking path lead to a ledge inside Fingal's Cave. Come in summer and you can also cross the island to a spot where curious puffins, who nest on the cliffs, will land on the clifftop only a few feet away from you. —*HH*

(i) **Staffa Nature Preserve** (© **44/844/493-2237;** www.nts.org.uk/Property/64/).

✈ Glasgow International (140km/87 miles).

🚆 Oban (83km/52 miles).

⛴ Boat tours run Apr–Oct. From Oban: **Gordon Grant Tours** (© **44/1681/700-338;** www.staffatours.com). From Iona: **Staffa Trips** (© **44/1681/700-358;** www.staffatrips.f9.co.uk). From Mull: **Turus Mara** (© **44/1688/400-242;** www.turusmara.com).

🛏 $$ **Argyll Hotel** (© **44/1681/700-334;** www.argyllhoteliona.co.uk). $ **St. Columba Hotel** (© **44/1681/700-304;** www.stcolumba-hotel.co.uk).

387 Otherworldly Landscapes

Sardinia

Nomad of the Mediterranean

Italy

Italy's second-largest island (after Sicily 331), and the western Mediterranean's most centrally located, Sardinia is a striking case of how both isolation and equidistance from some of Europe's most illustrious civilizations contrive to create a unique and separate culture. Sardinia may display certain influences of its neighbors across the sea—Spain, France, Italy, and North Africa—but the whole is an entirely different animal from any of them. The character of this strange, often wonderful island is truly insular. In 1921, D. H. Lawrence penned words that still ring true: *This land does not resemble any other place. Sardinia is another thing: enchanting space around and distance to travel, nothing finished, nothing definitive.*

First of all, take the scenery: Much of Sardinia is drop-dead gorgeous with a capital *G*, from the alpine peaks of the **Gennargentu** mountain range to formidable offshore islands like **Isola Tavolara,** to the Caribbean-colored seawater all over the island that draws hordes of summer vacationers. As stunning as they are, these natural elements don't seem to belong—at least coming from an Italian frame of mind, where Venice looks Venetian, Rome looks Roman, Tuscany fits your notions of all things "Tuscan," and so on. You may come to Sardinia not knowing what to expect, aesthetics-wise, and still find yourself surprised by the microcosm of landscapes on this 24,000-sq.-km (9,266-sq.-mile) island.

Thanks to hundreds of years of European maritime powers fighting for control of their ports, the coastal cities of Sardinia have some stellar examples of architecture, like the 14th-century Pisan forts in the capital of **Cagliari,** or the charming Catalan ensemble that is the northwestern city of **Alghero** (hands down, my favorite city on the island). By and large, however, Sardinia is the one Italian region that basically gives you a break from the museum-and-monument shuffle. Its only archaeological claims to fame are the beehive-shaped stone buildings called *nuraghi,* which date back several millennia. Thousands of these structures, whose use remains a mystery, exist on Sardinia, though the best is **Su Nuraxi di Barumini,** a UNESCO World Heritage Site.

The ace in the hole of Sardinian tourism is definitely *il mare.* The seacoast, with its crystal-clear water, is hard to resist. Most famous among Sardinia's summer destinations is the **Costa Smeralda** (Emerald Coast), stretching from Palau to Olbia in the northeast. The upper echelons of society and industry, like Italian Prime Minister Silvio Berlusconi, own villas here, in red-rock subdivisions that look uncannily like the American Southwest, and in synthetic towns like **Porto Cervo** and **Porto Rotondo,** international showgirls and soccer players drape themselves over the sun decks of yachts in the harbor. North of here is the more down-to-earth **La Maddalena** archipelago, with equally eye-popping Arizona-meets-the-sea geology. True Sardinia insiders scoff at the whole Costa Smeralda scene and urge vacationers to head for the (better) beaches elsewhere. The whole island is a Pandora's box of excellent places to spend a day in the sand, but one of my favorites is the neon-turquoise bath-water beach of **La Pelosa,** near Stintino at the northwest tip of Sardinia.

Trying to compare Sardinia to *la penisola* (mainland Italy) is wasted energy, and don't plan a trip here expecting to discover the newest frontier of untouristed Italy.

Sardinia.

This island, quite simply, does not match up with that romantic myth with which Italophiles are so in love. There are piazzas and cafes and wine bars here, but they're a lot sleepier. While Sardinians are quite friendly, it's a bit harder for a tourist to find that lively and inclusive community feel of so many other parts of Italy. The sheer size and diversity of Sardinia make it an enigma, and many travelers spend a lifetime trying to get to the heart of it. —*SM*

ⓘ www.sardegnaturismo.it.

✈ Cagliari-Elmas, Alghero-Fertilia, and Olbia (connections to Italy and Europe).

⛴ From several ports in Italy to Arbatax, Cagliari, Olbia, Palau, Porto Torres: Grandi Navi Veloci, Moby Lines, Tirrenia, Sardinia Ferries.

🛏 $$$ **El Faro Hotel,** Porto Conte, Alghero (✆ **39/079/942010;** www.elfarohotel.it). $$ **Monti di Mola,** Abbiadori, Porto Cervo (✆ **39/0789/96029**).

388 Otherworldly Landscapes

Chiloé

Time Passages

Chile

For centuries Chiloé, the largest island in the Chiloé archipelago, between 42 and 46 degrees south latitude off Chile's coast, has been a place of wonder. Its rolling green hills are shrouded with mist, giving the island a mystical air. It's divided by two peaks of coastal range and each offers its own delights; the west is dominated by beaches stretching for miles, otherworldly dunes, and temperate rainforests. Much of this area is protected as part of a national park, so its beauty is untouched. The east is dominated by pastureland, punctuated by several natural harbors and a number of smaller islands.

Visually appealing as it is, Chiloé is truly defined by its people, the hardy, character-rich Chilotes, who can still be seen plowing their fields with oxen or pulling in their catch of the day with old-fashioned nets. Life goes on pretty much as it has for centuries on this island—the second largest in Chile—giving visitors the feeling that they have gone back in time. Chiloé's isolation and resulting limited contact with the mainland have both allowed this island's unique way of life to be preserved and resulted in extreme poverty for many of its inhabitants. Most Chilotes rely on their livestock and what they can grow or catch to survive, and the majority of islanders count on a horse or boat for transportation.

When Spanish conquistadors settled here in the 16th century, they found the island inhabited by the Huiliche tribe, who continued their simple agricultural lifestyle of fishing and farming. Soon after, Jesuits arrived and established missions. Both groups were eventually forced off the island by natives, but their influence is still felt. The Spanish and natives married and the cultures merged, creating a tradition distinctly different from its mainland counterpart. The native faith is now a blend of Christianity and the island's traditional beliefs, which includes elements of witchcraft.

The beautiful **Bavarian, neoclassical-style churches** scattered throughout the island's many bays are the legacy of Catholicism introduced by the missionaries. Many of these architecturally important churches are World Heritage monuments. A close look inside each church offers numerous examples of techniques that were borrowed from shipbuilding, such as wooden pegs and joints instead of nails. The center of the roof, if imagined inverted, often resembles the hull of a boat, with three naves to a church. Moreover, nearly all the chapels in Chiloé face the water, with central towers that functioned as beacons for sailors.

Buses run in **Ancud** and **Castro,** the island's two major cities, as well as to the outdoors adventure spot **Chiloé National Park,** on the north coast. But the best way to get around the island is by car, stopping along the way to explore its bays, churches, and lookout points. (You will need to rent a car at the airport, in Puerto Montt or Puerto Varas, because there is no rental service available in Chiloé.) Keep in mind that the island's climate is cool and wet for most of the year (summer falls during the months of Jan and Feb), but with the right gear and spirit of adventure, you can take away memories of an island out of time. —*JD*

(i) www.chile-travel.com/chiloe.htm.

✈ Santiago.

⛴ From Pargua, Chile to Chacao port (35 min.).

🛏 $ **Hotel Casita Española,** Los Carrera 359 (✆ **56/65/632301;** www.hosteriadecastro.cl). $ **Hotel Galeón Azul,** av. Libertad 751 (✆ **56/65/622567;** www.hotelgaleonazul.cl).

Spiritual Centers **389**

Shikoku

Hiking the Way

Japan

Shikoku is the smallest of Japan's four main islands—but just try telling that to the footsore Buddhist pilgrims who've tramped its entire circumference. It's the most important pilgrimage in Buddhism, visiting 88 temples founded by the great Buddhist priest, poet, and scholar Kōbō Daishi. The founder of the Shingon Buddhist sect, Daishi—also known as Kūkai—was born an aristocrat on Shikoku in 774, but in his search for "the way" he became a wandering mountain priest for years. It's only fitting, therefore, that his legacy should be a thousand-mile-long hike.

Nestled in the Inland Sea, inside the curving southeastern coast of Honshu, Shikoku is mostly rural and mountainous; only since 1988 has it been connected to the larger island, by bridges to Okayama, Hiroshima, and Kobe. The traditional place for Japanese pilgrims, or *henro,* to start is actually on **Honshu,** at the monastery Kōbō Daishi founded on Mount Kōya, one of Japan's most sacred sites. After visiting Daishi's mausoleum there, you're supposed to hike back down the mountain and take a boat to Shikoku, landing in Tokushima.

The route then proceeds clockwise around Shikoku's coast, beginning in the town of **Naruto** (located today conveniently next to the bridge to Kobe) and completing the circuit back in Naruto again; those who began on Mount Kōya often return there to finish. In some areas, you'll visit a cluster of temples all in one day: Tokushima has four temples; Takamatsu, Saijo, and Zentsuji each have five; Imabari has six; and Matsuyama, the largest city on Shikoku, has eight. Even so, if you visit all 88 temples on foot—the purist's way—it would take around 2 months. The walking can be strenuous, too; given Shikoku's mountainous topography, nearly three-quarters of the temples are in the mountains, and a third of those are on mountaintops. That's why many modern pilgrims cover the longer and steeper stretches between temples by car, taxi, bus, or motorcycle; in fact, many take organized bus tours that speed through the whole circuit in 2 weeks. Even if you aren't doing the pilgrimage yourself, while on Shikoku you're bound to notice many pilgrims, who traditionally wear a white jacket and conical hat, and carry a walking stick and a little notebook to receive official stamps at every temple they visit. Many stay overnight in simple little B&Bs deliberately placed along the route, known as *minshuku*.

Pilgrims believe that visiting all 88 temples in order will elevate them from the cycle of reincarnation; another 20 smaller temples are added by many pilgrims to earn extra merit. Don't even consider doing a "greatest hits" version of the route; it's all 88 or nothing. Unlike other religious pilgrimages—to Mecca, for example or Jerusalem—this hike is not about your final destination but about the journey. What's striking about these Shikoku temples, actually, is how simple they are—not built for aristocrats, like some of Japan's more famous temples, but for ordinary folks. —*HH*

ⓘ www.wel-shikoku.gr.jp or www.shikokuhenrotrail.com.

✈ Tokushima, Takamatsu, or Matsuyama.

🚆 Tokushima or Matsuyama (6½ hr. from Tokyo by bullet train); Takamatsu (5 hr. from Tokyo by bullet train).

🛏 $$$ **ANA Hotel Clement Takamatsu,** 1-1 Hamano-cho, Takamatsu (✆ **877/424-2449** in the U.S. or 81/87/811-1111; www.ichotelsgroup.com). $ **Minshuku Miyoshi,** 3-7-23 Ishite, Matsuyama (✆ **81/89/977-2581**).

TOUR **Kinki Nihon Tourist** (✆ **81/3/3255-7137;** www.knt.co.jp).

Spiritual Centers

Iona

The Sacred Isle

Inner Hebrides, Scotland

When the outlaw Irish priest Colm Cille first arrived here in A.D. 563 with a dozen fellow monks, this mystical Druidic isle seemed a perfect home base. After all, they were men on a mission: to convert the pagan Scots to Christianity. While Colm Cille (later to be known as St. Columba) traveled tirelessly around Scotland, working miracles and founding churches, their island outpost evolved into a renowned center for classical learning—many believe the Book of Kells was painted here—throughout the Dark Ages.

The ascetic spirit of that early Christian community still hangs over this remote, treeless island. In summer, some 1,000 visitors a week step off the passenger ferry from the Isle of Mull (itself a 45-min. ferry trip from Oban), but they're mostly otherworldly sorts, intent on communing with ancient verities. You'll have to walk everywhere, though that's no hardship—the island is only 5.6km (3½ miles) long by 1.6km (1 mile) wide. The only village, **Baile Mor,** is a mere handful of houses and shops; sheep and cows wander freely about. Climb to the top of **Dun-I,** the hilltop ruins of an ancient Iron Age fort, and you can contemplate the ocean and the landscape in peace for hours.

St. Columba's original wattle-and-daub monastery grew to an entire complex, built with Norman-style solidity in the local pinkish granite. But over the years it was laid waste twice—first by 9th-century Norse invaders, then by the Reformation in 1560—

and it lay in ruins until the 20th century, when restoration efforts began. A new ecumenical religious group, the Iona Community, lives today on the grounds of the restored **Iona Abbey** (✆ **44/1681/700-512**), which encompasses the ruins of a Norman-era nunnery, the 11th-century St. Oran's Chapel, and square-towered Iona Cathedral, with its Norman arches and short round pillars. Despite the grand name, it's a surprisingly small and austere church, a jumble of styles from the 12th to the 16th century. Nearby, a grassy mound covers the ruins of the cell where St. Columba wrote and meditated. In front of the abbey stands one beautifully preserved Celtic stone cross, a lone survivor where hundreds once stood. Other relics are preserved in the abbey museum, set in the former infirmary of the monastery.

The monks of Iona played one other role: maintaining the eternal resting place of the kings of Scotland (lying over the water made it a safe place, where rival chieftains could not reach to desecrate their remains). Tradition claims that **St. Oran's Cemetery** holds the mossy graves—their inscriptions long ago obliterated—of 48 Scottish kings, including Macbeth and his rival Duncan.

You can learn more about the island's history at the **Iona Heritage Center** (✆ **44/1681/700-576**), set in an old parsonage between the nunnery ruins and the abbey. Interested visitors are welcome to stay overnight at the Abbey, to work, eat, and worship with the **Iona Community;** contact them at ✆ **44/1681/700-404** or www.iona.org.uk. —*HH*

ⓘ **Iona Community** (✆ **44/1681/700-404;** www.isle-of-iona.com).

✈ Oban (3 hr. from Glasgow).

⛴ Iona (10 min. from Fionnphort, Isle of Mull). **Caledonian MacBrayne ferries** (✆ **44/1688/302-017;** www.calmac.co.uk).

🛏 $$ **Argyll Hotel** (✆ **44/1681/700-334;** www.argyllhoteliona.co.uk). $ **St. Columba Hotel** (✆ **44/1681/700-304;** www.stcolumba-hotel.co.uk).

Spiritual Centers **391**

Patmos Island

Island of Churches

Greece

The lovely, unspoiled island of Patmos, situated 301km (187 miles) east of Piraeus, is sometimes called "The Jerusalem of the Aegean." It was here that St. John the Apostle, in exile and living in a cave, wrote the Book of Revelation in 95 A.D. The island is considered a sacred place, and religion plays a large role in its culture. Since the time of St. John, more than 300 churches have been built, one for every 10 citizens—of course, they attract many more people than that. Patmos has been a popular tourist destination for some time now, and beach resorts have sprung up to accommodate the many visitors. The tourists haven't changed the tenor of the island; however, first and foremost it is still a spiritual retreat.

Chora and Skala are the main towns on the island. **Chora** is home to its most famous attraction: the **Monastery of St. John,** a fortresslike structure constructed to deter pirate attacks. The walls reach over 15m (49 ft.) high and are made of thick, solid stone. Above the entrance is a small opening once used to pour hot oil or water onto the heads of intruders. Central to the monastery is its beautiful main chapel, with frescoes dating to the 12th century. It also houses a fabulous collection on Byzantine treasures. Like all of the island's places of worship, this monastery is Greek Orthodox.

About halfway down from the monastery is the **Cave of the Apocalypse,** where Saint John did his writing. The cave is encased with a sanctuary and surrounded by a convent. This is where St. John was said to have received visions from Christ that inspired his stories—it is also said that he heard God's voice through a cleft in the rock. At the cave's entrance you can see a mosaic representing his visions along with an indentation thought to be where St. John rested his head each night.

The port town of Skala, founded in the 16th century, was once one of the most important ports in the Mediterranean. Today, it offers amenities like shops, restaurants, hotels, and bars. It also boasts a nice, sandy beach about 200m (656 ft.) from the port.

Unlike most Greek islands, there isn't much nightlife here; clubs open for a few weeks in high season, and then close. Neither the people of Patmos nor its visitors are expected to spend their days in prayer, but the Patmians expect—and deserve—a heavy dose of respect for their traditions. Patmos is in many ways a more subdued, civilized alternative to major tourist destinations. Perhaps best of all are the island's simple pleasures, like walking on the unmarked donkey paths while church bells peel all around you. —*JD*

ⓘ **Tourism office,** in the port town of Skala (✆ **30/22470/31-666**).

✈ Athens to Samos, Kos, or Leros, then hydrofoil.

⛴ Ferry from Samos (3 hr.) Kos (2.5 hr.) Leros (40 min.); www.greeka.com/dodecanese/patmos/island/patmos-ferries.htm.

🛏 $ **Australis Hotel and Apartments,** Skala (✆ **30/22470/32-562**). $$ **Blue Bay Hotel,** Skala (✆ **30/22470/31-165;** www.bluebaypatmos.gr).

392 Spiritual Centers

Isla de Janitzio

Day of the Dead

Mexico

The first sight you'll see when you approach Isla de Janitzio in the Mexican state of Michoacán is its most famous: a giant statue of **Jose Maria Morelos,** the famous Mexican independence fighter. At 47m (156 ft.) high, it's hard to miss; with an arm raised high in the air, the iconic concrete statue looks out over surrounding Lake Pátzcuaro, where native Purpechan fisherman have fished for centuries. You can reach this small volcanic island on a day trip by boat, but when you get there, you'll have to navigate its narrow, picturesque streets by foot; no cars are allowed on the island. That's just as well, because the streets are dominated by tiny stalls selling food and colorful native crafts—half the fun is becoming part of the crowd.

There is no lodging on the island itself, but shelter can be found on nearby **Pátzcuaro,** a small colonial village about 20 minutes away by boat, known for its colonial architecture and also as the ferry port to the island. Once on land on Janitzio, you can enjoy stunning views from the top of the Morelos statue by taking the spiral staircase inside. The interior features murals chronicling Morelos's life, painted by the famous muralist Ramon Alba de la Canal. Although the steps are steep, it's

Isla de Janitzio.

worth the climb to see a visual history of Mexico's fight for independence. The giant peepholes in the statue's fist also offer stunning views of the island and surrounding Lake Pátzcuaro. The island is the largest in the lake, and is known for fresh *pescado blanco* (whitefish), a local delicacy. A highlight for many visitors is simply watching the island's fishermen dipping their delicate-looking butterfly nets in and out of the water to catch these fish.

Janitzio's biggest claim to fame, however, is as a destination spot for the celebration of ***Noche de los Muertos,*** or Day of the Dead, celebrated from October 31 to November 2. Since tourism is one of the main means of income for the island, visitors are welcomed to the festival, which honors loved ones who have passed away through candlelight vigils at the cemetery. Tombs are decorated for the events, and families gather to honor their ancestors. The main attraction takes place on November 1, when hundreds of candlelit boats arrive. Visitors carry the candles to the cemetery, where they observe a custom long practiced by the Catholic natives. Although the point is to honor the dead, it is by no means a somber celebration—alcohol flows freely.

Perhaps the biggest impression you'll take away on any trip to this island is made by its people, known as the Purepecha. They've managed to maintain their culture, traditions, and native dress despite outside influences, and many older residents have never left the island. By freely sharing their culture and traditions with visitors, they help make any trip here a personal and almost spiritual experience. *—JD*

ⓘ www.tourbymexico.com/michoa/michoa.htm.

✈ Pátzcuaro-Morelia Airport.

⛴ Pátzcuaro Pier (20 min.).

🛏 $ **Hotel Mansion Iturbe,** Portal Morelos 59, Pátzcuaro (✆ **52/434-342-0368**). $ **La Casa Encantata,** Dr. Cross #15, Pátzcuaro (✆ **52/434-342-3492;** www.lacasaencantada.com).

393 Historic Haunts

Roanoke Island

The Lost Colony

North Carolina, U.S.

Roanoke Island can lay claim to many American firsts: It's where the first English colony was established in the New World and it's where the first English baby was born in the New World. But Roanoke Island's claim to fame doesn't get the kind of fanfare extended to Plymouth, say, or Jamestown. That's because the colony of more than 100 settlers simply vanished from sight. Even today, more than 400 years later, the mystery of what happened remains unsolved.

The story goes something like this: In the race between England and Spain to claim America's riches, one of Queen Elizabeth's palace favorites, Walter Raleigh, sent out an intrepid band of settlers to put roots down in the New World. Captain John White, who would later plant the seeds for the first *permanent* colony in America at Jamestown, was the leader. Among the 17 women onboard was Smith's daughter, Eleanor Smith Dare, who would give birth in the New World to Virginia Dare.

Upon arrival on the shores of North Carolina in 1587, the colony built a palisades and encampment. Arriving too late to plant crops, the settlers struggled to prepare provisions for winter. Captain White decided to sail back to England for supplies, but when he returned, his country was at war with Spain. White was unable to return to the Roanoke Colony for more than 3 years. When he sailed back, in 1590, the settlers were gone, the structures dismantled. All that remained was the word croatan crudely carved into a post of the fort.

The settlement site, now the **Fort Raleigh National Park,** holds few clues to the colony's brief existence. It's a quiet, lovely place, where birds trill and sun-dappled oaks shade nature trails. Inside the park is an outdoor theater, with views of Roanoke Sound, where every summer Pulitzer Prize–winning playwright Paul Green's gripping dramatization of the colony and its disappearance, ***The Lost Colony*** (www.thelostcolony.org), is staged. Many actors got their start playing summer stock here, including Andy Griffith, Terence Mann, and Chris Elliot. Next door is the beautiful **Elizabethan Gardens** (✆ **252/473-3234;** www.elizabethangardens.org), which features an Elizabethan rose garden, a sunken garden, and a Shakespearean herb garden.

Elizabeth II ship and kayakers, Roanoke.

Island Hopping the Marquesas: Mystical Spires in the South Seas

Gothic peaks of volcanic rock rise straight out of the ocean, and there isn't an overwater bungalow in sight. The Marquesas are French Polynesia's odd man out, an island group of rugged terrain that bears little resemblance to the typical South Seas getaway. There are few sandy beaches here, no neon-bright turquoise waters of a lagoon, no honeymooners on package tours. Instead, the Marquesas offer soaring and lush mountainous scenery and a very back-to-basics travel experience. The Marquesas are for the adventurous and the flexible; getting here and around requires planning, and ultimately surrendering to island time (and the weather) in a major way. In fact, yachting is the best and most popular way to see the Marquesas. The two larger islands, Nuku Hiva and Hiva Oa, have the Marquesas' only international-level accommodations and broadest range of recreation and services, but if you embark on a jaunt to the wilder islands of the group, you'll find unforgettable encounters with primordial nature and centuries-old culture.

Waterfalls in the Marquesas.

Known in local dialects as Te Henua Enata ("Land of Men"), the Marquesas Islands are a 350km-long (217-mile) chain about 1,400km (870 miles) northeast of Tahiti 319. Of the 12 islands, only 6 are inhabited, with a total population of fewer than 9,000. (Before Europeans arrived here in the 16th c. and brought devastating diseases like smallpox with them, the native population was well over 100,000.) The islands' lofty interiors are littered with the overgrown remains of stone housing platforms that haven't been used in hundreds of years. That suggestive archaeology, combined with some of Polynesia's most impressive tiki sculptures, gives the Marquesas a mystical feel: The spirits of past generations are tangible here. Paul Gauguin came to the Marquesas to find the primitive life that inspired his art, and if Indiana Jones ever had a South Seas quest, the Marquesas would be a natural place to film.

Nuku Hiva and Hiva Oa are easily reached from Tahiti, as there are daily flights from Papeete. Less frequent air service connects Nuku Hiva and Hiva Oa with Ua Huka and Ua Pou, the only other islands with airstrips. For travel to any other Marquesan island, it's by sea only. The best way to island-hop in the Marquesas, unless you're on a yacht, is aboard the *Aranui 3,* a freighter–cum–cruise ship that sails from Rangiroa in Tahiti and makes a 15-day circuit of the Marquesas. The *Aranui 3* stops at all the islands listed here.

394 **Hiva Oa,** and the harbor town of Atuona, is many people's first port of call in the Marquesas, especially for sailboats making the crossing west over the Pacific. This is also the most historic island in the group, with giant stone tikis and maraes (ancient sacred sites), as well as the grave of painter Paul Gauguin, who died here in 1903. The excellent **Tohua Papa Nui (Paul Gauguin Cultural Center)** in Atuona provides context for his time here. Hiva Oa is blessed with untamed scenery and majestic views,

especially at Puamau Bay, a partially collapsed crater. Hiva Oa's Tehueto petroglyphs are the island's must-see attraction; you can get there by hiking, by horseback riding, or with an off-road vehicle and guide. A common side trip from Hiva Oa is the small island of 395 **Tahuata,** which is accessed strictly by boat (4km/2½ miles from Hiva Oa). Tahuata's villages, Vaitahu and Hapatoni, and warm people make for low-key exploring, and their expert bone carvings are authentic souvenirs. Even farther south, the island of 396 **Fatu Hiva** can be visited by boat from Hiva Oa (or aboard the *Aranui 3*). Fatu Hiva has stunning precipitous cliffs and a booming export business in tapa (cloth made from the bark of local trees like banyan). Hanavave valley is Fatu Hiva's showstopper and the main reason to make the trek out to this far-flung island: The valley is punctuated with tiki-shaped spires protruding from sharp ridges descending from the old crater wall.

Arguably the most beautiful island in the Marquesas, 397 **Nuku Hiva** is also the largest, and known for its arresting cliffs, cathedral spires of rock, and towering waterfalls. Mount Muake's steep slopes, rising abruptly to an elevation of 864m (2,835 ft.), form the backdrop to **Taiohae,** the administrative capital of the Marquesas and a lively port, especially during the yachting season. Nuku Hiva's gorgeous topography provides many opportunities for outdoorsy types to get out and explore, whether by 4x4 vehicle, sturdy Marquesan horse, or your own hiking feet. Given the rugged nature of the island's terrain, it's always best to go with a guide, which can be arranged at Nuku Hiva's one and only resort, the Keikahanui Nuku Hiva Pearl Lodge. Nuku Hiva's Taipivai Valley, a destination for many day-trippers from Taiohae, was the inspiration for Herman Melville's novel *Typee.* (He spent time here in 1842.) The seaside village of Hatiheu here is among the most picturesque in the South Pacific. For archaeology buffs, the area is filled with ancient petroglyphs and tiki.

Some 40km (25 miles) east of Nuku Hiva, 398 **Ua Huku** may not be blessed with the physical attributes of some other Marquesan islands, but it's a compelling stop for its rich artistic traditions. The handicrafts made here—most notably, the woodcarvings—are simply exquisite. Ua Huku's harbor town of Vaipaee is set in a dramatic fjord.

399 **Ua Pou,** south of Nuku Hiva, has the Marquesas' highest point, Mount Oave, at 1230m (4,035 ft.). Ua Pou owes its name (it means "the columns"), and its fame as poster child for the Marquesas' stunning scenery, to Mount Oave's spirelike thumbs of basalt, reminiscent of Moorea 86. —*SM*

(i) www.tahiti-tourisme.com.

Nuku Hiva and Hiva Oa are served by daily flights from Papeete, Tahiti. The other islands have less frequent interisland service on Air Tahiti.

Cruises offered by **Aranui 3** (www.aranui.com).

$$$ **Keikahanui Nuku Hiva Pearl Lodge,** Nuku Hiva (www.pearlresorts.com).

TOUR Tahiti Travels (www.tahititravels.com).

The physical evidence of the colony is ephemeral. In 1998, archaeologists uncovered the footprints of the settlement in 400-year-old postholes that trace the palisades surrounding the colony. Artifacts from the dig include a 10-karat gold signet ring from Elizabethan times. Climatologists studying the rings of ancient bald cypress trees nearby concluded that the summer the colonists arrived was a time of severe drought, which may have caused a fatal food shortage. Others theorize that the Spanish somehow massacred the group, or the colonists set out to sail home but were lost at sea. But the strongest theory is that the surviving members of a diminished colony were simply absorbed into the native Croatan tribes—perhaps the blue-eyed Lumbee tribe in Robeson County. A DNA project is underway to try to link the English colonists of Fort Raleigh to the current native populations.

A trip to Roanoke Island is not just time spent in a time warp reverie of Elizabethan England. The town of **Manteo** has been called "Mayberry by the Sea," and for good reason: It's the longtime home of Andy Griffith. Manteo has a sweet, small-town charm, with some of the area's most gracious inns. Visit Manteo's little waterfront, where you can board a replica of the *Elizabeth I,* the ship that brought the doomed colony to these shores 400 years ago. —*AF*

ⓘ www.nps.gov/fora or www.roanokeisland.net.

✈ Norfolk, Virginia.

1-hr., 40-min. drive from Norfolk.

$$ **Roanoke Island Inn,** 305 Fernando St., Manteo (✆ **252/473-5511;** www.roanokeislandinn.com). $$$ **White Doe Inn,** 319 Sir Walter Raleigh St., Manteo (✆ **800/473-6091** or 252/473-9851; www.whitedoeinn.com).

Historic Haunts

400

Haiti

Tropical Color Defined

Okay, so it might not be the first destination that comes to mind when you think of a Caribbean getaway. From poverty and corruption to riots and worse, Haiti is plagued with bad press, and parts of the island nation are downright dangerous. But for those willing to accept some of the very real risks associated with traveling here, intriguing Haiti rewards you with some of the most memorable travel experiences you'll ever have.

More than any other place in the Caribbean, Haiti has retained its wild, weird, and wonderful African cultural traditions. This is the home of **voodoo,** after all, and the existence of zombies—those dread souls conjured back from the grave to be the slaves of the living—is officially recognized by the government. Haiti is also the only nation where slaves staged a successful revolt against their oppressors; resourceful islanders achieved their independence from the French, in part, by fighting guerilla-style in the rainforest of the island. The slaves would play drums and sing to their gods, effectively terrifying the European soldiers.

Under colonial occupation, Haiti was called Saint-Domingue; when independence was won in 1804, the newly freed people renamed their country Haiti, from the indigenous Taino name *Ayiti,* meaning "Land of High Mountains." Much of the country, which occupies the western end of Hispaniola (the Dominican Republic 230 makes up the rest of the island), is blessed with gloriously rugged tropical terrain. Nowhere do Haiti's history and geography unite more dramatically than at **Citadelle La Ferrière.** This imposing fortress castle, set in an impossibly high and commanding position in the lush northern mountains, is the Caribbean's most wow-inducing man-made attraction. Built from 1805 to 1820, the Citadelle is a monument to Haiti's independence.

On the northern coast, the lazy town of **Cap-Haitien** is a must for a primer in colonial history and a great base for exploring the north part of the country, including its Atlantic-facing beaches. At the vertex of the two peninsulas that make up western Haiti, **Port-au-Prince** is the country's capital. Expect sensory overload as the traffic and local color here combine for fascinating, if chaotic, cultural encounters. Along the Caribbean (southern) side of the island, a number of laid-back towns make for low-key exploration and lazy beach days, but the handicrafts center of **Jacmel** is the prime draw along this coast. Vibrantly colored wood and papier-mâché objects, many designs informed by the voodoo culture of Haiti, can be found at reasonable prices.

In the days of piracy, Haiti was a major hangout for the buccaneers of the Caribbean. Nostalgic types looking for a now-safe enclave that evokes some of the romance and mystique of that era need look no further than rustic **Ile à Vache,** once a base for Captain Morgan himself, and where Jack Sparrow and Co. would look right at home.

Although Haiti has gotten more stable as of mid-2009, it's still wise to check out travel advisories, such as those posted on the U.S. State Department's website (www.travel.state.gov) before booking your trip. Although only a few tour operators currently offer Haiti itineraries, they may be the best way to go for a mixture of adventure and security. —*SM*

ⓘ www.haititourisme.org.

✈ Port-au-Prince, connections to Central and North America and the Caribbean.

🛏 $$ **Port Morgan,** Ile à Vache (✆ **509/921-0000;** www.port-morgan.com).

Historic Haunts

Delos Island

Temples of the Gods

Greece

When you step onto Delos Island, you'll find yourself in the most significant mythical site in all of Greece. It lies in the middle of a circular ring of islands known as the Cyclades, just 4.8km (3 miles) from the island of Mykonos 245, and it offers the visitor dazzling views of white marble monuments, many devoted to the god Apollo, who was thought to be born here along with his twin sister, Artemis. Because it was considered a holy site, no one was allowed to be born or die here. For centuries, pregnant women and the dying were transported to a nearby islet.

Today, the island abounds with monuments to Apollo and related gods, including the **Terrace of the Lions,** which originally featured 12 fierce lions flanking the path to the gate of the Venetian Arsenal. They stood in a row facing eastward, toward the Sacred Lake. The **Sacred Way** was the route taken to the Sanctuary of Apollo during the holy Delian festival. By following it, you'll see the remains of Apollo's sanctuary and temples. At the end of the path is the **Propylaea,** a tremendous marble gate that once opened onto the sanctuary. The island's museum is nearby and houses many artifacts from the ruined site. Also of note is the platform of the **Stoviadeion,** constructed in honor of Dionysus, the god of wine. The temple is known for its pillars supporting giant phalluses, the symbol of the god. Nearby is the **Sacred Lake,** once filled with swans that were thought to be oracles. Today, it's merely a circular indentation surrounded by a little wall—but is still considered a significant enough landmark to have other sites planned around it.

Not all of the island's history relates to the Greek Empire, which controlled the area from the 6th century B.C. to 315 B.C. Delos was a bustling commercial port and slave market when the Romans ruled it in the 2nd and 3rd centuries B.C. During this period the **Agora of the Competialists** was constructed to deities like Hermes, who was associated with commerce. Prosperity took a downfall when Mithridates of Pontus, an Asian Minor monarch at war with Rome, attacked in 88 B.C., looting the island and killing the inhabitants before leaving.

It's easy to get to Delos from Mykonos by excursion boat, but I recommend visiting early in the day before the crowds get too thick. Another factor to consider is that the island gets no shade, so the sun gets higher and hotter as the day wears on. It's wise to bring a hat, water, and plenty of sunscreen. *—JD*

ⓘ www.mykonos-web.com/mykonos/delos_history.htm.

Multiple options from Mykonos (30 min.).

$$ **Adonis Hotel,** 84600, Mykonos (✆ **30/22890/22-434;** www.mykonosadonis.com). $$ **Amazing View Hotel,** Agios Stefano beach, Mykonos (✆ **30/22890/22-053;** www.amazingviewhotel.com).

10 Island Cities

Capitals 402

Stockholm

The Stepping-Stone City

Sweden

Fourteen islands, scattered throughout the watery maze between Lake Mälaren and the Baltic Sea like steppingstones, make up the Swedish capital of Stockholm. Some are small and distinctly isolated; others are large and barely distinguishable as islands. But just about anywhere you turn in Stockholm, the backdrop involves the deep glittering blue water of the harbor, lined with striking architecture, making it one of the most beguiling cities in Northern Europe.

Stockholm's historic quarter is called **Gamla Stan,** and its cobblestone streets, lined with fairy-tale German architecture, are cloyingly picturesque. With the standard array of landmark churches, palaces, and museums, Gamla Stan is very touristy but still a must-see before you move onto the more vibrant parts of the real, modern Stockholm. Back across one of the three bridges that connect Gamla Stan to "mainland" Stockholm is the busy and well-groomed **Norrmalm,** Stockholm's commercial heart and a shopper's paradise, with venerable Swedish department store **N.K.** (Hamngatan 18–20) anchoring the retail offerings. Norrmalm is one of the poshest neighborhoods in the city, along with tony **Ostermalm** to the east, where you can browse around Scandinavia's top gourmet market, **Ostermalms Saluhalle** (Nybrogatan 31; www.saluhallen.com), located in a fortresslike neo-Gothic redbrick building that's been around since 1888. (If you've ever had a hankering to

Previous page: Times Square, Manhattan. Above: Gamla Stan, Stockholm.

try reindeer meat, now's your chance.) One of the best places to spend time for visitors and Stockholmers alike is the city's parks and recreation island, Djurgården 418. To the west, the mostly residential island-district of **Kungsholmen** is home to the imposing red-brick **Stadshuset** (City Hall), where the Nobel prize award banquet is held every year. The expansive lawn out front is a wonderful place to relax and watch the boat traffic on **Lake Mälaren.**

Södermalm ("south island") is to Stockholm as Brooklyn is to New York City. *Söder* is where the hip and bohemian boutiques and cafes are, but also where you'll find some of the city's oldest and most traditional eateries, like **Pelikan** (Blekingegatan 40), an atmospheric beer hall that makes Stockholm's best *kottbullar* (Swedish meatballs). Suspended over the **Slussen** locks between Lake Mälaren and the Baltic Sea (between Södermalm and Gamla Stan) is **Eriks Gondolen** (Stadtsgården 6), a touristy restaurant that nevertheless boasts one of the best views in Europe and provides a good overview of the city's countless waterways.

Summer is the absolute best time to appreciate the island-rich topography of Stockholm. On waterfront esplanades like **Strandvägen** and **Skeppsbron,** alfresco cafes spring to life and buzz with activity until the wee hours; it doesn't get dark until 1am or so, and the sun comes right back out a few hours later. Stockholmers hate to miss even 1 minute of the mild weather and plentiful light, creating a lively energy that permeates their city all season. —*SM*

ⓘ **Sverigehuset** (Sweden House), Hamngatan 27 (✆ **46/8/508-285-08;** www.stockholmtown.com).

✈ Stockholm Arlanda International Airport.

🛏 $$ **Radisson SAS Strand Hotel,** Nybrokajen 9 (✆ **46/8/506-640-00;** www.radissonsas.com). $$$ **Victory Hotel,** Lilla Nygatan 5 (✆ **46/8/506-400-00;** www.victory-hotel.se).

403 Capitals

Copenhagen

Danish Modern

Denmark

Like many medieval capitals, Copenhagen boomed around a harbor—the term *køben-havn* means "merchants' harbor"—with a strategic position guarding the Øresund, the main passage into the Baltic Sea. It's set on a large island, Zealand ("Sea Land"); the city itself is also a cluster of islands, either natural or set off by canals. One of its defining sights is a picture-book image of colorful houses lining the docks of **Nyhavn.**

Don't expect a quaint seafaring town, though. Even behind Nyhavn's simple facades lie hip boutiques, chic restaurants, and apartments gentrified well beyond any seaman's means. As the largest city in Scandinavia, lively Copenhagen—often called the "fun capital of Scandinavia"—is a culinary hot spot, a magnet for modern design, and a haven for freethinkers. (Visit the island **Christianshavn** to see the Free City of Christiania, founded in 1971, a complex of former army barracks where some 1,000 squatters live.) On one hand you can visit a world-class art museum, the **Ny Carlsberg Glypotek** (Dantes Plads 7); on the other you can tour the huge commercial brewery that subsidized it, the **Carlsberg Brewery** (11 Gamle Carlsberg Vej). In the **Assistens Kirkegård** (Nørrebrogade/Kapelvej 4), a wildly contrasting pair of literary heroes are buried: children's writer Hans Christian Andersen and the "father of existentialism," Søren Kierkegaard. While the **city museum** (Vesterbrogade 59) explores the life of Kierkegaard, it's Andersen's fairy-tale image that the city promotes, starting out with the wistful **Little Mermaid** statue on a rock in Copenhagen Harbor.

The prime exhibit for that fairy-tale image is **Tivoli Gardens** (Vesterbrogade 3; ✆ **45/33-15-10-01;** www.tivoligardens.com, open Apr–Oct), that most magical of amusement parks, with its profuse flower beds, fantasy pavilions, and tiny twinkling lights. Founded in 1843, Tivoli lies in the heart of downtown, and it's not just for kids and tourists—Copenhageners old and young attend regularly. Here you can ride a merry-go-round of tiny Viking ships, trundle in a cart past scenes from Andersen's fairy tales, or hurtle into the sky on Europe's tallest swing ride; it offers constant nighttime entertainment and some of the city's best restaurants.

As befits a fairy-tale sort of place, Copenhagen has not one but three royal castles: the rococo 18th-century **Amalienborg Palace,** where Queen Margrethe II lives; **Rosenberg Castle,** a monumental red-brick Dutch Renaissance pile built in 1633, where the royal family displays its dazzling possessions; and bulky gray Christiansborg Castle, where the Danish parliament, supreme court, and prime minister conduct the nation's business (the building dates to the 1920s, but its island, Slotsholmen, has been the nexus of Danish power since 1167).

Sociable, outgoing Copenhageners long ago took the Danish word *strøget,* which means "to stroll," and applied it to the longest pedestrianized street in Europe. Though the street name changes five times in a 1.2km (¾-mile) stretch, from the Rådhuspladsen (city hall square) to Kongens Nytorv (King's Square, at the top of Nyhavn), the retail buzz is constant, a parade of shops and cafes that includes several of Danish design's leading stores. It's anything but quaint, and it's quintessentially Copenhagen. —*HH*

ⓘ **Tourist office,** Vesterbrogade 4A (✆ **45/70/22-24-42** or 45/33/25-74-00; www.visitcopenhagen.com).

✈ Copenhagen Kastrup Airport.

🛏 $$ **Hotel Maritime,** Peder Skrams Gade 19 (✆ **45/33/13-48-82;** www.hotel-maritime.dk). $$$ **Kong Frederik,** Vester Voldgade 25 (✆ **45/33/12-59-02;** www.remmen.dk).

Capitals **404**

Saint Petersburg

The Spirit of the Czars

Russia

Czar Peter the Great had a brainstorm: What Russia needed was a new capital. A major seaport was essential, he knew, for his landlocked country to claim its place among the nations of Europe. And so in 1703 Peter the Great captured a chunk of marshy Baltic coast from Sweden and proceeded to build a glittering new capital there, with a network of canals draining the Neva River delta into a cluster of islands.

Moscow regained capital status after the Revolution in 1918, but the ghosts of the czars linger in Saint Petersburg, at elegant **Palace Square** (Dvortsovaya Ploshchad). Standing under the Alexander Column—a 600-ton monolith topped by a cross-carrying angel, commemorating the Russian victory over Napoleon—imagine all that this asymmetrical plaza has seen, from royal coaches pulling up to the baroque **Winter**

Palace on one side, to Communist solidarity marches in front of the long, curved **General Staff Building.** Through the grand courtyard of the Winter Palace today, you enter the **State Hermitage Museum** (✆ **7/812/710-9079;** www.hermitagemuseum.org), which houses the peerless art collection of the czars. The Hermitage's extravagantly decorated salons display an incredible catalog of Renaissance Italian art and loads of Dutch and Flemish masters; it has more French artworks than any museum outside of France.

If you stand on Strelka, a spit of land on Vasilievsky Island 419, you'll view a panorama of nearly every major landmark in Saint Petersburg—a classically harmonious assemblage of architecture, which luckily escaped the massive Stalin-era reconstruction that blighted many other Russian cities. Over 3 centuries, Saint Petersburg—dourly renamed Petrograd during World War I, and Leningrad from 1924 to 1991—gradually spread out from the south bank of the Neva, but under Peter the Great its center was the **Peter & Paul Fortress (Petropavlovskaya Krepost),** on Hare's Island (Zaichy Ostrov) across from the Winter Palace. The complex includes the **Peter and Paul Cathedral,** which holds the tombs of all Russian czars from Peter's day through the last czar, assassinated Nicholas II (he and his family were reburied here in 1997). Also at the fortress, the **Trubetskoi Bastion** housed such political prisoners as Fyodor Dostoevsky, Leon Trotsky, and Vladimir Lenin's brother.

You may also stroll around the formal gardens of the **Summer Palace;** glean literary insights at the **Dostoevsky House** (5/2 Kuznechny Pereulok) and **Nabokov House** (47 Bolshaya Morskaya Ulitsa) museums; walk along Nevsky Prospect, Saint Petersburg's greatest boulevard; and photograph the blindingly bright beveled domes of the Cathedral of the Saviour on the Spilled Blood, commemorating the spot where Czar Alexander II (who freed Russia's serfs in 1861) was assassinated in 1881. Exploring the city, you'll cross a lot of bridges—342 of them, many exquisitely designed and adorned with statues. If you're lucky enough to be here in June during White Nights, when the sun never dips below the horizon, perch on the quay at 2am to watch the Neva's drawbridges unfold in careful rhythm to allow nighttime shipping traffic through. Just be careful not to get caught on the wrong side of the river from your hotel! *—HH*

ⓘ **Saint-Petersburg information service** (✆ **7/812/380-2478;** www.saint-petersburg.com); also www.russia-travel.com.

✈ Pulkovo-2 International Airport (16km/10 miles).

🛏 $$$ **Corinthia Nevsky Palace,** 57 Nevsky Prospekt (✆ **7/812/380-2001;** www.corinthia.ru). $$ **Pulford Apartments,** 6 Moika Embankment (✆ **7/812/325-6277;** www.pulford.com).

405 Capitals

Singapore

Crossroads of Asia

With its steel skyscrapers, bustling street life, and sophisticated transit system, the historic district (downtown) of Singapore looks at first glance like any other thriving metropolis in any part of the world. But behind that familiar veneer lie centuries-old traditions—Eastern mysticism meets Western modernity—that are totally unique to

Singapore Night Market.

Singapore. Buddhist temples sit cheek by jowl with Islamic mosques, and sleek shopping malls lie just around the corner from the wonderful chaos and hawkers of Chinatown. Because English is so widely spoken here, it's not hard for an independent traveler to peel back the layers and get to know the place and its people. Asia can so often seem overwhelmingly foreign, even for the most seasoned of travelers; a few days in Singapore can be a blessed relief.

Thanks to a strategic location along the Strait of Malacca, at the southern tip of the Malay peninsula, Singapore has always been a place where foreign cultures have intersected. Chinese workers, Indian businessmen, and Arab merchants all put down roots here, and their presence is gloriously evident in the island's diverse architecture, ethnic enclaves, and religious buildings. But Singapore entered its most significant chapter of history when Sir Stamford Raffles established the island city as a trading center, a sort of way station between British interests in India and the Far East. Its early policy of free trade ensured Singapore a prosperity and cosmopolitan culture that has lasted for more than 200 years.

Singapore today is popular mostly as a 1- or 2-day stopover between Asian destinations. Even if you're disoriented by jet lag, Singapore is so compact and so well-organized, it's easy to see the island's highlights in a short time. If you're able to stay longer, you'll discover just how much this island city has to offer in the way of culture, nature, dining, and shopping.

A perfect place to begin any tour of the island is at the historic **Raffles Hotel** (see below). No other single structure in Asia better evokes the bygone romance of the Colonial era. In the hotel's atmospheric **Long Bar,** *punkahs* (leaf-shaped overhead fans) lazily nudge the air around, and you can sip a Singapore Sling in the very bar where it was invented. Everyone ends up on **Orchard Road** at some point: This buzzing retail strip has everything from electronics emporiums to glossy music stores blaring the latest Asian pop sensations to elegant department stores filled with designer fashions that most Western women can only dream of fitting into.

Many Asian cities tempt visitors with their street food, and Singapore's is some of the best, with greater variety—Chinese,

Malaysian, Indian, Indonesian, thanks to its multicultural heritage—and savory flavors and ingredients that are less frightening to Western palates. Street food can be found not actually on the street but in the city's "hawker centers." There are dozens of these citywide, each with their own ethnic bents and specialties, but a good place to start is at the venerable **Chinatown Food Centre,** where you can sample fried *hokkien mee* (noodles with prawns, cuttlefish, garlic and shrimp paste), the national dish of Singapore.

Singaporeans looking to impress out-of-towners always take their guests to the **Night Safari** (www.nightsafari.com.sg), without a doubt one of the absolute highlights of the city. When the sun goes down, visitors can see the fascinating nocturnal behavior of animals like rhinoceroses, giraffes, and hyenas in wonderful habitats that re-create the Himalayan foothills, the Southeast Asian rainforest, the African savanna, and the rivers of Nepal. Singapore isn't particularly known for its beaches (for that, go to nearby Malaysia), but if you are craving some sun and sand, the best place to go is **Sentosa island,** at the far southern tip of Singapore. —*SM*

ⓘ **Tourist office,** Orchard Rd. and Cairnhill Rd. (✆ **65/6736-2000;** www.visitsingapore.com).

✈ Singapore-Changi International.

🛏 $$$ **Raffles Hotel,** 1 Beach Rd. (✆ **65/6337-1886;** www.raffleshotel.com). $$ **Traders Hotel Singapore,** 1A Cuscaden Rd. (✆ **65/6738-2222;** www.shangri-la.com).

Showcases

Venice

The Adriatic Mirage

Italy

An island? Try 118 *separate* islands, dredged out of a marshy lagoon, shored up on wooden pylons, and linked by a devilishly intricate tapestry of bridges and boats. Other cities may have canals, but Venice makes an even bolder statement: It has *no streets at all,* only canals, more than 150 of them. Every time I visit Venice, I'm struck by the constant murmur of water lapping against stone; the very air feels magically moist against your skin. Then there's that faint scent of decay, a blend of rotting foundations, crumbling plaster, and sediment slushing around the canal floors. The sensory impact is unforgettable, and magical; it perfectly evokes the watery essence of the city.

Given its strategic position at the head of the Adriatic Sea, medieval Venice was a natural candidate to become a maritime power, Europe's gateway to the riches of Asia (it was no accident that Marco Polo came from a family of Venetian traders). In what is essentially still a Renaissance cityscape, you'll note exotic accents everywhere, from the glittering gold mosaics of the Byzantine-style **St. Mark's Basilica** (✆ **39/041/5225697**), to the Moorish facade of the **Doge's Palace** next door, to the fantastical decorations of the Venetian Gothic *palazzi* you glide past on a boat ride down the **Grand Canal.** Add to that a host of distinctly Venetian details—the dragon-prowed black gondolas navigating its canals, the candy-striped poles for docking them, the winged lion symbol that materializes everywhere—and it's like an art director's fever dream.

Its centerpiece, **Piazza San Marco,** is arguably the loveliest public space in the world, with subtly tapering loggias on either side framing the gold dome of St. Mark's at

Island Hopping Around the Venetian Lagoon: Watery Escapes from La Serenissima

Granted, the city of Venice 406 itself is already an island, or rather a massive cluster of islands linked with bridges. But this island city also has its own outlying islands, spattered around the lagoon and accessible only by boat. When the tourist crush around Venice's Piazza San Marco seems too much to bear, the islands offer a fantastic escape—quieter, more neighborhoody versions of Venice, each with its own distinct character.

Half- or full-day sightseeing cruises of the lagoon are one option, but for my money the best way to visit these islands is the way the locals do—by hopping on an ACTV vaporetto or waterbus from the city's northern bank, Fondamente Nuove. Go early in the day before the day-cruisers show up, or wait until late afternoon, when the light is gloriously mellow and the package hordes have piled back onto their boats.

Burano.

If tourists visit only one island, it's probably 407 **Murano,** the first stop on the vaporetto route, a 10-minute ride from Fondamente Nuove. It's not just convenience that brings visitors here—it's the amazing art glass turned out by the local glass blowers, who have centered Venice's craft on this island since their furnaces were banned from the mainland in 1291. I love to browse along the petite canals of Murano, lined with small shops and elegant galleries—you'll find everything from tiny animal sculptures and jewel-like beads, up to sets of richly colored glassware, intricately whorled paperweights, exquisite sculptures, and immense glittering chandeliers (don't worry about lugging large items in your suitcase—the galleries know just how to ship those delicate objects home for you). Check for the **"Vetro Murano Artistico"** decal in the shop window so that you won't be fobbed off with imported fakes. While you're on Murano, you can also marvel at historic glass pieces in the **Museo del Vetro di Murano** (Fondamente Giustinian 8), or take a short factory tour—several of the more commercial factories offer free walk-in tours, though be prepared for an aggressive sales pitch at the end. Don't pay the marked price on any ready-made item; bargaining is expected. Note that many factories shut down on weekends and in the month of August, though the shops remain open. If you're a serious collector, call for an appointment to visit the private **Barovier & Toso Museum** (Palazzo Contarini, Fondamenta Vetrai 28; ✆ **39/041/739049**).

When the shopping throngs start to overrun Murano, it's time to skip on to the next island on the ferry route, 408 **Burano,** traditionally home to Venice's lace-making trade. Even if you're not in the market for doilies, mantillas, or tablecloths, laid-back

Burano is a lovely place to visit: It's a stage set-perfect fishing village, its canals lined with small homes painted in bright shades of rose, azure, scarlet, buttercup-yellow, or grass-green. Naturally there's a lace museum, the **Scuola di Merletti di Burano** (Piazza Galuppi 187) in the center of the village; upstairs you can watch lace makers, mostly young women, at their painstaking work. Burano even has its own leaning tower, the crazily tilting campanile beside the **Duomo** on the same square as the lace museum. Relax over lunch at a local cafe, and then stop by one of the local bakeries to sample the island's addictive specialty, ring-shaped cookies known as *bussola*.

Even fewer tourists continue on to outlying 409 **Torcello** (total travel time from Fondamente Nuove: 45–50 min.), which suits the Venetians just fine—that way they can keep this rural refuge to themselves. Originally Torcello was more populous than Venice itself, until the surrounding lagoon turned to swamp in the 12th century; today it's sparsely inhabited and half-overgrown, refreshingly leafy and peaceful. From the ferry quay, a 15-minute stroll along the canal (arched over by the seemingly innocent Ponte Diablo, or Devil's Bridge) takes you to Torcello's chief sight, the glorious Byzantine-era **Cattedrale di Torcello,** also called **Santa Maria Assunta Isola di Torcello.** The wealth of glittering mosaics inside will dazzle you (check out the fire-and-brimstone *Last Judgment*). Climb the 11th-century campanile for a wonderful panorama of the island and the Lagoon. The crumbling stone seat in the square, dubbed Attila's Throne, was probably a bishop's ceremonial seat. Time your visit so that you can have dinner, or at least a late-afternoon drink, at the rustic-looking **Locanda Cipriani** (Piazza San Fosca 29; ✆ **39/041/730150;** www.locandacipriani.com), once one of Ernest Hemingway's favorite watering holes; it's a cousin to the famous Harry's Bar and Hotel Cipriani on the mainland, and even has a few bedrooms if you want to stay the night.

Save your poignant visit to the cemetery island, 410 **San Michele,** as a sightseeing add-on for a different day—only a short distance off Fondamente Nuove, it has its own vaporetto service, a quick 15-minute ride. The entire island is ringed with a neat brick wall, floating on the water like a cypress-crowned fortress of the dead, easily visible from mainland Venice. This graveyard island, founded in 1807 to eliminate the sanitary hazards of ground burials on the flood-prone mainland, is surprisingly unghoulish—ranks of white concrete mausoleums gleam in the sunlight, where nowadays, to save space, bones are deposited after 12 years in the ground. Prowl the older sections of the graveyard to find the final resting places of celebrities including composer Igor Stravinsky, poet Joseph Brodsky, choreographer Sergei Diaghilev, and poet Ezra Pound. The cacophony of Venice will seem miles away. —*HH*

ⓘ See Venice 406 for tourist office, getting there, and hotel information.

Gondolas on Venice's Grand Canal.

the upper end. Symmetry is beside the point—just off to the side, like an afterthought, is a perfect russet-brick bell tower; to the other side is a baroque clock tower where two mechanical Moors chime the hour. Most tourists are so dazzled by the place, they don't get much farther. But getting beyond San Marco is essential to understand Venice, even if that means getting lost in a maze of narrow stone passageways and high-arched bridges. Venice's art isn't just in the art museum—the **Galleria dell'Accademia** (Dorsoduro; www.galleriea ccademia.org) for the old Venetian masters, the **Collezione Peggy Guggenheim** (Dorsoduro 701; www.guggenheim-venice.it) for modern art—it's all over the place, in historic houses and especially in the city's churches, even the most obscure ones where you may be the only visitors. At the seaward tip of Castello you'll find the **Arsenale** (✆ **39/041/5200276**), the old naval arsenal, now a fascinating naval history museum; turn a corner in the middle of the San Marco district and you'll stumble upon the cramped white portico of **La Fenice** (San Marco 1965; www.teatrolafenice.it), the world-class opera house. Browse through street markets; encounter stray cats; buy a cone of gelato and stroll along the broad Giudecca Canal; peer through iron gates into back gardens; take a boat out to the Islands of the Venetian Lagoon (p. 420). In the end, it's the sheer Venice-ness of Venice you'll find—and remember forever. —*HH*

ⓘ **Tourist office,** Giardinetti Reali or 71F Piazza San Marco (✆ **39/041/5298710** or 39/041/5225150; www.turismovenezia.it).

✈ Aeroporto Marco Polo.

🛏 $$$ **Locanda Ai Santi Apostoli,** Strada Nuova, Cannaregio (✆ **39/041/5212612;** www.locandasantiapostoli.com). $$ **Pensione Accademia,** Fondamenta Bollani, Dorsoduro (✆ **39/041/5210188;** www.pensioneaccademia.it).

411 Showcases

Manhattan

Glittering Gotham

New York, U.S.

New York City may have five boroughs, but when most people say "New York," what they really mean is Manhattan, a skyscraper-loaded island muscling its way ahead of the rest of America. With a million and a half people crowded on its 23 square miles (60 sq. km), this narrow, rocky sliver of land has grown into one of the great cities of the world. It may not be the official capital of the United States—heck, it's not even the capital of New York State (Albany gets that honor)—but New York City is the country's biggest city, and in many respects its cultural and financial capital as well.

Being an island made Manhattan what it is today. Situated at the mouth of the Hudson River, it almost inevitably became a powerful port, but limited by its shores, it had to grow up, not out. Thanks to elevators, subways, and skyscrapers—not to mention the bridges and tunnels that funnel in suburbanites and outer-borough types—Manhattan supports an impressively dense population, made ever more diverse by waves of immigration. Despite the inevitable urban stresses, Manhattan's enormous wealth spins life here into another stratosphere.

With all those tall buildings, Manhattan has the world's most photogenic skyline. In Midtown, the most famous view is from the Art Deco **Empire State Building** (Fifth Ave. and 34th St.); you'll be 102 stories up, right among the skyscraper tops. But I prefer the sleeker deck 70 stories up at **Top of the Rock,** atop 30 Rockefeller Center (50th St. between 5th and 6th aves.), in the same building as **NBC Studios** and right next to **Rockefeller Plaza,** Sixth Avenue and 47th to 50th streets, a classic Manhattan scene where an immense golden Prometheus statue lounges over twirling ice skaters in winter and cafe tables in summer. Only a couple blocks west is **Times Square,** Broadway and 42nd to 45th streets, its dizzying razzmatazz of lit-up signs and theater marquees delivering a pure jolt of Manhattan's dynamic energy.

You can get around via clattering subway trains, iconic yellow taxicabs, touristy horse-drawn carriages, cheesy double-decker bus tours, or the goofy pedicabs that swarm around Midtown. You can even circumnavigate the island on narrated **Circle Line sightseeing cruises** (**© 212/563-3200;** www.circleline42.com). But my favorite way to explore this intensely compact city is simply to walk. Manhattan's apartment-dwelling, no-car-commuting population turns out on the streets, and there's something to gape at on every block—architectural landmarks, alluring shop windows, or the outrageous characters who thrive in a city that prizes individuality. Walking south from Midtown to the looming urban canyons of the financial district (aka **Wall Street**), you can explore the art galleries of **Chelsea,** the leafy brownstone streets of bohemian **Greenwich Village,** the exotic bustle of **Chinatown,** or the trendy boutiques of **SoHo**'s cast-iron loft buildings. North of Midtown, you can ramble through that surprising island of greenery, **Central Park,** 840 acres (340 hectares) of lawns, tree groves, statues, lakes, and ponds lying between the apartment buildings of the Upper West Side and the Upper East Side. Central Park is bracketed by the **Metropolitan Museum of Art** (on the park's east side at 81st St.) and the **American Museum of Natural History** (on the west side at 79th St.). Their world-class collections are pretty much what you'd expect in this world-class museum city. —*HH*

ⓘ **Tourist offices:** 810 7th Ave., 1560 Broadway, or 26 Wall St. (✆ **212/484-1222;** www.nycgo.com).

✈ John F. Kennedy International (15 miles/24km); Newark Liberty International (16 miles/26km); LaGuardia (8 miles/13km).

🛏 $$ **Milburn Hotel,** 242 W. 76th St. (✆ **800/833-9622** or 212/362-1006; www.milburnhotel.com). $$ **Washington Square Hotel,** 103 Waverly Place (✆ **800/222-0418** or 212/777-9515; www.washingtonsquarehotel.com).

Showcases

Miami Beach

Rat Pack Redux

Florida, U.S.

When I was a kid, in the late 1950s and early 1960s, Miami Beach seemed the epitome of vacation—America's Riviera, haunt of the Rat Pack, showman Jackie Gleason, and mobster Al Capone. Its long strip of barrier beach boasted massive resort hotels with fantasy architecture as exotic as their names (Eden Roc, Fontainebleau). When cheap airfares made overseas destinations—including the real Riviera—more available, Miami Beach's glory faded, only to roar back, phoenixlike, in the 1980s with the renaissance of formerly dowdy South Beach and its Art Deco hotels. If Miami Beach was hot at midcentury, by the dawn of the 21st century it was *white*-hot.

Distinct from mainland Miami, that great multicultural stew pot across Biscayne Bay, stylish Miami Beach is a separately incorporated city, tethered to the mainland by half a dozen causeways. Its spine, Collins Avenue, fronts nearly 10 miles (16km) of white-sand beach and blue-green waters from 1st to 86th streets; that strand continues north of Miami Beach proper through Surfside, ritzy Bal Harbour, and the adjacent barrier islands, the Sunny Isles. Although most of this stretch is lined with hotels and condos, there's plenty of public access to that hard-packed white-sand beach, continually replenished with (sadly, imported) sand.

That fabulous beach spawned Miami Beach, but nowadays beachcombing is beside the point. Lovely (and pricey) as those pastel-hued SoBe boutique hotels are, their rooms are often also tiny and minimally furnished. (I prefer to stay farther north and hit South Beach only when the mood strikes.) Hanging out in hip **South Beach** is all about seeing and being seen, with everyone from rock stars and fashion icons to club kids and trannies flocking to the bars, restaurants, and poolside lounges. Most night-lifers hop from bar to bar throughout the evening; perennial favorite haunts are the **Rose Bar at the Delano Hotel** (1685 Collins Ave.), the **SkyBar at The Shore Club** (1901 Collins Ave.), and the retro **Raleigh Bar at the Raleigh Hotel** (1775 Collins Ave.). Collins and Washington Avenues are the eye of the storm, but be forewarned: The scene doesn't even begin to buzz until 11pm.

Ocean Drive, Miami Beach.

Where there are fashionistas, there will be luxe shopping, and **Collins Avenue** has become Miami's designer-laden equivalent of New York's Madison Avenue. The **Lincoln Road pedestrian mall,** originally designed in 1957 by Morris Lapidus, is a little more low-rent and, frankly, I find it more fun. If you must have your Rodeo Drive experience, head north to Bal Harbour, and the exclusive **Bal Harbour Shops** mall (9700 Collins Ave.) can put a dent in your credit cards.

Fashion and food come first in South Beach, but culture is quickly catching up. Every December the popular Art Basel festival is held at the new **Collins Park Cultural Center,** a trio of modernist showpieces on Collins Park and Park Avenue between 21st and 23rd streets: the Bass Museum of Art, the Miami City Ballet Theater, and the Miami Beach Regional Library. The freshly restored **Colony Theater,** on Lincoln Road, is another Art Deco showpiece; meanwhile, touring Broadway productions appear at the aqua-tinted **Jackie Gleason Theater of the Performing Arts,** 1700 Washington Ave. *—HH*

ⓘ **Tourist office,** 1700 Convention Center Dr. (✆ **305/673-7400;** www.miamibeachfl.gov).

✈ Miami International Airport or Fort Lauderdale Hollywood International Airport.

🛏 $$ **Circa 39 Hotel,** 3900 Collins Ave. (✆ **877/824-7223** or 305/538-4900; www.circa39.com). $$ **South Seas Hotel,** 1751 Collins Ave. (✆ **800/345-2678** or 305/205-6195; www.southseashotel.com).

Showcases 413

Hong Kong
East Meets West
Hong Kong S.A.R., China

In its days as a British Crown Colony, Hong Kong was one of a kind—a seeming magic portal into the Far East, albeit one with English spoken everywhere and modern creature comforts at hand. Wooden boats bobbed in the harbor beside ocean liners, crumbling tenements leaned against modern high-rises, and rickshaws trundled past gleaming Rolls-Royces. The world held its breath in 1997 when, as per longtime agreement, this bustling financial capital reverted to China. So far, although real-estate development has run rampant—as in other island cities, land in Hong Kong has always been at a premium—the free-market lifestyle remains alive and well.

Though Hong Kong has expanded well beyond the central island, that postcard vista of Hong Kong's **Victoria Harbour,** bristling with skyscrapers, still promises glittering urban romance. The classic views are from the decks of the green-and-white **Star Ferry,** a 5-minute ride between Kowloon and Hong Kong Island's Central District across the ever-shrinking Victoria Harbour. An 8-minute ride on the **Peak tram**—the world's steepest funicular railway—takes you to the top of Victoria Peak, where there are spectacular views of the city below. The modern **Peak Tower** has a viewing terrace, as well as the obligatory set of tourist traps—a Madame Tussaud's, Ripley's Believe It or Not!, and the motion-simulator theater Peak Explorer. Many visitors prefer to get their views from the cliffside footpaths, where you can feel the expat British vibe of this exclusive residential enclave.

Hong Kong is a compact city—built up, not out—and well-served with public transportation. Get an Octopus card, which is good for all modes of transport: the Star Ferry, the MTR railway/subway, modern buses, and—the most atmospheric way to go—the rickety old double-decker trams around the northern end of Hong Kong Island. From your upper-deck seats, you'll see laundry hanging from second-story windows, signs swinging over the street, and markets twisting down side alleys.

Still a duty-free port, Hong Kong remains a shopping mecca, with great deals on designer clothes, jewelry, porcelain, watches, and many other luxury items. The epicenter is along Des Voeux Road in the Central Business District, where complexes such as **The Landmark,** the **Prince's Building, Alexandra House,** and **Chater House** offer the top designer boutiques, in buildings linked by elevated walkways. For only-in-Hong Kong local goods and souvenirs, try the little shops of teeming **Stanley Market,** on the southern shore of the island, or browse the still-colorful shopping streets of the Western District—Hillier Street, Bonham Strand, Man Wa Lane.

The push-and-pull between Chinese tradition and Western sophistication vitalizes Hong Kong's lively restaurant culture, which ranges from posh expense-account restaurants—often with killer views—to humble hole-in-the-wall noodle shops. For a real glimpse of old mercantile Hong Kong tradition, visit the Art Deco **Luk Yu Tea House** (24–26 Stanley St.; ✆ **852/2523-5464**), first opened in 1933, where businessmen still close their deals over dim sum and pots of tea, or the Western District's **Lin Heung Lau Tea House** (160–164 Wellington St., Sheung Wan; ✆ **852/2544-4556**), where the tea is still brewed in old-style lidded cups, rather than pots—another dying tradition in the scrum of modern Hong Kong. —*HH*

(i) **Tourist office,** Causeway Bay MTR (✆ **852/2508-1234;** www.discoverhongkong.com).

✈ Hong Kong International.

🛏 $$ **BP International House,** 8 Austin Rd., Tsim Sha Tsui, Kowloon (✆ **852/2376-1111;** www.bpih.com.hk). $$$ **Conrad International Hong Kong,** 88 Queensway, Pacific Place, Central District (✆ **800/CONRADS** [266-7237] in the U.S. and Canada, or 852/2521-3838; www.conradhotels.com).

414 Showcases

Salsette Island

Slumdogs & Millionaires

Mumbai, India

It's a wonder it hasn't sunk. Salsette Island, for its relatively diminutive size (438 sq. km/169 sq. miles), is the 14th most populous island in the world. Its entire southern tip is covered by the heaving urban agglomeration of Mumbai, home to more than 12 million people and one of the wildest, most overwhelming cities on planet Earth.

The 2008 film *Slumdog Millionaire* introduced world audiences to the geography and culture of Salsette and Mumbai. The gulf between social classes here will leave you agog: In ritzy neighborhoods like **Malabar Hill,** small apartments sell for over $1 million, while fully half of the city's population lives in shocking slum conditions, washing and bathing in the muddy rivers that still flow through Salsette. Glorious architecture from the period of British rule, as well as foul-smelling streets, form the backdrop to the vibrant daily life of Mumbai. Vanity and materialism, poverty and grit; they're all part of the whole.

Salsette originally consisted of dozens of smaller islands—its archaic name, *Sashti,* means "66 Villages"—separated by swampland. Fused together through massive land reclamation projects begun in the 18th century, by the early 1900s they had become one single island, divided from the mainland on the north by Vasai Creek and on the east by Thane Creek. (Today, it's easiest to get around the island by cab—don't even try to walk between far-flung sites.) The western edge of Mumbai fronts the Arabian Sea, making the city India's largest and most important port.

The city's most famous landmark, along with the **Gateway of India** arch on the waterfront, is its over-the-top train station, formerly known as Victoria Terminus but renamed **Chhatrapati Shivaji Terminus** (Dr. Dadabhai Naoroji Rd.) as part of 1996's nationalistic renaming binge (when Bombay was rechristened Mumbai). The ebullient Victorian/Italianate/Gothic Revival/Indian–style building will be familiar to those who've seen *Slumdog:* The final dance number, "Jai Ho," was shot here.

When Mumbaikars need a break from the chaos and claustrophobia of the city center, they head for the water: The pincer-shaped **Back Bay,** at Mumbai's southwestern tip, is home to **Chowpatty Beach.** The wind-swept promenade and all the permutations of humanity that populate it are a scene not to be missed. At night, Chowpatty's **Marine Drive** turns into the "Queen's Necklace," as all the fancy waterfront hotels and buildings turn on their twinkling lights. Mumbai is also the departure point for excursions to Elephanta Island 420, one of the sightseeing highlights of the region.

While Mumbai and its sprawl are the major tenant on Salsette, there are other areas to explore. **Borivali National Park** (aka Sanjay Gandhi National Park, named after the son of Indira Gandhi who was killed in a plane crash), in the central highlands, is a 104-sq.-km (40 sq. miles) nature reserve where visitors can come face to face with all kinds of Indian fauna, including the yawning big cats on the Lion Safari. A significant Buddhist complex, the ancient **Kanheri Caves,** is also in the park. Climb the aptly named "Highest Point Trail" to the highest point on Salsette Island and you can behold the amazing sprawl of Mumbai below—that is, if it's a clear day. —*SM*

ⓘ **Tourist office,** 123 Maharishi Karve Rd., Churchgate, Mumbai (✆ **91/22/2207-4333**).

✈ Sahar International Airport (30km/19 miles); Santa Cruz Airport (domestic flights; 26km/16 miles).

🛏 $$ **The Gordon House Hotel,** 5 Battery St., Apollo Bunder, Colaba (✆ **91/22/2287-1122;** www.ghhotel.com). $$$ **Taj Mahal Palace & Tower,** Apollo Bunder, Colaba (✆ **866/969-1825** in the U.S. and Canada, or 91/22/6665-3366; www.tajhotels.com).

11 City Islands

Magnets 415

Ile de la Cité

Center Stage on the Seine

Paris, France

On my first trip to Paris, a friend gave me one brilliant piece of travel advice. By all means see Notre-Dame, he said—that spectacular Gothic cathedral rising, all spires and gargoyles and flying buttresses, from this tiny island in the middle of the river Seine. But once you've appreciated its massive glories, dart down a side street to see Sainte Chapelle, the tiny royal chapel tucked away in a courtyard of the old Palais de Justice law courts. The two are so different—each beautiful in its own way—that you'll truly begin to understand the tapestry of contradictions that is Paris.

Ile de la Cité in the 4th arrondissement has long been considered the geographic heart of Paris—indeed, the heart of France, with all distances calculated from a bronze plaque at place du Parvis, officially named **Kilomètre Zéro.** The cathedral of **Notre-Dame** (6 place du Parvis Notre-Dame; www.notredamedeparis.fr), founded in the 12th century, has therefore stood center stage for much of France's history. Here Crusader knights prayed; citizens of the Revolution declared it a secular "temple of the people"; Napoleon crowned himself Emperor; and Victor Hugo's sad tale of a hunchback bell ringer thrilled 19th-century romantics. When Baron Haussmann redesigned Paris, he ordered the surrounding town houses torn down to showcase this architectural gem. It's a bit overwhelming to join the masses on the front plaza, everyone jostling to get his own snapshot of those amazing sculptured portals. Your photo will never equal professional shots, so why try? Admire them, identify the figures of the various saints and disciples and angels—and then duck inside, to prowl around the recesses of Notre-Dame's dusky, somber interior. Gaze upward to see the slender columns dissolving into that high cross-vaulted ceiling, rising (as its medieval workmen believed) like a prayer to God.

Standing inside Notre-Dame's huge nave, you can crane your neck to admire the stained glass of its north and west rose windows. But that's nothing compared to the windows of **Sainte Chapelle** (4 bd. du Palais; www.monum.fr), an architectural marvel for its time, designed to devote as much wall space as possible to stained glass. When the sun shines into this tiny church, the effect is breathtaking. Founded a century later than Notre-Dame, it had a very specific purpose—to house relics brought back from the Crusades by Louis XI. There are actually two levels—the servants' simple chapel below, and the royal chapel upstairs, still a relatively modest church, except when flooded with sapphire and ruby light from those amazing windows. (Prudently, the glass was removed for safekeeping during the Revolution and World War II.)

As the heart of medieval Paris, Ile de la Cité holds many other landmarks—the 19th-century **Hôtel Dieu** hospital, across from the cathedral; the gloomy medieval hulk of the infamous **Conciergerie** prison, on the north bank, where Louis XVI and Marie Antoinette awaited the guillotine; and, at the western tip of the island, the iconic **Pont Neuf** ("New Bridge"), the city's oldest bridge, opened in 1604 to link the Right and Left Banks. Right in the middle, look for French king Henri IV mounted on his bronze steed, forever observing the passing show of Paris. *—HH*

Previous page: Notre-Dame on Ile de la Cité.

ⓘ **Tourist office,** 25–27 rue des Pyramides, 1e (✆ **33/8/92-68-30-00;** www.parisinfo.com).

✈ De Gaulle (23km/14 miles) or Orly (14km/8⅔ miles).

🛏 $ **Hotel de la Place des Vosges,** 12 rue de Birague, 4e (✆ **33/1/42-72-60-46;** www.hotelplacedesvosges.com). $$ **La Tour Notre-Dame,** 20 rue du Sommerard, 5e (✆ **33/1/43-54-47-60;** www.la-tour-notre-dame.com).

416 Magnets

Museumsinsel

Sanctuary for Art

Berlin, Germany

Visitors seek many different Berlins—Cold War Berlin, Jewish Berlin, hipster post-Wall Berlin, 1920s decadent *Cabaret* Berlin. But if you're here for Museum Berlin, the repository of most of the country's art, you may get overwhelmed by the multitude of museums. That's when it's time to head to this island in the middle of the river Spree, where, with typical German efficiency, Berlin has bundled five of the most important museums together.

This island has been the heart of Berlin ever since the first settlements in the 13th century; for 5 centuries the Hohenzollerns ruled Prussia, and then all of Germany, from their castle here. In the early 1800s, Friedrich Wilhelm IV decided to dedicate the northern half of the island to the arts

Museumsinsel, Berlin.

and sciences. Its museums burgeoned along with an age of German power and prosperity, in which collectors amassed great art troves and German archaeologists conducted groundbreaking digs.

The approach to Museumsinsel is suitably impressive: You walk down Berlin's most iconic street, Unter den Linden, and cross the statue-lined Schlossbrücke (Castle Bridge). To the left is Berlin's cathedral, an oft-altered domed baroque church first built in 1750 (check out its stained-glass windows, royal tombs, and famous organ). To your right lies a construction site where layers of history intersect: The old Hohenzollern castle once stood here, but was torn down in the 1950s as a symbol of imperial decadence. The boxy modern Palast der Republik, the old GDR parliament building, replaced it, only to be demolished recently so the government can build a replica of the old castle.

Across the street from the cathedral, the Altes Museum (✆ **49/30/20-90-55-55**) stands in a beautiful 19th-century neoclassical structure, resembling a Greek Corinthian temple—a fitting home for Greek and Roman antiquities, a stunning array of Greek vases, and some exquisite bronze statues. Egyptian antiquities—including a colored bust of Nefertiti that has practically become Berlin's trademark—occupy the neoclassical Neues Museum across Bodestrasse. Past this you'll see the sandstone colonnades of the **Alte Nationalgalerie** (www.alte-nationalgalerie.de), known for its collection of 19th-century German and French Impressionists, as well as all that survives of Germany's early-20th-century art, which was mostly destroyed by the Nazis as "degenerate."

You have to walk up Kupfergraben to reach the bridge to the island's finest museum: the stolid **Pergamon Museum** (www.smb.museum), which was built in 1930 to show off the really big classical antiquities, including entire fragments of buildings. In the central hall you can't miss the ancient Pergamon Altar (180–160 B.C.), which is so large that a flight of 27 steps climbs from the museum floor to the colonnade. The south wing contains one of the largest collections anywhere of antiquities from ancient Babylonia, Persia, and Assyria, including the famous Ishtar Gate, dating from 575 B.C., and the throne room of Nebuchadnezzar. If you make it to the northern tip of the island, its curve commanded by the domed **Bode museum** (✆ **49/30/26-63-666**), you'll be rewarded with some stunning sculpture and Byzantine art. —*HH*

ⓘ **Tourist offices,** the Hauptbahnhof, Brandenburg Gate, Reichstag, and Neues Krarnzler Eck (✆ **49/30/25-00-24;** www.berlin-tourism.de).

✈ Berlin-Tagel.

🛏 $$ **Myers Hotel Berlin,** Metzer Strasse 26 (✆ **49/30/44-01-40;** www.myershotel.de). $$ **Sorat Ambassador Berlin,** Bayreuther Strasse 42 (✆ **49/30/21-90-20;** www.sorat-hotels.com).

Magnets **417**

Museumsinsel

Sprechen Sie Tech?

Munich, Germany

If the Prussians up in Berlin were going to dedicate an island to museums, the Bavarians over in Munich were bound to follow suit. Munich's Museumsinsel didn't happen until 1904, however, and German engineers propelled the project, not a high-minded German prince. As a result, this little island in the river Isar, in the heart of

The Deutsches Museum.

downtown Munich, has only one museum, and it's a technology museum—but oh, what a technology museum, the largest in the world.

I instantly felt at home at the **Deutsches Museum** (✆ **49/89/21791;** www.deutsches-museum.de), as if transported back to my childhood visits to Chicago's Museum of Science and Industry. The more I explored, though, the more I marveled at the historic nature of this collection, with many one-of-a-kind artifacts and priceless originals. Most of the inventions highlighted are German-made, but that's no surprise—Germans were at the forefront of most scientific developments in the 19th century. You'll see the first electric dynamo (built by Siemens in 1866), the first automobile (built by Benz in 1886), the first diesel engine (Diesel, 1897), and the laboratory bench where the atom was first split (Hahn and Strassmann, 1938). I was astonished to see an X-ray machine from 1895 and the first truly powerful refracting telescope, which discovered Neptune in 1846. The Deutsches Museum doesn't live in the past, either; there are huge exhibits on aerospace, computer science, and telecommunications as well.

Or so I saw on the brochure. Truthfully, the museum has so many objects on display, I had to be ruthlessly efficient during a visit with my family. We made a beeline for the areas we were most interested in: the agriculture-through-the-ages model farms; the mining section's models of coal, salt, and iron mines (always crowd pleasers); ciphering machines used in World War II to translate messages into the long-unbroken Enigma code; or the electric power hall, with gadgets that actually crank out bolts of lightning. My husband, the amateur astronomer, made sure we spent time in the astronomy exhibit, the largest in Europe, complete with a planetarium and a two-domed observatory with a solar telescope.

There's very little on the island except this museum, with its stout limestone towers and green copper roofs. Nearly a million and a half visitors per year wander amazed through these halls, and not all are schoolchildren by any means (though the hands-on nature of these exhibits definitely scores with kids). When you've had about as much beer-and-pretzel Bavarian cutesiness as you can take, a march through these halls of science makes a bracing antidote indeed—and a good window into what makes Germany tick. —*HH*

ⓘ **Tourist offices,** Marienplatz 2 or Bahnhofsplatz 2 (✆ **49/89/2339-6500;** www.munich-tourist.de).

✈ Franz-Josef-Strauss International (29km/18 miles).

🛏 $$ **Hotel Am Markt,** Heiliggeistrasse 6 (✆ **49/89/225014;** www.hotelinmunich.de). $$ **Hotel St. Paul,** St-Paul-Strasse 7 (✆ **49/89/5440-7800;** www.hotel-stpaul.de).

Magnets **418**

Djurgården

Sweden in Miniature

Stockholm, Sweden

Back in the late 16th century, you could come to Djurgården only as a hunting companion of the Swedish king, stalking the reindeer and elk in his royal game park. But at the dawn of the 19th century, the royal island of Djurgården, lying just east of the historic city center of Stockholm **402**, was shrewdly converted to a public pleasure ground, a rival to Tivoli Gardens in Copenhagen **403**. After all, why should the king and his cronies have all the fun?

You can get here by ferry (from Skeppsbron in the historic city center) or ride the historic blue tram down Ostermalm's broad boulevard Narvavågen and over the handsome Djurgårdsbron bridge, built for the 1897 World's Fair held on Djurgården. (Check out the four Norse gods on their lofty granite columns.) The island's newer attractions are on this western waterfront, formerly a naval base. First there's **Junibacken,** an indoor play land for children based on *Pippi Longstocking* and other stories by Astrid Lindgren. South of here, the immensely popular **Vasamuseet** (Galärvarvsvägen 14; ✆ **46/8/519-548-00;** www.vasamuseet.se) was built to contain the world's oldest boat: the warship *Vasa,* which was dredged up from the floor of Stockholm harbor in 1961. Built in 1628, the *Vasa* was designed to be the jewel of Sweden's navy—but the very day it was launched, it tragically sank, right in front of a cheering crowd of thousands. There's still something haunting about this ship, perched on its stand inside the museum, bristling with hundreds of baroque carvings and the massive guns that dragged it to its watery death. Across the road, the Renaissance-style **Nordiska Museet** (Djurgårdsvägen 6–16; www.nordiskamuseet.se), another legacy of the World's Fair, showcases Swedish cultural life, with a charming hodgepodge of artifacts: 16th-century dining tables, period costumes, dollhouses, textiles, Lapland fishing tools.

Following Djurgårdsvägen south, you may get distracted by the swings and roller coasters of **Gröna Lund,** Stockholm's pint-size amusement park, built in 1883. But the real prize is east of here: **Skansen** (Djurgården 49–51; www.skansen.se), the world's first open-air museum, opened in 1891 as a sort of Sweden in miniature. More than 150 dwellings from around Sweden were reconstructed here: windmills, manor houses, a pharmacy, a glass blower's forge, a blacksmith shop, and even a complete town quarter.

There's also a small zoo full of typically Swedish animals such as reindeer, elk, seal, lynx, brown bear, and wolverine. Originally an extension of the Nordiska Museet, Skansen has proven far more popular—for on the long golden days of a Scandinavian summer, it's much more fun to be outside.

And being outside is what Djurgården is all about. Waterfront promenades, woodland trails, bicycle paths—many locals spend the day here without visiting a single attraction. Hike around the **Rosendals Trädgård** (Rosendalsterrassen 12), laid out in the 1820s as the parkland of the pink hilltop Rosendal Palace; at least one example of every native Swedish tree grows here. The inner core of Rosendals Trädgård is, as the name suggests, a "trade garden"—a huge organic garden (with a casual cafe onsite) run by the Swedish Horticultural Society, where you can pick your own produce. How pastoral! *—HH*

ⓘ **Tourist office,** Hamngatan 27 (✆ **46/8/508-285-08;** www.stockholmtown.com).

✈ Stockholm Arlanda International Airport.

🛏 $$ **Clas på Hörnet,** Surbrunnsgatan 20 (✆ **46/8/16-51-30;** www.claspahornet.se). $$$ **Victory Hotel,** Lilla Nygatan 5 (✆ **46/8/506-400-00;** www.victory-hotel.se).

419 Magnets

Vasilievsky Island

Young & Hip in the Land of the Czars

Saint Petersburg, Russia

Vasilievsky Island may have the most dramatic view in all of Saint Petersburg 404: the panoramic vista of the Winter Palace complex, seen from Strelka, the eastern spit of land where the river Neva parts to swirl around this harborfront island. But that stunning architectural composition doesn't belong to the island; Vasilievsky itself has no such architectural pretensions. With its exposed location beset by winds and floods, Vasilievsky was instead relegated to scholars and students, becoming Saint Petersburg's version of the Latin Quarter. And that is its saving grace, for like student neighborhoods anywhere, it has a bohemian dynamic that's particularly refreshing to find in Russia. It's a great counterpoint to the stage-set czarist splendors and the kinetic New Russia bustle of Nevsky Prospect.

The university is still here, along with the Russian Academy of the Arts, along the Universitetskaya Embankment. The island also has, as you'd expect, a handful of museums, including the grand neoclassical **Naval Museum** right on Strelka (look for the red Rostrol Columns outside on Birzhevaya Square, bristling with the black prows of captured foreign ships). Even more intriguing is the **Kunstkamera,** around the bend at 3 Universitetskaya Embankment, a museum built by Peter the Great some 300 years ago to introduce Russia to what was then modern medical science. The real reason most people visit is to be grossed out by its anatomical specimens—deformed animals, human body parts floating in jars of formaldehyde, abnormal fetuses and diseased babies preserved for centuries. The worn stone steps and flaking paint of this elderly building only add to the creepiness—it's like a scene from a Tim Burton movie. Farther up the embankment the trim yellow Menshikov Palace (Universitetskaya Embankment 15), originally built as one of Peter the Great's many residences, now operates as an outpost of the Hermitage. And while you're here, continue west a few streets to the 6th Line (confusingly, the east side of a street also called 7th Line) to be dazzled by the magnificent gilded iconostasis of the ornate **Andreevsky Cathedral.**

But all that is mere sightseeing; the essence of Vasilievsky lies in its funky shops and hip little restaurants, with their ironic arched-eyebrow sensibility. Check out the not-for-real-reading bookshelves that line **Akademiya** (62 Birzhevoy Proezd); the artful re-creation of Francophile 19th-century Russia at **Staraya Tamozhyna** (1 Tamozhenny Pereulok); or the satiric pop references of busy **Russky Kitsch** (25 Universitetskaya Embankment). Though four bridges arch over the Neva, connecting Vasilievsky to the "mainland" within a couple minutes' walk, it still seems buffered from Saint Petersburg's pomp and circumstance. Until recently few tourists wandered its streets, with their slightly shabby 18th-century facades; though the student quarter has now been colonized by hipsters, wander west and you'll find an almost Dickensian district of run-down factories and warehouses. This is where, in the 19th century, Russia scrambled to catch up to the Industrial Revolution. As the factory workers mingled with nearby students, Vasilievsky became a stew of radical ideas—an underground side of Russian history you'll spy only here. —*HH*

ⓘ **Information service** (✆ **7/812/380-2478;** www.saint-petersburg.com); also www.russia-travel.com.

✈ Pulkovo-2 International Airport (16km/10 miles).

🛏 $$$ **Corinthia Nevsky Palace,** 57 Nevsky Prospekt (✆ **7/812/380-2001;** www.corinthia.ru). $$ **Pulford Apartments,** 6 Moika Embankment (✆ **7/812/325-6277;** www.pulford.com).

Magnets **420**

Elephanta Island

The Hindu Caves of Old Bombay

Mumbai, India

Taking the boat to Elephanta Island from the dock in front of the Gateway of India is the classic day excursion from Mumbai 414—you take it as much to escape the city's chaos as you do to visit the island's fantastic Hindu temple caves. The whole experience is wonderfully evocative of old Bombay, from the balustraded wooden ferries to the *Indiana Jones* atmosphere of the temples themselves.

After an hour-long journey across the muddy-brown harbor of Salsette Island, Mumbai, during which local guides deliver some informative remarks about the history and significance of what you'll be seeing on the island, the boat pulls up to the Elephanta jetty. A narrow-gauge train brings you in from the pier, but to reach the caves, which lie in the middle of the 16-sq.-km (6¼-sq.-mile) island, you must climb a long stone staircase. This can be done under the power of your own quadriceps or, for the full colonial experience, by hiring a palanquin (a sedan chair carried by four men) for a small fee. Monkeys run amok on Elephanta Island and will gladly pose for pictures if you lure them with a small nibble, but be careful not to leave valuables lying around—the little simians are notorious petty thieves.

The **temples of Elephanta** were carved between the 5th and 8th centuries A.D.—though some scholars suggest a later date, from the 9th to 13th centuries—and were declared a UNESCO World Heritage Site in 1987. Entrance is via a monumental hall that houses the enormous 6.3m-tall (21-ft.) **Trimurti** (three-headed) statue of Shiva: The forward-looking face, benign and meditative, is Shiva as the Protector (Vishnu); the youthful face on the right side is Shiva as the Creator (Vamadeva or Brahma); the left-looking face, angry and mustachioed, with serpents for hair, is Shiva as the Destroyer (Bhairadeva or Rudra). The rest of the cave complex, which was excavated and decorated entirely by hand tools, covers a massive 14,504 sq. km (5,600 sq. miles). Its many halls, courtyards, and vestibules each have evocative stone pillars and wall reliefs depicting Shiva's various accomplishments.

Elephanta, which is properly called Gharapuri island in Marathi, got its present name only in the 17th century, when Portuguese explorers found a basalt sculpture of an elephant near the entrance of the caves. The sculpture has long since been removed and now resides in the Victoria Gardens of Mumbai Zoo.

Try to time your visit for the afternoon (the last ferries leave Mumbai for Elephanta at 2:30pm) so that when you return, you'll enjoy the visual treat of the sun setting over the Mumbai skyline. After disembarking at the Gateway of India, head across the way to the Taj Mahal Hotel, on the mend and still Mumbai's grande dame after the attacks of November 2008, for a celebratory cocktail. *—SM*

ⓘ **Tourist office,** 123 Maharishi Karve Rd., Churchgate, Mumbai (✆ **91/22/2207-4333**).

✈ Sahar International Airport (30km/19 miles) or Santa Cruz Airport (domestic flights; 26km/16 miles).

🛏 $$ **The Gordon House Hotel,** 5 Battery St., Apollo Bunder, Colaba (✆ **91/22/2287-1122;** www.ghhotel.com). $$$ **Taj Mahal Palace & Tower,** Apollo Bunder, Colaba (✆ **866/969-1825** in the U.S. and Canada, or 91/22/6665-3366; www.tajhotels.com).

421 Magnets

Koh Rattanakosin

Splendid Wats & Palaces

Bangkok, Thailand

Chalk it up to disorientation by tuk-tuk—or just too much sensory stimulation in the pulsating capital of Thailand—but few visitors to Bangkok's most famous temples and palaces know that these postcard-staple sights actually lie on an island. Koh Rattanakosin (Rattanakosin Island) is the oldest and most monumental part of Bangkok, nestled on the eastern bank of the Chao Phraya River's grand mid-city curve, and hemmed in by 18th-century canals (some now filled in) along its western boundary.

Along with long-tail boat cruises and the floating markets, the de rigueur tourist attractions of Bangkok are rounded out by a handful of eye-popping Buddhist wats (temples) and one very over-the-top Royal Palace. The majority of these lie on Rattanakosin, as the past rulers of Siam clearly recognized the dramatic effect of building such statement-making civic structures along the most heavily trafficked stretch of the river. Occupying much of the riverside skyline on Rattanakosin, which can be explored on foot or by tuk-tuk, is the 18th-century **Phra Borom Maha Ratcha Wang** (Royal or Grand Palace), which was the residence of the Thai monarchs until the mid–20th century. The complex consists of a succession of Renaissance-inspired marble buildings,

A stupa at the Grand Palace.

capped rather incongruously by traditional Thai rooflines. With its gilt gables and ornate *chedis* (stupas), the palace looks like an Italian government building dressed up to go to a Siamese-themed costume party.

Within the palace complex, which is still actively used by the Thai government for cultural and educational programs, lies the **Temple of the Emerald Buddha (Wat Phra Kaew).** This is the most sacred Buddhist temple in Thailand and the official place of worship for the royal family. King Rama I, who established the capital of Thailand in Bangkok in 1782, had the temple built to house the "emerald Buddha" statue that he had taken from Vientiane in Laos. Yet for all the fuss over him, the Buddha is made of jade, not emerald, and stands only 45cm (18 in.) tall—rather diminutive for all the bombastic gold stupas and spires built around him!

The most impressive and most memorable stop on the sightseeing circuit of Bangkok, however, is **Wat Po (the Temple of the Reclining Buddha),** which lies a few blocks away from the Royal Palace complex on the southern part of Rattanakosin. With a sacred precinct covering 8 hectares (20 acres), this wat is the largest in Bangkok. The cult statue of the languid Buddha—who is depicted in the moment of his extremely chilled-out passage to nirvana—does not disappoint. The Buddha is a whopping 46m (151 ft.) long and 15m (49 ft.) high, plated entirely in gold. Most extraordinary of all are the bottoms of his feet, which greet visitors like a wall of gold inlaid with mother-of-pearl—with 10 rounded toes at one end. The detailed scenes carved into his soles relate the 108 auspicious characteristics of the Buddha. The grounds of Wat Pho also contain a massage school, making this a good place to get an inexpensive rubdown. —*SM*

ⓘ www.bangkoktourist.com.

✈ Bangkok-Suvarnabhumi International (25km/16 miles).

🛏 $$$ **The Mandarin Oriental,** 48 Oriental Ave. (✆ **66/2/659-9000;** www.mandarinoriental.com/bangkok). **Shangri-La Hotel,** 89 Soi Wat Suan Plu (✆ **800/942-5050** in the U.S. and Canada or 66/2/236-7777; www.shangri-la.com).

422 Magnets

Odaiba

Over the Rainbow

Tokyo, Japan

Much as I love the old-Edo side of Japan—its Zen monasteries, tea ceremonies, and delicately composed gardens—I'm just as easily sucked into its edgy modern buzz, a jumble of cultural kitsch and high-tech trendiness. Nowhere is this side of Tokyo more evident than on Odaiba, a man-made harbor island anchored to the city by the soaring span of the Rainbow Bridge.

Formerly a set of 19th-century waterfront gun emplacements, in the 1980s Odaiba was filled in and on course to become an ambitious futuristic residential community—until Japan's economic bubble burst. New investors reinvented the island as an entertainment destination, and it finally took off, attracting the Fuji Television studios, the Tokyo Big Sight convention center, and the Telecom Center (from its observation deck you can see Mount Fuji on a clear day). For tourists, Odaiba functions as a sort of wired-up Disneyland, with a monorail linking kitschy features like a replica Statue of Liberty, the immense Daikanransha observation wheel, a Venice-themed shopping mall, a Hong Kong–themed food court, and **Oedo Onsen Monogatari** (2-57 Oumi; © **81/3/5500-1126;** www.ooedoonsen.jp/higaeri/english), a re-creation of an Edo Period hot springs resort, where visitors can soak in various types of baths fed by hot springs discovered deep beneath the harbor.

Odaiba's top lure for visitors may be **Miraikan,** Japan's National Museum of Emerging Science and Innovation (2-41 Aomi; © **81/3/3570-9151;** www.miraikan.jst.go.jp), a sleek assembly of hands-on exhibits, virtual reality rides, and a state-of-the-art planetarium. Alongside earnest

Odaiba and the Rainbow Bridge.

exhibits on environmental science and genomes, Miraikan shows off cutting-edge achievements of Japanese technology, from micromachines to robotics; one of its most popular attractions is stump-the-robot demonstrations starring ASIMO, the famed intelligent robot. The nearby **Museum of Maritime Science** (3-1 Higashi-Yashio; ✆ **81/3/5500-1111**) occupies a modern white building with a majestic shiplike prow. Among its displays of historic seafaring relics are a number of ships of all sizes, moored to the wharves outside the museum.

Two other attractions aren't educational, but are sure to be a hit with the kids. The first is **Megaweb,** 1 Aomi (✆ **81/3/3599-0808;** www.megaweb.gr.jp), a sprawling amusement park, which is actually a Toyota showroom—but who cares? The commercial message is sweetened with virtual thrill rides, driving simulators, a 3-D motion theater, and driverless electric commuter cars. You can top off the day at **Joypolis Sega** (Tokyo Decks mall; ✆ **81/3/5500-1801**), Tokyo's most sophisticated virtual amusement arcade, brought to you by—you guessed it—Sega. There are virtual reality video games where players try their hands at bobsledding and other action sports. You can even take a 3-D virtual sightseeing tour of Tokyo, careening around the "sights" in seats that lurch and tilt to the action on the screen.

Although there is a patch of greenery left at the top of the island, near the bridge, Odaiba is mostly paved and built up, with striking modern architecture (except for the stage-set historic fakes). It may not be a haven for tuning out, but it's a great place to plug in—with all batteries included. —*HH*

ⓘ www.tcvb.or.jp.

✈ Narita International (66km/41 miles).

🛏 $$$ **Hotel Nikko Tokyo,** 1-9-1 Daiba, Minato-Ku (✆ **800/645-5687** in the U.S. and Canada, or 81/3/5500-5500; www.hnt.co.jp). $$ **Park Hotel Tokyo,** 1-7-1 Higashi Shimbashi, Minato-ku, Ginza (✆ **81/3/6252-1111;** www.parkhoteltokyo.com).

Magnets **423**

Cockatoo Island

Dirty Work

Sydney, Australia

If you're imagining a sylvan, parklike setting filled with cooing, white-feathered cockatoos, think again. Cockatoo Island is a park all right—but this ultraurban setting, enveloped in the metropolitan sprawl of Sydney, Australia, is a gritty living remnant of the Industrial Age.

Set at the confluence of the Parramatta and Lane Cove rivers, Cockatoo is the largest island in Sydney Harbour. During the building of Sydney in the mid–19th century, it was where much of the country's dirty work was carried out. The island was home to massive industrial workshops and shipyards where merchant ships, aircraft carriers, and steel warships were hammered and bolted. It was also a penal colony where convicts were put to hard labor, and something of a lost-child repository, where orphaned and homeless children were delivered to chilly reformatories. Two large dry docks were built here, one constructed entirely by prison labor in 1857. For much of the 20th century, Cockatoo Island was the site of one of the country's largest shipbuilding yards.

So what's with the name? Long before the island was built up, Cockatoo was indeed the habitat of the sulphur-crested cockatoo. The large white (and very vocal) cockatoo thrived here in this isolated habitat, along with red gum trees. Today both are gone, replaced by large Moreton Bay fig trees and bats.

The rebirth of Cockatoo Island as a cultural and historical arm of the city of Sydney is already underway. Under the management of the Sydney Harbour Federation Trust, the island's Industrial Age sites—piled high with century-old cranes, jetties, and machinery—are being rehabbed and restored as historic relics from the country's early days. Against the evocative backdrop, arts and entertainment events are also on the calendar, including an international music festival that drew 20,000 people in its inaugural year. Cockatoo is even up for consideration for World Heritage Site status.

It's easy to get around this 18-hectare (44-acre) island on foot, and there's no entrance fee. Pick up a map (or audio tour and headphones) for a self-guided tour at the **Cockatoo Island Muster Station.** Guided tours are given twice on Sundays. Don't forget your camera; the views of Sydney and the harbor are magnificent. But the immense industrial sites have their own photogenic allure—particularly at night, when seen against a backdrop of glittering city lights. Fortunately, camping is now allowed on Cockatoo at 135 unpowered (tents only) sites, and you can rent a tent and camping equipment on the island. Sleeping under the stars—and towering cranes—should make for an unforgettable night in the urban wilderness. —*AF*

ⓘ www.cockatooisland.gov.au.

✈ Sydney.

Sydney Ferries (✆ **61/2/131 500;** www.sydneyferries.info). From Circular Quay, 10 min.

$ **Cockatoo Island camping:** www.cockatooisland.gov.au. $$$ **Sir Stamford at Circular Quay,** 93 Macquarie St., Sydney (✆ **61/2/9252 4600;** www.stamford.com.au).

424 Magnets

Liberty & Ellis Islands

Gateway to America

New York, New York, U.S.

The icon to end all icons, the Statue of Liberty isn't just New York City's trademark image—it is recognized around the world as the symbol of American freedom. Of *course* you have to visit it while you're in New York City, right? Well, I'll confess, I lived in New York for 15 years before I finally visited Lady Liberty on Liberty Island, on a summer afternoon with my then-10-year-old son. I can't imagine why I waited that long. It's a great half-day excursion from the skyscraper canyons; what's more, it's the city's greatest two-for-one deal, for the same ferryboat takes you to Ellis Island.

The **Statue of Liberty** (or, as she is officially known, Liberty Enlightening the World) is impressive enough from across the harbor, but close up—man, this chick is BIG. Don't be surprised if you feel overwhelmed, staring up at her stately toga-clad physique. Lady Liberty weighs in at 225 tons of hammered copper, oxidized as planned to a delicate pale green, and her nose alone is 4½ ft. (1.4m) long. Given to the United States by France, she has presided over the harbor since 1886 as a symbol of America's stature as a nation of immigrants. It's worth the trip just to stroll around Liberty Island and gaze out over the harbor. To go inside the statue, however, make sure you have a monument access ticket; a limited number of tickets now also grant access to the crown at the top, which was closed for several years. Reserve your ferry tickets in advance to guarantee monument access (✆ **877/523-9849;** www.statuecruises.com). Even if you don't go all the way to the top, you can explore the promenade or go to the 10th-floor observatory for fascinating historic exhibits and a peek through a glass ceiling into her ingenious steel skeleton, designed by Gustave Eiffel of Eiffel Tower fame.

But you know what? Much as my son and I loved the Statue of Liberty, we were unexpectedly blown away by our next stop, Ellis Island. From the mountain of ragtag luggage stacked right inside the front doors, upstairs to the cramped dormitories and medical examination rooms (cough the wrong way and you could be sent right back to Europe), to glass cases crammed with immigrants' old-country family heirlooms, the **Ellis Island Immigration Museum** brings history to life. From 1892 to 1954, this was America's main immigration port of entry, where successive waves of new Americans first set foot on the soil of their new homeland. Prepare to be awed by the second-floor Registry Hall, its soaring vaulted ceiling faced with white tile, where new arrivals shuffled along in tediously long lines to be interviewed by immigration officials. (Cue up the theme from *The Godfather, Part II.*) On the Wall of Honor outside, some 420,000 immigrants' names are inscribed in steel. There are hands-on exhibits, films, live plays, computer stations where you can examine ship manifests—2 hours is barely enough to do this place justice.

Both sights are free; you pay only for the boat ride (and there's no other way to get here). Ferryboats make frequent trips, running a 35-minute loop from Battery Park to Liberty Island to Ellis Island and back to Battery Park; from New Jersey you can board ferries in Liberty State Park. —*HH*

ⓘ **Liberty Island** (✆ **212/363-3200;** www.nps.gov/stli). **Ellis Island** (✆ **212/363-3200;** www.nps.gov/elis).

✈ John F. Kennedy International, Newark Liberty International, or LaGuardia.

🛏 $$ **Milburn Hotel,** 242 W. 76th St. (✆ **800/833-9622** or 212/362-1006; www.milburnhotel.com). $$ **Washington Square Hotel,** 103 Waverly Place (✆ **800/222-0418** or 212/777-9515; www.washingtonsquarehotel.com).

The Statue of Liberty on Liberty Island.

425 Magnets

Mud Island

Ode to Old Man River

Memphis, Tennessee, U.S.

Like its namesake in Egypt, the city of Memphis, Tennessee, is first and foremost a river town. Everything that makes it a great city—its blues, its rock-and-roll music (viva Elvis!), its civil rights history, its barbecue—stems from its character as a river port, and therefore a cultural melting pot. Several museums along the course of the mighty Mississippi claim to define this great river, but I'll cast my vote for Memphis's candidate: Mud Island River Park.

Aptly named Mud Island didn't always exist—it first started to build up, an accretion of river sand and sediment, around 1900. As it filled in and became permanent land, it eventually began to meld into the mainland; the Wolf River which now divides it from the rest of Memphis is a carefully maintained canal (a monorail track arches overhead, handily zipping visitors to the island from downtown Memphis). But that kind of transformation is par for the course along the muddy meander of the Mississippi. That's why it's especially appropriate that this more-or-less-real island should feature a museum celebrating the Mississippi River.

It's also appropriate that the heart of this museum is outside, in a 52-acre (21-hectare) park trailing the length of the island, along its riverbank side. There you'll find **River Walk,** a 5-block-long scale model of 900 miles (1,448km) of the Mississippi River, from Cairo, Illinois (where the confluence of the Ohio and the Mississippi creates a truly majestic river), down to New Orleans and the Gulf of Mexico. Carving its course through a long paved plaza, the water of the "river" flows past little street grids representing various river towns; informative plaques discourse on the river's geology and history. While strolling along River Walk is free, it'll probably get you interested enough to pay the admission fee to go through the adjacent **Mississippi River Museum,** 125 N. Front St. (✆ **800/507-6507** or 901/576-7241; www.mudisland.com). The most fun exhibits here are the huge aquarium tank, the massive red riverboat paddle wheel, a trove of music artifacts, and dioramas of riverboat gamblers, levee builders, and the great bard of the Mississippi River, Mark Twain.

At any rate, River Walk should tempt you to get onto the water, which you can do by renting kayaks at the park concession to explore the calm harbor, or by renting paddle boats to navigate River Walk's acre-large model of the Gulf of Mexico. You can also rent bicycles to cruise along the shore path. Given the typical humid swelter of a Memphis summer day (Mud Island is open Apr–Nov), these offer heavenly opportunities to catch a few river breezes. Naturally, this being Memphis, there's a music hook too: On summer evenings, the **Mud Island Amphitheater** hosts touring acts that have ranged in the past from Smashing Pumpkins to Fall Out Boy and from Willie Nelson to Norah Jones. —*HH*

ⓘ **Tourist office,** 47 Union Ave. (✆ **800/8-MEMPHIS** [863-6744] or 901/543-5300; www.memphistravel.com).

✈ Memphis International.

🛏 $$$ **The Peabody Memphis,** 149 Union Ave. (✆ **901/529-3677;** www.peabodymemphis.com). $$ **Wyndham Gardens Hotel,** 300 N. 2nd St. (✆ **901/525-1800;** www.wyndham.com).

Magnets 426

Watson Island

Welcome to the Jungle

Miami, Florida, U.S.

For years, I'd read about Parrot Jungle, touted as a charmingly ramshackle Miami attraction with an authentic old-Florida vibe, like Gatorland, Cypress Gardens, or Weeki Watchee Springs. I'm a sucker for these relics from the early days of mass tourism. I kept telling myself I had to get down there and see it, before it was gobbled up by rampaging south Florida development.

No sooner had my family finally booked a Miami vacation than I discovered that Parrot Jungle had closed—or, at any rate, moved from that junky old site to a brand-spanking-new spot on Watson Island, just off MacArthur Causeway in the middle of Biscayne Bay. Several such man-made islands prop up the causeways that tether Miami Beach 412 to mainland Miami, most of them exclusive residential enclaves like Star Island, Hibiscus Island, Palm Island, and the Venetian islands. The online travel blogs I read griped that Parrot Jungle had lost its soul.

Steeled for disappointment, I took my then-7-year-old daughter to the new Parrot Jungle—since renamed **Jungle Island** (✆ **305/400-7000;** www.jungleisland.com)—and I have to admit, we had a ball. Though the lush tropical plantings hadn't quite grown in yet, the birds and other wildlife seemed happy in their "soulless" (and probably more humane) new quarters. Meandering pathways, ponds and streams, rocky outcrops, pavilions for animal demonstrations—it seems roomy indeed, though not too big to cover in half a day. The name change makes sense—besides the original parrots, this avian collection now includes penguins, emus, owls, even a vulture and condor, along with the standard Florida flamingo pond. Mammals have been added to the mix as well, with a host of jungle primates—orangutans, chimpanzees, gibbons, lemurs—as well as nonjungly species like llamas and kangaroos, all in suitably naturalistic fake habitats. Since we came, the tiger population of the park has added Hercules, an immense "liger" (offspring of a lion and tiger—and you thought Napoleon Dynamite had made that up!), as well a private white-sand beach on the bay, a splendid way to take advantage of that island location.

On the south side of the causeway, check out the **Miami Children's Museum** (✆ **305/373-5437;** www.miamichildrensmuseum.org), with loads of lively interactive exhibits in a nautical-looking building (portholes, wave-curved roofline) fronted by what looks like a giant traffic cone. We didn't expect to find a child pleaser like that next door to Parrot Jungle—and unfortunately we hadn't set aside enough time to explore it. "Next time," I promised my daughter. Well, she's 14 now and I suspect she's outgrown the Children's Museum. But maybe now we could add on the nearby **Ichimura Miami-Japanese Garden** (✆ **305/960-4639;** www.jgarden.org/gardens.asp?ID=290), an acre full of stone lanterns, bamboo groves, rock gardens, and koi ponds, perfect for serene meditation.

With a proposed new marina-hotel-entertainment complex in the offing, Watson Island may someday lose its laid-back quality, that sense of being a safe buffer zone between the two Miamis. No doubt the bloggers will lament that too. *—HH*

ⓘ **Tourist office,** 1700 Convention Center Dr. (✆ **305/673-7400;** www.miamibeachfl.gov).

✈ Miami International Airport or Fort Lauderdale Hollywood International Airport.

🛏 $$ **Circa 39 Hotel,** 3900 Collins Ave. (✆ **877/824-7223** or 305/538-4900; www.circa39.com). $$ **South Seas Hotel,** 1751 Collins Ave. (✆ **800/345-2678** or 305/205-6195; www.southseashotel.com).

427 Magnets

Ile Sainte-Hélène & Ile Notre-Dame

Beaucoup Recreation

Montreal, Canada

Counting among their attractions a Biosphere, an amusement park, a casino, and Olympic-caliber sports facilities, Montreal's richest repositories of recreational opportunities are its two playground-islands in the middle of the St. Lawrence river, Ile Sainte-Hélène and Ile Notre-Dame. Significantly developed for Montreal's Expo 67, they remain prime destinations for Montrealers in the 21st century.

Ile Sainte-Hélène has long been a fixture in Montreal's history. Following the War of 1812, defenses such as a fort, a powder house, and a blockhouse were built here to protect the city. Some of these remains can be explored at the **Fort de l'Ile** historic site and accompanying **David M. Stewart Museum** (Vieux Fort; www.stewart-museum.org), where reenactments are staged and a noonday gun salute is shot every day. While the island was converted into parkland in 1874, Ile Sainte-Hélène returned to military duty in World War II, when prisoner-of-war camps were established here in the early 1940s.

The Expo 67 world's fair to celebrate Canada's centennial signaled the island's heyday. For all the fair's ambitious displays and pavilions, Ile Sainte-Hélène was greatly enlarged and merged with smaller islands around it, while its neighbor across the narrow Le Moyne channel, Ile Notre-Dame, was built entirely from scratch, using 15 million tons of rocks excavated for tunnels for the Montreal Metro in 1965. The **La Ronde amusement park** (22 Chemin Macdonald; www.laronde.com) was built on Sainte-Hélène for the exposition; today operated by Six Flags, it offers world-class roller coasters and thrill rides.

Most of the Expo 67 pavilions were dismantled in the years following the fair; the pavilions of France and Quebec became Ile Notre-Dame's **Montreal Casino** (www.casinosduquebec.com/montreal), and the American pavilion became Ile St. Helene's **Biosphere** attraction (http://biosphere.ec.gc.ca), which has

Ile Sainte-Hélène's Biosphere.

exhibits on environmental issues. Much of the islands' real estate was also requalified as competition space for the 1976 Montreal Summer Olympics, most notably a **rowing and canoeing basin** on the east side of Ile Notre-Dame, still the largest artificial rowing basin in North America. The extensive **Aquatic Complex** also remains an important training facility for competitive swimmers and divers.

Today, with lakes and green areas galore, iles Sainte-Hélène and Notre-Dame make up one of the city's largest and most well-used parks, **Parc Jean-Drapeau,** easily accessible by metro from central Montreal. In winter, visitors can cross-country ski or snowshoe through the park's wilder areas, and ice-skating rinks are set up either on the frozen-over rowing basin or near the metro station on Ile Sainte-Hélène. In summer, an **artificial beach** on Ile Notre-Dame has watercraft rentals and sand volleyball courts. A few times a year, the general peace and quiet of the island is interrupted by the roar of engines for Formula 1 and NASCAR races held at Ile Notre-Dame's **Circuit Gilles Villeneuve;** and by the overhead explosions of **L'International des Feux Loto-Québec** (Montreal Fireworks Festival, June–Aug), one of the most important pyrotechnics display-competitions in the world, taking place at La Ronde amusement park. *—SM*

ⓘ **Tourist offices:** Parc Jean-Drapeau metro station on Ile Sainte-Hélène; Passerelle du Cosmos on Ile Notre-Dame (✆ **514/872-6120;** www.parcjeandrapeau.com).

✈ Montreal-Trudeau International (20km/12 miles).

🛏 $$ **Auberge Bonaparte,** 447 St.-François-Xavier (✆ **514/844-1448;** www.bonaparte.com). $$$ **Hôtel Le St-James,** 355 rue St-Jacques oust (✆ **866/841-3111** or 514/841-3111; www.hotellestjames.com).

Magnets 428

Granville Island

From Factory to Funky

Vancouver, B.C., Canada

Back in the 1970s, Granville Island had become a problem—a derelict industrial district rusting away on its man-made island in False Creek, that long inlet that almost severs downtown Vancouver from the mainland. Lying in the shadows underneath the Granville Bridge, its warehouses, sheds, foundries, and empty factories were nothing but an eyesore.

Twenty-five years later, Granville Island is one of the most successful urban renewal projects ever. Potters, weavers, painters, printmakers, jewelry makers, glass blowers—even a microbrewery and an artisanal sake maker—have taken over those high-ceilinged industrial spaces. The outdoor decks of trendy restaurants overlook the waterfront. Small theaters and outdoor performance spaces produce an almost continuous stream of entertainment. A sprawling marina on the island's southwest, close to the open waters of English Bay, is filled with pleasure craft as well as kayaks, canoes, and paddle boats for hourly rentals.

You can take a ferry from downtown, or come by land from the south, over the Anderson Street causeway, which runs directly underneath Granville Bridge—look for the red neon Granville Island sign welcoming you onto the island. ***Warning:*** Parking can be scarce; walk or bike over if you can. Most first-time visitors begin at the **Granville Island Public Market** (1669 Johnston St.), where the ferries dock, on the island's northwest waterfront. In a series of cavernous sheds, Granville Market's lineup of stalls is proof positive of Vancouver's vibrant foodie scene—a tasty mix of locavore produce, organic cheeses, grass-fed beef, free-range poultry, and fresh-off-the-boat seafood alongside Asian imports, Italian pastas, German delis, and specialty shops that express the multicultural richness of this Pacific Rim capital. Roam the market stalls for sandwiches, sausages, or oven-warm bread, and then head for the outdoor seating areas, where you can enjoy a view of tugboats, sailboats, and ferries while buskers perform and seagulls swoop in for treats.

Next to the market, two other industrial buildings have been turned into mini-malls with an arts-and-crafts bent—the **Creekhouse** on Johnston Street (under the bridge) and the **Net Loft** on Duranleau Street. Across Duranleau, a sizable cluster of sheds is now the shipshape **Maritime Market,** where the shops sell everything from boating equipment to yachting fashions. Check out the art exhibits and galleries in the **North Building** (1399 Johnston St.), and then stroll around the adjoining side streets—Cartwright Street, Old Bridge Street, narrow Railspur Alley—to find artist's studios and galleries. More important, drink in the overall Granville aesthetic vibe—funky signs, cheery paint jobs, hanging flowerpots, all of it transforming urban grit (there's still a cement company on the waterfront) into hipster coolness.

If you've got kids in tow, stop off at the **Kids Market** at the foot of Anderson Street, where all the shops cater to youngsters. Then head up Cartwright Street to the free **Granville Island Water Park and Adventure Playground** (1496 Cartwright St.), where the kids can while away warm afternoons with water guns, sprinklers, wading pools, and water slides. —*HH*

(i) **Granville Island Information Centre,** 1592 Johnston St. (✆ **604/666-5784;** www.granvilleisland.com).

✈ Vancouver International.

⛴ From various North Shore docks, 5–20 min: **Aquabus** (✆ **604/689-5858;** www.theaquabus.com) or **False Creek Ferries** (✆ **604/684-7781;** www.granvilleislandferries.bc.ca).

🛏 $$ **Granville Island Hotel,** 1253 Johnston St., Granville Island (✆ **800/663-1840** or 604/683-7373; www.granvilleislandhotel.com). $$ **Robsonstrasse Hotel,** 1394 Robson St. (✆ **888/667-8877** or 604/687-1674; www.robsonstrassehotel.com).

429 Parks

Margit-sziget

Where Buda & Pest Meet

Budapest, Hungary

In 1873, the flat plain of Pest and the hilly precincts of Buda were officially yoked together, for better or worse, as one city: Budapest. Facing each other across the Danube River, the two halves of Hungary's capital have not always seemed compatible. But the distinctions between Buda and Pest seem to melt away on Margit-sziget, a serene wooded island set exactly halfway between them, in the middle of the Danube between the Árpád and Margit bridges.

Originally known as Rabbit Island, this Danube island was long ago a stronghold of the Crusader knights of St. John. In the 13th century, Princess Margaret, daughter of Bela IV, founded a cloistered Dominican convent here; a cluster of religious establishments located on the island by the

Margit-sziget and Budapest.

16th century were all abruptly destroyed during the Ottoman wars (a few church ruins survive). In the 19th century, Rabbit Island was greatly enlarged when it was combined with two other neighboring islands, part of an ongoing quest to control the Danube's periodic floods.

In 1908, Margit-sziget was declared a public park for the newly united city of Budapest. Amenities were loaded on over the years—**Palatinus,** a huge open-air swimming complex; a tennis stadium; an athletics center; a rubberized jogging track circling the 2.3km-long (1½-mile) island. Amid flower plantings and stands of century-old sycamore trees, there's a charming Japanese garden, complete with fish pond, and a small petting zoo. A stunning castellated water tower rises above the dense treetops; by the Margaret Bridge, the landmark **Zenélő szökőkút fountain** sprays and sparkles to the accompaniment of music and nighttime light shows. An open-air theater, clubs, restaurants—eventually every Budapester is lured here for some sort of pleasure. And it's not just locals: There are two hotels at the island's northern tip—the venerable resortlike **Grand Hotel Margitsziget** and its more modern sister hotel, the **Thermal Hotel Margitsziget,** where guests of either hotel can enjoy a host of spa services as well as extensive thermal baths (Budapest has long been famous for its hot springs).

Though both Árpád and Margit bridges touch the island, you can't bring a car here—the only cars allowed are on official business. You can rent small electric cars for use on the island, though most visitors seem to prefer the ubiquitous four-seater cycles. It's a choice spot for bicycling—considering the frantic nature of Budapest's traffic, it's probably the only really safe biking place in the city. Bring a picnic, sunbathe on the lido, or just stroll along in the deliciously cool shade of those venerable trees. The nuns may be gone, but the sense of tranquillity on Margaret Island lives on. *—HH*

ⓘ **Tourist office,** V. Sütő u. 2 at Deák square (✆ **36/1/322-4098** or 36/1/438-8080; www.budapestinfo.hu).

✈ Budapest.

🛏 $$ **Hotel Erzsébet,** V. Károlyi Mihály u. 11–15 (✆ **36/1/889-3700;** www.danubiusgroup.com). $$ **Hotel Papillon,** II. Rózsahegy u. 3/b (✆ **36/1/212-4750;** www.hotelpapillon.hu).

430 Parks

Cagarras Islands

Off the Shores of Ipanema

Rio de Janeiro, Brazil

Rio de Janeiro may be best known to travelers for its wild beach life and unhinged party scene, but for outdoor enthusiasts, one of Rio's top insider secrets is the little, uninhabited archipelago lying just 5km (3 miles) off legendary Ipanema Beach. The Cagarras Islands (Ilhas Cagarras in Portuguese) are a wildlife refuge for sea gulls and other marine birds, and you can frequently spot—or swim among—dolphins in the waters offshore.

Five islands make up the *arquipélago,* and their rounded grey-stone contours make them look like oversized pebbles—albeit stained with guano and vegetation—that have been gently deposited in the sea. **Ilha Cagarra,** the island group's namesake, is the tallest (79m/259 ft.) and most visible from land. Though the rock faces of the island are quite steep, they shelter an enormous number of marine avifauna, from seagulls to boobies to frigate birds, who build their nests here each year. **Ilha das Palmas** owes its name to the dense growth of palm trees, and its vegetation is the lushest in the archipelago. The longest island in the chain is **Ilha Comprida** ("Trousers Island"), and its calm beach makes it the preferred point of landing for tourist boats and dive charters. Unfortunately, many visitors don't pick up their trash, so there's often an annoying colony of buzzards to greet newcomers. Dolphins are particularly common in the waters off Comprida, and divers are attracted to the island's underwater sights, including a recent shipwreck. **Laje da Cagarra** is the island facing Copacabana fort, nearest to the mainland, and not typically accessible to visitors: The waters here are difficult to navigate, as testified by the many vestiges of shipwrecks among the rocks. The final island in the group, **Ilha Filhote,** is hidden from shore by the mass of Ilha Cagarra; it has a small natural pool that comes and goes with the tides.

Unless you have arranged private sea transportation (see below for info on customized excursions), organized boat tours leaving from Marina da Glòria—either diving- and wildlife-specific day trips, or general offshore excursions that also take in sights like Copacabana Beach and Sugarloaf Mountain from the water—are generally the only way to get to the Cagarras islands. While many of these trips allow you to disembark, hike, and swim on the islands, there are no overnight facilities or restaurants on any of the Cagarras. —*SM*

ⓘ www.braziltour.com.

✈ Rio de Janeiro-Galeão.

Customized excursions can be arranged through **Tropical Cruises** (✆ **55/21/9963-6172;** www.tropicalcruises.com.br).

$$$ **Copacabana Palace,** av. Atlântica 1702, Copacabana, Rio de Janeiro (✆ **55/21/2548-7070;** www.copacabanapalace.orient-express.com). $$ **Hotel Florida,** Rua Ferreira Viana 81, Flamengo, Rio de Janeiro (✆ **55/21/2195-6800;** www.windsorhoteis.com).

Parks 431

Centre Island

Hiawatha's Island

Toronto, Canada

The 10-minute ferry ride across Toronto Harbour to visit the Toronto Islands is a classic Toronto getaway—the city's dramatic skyline, dominated by the CN Tower, slides away behind you, while this cluster of green islands rises up out of the lake to greet you.

Early native American residents knew that this shifting mass of sandbars and marshes, the storm-broken remains of a long, curving peninsula, was the best place to cool off in summer along the shores of Lake Ontario. For years, the European settlers referred to it as Hiawatha's Island. Soon enough, though, Torontonians were making their way over to the lake islands too. By the late 1800s, elegant Victorian-style summer homes lined Lake Shore Avenue, which connects several of the more residential islands. Yacht clubs, theaters, restaurants, dance halls, a ball stadium (where Babe Ruth hit his first home run!)—the Toronto Islands bustled with entertainment. Many of these facilities and most of the houses were torn down in the 1950s and 1960s when the city decided to make the islands a more pastoral public park, but a handful of homes survive, including a vintage cottage community preserved on the eastern end, **Ward's Island.**

For the casual visitor, the place to go is 243-hectare (600-acre) **Centre Island Park** (which, naturally, lies at the center of the cluster). Car-free Centre Island is perfect for cycling, in-line skating, strolling, and picnicking, all with that skyline panorama as a backdrop. Most of Centre Island is parkland, crisscrossed by shaded paths and quiet waterways; pedestrian

View from ferry to Centre Island.

bridges lead to some of the neighboring islands, if you want to have a more secluded picnic. On the south side of the island you'll find sandy **Centre Island Beach;** at the **City of Toronto Boathouse** (© **416/397-BOAT** [397-2628]), you can rent canoes, rowboats, and pedal boats for exploring the quiet waterways between the various bits of islands.

Families usually head straight for the old-fashioned amusement park **Centreville** (© **416/203-0405;** www.centreisland.ca), which has been around since 1966. Open from early May to Labor Day, Centreville keeps things wholesome and clean—instead of neon signs and thrill coasters, its main feature is a turn-of-the-20th-century village complete with a shop-lined Main Street, firehouse, and petting farm. As far as rides go, Centreville's are sweet and low-key—antique cars, fire engines, a minitrain, a flume ride, an authentic 1890s carousel, bumper boats, twirling teacups, and picturesque swan boats circling a lagoon.

Busy as the island may get on your typical sunny summer weekend, that's nothing compared to the crowds that come here every June for the annual 2-day **Toronto International Dragon Boat Race Festival** (© **416/595-0313;** www.dragonboats.com). First run in 1989, the Dragon Boat races—sponsored by Toronto's substantial Chinese community—have become one of the city's most popular festivals, with some 200 boats now competing in front of more than a hundred thousand cheering spectators. *—HH*

ⓘ **Tourist office,** 207 Queens Quay West (© **800/499-2514** or 416/203-2500; www.seetorontonow.com).

✈ Toronto International.

⛴ 10-min. ride from the Bay St. docks, by Queens Quay (© **416/392-8193**).

🛏 $$ **The Drake Hotel,** 1150 Queen St. W. (© **416/531-5042;** www.thedrakehotel.ca). $$$ **Le Royal Meridien King Edward,** 37 King St. E. (© **800/543-4300** or 416/863-9700; www.starwoodhotels.com).

432 Parks

Theodore Roosevelt Island

The Rough Rider's Refuge

Washington, D.C., U.S.

Let the other American presidents—Lincoln, Jefferson, Washington, FDR—have their dignified neoclassical monuments near the well-groomed Mall in downtown Washington, D.C. For the nation's 26th president, Theodore Roosevelt, this is a far more fitting memorial: a densely wooded marshy island in the middle of the Potomac, overrun with rabbits, chipmunks, owls, foxes, muskrats, turtles, and groundhogs. Under Roosevelt's leadership, the United States set aside a total of 234 million acres (98 million hectares) of public lands for forests, national parks, wildlife and bird refuges, and monuments—quite an impressive record. The least we could do is devote a wildlife island to our greenest president ever.

Getting here requires the sort of tenacity that T. R. himself would have admired: There's only one footbridge, connecting the island to the western bank of the Potomac, at Arlington, Virginia. (No cars or bicycles are allowed on the island.) Technically it's part of the George Washington Memorial Parkway, with its own parking lot off the parkway's northbound lane, just past the Theodore Roosevelt Bridge. Leave your car there, at the Virginia end of the bridge, and hike over the bridge—you'll be amazed at how effectively the thick vegetation screens out the whizzing parkway traffic and the general hyperbolic energy of the nation's capital.

Three loops of **walking trails,** 2½ miles (4km) in total, wind through the 90-acre (36-hectare) island's various habitats—woods, uplands, and swamp (that part of the trail turns into a boardwalk). It's a complex ecosystem in which cattails, arrow arum, and pickerelweed grow in the marshes, and willow, ash, and maple trees root on the mud flats. Bring your binoculars and you may score some surprising bird sightings, considering how close you are to Reagan National Airport and the Pentagon. (Well, maybe the hawks commute here from the Pentagon.) In the heart of the island stands a giant **bronze statue of Roosevelt,** depicted in a dynamic pose with his arm raised emphatically, as if leading the charge up San Juan Hill all over again. Around it are set a few marble plinths engraved with Roosevelt quotes about conserving the environment.

As for the greenest First Lady—Lady Byrd Johnson, whose 1960s highway beautification campaign replaced billboards with flowerbeds across America—follow the paved Mount Vernon Trail south from Theodore Roosevelt Island's parking lot and you'll soon arrive at neighboring Columbia Island, now called **Lady Bird Johnson Island** in her honor. The Lyndon Baines Johnson Memorial Grove here is a stunning picnic spot with postcard views of the Tidal Basin monuments and, in the distance, the gleaming dome of the U.S. Capitol. —*HH*

ⓘ **Tourist information** (✆ **703/289-2500;** www.nps.gov/this).

✈ Reagan Natl (3 miles/4.8km); Dulles International (26 miles/42km); Baltimore-Washington International (35 miles/56km).

Footbridge from Arlington, Virginia.

$$ **Four Points by Sheraton,** 1201 K St. NW (✆ **202/289-7600;** www.fourpoints.com/washingtondcdowntown). $$ **Georgetown Suites,** 1111 30th St. NW (✆ **202/298-1600;** www.georgetownsuites.com).

Parks **433**

Belle Isle

Detroit's Tarnished Jewel

Detroit, Michigan, U.S.

Talk about pedigrees. This 983-acre (398-hectare) island park in the Detroit River was laid out in the 1880s by the great American landscape architect Frederick Law Olmsted. Several of its showpiece buildings were designed by Albert Kahn, big-money Detroit's architect of choice in the early 20th century. Noted Beaux Arts architect Cass Gilbert designed the exuberant Scott Fountain you see as you first cross the bridge onto the island, festooned with over a hundred water spouts shaped like human and animal heads.

Anyone who reads the newspapers, however, knows that Detroit has fallen on hard times. With the city's long-awaited renaissance stalled yet again, the beauties of Belle Isle (a 10-min. drive from Cadillac Square in downtown Detroit) are crying out for attention.

On the one hand, Belle Isle performs the role of any urban park, by providing

Detroit's citizens with recreational amenities—ball fields, tennis and handball courts, picnic shelters, a huge playground, a golf course, fishing piers, a water-slide pool, and Detroit's only public beach. Paved roads and paths, winding through Olmsted's artfully variegated landscape, welcome joggers, cyclists, and inline skaters. On any given summer weekend, the drives are choked with traffic—that's how popular it is.

But in its heyday—back when Detroit was the Motor Capital of the World—Belle Isle was so much more. When the city fathers renamed Hog Island as Belle Isle—"beautiful island"—in 1879, they also hired Olmsted to give it a flair worthy of Paris. Its stylish Spanish-style Casino, now a rentable event space near the Scott Fountain, was one of the world's most glamorous pavilions. The Detroit Zoo occupied a smart set of Tudor-style buildings here until it moved to larger quarters in 1928. Concerts at the Remick Music Shell, ice-skating at the Flynn Pavilion, boating events at the Detroit Boat Club (the oldest boat club in the United States)—all are things of the past, their graceful buildings mere shells. Even the striking 1904 Belle Isle Aquarium—the oldest continuously operating public aquarium in North America—was closed in 2005 due to budget cuts, though conservationists are still fighting to have it reopened.

Though there's a weird romance to all those decaying buildings, several gems remain. In the middle of the island, the **Whitcomb Conservatory** (✆ **313/821-5428**), designed in 1904 as Albert Kahn's homage to Monticello, lofts its glass dome over palm trees, cacti, ferns, tropical plants, and a world-class orchid display. Every half-hour, the sound of brass bells rings out from the 85-feet-high (26m) Carillon Tower. On the south shore, the **Dossin Great Lakes Museum** (✆ **313/852-4051;** Strand Dr.; www.glmi.org) conveys the history of Great Lakes shipping. On the eastern end, a herd of fallow deer that once ran wild over the island is safely enclosed in the **Belle Isle Nature Zoo** (✆ **313/852-4056;** Lakeside Dr.; www.detroitzoo.org). The venerable Detroit Yacht Club, founded in 1868, is still quartered on the north side of the island. And the beacon goes on shining from the Livingstone Memorial Lighthouse (another Kahn design), an elegantly decorated shaft of Georgia marble guarding the mouth of the Detroit River. —HH

ⓘ **Belle Isle information** (✆ **313/628-2081**). **Detroit tourist office,** 211 W. Fort St. (✆ **800/DETROIT** [338-7648] or 313/202-1800; www.visitdetroit.com).

✈ Detroit Metropolitan Airport (35 miles/56km).

🛏 $$$ **Detroit Marriott at the Renaissance Center,** 400 Renaissance Center (✆ **888/228-9290** or 313/568-8000; www.marriott.com). $$ **The Inn on Ferry Street,** 84 E. Ferry St. (✆ **313/871-6000;** www.theinnonferrystreet.com).

Parks

Angel Island

Ellis Island by the Golden Gate

San Francisco, California, U.S.

They call it the City by the Bay for good reason. When you visit San Francisco you'll be treated to panoramas of San Francisco Bay from every perspective—the Golden Gate Bridge, the top of Coit Tower, the lawns of the Presidio, the hilly peaks of the cable car lines, the tourist-thronged piers of Fisherman's Wharf. How

Island Hopping the Aeolian Islands: La Vita Lava

This remote archipelago is beautiful in a rugged, wind-swept way, not surprising for a place built on fire and smoke. Here great granite rocks stand guard over cobalt-blue harbors, and volcanoes spit out plumes of smoke and fiery ash. This is where Ingrid Bergman famously discovered her inner Italian and where the blooms of wild capers—"the orchids of the Aeolians"—perfume the countryside.

Located in the Tyrrhenian Sea just north of Palermo, Sicily, the eight Aeolian Islands are the emergent tips of undersea volcanoes, the bones of these islands fashioned over a period of 260,000 years of volcanic mischief. Today the rough edges are softened by a coat of velvety green, cinematically set against blue sea and sky. It's quite a picture.

435 **Lipari** is the largest and most developed island, with a rare white-sand beach in **Spiaggia Bianca.** 436 **Stromboli** is the most distant and volcanically active island, essentially a 924m (3,031-ft.) mountain of muscular rock and molten lava—the second-largest active volcano in Europe, after Mount Etna. Stromboli is an atmospheric place, with black-sand beaches and black-clad Italian grandmothers climbing steep cobblestoned alleyways. It takes 3 hours to hike up to the lip of the volcano's **Gran Cratere,** where you can stare down into bubbling pools of superheated lava. Guides are essential; **Magmatrek** (Via Vittorio Emanuele; ✆ **39/90/9865768;** www.magmatrek.it) offers volcano excursions on Stromboli and other islands.

437 **Vulcano,** with its brooding, potentially volatile cone, perpetual smell of sulfur, and therapeutic mud baths, is the island closest to the Sicilian "mainland." Tiny 438 **Panarea** has become a trendy spot for international scenesters and the paparazzi who follow them; the island's whitewashed houses and picturesque harbor give it a Greek Island feel. 439 **Salina,** the chain's second-largest island, is lush and green; vineyards carpet curving slopes, and aromatic capers grow everywhere. Salina starred in the charming 1994 film *Il Postino;* you may remember the protagonist tootling around the island on a bicycle amid astonishing sea views. (The remaining islands—**Filicudi, Alicudi, and Basiluzzo**—are visited mainly by day-trippers.)

A dock in Lipari.

The islands may be remote, but they have been discovered. The larger islands are popular holiday destinations in summer, when the ferries from Sicily swell with visitors; it's estimated that the islands draw some 200,000 people annually. Many are there to see the nightly fireworks from the volcano on Stromboli. The islands provide a rich textbook for volcanologists and geologists studying the development of volcanic landforms. It's such an important spot for scientists and researchers that in 2000 the entire Aeolian "volcanic arc" was named a UNESCO World Heritage Site.

The scenery is beautiful, no doubt, but the Aeolians have been able to maintain their natural good looks by keeping commercial overdevelopment at bay with tight building restrictions and codes. Which makes these islands a pleasure to visit, with small villages, few roads, friendly people—everything on a smaller, more human scale except for the staggering scenery. Only 10,000 people make their permanent homes on these islands.

Unless you're a volcanologist, you won't want to spend your entire vacation staring into the crater of a volcano, however. Seeing these gorgeous islands from the water is simply a must. You can take a minicruise with **Taranto Navigazione** (✆ **39/90/9223617;** www.tarantonavigazione.it), which offers trips out of Lipari and Vulcano; one excursion, "Stromboli by Night," gives you a wonderful wide-angle view of volcanic pyrotechnics against the blue-black sky. Or have your hotel arrange a modest excursion with a local boatman. He might even cook a simple lunch of pasta and put down anchor to let you swim or snorkel in a warm blue grotto, enveloped by ancient rock. —*AF*

ⓘ www.regione.sicilia.it/turismo and www.comunelipari.it.

✈ Sicily.

Ferries and hydrofoils service all of the Aeolian Islands from the port of Milazzo, on the northeastern coast of Sicily (32km/20 miles) west of Messina; summer ferries travel between Messina and Palermo, Reggio Calabria, and Naples. Both **Società Siremar** (✆ **39/90/9283242;** www.siremar.it) and **Ustica Lines** (✆ **39/90/9287821;** www.usticalines.it) operate ferry and hydrofoil routes.

$$$ **Capofaro Malvasia & Resort,** Via Faro 3, Salina (✆ **39/90/9844330;** www.capofaro.it). $$ **Sirenetta Park Hotel,** Via Marina 33, Stromboli (✆ **39/90/986025;** www.lasirenetta.it).

much better it is, though, to get on a ferry and charge out into the water to see it for yourself.

While most tourists fixate on the drama of Alcatraz Island 357, there's really more to do on Angel Island, the Bay's largest islet. Now a tranquil state park, Angel Island has its own complicated history: It's been a Miwok Indian hunting ground, a Civil War encampment, a medical quarantine station during the Spanish-American War, a discharge depot during World War I, a POW camp during World War II, a 20th-century immigration station, and a Nike Missile Base from 1955 to 1962. Many visitors graze the surface of the island's history by taking an open-air tram tour of the island, which lasts about an hour. But if you're a real history buff like me, stop by the Cove Café visitor desk to book a guided tour of the freshly restored **U.S. Immigration Station.** From 1910 to 1940, this station—the "Ellis Island of the West"—saw Chinese immigrants detained for weeks or even months, trying to gain entry to this country despite harsh laws designed to keep them out. How tantalizing it must have been to be penned on this tiny island, with the promised land of San Francisco so visible just across the water. You can still see faded Chinese characters on some of the walls of the barracks where immigrants wrote poignant poems during their long sequestration.

Most Angel Island visitors today, however, have recreation on their minds. Flocks of picnickers converge on the large green lawn that fronts the docking area at Ayala Cove; visitors with a little more energy may hike, mountain bike, or even kayak around the island. Of the island's 12 miles (19km) of hiking and bike trails, the classic circuit is to follow the 5-mile (8km) **Perimeter Road** around the island's shore. Several turnoffs lead to the top of Mount Livermore, 776 feet (237m) above the bay (if you didn't bring your mountain bike, you can rent one by the docks). Though the island has no hotels, you can camp overnight; make reservations in advance (✆ **800/444-7275;** www.reserveamerica.com).

To be really hip, opt for a guided 2½-hour **Segway tour** (✆ **415/897-0715;** www.acteva.com; available Mar—Nov). Or if you really want to brave the waters, head up to Sausalito and take a half-day naturalist-guided **sea-kayak tour** down to Angel Island (**Sea Trek,** ✆ **415/488-1000;** www.seatrekkayak.com). *—HH*

ⓘ **Tourist info** (✆ **415/897-0715;** www.angelisland.com).

✈ San Francisco International (14 miles/23km).

⛴ From Pier 41 (Fisherman's Wharf), **Blue & Gold** ferries (✆ **415/705-8200;** www.blueandgoldfleet.com). From Tiburon, **Tiburon-Angel Island** ferries (✆ **415/435-2131;** www.angelislandferry.com), 15 min.

🛏 $$$ **Hotel Adagio,** 550 Geary St. (✆ **800/228-8830** or 415/775-5000; www.thehoteladagio.com). $ **Hotel des Arts,** 447 Bush St. (✆ **800/956-4322** or 415/956-3232; www.sfhoteldesarts.com).

440 Parks

Georges Island

The Harbor Master

Boston, Massachusetts, U.S.

Yes, there was that little incident in 1773 when a crew of outraged Bostonians dumped shipments of English tea into the waters of Boston Harbor. But by and large, this New England capital treasures its famous harbor, which once brought in great catches of codfish and whale blubber. Nowadays, the catch is more likely to be tourists visiting the New England Aquarium and the Faneuil Hall Marketplace, but the wharves remain one of Boston's most vital areas.

While most Bostonians have admired the Inner Harbor from its piers, strangely enough, no one I know ever visits the Outer Harbor, a huge basin cupped between the North Shore (Winthrop neck) and the South Shore (the Hull promontory). Whale-watching cruises constantly glide right past the 30-odd little islands that dot the Outer Harbor, their passengers completely unaware of the islands' natural beauties and historic features. Granted, the Harbor Islands were set up as a national recreation area only fairly recently, in 1996. But *still.*

Oh, if they only knew what they were missing! Ferries from Long Wharf stop at two islands in the group: Spectacle Island (10 min. from shore) and, farther out, Georges Island (25 min. from shore). Recently opened **Spectacle Island** is artificial, being the place where the city piled all the dirt from Boston's everlasting downtown construction project, the Big Dig. Being so close to shore, though, it's a fun place to swim or hike around, with the Boston skyline constantly in view.

Georges Island, though, is the real deal. Set out in the mouth of the Outer Harbor, it was naturally a strategic defense spot, and most of this 39-acre (16-hectare) island is occupied by **Fort Warren,** a national historic landmark built between 1833 and 1847. Rangers lead guided tours of this bunkered granite stronghold, which served as a Civil War prison and remained active up through World War II. Stroll along the island's stone ramparts to drink in the wide-view panorama of Boston. With its velvety green sloping lawns and stands of horse chestnut and apple trees, it's a fine place for picnicking or flying a kite.

It's also the jumping-off place for free water taxis to various other islands in the group, several of which offer campsites for overnight stays. **Bumpkin Island,** once site of a children's hospital, has shelling beaches and wildflower meadows; **Lovell Island** is popular with campers, who explore its dunes, tide pools, and ruined fort; wooded **Grape Island** is a fine place for bird-watching; **Peddocks Island** offers rocky beaches, marshes, and woods to explore, as well as another abandoned fort and a few summer cottages. Special cruises also visit the lighthouse on way-out **Brewster Island** or the rolling hills and salt marshes of large, close-to-shore **Thompson Island.**

In summer, boats also depart from the South Shore towns of Hingham, Quincy, and Hull. So really, Beantowners, you've got no excuse anymore. . . . —*HH*

ⓘ **Boston Harbor Islands NRA visitor center,** Long Wharf (✆ **617/223-8666;** www.nps.gov/boha). **Friends of the Boston Harbor Islands** (✆ **617/740-4290;** www.fbhi.org).

✈ Boston Logan International.

⛴ From Long Wharf, 30 min; **Harbor Express** (✆ **617/222-6999;** www.harborexpress.com).

🛏 $$$ **The Charles Hotel,** 1 Bennett St., Cambridge (✆ **800/882-1818** or 617/864-1200; www.charleshotel.com). $$ **Harborside Inn,** 185 State St., Boston (✆ **617/670-6015;** www.harborsideinnboston.com).

Enclaves 441

Bainbridge Island

Puget Sound Surprise

Seattle, Washington, U.S.

It was just an excuse, really, to board a ferry and cruise out over Puget Sound, which had been beckoning us ever since we arrived in Seattle. There was nothing my family and I particularly wanted to *see* on Bainbridge Island.

Mesmerized by that gloriously scenic half-hour ferry ride, though, we weren't just going to turn around and take the ferry straight back to the city—no way! So we tramped uphill from the docks to the historic village of Winslow and—well, in no time we began to go native.

Bainbridge Island has been a lot of things in its time—a Suquamish Indian community, a late-19th-century powerhouse for lumber mills and shipyards (back then it was more populous than Seattle), an agricultural locale known for its superb hops and strawberries, and a strategic World War II site for naval communications. It's really closer to the Kitsap peninsula than it is to Seattle, just a minute's drive over the Agate Pass bridge. But as Seattle grew into the great metropolitan sprawl it is today, the natural beauty of Bainbridge Island made it a particularly desirable Seattle suburb—who wouldn't want to commute every day by ferry instead of by car?—with a population of around 22,000, dispersed around this never-crowded island. It still has a countercultural vibe, thanks to the number of artists who located here; check out the **Bainbridge Arts and Crafts Gallery** (151 Winslow Way E.) to get a sampling of regional artists. It's also comfortably multicultural, thanks to that early industry, which attracted many Japanese-American and Filipino families here several generations ago. Among the cafes on Madison Avenue and Winslow Way we saw a cosmopolitan lineup of restaurants, including Thai, Mexican, Indian, and Japanese places. If only we'd arrived early enough for lunch, or hadn't already planned to be back in Seattle for dinner!

Well, that's the way it sometimes goes when you're traveling: It's the unexpected places that bowl you over. We were lucky enough to be there on a day when the **Bainbridge Island Historical Society museum** (215 Ericksen Ave. NE; www.bainbridgehistory.org) was open, and we managed to stock up on treats at **Island Ice Cream** (584 Winslow Way) and **Bainbridge Bakers** (140 Winslow Way E.). But before we left, I'd already started my list of things we have to do next time—like renting kayaks to paddle around **Blakely Harbor,** a tranquil beach and wetlands on the former site of one of the world's biggest lumber mills. Or taking a taxi from the ferry north to the **Bloedel Reserve,** a former estate with 150 stunning acres of woods, waterfalls, rainforest glens, and formal gardens (advance reservations required—now they tell me!—at ✆ **206/842-7631** or www.bloedelreserve.org). Or joining a wine tasting at the **Bainbridge Island Vineyard,** 682 State Hwy. 305 (✆ **206/842-9463**), or scheduling our trip to coincide with one of the annual **artists' Studio Tours** (www.bistudiotour.com)—well, it's a surprisingly long list. . . . *—HH*

ⓘ **Tourist office,** 590 Winslow Way E. (✆ **206/842-3700;** www.bainbridgechamber.com).

✈ Seattle-Tacoma International.

⛴ **Washington State Ferries** (✆ **800/843-3779** or 206/464-6400; www.wsdot.wa.gov/ferries), 35 min. from downtown Seattle.

🛏 $$ **Best Western Bainbridge Island Suites,** 350 NE High School Rd. (✆ **866/396-9666** or 206/855-9666; www.bestwestern.com/bainbridgeislandsuites). $$$ **The Eagle Harbor Inn,** 291 Madison Ave. S., Winslow (✆ **206/842-1446;** www.theeagleharborinn.com).

442 Enclaves

Vashon Island

Lavender, Monks & Bikes in Trees

Seattle, Washington, U.S.

Farther up the Puget Sound, Vashon Island is about the same size as Bainbridge Island 441, but it has about half as many people. That's a significant statistic. Though it's not much farther from Seattle, Vashon Island feels a lot more remote, and determinedly rural. Yes, a fair percentage of the island's residents commute to work in Seattle and Tacoma, but they tend to regard themselves as back-to-nature types. Three different ferry routes connect Vashon to the big cities, yet it still doesn't have a bridge to the nearby Kitsap Peninsula. You get the idea that Vashonites would like to keep it that way.

Vashon concentrates most of its commercial action in low-rise Vashon Town, midway down the island, leaving the rest of the island to woods and rural landscape. There are still farms here, even though they mostly just provide the locavore residents with their organic produce, milk, and eggs. The biggest event on the calendar is the annual July Strawberry Festival, which is still going strong after 100 years. (If you miss the Strawberry Festival, maybe you'll make it for the annual Lavender Farm weekend, which tours half a dozen local lavender farms.)

So naturally, the main things visitors do on Vashon Island involve being out-of-doors. (That's after you've visited the local landmark **Bike in Tree,** just off 20312 Vashon Hwy. SW, where an abandoned kid's red bike has grown into the trunk of a giant tree.) Vashon's squiggly coast gives it an extraordinary 45 miles (72km) of shoreline, deeply indented from the south by Quartermaster Harbor, which severs the island into two parts, Vashon Island and Maury Island. (Once separate except at low tide, the two islands were connected by the U.S. Corps of Engineers many years ago.) Kayaking is a great way to explore the thickly wooded shoreline—you can start out at the **Vashon Kayak Center** (✆ **206/463-9257**) in Jensen Point Park on the Burton Peninsula, located deep in Quartermaster Harbor.

The whole island has been declared an equestrian community, with most roads designed to be horse-friendly. In the heart of the island, an entire park, **Paradise Ridge** (SW 220th St.), has been created on a 43-acre (17-hectare) parcel that was once a NIKE missile site. Its cross-country jumping course is also accessible for mountain bikers and hikers. There are also horse trails at **Point Robinson Park** (technically on Maury Island), near the historic 1885 lighthouse, where a beach and a bird-rich saltwater marsh offer dramatic views of Tacoma and Mount Rainier.

As if to prove what a quiet haven this island is, there's even a Russian Orthodox monastery on 16 acres (6.5 hectares) of Maury Island—the **All Merciful Saviour Monastery,** one of the few in North America, which was founded in 1986. The monks endured a brief moment of fame when they were sued by Starbucks for innocently marketing a coffee with a name that the giant chain had already trademarked. To visit the monastery, contact the monks at ✆ **206/463-5918** or www.vashonmonks.com. —*HH*

ⓘ **Tourist office** (✆ **206/463-6217;** http://vashonchamber.com).

✈ Seattle-Tacoma International.

⛴ **Washington State Ferries** (✆ **800/843-3779** or 206/464-6400; www.wsdot.wa.gov/ferries), 15-min. car ferry from west Seattle, 35 min. from Pier 50 (foot passengers only).

🛏 $ **AYH Ranch Hostel/Lavender Duck Inn,** 12119 SW Cove Rd. (✆ **206/463-2592;** www.vashonhostel.com). $$ **Point Robinson Keepers Quarters,** Point Robinson Lighthouse (✆ **206/463-9602;** www.vashonparkdistrict.org).

Enclaves **443**

Bowen Island

Small Town Island

Vancouver, B.C., Canada

Who knew that just minutes away from the vibrant city streets of Vancouver, British Columbia, is Canada's own version of Mayberry?

This idyllic little island municipality of some 3,500 permanent residents is just a 20-minute ferry ride from downtown Vancouver. Stepping off the ferry, you'll find yourself in aptly named **Snug Cove,** Bowen Island's only town—a name that practically wraps itself around you in a cozy welcome. If you're looking for extreme sports or high-gloss nightlife, then earthy, homey Bowen Island is not the spot for you. But if you're attracted to a friendly, picturesque little community with a mellow, bohemian feel and a nicely percolating arts scene—and one that happens to be surrounded by silky blue harbor waters—then head straight here, whether for a day trip or a leisurely, relaxing weekend.

Of course, Bowen Island hasn't escaped the imagination of filmmakers, who have made Vancouver one of the world's most active movie sets. The little cottages, century-old buildings, and flower gardens of Bowen Island have been the backdrop for some 20 movies and one of the stars of the short-lived CBS prime-time thriller *Harper's Island.* Craggy and green, Bowen Island, aka "The Rock," comes by its cinematic good looks naturally, since it's blessed with the lushly forested, undulating terrain of the Pacific Northwest.

Bowen Island has always enjoyed the good life, moving easily over the years from wilderness to resort community, with a few logging and factory stints in between. At the turn of the 20th century, the island was the site of a vacation resort operated by the Union Steamship Company. These days, however, a serious resident arts community thrives on Bowen. Visit the work of a collective of local artists at the **Arts Pacific Cooperative Guild** in Artisan Square (www.artisansquare.com), a 15-minute walk from the ferry dock at Snug Cove.

Bowen is also a real outdoorsman's paradise, with plenty of wilderness to explore—the island has 650 acres (263 hectares) of dedicated parkland and numerous trails to hike (a trail map is available from Tourism Bowen; see below). **Bowen Tours** (✆ **604/314-1712**) leads a variety of guided walks, ranging from historical walking tours to wildlife-spotting outings to strenuous climbs up the island's central peak, Mount Gardiner. You can also rent kayaks and skim the waters ringing the island; contact **Bowen Island Sea Kayaking** (✆ **800/60-KAYAK** [605-2925]; www.bowenislandkayaking.com). *—AF*

ⓘ **Tourism Bowen** (✆ **604/947-9024;** www.bowenisland.org).

✈ Vancouver.

⛴ 20 min. from Horseshoe Bay, Vancouver. **B.C. Ferries** (✆ **888/BC-FERRY** [223-3779]; www.bcferries.com).

🛏 $$ **Island Thyme Bed & Breakfast,** 967 Windjammer Rd. (✆ **604/947-0191;** www.artistinthegarden.ca). $$ **The Lodge at the Old Dorm,** 460 Melmore Rd. (✆ **604/947-0947;** www.lodgeattheolddorm.com).

Enclaves

Coronado Island

Some Like It Hot

San Diego, California, U.S.

Maps will tell you that Coronado isn't really an island; it's a peninsula, anchored to the mainland by a long tenuous southern strip of barrier beach called the Silver Strand. But that's a mere technicality. San Diegans still refer to it as Coronado Island; and it sure *feels* like an island, floating serenely on the other side of San Diego Bay from downtown San Diego. Dotted with palm trees, sailboats bobbing in its marina, cool breezes and gentle surf caressing its broad white Pacific beach—it seems such a world apart.

I had never seen the classic comedy *Some Like It Hot* the summer I first visited Coronado. But even at age 12, I could tell that there was something special about the Hotel Del Coronado, with its white Victorian turrets, red roof, and long ocean-view veranda: It's the quintessential seaside villa, writ large. (In the movie, the resort is supposed to be in Florida, but never mind.) It's said that Coronado resident L. Frank Baum based the Emerald City in *The Wizard of Oz* on the Hotel Del, and I believe it. Frolicking on that spectacular beach, my siblings and I knew for sure that we'd left the Midwest behind. Naturally, I had to bring my own kids here years later—and the Hotel Del was one of those rare revisited childhood memories that did not disappoint. In fact, through the hotel's kids program, my children took a ghost tour of the hotel's nooks and crannies, then roasted marshmallows on the beach—making me very jealous. (Why do kids get to have all the fun?)

On my first visit, we arrived by a poky little ferry (see—it must be an island!). Only a couple years later, however, the majestic 2¼-mile (3.6km) swoop of the Coronado Bridge was erected over the Bay, rising high over the water so that navy ships could pass underneath. The views from the bridge are so spectacular—you can even see Mexico in the distance—it's hard to keep your eyes on the road. Though Coronado has become much more accessible to the mainland, it hasn't lost its air of a protected enclave;

Hotel del Coronado.

it's still its own separately incorporated city, independent of San Diego. Such serenity doesn't come cheap, however. We rented bikes at the hotel to pedal around its quiet streets, and saw some very pricey real estate tucked away on small, exquisitely maintained lots. Orange Avenue, Coronado's palm-lined main street, is a delightfully walkable succession of tony shops and smart little restaurants—but nothing too flashy, not in this bastion of Republicanism. (Many residents are retired officers from the naval air station on the north side of the island.) Coronado's "downtown" has the sort of cozy small-town ambience I'd never have expected in southern California. No wonder this Midwestern kid still loves the place, 40 years later. —*HH*

ⓘ **Tourist office,** 1100 Orange Ave. (✆ **866/599-7242** or 619/437-8788; www.coronadovisitorcenter.com).

✈ San Diego.

⛴ 15 min. from Broadway Pier, San Diego (✆ **619/234-4111;** www.sdhe.com).

8 miles/13km drive from San Diego.

🛏 $ **The Coronado Village Inn,** 1017 Park Place (✆ **619/435-9318;** www.coronadovillageinn.com). $$$ **Hotel del Coronado,** 1500 Orange Ave. (✆ **800/468-3533** or 619/435-6611; www.hoteldel.com).

Enclaves **445**

Goose Island

Old Irish Industry

Chicago, Illinois, U.S.

Waterfront property on the Chicago River. Abandoned buildings from the 19th century and empty lots. In the late 1980s, residential real estate developers licked their lips as they eyed industrial Goose Island as a derelict that could be rehabilitated. The only island in the Chicago River stood poised to become a trendy address for the affluent of the Windy City, something akin to New York's Williamsburg, and shiny new luxury lofts would breathe new life into an area where both businesses and residents were dwindling.

The lofts were never built. In 1990, Chicago Mayor Richard Daley designated Goose Island as a Planned Manufacturing

District, barring residential development. The island is now largely given over to industrial parks, though **Kendall College** (a business, hospitality, culinary, and education school) occupies the southern end. The school has the top-ranked culinary program in the Midwest, and visitors can sample the students' gourmet skills at **The Dining Room at Kendall College** (900 N. North Branch St.; ✆ **866/667-3344**). At only 160 acres (65 hectares), Goose Island remains a quirky pocket of central Chicago, free—at least temporarily—of the gentrification of its adjacent neighborhoods.

Poll most any Chicagoan, however, and they might not even be able to tell you that there is an island in their city's river, although the name Goose Island is likely to ring a bell as a local **microbrewery and pub** (www.gooseisland.com). Goose Island—the landform, not the beer—was created when the North Branch Canal was dug in the 1850s, along what is now the east side of the island (bordering the Near North Side). The origins of the name are a bit foggy, but the avian moniker may come from the fact that when Irish immigrants moved here after the potato famine, they grew crops and kept farm animals on the island; geese may have been among their livestock.

During the time of the Irish settlement here, Goose Island was a place where relations were tight; everyone knew each other's name and business. By the end of the 1800s, however, this part of Chicago had fallen on hard times, and the Irish of Goose Island relocated. The early-20th-century construction of a railway track and train yard down the north-south axis of the island—to ease transport logistics from river to rail—seemed to seal Goose Island's fate as an industrial center where housing and families were increasingly marginalized. A few residents held out over the decades, but by the 1980s, only one inhabited house remained. Whether Goose Island ever flourishes again as a community will depend on future municipal legislation: Plenty of neighbors want the industrial parks gone; however, those manufacturing plants provide important jobs for the local economy.

North-south–running North Halsted Street connects Goose Island with "mainland" Chicago, while West Division Street cuts across the island from east to west. The "El" does not stop on Goose Island, but you can take the #70 Division Street bus and the #8 Halsted bus there. —*SM*

ⓘ www.explorechicago.org.

✈ Chicago O'Hare or Midway International airports.

🛏 $$$ **Hotel Monaco,** 225 N. Wabash, Chicago (✆ **312/960-8500;** www.monacochicago.com).

Enclaves

City Island

A Bit of Maine in the Bronx

New York, New York, U.S.

What a humdrum name for one of New York City's most atmospheric—and little-known—neighborhoods. Down at South Street Seaport, you'll see a museum version of the great historic port of New York; up in the Bronx at City Island, you'll see real fishermen and boatyards, a seafaring community so authentic you'd swear the Cross Bronx Expressway had zipped you straight up to New England.

That seafaring air comes naturally, considering City Island's location, surrounded by Long Island Sound and Eastchester Bay. It was just far enough north of Manhattan that the early Dutch settlers let it slip into English ownership. In the late 1700s, its private owners tried to develop it as a commercial rival to Manhattan. Thanks to the disruptions of the Revolutionary War, that never came to pass, but the shipbuilding and oystering industries never left. Though it's geographically closer to Westchester County—you have to drive through a bit of Pelham to get here—City Islanders voted to be part of New York City in 1896. During both world wars, the island's boatyards produced minesweepers, tugboats, and landing craft; in times of peace, they turned to yachts (no less than seven Americas Cup winners were built here). Even today, there are no fewer than six yachting and boating clubs on this tiny island.

From the expanse of Pelham Bay Park (which, by the way, has a superb public golf course), you cross over a green steel bridge so short, you barely know you've left the mainland. But what you will notice right away is the swift change in atmosphere, to a quiet village ambience that's the antithesis of nearby Bronx condo projects. Seafood restaurants and bars line the few sign-cluttered blocks of the island's spine, City Island Avenue. (Classics include **Johnny's Reef,** 2 City Island Ave., ✆ **718/885-2090; Neptune Inn,** 35 City Island Ave., ✆ **718/885-1168;** and **Sammy's Fish Box,** 41 City Island Ave., ✆ **718/885-0920**). Small side streets on either side run a block to the ocean and then stop. The lots are tiny, their jaunty little houses crammed close together, with neighborly railed porches and picket fences; a few larger Victorians ramble along the Long Island Sound side. The island's shores are rimmed with docks and small boats, and marinas and boat sheds crop up everywhere. Charter yachts and fishing expedition boats are easily booked for an afternoon out on the water. On West Ditmar Street, a small patch of wetlands has been set aside as a birding preserve, but the island's most surprising avian population is the number of little green parrots that perch on street signs and telephone wires, descendants of escaped pet birds.

There's nothing pretentious about City Island; the water views come in snatches, not great sweeping vistas, and instead of a country club–like refinement, you'll encounter the gear and tackle of working fishing boats. But in the feverish scrum of this great metropolis, this dowdy little fishing village offers something even rarer: a breath of (literally) fresh air. *—HH*

ⓘ **City Island Museum,** 190 Fordham St. (✆ **718/885-0008;** www.cityisland museum.org); also www.cityisland.org.

✈ John F. Kennedy International, Newark Liberty International, or LaGuardia.

3-mile/4.8km drive from Pelham Bay Park.

$$ **Le Refuge Inn,** 586 City Island Ave. (✆ **718/885-2478;** www.lerefugeinn.com).

Enclaves 447

Eel Pie Island

The Music & the Memories

London, England

Nowadays, there's very little demand for eel pies, that quintessential 19th-century London street food. The "ick" factor has banned eel pies from the modern menu, but the name of that once-popular savory snack lives on in this island snuggled into a bend in the Thames, west of London proper. Though it borders on the snooty residential neighborhoods of Twickenham, Eel Pie Island is a very different kettle of fish indeed.

The history of Eel Pie Island is, in a way, London's cultural history in a nutshell. Even though you could get here only by boat, pubs on this island—or ait, as Thames islands are termed—were serving river traffic as early as 1780. It got its current name in the mid-1800s from the popular Eel Pie Hotel, known for the delectable eel pies it served up to Thames boating parties. Charles Dickens wrote the first chapter of *Little Dorrit* while staying at the hotel. After the eel population was depleted, the emphasis shifted to the three-story hotel's ballroom, which boasted a fine sprung floor, drawing crowds during the tea-dance craze of the 1920s and 1930s.

In the 1950s, just around the time that an arched footbridge to the Twickenham shore was finally built, the hotel became a trad jazz venue when that was all the rage. Then, as in jazz clubs all over the country, the Eel Pie Club stage was taken over by scruffy young rock-and-roll bands in the early 1960s. The Rolling Stones, the Yardbirds, John Mayall's Bluesbreakers, and Pink Floyd all played some of their first gigs at the **Eel Pie Club** between 1962 and 1967; it was such a seminal rock venue that Pete Townshend of The Who named both his record studio and his music publishing company after it, even though they were headquartered inland in Twickenham. Closed in 1967, the dilapidated Eel Pie Club in 1970 became a notorious hippie squat, and mysteriously burned down in 1971.

Crossing that arched footbridge from Twickenham to visit Eel Pie Island today is a much more mellow experience. The shores are lined with small boats and docks; there's been a working boatyard here for years, along with the boathouses of the **Twickenham Rowing Club** and **Richmond Yacht Club.** It doesn't take long to tramp from one end of the island to the other, both ends being nature reserves overrun with scrubby trees and tangled

Footbridge to Eel Pie Island.

undergrowth. There are only about 50 small houses on the ait, most of them quirky and ramshackle; it's a close-knit community that tends to attract artists and craftspeople. Of course there are no cars, which somehow seems to fit the countercultural aura that still hangs over this place. The music scene may have moved on, but on a misty morning, bathed in silvery river light, visiting this oddly named island is still quite a trip. —*HH*

ⓘ **Tourist office,** 44 York St., Twickenham (✆ **44/20/8891-7272**).

✈ Gatwick Airport (1.5km/1 mile), Heathrow (18km/11 miles).

🛏 $$ **The Alexander Pope Hotel,** Cross Deep, Twickenham (✆ **44/20/8892-3050;** www.popesgrotto.co.uk).

Enclaves 448

Isola Tiberina

Chosen by the God of Medicine

Rome, Italy

In 291 B.C., a plague swept through Rome. Hundreds fell ill and died, and the population might have been decimated—or so legend has it—had something fortuitous not happened on the island in the middle of the river Tiber. To stop the plague, the Roman high priests had sent for a statue of the god of medicine, Aesculapius, from Greece. As the ship carrying the statue made its way up the Tiber, a snake slithered off the ship, into the water, and onto the shores of Isola Tiberina (Tiber Island). The Romans, of course, were no dummies; they recognized this snake as the animal incarnation of Aesculapius, who was clearly indicating his will that his temple be built on the island. Sure enough, the temple of Aesculapius was built on Tiber Island, and good health was restored to Rome.

Some 2,300 years later, Tiber Island—the only island in Rome—is still a sanctuary of medicine. Colorful folklore aside, the island's isolation from the densely populated city made it a natural location for the quarantine and treatment of the contagiously ill. There are no residential buildings here, just hospitals and churches. The main structure here is the **Fatebenefratelli** ("Do-Good Brothers") **hospital.** This being Rome, there's also a Catholic church on the island, the basilica of **San Bartolomeo all'Isola,** which stands more or less on the spot where the temple of Aesculapius stood in ancient times. The temple is long gone, but there is one surviving bit of open-air archaeology here: Along the southeast side of the lower esplanade of the island, remnants of a **travertine ship's hull** are clearly visible. Look closely and you'll even see the caduceus symbol of Aesculapius carved into the rock. These vestiges date from ancient Roman times, when the entire island was sculpted to look like the ship that brought the god of medicine to Rome.

Tiber Island is a mere sliver of land, connected to the Jewish Ghetto by the 62 B.C. **Ponte Fabricio,** Rome's oldest bridge, and to Trastevere by the (reconstructed) Ponte Cestio. The Tiber River is a sluggish, greeny-brown waterway that, despite its illustrious history in the founding and development of Rome, is far from impressive today. In short—don't expect anything like Paris's monumental Ile de la Cité 415 in the Seine. Still, Isola Tiberina has a fair amount of rustic Roman charm in its ocher-washed buildings and evocatively unkempt vegetation. The only restaurant on the island is the old-school trattoria **Sora Lella.** Next door, there's a *gelateria* that gets a lot of traffic during the Sunday *passeggiata* (traditional stroll though central Rome). In summer, the stalls and screens of the **Isola del Cinema** outdoor film festival are set up on the lower esplanades, creating a festive atmosphere. —*SM*

ⓘ www.romaturismo.com or www.isolatiberina.it.

✈ Fiumicino–Leonardo Da Vinci International Airport, or Ciampino Airport.

Ponte Fabricio (pedestrian only) or Ponte Cestio.

$ **Arco del Lauro,** Via dell'Arco dei Tolomei 27, Trastevere (✆ **39/346/2443212;** www.arcodellauro.it). $$$ **Hotel Ponte Sisto,** Via dei Pettinari 64, Rome (✆ **39/06/6863100;** www.hotelpontesisto.com).

449 Enclaves

Ile St-Louis

Aristocratic Hideaway

Paris, France

All those tourists milling around the plaza in front of the cathedral of Notre-Dame on Ile de la Cité 415—how few of them ever circle behind the flying buttresses, wander through the cathedral gardens, and walk 60m (197 ft.) across Pont St-Louis to Paris's *other* central island, Ile St-Louis.

After all, what is there to see there? Named after France's sainted King Louis IX, who died of plague while off fighting the Crusades, this residential Seine island is about half the size of its more famous neighbor, and far more tranquil. When Ile de la Cité had churches and royal dwellings and law courts, Ile St-Louis was a cow pasture and sometime jousting ground; Louis IX would slip over from Ile de la Cité in the evenings to read and pray, while in a later era aristocrats came at dawn to fight duels. Finally, in the 17th century, houses were built here, all at once, giving the island a remarkable architectural unity of matching mansard roofs, tiny gables, and serried windows. Most of the island's 6,000 residents today occupy these beautiful antique stone town houses with charming courtyards, properties that are among the most prime real estate in Paris.

While there are few attractions per se, anyone can visit this aristocratic enclave—to stroll the shady promenades of its tree-lined northern quays, Quai de Bourbon and Quai de Anjou; to admire the Seine panorama from green square Barye in the southeastern corner; or to browse through the many high-end antiques shops or pass time in the charming restaurants and cafes along the main street, rue St-Louis-en-l'Ile. I have to admit that that is what first drew me across the bridge onto this island—the promise of a luscious, creamy glacé at **Berthillon** (29 rue St-Louis), where some of the planet's best ice cream has been whipped up daily since 1954.

As you wander around, look for plaques on the facades to identify the celebrities who once lived here—scientist **Marie Curie** at 36 quai de Béthune; **Camille Claudel** (Rodin's mistress) at 19 quai de Bourbon; the writer **Voltaire** at the Hôtel Lambert, 2 quai d'Anjou; painter/sculptor/lithographer **Honoré Daumier** at 9 quai d'Anjou. At 29 quai d'Anjou, **Ezra Pound** ran the Three Mountain Press, which published works by **Ernest Hemingway** and other expatriate writers. The city-owned **Hôtel de Lauzun** (17 quai d'Anjou) has the most checkered history of all, from its first owner, the aristocratic embezzler Charles Gruyn des Bordes, down to its 19th-century incarnation as a hashish club where the poet **Baudelaire** did "research" for his symbol-laden poetry. On a summer weekend you may see wedding parties posing on the steps of the baroque white church of **St-Louis-en-l'Ile** (19 bis rue St-Louis-en-l'Ile). Nearby, a 1926 plaque declares IN GRATEFUL MEMORY OF ST. LOUIS IN WHOSE HONOR THE CITY OF ST. LOUIS, MISSOURI, U.S., IS NAMED. —*HH*

ⓘ **Tourist office,** 25–27 rue des Pyramides, 1e (✆ **33/8/92-68-30-00;** www.parisinfo.com).

✈ De Gaulle (23km/14 miles), Orly (14km/8⅔ miles).

🛏 $$$ **Hôtel des Deux-Iles,** 59 rue de St-Louis-en-Ile, 4e (✆ **33/1/43-26-13-35;** www.deuxiles-paris-hotel.com). $$ **Hôtel Saint Louis,** 75 rue de St-Louis-en-Ile, 4e (✆ **33/1/46-34-04-80;** www.hotelsaintlouis.com).

Enclaves 450

Suomenlinna

Northern Naval History & a Picnic

Helsinki, Finland

A day trip to this fortress "archipelago," just across the harbor from the capital city of Helsinki, is one of the cultural highlights of visiting Finland. In fact, what makes Suomenlinna such a pleasure is that it offers a little something for everyone: History buffs can brush up on their Scandinavian naval lore; for those interested in architecture, the original fortress buildings here are kept in immaculate condition and provide a fascinating look at 17th- and 18th-century military construction; finally, nature lovers can go for a stroll around the wilder parts of Suomenlinna and see native Finnish flora and fauna.

Suomenlinna is not one single island but a string of linked, smaller landmasses (linked by bridges and walkways) that together cover an area of 80 hectares (198 acres). The islands were originally founded as a **fortress site** in 1748 by the Swedish and called Sveaborg, meaning "fortress of Svea." Suomenlinna was also known by its Finnish name Viapori until the early 20th century, when the patriotic, current name (Suomenlinna means "castle of Finland") replaced it for nationalistic reasons. Over the centuries—during the Swedish period as well as the Russian era, when Suomenlinna was taken and fortified as a counterpart to Kronshtadt naval base 333—the linked islands of Suomenlinna have protected the strategic city of Helsinki with their star-shaped bastions and heavy

Suomenlinna fort.

artillery capability. During Suomenlinna's heyday, more than 100 cannons were at the ready to defend the islands and sea approaches to Helsinki. No longer in use as an active fortress, Suomenlinna became a UNESCO World Heritage Site in 1991. In the 18th-century dry dock, where battleships were once built and repaired, there's now a facility for restoring old wooden sailboats. One of the islands, Pikku Mustasaari, is home to the Finnish Naval Academy (off-limits to the public).

Today, Suomenlinna is Helsinki's most treasured mild-weather picnic spot, as it's just a 15-minute ferry ride from the city's Market Square. Extensive nature paths on Suomenlinna take you past migratory birds' habitats, including the nesting sites of swans and barnacle geese. Summer is the best time to visit Suomenlinna (and that goes for all Scandinavian islands, in my opinion) as it stays light until about midnight and there are all kinds of cultural events organized for Suomenlinna's summer program. In the islands' open-air spaces, you'll find all kinds of concerts and the **Viapori Jazz Festival,** and children's theater performances are staged. With several dining and drinking establishments—both traditional and more modern—on Suomenlinna, and ferries running until 2am, you might end up spending more time here than in Helsinki. —*SM*

ⓘ ✆ **358/09/684-1880;** www.suomenlinna.fi.

✈ Helsinki (17km/11 miles), then ferry.

⛴ **Helsinki City Transportation Ferries,** 15 min. from Helsinki's Market Square (Kauppatori; ✆ **358/09/010-0111**).

🛏 $$$ **Hotel Glo,** Kluuvikatu 4 (✆ **358/09/5840-9540;** www.palacekamp.fi).

12 Island Nations

451 Archipelagos

Malta

Crossroads of the Mediterranean

Walking the streets of most any Maltese town, you get the vague sense that you're in some kind of greatest hits of European architecture—a little London here, echoes of Paris there, maybe a touch of Rome in that baroque church facade. And it's no wonder: For several thousand years, this strategic little archipelago has been one of the Mediterranean's busiest steppingstones. The Phoenicians, the Carthaginians, the Romans, the knights of St. John, the French, and the British all swept in from their respective compass points and left indelible reminders of their conquests. (From all those competing cultures, Malta forged its own idiosyncratic language, a sort of hypnotic mix of Arabic and Italian.) Having won its independence from the United Kingdom in 1964 and acceded to the European Union in 2004, Malta today is a modern and well-run island nation, with its illustrious laurels of history on full view.

If possible, come to Malta by sea, to the port of **Valletta;** if you do come by air, plan to take a harbor cruise soon upon arrival. Hemmed in by the imposing Fort St. Elmo and Fort Ricasoli, Valletta's **Grand Harbor** is a stunning tableau of honey-colored stone bastions and church tops. Once in Valletta, make a beeline to the **Malta Experience** (© **356/21243776;** www.themaltaexperience.com), an "audiovisual spectacular" that dynamically presents the islands' 7,000 years of history in 45 compelling minutes.

Sights related to the Knights of Malta (full name: Order of the Knights of the Hospital of St. John in Jerusalem), who occupied Malta for several centuries, are also sprinkled throughout Valletta. (They're all clearly marked for tourists.) Charged with defending Christianity against the Ottoman Empire, the Knights withstood a massive siege by Suleiman the Magnificent's soldiers in 1565. Though Napoleon eventually ousted them from this island in 1798 (they're now headquartered in Rome, Italy), you'll still see the Knights' well-known ancient symbol—the eight-pointed cross, aka the Maltese cross—all around the country, including on Maltese money. The walled city of **Mdina,** on Malta proper, is superbly evocative of the island's medieval era. Descendants of the noble families—Norman, Sicilian, and Spanish—that ruled Malta centuries ago still inhabit the patrician palaces that line the shady streets here.

In summer, the coastal resort towns of **Sliema** and **St. Julian's,** just outside Valletta, come alive with holidaymakers and yachtsetters, and the cafe-filled promenades fronting the teal sea are the epitome of the Mediterranean good life. The best beaches are scattered along the western tip of the island—Ghajn Tuffieha, Golden Bay, Paradise Bay, Armier, and Mellieha Bay.

For those with a hankering for the ancient and mysterious, Malta's best attraction lies on **Gozo** (part of Malta's seven-island archipelago, accessible as a day trip by ferry from Valletta). The enigmatic megaliths of **Ggantija** here are the oldest free-standing temples in the world, predating even the Egyptian pyramids by at least a millennium. —*SM*

Previous page: A Papau New Guinean.

A dock in Malta.

ⓘ **Tourist office,** 1 City Arcades, City Gate, Valletta (✆ **356/22-915440;** www.visitmalta.com).

✈ Malta International (10km/6 miles from Valletta).

⛴ From Naples, 10 hr. (**Grimaldi Lines;** www.grimaldi-lines.com); Genoa, 13 hr.; and Palermo, 12 hr. (**Grandi Navi Veloci;** www.gnv.it).

🛏 $$$ **Hotel Phoenicia,** Valletta (✆ **356/21-225241;** www.phoeniciamalta.com). $$$ **Westin Dragonara Resort,** St. Julian's (✆ **356/21-381000;** www.westinmalta.com).

Archipelagos 452

The Philippines

Spain's Legacy in the Tropics

As an island nation, the Republic of the Philippines isn't messing around. The country counts 7,107 islands in the western Pacific and a population of 91 million. If those islands were one contiguous landmass, it would be about two-thirds the size of California—with about three times the population. Getting around the archipelago, however, is no easy feat: To see the highlights of the Philippines, you'd better develop a good set of sea legs, an intrepid attitude toward dodgy-looking airplanes, and a whole lot of patience for the Filipino stance on punctuality (that is, that it's overrated).

Most travelers will start in **Manila,** the country's capital. Manila is a crazy, throbbing city with plenty of culture—it has some of the hottest nightlife in Asia and a wealth of historical sights from the country's Spanish colonial past in the walled district of Intramuros. But chances are, you're coming to the Philippines not for its urban chaos but for its natural wonders. From Manila, take a day trip to **Mount Pinatubo,** the 1,485m (4,872-ft.) volcano that made headlines in 1991 when it erupted in colossal, spectacular fashion. The crater is now a lake, and courageous travelers can even swim inside it. The greatest treasure of this area, however, is the **Banaue Rice Terraces,** what many rightly call the eighth wonder of the world. Covering a massive 10,000 sq. km (3,860 sq. miles) of undulating topography, the terraces were carved thousands of years ago and employ highly sophisticated irrigation and engineering techniques.

When you want to swim, sunbathe, or snorkel along the archipelago, the Philippines have a number of resort areas. **Boracay** island, which has 4km (2½ miles) of pristine white-sand beach that squeaks underfoot, is justly celebrated as the country's single best beach area, with luxury hotels and happening nightlife. At the northern tip of Palawan island (across the Sulu Sea to the west), **El Nido** is a tropical paradise with staggering limestone formations in the water offshore. World-class dive spots abound in the archipelago: Go to **Sorsogon** to see whale sharks, or **Subic Bay** or **Busuanga** island for submerged World War II wrecks.

The island of **Bohol,** in the central Visaya cluster of islands, isn't so much a beachy place as a trove of land-based treasures, like the famed **Chocolate Hills** (the limestone turns from beige to deep brown depending on the season) and **Sikayuna National Park,** the endemic home of one of the world's smallest monkeys, the tarsier, which is no bigger than your fist.

The Philippines were a Spanish territory from the 16th to the 19th century, and the

Mount Pinatubo Crater Lake.

legacy of that occupation is everywhere. Ninety percent of the population is Roman Catholic, and nearly all citizens—most of whom are ethnically descended from Taiwanese aborigines—have a Spanish surname. And then there's the food: Filipino cuisine is famously cross-cultural, with *lumpia* (vegetable-stuffed rolls) of the Southeast Asian tradition and pansit noodles derived from Chinese cooking, alongside many dishes with a European or Hispanic flair. The de facto national dish is *lechon* (suckling pig roasted on a spit), hailed by Anthony Bourdain as the king of all pig dishes worldwide. —*SM*

ⓘ www.tourism.gov.ph, www.philtourism.com, or http://tourism-philippines.com.

✈ Manila-Ninoy Aquino International.

🛏 $ **Dave's Straw Hat Inn,** Boracay (✆ **63/36-288-5465;** www.davesstrawhatinn.com); $$ **El Nido Resorts,** El Nido (✆ **63/2-894-5644;** www.elnidoresorts.com).

Archipelagos **453**

Tonga

Tonga Time

Adjusting to island time is one thing, but acclimating to laid-back Tonga Time is another (maddening? refreshing?) aspect of visiting this beautiful, remote South Seas archipelago. Planes leave 2 hours later—or 2 hours earlier—than scheduled; service can be genial but indifferent.

The Kingdom of Tonga is the only South Pacific nation that was never fully colonized by a Western power, and this tight-knit, family-oriented community has retained its indigenous Polynesian culture through 3,000 years of human settlement. An underdeveloped tourism infrastructure—that Tonga Time factor again?—means that it's not overrun with tourists. Domesticated pigs roam the islands, sometimes outnumbering the people. Most every night, Tongan men—mellow to begin with—drink large quantities of kava, a tranquilizing beverage made from the kava plant (women are not allowed to drink kava).

Tonga is composed of five island groups—Tongatapu, Ha'apai, Vava'u, Eua, and Niua—which were united as one kingdom in 1845. Of a total 176 islands and islets, only 36 are inhabited. A quarter of all Tongan citizens live in **Nuku'alofa,** the capital, located on the main island of **Tongatapu.** Nuku'alofa has most of the country's accommodations and tourist businesses, but much of its central business district was burned to the ground during pro-democracy riots in 2006, triggered by the death of much-loved King Tupou IV, who had ruled Tonga for 41 years. Tonga, a constitutional monarchy since 1875, remains the only monarchy in the Pacific, but in 2008 the newly crowned king relinquished much of his power to pave the way for a fully democratic government.

Other attractions on Tongatapu include the **Ha'amonga Trilithon,** a mysterious and massive stone arch that has been called "the Stonehenge of the South Pacific"; the **Blow Holes,** spewing fountains of water along the rocky southern coast; and **Captain Cook's Landing Place,** where Captain James Cook landed on April 30, 1777.

Whereas Tongatapu and Ha'apai are low-lying coral islands, with superb snorkeling and diving spots, lovely **Vava'u** is classic Polynesia—mossy volcanic peaks set against a blue sky. It's a sailor's paradise, where you can explore exquisite white-sand islets and secluded coves in near-perfect sailing (and snorkeling) conditions. Charter a yacht in Vava'u with **The Moorings** (✆ **676/70-016**), or hire a fully crewed sailing yacht for multiday outings with **Melinda Sea Adventures** (✆ **676/70-975;** www.sailtonga.com). The warm tropical waters of Tonga are also prime breeding grounds for Southern humpback whales; you may actually swim with the whales during a day trip with **Sailing Safaris** (✆ **676/70-650;** www.sailingsafaris.com), operating out of Vava'u.

If you're traveling by boat, build time into your schedule for getting from one island group to another (it can take at least half a day). The most expeditious way to get around is to fly (**Chathams Pacific Airline;** ✆ **676/28-852;** www.chathamspacific.com). You can also travel by ferry from Tongatapu to Ha'apai (**MV *Olovaha;*** ✆ **676/23-853**) and Vava'u (**MV *Pulupaki;*** ✆ **676/23-855**) once a week.

Keep in mind that Tongans are staunch churchgoing Christians, and modesty of dress is recommended for all visitors; swimsuits, skimpy clothing, and going shirtless should be relegated to the beach and pool. —*AF*

ⓘ **Tonga Visitors Bureau** (✆ **676/25-334;** www.tongaholiday.com).

✈ Fua'amotu International Airport (21km/13 miles south of Nuku'alofa).

🛏 $$ **Matafonua Lodge,** Foa Island, Ha'apai Island Group (✆ **676/69-766;** www.matafonua.com). $$$ **The Tongan Beach Resort Vava'u,** Neiafu, Vava'u (✆ **676/70-380;** www.thetongan.com).

Archipelagos

Palau

The Ace of Aquatic Life

Best known for its spectacular diving, and for its stint as a *Survivor* host island, Palau landed in the headlines for another reason with the political events of June 2009. That's when this tiny Micronesian nation agreed to take 17 Uighur (Chinese Muslim) detainees from Guantánamo Bay off the U.S.'s hands, at least temporarily, in exchange for millions of dollars in aid. That might not have been the best marketing tactic for this country of 20,000 people, who largely depend on revenues from international tourists drawn to Palau's otherworldly natural attractions. Commentators had a field day, however, with jokes about the Uighur prisoners' luck—considering their dry and mountainous homeland—upon being relocated to such a tropical paradise.

Most travelers who make it to Palau—which is located about halfway between the Philippines 452 and Guam 456—come for the diving, and specifically for the aquatic splendors of the Rock Islands 45, a chain of hundreds of mushroomlike formations (think *The Smurfs Go to the South Seas*) covered by lush jungle vegetation. The Rock Islands are usually reached by day excursions from **Koror,** Palau's chaotic capital. Along with the other two islands that Koror State comprises, Malakal and Arakebesang, this is where most hotels, restaurants, shops, and services are in Palau. **Malakal** has an important harbor from which many excursions depart, while lush **Arakebesang** is home to the five-star Palau Pacific Resort. Koror Island itself has two spectacular waterfalls, and many outfitters organize day hikes to the **Ngardmau waterfall** on Palau's tallest peak, Mount Ngerchelechuus, and to the **Ngatpang waterfall** on the Tabecheding River.

North of Koror and within easy day trip distance is the time warp island of **Babeldaob,** the largest island in the Palau archipelago, where you can gaze at mysterious stone monoliths, walk ancient footpaths, and visit *bai* (men's meeting houses, with traditional stories carved in their wooden beams and gables).

Rounding out the Palauan archipelago to the south are the islands of Peleliu and Angaur. (For the most authentic experience, take the ferry from Koror to reach these.) Peaceful and rustic **Peleliu** belies its grisly war history: More than 15,000 men were killed here in 1944 and there are still war relics aplenty hidden in the jungle foliage. On **Angaur,** monkeys outnumber people by a huge margin, and there are sunken tanks in the harbor and warplanes overgrown with vegetation in the interior. Which Palauan island, if any, the Gitmo Uighurs resettle on remains to be seen. —*SM*

ⓘ www.visit-palau.com.

✈ Palau International, Airai (30 min. to Koror).

🛏 $$$ **Palau Pacific Resort,** Arakebesang (✆ **680/488-2600;** www.palauppr.com).

Going It Alone **455**

Iceland

Land of Fire & Ice

When you get off the plane at Keflavik Airport, it's clear right away: You're not in Kansas anymore. Steam whiffs out of cracks in the treeless basalt plain; the air has a definite sulfuric tang. Iceland is perched right on a geologic hot spot, with its geysers and volcanoes constantly rumbling. The same forces that heaved this quirky island up out of the Atlantic in the first place are still at work, shifting and reshaping its stony terrain.

The Blue Lagoon.

Long ago, when the first Danish Vikings landed here, they didn't dream up any evocative name for it—they just called it Island. In English, however, it came out as Iceland, and ever since, English-speaking schoolchildren have imagined it as a land of glaciers and polar snowdrifts. In fact Iceland isn't icy at all. Between the hot springs bubbling beneath its crust and the warming effects of the Atlantic Current, it's surprisingly temperate for an island this far north.

Iceland's capital, **Reykjavik,** is one of my favorite cities in the world. It looks like an overgrown fishing village, with its colorfully painted boxy houses—most made of corrugated iron, a must in this timberless land—surrounding a harbor full of fishing boats. Yet I find it a refreshingly cosmopolitan city, with small cutting-edge museums, trendy shopping, a lively dining scene, and thriving nightlife. Don't expect fusty palaces or a crumbling medieval core—Reykjavik was founded only in the late 1700s, and as a longtime Danish colony (it won its independence only in 1944), it's never had resident royals.

There are two classic day trips out of Reykjavik. Forty minutes southwest of the city, you can bob around the warm turquoise waters of the **Blue Lagoon** spa complex (240 Grindavik; ✆**354/420-8800;** www.bluelagoon.com), incongruously sunk into a lava field, fringed by black-sand beaches and tumbled chunks of volcanic rock. An hour's drive southeast, in Selfoss, you'll find the ancient meeting place of the world's first parliament, the Althing, at **Thingvellir** (✆ **354/482-2660;** www.thingvellir.is). There are few historic buildings left in this mossy lakeside dell, but the visitor center helps you re-create the scene in your imagination. An Icelandic flag marks the site of the Law Rock (Lögberg), where the elected Speaker of the Law announced new rulings; grass-covered mounds cover the ancient market stalls that sprang up each summer when the Althing was in session.

Other excursions depend on your interests—pony trekking, whale-watching, puffin spotting on the sea cliffs, salmon fishing in glacial streams, and golf on more than 50 challenging courses (you can play around-the-clock during the summer's midnight sun). Hiking through the central highland's unearthly volcanic landscapes is a special treat—after soaking in the bathtub-warm natural thermal pools of **Landmannalaugar,** hike into the weirdly colored mountains of the surrounding **Fjallabak Nature Reserve,** staying overnight at mountain huts run by the **Iceland Touring Association** (Ferdafélag Islands; ✆**354/568-2533;** www.fi.is). The 3- to 4-day walk from Landmannalaugar to the wooded nature reserve of **Þórsmörk** is the premier hike in Iceland. —*HH*

ⓘ**Reykjavik tourist office,** Aðalstræti 2 (✆ **354/590-1550;** www.visitreykjavik.is); also www.visiticeland.com.

✈ Keflavik International Airport.

🛏 $$ **Hotel Bjork,** Brautarholt 22–24, Reykjavík (✆ **354/511-3777;** www.bjorkhotelreykjavik.com). $$ **Hotel Vik,** Síðumúla 19, Reykjavík (✆**354/588-5588;** www.hotelvik.is).

456 Going It Alone

Guam

America in Asia

Often it seems no more than a handy comedy-routine punch line—Guam, the United States' least-known overseas territory. Back in 1898, when the United States took Guam from Spain during the Spanish-American War, it made strategic sense for the budding superpower to have a presence in the Western Pacific. The U.S. fought fiercely to retain the island in World War II, when the Japanese occupied it. Ironically, while the U.S. maintains a strong military presence on the island, today the Japanese are back in full force—as tourists.

It makes sense for Japanese travelers to visit Guam—the largest island in Micronesia, Guam is much closer to Japan than Hawaii is, yet it offers a full spectrum of American-style amenities. The tourist hub city of **Tumon** has a broad white-sand beach lined with Miami-esque hotels, duty-free shopping malls, Vegas-like entertainment, and an aquarium. Ten golf courses around the island cater to golf-crazy Japanese.

But there's a lot more to this island than its "America in Asia" profile. Guam has a long colonial history—first visited by Magellan in 1521, settled by Spanish missionaries in 1668, a major stop for Spanish trading galleons between the Philippines 452 and Mexico—and that history is strikingly evident in the capital, **Hagåtña** (formerly Agana), with its stone bridges, the 17th-century Dulce Nombre de Maria cathedral, and the graceful colonial buildings of the **Plaza De España.** (Of course, there's also a bizarre replica Statue of Liberty overlooking the bay at Paseo de Susana.) Hagåtña also showcases the indigenous Chamorro culture, one of Micronesia's most interesting societies: The public market at **Chamorro Village** (next to Paseo de Susana) sells traditional Chamorro clothing and crafts—handwoven textiles, intricate woodcarving, baskets—and tempting aromas rise from food stands where seafood stews, fried chicken, and other local delicacies are sold. In **Latte Park,** a set of eight massive stone pillars known as lattes has been assembled. Originally pillars of Chamorro chiefs' houses, they're capped with rounded "heads" of dark coral limestone that have a brooding mystery about them, almost like the moais of Easter Island 375.

Ringed by coral reefs, frequently swept by typhoons, Guam fills all those tropical paradise cliches: patches of dusky forest, extinct volcanoes turned to grassy rounded hills, and gorgeous waterfalls (try Talofofo Falls on the Ugum River, accessed via cable car—this park also includes the fascinating **Yokoi's Cave,** a Japanese soldier's hideout from World War II). Plumeria, jasmine, and ginger perfume the air, and brilliantly colored bougainvillea—Guam's territorial flower—blooms everywhere, alongside red-and-orange summer bursts of blossom on the aptly named flame trees. Coconut palms and mango trees are interspersed with the majestic spreading branches of banyan trees.

To explore on foot, join a public hike with **Guam Boonie Stompers** (✆ **671/653-2897;** davelotz@ite.net), who set out Saturday mornings from Chamorro Village. For snorkeling and windsurfing, head for Merizo, a fishing village on Guam's southernmost tip, where a ferry will take you to Cocos Island**,** a 40-hectare (100-acre) islet with a day resort set up along a pristine turquoise lagoon. *—HH*

ⓘ **Tourist office,** 401 Pale San Vitores Rd., Tumon (✆ **671/646-5278;** www.visitguam.org).

✈ Antonio B. Won Pat International Airport.

🛏 $$ **Hilton Guam,** 202 Hilton Rd., Tumon (✆ **800/445-8667** or 671/646-1835; www1.hilton.com). $ **Ohana Bayview Guam,** 1475 Pale San Vitores Rd., Tumon (✆ **866/968-8744** or 671/646-2300; www.ohanahotels.com).

Going It Alone 457

The Isle of Man

The Seven-Kingdom View

From the peak of Snaefell—the highest point of the Isle of Man—it's said that you can see seven kingdoms: Scotland, Ireland, England, Wales, Man, Neptune, and Heaven. Set amid fierce tidal currents in the middle of the Irish Sea, the Isle of Man was ruled at various times by all those neighbors—Celts, Vikings, the English, the Scottish—yet was isolated enough to remain feisty and independent (smuggling was nearly as big an industry as fishing). Today it is technically a "self-governing Crown dependency"—the British Queen rules as the Lord of Mann, but the island has its own parliament, the Tynwald, as well as its own language (Manx Gaelic) and flag, adorned with a bizarre symbol of three rotating human legs.

Keep your eyes open and the layers of Manx history peel back like layers of an onion. Scattered around this 52km-long (32-mile) island you'll find the Neolithic chambered tomb of **Cashtal yn Ard** near Maughold, the megalithic burial site **Meayll Circle** near Cregneash, the remains of Celtic hill forts, and Viking stone crosses, decorated with mingled symbols of both Celtic Christianity and Norse mythology. Though the 11th-century **Peel Castle** in Peel is now a picturesque sandstone ruin, you can tour the limestone battlements of **Castle Rushen,** built for English kings overlooking the harbor in Castletown. Also in Castletown, don't miss the **Nautical Museum,** a trove of artifacts illuminating the island's fishing (and smuggling) history. The thatched white-washed cottages of Cregneash's **National Folk Museum** demonstrate the farming heritage of Manx crofters; in Laxey, the Mines Trail and the **Laxey Wheel** (the world's largest working water wheel) shed light on the island's 19th-century lead- and zinc-mining past. In the Victorian era, Man was also a popular summer resort—visit the **Grove Museum** up in Ramsey, a perfectly preserved Victorian family home, or (weekends only) the vintage **Camera Obscura** on Douglas Head, a quaint round pavilion on a cliff that provides a 360-degree view.

For many visitors, the Isle of Man's quirky history comes second to its natural beauty. They challenge themselves to climb to the top of Snaefell (you can also cheat and zip up to the summit on the vintage **Snaefell Mountain Railway** from Laxey—one of several Manx trains that inspired Thomas the Tank Engine's fictional Island of Sodor). They spend a week hiking the 153km (95-mile) **Raad ny Foillan** ("Way of the Gull") walking trail, which circles the spectacular coastline from the long beaches of the north to the sheer seaview cliffs of the south. Divers love to explore the many shipwrecks and rich marine life—abundant porpoises, huge basking sharks, seals, and Minke whales. Bird-watchers take excursions (ferries leave daily Apr–Sept from Port Erin; ✆ **44/1624/832339**) to the British Bird Observatory on the **Calf of Man,** the tiny islet off Man's southernmost tip, a sanctuary with extensive seabird colonies and a nonstop flow of migrating birds every spring through summer. You may even stay overnight with the park wardens in summer—contact **Manx Heritage** at ✆ **44/1624/648000.** —*HH*

ⓘ **Tourist office** (✆ **44/1624/686801;** www.visitisleofman.com).

✈ Isle of Man airport, Ronaldsway.

⛴ Douglas, 2½ hr. from Liverpool, 3½ hr. from Heysham, 3 hr. from Dublin, 3 hr. from Belfast (summer only). **Isle of Man Steam Packet Company** (✆ **44/1624/661661;** www.steam-packet.com).

🛏 $$ **Arrandale Hotel,** 39 Hutchinson Sq., Douglas (✆ **44/1624/674907;** www.arrandale.com). $$ **Welbeck Hotel,** Mona Dr., Central Promenade, Douglas (✆ **44/1624/675663;** www.welbeckhotel.com).

Going It Alone

458

Bahrain

Modern Attitudes & Ancient Culture

Cosmopolitan, progressive, and liberal: These aren't words one normally associates with the Middle East, yet this island nation of 655 sq. km (253 sq. miles) in the heart of the Arabian Gulf manages to be all three. Floating in a finger of the Persian Gulf between the east coast of Saudi Arabia and the peninsula of Qatar, Bahrain is the banking and financial capital of the Arab world; expatriates compose more than a third of its population, and relatively open attitudes and relaxed social norms prevail—extremists and zealots are hard to find in mostly Muslim Bahrain. In contrast to Dubai, the westernized United Arab Emirate with which it's often compared, Bahrain has a more authentic feel, with a strong cultural heritage; the atmosphere of the place isn't nearly so dominated by over-the-top oil riches.

The kingdom is actually an archipelago comprising Bahrain island (the largest and most populated, and where the sites listed here are located), Muharraq (where the airport is), Umm an Nasan, Sitrah, and Hawar 108. In Arabic, the name Bahrain means "two seas," referring to the sweetwater springs that bubble up in the shallow, salty ocean water offshore. This unique phenomenon played an important role in the commercial history of the island, as the pearls harvested here are given a special luster and color by the mixing of the waters. For centuries, pearls gave Bahrain its wealth; the Al-Khalifa family, who rule Bahrain today, came here in the 18th century to deal in oysters and pearls. Historians describe the heyday of the pearl trade in Bahrain as something akin to court life in Renaissance Italy, with cosmopolitan ruling families comparable to the Medicis and Borgias.

In antiquity—as attested by myriad tomb and temple remains poking up out of the sand—Bahrain was home to a sophisticated ancient civilization, the Dilmun, which flourished on the island for several millennia B.C. Most of the artifacts uncovered from the Dilmun period are now in the **Bahrain National Museum,** a striking series of modern exhibition buildings along the water, but there are impressive Dilmun remains at the **Qal'at Al-Bahrain,** on Bahrain's north coast, a UNESCO World Heritage Site. Experts believe that this was the capital of the Dilmun world; it was later fortified and given a moat during the 16th-century Portuguese occupation of Bahrain.

Bahrain was the first Arabian Gulf country to discover oil, in 1932, at a desolate place in the island's reliefless desert interior—a momentous spot marked by the **Oil Museum,** near Awali. Luckily, "black gold" sputtered up just as the world pearl market was bottoming out, and oil revenues assured Bahrain's continued prosperity.

In the capital city of **Manama,** the Juffair district, built on reclaimed land, is a Disney-esque hive of entertainment venues for visiting Saudi weekenders and American service members (Bahrain is the U.S. Navy's Arabian Gulf headquarters). Just north of the airport on Muharraq island, the ersatz "archipelago" known as the **Amwaj Islands** (also made from dredged-up land) is the hottest real estate in Bahrain, with Miami Beach–meets–the Middle East architecture. (The late Michael Jackson once owned property here.)

Bahrain is connected to the mainland of Saudi Arabia by the 25km-long (16-mile) King Fahd Causeway, and will be linked to its eastern neighbor Qatar by the planned Qatar–Bahrain Friendship Bridge (to be completed sometime in 2013), with a span of 40km (25 miles) and a price tag of over $3 billion.

The best way to get around Bahrain, which has good roads and signage, is by rental car. Otherwise, consider booking a tour with **Arab World Tours** (✆ **973/1763-7737;** www.bahrainguide.org), which has a number of general island-introduction and theme-based itineraries. —*SM*

ⓘ www.bahraintourism.com.

✈ Bahrain–Al Muharraq International (8km/5 miles from Manama).

🛏 $ **Best Western Juffair,** 676 Rd. 4015, Manama (✆ **973/1782-7600;** www.bestwesternjuffair.com). $$$ **Gulf Hotel Bahrain,** Bani Otbah Ave., Manama (✆ **973/1771-3000;** www.gulfhotelbahrain.com).

459 Going It Alone

Mauritius

Sophisticated Paradise

Blessedly isolated in the Indian Ocean, 2,000km (1,243 miles) east of mainland Africa, Mauritius may be tiny, but there's never a shortage of things to do. With a coastline ringed by coral reefs, and calm, clear, shallow lagoon waters, the island is ideal for all sorts of watersports; the unspoiled interior offers sights of spectacular natural beauty as well. Tourism on Mauritius is a relatively new phenomenon, however—the government began promoting it when their traditional sources of revenue, sugar and textiles, flattened in the 1970s and 1980s—and so far it's definitely geared toward the higher-end traveler.

Grand Baie, on the north coast, is ground zero for holidays on Mauritius; here you'll find the widest array of accommodations and the best restaurant and nightlife scene. The beaches are better, however, near the up-and-coming resort areas **Pereybere** and **Trou aux Biches.** Also on the north coast is historic **Cap Malheureux,** where the French surrendered the island to the invading British in 1810. **Flic en Flac,** on the west coast, is the other well-established resort area, with *casuarinas* framing the sand; on the east coast, exclusive **Belle Mare** and laid-back **Trou d'Eau Douce** are where the big spenders choose to stay. Trou d'Eau Douce is also the point of departure for Mauritius's most popular day trip—to the beach-paradise island of **Ile aux Cerfs.**

Nature enthusiasts will want to explore **Black River Gorges National Park** (think tropical forests and monkeys) and the **SSR Botanical Garden** in Pamplemousses, home to giant water lilies and rare palms. Inland **Casela Nature Park** offers lion walks and cheetah encounters. In the southwest, **Chamarel** is touted for its "colored earths"—soils of varying hues that look much more vibrant in postcards than in reality—but the real highlight here is the multistranded, 83m-high (272-ft.) waterfall. Along the rugged south coast, the island's most scenic drive runs from **Baie du Cap** to **Souillac,** past basalt cliffs and coves. On the southeast, **Blue Bay** is one of Mauritius's best beaches for windsurfing and sailing; the nearby fishing village of **Mahébourg** is quirky and charming.

Mauritius today is an amalgam of Creole, Indian, Chinese, and French peoples (there was never an indigenous population), with Creole and French the dominant flavors. While the main island of Mauritius

Island Hopping the Cape Verde Islands: Land of Mountains, Desert & Sea

Like many nations in Africa, Cape Verde was for centuries a colonial outpost. This volcanic archipelago lying 644km (400 miles) off the West African coast was finally granted independence in 1975. Unlike many former colonies in Africa, however, Cape Verde has gone from colony to independent nation with relative ease. In the words of the U.S. Secretary of State Hillary Clinton, who visited Cape Verde in the summer of 2009: "Few places demonstrate the promise of Africa better than Cape Verde. No place has put it all together, with . . . a democracy that is delivering for its people, lifting them out of poverty, putting them now in a category of middle-income countries in the world."

Cape Verde (*Cabo Verde* in Portuguese) is located off the coast of Senegal in the east Atlantic Ocean; its 10 islands and 8 islets cover just 4,000 sq. km (1,544 sq. miles). Although it's roughly the size of Rhode Island, Cape Verde has a remarkably diverse topography, an unspoiled landscape that includes striking volcanic peaks, arid salt flats, and sun-splashed golden beaches; on one island, Santo Antão, a high ridge separates two entirely different terrains and climates. The islands are generally warm and dry year-round.

The country is making a big push to tap into its considerable tourism potential, an effort that got a tremendous boost in 2009, when the old capital city of **Cidade Velha,** on the island of Santiago, was named a UNESCO World Heritage Site. The city, formerly known as Ribeira Grande, was founded by Portuguese colonists in the 15th century and contains the remains of a royal fortress, two churches, a city square—even a centuries-old pillory.

Children on the Cape Verde Islands.

Cape Verde was uninhabited when Portuguese settlers arrived here in 1462, and it remained, for the most part, a Portuguese colony for more than 500 years. The Portuguese used Cape Verde as a distribution point for slave traffic out of West Africa, and later as an important refueling stop for sailing ships and their crews (just as it would serve centuries later as an important air and sea refueling site). To meet the needs of its burgeoning armada, the Portuguese planted crops and imported slaves to work the plantations. Over time, many Cape Verdeans left home to work as ship crew or escape impoverishing conditions, and the population dwindled.

Today some 71% of Cape Verdeans are Creole, people of mixed black African and Portuguese descent. The Cape Verde culture is a fascinating blend of European and African influences. Of all the islands, the mountainous 460 **São Vicente** may have the most European feel. The island's cobblestoned capital, **Mindelo,** contains a treasure-trove of colonial architecture. This is the home of *morna,* the lyrical music of Cape Verde, and the mistress of *morna* Césaria Evora. *Morna* is lovely and elegiac, the mournful lament of countrymen far from home. The island also has nice swimming beaches in **Baia de Salamansa** and **Baia das Gatas.**

461 **Santiago,** the largest island, is the home of the capital city, Praia. The city has a West African sensibility, where markets sell local crafts and fruit, and discos fill the night air with music. The island terrain is varied; volcanic peaks snake down to gorgeous beaches ideal for swimming and sunbathing. Don't miss a trip to the 15th-century colonial city of Cidade Velha (see above).

Flat and blanketed in sand dunes, the islands of 462 **Boa Vista** and 463 **Sal** have beautiful white-sand beaches rimmed by turquoise seas. These idyllic beaches—literally oases in an arid dunescape—are what is bringing visitors to the islands, many of them on winter-break package tours from England and Europe who are looking for a quieter and less trammeled alternative to sunny spots like Tenerife. (Many hope, then, that the development of big, bland, all-inclusive resorts on island beaches does not continue apace.) The beautiful white-sand beaches and warm blue seas on the island of 464 **Maio** are empty and secluded—the island is accessible only by ferry or puddle jumper.

Remote 465 **Santo Antão** has two distinct landscapes. A ridge in the island's center separates desert on one side and lush vegetation on the other, a scented, cliffside garden filled with acacia, pine, and eucalyptus. Some writers have compared the terrain to that of rural Cuba, and a mind-set similarly mired in the 1950s. —*AF*

ⓘ www.governo.cv.

✈ Sal international airport via London (5½ hr.).

🛏 $$ **Hotel Morabeza,** Sal Island (✆ **238/242-10-20;** www.hotelmorabeza.com).

TOUR Barracuda Tours (✆ **238/242-20-33;** http://db.barracudatours.com) can arrange 7-night itineraries on multiple islands or specific activities.

Mauritius.

is where most visitors go, there are also three other, farther-flung landmasses—Rodrigues, St. Brandon, and the Agalega islands—that are part of the Republic. First settled by the Dutch in 1568, the island chain reached its heyday under French rule (1715–1810), when sugar plantations flourished and Mauritius was a significant port of call for ships sailing between Europe and Asia. African slaves brought here to work the plantations developed their own traditions, including the still-popular sega music and dance (a sort of drum-and-triangle-based reggae).

Mauritius's most famous resident, however, may have been the flightless dodo bird, a rare endemic species discovered here by the first Dutch visitors and soon driven to extinction by the settlers' wild pigs and macaques. A perfectly intact dodo skeleton is preserved at the otherwise missable **Natural History Museum** in Port Louis—its oversized bill and witless aspect are still fascinating, all these centuries later. —*SM*

(i) **Tourist office,** 5 President John Kennedy St., Port Louis (✆ **230/210-1545;** www.mauritius.net); also www.tourism-mauritius.mu.

✈ Sir Seewoosagur Ramgoolam-Plaisance International Airport, Plaine Magnien.

🛏 $$$ **Four Seasons Resort at Anahita,** near Trou d'Eau Douce (✆ **230/402-3100;** www.fourseasons.com/mauritius).

466

Bermuda

Little Britain

Looking out the window as my plane made its descent into Bermuda, I had to catch my breath—the waters really were turquoise, the sands really pink. No wonder Shakespeare was inspired to write *The Tempest* by accounts of this newly discovered island; no wonder it's an enduringly popular honeymoon destination.

Besides the honeymooners, most visitors land on Bermuda as part of a cruise itinerary; they spend a few hours on shore excursions, then hop back on the ship and leave. What a pity. For me, visiting Bermuda is like slipping into a little slice of the British Empire, albeit one where the policemen wear (Bermuda) shorts. Bermudans—including many black descendants of former African slaves—steadfastly adhere to British customs, from afternoon tea to judges in powdered wigs to driving on the left. (Visitors aren't allowed to rent cars, though—you'll have to get around by taxi, motor scooter, or bike.) Self-governing since 1957, Bermuda in 1995 voted to remain a British overseas territory; those British connections run deep.

Settled by shipwrecked English sailors in 1609, Bermuda became a British colony in 1620; its parliament is the oldest in the Commonwealth. It remained loyal to the

Crown when its fellow North Americans declared their independence, and as a result became a significant mid-Atlantic naval base (check out the massive **Royal Naval Dockyard** in Sandys Parish, occupied by the British navy 1809–1951). Thanks to its strategic offshore position, Bermuda got involved in blockade running in the Civil War, rumrunning during Prohibition, and anti-Nazi spying during World War II—all the fun stuff.

Spend some time walking around Bermuda's original capital, **St. George,** which lies at the eastern end of this fishhook-shaped island (actually a string of islands, connected by bridges and ferries). The 17th-century stocks on King's Square make an obvious photo op, but also investigate the narrow cobblestone lanes, where you'll find sights like the Italianate **Old State House** (Princess St.), constructed in 1620, the oldest stone house on Bermuda; **St. Peter's Church** (Duke of York St.), founded in 1620, the oldest Anglican Church in the Western Hemisphere; or the **Old Rectory** (Broad Alley), built by a former pirate in 1705.

Since 1815, Bermuda's capital has been the more central town of **Hamilton.** (Don't miss taking a boat tour of its glorious protected harbor.) Dubbed the "show window of the British Empire," Hamilton's Front Street is a tourist magnet for its chic shops and restaurants. Farther east, in Smith's Parish, the island's most striking historic home, **Verdmont** (Verdmont Lane), built in 1710, is a pitch-perfect version of an English manor house.

During my last visit, I biked along a section of the Bermuda Railway Trail, which runs the length of the island, and found myself cycling up and down the hills of Devonshire Parish, past distinctly English cottages surrounded by flower gardens. Bermuda's British character also comes out in its impressive string of eight manicured golf courses. But there's one important difference between Britain and Bermuda: those incredible pink beaches—try **Horseshoe Bay Beach** or **Elbow Beach**—where you can score a very un-British suntan before heading home. *—HH*

Tourist offices, airport, cruise ship terminal, Royal Naval Dockyards, and off Water Street Plaza in St. George's (**441/297-8000;** www.bermuda.com).

Bermuda International Airport, St. George's.

$$$ **Fairmont Southhampton,** 101 South Rd., Southhampton (**800/257-7544** in the U.S. and Canada, or 441/238-8000; www.fairmont.com). $$ **Rosemont,** 41 Rosemont Ave., Pembroke Parish (**800/367-0040** in the U.S., 800/267-0040 in Canada, or 441/292-1055; www.rosemont.bm).

Preserving the Old Ways

Barbados

Blissful Beaches

Its beachscapes are the stuff of travel magazine spreads and office PC screensavers: perfect bays of pink-white sand, dappled by casual groves of wind-bent palms, unsullied turquoise water lapping gently at the shore. But Barbados offers more than cocooned, bland beachside bliss. An independent nation since 1966, the island retains a strong British influence from centuries as a crown colony. Barbados has historical attractions that transport you right back to the 17th-century sugar-plantation era, but the island also holds its own in the natural-splendors department, with lush gardens and dramatic topography—all set to a soundtrack

A fort on Barbados.

of steel drums (or native daughter Rihanna) and lubricated by tropical rum drinks.

Lima bean–shaped Barbados has three distinct coasts, which are important to keep straight when you're booking accommodations. The convex **west coast** (facing the Caribbean Sea) is also known as the Gold or Platinum Coast; this is where all the big-name, ritzy resorts are, and the sea is like a great turquoise bathtub. The **south coast** is where you'll find some of the island's most picturesque beaches, like Crane Beach, set below a cliff and the classy Crane Hotel; and Bottom Bay, lined with tall coconut palms that are the arboreal equivalent of leggy models posing for a photo shoot. The south also offers entertainment venues from relaxed to rowdy, concentrated in the restaurant and nightlife strip known as St. Lawrence Gap. The **east coast** is Barbados at its wildest; Atlantic waters regularly lash at the rocky shores, making it the least attractive part of the island for swimmers but the best for hiking, nature appreciation, and general solitude.

One of the best ways to get acquainted with Barbados's varied coastline is to take a **catamaran cruise** around the island. The full-day tours offered by superfriendly **Cool Runnings** (✆ **246/436-0911;** www.coolrunningsbarbados.com) in Bridgetown include stops to swim with sea turtles and snorkel among shallow shipwrecks. To see the island from a land perspective, try one of the free Sunday-morning hikes offered by the Barbados National Trust, or hit the rugged trails of the east coast; it's filled with fabulously panoramic spots for a picnic.

At the "crest" of the lima bean (on the island's southwest coast), **Bridgetown** is the capital and largest city on Barbados. Visitors come here to see its historical forts and places of worship, but few stay in Bridgetown overnight—the beachy island rhythms are elsewhere. The interior of Barbados draws travelers with evocative colonial sights like **Sunbury Plantation House** (✆ **246/423-6270**) and natural wonders like **Harrison's Cave** (✆ **246/438-6640**), the number one tourist attraction on Barbados. After a day of culture- and nature-touring, it'll be time for well-earned rum libations and some fresh fish at one of the colorful beach shacks on the west coast: Try **John Moore Bar,** in Weston

(✆ **246/422-2258**), or **Fisherman's Pub & Beach Bar,** in Speightstown (✆ **246/422-2703**). *—SM*

ⓘ www.visitbarbados.org.

✈ Barbados–Grantley Adams, on the south coast.

🛏 $$ **The Crane,** St. Philip (✆ **246/423-6220;** www.thecrane.com). $$ **Divi Southwinds Beach Resort,** South of Bridgetown/ The South Coast (✆ **800/367-3484** in the U.S., or 246/428-7181; www.diviresorts.com).

468 Preserving the Old Ways

São Tomé & Príncipe

The Leve-Leve Life

Imagine a lush tropical island with crystal-clear seas, palm-fringed beaches, and densely green volcanic slopes. A place where you can sip some of the best coffee in the world and savor fine chocolate, both produced from crops grown in the island's nutrient-rich volcanic soil. A place where once-grand colonial plantations overlook patchwork fields of emerald green. Think you'll have to fight off the hordes of tourists clamoring to rent out a piece of this paradise? Think again.

São Tomé and Príncipe compose one of the last undiscovered paradises on Earth. Tourism is in its infancy on these remote West African islands, but the country's infrastructure is solid and visitors are greeted with warmth and native hospitality. You'll find the local philosophy, *leve-leve*—"slowly, slowly"; take it easy, sit back and enjoy—infectious.

Located about 200km (124 miles) off the west coast of central Africa in the Gulf of Guinea, the equatorial islands of São Tomé and Príncipe form one African country, The Democratic Republic of São Tomé and Príncipe (a long name for Africa's second-smallest nation). This Portuguese-speaking nation was a colony of Portugal for nearly 500 years until it gained independence in 1975. In fact, Portuguese explorers were its first inhabitants, at the time when the islands were little more than a dense tangle of rainforest. The Portuguese recognized the explosive growth potential in the fertile soil and planted large sugar plantations. They imported slaves from West Africa to work the plantations; when sugar proved no longer economically viable, they replaced it with coffee and cocoa crops. Even though slavery was officially banned in 1876, forced labor kept former slaves from gaining their freedom. Riots broke out in protest in 1953 (with many laborers killed), but it wasn't until 1974 that Portugal finally relinquished its hold over the colony.

São Tomé and Príncipe are known for their exotic flowers, beautiful white- and black-sand beaches, ruggedly handsome interior, and significant cultural heritage. The pristine waters surrounding the island are largely unexplored; there's a high level of endemic flora and fauna, due to the islands' geographic isolation. You'll find reminders of the nation's colonial history all around, in the faded elegance of **São Tomé Town** and several former plantation houses *(rocas)*.

Príncipe, roughly half the size of São Tomé, is even more laid-back, with beautiful beaches; **Banana Beach** is particularly striking, with an expansive curve of beige sand licked by blue surf. The offshore waters of Príncipe teem with blue marlin, sailfish, and other big game fish—peak fishing season runs May through mid-October. Arrange a fishing charter, scuba excursion, or island tour with **Club Maxel** (✆ **239/904-424;** http://clubmaxel.st). One tour operator that offers multi-day trips to the region is **Africa's Eden** (✆ **31/26-370-5567;** www.africas-eden.com), which leads island, nature, and wildlife tours. —*AF*

ⓘ www.saotome.st.

✈ São Tomé International Airport, then commuter plane (**SCD Aviation;** www.navetur-equatour.st; 35 min.) to Príncipe.

🛏 $$$ **Bom Bom Island Resort,** Príncipe (✆ **31/26-370-5567;** www.africas-eden.com/Bom-Bom-Island-Resort.asp). $$$ **Pestana Equador,** Ilhéu das Rolas (✆ **239/261-196;** www.pestana.com).

Preserving the Old Ways

Papua New Guinea

Primitive Peoples & Unfettered Nature

It has a population of more than six million and occupies one-half of the second-largest island in the world, yet Papua New Guinea remains one of the least explored, least touristed nations anywhere. As the eastern tenant of the island of New Guinea (total area: 786,000 sq. km/303,476 sq. miles; the other half is taken up by the Indonesian province of Irian Jaya), Papua New Guinea is home to more than 800 indigenous peoples and discrete languages. Culturally, it's one of the wildest places in the world.

Venture away from the gritty capital of **Port Moresby**—and I do mean venture; tourist infrastructure and amenities are few in this land, so it's best to get around with a tour operator—and you'll discover just how diverse, ethnically and ecologically, this little-known country really is. If you've ever seen the Travel Channel's *Living with the Kombai Tribe,* about Papua New Guinea's primitive tree people, you already have some idea that this is truly another world. Rigid tribal rules, masks, and body paint are not just cultural archives trotted out for visitors' benefit, but represent the only life that many people of these tribes know.

Hands down, Papua New Guinea's biggest attraction for foreign visitors is the **Kokoda Track,** a 96km-long (60-mile) single-file footpath that crosses the Owen Stanley mountains between the southern and northern shores of the island. During the Pacific campaign of World War II, parts of the track saw bloody battle in 1942 between Japanese and Australian forces. The trek is one of the world's great hikes, but a serious undertaking that should be approached with every cautionary measure: Contact the **Kokoda Track Authority** (✆ **675/325-1887;** kokodatrackauthority@global.net.pg) for more details and to arrange guides and porters. Depending on your fitness level, the trek can take anywhere from 4 to 10 days (it's all bush camping along the way—there are no cushy lodges), though seasoned locals can breeze across the 2,000m-high (6,562-ft.) mountain passes in 3 days.

From an ecological perspective, Papua New Guinea is among the richest habitats in Oceania, with a diversity of flora and fauna—both on land and undersea—that rivals that of Australia and other, more well-known Micronesian destinations. Throughout the country, dozens of dive operators offer land-based day trips or multiday excursions to phenomenal reefs, coral walls and gardens, and an incredible number of sunken World War II wrecks. **Rabaul, Kavieng, Madang,** and **Milne Bay** are the top spots for immersing yourself among Papau New Guinea's vivid

Locals on Papua New Guinea.

marine life and fascinating relics. Australian operator **Diversion OZ** (✆ **61/7/4039 0200;** www.diversionoz.com) is a reputable outfitter with a variety of trip options.
—*SM*

ⓘ www.pngtourism.org.pg.

✈ Port Moresby International.

🛏 $$ **Madang Resort Hotel,** book through Melanesian Tourist Services (✆ **675/854-1300;** www.mtspng.com).

470 Hot Spots

Madagascar

Land of the Lemurs

As the fourth-largest island in the world, Madagascar—or to use its old name, the Malagasy Republic—was always a prize worth winning, from its days as a British protectorate to its annexation by France in 1883. Though it has been independent since 1960, this largely poor island nation has been plagued with coups and power struggles—most recently in 2009, when President Marc Ravalomanana was forced out of office by Andry Rajoelina, former mayor of the capital city Antananarivo. International mediators stepped in and are monitoring Rajoelina's transitional government as it prepares the country for democratic elections, no later than November 2010. Check your country's travel warnings for updates.

If Madagascar could only quell its political turmoil, this Indian Ocean island, off Africa's east coast, could rival the Galápagos (p. 100) as one of the world's top ecotourism destinations. Despite wide deforestation and slash-and-burn agriculture—the bane of many developing countries—what remains of the country's dense interior woods and tropical rainforest is like a Noah's ark of rare species. A hefty 5% of the world's species live here—and nearly 75% of those species live nowhere else. You'll see the glorious yellow comet moth with its 20cm (8-in.) tail, the sticky-pawed tomato frog, neon-green day geckos, petite chameleons less than an inch long, spiny insect-gobbling tenrecs, and leathery-winged flying foxes. Though Madagascar has only 258 bird species, nearly half of them are also unique to the island, including the pheasantlike ground birds known as couias. The only amphibians here are frogs—but there are 300 species of them, nearly all endemic. And do you want to talk **lemurs?** Madagascar has cornered the market on lemurs; no other country has any native lemurs at all. In Madagascar, though, lemurs seem to drip from the trees, in both the rainforest and the western dry forest. They come in all shapes and color and sizes, resembling pandas, raccoons, monkeys, rats, bats, whatever you can imagine.

Lemurs on Madagascar.

Andasibe-Mantadia National Park, a 3-hour drive from Antananarivo, is the most accessible wildlife preserve, known especially for the black-and-white lemur called the indri, whose cry is uncannily like a whale song. Farther south along Route 7 lies the country's most developed rainforest park, **Ranomafana** (60km/37 miles from Fianarantosa), a romantic terrain of rocky slopes, waterfalls, and moss-draped trees. Continue south for **L'Isalo National Park,** which offers an entirely different experience, where you can hike around tapia forests, narrow canyons, and sheer sandstone crags. On the east coast near Morondava, you can gape at the **Avenue of the Baobabs,** a remarkable collection of those upside-down tropical trees, another of Madagascar's specialties.

Even if you're normally a go-it-alone traveler, it's advisable to take an organized tour to Madagascar, especially if you want to move around the countryside—local roads are spotty at best, and booking hotels can be a gamble. You'll need local guides, anyway—how else will you tell all the different lemurs apart? *—HH*

(i) www.parcs-madagascar.com or www.wildmadagascar.org.

✈ Antananarivo.

🛏 $$$ **La Varangue,** 17 Rue Printsy Ratsimamanga, Antananrivo (✆ **261/20/225-5230;** www.tana-hotel.com). $$ **Setam Lodge**, 56 Ave de 26 Juin, Ranomafana National Park (✆ **261/20/243-1071;** www.setam-madagascar.com).

TOUR **Ilay Tours** (✆ **261/20/223-9036** or 33/1/4253-7161 [France]; http://madagascarilaytours.com). **Madagascar Travel** (✆ **44/20/7226-1004** [U.K.]; www.madagascar-travel.net).

471 Hot Spots

Cyprus

A Country Divided

The sun shines almost all the time on this beautiful, light-filled island—what else would you expect of the birthplace of Aphrodite? Rich in antiquities, World Heritage Sites, lovely beaches, medieval castles, and warm, welcoming people, Cyprus is one of the gems of the Mediterranean.

Roughly the size of the state of Connecticut, Cyprus is officially European and a member of the European Union. But the third-largest island in the Mediterranean Sea also lies just 81km (50 miles) from Syria. Its food—figs, olives, dates, almonds, hummus, and stuffed vine leaves—has a distinctively Middle Eastern bent. Like its neighbors the Greek Isles, Cyprus enjoys a thoroughly Mediterranean sensibility, with a similar landscape, climate, history, and culture.

In truth, Cyprus is unofficially two nations. Long fought over and conquered by various civilizations, Cyprus won its independence from Great Britain in 1960. In the 1970s clashes between the ethnic Greek majority and Turkish settlers came to a head with a failed coup attempt by Greek nationalists and the invasion of northern Cyprus by Turkish troops. Today, the country's southern two-thirds is the internationally recognized Republic of Cyprus and occupied by Greek Cypriot nationalists. The northern third of the island is the Turkish-occupied area, a "country" recognized only by Turkey. A UN Green Zone separates the "border" and even splits the capital city, Nicosia, right down the middle—the last capital in the world so divided.

Moving between the two regions is becoming easier as hostilities have subsided—although it's recommended that citizens from non-E.U. countries enter Cyprus through one of the officially recognized entry points in the south. The differences between north and south can be stark. Southern Cyprus is being developed at a rapid pace (it's a popular second-home market for British citizens), while the Turkish area feels stuck in a time warp. Many important archaeological sites are located in the north, but the tourism infrastructure is nowhere near as advanced as that in the south.

The best way to get around Cyprus is by rental car. Start exploring in **Nicosia** (also known as Lefkosia), where the capital's elegant Old City is ringed by a star-shaped 16th-century Venetian wall. The **Cyprus Museum,** 1 Museum St. (✆ **357/22-865864**), displays artifacts and antiquities that trace civilization on Cyprus from the Neolithic age to the early Byzantine period (around the 7th c. A.D.).

The ruins of the ancient city-state of **Salamis,** on Cyprus' northeast coast (6km/3¾ miles north of Famagusta) are amazingly preserved—the result, experts say, of being buried under sand for much of medieval times, when many ancient sites were dismantled for stone to be used in castle construction. The **Kyrenia mountain range** in northern Cyprus is something of castle country, in fact, with imposing fortresses from the Middle Ages topping craggy cliffs; the castles of **Bufavento, St. Hilarion,** and **Kantara** were built along the range to defend against Arab invasions.

If you're looking for a happening beach resort with good, clean beaches, check out **Ayia Napa,** located in the non-Turkish section of the Famagusta District; this former fishing village is now a buzzing resort town, with multistory hotels, cafes, nightclubs, and a dizzying array of watersports activities. —*AF*

The Cyprus waterfront.

ⓘ www.visitcyprus.org.cy or www.cyprus.com.

✈ Larnaca International Airport.

🛏 $$$ **Anesis Hotel,** Ayia Napa (✆ **357/23-721104;** http://anesishotel.com). $$ **The Classic Hotel,** 94 Rigenis St., Nicosia (✆ **357/22-664006;** www.classic.com.cy).

Hot Spots 472

Sri Lanka

The Mystique of Old Ceylon

Sri Lanka's archaic name, Ceylon, still best evokes the incredible allure of this destination—a land of tea plantations, colonial hill stations, lush jungles, and Buddhist antiquities. Certainly, this teardrop-shaped island nation off the coast of southern India is still recovering from the devastating 2004 tsunami and from years of insurgency by the separatist militant Tamil Tigers. But for adventurous travelers, exotic Sri Lanka richly satisfies the senses.

On the eastern coast, the capital city of **Colombo** is busy and hot, yet far greener and more manageable than other Asian capitals. All over Colombo, romantic vestiges of the colonial era—Portuguese, Dutch, and British—still stand, cheek by jowl with modern skyscrapers and air-conditioned shopping malls. Among these landmarks, don't miss the Governor's Mansion (housing the **Sri Lankan Museum**), the old **Parliament Building,** and the splendidly evocative seaside hotel, the **Galle Face.**

The stunning, monument-studded hill country of the interior is known as the **Cultural Triangle,** at the heart of which lies the island's ancient capital, **Kandy,** a UNESCO World Heritage Site. Kandy's biggest draw is the Dalada Maligawa, or Temple of the Sacred Tooth Relic of the Buddha, enshrining a relic brought to Sri Lanka in the 4th century A.D. North of Kandy, the center point of Sri Lanka is **Dambulla Vihara,** a town built around a huge, isolated rock mass, into the top of which there is an ancient Buddhist cave temple with extensive reliefs and frescoes. At the 11th-century city of **Polonnaruwa** (east of Dambulla), check out the **Gal Vihare** archaeological site, with its colossal granite carvings of the Buddha. Rising out of the dense vegetation between Dambulla and Polonnaruwa, the remarkable **Sigiriya Rock** is home to 5th-century frescoes, water gardens, and ruins of a royal palace fortress. The top of the Cultural Triangle is the sacred city of **Anuradhapura,** with its palaces and monasteries built around the much-revered Bo Tree (Buddha's fig tree of enlightenment).

Another favorite escape from Colombo is the hill town of **Nuwara Eliya,** in the heart of Ceylon tea country. It still recalls its British colonial heyday, with Queen Anne and Victorian architecture and English-style gardens. Near here is the Horton Plains plateau and famed **World's End** precipice—a 1000m/3,280-ft. drop-off before a sea of lush tropical flora.

Seekers of warm, Indian Ocean waters and palm-fringed beaches gravitate to the coastline south of Colombo. **Hikkaduwa** is the most developed beach resort area; its shore breaks and reefs attract surfers and divers from all over the world. The other great Sri Lankan surfing spot is budget-traveler mecca **Arugam Bay,** where elephants roam freely on the beach. Sri Lanka's top wildlife attractions are the **Pinnawela Elephant Orphanage,** home to a protected colony of pachyderms, and **Yala National Park,** where if you're lucky you may sight an elusive leopard.

Note: Before planning a trip to Sri Lanka, check for travel advisories. Though the Tamil Tiger conflict had ended as of May 2009, much of the north and east of the island remains war-torn and may be unsafe. In general, it's best to get around with private tours and charters and avoid public transportation. —*SM*

(i) www.srilankatourism.org.

✈ Bandaranaike International Airport (35km/22 miles north of Colombo).

🛏 $$$ **Galle Face,** 2 Galle Rd., Colombo (✆ **94/52/12541010;** www.gallefacehotel.com). $$ **Tea Factory,** Nuwara Eliya (✆**94/52/2229600**).

TOUR Imaginative Traveler (www.imaginative-traveller.com).

13 Ends of the Earth

473 Walk with the Animals

The Falkland Islands

Penguin Paradise

Say "Falkland Islands" and most folks immediately flash to 1982, when Argentina launched a quixotic invasion of this virtually unknown British possession, 483km (300 miles) off Argentina's Atlantic coast. The spectacle of Great Britain flexing its military power to protect such a distant and seemingly insignificant bit of territory provided an irresistible target for late-night TV comedians for months.

But say "Falkland Islands" to an ornithologist and he'll see something way different: a sunny vision of penguins, seals, and albatrosses, frolicking on unspoiled rocky islands. Often lumped into an Antarctic cruise itinerary, the Falklands—also known as the Malvinas—deserve a visit on their own merits. Individual tourists (there aren't many) can fly in from Santiago, Chile, though there is also a weekly RAF charter from the U.K.; note that you must have accommodations booked before you enter the country. As far south as it is, the Falklands archipelago (comprising the two main islands of East and West Falkland and a few hundred smaller islands) is still in the temperate zone, with temperatures similar to London's; even in the depths of winter the sun shines at least 6 hours a day. Instead of daredevil glacier climbing, Falklands visitors enjoy more contemplative pursuits such as photography, birding, cross-country tramping, horse trekking, and trout fishing.

Penguins are the stars of the show, with no fewer than five varieties colonizing the islands' white sandy beaches: **Gentoo, Magellanic, Macaroni, Rockhopper,** and **King penguins.** Sea lions, fur seals, and elephant seals hide in the tall tussac grass, alongside tiny spiky tussac birds; rare seabirds such as the black-browed albatross, the giant petrel, and the striated caracara (known here as the Johnny rook) roost on tiny rocky sanctuaries scattered around East and West Falkland. Local tour operators will help you organize the 4WD vehicles or small planes you may need to reach the more remote wildlife spots.

The Falklands have their own defiantly unglitzy charm, the no-nonsense air of a distant outpost where the settlers simply soldier on. Residents cling to a sense of Empire, with the Union Jack proudly on display. The port town of **Stanley** (or, as Falklanders call it, simply Town) on East Falkland has a Victorian air, though most houses sport gaily colored tin roofs that look more like Reykjavik than Dover. Yes, there are a golf course, a race course, a fish and chips shop, and an **Anglican cathedral**—the most southerly cathedral in the world—but the whalebone arch in front of the cathedral reminds you of the town's days as a whaling port. You'll also see oil rigs pumping away offshore, which solves the mystery of why Britain went to war in 1982.

As plans to develop that oil proceed apace, environmentalists scramble to assess the impact on the islands' extraordinary wildlife. The landscape is scrubby, heathy, a hardy terrain of eroded peat and rocky scree, where dwarf shrubs stand in for trees. But those penguins, they think it's paradise—and naturalists would like to keep it that way. —*HH*

ⓘ **Jetty Visitor Centre** (✆ **500/22215;** www.visitorfalklands.com).

✈ Mount Pleasant military base (60km/37 miles from Stanley).

Previous page: Nuuk, Greenland.

🛏 $$ **Malvina House Hotel,** 3 Ross Rd., Stanley (✆ **500/21355;** www.malvinahousehotel.com). $$ **Upland Goose Hotel,** 22 Ross Rd., Stanley (✆ **500/21455;** www.the-falkland-islands-co.com).

TOUR Falkland Islands Holidays (✆ **500/22622;** www.falklandislandsholidays.com). **International Tours and Travel** (✆ **500/22041;** www.falklandstravel.com). **Lindblad Expeditions** (✆ **800/EXPEDITION** [397-3348] in the U.S., or 212/765-7740; www.expeditions.com).

Walk with the Animals 474

Malpelo Island

Swimming with Sharks

Colombia

From the sea, Malpelo looks like something out of a classic 007 movie—the remote Pacific hideout where the over-the-top villain plots some dastardly scheme from within a rocky fortress. The island's profile is so sinister it's almost campy: The "shoreline" consists of sheer cliffs, and the island's highest peak, **Cerro de la Mona,** looms 376m (1,234 ft.) above like a glowering overlord. The entire surface of Malpelo, a scant 350 hectares (865 acres), is harsh grey lavic rock, practically devoid of vegetation. And for 10km (6 miles) in every direction, the waters around Malpelo are a UNESCO sanctuary where some of the ocean's most menacing-looking creatures circle and feed. Yet it's thanks to this teeming and diverse population of sharks that Malpelo is one of the top scuba diving destinations in the world.

Sharks swimming by Malpelo Island.

The miniscule above-water peak of an enormous undersea mountain that extends for 3.2km (2 miles) to the floor of the Eastern Pacific Ocean, Malpelo is located 506km (314 miles) off the western coast of Colombia. Because of its extreme isolation and the government permits required to visit Malpelo, most people travel there on organized diving trips that include Costa Rica's Coco Island 90, another phenomenal dive site.

Massive, spectacular sea caves, where smaller fish seek harbor from rough mid-ocean conditions, are what make Malpelo and its offshore rock stacks such a consistently thrilling place to dive. These ecological conditions are a magnet for the shark species so frequently seen here, and at relatively shallow depths. Visibility underwater is generally excellent. There are more than 500 scalloped hammerheads swimming around Malpelo, as well as silky sharks, bull sharks, white-tip sharks, manta rays, barracuda, and an astounding number of moray eels. It's also one of few places in the world where the rare small-tooth **sand tiger shark** is commonly seen, off a rock wall known as "Monster Face." More friendly-faced creatures in the vicinity include dolphins, sea turtles, and the occasional humpback whale on migratory routes. The prehistoric hammerheads, which measure up to 4.2m (14 ft.) in length and swim in formidable synchronized matrices—a dazzling sight for divers—may look monstrous, but neither they nor any of the other species off Malpelo are aggressive toward humans.

Unless you're an experienced and intrepid diver (there are strong currents to contend with in addition to the toothy sea life), there's no reason to visit Malpelo. The island's name is a corruption of the Latin nickname a sailor once gave this barren rock: *malveolus,* or "inhospitable," which pretty well sums up the above-water aspect of the place. The island—"rock" is more like it—is uninhabited by humans except for a small Colombian navy garrison. Some other fauna, however, are perfectly suited to this seemingly hostile environment: A colony of some 25,000 Nazca, or **masked boobies,** thrives on tiny Malpelo, and there are a number of endemic species, including lizards and crabs, that live on the algae and lichens that grow on the crags. —*SM*

ⓘ http://whc.unesco.org/en/list/1216.

✈ San Jose International, Costa Rica. Diving trips depart from Puntarenas, Costa Rica.

TOUR Undersea Hunter, Puntarenas, Costa Rica (✆ **506/2228-6613;** www.underseahunter.com).

475 Walk with the Animals

Herschel Island

Whaling Ghost Town

Canada

It's deserted today except for the formidable exemplars of Arctic wildlife that spend part of the year here, but this 117-sq.-km (45-sq.-mile) island on the top shelf of the North American continent was, for a very brief period in the late 19th century, a place that saw a lot of action. In the heyday of whaling, Herschel Island was an important harbor and wintering site for whale ships and their crews, who built everything—from ball fields to ballrooms—they needed to make this island of tundra feel more like home. What brought them to this remote part of the globe was the bowhead whale, a baleen species that, by that time, existed only in the Beaufort Sea off the north coast of Yukon. But when, in the early 20th century, the advent of petroleum made whale oil obsolete, the whalers left Herschel, and the native Inuvialuit people soon followed suit, returning the island to the bears, caribou, and other fauna that thrive in the harsh conditions of the far north.

The Inuvialuits, Inuits descended from the Thule people, called Herschel Qikiqtaruk ("island"). The island is now designated as Herschel Island Qikiqtaruk Territorial Park, administered by the Government of Yukon. Although nominally protected as a national park, Herschel is very much under threat from climate change. Ice in the Arctic region is melting fast, and the rising sea levels are encroaching on the shorelines of much of this part of the world. Herschel's cultural heritage sites—including the archaeology of its whaling buildings at the European-American settlement of **Pauline**

Cove, as well as Inuvialuit structures and graves—will disappear underwater unless they're moved. The World Monuments Fund has placed Herschel on its 100 Most Endangered Sites list; in the meantime, the island is a likely candidate to become a UNESCO World Heritage Site, for both its cultural and its natural assets.

On the trip to Herschel Island from the mainland, a near-encyclopedic sampling of Arctic mammals can be seen here at various times of the year. Porcupine caribou are a common sight, and moose and musk oxen are also present. Black bears, polar bears, and grizzlies are all known to have dens on the island. **Beluga and bowhead whales** still swim in the Beaufort Sea offshore, unharried by the whalers' harpoons.

For visitors, getting to Herschel Island, even though it's only 6.4km (4 miles) from the mainland of Yukon and 72km (45 miles) from the north coast of Alaska, is a challenge. There are no regularly scheduled flights or boat services here, but charters can be arranged and kayakers traveling the Firth river can stop here. —*SM*

ⓘ www.environmentyukon.gov.yk.ca.

Charters from Inuvik (250km/155 miles away).

Boat charters only.

$ Camping; see the Environment Yukon website above for details.

TOUR Arctic Nature Tours, Inuvik (✆ **867/777-3300;** www.arcticnaturetours.com). **Uncommon Journeys,** Whitehorse (✆ **867/668-2255;** www.uncommonyukon.com).

Walk with the Animals **476**

North Uist

Next Stop, Canada

The Outer Hebrides, Scotland

The Western Isles aren't exactly the most far-flung of Scotland's islands—that honor goes to the Shetlands (p. 234)—but stand on the rocky headlands of Balranald, looking west onto the cold, grey North Atlantic, and you feel like you're hanging onto the rim of the continent. This wind-swept, waterlogged island is the last stop before Newfoundland; no wonder so many birds end their westward flights on North Uist's long white beaches.

The bird-watching here is simply spectacular, especially on that wild western side of the island. Follow the nature trail through **Balranald Nature Reserve** (visitor center at Goulat; ✆ **44/1463/715000**) and you'll see the amazing bird life of the machair, a uniquely Scottish sort of plain. With its rich tapestry of summer flowers—wild pansies, poppies, marigolds, marsh orchids, eyebrights, silverweed, daisies, purple clover—the machair is a peaty low-lying pasture that takes over a beach after a drop in sea level creates a new beach. Being so close to the sea, it attracts both shorebirds—ringed plovers, redshanks, oystercatchers, greylag geese, and barnacle geese—and meadow species like twites, skylarks, meadow pipets, corn buntings, and a whopping number of **corncrakes,** one of Europe's most endangered species. From mid-April to early August, you can hear its spooky rasping call everywhere, especially at night.

It's hard to believe that human beings have persisted on this remote isle for so many centuries, long before steamboats could cross over from the Inner Hebrides and the mainland, and long before causeways were built to link North Uist with its Hebridean neighbors Grimsey, Benbecula, and South Uist. But signs of ancient habitation are everywhere, blessedly undisturbed by later development. (North Uist's population has been dwindling for years; there are currently only about 1,200 residents on this 21km/13-mile-long island.) Northwest from the ferry port of Lochmaddy, the hamlet of Blashaval features a trio of standing stones that legend claims were three actual men from Skye 329, who were turned to stone by a witch for deserting their wives. South from Lochmaddy, on the slopes of the mountain **Ben Langass** is a beautifully preserved chambered cairn thought to be nearly 5,000 years old, as well as the dramatic stone circle Pobull Fhinn. Farther south, just before you reach the causeway to Grimsey, in the hamlet of **Carinish** you can see the Carinish Stone Circle and the ruins of a 13th-century monastery that includes Trinity Temple (Teampull na Trionad in Gaelic), founded by Beathag, the first prioress of Iona.

The low-lying eastern side of the island is peppered with so many little lakes, it seems almost more water than land—but all the better for anglers, who come here for possibly the best sea trout fishing in the country, as well as brown trout and salmon. As for other outdoor sports like rock climbing and kayaking, you'll get all the help you need from the **Uist Outdoor Centre** in Lochmaddy (✆ **44/1876/500-480;** www.uistoutdoorcentre.co.uk), right near Lochmaddy's surprisingly sophisticated museum and art gallery, **Taigh Chearsabhagh** (✆ **44/1876/500-293;** www.taigh-chearsabhagh.org). —*HH*

ⓘ www.isle-of-north-uist.co.uk.

✈ Benbecula (16km/10-mile drive from North Uist).

Lochmaddy (from Skye), 1 hr., 45 min. **Caledonian McBride ferries** (www.calmac.co.uk).

$$ **Langass Lodge,** Locheport (✆ **44/1876/580-285;** www.langasslodge.co.uk). $ **Lochmaddy Hotel,** Lochmaddy (✆ **44/1876/500-331;** www.lochmaddyhotel.co.uk).

Walk with the Animals

Socotra

Frankincense & Myrrh

Yemen

Otherworldly and enchanting, Socotra has long been described as a forgotten Eden. A rocky archipelago in the northwestern Indian Ocean off the Horn of Africa, Socotra is composed of one large island (Socotra) and three smaller islands. At 250km (155 miles) long, Socotra is the largest island in the Middle East and also the most isolated, believed to have separated from the mainland millions of years ago.

Extreme isolation has resulted in endemic species little changed from the ancient flora and fauna of the Mesozoic period. This "Galapagos of the Indian Ocean" has been called one of the 10 most richly biodiverse places on the planet; 37% of Socotra's 825 plant species, 90% of its reptile species, and 95% of its land snail species occur *nowhere else on earth.* It's a beautiful and bizarre landscape of old and new, with umbrella-shaped dragon's blood trees (which bleed red sap) and frankincense forests, as well as introduced species such as goats and donkeys. The terrain veers from tropical desert to limestone plateau to dramatic mountain ranges. The marine waters surrounding the archipelago are filled with 253 species of reef-building corals, 730 species of coastal fish, and 300 species of crab, lobster, and shrimp; the **deep-water diving** is world-class.

Island Hopping the Aleutian Islands: North to Alaska

Alaska's Aleutians consist of more than 300 volcanic islands—part of the "Pacific Ring of Fire" that extends over 1,000 miles (1,610km) into the Pacific Ocean from Alaska. This vast archipelago is divided into several strings of islands, all of which are actually the tops of submerged volcanoes. Most share in common a rugged landscape of lush green tundra blanketed with grasses and wildflowers. The Aleutians are now part of the **Alaska Maritime National Refuge,** attracting hardy visitors who don't mind the frequent rainstorms and wind.

In the summer, a ferry runs every 2 weeks from the mainland city of Homer out to the Aleutian island of 478 **Unalaska** with stops in several remote Native communities along the way. Contact **Alaska Marine Highway System** (✆ **800/642-0066;** www.dot.state.ak.us/amhs/index.shtml). To fly to a roadless village, or to fly between most towns without returning to a hub, you can also take a small, prop-driven plane with an Alaska bush pilot at the controls. To find a bush pilot, inquire at the Homer visitor center. Unalaska Island, the hub of the island chain and the nation's largest fishing port, provides a wealth of outdoor activities and fascinating landmarks. Some of its hiking trails were forged by natives thousands of years ago. A visit here would not be complete without a trip to the **Holy Ascension Cathedral,** a 19th-century white church, and **Sitka Historic National Park,** the site of clashes between Russian troops who sought to claim the Pacific Northwest for Russia and the native Tlingit forces who fought them.

479 **Amaknak Island** affords great views of active **Makushin Volcano,** the fourth-highest point in the Aleutians, and attracts mountain climbers from around the world. The island is actually an islet in Unalaska Bay, just northeast of Unalaska Island. It's home to more than 2,500 people, making it the most populated island in the chain. The U.S. Navy used Amaknak as a site for a radio station in the 1930s. The largest island in the chain, covering over 1,571 sq. miles (4,069 sq. km), is 480 **Unimak Island.** It is the site of **Mount Shishaldin,** one of the 10-most-active volcanoes in the world, and is largely uninhabited: The 2000 census counted only 64 people, all living on the eastern end of the island in the city of False Pass. Much larger is the population of brown bears and caribou that roam the wilderness. Also worth checking out is **Fisher Caldera,** a volcanic crater marked by volcanic cones and lakes.

In a single day, you can observe murres, kittiwakes, puffins, and gulls at 481 **Bogoslof Island,** a bird-watcher's dream. Theodore Roosevelt dedicated it as a sanctuary for bird and marine life, and it astonishes with its diversity. The name Bogoslof comes from an Aleutian word meaning the "voice of god," earning its name when a volcanic eruption lifted the land from the Bering Sea in the late 18th century. The island's volcano remains active and has long fascinated geologists. *—JD*

ⓘ www.unalaska.info/tourism.htm.

✈ Homer or Barrow.

TOUR Victor Emanuel Nature Tours (✆ **800/328-8368;** www.ventbird.com).

The island was granted World Heritage Site status in 2008 by UNESCO, which cited Socotra's importance to the Horn of Africa's biodiversity hot spot. It's an ecotourist's dream, and with tourism in its infancy and a solid stewardship in place (three-quarters of the island is protected), it looks like sustainable tourism has a good chance to succeed here.

Socotra has one foot in the Arab world and another in Africa. Its populace is of mixed Arab, Somali, and South Asian origins. The rural areas are populated by fishermen descended from ancient South African tribes and seminomadic pastoralists raising goats, sheep, cattle, or camels and cultivating date palms. Fishing from small boats, natives pull in shark, king fish, and tuna, which are salted or dried and sold on the mainland.

As remote and ancient as the island feels today, Socotra was once a vital trading post whose harbor welcomed ships from around the world. The island supplied an abundance of rare frankincense, myrrh, dragon's blood, and aloe, all valuable and rare commodities that drew trading ships by the hundreds to Socotra ports. Sailors and globe-trotters have long known of the island—it was mentioned in a 1st-century-B.C. Greek navigational aid and in *The Travels of Marco Polo.* More recently, the country was a British protectorate for 80 years until 1967, when Southern Yemen gained full independence.

A good way to see Socotra is by guided tour. Ecotourism outfit **Socotra Adventure Tours** (✆ **967/5-660136;** www.socotraislandadventure.com) specializes in customized tours and nature, wildlife, birding, and cultural trips and will set up accommodations and transportation. —*AF*

ⓘ www.socotraisland.org.

✈ Yemania Airlines flies between Sana'a-Mukkala and Socotra (3 hr.).

🛏 To arrange lodging in a guesthouse, overnight camping, and tours, contact the **Socotra Ecotourism Society** (✆ **967/5-660253;** www.socotraisland.org).

TOUR See Socotra Adventure Tours info above.

482 Walk with the Animals

Wrangel Island

Arctic Circle Refuge

Russia

Northwest of the Bering Strait, the arctic winters are long, and I mean loooooong. For 2 months, November 22 to January 22, the sun never rises at all. A lonely landmass in the Chukchi Sea, Wrangel Island lies shrouded in snow until June, an icy wind moaning overhead.

And yet the sun does return every spring, and when it does, it's miraculous. Tens of thousands of **migratory birds**—black-legged kittiwakes, pelagic cormorants, glaucous gulls—arrive to nest on the jagged cliffs. Ringed seals and bearded seals dip their snouts through holes in the ice, hungry for fish. Walruses lumber out onto narrow spits to give birth. Female **polar bears** emerge drowsily from their winter dens, newborn cubs snuffling in their wake. Arctic foxes scavenge the rocky beaches, where snowy owls swoop down on unsuspecting lemmings.

A few months later, in the summer, the tundra teems with life. Rivers, swelled with snowmelt, gush through the narrow valleys, and the last remaining Russian population of **snow geese** paddles around glacial lakes in the island's interior. Brilliantly colored Arctic wildflowers mantle the slopes in shades of pink and yellow. Shaggy musk oxen browse sedges and grasses of the ancient tundra, a relic of the Ice Age. The walruses bask on ice floes and rocky spits, going through their annual breeding rituals. It's a sight to see—but very few travelers ever get the chance.

Located 193km (120 miles) off the coast of Siberia, right on the 180-degree line that divides the Western and Eastern hemispheres, Wrangel Island became designated as a nature reserve (or *zapovednik*) in 1976 to protect the delicate Arctic ecosystem, in particular the snow geese and polar bear, who were being hunted to death. There are no lodgings on the island—a small research base is the only habitation—so the only way to visit is on a ship (and an icebreaker at that), with smaller craft for shore visits. Wrangel is typically one stop on a Bering Strait voyage that also includes the Kuril Islands and Kamchatka. On your way through the strait, you'll also have a good chance of sighting minke, gray, and even beluga whales. These are long, expensive, summer-only expeditions, and few companies run them—if you see one offered (there were two in July–Aug 2009), jump on it. —*HH*

ⓘ and **TOUR Polar Cruises** (✆ **888/484-2244** or 541/330-2454 [both in the U.S.]; www.polarcruises.com).

Walk with the Animals **483**

Christmas Island

The Indian Ocean's Galápagos

Australia

A mere speck in the wide expanse of the Indian Ocean, Christmas Island's 135 sq. km (52 sq. miles) consist of rugged cliffs and dense rainforest. It's several thousand kilometers from here to the country it belongs to, Australia, and some 300km (186 miles) to the nearest landmass, Java 346: Given the tiny size and extreme isolation of Christmas Island, the few human inhabitants here must have a serious resistance to island fever. For the endemic flora and fauna of Christmas Island, however, being this far-flung, uninfluenced by other ecosystems, has been a boon. Uninhabited until the late 1800s, Christmas Island is a naturalist's delight, with many wonders of evolution comparable to what Darwin famously found in the Galápagos Islands (p. 100).

Christmas Island was named in 1643 when Captain William Mynors of the British East India Company landed here on December 25. The first scientific explorations of the island, however, were not carried out until the latter part of the 19th century, when researchers collected specimens of Christmas Island's curious animal and plant life. It wasn't until 1888, however, when large quantities of pure phosphate were discovered here, that Christmas Island was annexed by the British Crown and exploited for its mineral wealth (phosphate is used in fertilizers). More than a century of mining later, Christmas Island's phosphate stores are nearing depletion, and some of the fauna identified by those early scientists, like two endemic species of rat and some birds and bats, have now gone extinct because of human presence.

Thankfully, many conservation measures are present on the island, which has been an Australian territory since 1958, and 63% of the island has been protected as **Christmas Island National Park** (www.environment.gov.au/parks/christmas) since the 1980s. Several destinations around the mostly cliff-fringed island offer wonderful wildlife viewing, such as the acrobatic displays of boobies and the endemic Christmas Island frigate bird at **Margaret Knoll.** At **Dolly Beach,** sea turtles nest against a tropical-paradise backdrop of sugary sand and overhanging coconut palms.

For their spectacular breeding ritual here, Christmas Island's most fascinating creatures are without a doubt the **red crab.** Every year, at the start of the wet season, more than 100 million of these brightly colored crustaceans make their way down from the mountain rainforests of Christmas Island to the sea, where they release their eggs. During the migration, which can last up to 18 days, many island roads are closed, or the crabs' path is carefully diverted, to protect them from being crushed by vehicles or trampled.

The only inhabited part of Christmas Island is called the **Settlement,** occupying the northeast tip of the island. The harbor here is known as **Flying Fish Cove,** where you'll find colorful local culture, the island's few accommodations and restaurants, and a great beach for barbecuing, swimming, snorkeling, and shore diving among tropical fish and the occasional whale shark.

Among Australians, Christmas Island is also known for its immigrant detention center, only one of two such facilities in the entire nation where illegal refugees are held by border patrol authorities. The center has recently been under fire by human rights groups for its antiquated security measures. —*SM*

(i) ✆ **61/8/9164 8362;** www.christmas.net.au.

✈ Christmas Island, connections to Perth, Australia, and to Kuala Lumpur, Malaysia.

🛏 $$$ **The Sanctuary,** The Settlement (✆ **61/8/9164 8382;** www.christmas.net.au/accom_sanctuary.html).

TOUR Christmas Island Expeditions (✆ **61/8/9164 7168;** www.christmasisland expeditions.com/index.html).

484 Remarkable Ecosystems

Grande Terre

Desolation Island

Kerguelen Islands

It's at the southern end of the Indian Ocean, about 5,000km (3,100 miles) from civilization and—to make it even more forbidding—bitter cold, windy, and barren. The 300-island Kerguelen archipelago lies just outside the Antarctic Circle but is missing little of the Antarctic's icy frigidity. **Grand Terre,** the Kerguelens' largest island, is roughly the size of Delaware. Its rugged terrain, replete with ice-covered mountains, glaciers, and a ragged, jagged coastline, is home to penguins, fur and elephant seals, and few other inhabitants. No trees grow on Grand Terre, and the wind blows almost constantly from the west. Precipitation in the form of snow or rain falls 300 days out of every year.

It's not called Desolation Island for nothing.

This volcanic archipelago was first discovered in 1772 by 18th-century French explorers; the islands, which remain a French offshore territory, were long the domain of whalers and sealers who hunted the native species nearly to extinction. Today the Kerguelen whale and seal populations are back to healthy numbers. They share the island with a band of feral cats, descendants of ship cats who kept the rodent population under control (unfortunately, the cats are now working on the petrel population—and eradication programs have so far been unsuccessful). The island also has a number of feral rabbits and feral sheep—both introduced during various settlements. When it comes to human inhabitants, the island numbers around 100, most of them researchers at Grande Terre's scientific stations (including a permanent weather station).

The Grande Terre landscape is both barren and spectacular, with gray mountains rising out of the sea and blue ice sparkling against blue sky. The highest point on the island is **Mount Ross,** which has an elevation of 1,850m (6,070 ft.). But perhaps the most stunning sight is the **Cook Glacier,** which covers approximately 550 sq. km (212 sq. miles)—it once blanketed the entire island.

Although the islands have no trees, in the warmer months low shrubs, grasslands, mosses, and lichens blanket the tundra. But the most unique plant species on the island is actually an edible one. For hundreds of years, mariners have kept scurvy at bay by eating the indigenous **Kerguelen cabbage,** rich in vitamin C.

Grand Terre is not an easy place to access. As one blogger put it, if you want to get to the Kerguelen Islands, "mounting an expedition might be helpful." Otherwise, look for Desolation Island (Grande Terre, that is) in one of several books inspired by it, including Jules Verne's *Le Sphinx des Glace (An Antarctic Mystery),* which has a whole chapter devoted to exploring the island. And keep an eye out for future tours with **Adventure Associates** (www.adventure-associates.com). —*AF*

ⓘ www.taaf.fr.

Remarkable Ecosystems **485**

Montagu Island

Fire & Ice

South Sandwich Islands

Something interesting always happens when fire meets ice. On Montagu Island, off the Antarctic coast, ice and cold have been a constant—that is, until that day in 2005 when rumblings from below turned up the heat. When Mount Belinda blew its volcanic top, it was a momentous occasion for science—rarely have scientists been able to monitor the effects of a live volcanic eruption under sheets of ice. News reports of the satellite data told of "a large and fast flowing lava flow that is pouring into the sea like a huge waterfall."

It was also a momentous occasion for Montagu Island, which grew a whopping 20 hectares (49 acres) in less than a month as the lava was cooled by the ice and formed a solid mass.

Few people were around to see this phenomenon, however. Montagu is seriously remote and completely uninhabited—not surprising, since it's a supremely inhospitable place: Ninety percent of the island is sheathed in permanent ice. Even the Antarctic fur seals that breed in the waters surrounding the island go elsewhere to hang out; Montagu's slopes are so steep and its surfaces so icy it makes for tough going.

What actually lives on this Mars-like terrain? The South Sandwich archipelago—specifically Zavadovski Island—is the terrain of two-thirds of the world's population of **chinstrap penguins,** easily recognizable by their narrow black band that closely resembles a helmet's chin strap. In addition, the island has a variety of mosses, lichens, and flowering grasses.

Montagu Island is the largest of the South Sandwich Islands, a British Overseas Territory some 2,000km (1,243 miles) from the Antarctic continent. **Mount Belinda,** at 1,371m (4,498 ft.), is the highest point on the island archipelago. The South Sandwich Island chain is an arc of 11 emergent volcanoes, most of which are active.

Captain James Cook spent most of his career cruising the sun-dappled South Pacific, naming the Hawaiian islands the Sandwich Islands after his friend and patron John Montague (1718–92), the Fourth Earl of Sandwich. But it's clear that Cook got around: In his search for the "South Continent," he headed into colder, rougher seas and discovered these windswept, glaciated volcanic islands off the coast of Antarctica 486 in 1775; he named them "Sandwich Land." The archipelago Cook deemed "the most horrible coast in the world" was eventually called the South Sandwich Islands.

Bleak and forbidding as they are, the South Sandwich Islands are an increasingly popular draw for cruise ships (those chinstrap penguins floating on blue icebergs make for great photo ops). Montagu, however, is nearly impossible to explore by boat; it has no harbor to speak of, and moorings are extremely difficult along its rocky coast. A handful of scientific research stations have been set up on neighboring islands in the past, but the monitoring of volcanic activity is done largely through satellite imagery.

Poet Robert Frost once pondered whether the world would end in fire or ice. On Montagu Island, however, the marriage of fire and ice shows us how the world begins. —*AF*

(i) www.antarctica.ac.uk.

TOUR Arctic & Antarctic Collection (© **866/256-2765** in the U.S. and Canada; www.arcticantarcticcollection.com) offers cruises that include a possible landing (weather permitting) on Montagu Island.

486 Remarkable Ecosystems

Antarctica

The White Continent

To call it an island is, well, a bit insulting. Of the world's seven continents, Antarctica is the fifth largest (ahead of Europe and Australia), with 14 million sq. km (5.4 million sq. miles) of area draped over and around the South Pole. The majority of Antarctica is covered by a sheet of ice so massive that it composes 70% of the world's fresh water. Girded by the frigid and formidable seas of the Southern Ocean, studded with jagged icebergs and glaciers, and home to astonishingly adapted endemic wildlife, Antarctica truly is the ultimate "ends of the earth" destination. A trip to the White Continent is time-consuming and costly, but it's an unforgettable, once-in-a-lifetime experience, one that reminds you just how untamed parts of the planet still are, and how small we humans are by comparison.

Antarctica doesn't belong to any one nation, though several have made territorial claims over parts of the continent in the past. The Antarctic Treaty of 1959, signed by the countries with a history of exploration there, ensures that the continent will not be exploited for military or mining use, and that research stations—there are dozens, operated by various countries—promote the ecology of Antarctica. Much of the vast interior of the continent remains unexplored, and expeditions to the South Pole are still very much extreme undertakings. It is the coldest, windiest place on earth, but for all its

A penguin on Antarctica.

watery, icy geography, Antarctica is actually considered a desert, as it receives only 20cm (7¾ in.) of precipitation on average each year. There is no permanent population of humans here, though about 1,000 people staff the research stations during the Austral summer.

For the traveler lucky enough to come here, visiting Antarctica is a ship-based affair that will take you around the **Antarctic Peninsula.** The Peninsula is the gnarled finger that stretches up from the central mass of Antarctica toward the next nearest continent, South America, which lies some 1,288km (800 miles) away across the heavy seas of the Drake Passage. The Peninsula is also the Antarctica of nature programs, where the opportunities for seeing wildlife are as stunning as the exotic scenery. At the northern tip of the Peninsula is **Hope Bay,** familiarly known as "Iceberg Alley" for the extraordinary hunks of ice and snow floating in the waters here. The **Lemaire Channel** is perhaps the greatest visual icon of Antarctica, a narrow passage where towering cliffs drop straight down into the glassy, blue-black water, and melted cavities in the ice create a gorgeous palette of cool aqua tones. **Paradise Harbor** is another amazing spot for laying your eyes on Antarctic icebergs, which frequently calve before your eyes at the far end of the bay.

On the ice floes here, the animal life is abundant, with seals, penguins, and whales (and unseen krill below) all playing their part in the food chain. The two-cabin town of **Port Lockroy** is home to the old British research station, now defunct except for a post office and gift shop. The Brits who staff the outpost live amid a sizable gentoo penguin colony, and the sociable birds are known to sleep—and perform other bodily functions—inside the cabins if the doors are left open!

After navigating the highlights of the Peninsula, many ships make their way east and north across the **Weddell Sea,** with its teeming populations of penguins and seals and treacherous ice-filled waters, toward Elephant Island and South Georgia Island 488. This leg of the journey traces the legendary voyage of Ernest Shackleton, whose ship *Endurance* became trapped in Weddell Sea pack ice in 1915. —*SM*

ⓘ www.iaato.org or http://antarcticconnection.com.

TOUR Antarctic Shipping S.A. (✆ **877/972-3531** in the U.S.; www.antarcticacruises.com.ar). **Lindblad Expeditions** (✆ **800/EXPEDITION** [397-3348] in the U.S.; www.expeditions.com).

487 Historic Frontiers

Isla Grande de Tierra del Fuego

El Fin del Mundo

Argentina and Chile

Several centuries ago, the only inhabitants of the southern extremity of South America were the native Yahgan Indians. To survive in the inhospitable climate of this land, the Yahgans made ample use of fire. The campfires continuously burning here were so numerous and so bright that when the first Europeans to explore the region saw them from the sea, they called the whole place *Tierra del Fuego* ("Land of Fire"). Today, the name Tierra del Fuego applies to the group of islands that make up the southern tips of both Argentina and Chile. Isla Grande—as its name suggests—is the largest landmass in the archipelago, with territories belonging to both those countries.

The word "southernmost" is proudly applied to many attributes of Isla Grande: It's the southernmost part of the Patagonia region (the Patagonia ecotourism base town of Punta Arenas is just across the Strait of Magellan from the island) and claims to have the "southernmost city in the world" in Ushuaia, Argentina (Puerto Williams in Isla Navarino 499 contests that claim). **Ushuaia,** a former penal colony, is the main embarkation point for ship expeditions to the Southern Ocean sites of Antarctica 486, the Falklands 473, and South Georgia 488. The principal attraction of the town itself is the **Museo del Fin del Mundo** (Maipú 175; ✆ **54/2901/421-863**), with interesting exhibits on the indigenous peoples and nature of Tierra del Fuego and fascinating navigation artifacts and records. Besides those passengers who spend a day here en route to the Drake Passage and the Antarctic region, Ushuaia and Isla Grande don't get much tourism. The 48,000-sq.-km (18,533-sq.-mile) island's terrain is mostly mountainous, and there are some oil and natural gas deposits in the northern part of the island.

Not far from Isla Grande, though it's actually a separate small island in the Tierra del Fuego group, is the real southernmost tip of South America and one of the most fabled sites in the story of seafaring: **Cape Horn** (Cabo de Hornos). Before the opening of the Panama Canal in 1914, rounding "the Horn" was the only way for ships to get between the Atlantic and the Pacific Oceans, and its hostile waters were—and still are—notorious for the challenges they posed to sailors. Strong winds and currents, enormous waves, and even icebergs sent many a seaman to his watery grave. —*SM*

An iceberg in Tierra del Fuego.

ⓘ www.e-ushuaia.com.

✈ Ushuaia, connections to major South American airports.

🛏 $$ **Tierra de Leyendas,** Calle Tierra de Vientos 2448 (✆ **54/2901/443-565;** www.tierradeleyendas.com.ar).

TOUR **Abercrombie & Kent** (✆ **800/554-7016** in the U.S.; www.abercrombiekent.com). **Lindblad Expeditions** (✆ **800/EXPEDITION** [397-3348] in the U.S.; www.expeditions.com).

Historic Frontiers **488**

South Georgia

Shackleton Lore & Unbridled Wildlife

The most heroic journey in the history of southern Ocean exploration, that of Ernest Shackleton and the crew of *Endurance,* owes a major debt of gratitude to South Georgia. When Shackleton's ship became trapped and crushed by pack ice off the Antarctic peninsula, he sailed a 6.6m (22-ft.) sailboat 1,127km (700 miles) across the open sea to South Georgia and found help at a whaling station here. It's no small irony that one of the farthest-flung, least-hospitable islands on the planet provided the happy ending for Shackleton's incredible voyage.

Almost 2,093km (1,300 miles) from Cape Horn and 4,830km (3,000 miles) from the Cape of Good Hope, South Georgia lies a third of the way between the southern tips of South America and Africa. Like a whalebone floating in the sea, crescent-shaped South Georgia arcs from west to south, some 170km (106 miles) long by 40km (25 miles) wide at its fattest point. The rugged topography of the island, a British territory, is immediate: Great ice- and snow-capped peaks shoot up within meters of the shoreline, giving the island an unforgettable Alps-of-the-Southern-Ocean aspect, a formidable sight in the midst of so much open, and often angry, ocean. The highest mountains reach elevations of more than 2,100m (6,890 ft.), their deep gorges filled with glaciers. Massive icebergs float in the waters just off South Georgia. The south-facing curve of the island bears the brunt of prevailing westerly winds from the Scotia Sea, while the north-facing side of the island offers some protected bays, many with now-defunct whaling stations. When Shackleton and his companions landed on South Georgia in May of 1916, it was at **King Haakon Bay** on the harsh southern coast; the men then made the 35km (22-mile) trek overland to Stromness whaling station, where they found help and borrowed a ship from the Norwegian community there.

The Shackleton history aside, wildlife is the marquee attraction for the roughly 2,000 visitors who make it to South Georgia annually (the island is visited almost exclusively by expedition cruises to the Antarctic region, which are quite expensive and lengthy—at least $14,000 for 25-day expeditions). It may be a hostile environment for people, but if you're a fur seal or a king penguin, South Georgia is the Big Apple, pulsing with huge populations of some of the world's most fascinating creatures. The fierce **Antarctic fur seal** is present here in the millions (95% of the entire species lives on South Georgia), and the island lays claim to a penguin colony of mind-boggling scale at **St. Andrews Bay,** where more than 100,000 pairs of **king penguins** fill the shore with their waddling, bellowing, and malodorous guano. At the king penguin rookery of **Salisbury Plain,** the scene of easy-to-anthropomorphize birds—dirty, disheveled, and socializing around tussock grass-covered knolls—look like a rock music festival. The jumbo jet of seabirds, the **wandering albatross** (it has the longest wingspan of any bird species—up to 3.6m [12 ft.]—and a cruising range of over 16,100km/10,000 miles) also breeds on South Georgia and its neighboring islets.

During the whaling and sealing era on South Georgia, which was shut down in 1966, some 2,000 Norwegian and British transplants lived on the island. (The Norwegians introduced reindeer to South Georgia, and the animals thrive here to this day, though it's an ecologists' debate about whether they should remain.) These days, there is no permanent population on South Georgia, though the British **King Edward Point Research Station** (www.antarctica.ac.uk) is staffed during the austral summer. Visitors can tour the museum town of **Grytviken,** a partially restored Norwegian whaling station with cottages in a Scandinavian palette of red and orange and evocatively decayed remnants of whale-oil processing equipment.

Grytviken is also the site of Ernest Shackleton's final resting place. In 1922, several years after the *Endurance* saga, Shackleton returned to South Georgia on what would be his final expedition: The legendary leader and captain died of a heart attack, at the age of 47, onboard a ship in the waters just off the island. He is buried in a poignantly simple grave, surrounded by a white fence and low native grass, on this most remote outpost of the Southern Ocean. —*SM*

ⓘ www.sgisland.gs.

TOUR Cheesemans (✆ **800/527-5330** in the U.S.; www.cheesemans.com). **Lindblad Expeditions** (✆ **800/EXPEDITION** [397-3348] in the U.S.; www.expeditions.com).

489 Historic Frontiers

Guadalcanal

In the Theater of War

Solomon Islands

The tipping point in the World War II struggle between the U.S.-led Allies and the Japanese came amid ferocious fighting in and around the tangled jungles of this tropical South Pacific island. Some 38,000 lives were lost on both sides in the epic 1942 Guadalcanal campaign, and so many ships were sunk that the waters surrounding the island were nicknamed Iron Bottom Sound. It was to be the war's bloodiest campaign but also one of the most important: By forcing their enemies to give up control of this strategic prize, the Allies succeeded in halting the Japanese advance in the South Pacific.

Guadalcanal, a province and one of the six largest islands in the 992-island Solomon Islands archipelago, is the home of the nation's capital, **Honiara,** and the island chain's main port of entry. You may want to hire a rental car or taxi once you get to Honiara to get around, but you can also take the public buses that run along the main road (Mendana Ave.).

Like its sister islands, Guadalcanal is volcanic in origin and largely mountainous, blanketed in dense tropical vegetation and threaded with rivers and streams. The waters surrounding Guadalcanal are typical of the South Pacific: warm, blue, and clear, with superb diving and snorkeling opportunities. The rich array of marine life includes angelfish, parrotfish, barracuda, and large pelagics. One outfit that offers dive trips on live-aboard boats is **Bilikiki Cruises,** which operates out of Honiara (✆ **800/663-5363** in the U.S. and Canada; www.bilikiki.com). The top sites for snorkeling are **Tavanipupu,**

Tawahi, and **Bonege Beach.** The starry South Sea skies are spectacular, too, with the **Southern Cross** constellation twinkling in the black night.

But for many visitors, the World War II sites are what brings them to Guadalcanal, places with names like **Edson's Bloody Ridge, Galloping Horse,** and **Skyline Ridge.** You can actually see the remains of foxholes and ration tins on **Hill 66;** Japanese propellers and guns at **Henderson Field;** and Japanese mass graves at **Edson's Ridge.** The **Guadalcanal Foundation** (www.guadalcanal.com.sb) offers guided tours of the major war sites on the island, including **Red Beach,** site of the Allies' original amphibious landing on Guadalcanal in May 1942. The Allies' aim was to blunt the Japanese advance into the South Pacific. After 6 months of fierce fighting, Allied forces were able to secure Guadalcanal and halt the Japanese army from expanding their conquests in the Pacific. It was to be a pivotal point in the war against a superbly trained enemy.

The Solomon Islands have been inhabited for thousands of years, and many Melanesian (West Pacific) islands can trace their ancestry here. Today, most of the islanders still live on traditional subsistence farming in small villages and islands. The most common language spoken among the locals is Melanesian pidgin, a mix of Melanesian and English. —*AF*

ⓘ www.visitsolomons.com.sb.

✈ Honiara International Airport (11km/ 6¾ miles east of Honiara) from Nadi, Fiji; Brisbane, Australia; or Port Moresby, Papua New Guinea.

🛏 $$$ **King Solomon Hotel,** Honiara (✆ **677-21205;** www.kingsolomonhotel.info).

TOUR South Seas Adventure (www.south-seas-adventures.com).

Historic Frontiers **490**

Vanuatu

The Happiest Place on Earth

The remote ends of the earth aren't necessarily barren and inhospitable; in fact, some are downright alluring. On the sunny tropical isles of Vanuatu, you're pretty far away from the rest of the world: The 83-island archipelago, steppingstones along a volcanic ridge stretching for 800km (497 miles) across the South Pacific, lies halfway between Australia and Hawaii—it's a hike to get *anywhere* from here. But who cares, when you have sparkling blue lagoons to paddle around in, spectacular dive sites to explore, and soft breezes to mop your brow as you sunbathe on a crescent of sugary white sand?

Its remote location apparently has no bearing on the happiness quotient of its inhabitants, either. Pitted against the biggest nations in the world in a 178-nation "happiness index," the Republic of Vanuatu topped them all. The index, compiled by an economic think tank in 2006, measured a nation's consumption levels, life expectancy, and happiness, rather than yardsticks of national economic wealth such as GDP. By these indicators, little Vanuatu was deemed the happiest place on earth. (The U.S. came in 150th and Britain 108th.)

Life, it appears, is good on this island nation, a classic Polynesian landscape of volcanoes, tropical rainforests, silky white beaches, and dramatic waterfalls, where kava is the drink of choice. With a close-knit community of some 200,000 inhabitants living on 12,173 sq. km (4,700 sq. miles) of land, Vanuatu subsists on farming and, increasingly, tourism. Most of the inhabitants are native Melanesian, and the three languages most commonly spoken are English, French, and Bislama, a pidgin English. **Efate** is the main island and the site of the nation's capital, **Port Vila** (it has a lovely deep-water harbor). **Espiritu Santo** is Vanuatu's largest island and has many of the country's top dive sites.

Until 1980, when the nation gained its independence from a joint British-French cabal known as the Condominium, Vanuatu was known as New Hebrides. First colonized 3,000 years ago by Polynesians who traveled from the Solomon Islands in sailing canoes, Vanuatu was not settled by European colonists until the late 18th century. Christian missionaries showed up in the 19th century, introducing diseases like measles and smallpox to the native population, which killed many. But by the next century, for better or worse, much of the nation had been converted.

In World War II, the islands were "invaded" by American forces, there to wage a counteroffensive against the Japanese, who had taken over the nearby Solomon Islands. The Americans rapidly built a wartime infrastructure—roads, airstrips, hospitals, barracks—and employed islanders in their efforts. Today, wartime detritus is still scattered about the islands *and* in the waters surrounding the islands. It seems that once the war was over, the Yanks offered to sell perfectly good trucks, machinery, cranes, and office machinery to the islanders for 7 cents on the dollar. Despite the fire-sale prices, however, the French/British Condominium balked—so the Americans simply bulldozed most of it straight into the Pacific.

Vanuatu locals.

The most spectacular World War II relic here is the 21,000-ton luxury liner ***SS President Coolidge,*** which had a brief wartime stint as a transport ship until it was sunk by mines planted in the channel leading into Espiritu Santo. The *Coolidge* is the largest wreck of World War II, and a fantastic dive site for divers. —*AF*

ⓘ http://vanuatu.travel.

✈ Port Vila, Efate Island (direct flights from Australia, New Zealand, Fiji, Noumea, and the Solomon Islands).

🛏 $$$ **Chantilly's on the Bay,** Port Vila, Efate (✆ **678/27079;** www.chantillysonthebay.com). $$$ **Eratap Beach Resort,** Efate (✆ **678/5545007;** www.eratap.com).

Historic Frontiers

Faial

Last Stop Before the Open Atlantic

The Azores, Portugal

Whether for exploration or commercial pursuits, in the 19th century there was one port that practically all ships bound for the Americas from Europe called at for provisioning before crossing the Atlantic: Faial, in the Portuguese island chain of the

Island Hopping the Cook Islands: Truly Cast Away

In the 18th century, the legendary Captain Cook made navigation history sailing all over the South Seas, to improbably far-flung islands of often-miniscule dimensions. It's only fitting that the most strewn-out group of islands he visited—with landmasses totaling a tiny 240 sq. km (93 sq. miles) over 2 million sq. km (roughly 1 million sq. miles) of the Pacific—bears his name. The Cook Islands are castaway perfection, with brilliantly colored lagoons and endless settings in which to find complete relaxation, but they're far from being a blank slate of white sand, turquoise water, and swaying palms: The Cooks have some of the richest traditions of any Polynesian culture, and a cast of local characters that overwhelm visitors with warmth and inclusiveness. The 15 islands that make up the Cooks are divided between the Southern Group, where most people travel and where most islanders live, and the Northern Group, which is minimally developed for tourism and very hard to reach. Given the distances between the Southern and Northern Group (1,160km/721 miles), "island hopping" here takes on a whole new meaning. Of the islands listed here, only Manihiki is in the Northern Group.

In tourism terms, going to the Cook Islands usually means going, at the very least, to 492 **Rarotonga,** the gorgeous capital island. Rugged Rarotonga has opportunities for land-based recreation and sublime isolation, like the trek across the island's interior to the iconic rock known as **Te Rua Manga** (the Needle), as well as plenty of watersports from the beaches that line its 32km (20-mile) perimeter. **Avarua** is Rarotonga's commercial center, with just enough bustle to keep anyone from getting island fever, while **Muri Beach** is where the best resorts are clustered. Rarotonga is the Cook Islands' all-arounder, with the widest range of scenery, things to do, places to eat, accommodations, and transportation connections.

Snorkeling in the Cook Islands.

The next-most-frequented Cook Island after Rarotonga—and, really, a required stop for anyone who makes it all the way out here—is the atoll of 493 **Aitutaki** (www.aitutaki.com). It's the stuff your wildest tropical dreams are made of: Aitutaki's trump card, and what will take your breath away as it comes into view on the flight from Rarotonga, is its lagoon. Shaped like an arrowhead, with barrier reef on two sides and a string of *motus* (uninhabited islets) on the other, Aitutaki's triangular lagoon is an otherworldly shade of turquoise that strikes an amazing contrast with the cobalt ocean all around. Aitutaki has a handful of upscale boutique resorts that organize excursions out into the lagoon, whether it's snorkeling, kayaking, or simply cruising across the amazingly clear water. Fans of reality TV may recognize Aitutaki's lagoon from the 13th season of *Survivor.* The Cook Islands installment of the show was filmed here.

To delve deeper into the Cook Islands, you might next choose to visit 494 **Atiu,** a more traditional island where tourism is a bare-bones affair. Atiu is surrounded, as many of the Cook Islands are, by *makatea,* or a raised wall of fossilized coral. Dozens of fascinating caves, each with their own intricate legends, exist among the coastal ***makatea* cliffs,** which provide a habitat for the island's unusual bird populations. The must-do cultural activity of Atiu is to go to a *tumunu,* a gathering in which the local orange-based bush beer is drunk, accompanied by prayer, ceremonial drums, traditional song and dance, and unforgettable socializing with real locals. Of the six *tumunu* on Atiu, Aretou is the most popular with visitors, meeting at dusk every day except Sunday. Captain Cook landed at Atiu's **Orovaru Beach** in 1777.

Cook Islands beach.

The *makatea* cliffs of 495 **Mangaia,** the oldest island in the Cooks, are even more spectacular than Atiu's, with sheer drops of up to 60m (197 ft.) in some parts of the island's ring wall of fossilized coral. Mangaia has some of the Cook Islands' best caves, whose labyrinthine chambers can be explored by good old-fashioned torchlight. Filled with impressive stalactites and stalagmites, these subterranean areas have been used as burial sites for past generations of islanders. A sense of quiet mystery pervades peaceful Mangaia, and longtime residents believe their island to be haunted.

In order to experience the true remoteness of the Cook Islands, travel to the Northern Group. (Note that this is a costly and time-consuming affair; the 4-hr. flight from Rarotonga is operated only when there's enough demand to fill the plane.) Of the Northern islands, 496 **Manihiki** is the most interesting and accessible for visitors. Barely an island, Manihiki is a quadrilateral of land strips and *motus* that enclose a beautiful lagoon where sought-after Cook Island black pearls are cultured. Nearly all the population of Manihiki is involved in the pearl business, and it's fascinating to watch a typical day unfold on the lagoon. Tropical fish abound in the crystal-clear waters here, making for excellent swimming and snorkeling.

All interisland travel in the Cook Islands is by air, through Rarotonga. —*SM*

(i) www.cookislands.travel or www.atiu.info.

✈ Rarotonga, connections to New Zealand and Tahiti.

🛏 $$ **Etu Moana,** Aitutaki (✆ **682/31458;** www.etumoana.com). $$$ **Pacific Resort,** Muri Beach, Rarotonga (✆ **682/20427;** www.pacificresort.com).

TOUR South Pacific Custom Travel (✆ **866/770-3711** in the U.S.; www.southpacificcustomtravel.com).

Azores. Whaling vessels, laden with their harvests of blubber, spermaceti, and ambergris, stopped in Faial upon returning from the whale-rich waters off North and South America and used the island's whale-product processing plants to turn their hauls into marketable goods. Similarly, cargo ships carrying oranges to the Americas employed Faial as a way station—the last outpost before embarking on thousands of miles of landless ocean. Although that romantic era of sea travel may be long gone, the port of **Horta** bears testimony to Faial's illustrious place in the history of Atlantic navigation. Seafaring runs deep in the DNA of this island.

The westernmost of the central cluster of Azores islands, Faial (sometimes spelled *Fayal*) lies approximately one-third of the way between the western coast of the European continent and the eastern seaboard of the United States. With an area of only 174 sq. km (67 sq. miles), Faial is diminutive, though the calderas and peaks of its volcanic interior make for some striking terrain. Violet-petaled hydrangeas bloom all over the island, earning Faial the nickname *Ilha Azul* ("Blue Island"). The port town of Horta is Faial's only large town (pop. 7,000), and sits on the protected eastern side of the polygon-shaped island.

Whereas a century ago, you would have found **Horta marina** full of whalers and sailors whooping it up after months or years at sea, the scene today is a bit more genteel. Pleasure yachts bob in the harbor, as Faial is still an important stopping point for anyone sailing across the wide Atlantic, and it's become a superstitious tradition for all boat crews to leave a souvenir of their time on Faial in the form of a small painting, with their vessel's name and dates of travel, on the concrete wall of the port. Faded Beaux Arts houses on the cobblestoned streets of Horta recall centuries of exposure to the elements, and at small museums dedicated to the bygone practices of whaling and scrimshaw art, vestiges of Faial's past are preserved for visitors' edification. A required stop on any walking tour of Horta is **Café Sport** (Rua Tenente Valadim 9; ✆ **351/292/292327;** www.petercafesport.com), a wood-paneled bar festooned with maritime regalia. It's admittedly touristy, but there are usually a few genuinely salty types, young and old, humble and cosmopolitan, dressed in appropriately nautical striped sweaters, exchanging sailing stories. Faial's seafaring traditions come to a climax during the **Semana do Mar** ("Week of the Sea"), a festival in early August featuring a colorful regatta between Faial and the neighboring island of Pico.

Thanks to its strategic position between Europe and the Americas, Faial has played a significant role not only in seaborne navigation but also in the history of communication and early aviation. In 1893, submarine cable was laid between Faial and Lisbon, heralding the era of the trans-Atlantic telegraph. In 1929, Pan American Airways hired one Charles Lindbergh to do some reconnaissance on Faial, to determine whether the island and Horta held any interest for passengers as a stopover en route between Europe and America. Lindbergh gave it the thumbs up, and from 1939 to 1945, the great clippers of Pan Am landed in Faial on their way back and forth across the Atlantic. Even though modern jets now touch down here, Faial's sense of remoteness, clinging to the edge of the ocean "frontier," remains. —*SM*

ⓘ www.azores.com.

✈ Faial (10km/6 miles from Horta), connections to other Azores islands and mainland Portugal.

⛴ **Transmaçor** (✆ **351/292-200-380;** www.transmacor.pt), service within central Azores group only.

🛏 $$ **Pousada de Santa Cruz,** Horta (✆ **351/292-202-200;** www.pousadas.pt).

497 Real Adventures

Victoria Island

Land of Arctic Lakes

Canada

This vast expanse of land stretches far and wide; by dint of its sheer size, Victoria Island should have a Texas-style bigger-is-better swagger. But Canada's second-largest island and the world's eighth-largest island is a hushed landscape of barren, sparsely inhabited wilderness, rusting mining camp detritus, and abandoned trading posts from the days of the fur trade.

This remote island lies in the Canadian High Arctic Archipelago and borders Canada's Northwest Territories, some 2,000km (1,243 miles) from the city of Victoria, BC. Much of it is native tribal land: The western third of the island belongs to the Inuvik Region in the Northwest Territories, and the southern and eastern sections are part of Nunavut's Kitikmeot Region.

Large fields of tundra are dotted with waving grasses and puffs of wildflowers, the white blooms known as "Arctic cotton." Icy rivers course through badlands and around buttes. The area is home to an amazing variety of wildlife, including caribou, musk ox, arctic and red fox, polar bears, wolves, beluga and bowhead whales, ringed and bearded seals, king and common eider, tundra swans, yellow-billed Pacific loons, sandhill cranes, and peregrine falcons.

The island is also one of those way-off-the-beaten-path destinations that give adventure travel a real edge. A handful of outfitters offer true wilderness trips onto the island, with pristine whitewater rafting on Class II and III rapids and hiking on otherworldly terrain—no trails, thank you; you follow in the footsteps of practically no one. Anchorage, Alaska–based **Equinox Wilderness Expeditions** (✆ **604/222-1219;** http://equinoxexpeditions.com) offers award-winning (and fairly unscripted) itineraries canoeing the rapids of the Kuujjua River in Norwegian-crafted canoes.

Hundreds of lakes and rivers crisscross the island, brimming with record-breaking Arctic char and lake trout. The lakes are so clean and crystal clear that it's said you can spot fish from a plane. Many of the island lodges offer **fly-fishing packages** that arrange for guests to fish in a different lake or stream every day—delivered there by pilots who also double as expert fly-fishing guides. Many lodges offer customized naturalist tours, where you can hike on the flower-filled tundra, cruise in a boat on a lake alongside swimming caribou, or even stay in an outpost camp to the sounds of baying Arctic wolves.

Of course, a visit to Victoria Island is highly dependent on the weather. With a location that lies 483km (300 miles) north of the Arctic Circle, summer is the season to come, and it's a short 3 months to get in a lot of adventuring—so book your spot early. *—AF*

✈ Inuvik or Cambridge Bay, Nunavut.

🛏 $$ **Arctic Islands Lodge,** Cambridge Bay (✆ **867/983-2345;** www.cambridgebayhotel.com). $$$ **High Arctic Lodge,** Penticton (✆ **800/661-3880;** www.higharctic.com).

TOUR Equinox Wilderness Expeditions (see above).

Real Adventures 498

Maria Island

Tasmania's Secret Hideaway

Tasmania, Australia

For many travelers, going to Australia can feel like traveling to the end of the earth—but if you really want to explore the edge of the world, consider this scenario. First, you catch a plane or an overnight ferry from Melbourne to Australia's smallest state, the sparsely populated island of Tasmania 236, off the country's southern coast; then you catch another ferry that carries you from Tasmania's eastern shoreline several miles out to sea, across a strait known as the Mercury Passage, to a little figure-eight-shaped island where the only settlement is a ghost town. This is where Tasmanians themselves go to get in touch with nature.

This lovely and remote spot is Maria Island—and if you're planning to check it out, be sure to stock up on supplies and rented bikes ahead of time, because Maria Island has no vehicular traffic, no shops, no electricity, and no permanent residents other than the few Tasmania Parks & Wildlife Service employees who watch over the hilly, 19km-long (12-mile) island and its wildlife inhabitants.

Wallabies on Maria Island.

During Australia's summer holidays, several hundred visitors a day take the 35-minute ferry ride to **Darlington,** the abandoned city on Maria Island's northern tip. When they arrive, they're greeted by a recreational and historical wonderland. Bike paths run the length and width of the island, allowing those with the energy and desire to sample the island's diverse flora and fauna in full (for a bike-route map, go to the Parks & Wildlife Service website; see below). The island's native wombats and Tasmanian pedamelons (both plant-eating marsupials) were joined in the early 1970s by several species imported from the Tasmanian mainland, including the Eastern grey kangaroo, the red-necked wallaby, and the Tasmanian devil.

Maria Island is also known for its bird population—it's one of the last refuges of the endangered forty-spotted pardalote, the Cape Barren goose, and the sea eagle. **Haunted Bay,** on the island's southern end, is famous for its fairy penguins, whose mournful calls gave the bay its name.

The national marine park that extends for a kilometer off Maria Island's coast is a vibrant ecosystem of fish, seals (four species), dolphins, and birds. The island is on the whale migration route as well, with Southern Right whales, pilot whales, and humpback whales making regular appearances.

The island is also rich in history, both natural—within walking distance of Darlington you'll encounter both limestone **Fossil Cliffs** and sandstone **Painted Cliffs,** known for their stunning iron oxide patterns—and human. The island has gone through a number of settlement phases, starting as a basic camp for whalers and sealers in the early 1800s (the stench of boiling whale blubber forced the camp elsewhere) and then becoming a convict colony in the 1820s. During the island's industrial phase, work revolved around a cement factory, and visitors stayed at the truly grand **Grand Hotel,** a French chalet–style structure complete with dining and billiards rooms. It was built by an Italian entrepreneur who hoped to develop Maria Island as a tourist destination as well as a production center for wine and silk. The island's romantic billing as the "Riviera of Australia" never quite took hold, and by the time of the Great Depression, islanders had turned to farming and fishing. Maria Island was designated a national park in 1972.

The Grand Hotel may lie in ruins today, but many other historic sites have been recycled. A number of the old family farms now feature campsites, while the former penitentiary in Darlington has been transformed into a rustic (read: bare-bones) lodging, with rooms with bunk beds and wood heaters for rent (book through the Tasmania Parks & Wildlife Service; see below).

If it all seems a little 19th-century, that's only fitting: After all, what better way to recall a time when Maria Island tried to bring the edge of the world a step or two closer? —*AF*

(i) **Tasmania Parks & Wildlife Service:** www.parks.tas.gov.au/index.aspx?base=3495 and www.discovertasmania.com/us.

✈ Hobart (2 hr. away).

⛴ Triabunna (90 min. from Hobart): **Maria Island Ferry & Eco Cruises** (✆ **61/4/1974 6668;** www.mariaislandferry.com.au; 35 min.).

🛏 **Tasmania Parks & Wildlife Service** (✆ **61/3/6257 1420;** www.parks.tas.gov.au/index.aspx?base=3503).

499 Real Adventures

Isla Navarino

The Bottom of the World

Chile

It is a certain kind of traveler who seeks out a place like Isla Navarino. Remote and sparsely populated, it has plenty to recommend it: dramatic landscapes, thrilling sea passages, and, in **Puerto Williams,** a self-declared southernmost town in the world (that title is under dispute with Ushuaia in Tierra del Fuego 487). Isla Navarino lies at the tail end of Chilean Patagonia. It's just north of Cape Horn, the southernmost point of South America and the place where the Atlantic and Pacific meet, spectacularly. Next stop: Antarctica 486.

Isla Navarino is not an easy island escape. It takes a lot of effort to get here, and once you do, don't expect to be pampered. Tourism is in its raw early stages. The towns have a deserted, tucked-in feel, with wooden bungalows topped with corrugated iron roofs. The weather can be wildly unpredictable—sun out one minute, snowing the next (even in summer), winds blowing crazily—so that even a leisurely hike can turn into extreme sport. A trip to Isla Navarino is usually a mix of serious outdoor adventure and sedate explorations of the little island towns. What won't let you down is the stunning scenery: from unspoiled forests to glaciers and Chilean fjords framed by towering granite needles called the "Teeth of Navarino."

To hikers, Isla Navarino is one of trekking's holy grails. The island rises in the center, around which are coiled hiking trails of low and high intensity through a landscape of almost grave purity. The 5-day hiking circuit around the peaks of Navarino is known as the **Dientes de Navarino,** or "The Dientes Circuit." Hikers camp around pristine lakes and streams that trickle down the mountains. The landscape is little changed since Charles Darwin hiked these hills in 1832 on an expedition aboard the British survey ship the HMS *Beagle*.

You can get here by air—Puerto Williams has a small airport—or by ferry from Punta Arenas, some 346km (215 miles) away (you first fly to Punta Arenas from Santiago); the scenic ferry ride gets you there in a day and a half. The Patagonian airline **Aerovias DAP** (✆ **56/61/616100;** www.aeroviasdap.cl) has daily 1-hour flights from Punta Arenas into Puerto Williams. You can also take a little boat from Ushuaia, Argentina. But perhaps the best way to see the island and its amazing surrounds is by small cruise ship. **Victory Adventure Expeditions** (www.victory-cruises.com) has two full-service 100-passenger cruise ships, M/V *Mare Australia* and M/V *Via Australis,* that have regular itineraries including Cape Horn and Tierra del Fuego.

Puerto Williams is a town of about 2,400 people, many of them members of the Chilean navy. It is within shouting distance of the stunning Tierra del Fuego in Argentina, separated from the Chilean town by the narrow Beagle Channel. Magellan discovered Tierra del Fuego and its snowy peaks on his expedition to find a route to the East. The Magellan Strait, which rounds the imposing rocky promontory known as Cape Horn, opened up trade between East and West.

Cape Horn marks the southernmost point of South America and extends into the Drake Passage, the Antarctic strait connecting the south Atlantic and south Pacific oceans. This is one of the most dangerous sea passages on the planet—winds swirl, currents collide, and icebergs lurk beneath the water. Rounding "the Horn" is one of the world's last great ocean adventures. As Darwin wrote of the Horn in 1832: "On our weather-bow this notorious promontory in its proper form—veiled in a mist, and its dim outline surrounded by a storm of wind and water. Great black clouds were rolling across the heavens, and squalls of rain, with hail, swept by us. . . ."

Isla Navarino also has significance in the archaeological and anthropological worlds—it's the site of the last vestiges of the indigenous Yahgan culture, the native tribe that so fascinated early explorers. The last member of the tribe who speaks the language lives on the island. Christina Calderón lives in Villa Ukikia, a 10-minute walk from Puerto Williams (some blogs have reported that you may actually have to pony up some cash to hear her speak). Yahgan is a language isolate, which means it has no discernible genetic connection to any other language; when it's gone, it's gone forever.

Whether you've chanced the perilous Cape Horn or hiked the needles of Navarino, a night in Puerto Williams is not complete without a drink around the wood fire at the town's "yacht club," a cozy lounge inside the pilothouse of a junky old Swiss freighter (the *Micalvi*) listing dockside in a sheltered inlet. At the **Club de Yates Micalvi** (✆ **56/61/621020**), you may be hobnobbing with ship captains and crew on refueling stops, yachties preparing to round the Horn, off-duty Chilean naval personnel, and intrepid travelers from around the world—it's a warm, lively escape from the cold, lit with the *frisson* of being with fellow adventurers at a real crossroads of the world. —*AF*

ⓘ www.visit-chile.org.

✈ Punta Arenas (346km/215 miles).

Turismo Comapa (www.comapa.com) or **Victory Adventure Expeditions** (www.victory-cruises.com).

$ **Bella Vista Hostal,** Puerto Williams (http://cape-horn.net/bella_vista_hostal.html). $ **Lodge Lakutaia,** Puerto Williams (✆ **56/61/621721;** www.lakutaia.cl/).

TOUR Victory Adventure Expeditions (see above).

500 Real Adventures

Greenland

Icy Nomad of the North Atlantic

Among those ostensibly no-man's-land-masses that transatlantic flights pass over between North America and Europe, Greenland seems the most unlikely travel destination in and of itself. Iceland 455, maybe. But Greenland? It's the world's largest island that isn't a continent in its own right (about a quarter of the size of Australia), with a coastline as long as the equator. The bulk of the island lies above the Arctic Circle, and for all those terrific statistics and surface area, only 57,000 people live here, almost all of them Inuit, and concentrated on the marginally hospitable west coast. Eighty-one percent of Greenland is covered by an ice sheet, and if it were to melt, sea level worldwide would rise by 7m (23 ft.).

Greenland may be the least densely populated country in the world, but its being inhabited at all boggles the mind. If you're looking for one of the planet's most out-there travel experiences, book the next flight (flights are operated from Iceland and Denmark, of which Greenland remains part, though the island is making major progress toward independence). Your port of entry will be **Kangerlussuaq** on the west coast, and from there, you can connect to helicopter or small plane transport to other destinations in the country. There are very few roads on Greenland, and four sets of traffic lights on the entire 2,166,086-sq.-km (836,330-sq.-mile) island. The capital city of **Nuuk** (formerly called Godthab by Danes) is a booming metropolis of 17,000 souls.

Dog sledding on Greenland.

Greenland's greatest natural attraction is the **Ilulissat Ice Fjord,** a UNESCO World Heritage Site on the west coast, where the **Sermeq Kujalleq** glacier meets the sea in often-spectacular fashion. Sermeq Kujalleq is one of the fastest and most active glaciers in the world, calving over 70 cubic km of ice annually, a rate that has sped up significantly in the past decade due to climate change in the Arctic. For now, however, Greenland is still connected to the North Pole by ice, which makes it—you guessed it—the home island of Santa Claus (read more at www.santa.gl).

Besides the sublime quiet and majesty of nature here, perhaps the most quintessential Greenlandic experience is going for a **dog sled trip.** In the east and north of Greenland, some 29,000 sled dogs (one for every two residents of the whole island) are a vital, if pungent, form of transport in the winter; dog sleds always have the right of way. A number of tour outfitters also go on rip-roaring journeys over the ice and snow. Greenland sled dogs, which usually work in teams of 12 to 15 dogs per sled, are a unique breed descended from wolves and cannot bark; they howl instead.

Getting into the local way of life in Greenland represents some challenges; first and foremost of course are the harsh territory and weather. Then there's the Inuit food: The national dish of Greenland is boiled seal meat with rice and onions *(suaassat),* while a local gourmet deli item is *mattak* (raw whale skin with a thin layer of blubber).

So why is it called "Greenland" when it's mostly covered by white? The etymology of the island's name is a matter of debate: Some chalk it up to the Viking explorer Erik the Red, who might have given it this name as a sort of tongue-in-cheek way of attracting settlers from Iceland. More likely, Greenland is a corruption of *Hronland,* which meant "Land of the Whales" in ancient Norse. —*SM*

ⓘ www.greenland.com.

✈ Kangerlussuaq, flights from Reykjavik, Iceland, and Copenhagen, Denmark.

TOUR Greenland Explored (✆ **44/2921/251515;** www.greenlandholiday.com).

Indexes

Geographical Index

Alphabetical Index

Photo Credits

p. 1: Outer Banks Visitors Bureau; p. 2, bottom: Courtesy of Tourism Queensland; p. 8, top left: Bahamas Ministry of Tourism; p. 11, top: Rachel Falk; p. 16, top left: Cayman Islands Department of Tourism; p. 19, bottom: Lee County VCB/www.FortMyersSanibel.com; p. 28, top: Nevis Tourism Authority; p. 29, bottom: Courtesy of the South Padre Island CVB; p. 35, top: Gothenburg/Göteborg and Västsverige/West Sweden; p. 36, middle: Bahamas Ministry of Tourism; p. 38, bottom: U.S. Virgin Islands Tourism Board; p. 42, top: Tony Rath of Tony Rath Photography/www.tonyrath.com; p. 47, bottom: Topel Kommunikation GmbH Topel, Dirk/GNTB; p. 50, bottom: Marco Garcia; p. 57: Photo courtesy of Tahiti Tourisme; p. 59, bottom: Grenada Board of Tourism; p. 61, top: Tourism PEI/John Sylvester; p. 66, top: Image supplied by Tresco Estate; p. 70, top: Ryan Candee; p. 73, bottom: Courtesy of SCPRT/Photo by Perry Baker; p. 76, top: Photo courtesy of Tahiti Tourisme; p. 81, bottom: K.P.V.B.; p. 84, top: Kaster, Andreas/GNTB; p. 88, top left: Garden Island Photography/Dana Nadeau; p. 89, bottom: Saint Lucia Tourist Board; p. 93: Tourism Australia; p. 95, bottom: Robert Delfs, courtesy of PT. Putri Naga Komodo; p. 100, middle: Kleintours; p. 101, bottom right: Metropolitan Touring; p. 105, bottom: Images New Zealand; p. 111, bottom right: Heather Garrett/Zelinka Priamo Planners; p. 115, top right: Cayman Islands Department of Tourism; p. 116, bottom: PromPeru–North America; p. 118, top: Tourism Queensland; p. 121, bottom: EMBRATUR; p. 126, top: National Park Service; p. 127, bottom: Utah State Parks; p. 132, top: Aviatur; p. 134, bottom left: Ian Trafford and Images New Zealand; p. 138, middle: K.P.V.B.; p. 144: Michael Melford; p. 145, bottom: Images New Zealand; p. 148, top: Seurasaari Foundation; p. 152, bottom left: Image Source Pink/Alamy; p. 155, bottom: Howie Garber/Danita Delmont Stock Photography; p. 159, top: Åland Tourist/Hannu Vallas; p. 167, top: Courtesy of SCPRT/Photo by Perry Baker; p. 168, bottom: Marco Garcia; p. 171, bottom: Jennifer Reilly; p. 176, middle: Corbis Premium RF/Alamy; p. 182, top: German National Merten, Hans Peter Tourism Board; p. 185, bottom: Scarborough–Tobago/TDC (Tourism Development Company); p. 189, bottom: Miyagi Prefecture Industry Department, Tourism Division; p. 194: Onne van der Wal/www.vanderwal.com; p. 196, bottom: Lawrel Strauch Spera/Nantucket Chamber; p. 198, top: Richard Graves; p. 201, top: Courtesy of Tahiti Tourisme; p. 206, middle: C H and Innovation Norway; p. 207, middle: C H and Innovation Norway; p. 209, top: Sea Island Resorts; p. 210, bottom: Georgia Department of Economic Development; p. 213, bottom: Jason Gonzalez; p. 217, top: John Cole; p. 223, bottom: Kenya Tourist Board; p. 228, top: Jennifer Reilly; p. 231, bottom right: Georgios Makkas/Panos; p. 233, top: The Dominican Republic Ministry of Tourism; p. 236, bottom: Tourism Tasmania and George Apostolidis; p. 242, bottom left: Bahamas Ministry of Tourism; p. 244, top: National Park Service; p. 245: Bahamas Ministry of Tourism; p. 247, bottom right: Croatian Tourist Board and Juraj Kopač; p. 256, top left: Isle of Wight Council/www.islandbreaks.co.uk; p. 259, top: Sylvie Murphy; p. 261, bottom: California Travel & Tourism Commission; Robert Holmes; p. 264, top: Aruba Tourism Authority; p. 266, top left: Chukka Caribbean Adventures; p. 267, bottom: Kristin Mills; p. 271, top: Mexico Tourism Board; p. 272, middle: Courtesy of Tourism Queensland; p. 277: Steve Terrill; p. 279, bottom: Courtesy of michigan.org; p. 281, bottom: Jack Brink; p. 284, top: Courtesy of SCPRT/Photo by Perry Baker; p. 288, top: Vermont Dept. of Tourism & Marketing; p. 295, top: Photo by George Fischer for 1000 Islands International Tourism Council; p. 298, top: Marco Garcia; p. 302, top: Sergi Camara; p. 305, top: Greek National Tourism Organization, Archives; p. 308, bottom: Mexico Tourism Board; p. 315, top: Georgia Department of Economic Development; p. 316, bottom: San Juan Islands Visitors Bureau; p. 318, bottom left: National Park Service; p. 321, top: Hokkaido Tourism Bureau; p. 323: William Villalobos; p. 325, bottom: Jennifer Reilly; p. 328, bottom: Peter Grant; p. 330, top: Courtesy of SCPRT/Photo by Perry Baker; p. 331, middle: Croatian National Tourist Board and Josip Madračevi; p. 333, bottom: Images courtesy of VisitGuernsey; p. 337, bottom right: Giuseppe Piazza; p. 341, top: Debra Hunter;

p. 346, top left: Georgia Department of Economic Development; p. 350, bottom: Curacao Tourism Corporation; p. 352, top: Newfoundland and Labrador Tourism; p. 359, bottom right: Bahamas Ministry of Tourism; p. 363, top: Galveston Island Convention & Visitors Bureau; p. 369, top right: Courtesy Alcatraz Cruises; p. 370, bottom left: Gareth McCormack/Alamy; p. 375, bottom: GNTB/Werner H. Müller; p. 377, top: Courtesy of the Martha's Vineyard Chamber of Commerce/Heather Goff; p. 380, top: Sylvie Murphy; p. 384, top: Rich Ryzman, Isles of Shoals Steamship Co., Marketing Manager, 2007; p. 387: Jack Brink; p. 389, bottom: Courtesy of Tahiti Tourisme; p. 392, middle: PromPeru–North America; p. 393, middle: PromPeru–North America; p. 396, top: Michael McLaughlin; p. 400, bottom: Sylvie Murphy; p. 406, top: Mexico Tourism Board; p. 407, bottom right: Outer Banks Visitors Bureau; p. 408, middle: Courtesy of Tahiti Tourisme; p. 413: Erik Rank; p. 414, bottom: Nicho Södling; p. 418, top: Singapore Tourism Board; p. 420, middle: Sylvie Murphy; p. 422, top: Jack Brink; p. 425, top: Greater Miami Convention & Visitors Bureau/www.gmcvb.com; p. 429: William Villalobos; p. 431, bottom: GNTB/Merten, Hans Peter; p. 433, top: GNTB/Andrew Cowin; p. 438, top left: Jennifer Reilly; p. 439, bottom: JNTO; p. 442, bottom: Rob Flynn; p. 445, bottom right: Environment Canada's Biosphère; p. 448, top: Tourism Office of Budapest; p. 450, bottom: Tourism Toronto; p. 454, bottom left: Kim Hart; p. 462, top left: California Travel & Tourism Commission; Robert Holmes; p. 465, top right: www.visitrichmond.co.uk/Ken McKenzie; p. 468, bottom: Esko Jämsä/Governing Body of Suomenlinna; p. 470: PNG Tourism Promotion Authority; p. 472, top: Malta Tourism Authority; p. 473, bottom: Philippine Department of Tourism; p. 476, bottom left: Iceland Tourist Board; p. 482, bottom left: Angelo Tondini; CuboImages srl/Alamy; p. 484, top left: Mauritius Tourism Promotion Authority; MPTA/www.fotoseeker.com; p. 486, top: Barbados Tourism Authority/Mike Toy; p. 489, top: PNG Tourism Promotion Authority; p. 490, bottom left: Rhett Butler; p. 492, top: Cyprus Tourism Organization; p. 494: Karsten Bidstrup/Greenland Tourism & Business Council; p. 496, bottom left: Aviatur–Fundacion Malpelo; p. 506, top left: Gentileza TurismoChile; p. 507, bottom right: Gentileza TurismoChile; p. 511, top right: Vanuatu Tourist Office; p. 512, middle: Cook Islands Tourism Corporation; p. 513, middle: Cook Islands Tourism Corporation; p. 516, bottom left: Tourism Tasmania Copyright; George Apostolidis; p. 519, bottom: Filippo Barbanera/Greenland Tourism & Business Council